OPERATIONAL AMPLIFIERS AND THEIR APPLICATIONS

[For B.Sc. (Hons.), B.E. (Electrical, Electronics, Instrumentation Computer Engineering) and degree Syllabus of Applied Sciences]

Dr. SUBIR KUMAR SARKAR

Professor, Department of Electronics and
Telecommuni... ...gineering,
...ity

S. CHAND & COMPANY LTD.

(AN ISO 9001 : 2000 COMPANY)

RAM NAGAR, NEW DELHI-110 055

S. CHAND & COMPANY LTD.

(An ISO 9001 : 2000 Company)

Head Office: 7361, RAM NAGAR, NEW DELHI - 110 055
Phone: 23672080-81-82, 9899107446, 9911310888
Fax: 91-11-23677446
Shop at: **schandgroup.com**; e-mail: **info@schandgroup.com**

Branches :

AHMEDABAD : 1st Floor, Heritage, Near Gujarat Vidhyapeeth, Ashram Road, **Ahmedabad** - 380 014, Ph: 27541965, 27542369, ahmedabad@schandgroup.com

BANGALORE : No. 6, Ahuja Chambers, 1st Cross, Kumara Krupa Road, **Bangalore** - 560 001, Ph: 22268048, 22354008, bangalore@schandgroup.com

BHOPAL : 238-A, M.P. Nagar, Zone 1, **Bhopal** - 462 011, Ph: 4274723. bhopal@schandgroup.com

CHANDIGARH : S.C.O. 2419-20, First Floor, Sector - 22-C (Near Aroma Hotel), **Chandigarh** -160 022, Ph: 2725443, 2725446, chandigarh@schandgroup.com

CHENNAI : 152, Anna Salai, **Chennai** - 600 002, Ph: 28460026, 28460027, chennai@schandgroup.com

COIMBATORE : Plot No. 5, Rajalakshmi Nagar, Peelamedu, **Coimbatore** -641 004, (M) 09444228242, coimbatore@schandgroup.com

CUTTACK : 1st Floor, Bhartia Tower, Badambadi, **Cuttack** - 753 009, Ph: 2332580; 2332581, cuttack@schandgroup.com

DEHRADUN : 1st Floor, 20, New Road, Near Dwarka Store, **Dehradun** - 248 001, Ph: 2711101, 2710861, dehradun@schandgroup.com

GUWAHATI : Pan Bazar, **Guwahati** - 781 001, Ph: 2738811, 2735640 guwahati@schandgroup.com

HYDERABAD : Padma Plaza, H.No. 3-4-630, Opp. Ratna College, Narayanaguda, **Hyderabad** - 500 029, Ph: 24651135, 24744815, hyderabad@schandgroup.com

JAIPUR : A-14, Janta Store Shopping Complex, University Marg, Bapu Nagar, **Jaipur** - 302 015, Ph: 2719126, jaipur@schandgroup.com

JALANDHAR : Mai Hiran Gate, **Jalandhar** - 144 008, Ph: 2401630, 5000630, jalandhar@schandgroup.com

JAMMU : 67/B, B-Block, Gandhi Nagar, **Jammu** - 180 004, (M) 09878651464

KOCHI : Kachapilly Square, Mullassery Canal Road, Ernakulam, **Kochi** - 682 011, Ph: 2378207, cochin@schandgroup.com

KOLKATA : 285/J, Bipin Bihari Ganguli Street, **Kolkata** - 700 012, Ph: 22367459, 22373914, kolkata@schandgroup.com

LUCKNOW : Mahabeer Market, 25 Gwynne Road, Aminabad, **Lucknow** - 226 018, Ph: 2626801, 2284815, lucknow@schandgroup.com

MUMBAI : Blackie House, 103/5, Walchand Hirachand Marg, Opp. G.P.O., **Mumbai** - 400 001, Ph: 22690881, 22610885, mumbai@schandgroup.com

NAGPUR : Karnal Bag, Model Mill Chowk, Umrer Road, **Nagpur** - 440 032, Ph: 2723901, 2777666 nagpur@schandgroup.com

PATNA : 104, Citicentre Ashok, Govind Mitra Road, **Patna** - 800 004, Ph: 2300489, 2302100, patna@schandgroup.com

PUNE : 291/1, Ganesh Gayatri Complex, 1st Floor, Somwarpeth, Near Jain Mandir, **Pune** - 411 011, Ph: 64017298, pune@schandgroup.com

RAIPUR : Kailash Residency, Plot No. 4B, Bottle House Road, Shankar Nagar, **Raipur** - 492 007, Ph: 09981200834, raipur@schandgroup.com

RANCHI : Flat No. 104, Sri Draupadi Smriti Apartments, East of Jaipal Singh Stadium, Neel Ratan Street, Upper Bazar, **Ranchi** - 834 001, Ph: 2208761, ranchi@schandgroup.com

VISAKHAPATNAM: Plot No. 7, 1st Floor, Allipuram Extension, Opp. Radhakrishna Towers, Seethammadhara North Extn., **Visakhapatnam** - 530 013, (M) 09347580841, visakhapatnam@schandgroup.com

First Edition 1999
Revised Edition 2003
Revised Edition 2010

ISBN : 81-219-1779-4 **Code :** 10A 190

PRINTED IN INDIA

By Rajendra Ravindra Printers Pvt. Ltd., 7361, Ram Nagar, New Delhi -110 055 and published by S. Chand & Company Ltd., 7361, Ram Nagar, New Delhi -110 055.

Dedicated to my father

Late Girish Chandra Sarkar

PREFACE TO THE REVISED EDITION

The operational amplifier is really a versatile device. IC operational amplifier has appeared as an inexpensive and effective tool for handling circuit design problems. The author is acutely aware of the rapid advances being made in electronic engineering. The text is based on a series of Lecture courses given by the author at Bengal Engineering College (Deemed University) to undergraduates. This textbook is aimed to benefit electronics, electrical computer, control, communication engineering students and partly for undergraduate and postgraduate students of physics. However, practising engineers who feel the need for retraining should also find it helpful.

Many textbooks describe the theory in great detail and not without some degree of complexity. Other engineering texts merely provide a cursory description. The present book is an attempt to close the gap between the two extremes.

This book is suitable for one semester course on operational amplifiers. Some modern aspects of op amps have also been incorporated for the benefit of the students. These days quite a number of the students are unable to keep pace with the teacher. Hence "Self study" textbooks have become essential. This book provides a unified approach to conceive and understand the basic principle of operational amplifier, internal construction, and applications. The conversational style of language is intentionally accepted to make the reader feel that the teacher is always close to him, and will come to his assistance whenever needed. The various chapters are based on the functions, rather than on the inventional approach. The data sheets and application notes of some of the very popular operational amplifiers together with pin configuration are provided. Each chapter contains worked examples and provides exercises followed by objective type questions like true-false, one word type, fill in the blank and multiple choice type. A widely used program for the automatic analysis of circuit is the Simulation Program with Integrated Circuit Emphasis (SPICE) has been used to analyse the circuit containing operational amplifiers. This program is capable of performing the dc, ac and transient analysis of circuits containing dependent and independent source and other electronic components. A chapter for laboratory experiments with all details is included in the book.

I am deeply indebted to the Head of the Department, Department of Electronics and Telecommunication Engineering, and Dr. S.M. Chatterjee, Vice-Chancellor, Bengal Engineering College (Deemed University), for their encouragement. I am also grateful to my colleagues, in particular to Prof. S. K. Ghosh.

I am obliged to my dear friend Dr. R.N. Bera of Institute of Radiophysics and Electronics, University of Calcutta, for many enjoyable and useful discussions. I am indebted to my wife, Mrs. Bani Sarkar, and my sons, Sri Souvik Sarkar and Surjadya Sarkar for their encouragement and steadfast support. I am thankful to a large group of my students. I am also thankful to my brother-in-law Sri Subasish Basu, for his help.

Lastly I am thankful to Govt. of West Bengal for permitting me to publish this book and to M/s S. Chand and Company Ltd. for publishing this book in such a nice form and in a record time.

Suggestions for further improvement will be gratefully acknowledged.

AUTHOR

CONTENTS

1. DIFFERENTIAL AMPLIFIER **1 – 31**

1.1 Introduction 1
1.2 Parameters of Differential Amplifier 1
1.3 Common Mode Rejection Ratio 2
1.4 Applications of Differential Amplifier 3
1.5 Circuit Configurations of Differential Amplifier 3
1.6 A.C. Analysis of the Differential Amplifier 4
1.7 Differential Amplifer with a Constant Current Stage 9
1.8 Transfer Characteristics of the Basic Differential Amplifier 11
1.9 Differential Amplifier with FET 18
1.10 Cascading of Differential Amplifier 21
1.11 Effects of Cascading 22
1.12 Comparison of Different Configurations of Differential Amplifier 22
Solved Problems 22

2. OPERATIONAL AMPLIFIER **32 – 63**

2.1 Introduction 32
2.2 Generations of Operational Amplifiers 32
2.3 Designations for Operational Amplifiers 35
2.4 Pin Configuration and Different Packages of IC Operational Amplifier 36
2.5 Special Operational Amplifiers 37
2.6 Ordering Information for IC Operational Amplifier 37
2.7 Identification of Operational Amplifier 37
2.8 Selection of Right Operational Amplifier for the Right Job 38
2.9 Block Diagram of a Typical Operational Amplifier 38
2.10 Circuit Symbol of Operational Amplifier 39
2.11 Need of Power Supplies for Operational Amplifier 39
2.12 Characteristic Features of an Ideal Operational Amplifier 40
2.13 Detailed Circuit Description of Operational Amplifier 741 41
2.14 Basic Operational Amplifier 42
2.15 Virtual Ground 42
2.16 Some Important Terms of Operational Amplifier 43
2.17 Offset Correcting Resistor 48
2.18 Effect of Voltage and Current Drifts 50
2.19 Characteristics of Practical or Non-Ideal Operational Amplifier 51
2.20 Gain Bandwidth Product 51
2.21 Feedback in Operational Amplifier Circuits 52
2.22 Closed-Loop Voltage Gain 52
2.23 Closed-Loop Gain A_{cl} in terms of Open Loop-Gain (A) 53
2.24 Input Resistance with Feedback 53
2.25 Output Resistance with Feedback 54
2.26 Bandwidth with Feedback 54

2.27 The Effect of Feedback on Total of Output Offset Voltage 55
Solved Problems 56

3. BASIC OPERATIONAL AMPLIFIER CIRCUITS 64 – 110
3.1 Introduction 64
3.2 Inverting Operational Amplifier Circuit 65
3.3 Non-Inverting Operational Amplifier Circuit 65
3.4 Voltage Follower Circuit Using Operational Amplifier 66
3.5 Summing Amplifier (Adder/Subtractor Circuit) 67
3.6 Difference Amplifier 68
3.7 Multiplier Circuit Using Operational Amplifier 69
3.8 Negative Resistance Converter 70
3.9 Instrumentation Amplifier 71
3.10 Transresistance Amplifier 72
3.11 Transconductance Amplifier 73
3.12 Current Amplifier 74
3.13 Controlled Source Representation of Different Operational Amplifier Configurations 75
3.14 Comparators 77
3.15 Log and Antilog Amplifiers 78
3.15 (*a*) Log Amplifier and Multiplication 79
3.16 Control of Gain Polarity 81
Solved Problems 81

4. FREQUENCY RESPONSE AND COMPENSATION OF OPERATIONAL AMPLIFIER 111 – 124
4.1 Introduction 111
4.2 Stability in Operational Amplifier Circuit 112
4.3 (a) Frequency Response 113
(b) Phase Response 114
4.4 Frequency and Phase Response of Operational Amplifier 114
4.5 Oscillation and Precaution 114
4.6 Stability of Amplifiers 115
4.7 Methods of Frequency Compensation 116
4.8 Miller Effect Compensation 117
4.9 Feedforward Compensation 118
4.10 Effects of Stray Capacitance on Circuit Instability 118
4.11 More About the Compensation for Stray Capacitance 119
4.12 Effect of Load Capacitance on Circuit Instability 120
4.13 How to Improve Stability with Capacitive Load 120
4.14 Frequency Compensation Using Input Impedance Modification Technique 121
4.15 Some Important Terms Compensation Recommended by Manufacturers 123
4.16 Precautions to be Taken for Better Stability 123

5. SIGNAL CONDITIONING CIRCUITS 125 – 139
5.1 Introduction 125
5.2 Integrator Circuit 125

5.3 Noninverting Integrator 127
5.4 Setting of Initial Condition 128
5.5 Other Practical Considerations 128
5.6 Integrator with Bias Current Compensation 129
5.7 Integrator with Feed Forward Frequency Compensation 129
5.8 Integrator with Two Operational Amplifier 130
5.9 Double-Integrator Circuit Using Single Operational Amplifier 131
5.10 Some Specialised Integrator Circuits 133
5.11 Differentiator Circuits 134
5.12 Practical Differentiator 136
5.13 Some Specialised Differentiators 137

6. ACTIVE FILTER CIRCUIT 140 – 168
6.1 Filters 140
6.2 Advantages of Active Filters 140
6.3 Applications of Active Filters 141
6.4 Filter Classification 141
6.5 Butterworth, Chebysher and Caucer Filters 142
6.6 Low Pass Filter (Butterworth) 144
6.7 Frequency Scaling 146
6.8 Advantages of Higher Order Filters 147
6.9 High Pass Filter (Butterworth) 147
6.10 Band Pass Filter (BPF) 149
6.11 Band Stop Filter 151
6.12 Notch Filters 152
6.13 All Pass Filters 153
6.14 Characteristic Impedance of Active Filters 156
Solved Problems 157

7. NOISE CONTROL IN OPERATIONAL AMPLIFIER 169 – 180
7.1 Introduction 169
7.2 Noise Associated with Differential Amplifier (Operational Amplifier) 169
7.3 Equivalent Input Noise for BJT Differential Amplifier 171
7.4 Noise Characteristic of a BJT Differential Stage 175
7.5 Equivalent Input for FET Differential Amplifier 175
7.6 Optimum Noise Performance Conditions 178
7.7 Noise in Cascaded Operational Amplifiers 179

8. OPERATIONAL AMPLIFIER APPLICATIONS 181 – 201
8.1 Introduction 181
8.2 Audio Mixer Using Operational Amplifier 181
8.3 Active Voltage Divider 182
8.4 Equilizers Using Operational Amplifier 183
8.5 Audio Tone Control Using Operational Amplifier 185
8.6 Operational Amplifier Operated Photo Electric Relay 186
8.7 Photovoltaic Light Sensors Using Operational Amplifier 187
8.8 High Precision Voltage Sources Using Operational Amplifier 187

8.9 Resistance Temperature Sensor 187
8.10 Signal Rectification Using Operational Amplifier 188
8.11 Variable Voltage Power Supply 189
8.12 High Voltage Power Supply Using Operational Amplifier 190
8.13 High Performance Series Regulator 193
8.14 OP AMP in Over Current Protection Circuit 194
8.15 Foldback Current Limiting in a Series Regulator 195
8.16 Operational Amplifier as a Phase Detector 195
8.17 Operational Amplifier Electronic Thermometers 197
8.18 Operational Amplifier in Medical Electronic Monitoring System 199
8.19 Operational Amplifier as a Power Amplifier 200

9. MORE OPERATIONAL AMPLIFIER APPLICATIONS 202 – 228

9.1 Introduction 202
9.2 Quadrature Oscillator 202
9.3 Wien Bridge Oscillator 203
9.4 Zero Crossing Detector 205
9.5 Phase Shift Oscillator 210
9.6 Wave Form Generation 212
9.7 Sawtooth Wave Generation Using Operational Amplifier 214
9.8 Generation of Sine Wave From Square Wave Using Operational Amplifier 215
9.9 Schmitt Trigger Circuit 216
9.10 Applications of Operational Amplifier as A/D and D/A Convertors 218
9.11 Multiplication of Capacitance Using Operational Amplifier 223
9.12 Simulation of Inductance Using Operational Amplifier 224
9.13 Special Operational Amplifier Circuit for Capacitance Multiplier 225

10. APPLICATION OF SPICE & PSPICE IN THE ANALYSIS OF OPERATIONAL AMPLIFIER CIRCUITS 229 – 252

10.1 Introduction 229
10.2 SPICE/PSPICE General Description 229
10.3 Working Principle of SPICE/PSPICE 230
10.4 Rules Regarding SPICE/PSPICE 230
10.5 Some Special Statements 233
10.6 SPICE Analysis for Purely Resistive Circuit 234
10.7 SPICE Analysis to Find the Thevenin and Norton Equivalents Across the Terminal (a, b) 235

Solved Problems 237

11. PRACTICAL EXPERIMENTS ON OPERATIONAL AMPLIFIERS 253 – 294

11.1 Experiment

(*i*) To Study the Unity Gain Buffer Using Operational Amplifier
(*ii*) To Measure Input Resistance (R_i) of Operational Amplifier
(*iii*) To Measure the Output Resistance (R_o) of Operational Amplifier
(*iv*) To Study the Frequency Response of an Operational Amplifier and Calculation of Gain Bandwidth Product 253

11.2 Experiment to Study the Adder Circuit Using Operational Amplifier 260
11.3 Experiment to Study the Integrator Circuit Using Operational Amplifier 263
11.4 Experiment
(*i*) To Study the Operation of a Differentiation Circuit Using Operational Amplifier
(*ii*) To Study the Frequency Response of Differentiator
(*iii*) To Study the Input and Output Waveform Whether the Output Waveform is the Derivative of Input or Not 266
11.5 Experiment to Study the Comparator Circuit Using Operational Amplifier 270
11.6 Experiment to Study the Cascade Amplifier by Using Operational Amplifiern 271
11.7 Experiment to Study Schmitt Trigger Circuit by Using Operational Amplifier 275
11.8 Experiment to Study the Frequency Response of Low Pass Filter 279
11.9 Experiment to Study the Frequency Response of High Pass Filter 284
11.10 Experiment to Study the Frequency Response of Band Pass Filter 286
11.11 Experiment
(*i*) To Study Gain Polarity Control by Operational Amplifier
(*ii*) To Study Some Oscillators Phase Shift Oscillator 289

EXTRA PROBLEMS ON OPERATIONAL AMPLIFIER CIRCUITS **295–332**
Problems on Transient Response 298
Problems on Filters 305
REVIEW QUESTIONS AND ANSWERS **327 – 352**
MULTIPLE CHOICE QUESTIONS **353 – 369**
ADDITIONAL MULTIPLE CHOICE QUESTIONS **370 – 375**
APPENDIX – A: **376 – 377**
APPENDIX – B: **378 – 378**
APPENDIX – C: **378 – 379**
APPENDIX – D: **379 – 397**
INDEX **399 – 402**

1

DIFFERENTIAL AMPLIFIER

1·1. Introduction. 1·2. Parameters of Differential Amplifier. 1·3. Common Mode Rejection Ratio. 1·4. Applications of Diff. Amp. 1·5. Circuit Configuration of Diff. Amp. 1·6. AC Analysis of the Diff. Amp. 1·7. Diff. Amp. with a Constant Current Stage. 1·8. Transfer Characteristics of the Basic Diff. Amplifier 1·9. Diff. Amp. with JFET. 1·10. Cascading of Diff. Amp. 1·11. Effects of Cascading 1·12. Comparison of Different Configurations of Diff. Amp. Solved Problems. Review Questions.

1·1. INTRODUCTION

Differential amplifier (DIFF. AMP) is the basic stage of an integrated operational amplifier with differential input. Hence detailed discussion of differential amplifiers prescribes the ground work for analysis and design procedure for the operational amplifiers. Moreover, the analysis of differential amplifier provides the following:

- clarifies the operation of the operational amplifiers.
- easy understanding of the characteristics of the operational amplifiers.
- ways of checking parameters of operational amplifiers (like inputs, output, impedance and voltage gain).

A differential amplifier is often used to amplify the difference between two signals. It can eliminate signals common to both inputs, specially noise. It can also be used as a phase-splitting amplifier. Moreover, it can be used in many physical measurements where response from dc to many megahertz is needed.

1.2. PARAMETERS OF DIFF. AMP.

Figure 1.1 depicts a differential amplifier formed by a linear active device. For the analysis of the parameters of the DIFF AMP it is assumed that it is an ideal one. Now question may come about the definition of an ideal DIFF AMP. A DIFF. AMP is defined to be an ideal one if any signal which is common to both inputs has no effect on the output voltage.

For an ideal DIFF AMP,

$$v_o = A_d(v_{\text{in}1} - v_{\text{in}2}) \quad ...(1.2.1)$$

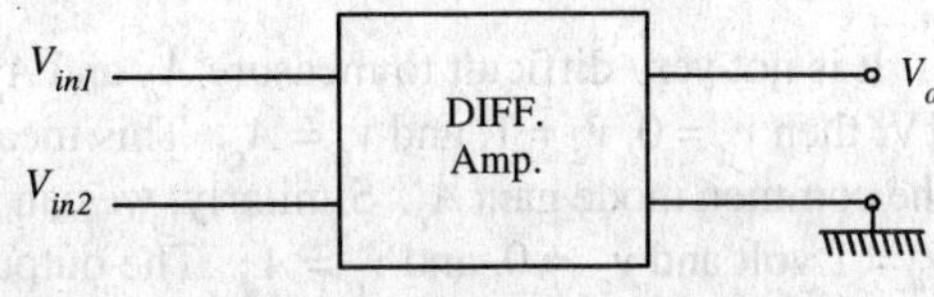

Fig. 1.1

Here A_d is the gain of the differential amplifier. But a practical differential amplifier does not follow the eq. (1.2.1). This is due to the fact that the output is not only controlled by the difference signal v_d of the two input signals, but also depends upon the average level v_c, where v_c is called common-mode signal and expressed as

$$v_c = \frac{1}{2}(v_{\text{in}\,1} + v_{\text{in}\,2}) \qquad ...(1.2.2)$$

Thus, if one signal is 50 μV and the other signal is –50μV, the output will not be exactly the same as if $v_{\text{in}\,1}$ = 550 μV *and* $v_{\text{in}\,2}$ = 650 μV, *even though the difference is same in both the cases and equal to 100* μV.

1·3. COMMON MODE REJECTION RATIO

As nothing is really ideal, identical input signals may create an output with the same input on both terminals. It is called common mode. The capacity of the differential amplifier to cancel out these identical signals is called common mode rejection. Common mode rejection is its ability to reject a common-mode signal-one common to both inputs.

It is easy to see the practical importance of rejecting common-mode signal. Common-mode rejection ratio is a measure of a differential amplifier's capacity to eliminate common signals. It is abbreviated as CMRR.

$$\text{CMRR} = \frac{\text{Difference signal gain } (A_d)}{\text{Common signal gain } (A_c)} \qquad ...(1.3.1)$$

The higher the CMRR, the better the differential amplifier is of eliminating common signals. This is because there always remains some kind of noise present on the signal lines and it is not expected that this noise be amplified and appear in the output. The CMRR is generally expressed in dB and denoted by ρ,

$$\rho = 20 \log_{10} (A_d / A_c) \qquad ...(1.3.2)$$

From Fig. 1.1 it can be written that

$$v_o = A_1\, v_{\text{in}\,1} + A_2\, v_{\text{in}\,2} \qquad ...(1.3.3)$$

In the above eqn. A_1 (A_2) represents the voltage amplification from input 1(2) to the output under the condition that input 2(1) is grounded.

It is already known

$$v_d = v_{\text{in}\,1} - v_{\text{in}\,2} \text{ and } v_c = \frac{v_{\text{in}\,1} + v_{\text{in}\,2}}{2}$$

$$\therefore \qquad v_{\text{in}\,1} = v_c + v_d / 2 \text{ and } v_{\text{in}\,2} = v_c - v_d / 2 \qquad ...(1.3.4)$$

Then from eqns (1.3.3) and (1.3.4), we get

$$v_o = A_d\, v_d + A_c\, v_c \qquad ...(1.3.5)$$

where $\quad A_c = A_1 + A_2$ and ...(1.3.6)

$$A_d = \frac{1}{2}(A_1 - A_2)$$

It is not very difficult to measure A_d and A_c. A_c can be measured directly by setting $v_{\text{in}\,1} = v_{\text{in}\,2}$ = 1V, then $v_d = 0$, $v_c = 1$, and $v_o = A_c$. This means the output voltage now is a direct measurement of the common mode gain A_c. Similarly, we can measure A_d directly by making $v_{\text{in}\,1} = 0.5 = -v_{\text{in}\,2}$ then v_d = 1 volt and v_c = 0, and $v_o = A_d$. The output voltage is a direct measurement of difference mode gain A_d for the difference signal.

Now Eq. (1.3.5) and the definition of CMRR will give

$$v_o = A_d\, v_d \left(1 + \frac{A_c}{A_d} \cdot \frac{v_c}{v_d}\right)$$

$$= A_d\, v_d \left(1 + \frac{v_c}{\rho\, v_d}\right) \qquad ...(1.3.7)$$

It is evident from eq. (1.3.7) that ρ should be large compared to the ratio of the common mode signal to the difference mode signal. This is because there is always some kind of noise on the signal lines. Moreover it is undesirable that this noise be amplified and present in the output. This noise is virtually eliminated in the differential amplifier.

1·4. APPLICATIONS OF DIFF. AMP.

Differential amplifier has vast applications such as (1) a phase-splitting amplifier, (2) used to amplify the difference between two signals, (3) used to eliminate signals common to both inputs, particularly noise.

1·5. CIRCUIT CONFIGURATIONS OF DIFF. AMP.

There are several differential amplifier configurations, one such configuration is Dual-input, balanced output Differential Amplifier. It is also called symmetrical emitter coupled difference amplifier. Such a configuration is shown in the Fig. 1·2.

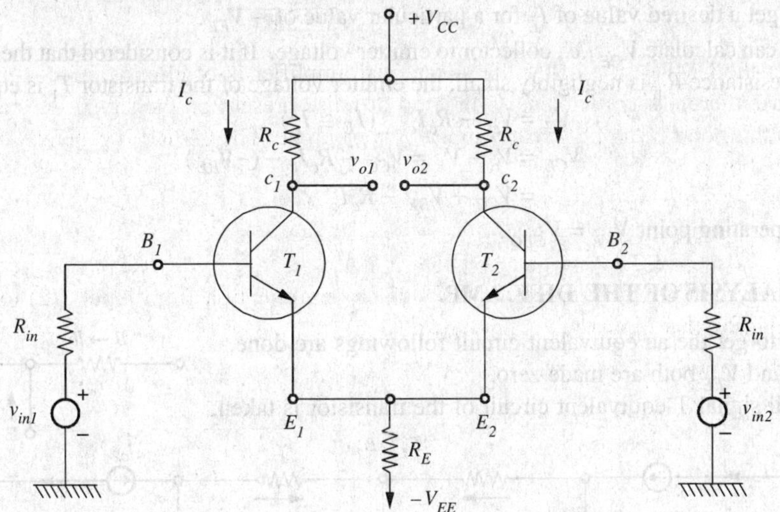

Fig. 1.2. Symmetrical emitter coupled Diff. Amp.

In Fig. 1.2, $v_{\text{in }1}$ and $v_{\text{in }2}$ are the two input signals. v_{o1} and v_{o2} are the output signals. Final output is measured between c_1 and c_2 and is ($v_{o1} \sim v_{o2}$). c_1 and c_2 are all at the same *dc* potential. As either c_1 or c_2 has the same *dc* potential with respect to ground, the output is referred to as a balanced output.

In order to determine the operating points *i.e.*, V_{CEQ} and I_{CQ} for the present configuration of differential amplifier, dc equivalent circuit is essential. Input signals $v_{\text{in }1}$ and $v_{\text{in }2}$ are made zero individually to get the dc equivalent circuit keeping dc sources as usual.

Now if Kirchhoff's voltage law is applied to the base emitter circuit of the transistor T_1 in Fig. 1.2(*a*) with $v_{\text{in }1} = v_{\text{in }2} = 0$, we get

$$-V_{EE} + V_{BE} + R_{in}\, I_B + R_E\,(2I_E) = 0 \qquad ...(1.5.1)$$

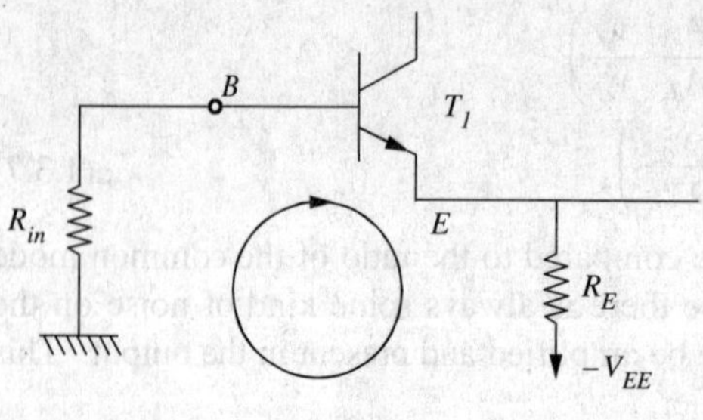

Fig. 1.2(*a*)

Assuming $h_{re} \cong 0$ *i.e.*, $I_c \cong I_E$

$$I_E = \beta I_B \qquad ...(1.5.2)$$

Hence from eqn. (1.5.1)

$$V_{EE} - V_{BE} - 2 I_E R_E - R_{in} \frac{I_E}{\beta} = 0$$

or
$$I_E \left(2R_E + \frac{R_{in}}{\beta} \right) = V_{EE} - V_{BE}$$

$$\therefore \quad I_E = \frac{V_{EE} - V_{BE}}{2 R_E + R_{in} / \beta} \qquad ...(1.5.3)$$

where V_{BE} is the emitter-base cut in voltage for the transistor. Normally

$$2 R_E >> \frac{R_{in}}{\beta}$$

Then eqn. (1.5.3) can be reduced to

$$I_E = \frac{V_{EE} - V_{BE}}{2 R_E} \qquad ...(1.5.4)$$

At the operating point $I_E = I_{CQ}$.

From the equation it is evident that emitter current is independent of R_c. Hence by selection of R_E, we can get a desired value of I_E for a particular value of $- V_{EE}$.

Now we can calculate V_{CE} *i.e.*, collector to emitter voltage. If it is considered that the voltage drop across the resistance R_{in} is negligibly small, the emitter voltage of the transistor T_1 is equal to $- V_{BE}$.

$$V_C = V_{cc} - R_c I_c \quad (I_E \cong I_c) \qquad ...(1.5.5)$$

$$V_{CE} = V_c - V_E = V_{CC} - R_c I_c - (-V_{BE})$$

$$= V_{CC} + V_{BE} - R_c I_c \qquad ...(1.5.6)$$

At the operating point $V_{CE} = V_{CEQ}$.

1·6. AC ANALYSIS OF THE DIFF. AMP.

In order to get the ac equivalent circuit followings are done.

(*i*) V_{CC} and V_{EE} both are made zero.

(*ii*) Small signal T-equivalent circuit of the transistor is taken.

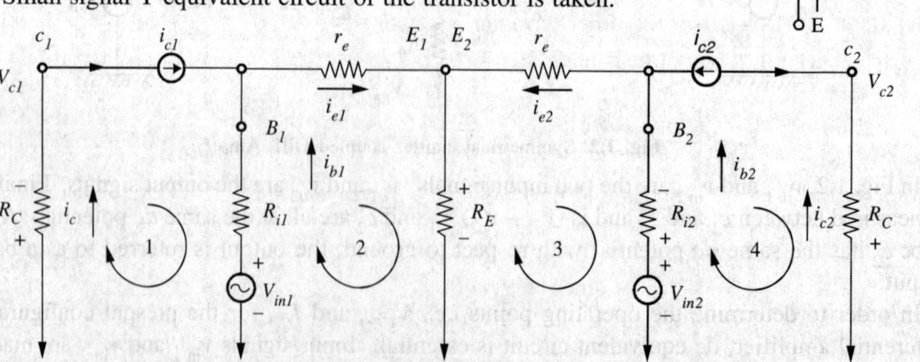

Fig. 1.3. AC equivalent circuit for the DIFF. AMP.

Calculation of Differential Input Resistance (R_{in})

From Fig. 1.3, by applying Kirchhoff's voltage law we get (Assuming $I_{E1} = I_{E2}$, $r_{e1} = r_{e2} = r_e$)
(*re* = *ac* emitter resistance. *gm* = transconductance).

$$R_{i1}\, i_{b1} + r_e\, i_{e1} + R_E(i_{e1} + i_{e2}) - V_{\text{in }1} = 0 \qquad \text{...(1.6.1)}$$
$$R_{i2}\, i_{b2} + r_e\, i_{e2} + R_E(i_{e1} + i_{e2}) - V_{\text{in }2} = 0 \qquad \text{...(1.6.2)}$$

We know that $i_{b1} = i_{e1} / \beta_{ac}$ and $i_{b2} = i_{e2} / \beta_{ac}$

$$R_{i1}\frac{i_{e1}}{\beta_{ac}} + r_e\, i_{e1} + R_E(i_{e1} + i_{e2}) - V_{\text{in }1} = 0$$

$$R_{i2}\frac{i_{e2}}{\beta_{ac}} + r_e\, i_{e2} + R_E(i_{e1} + i_{e2}) - V_{\text{in }2} = 0$$

As $\frac{R_{i1}}{\beta_{ac}}$ and $\frac{R_{i2}}{\beta_{ac}}$ are very small and hence can be neglected.

$$\therefore \quad V_{\text{in }1} = R_E i_{e2} + (r_e + R_E) i_{e1} \qquad \text{...(1.6.3)}$$
$$V_{\text{in }2} = R_E i_{e1} + (r_e + R_E) i_{e2} \qquad \text{...(1.6.4)}$$

We can express in determinant form like this

$$\begin{bmatrix} R_E + r_e & R_E \\ R_E & r_e + R_E \end{bmatrix} \begin{bmatrix} i_{e1} \\ i_{e2} \end{bmatrix} = \begin{bmatrix} V_{\text{in }1} \\ V_{\text{in }2} \end{bmatrix}$$

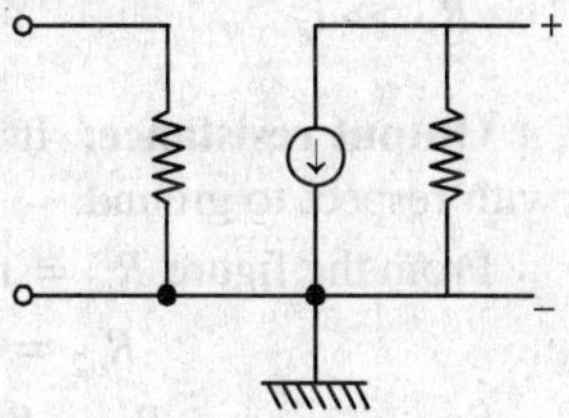

small-signal model (π model)

Let
$$\Delta = \begin{vmatrix} R_E + r_e & R_E \\ R_E & r_e + R_E \end{vmatrix}$$

Hence
$$i_{e1} = \frac{\begin{bmatrix} V_{\text{in }1} & R_E \\ V_{\text{in }2} & r_e + R_E \end{bmatrix}}{\Delta} = \frac{V_{\text{in }1}\,(r_e + R_E) - V_{\text{in }2}\, R_E}{(r_e + R_E)^2 - (R_E)^2} \qquad \text{...(1.6.5)}$$

and
$$i_{e2} = \frac{\begin{bmatrix} r_e + R_E & V_{\text{in }1} \\ R_E & V_{\text{in }2} \end{bmatrix}}{\Delta} = \frac{V_{\text{in }2}\,(r_e + R_E) - V_{\text{in }1}\, R_E}{(r_e + R_E)^2 - (R_E)^2} \qquad \text{...(1.6.6)}$$

Calculation of input impedances

Let us define the differential input resistance. It is the equivalent resistance which is measured at either input terminal when the other terminal is grounded.

So R_{in1} = Differential input resistance seen from the input signal source V_{in1}.

$$\therefore \quad R_{in1} = \left|\frac{V_{\text{in }1}}{i_{b1}}\right|_{V_{\text{in }2} = 0} = \left|\frac{V_{\text{in }1}}{i_{e1} / \beta_{ac}}\right|_{V_{\text{in }2} = 0} \qquad \text{Since } i_{b1} = \frac{i_{e1}}{\beta_{ac}}$$

Putting the value of i_{e1} from Eqn. (1.6.5) we get

$$R_{\text{in }1} = \frac{\beta_{ac}\, V_{\text{in }1}}{\dfrac{V_{\text{in }1}\,(R_E + r_e)}{(R_E + r_e)^2 - R_E^2}} \qquad \text{since } V_{\text{in }2} = 0$$

$$\therefore \quad R_{\text{in }1} = \frac{\beta_{ac}\, V_{\text{in }1}\,\{(R_E + r_e)^2 - R_E^2\}}{V_{\text{in }1}\,(R_E + r_e)}$$

$$= \beta_{ac}\left\{\frac{R_E^2 + 2\,R_E\, r_e + r_e^2 - R_E^2}{R_E + r_e}\right\}$$

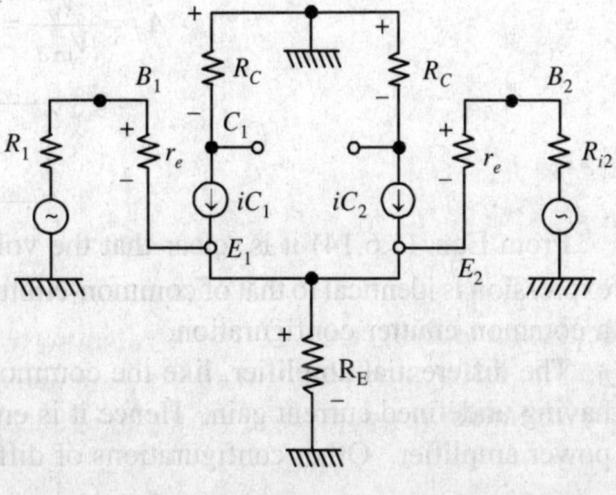

$$= \frac{\beta_{ac}\,(2R_E + r_e)r_e}{r_e + R_E} \quad ...(1.6.7)$$

Normally it is seen that $R_E >> r_e$. So $2R_E + r_e \cong 2R_E$ and $r_e + R_E \cong R_E$.

Eqn. (1.6.7) reduces to $R_{\text{in }1} = \dfrac{2\beta_{ac}\, r_e\, R_E}{R_E}$

$$\therefore \quad \boxed{R_{\text{in }1} = 2\beta_{ac}\, r_e} \quad ...(1.6.8)$$

In the same way $\quad R_{\text{in }2} = \left|\dfrac{V_{\text{in }2}}{i_{b2}}\right|_{V_{\text{in }1}=0} = \left|\dfrac{V_{\text{in }2}\,\beta_{ac}}{i_{e2}}\right|_{V_{\text{in }1}=0}$

Taking the values of i_{e2} we get from Eqn. (1.6.6) and assuming

$$R_E >> r_e \qquad \boxed{R_{\text{in }2} = 2\beta_{ac}\, r_e} \quad ...(1.6.9)$$

Output resistance: It is the equivalent resistance which is measured at either output terminal with respect to ground.

From the figure R_{o1} = resistance between the collector C_1 and ground = R_c

R_{o2} = resistance between the collector C_2 and ground = R_c

So $\quad R_{o1} = R_{o2} = R_c$

Voltage gain: The differential voltage gain $A_d = \dfrac{V_o}{V_{\text{in }d}}$ ...(1.6.10)

where $V_{\text{in }d}$ = difference in the input signals.

$$\therefore \quad \boxed{v_0 = i_{c1}\,R_c - i_{c2}\,R_c} \quad ...(1.6.11)$$

$$= R_c\,(i_{c1} - i_{c2}) \text{ as } i_e \cong i_c$$

$$= R_c\,(i_{e1} - i_{e2}) \quad ...(1.6.12)$$

Putting the values of i_{e1} and i_{e2} from Eqns. (1.6.5) & (1.6.6) in Eqn. (1.6.12) we get

$$V_o = \frac{(r_e + 2R_E)(V_{\text{in }1} - V_{\text{in }2})}{r_e\,(r_e + 2R_E)} \cdot R_c$$

$$= \frac{R_c}{r_e}(V_{\text{in }1} - V_{\text{in }2}) \quad ...(1.6.13)$$

$$\therefore \quad A_d = \frac{V_o}{V_{\text{in }d}} = \frac{\frac{R_c}{r_e}(V_{\text{in }1} - V_{\text{in }2})}{V_{\text{in }1} - V_{\text{in }2}} = \frac{R_c}{r_e}$$

$$\therefore \quad \boxed{A_d = \frac{R_c}{r_e}} \quad ...(1.6.14)$$

From Eqn. (1.6.14) it is clear that the voltage gain is independent of R_E. Moreover the gain expression is identical to that of common-emitter amplifier. This is because the DIFF. AMP. employs a common-emitter configuration.

The differential amplifier, like the common-emitter amplifier, is a small signal amplifier. It is having undefined current gain. Hence it is employed as a voltage amplifier but not as a current or power amplifier. Other configurations of differential amplifiers are

(1) Dual input, unbalanced output Differential Amplifier:

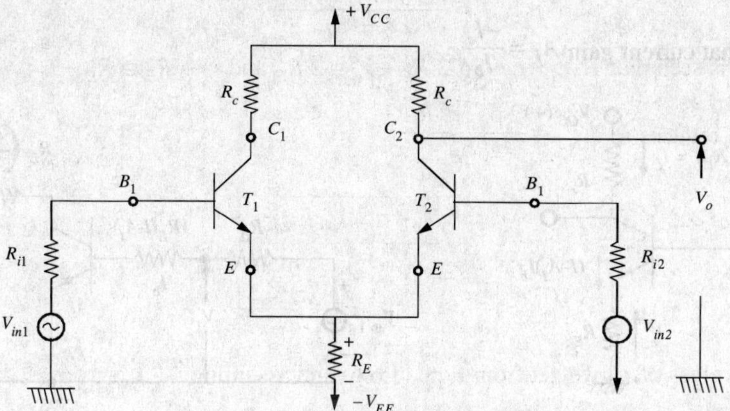

Fig. 1.4. Dual-input, unbalanced output DIFF. AMP.

(2) Single input, balanced output Differential Amplifier.

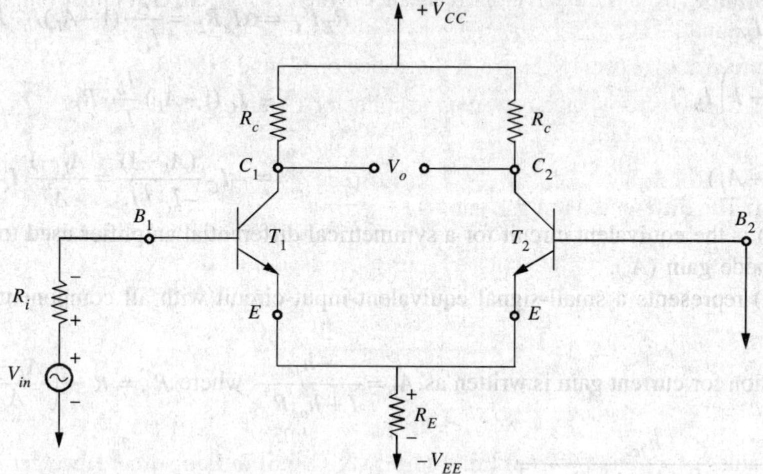

Fig. 1.5.

(3) Single input, unbalanced output Differential Amplifier.

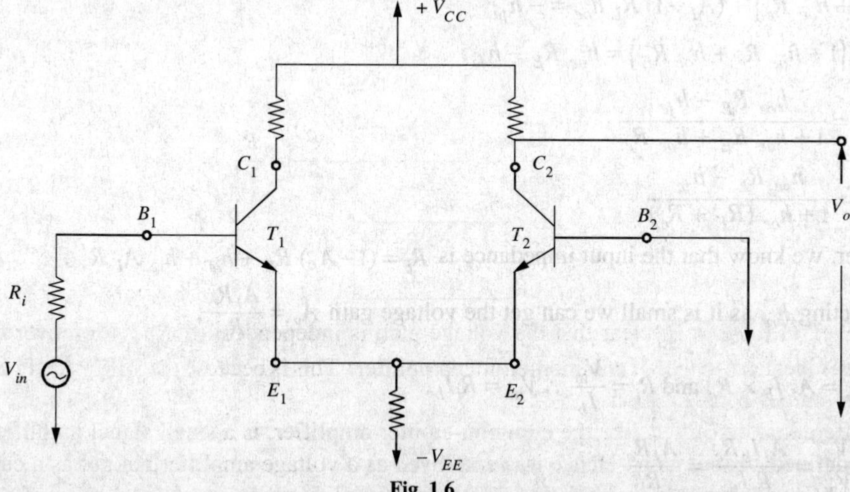

Fig. 1.6.

Calculation of A_c & CMRR

We know that current gain $A_I = \dfrac{-I_e}{I_b}$

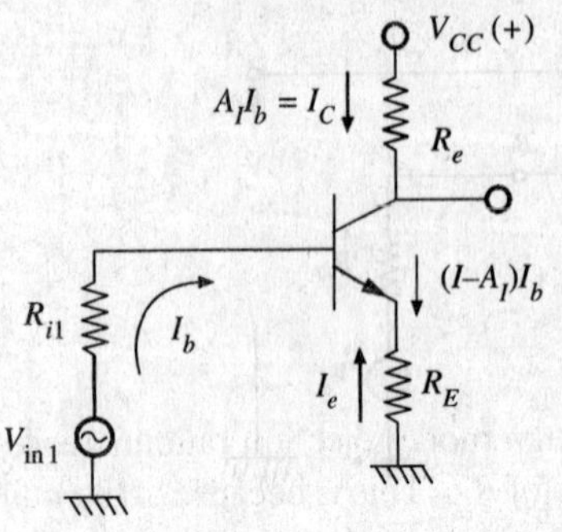

Fig. 1.6(*a*)

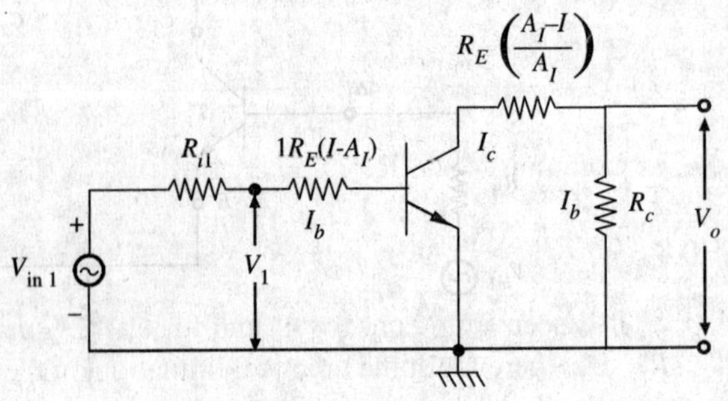

Fig. 1.6(*b*) Small signal equivalent ckt.

$$\therefore I_e = I_c + I_b$$

$$= \left(\frac{I_c}{I_b} + I\right) I_b$$

$$= I_b\,(I - A_I)$$

$$R_E I'_C = \alpha I_e R_E = \frac{I_C}{I_C} \cdot (1 - A_I) I_b \cdot R_E$$

$$= I_C (1 - A_I) \frac{I_b}{I_e} \cdot R_E$$

$$= -I_C \frac{(A_I - 1)}{-I_C / I_b} = \frac{A_I - 1}{A_t} I_C$$

Fig. 1.6.*x*(*a*) is the equivalent circuit for a symmetrical differential amplifier used to determine the common mode gain (A_c).

Fig. 1.6.*x*(*b*) represents a small-signal equivalent input circuit with all components reflected into the base.

The expression for current gain is written as $A_I = \dfrac{-h_{fe}}{I + h_{oe} R'_c}$ where $R'_c = R_c + \left(\dfrac{A_I - I}{A_I}\right) R_E$

$$\text{So } A_I = -\frac{h_{fe}}{1 + h_{oe}\left[R_c + \dfrac{A_I - 1}{A_I} R_E\right]}$$

$$A_I\,\{1 + h_{oe}\,R_c\} + (A_I - 1)\,R_E\,h_{oe} = -\,h_{fe}$$

$$\text{or } A_I\,\{1 + h_{oe}\,R_c + h_{oe}\,R_E\} = h_{oe}\,R_E - h_{fe}.$$

$$\text{or } A_I = \frac{h_{oe}\,R_E - h_{fe}}{1 + h_{oe}\,R_E + h_{oe}\,R_c}$$

$$= \frac{h_{oe}\,R_E - h_{fe}}{1 + h_{oe}\,(R_E + R_c)}$$

Further, we know that the input impedance is $R_i = (1 - A_I)\,R_E + h_{ie} + h_{re}\,A_I\,R'_c$.

Neglecting h_{re} as it is small we can get the voltage gain $A_v = \dfrac{A_I R_c}{R_i}$.

For $V_o = A_I\,I_b \times R_c$ and $R_i = \dfrac{V_{in}}{I_b}$ $\therefore V_{in} = R_i I_b$.

$$A_v = \frac{V_o}{V_{in}} = \frac{A_I I_b R_c}{R_i I_b} = \frac{A_I R_c}{R_i}$$

If $V_{in\,1} = V_{in\,2} = V_{in}$. So, $V_d = O$ hence $A_d = 0$.

$\therefore$ [Neglecting h_{re}] and including R_{in}.

So, $A_c = \dfrac{A_I R_c}{R_i}$.

$$A_c = \frac{\left(2 R_E\, h_{oe} - h_{fe}\right) R_c}{2 R_E (I + h_{fe}) + (R_s + h_{ie})(2 R_E h_{oe} + 1)} \qquad \ldots 1.6.15$$

Common Mode Rejection Ratio (ρ) CMRR:—

$$CMRR = \frac{A_d}{A_c} = \frac{R_c}{r_e} \times \frac{2 R_E\,(I + h_{fe}) + (R_{in} + h_{ie})(2 h_{oe}\, R_E + 1)}{(2 h_{oe}\, R_E - h_{fe})\, R_c} \qquad \ldots 1.6.16$$

It is seen from eqn. for A_c and for $CMMR$ that the common mode rejection ratio increases with R_E. But there are some practical limitation on the magnitude of R_E. This is because of the quiescent dc voltage drop across it by the quiescent current at its proper valuc, when the emitter supply V_{EE} must become larger if R_E is increased. Again in case the operating currents of the transistors are allowed to decrease, h_{ie} will increase and β will decrease. From the equation it is clear that both of these effects will tend to decrease the CMRR. Hence the DIFF. AMP. will deviate from ideal one. Solution of such a crucial problem is to replace R_E by a transistor circuit which behaves like a constant current stage, so that quiescent conditions for T_1 and T_2 are kept the same as the original circuit. Operation of such a system is explained in the next article.

1·7. DIFF. AMP. WITH A CONSTANT CURRENT STAGE

Fig. 1.7 represents such an arrangement.

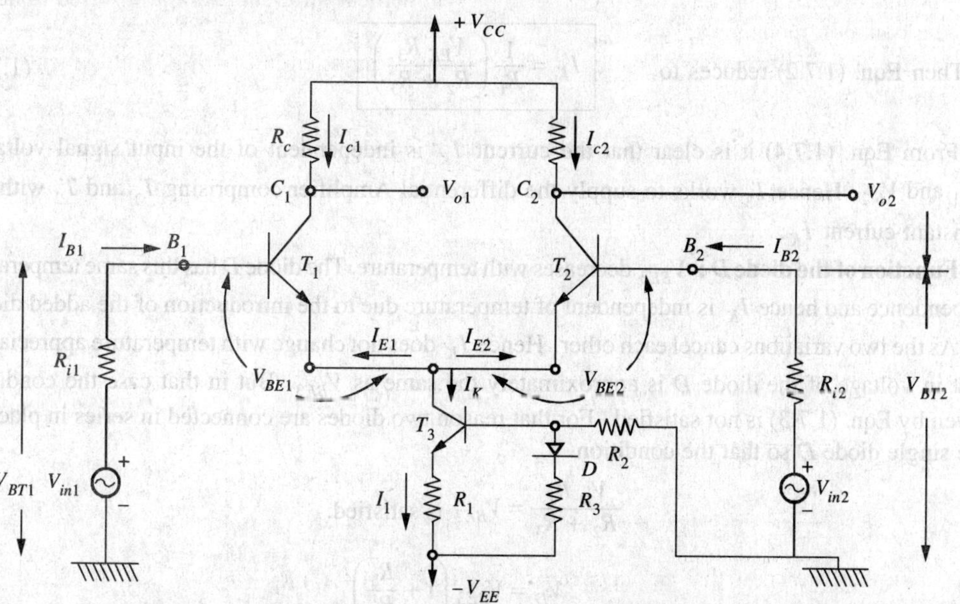

Fig. 1.7. DIFF. AMP. with a constant current stage.

The above arrangement provides a very high effective emitter resistance R_E for the two transistors T_1 and T_2. R_E is also the effective resistance looking into the collector of transistor T_3, it can be written as $R_o = \dfrac{1}{h_{oe}} \cdot \dfrac{(1+\beta)\, R_E + (R_{i1} + h_{ie})(1 + h_{oe}\, R_E)}{R_E + R_{i1} + h_{ie} - h_{re}\, \beta / h_{oe}}$. (Assuming that $R_{i1} = R_{i2}$).

$$R_o \text{ or } \frac{1+\beta}{h_{oe}} + \frac{(R_{i1}+h_{ie})(1+h_{oe}\,R_E)}{h_{oe}\,R_E}$$

$$\cong \frac{1}{h_{ob}} + (R_{i1}+h_{ie})\left(1+\frac{1}{h_{oe}\,R_E}\right) \text{ for } R_E >> R_{i1}+h_{ie}; h_{fe}=\beta.$$

R_{i1} = Source resistance, $h \rightarrow$ transistor's hybrid parameters.

Now if $R_E = R_{i1} = 1\,\text{K}$ (say), and put the hybrid parameters from the table 1 it is seen that $R_o = 817$ K. This indicates that with small value of R_1 we can get high effective value of R_E.

Now we are to show that the transistor T_3 operates as an approximately constant current source, subject to the condition that the current flowing through the base of T_3 is negligibly small. Otherwise, the change in current value will produce change in $V_{CE}Q$ and I_{ces}.

With the application of Kirchhoff's voltage law to the base circuit of T_3 it can be seen

$$I_1\,R_1 + V_{BE3} = V_D + (V_{EE} - V_D)\frac{R_3}{R_3+R_2} \quad \text{...(1.7.1)}$$

where V_D represents diode voltage.

If the current in the base of T_3 is negligible then $I_K = I_1$ (*i.e.*, $I_E = I_c$)

$$I_K = I_1 = \frac{1}{R_1}\left(\frac{V_{EE}\,R_3}{R_2+R_3} + \frac{V_D\,R_2}{R_2+R_3} - V_{BE3}\right) \quad \text{...(1.7.2)}$$

Now parameters of the circuit are chosen such that

$$\frac{V_D\,R_2}{R_2+R_3} = V_{BE3} \quad \text{...(1.7.3)}$$

Then Eqn. (1.7.2) reduces to

$$\boxed{I_K = \frac{1}{R_1}\left(\frac{V_{EE}\,R_3}{R_2+R_3}\right)} \quad \text{...(1.7.4)}$$

From Eqn. (1.7.4) it is clear that the current I_K is independent of the input signal voltages V_{in1} and V_{in2}. Hence T_3 works to supply the differential Amplifier comprising T_1 and T_2 with the constant current I_K.

Function of the diode *D*: V_{BE3} decreases with temperature. The diode D has this same temperature dependence and hence I_K is independent of temperature due to the introduction of the added diode.

As the two variations cancel each other. Hence I_K does not change with temperature appreciably. Cut in voltage of the diode D is approximately the same as V_{BE3}. But in that case the condition given by Eqn. (1.7.3) is not satisfied. For that reason two diodes are connected in series in place of the single diode D so that the condition

$$\frac{V_D\,R_2}{R_2+R_3} = V_{BE3} \text{ is satisfied.}$$

$$V_D = V_{BE3}\left(1+\frac{R_3}{R_2}\right)$$

Here although we have considered that T_1 and T_2 are identical. Also T_3 is a true constant current source. Under that ideal condition, $A_c = 0$, $V_{\text{in}\,1} = V_{\text{in}\,2} = V_{\text{in}}$. Then as *it* is a symmetric circuit $I_{c1} = I_{c2}$. As the total current increase $I_{c1} + I_{c2} = 0$ if I_g = constant, so $I_{c1} = I_{c2} = 0$.

$$A_c = \frac{V_{o2}}{V_{\text{in}}} = \frac{-I_{c2}\ R_c}{V_{\text{in}}} = 0.$$

DIFF. AMP can be cascaded to get large amplifications for the difference signal.

1·8. TRANSFER CHARACTERISTICS OF THE BASIC DIFF. AMP.

In order to realize the advantages as well as the limitations of DIFF. AMP it is better to examine the transfer characteristics of the DIFF. AMP. It is the plot of the collector current ($I_{c1} = I_{c2} = I_c$) versus the difference of the voltages between the bases of T_1 and T_2 of Fig. 1.7.

When the base voltage of transistor T_1 is below the cut off value of T_1, all the current I_K will flow through T_2. As base voltage increases and goes above the cut off value, the current in T_1 increases. But, on the other hand, the current in T_2 decreases, and the sum total of the currents in the two transistors is equal to I_K. If the output can follow the input over the range ΔV_o.

Then
$$\Delta V_o = R_c\ I_K$$

Now from Fig. 1.7, we can write

$$I_{E2} + I_{E1} = -I_K \text{ and } V_{B1} - V_{B2} = V_{BE1} - V_{BE2}$$

$$I_E = I_{EM}\ e^{eV_{BE}/k_BT} \qquad \text{...(1.8.1.)}$$

where k_B = Boltzman's constant, I_{EM} is expressed in terms of E bers-Mol parameters.

$$I_{E1} = I_{EM}\ e^{VB1/V_T},\ I_{E2} = I_{EM}\ e^{VB_2/V_T} \text{ As } I_{E1} + I_{E2} = -I_K$$

$$\therefore I_{EM}\,(e^{V_{B1}/V_T} + e^{V_{B2}/V_T}) = -I_K \ \therefore I_{EM} = \frac{-I_K}{e^{V_{B1}/V_T} + e^{V_{B2}/V_T}}$$

$$I_{C_1} = -I_{E_1} = -I_{EM_c}\ V_{B_1}/V_T = \frac{I_K\ e^{V_{B_1}/V_T}}{e^{V_B/V_T}\left[1 + e^{(V_{B_2} - V_{B_1})/V_T}\right]}$$

$$I_{C_1} = -I_{E_1} = \frac{I_K}{1 + \exp\left(V_{B_2} - V_{B_1}\right)/V_T}$$

As T_1 and T_2 are matched transistors, so we can write

$$I_{c1} \cong -I_{E1} = \frac{I_K}{1 + \exp\{-(V_{B1} - V_{B2})\,e/k_BT\}} \qquad \text{...(1.8.2)}$$

and
$$I_{c2} \cong -I_{E2} = \frac{I_K}{1 + \exp\{-e(V_{B2} - V_{B1})/k_BT\}} \qquad \text{...(1.8.3)}$$

$$I_{c1}/I_K = \frac{1}{1 + \exp\{-V_{\text{ind}}/V_T\}}$$

where $V_{\text{ind}} = V_{B1} - V_{B2},\ \frac{k_BT}{e} = V_T$ and ...(1.8.4)

$$I_{c2}/I_K = \frac{1}{1 + e^{V_{\text{ind}}/V_T}}$$

The transfer characteristics for I_{c1}/I_K. Vs. = V_{ind} and I_{c2}/I_K. Vs. V_{ind} are plotted in Fig. 1.8.

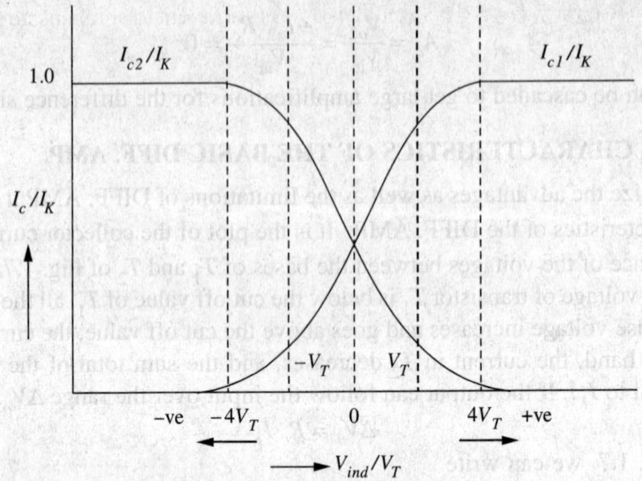

Fig. 1.8. Transfer characteristic of Diff. Amp.

The transconductance g_{md} of the differential amplifier in respect to the differential input voltage is obtained by differentiating I_{c1} with respect to $V_{in\,d}$.

$$g_{md} = \frac{dI_{c1}}{dV_{ind}} = \frac{I_K}{V_T}\,\frac{e^{-V_{ind}/V_T}}{(1+e^{-V_{ind}/V_T})^2} \quad ...(1.8.5)$$

If $$V_{ind} = 0 \text{ i.e., } V_{B_1} = V_{B_2}$$

$$g_{md} = \frac{I_K}{V_T}\cdot\frac{1}{4} = \frac{I_K}{4\,V_T} \quad ...(1.8.6)$$

Let us now comment about the characteristic.

1. Within the range of $V_{ind} = \pm V_T$, the DIFF. AMP shows a linear variation between the normalized collector current and differential input voltage V_{ind}.
2. When V_{ind} exceeds $\pm 4V_T$, very little further variation (increase) in the output is possible. Hence DIFF. AMP is a very good limiter.
3. The slope of the curves determines the transconductance. Hence from the curves it is clear that g_{md} starts its variation from zero, reaches a maximum of $I_K / 4V_T$ at $I_{c1} = I_{c2} = \frac{1}{2}I_K$. Thereafter it again reaches to null value.
4. The value of g_{md} is a linear function of I_K. This is because the output voltage change is expressed as $= g_{md}\ R_c\ (V_{ind})$. ...(1.8.7)
5. The differential gain can be changed by varying the value of the current I_K. Hence automatic gain control is possible with the DIFF. AMP.

1. Balanced differential amplifier

It is expected that transistors (T_1 & T_2) are to be identical in all respects. But in majority of times this is not the case. The transistors have different characteristics and as such they have different emitter currents $\left(I_{EQ_1} \neq I_{EQ_2}\right)$. So the differential amplifier will lose its balancing. To restore the balance, a small resistor ($R_B \cong 100\Omega$) is connected between the emitters of the transistors and the resistor is set such that $I_{EQ_1} = I_{EQ_2}$. This small resistor is sufficient to compensate for wide differences between h_{fe_1} and h_{fe_2}.

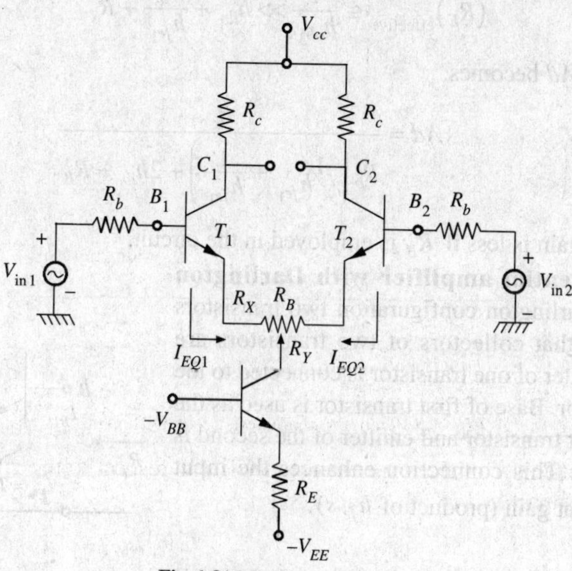

Fig. 1.8(*a*) Balance control.

At balance condition it is expected that there will be the same voltage when taken around the base-emitter loop of either T_1 or T_2 provided $V_{in_1} = V_{in_2} = 0$.

Thus we can write:

$$\left(\frac{R_b}{h_{fe_1}} + R_x\right) I_{EQ_1} + V_{BE_1} = \left(\frac{R_b}{h_{fe_2}} + R_y\right) I_{EQ_2} + V_{BE_2} \qquad \ldots(1.1)$$

when $\qquad V_{BE_1} = V_{BE_2}$, then $I_{EQ_1} = I_{EQ_2}$.

So the equation 1.1 reduces to

$$\frac{R_b}{h_{fe_1}} + R_x = \frac{R_b}{h_{fe_2}} + R_y$$

$$\therefore \qquad R_y - R_x = R_b\left(\frac{1}{h_{fe_1}} - \frac{1}{h_{fe_2}}\right) \qquad \ldots(1.2)$$

As $R_x + R_y = R_B$, the balance is attained when

$$R_y = \frac{R_B}{2} + \frac{R_b}{2}\left(\frac{1}{h_{fe_1}} - \frac{1}{h_{fe_2}}\right) \qquad \ldots(1.3)$$

and

$$R_x = \frac{R_B}{2} - \frac{R_b}{2}\left(\frac{1}{h_{fe_1}} - \frac{1}{h_{fe_2}}\right). \qquad \ldots(1.4)$$

Problem. Find the balancing resistors when $h_{fe1} = 60$ and $h_{fe2} = 180$, $R_B = 2 \cdot 2K$, (range of R_B & R_x and R_y are to be calculated).

Loss of current gain due to balancing: When we include the balancing resistor it ensures the symmetrical operation of the differential amplifier but it results a loss in current gain.

When the balancing resistor ($R_B = R_x + R_y$) is adjusted for balance and the effective emitter resistor is very large,

$$(R_E)_{\text{effective}} \cong \frac{1}{h_{ob_3}} >> h_{ib_1} + \frac{R_b}{h_{fe_1}} + R_x$$

Under this condition Ad becomes:

$$Ad = \frac{R_c}{R_b\left(\frac{1}{h_{fe_1}} + \frac{1}{h_{fe_1}}\right) + 2h_{ib} + R_B}$$

This ensures that gain is less if R_B is employed in the circuit.

Problem. Differential amplifier with Darlington configuration: In Darlington configuration two transistors are connected such that collectors of two transistors are twisted together, emitter of one transistor is connected to the base of other transistor. Base of first transistor is used as the base of the equivalent transistor and emitter of the second is taken as the emitter. This connection enhances the input impedance and current gain (product of h_{fe} s).

Fig. 1.8(*b*)

This current gain

$$A_I = \frac{I_c}{I_{B_1}} = \frac{I_{c1} + I_{c2}}{I_{B_1}}$$

$$= \frac{\alpha\, I_{E_1}}{I_{B_1}} + \frac{\alpha\, I_{E_2}}{I_{B_1}}. \qquad (\alpha\text{s's are taken as the same})$$

$$\frac{I_{E_2}}{I_{B_1}} = \frac{I_{E_2}}{I_{B_2}} \times \frac{I_{B_2}}{I_{E_1}} \times \frac{I_{E_1}}{I_{B_1}} = (h_{fe} + 1) \times 1 \times (h_{fe} + 1)$$

$$= \left(h_{fe} + 1\right)^2 \qquad [h_{fe}\text{'s are taken same for both } T_1 \;\&\; T_2]$$

Similarly

$$\frac{I_{E_1}}{I_{B_1}} = \left(h_{fe} + 1\right)$$

$\therefore$

$$A_I = \frac{\alpha\, I_{E_1}}{I_{B_1}} + \frac{\alpha\, I_{E_2}}{I_{B_1}} = \alpha\,(h_{fe} + 1) + \alpha\,(h_{fe} + 1)^2$$

$$= \alpha\left(h_{fe} + 1\right)^2 + \alpha\left(h_{fe} + 1\right) = \alpha\left(h_{fe} + 1\right)\left\{h_{fe} + 2\right\}$$

$$\boxed{A_I \cong \alpha\, h_{fe}^2.} \qquad [\text{as } h_{fe} >> 1 \text{ or } 2]$$

Input impedance: From the above figure,

$$R_i = h_{ie_1} + \left(h_{fe} + 1\right) h_{ie_2}$$

But

$$h_{ie} = \left(h_{fe} + 1\right) V_T / I_{EQ}$$

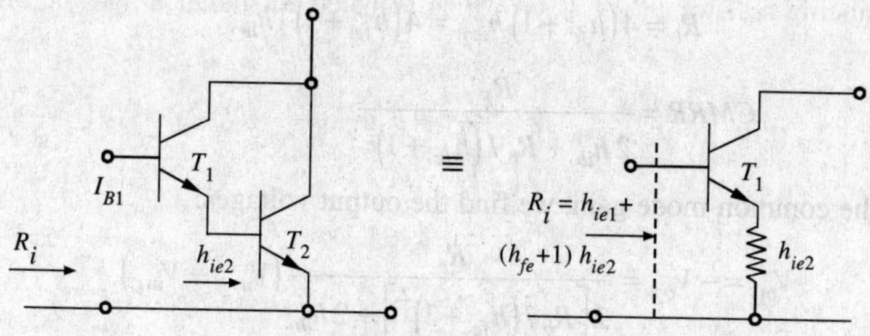

Fig. 1.8(*c*)

$$\therefore \qquad R_i = \frac{(h_{fe}+1)V_T}{I_{EQ_1}} + \frac{(h_{fe}+1)^2}{I_{EQ_2}} V_T.$$

(Assumed $h_{fe_1} = h_{fe_2}$)

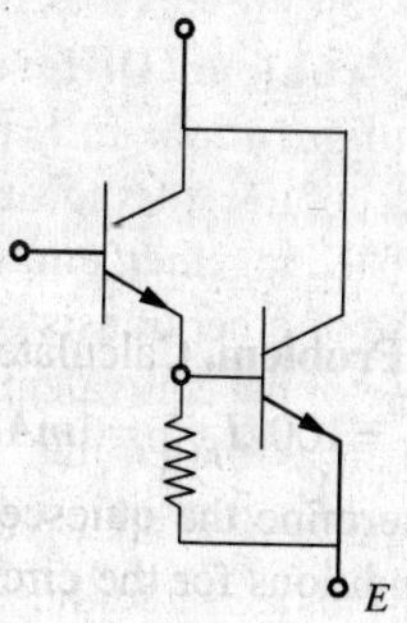

But
$$I_{EQ_1} = \frac{I_{EQ2}}{h_{fe}+1} \text{ As } I_{E_1} = I_{B_2}.$$

$$R_i = \frac{(h_{fe}+1)^2 V_T}{I_{EQ_2}} + \frac{(1+h_{fe})^2 V_T}{I_{EQ_2}}$$

$$= \frac{2(h_{fe}+1)^2 V_T}{I_{EQ2}}$$

$$= 2(h_{fe}+1) . \left\{ \frac{(h_{fe}+1) V_T}{I_{EQ_2}} \right\}$$

Fig. 1.8(*d*)

Then
$$R_i = 2\left(h_{fe}+1\right) h_{ie_2}$$

It can be concluded that the input impedance is enhanced.

Now, let us go to our original problem of differential amplifier (as shown in the following figure).

The differential input impedance between the bases of T_1 and T_4 is

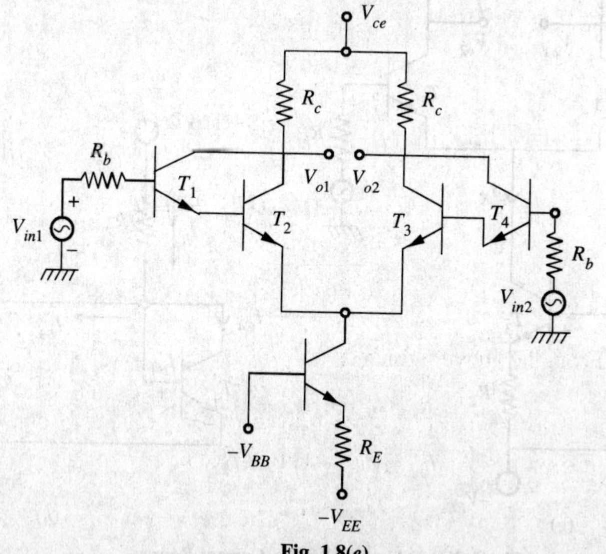

Fig. 1.8(*e*)

$$R_i = 4(h_{fe}+1)\,h_{ie_2} = 4(h_{fe}+1)^2\,h_{ib_2}.$$

$$CMRR = \frac{R_E}{2h_{ib} + R_b/(h_{fe}+1)^2}$$

If we neglect the common mode gain, we find the output voltages:

$$V_{o_1} = -V_{o_2} = \frac{R_c}{2\left[R_b/(h_{fe}+1)^2\right] + 2h_{ib}}\left(V_{in_2} - V_{in_1}\right)$$

Problem. Calculate R_i if $h_{fe} = 100$, $I_{EQ_2} = 1mA$ and also determine the quiescent operating conditions for the circuit given.

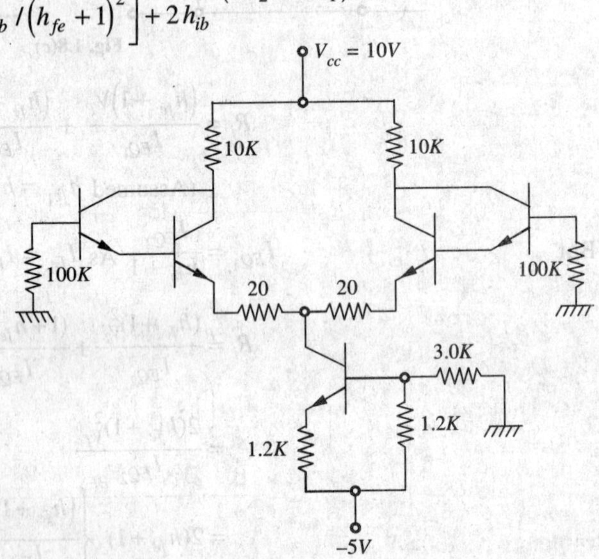

Fig. 1.8(*f*)

Differential Amplifier using a Widlar Current Source.

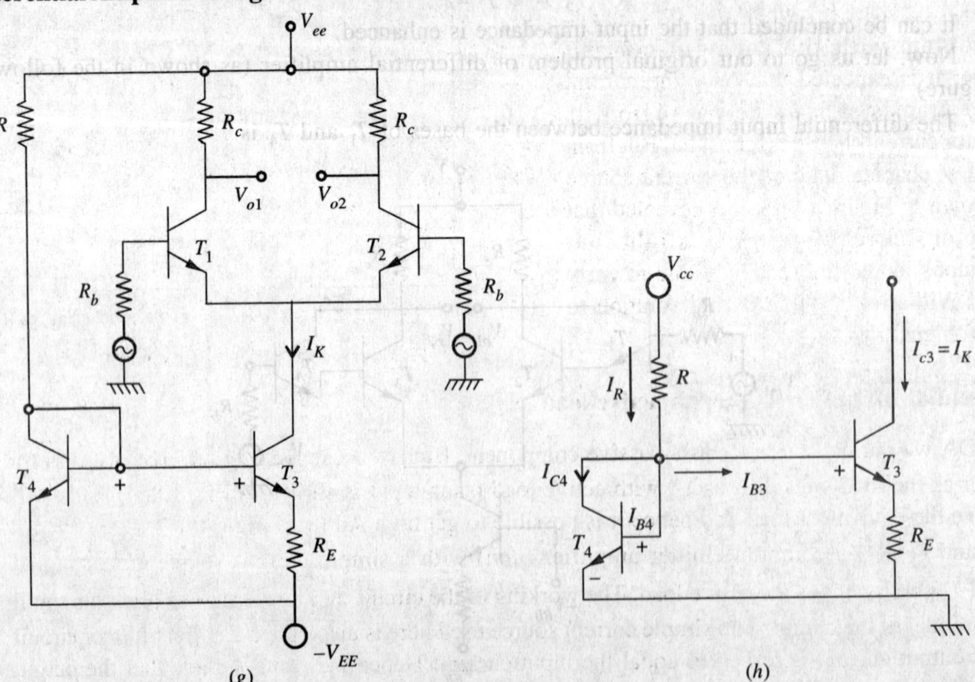

Fig. 1.8(*g*) DA using Widlar Current Source.

A differential amplifier is normally fabricated by integrated circuit. In integrated circuit, realisation of too large resistance is difficult. To get low resistance for low-valued current sources, the modified circuit is first proposed by Widlar and called Widlar Current Source (as shown in Figure 1.8(*g*). Let us make an analysis of such a circuit. To determine the circuit parameter let us analyse the circuit separately.

From Figure 1.8(*h*) using *KVL* we get.

$$V_{BE_4} = V_{BE_3} + \left(I_{B_3} + I_{C_3}\right) R_E \qquad \text{...1.8g.1}$$

$$\frac{I_{C_4}}{I_{C_3}} = e^{\left(V_{BE_4} - V_{BE_3}\right)/V_T} \qquad I_C = I_{EMe}{}^{V_3/V_T} \qquad \text{...1.8g.2}$$

$$\log c \frac{I_{C4}}{I_{C3}} = \frac{V_{BE4} - V_{BE3}}{V_T}$$

$$R_E = \frac{V_T}{I_{c3}\left(1+\frac{1}{\beta}\right)} \log_e \frac{I_{C_4}}{I_{C_3}} \left(\text{as } I_{B_3} = \frac{I_{C_3}}{\beta}\right) \qquad \text{...1.8g.3}$$

$$\therefore \quad I_R = I_{C_4} + I_{B_4} + I_{B_3} = I_{C_4}\left(1+\frac{1}{\beta}\right) + \frac{I_{C_3}}{\beta}$$

$$= I_{C_4}\left(1+\frac{1}{\beta}\right) \text{ as } I_{C_4} > I_{C_3}.$$

$$\therefore \quad I_{C_4} = \frac{\beta}{\beta+1} \cdot I_R = \frac{\beta}{\beta+1} \cdot \frac{V_{CC} - V_{BE_4}}{R} = \frac{V_{CC} - V_{BE_4}}{R} \text{ as } \beta >> 1.$$

Problem. For a 60μ*A* current source, with $R = 6{\cdot}8K$, $V_{cc} = 15V$, $V_{BE_4} = 0.715V$, and $\beta = 80$. Calculate I_{C_4} and R_E.

Problem with the constant current source: It is expected that once the current source transistor is in active region its collector current should be constant. But from the $I - V$ characteristic of the current source (as shown in Figure 1.8(*i*), it is revealed that collector current shows a slight but continuous increasing tendency due to early effect. Widlar circuit is a partial solution to this problem.

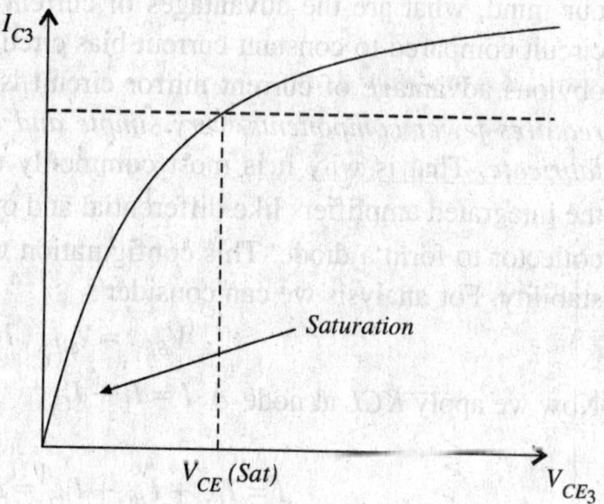

Fig. 1.8(*i*) *I-V* ch. of the current source.

Differential Amplifier (DA) with active load

In DA we normally use R_C as a passive component. But if we use a current source instead of a resistor as the load we call it a DA with active load [such a ckt is shown in Fig. 1.8(*j*)]. This will improve the equivalent load and hence it is possible to get high Ad (*also high Ac*)

T_1 and T_2 act as common emitter amplifier (*npn*) with a simple current source consisting of T_3 and T_4 (both *pnp*) as the active load. The working of the circuit will be clear if we draw the small signal model of the circuit. The simple current source used here is also called a current mirror circuit whose output current is forced to equal the input current. Hence we can conclude that the output current in a current mirror circuit is a mirror image of the input current. Figure 1.8(*i*) represents a current mirror circuit.

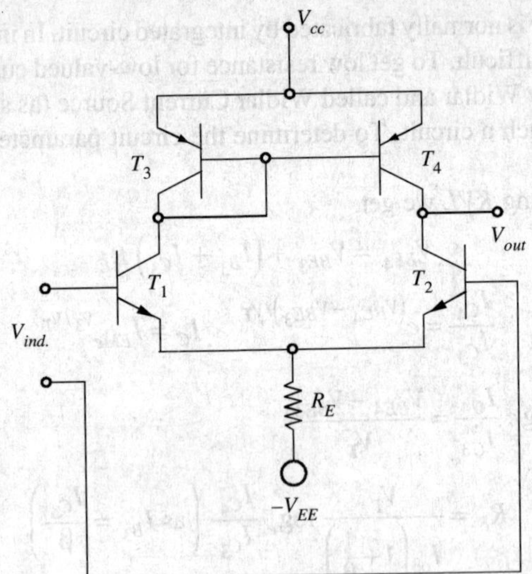

Fig. 1.8(*j*) DA with active load.

In the curcuit, if current I is set up the current I_{C_2} will be automatically adjusted to nearly equal to I. This is why current mirror circuit is also called a special case of constant current bias and therefore can be employed to establish constant emitter currents in different amplifier stages. Then question comes into our mind, what are the advantages of current mirror circuit compared to constant current bias circuit? The obvious advantage of current mirror circuit is that *it requires fewer components, very simple and easy to fabricate*. That is why it is most commonly used in the integrated amplifiers like differential and operational amplifiers. Here base of T_1 is sorted to its collector to form a diode. This configuration will help to get the desired collector current thermal stability. For analysis we can consider

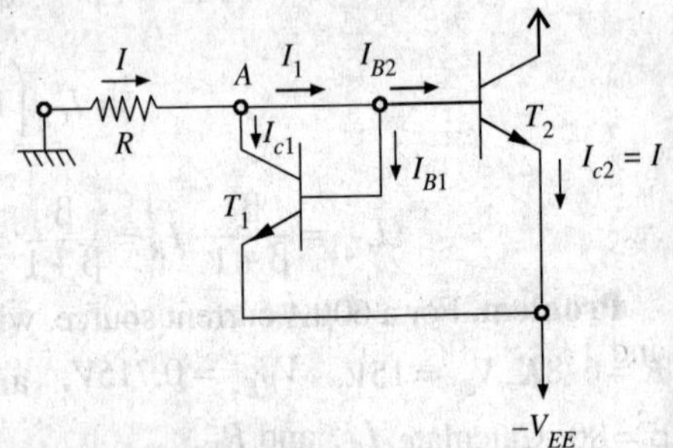

Fig. 1.8(*k*) Current mirror circuit.

$$V_{BE_1} = V_{BE_2},\ I_{B_1} = I_{B_2},\ I_{C_1} = I_{C_2}.$$

Now we apply *KCL* at node $A, I = I_1 + I_{C_1}$

$$\therefore \qquad I = I_{C_1} + I_{B_1} + I_{B_2} = I_{C_2} + 2I_{B_2} = I_{C_2} + 2\left(\frac{I_{C_2}}{\beta_{dc}}\right).$$

$I = I_{C_2}\left(1 + \frac{2}{\beta_{dc}}\right) \cdot \cong I_{C_2}$ (as β_{dc} is much larger. Applying the *KVL* in the base-emitter loop of T_2 we get $-R_I - V_{BE_2} + V_{EE} = 0$. $\therefore I = \dfrac{V_{EE} - V_{BE_2}}{R}$. The proper adjustment of R will give a good current mirror circuit. Note that for current mirror circuit transistors should be identical.

1·9. DIFFERENTIAL AMPLIFIER WITH JFET

Figure 1·9 represents a JFET differential amplifier with Zener constant current source.

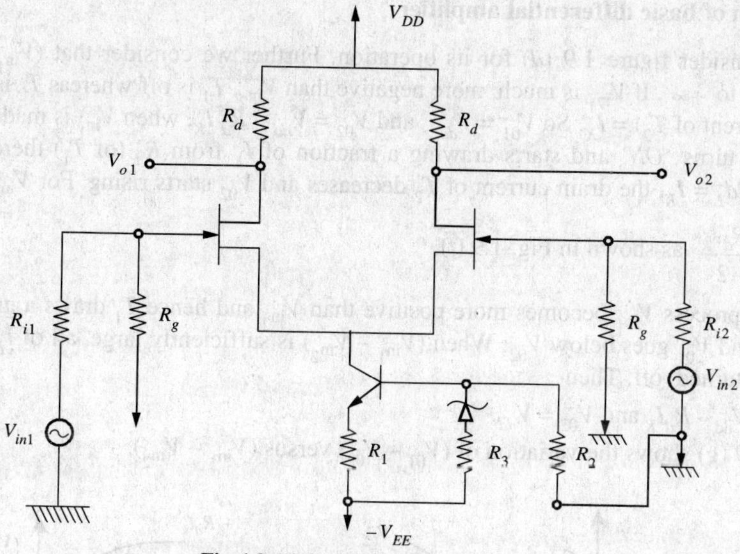

Fig. 1.9. JFET DIFF. AMP.

BJT FET

$$R_c = R_d$$

$$r_e = \frac{1}{g_m}$$

$$A_d = \frac{V_o}{V_{ind}} = \frac{R_d}{1/g_{md}} = g_{md}\, R_d$$

Various configurations of *JFET* based differential amplifiers are shown in Fig. 1.9 (*b*), 1.9 (*c*), and 1.9 (*d*). Fig. 1.9 (*e*) represents the input-output characteristics (common mode).

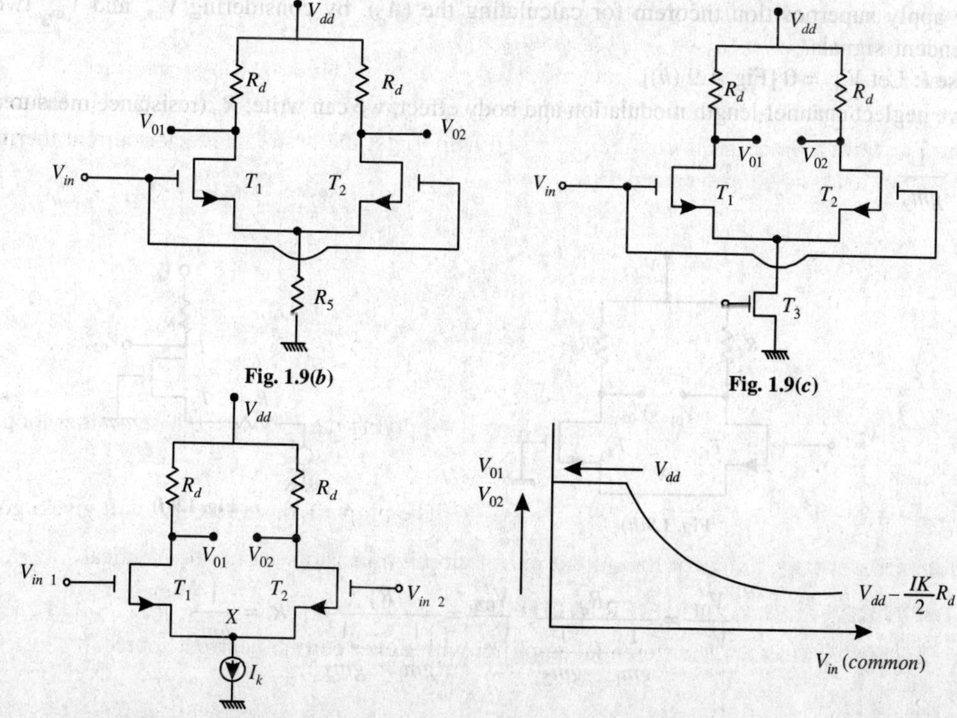

Fig. 1.9(*b*)

Fig. 1.9(*c*)

Fig. 1.9(*d*) Basic differential Amplifier

Fig. 1.9(*e*)

Operation of basic differential amplifier

Let us consider figure 1.9 (*d*) for its operation. Further we consider that $(V_{in_1} - V_{in_2})$ can vary from $-\infty$ to $+\infty$. If V_{in_1} is much more negative than V_{in_2}, T_1 is off whereas T_2 is '*ON*' making Id_2 (drain current of T_2) = I_K. So $V_{01} = V_{dd}$ and $V_{02} = V_{dd} - R_d I_K$, when V_{in_1} is made closer to V_{in_2}, T_1 gradually turns '*ON*' and starts drawing a fraction of I_K from R_d (of T_1) thereby lowering V_{01}. As $Id_1 + Id_2 = I_K$, the drain current of T_2 decreases and V_{02} starts rising. For $V_{in_1} = V_{in_2}$, $V_{01} = V_{02}$ $= V_{dd} - \frac{R_d I_k}{2}$ as shown in Fig. 1.9 (*f*).

In the process V_{in_1} becomes more positive than V_{in_2} and hence T_1 draws a greater current than does T_2 and V_{01} goes below V_{02}. When $(V_{in_1} - V_{in_2})$ is sufficiently large, all of I_K flows through T_1 and T_2 is turned off. Then

$V_{01} = V_{dd} - R_d I_K$ and $V_{02} = V_{dd}$.

Fig 1.9 (*g*) shows the variation of $(V_{01} - V_{02})$ versus $(V_{in_1} - V_{in_2})$.

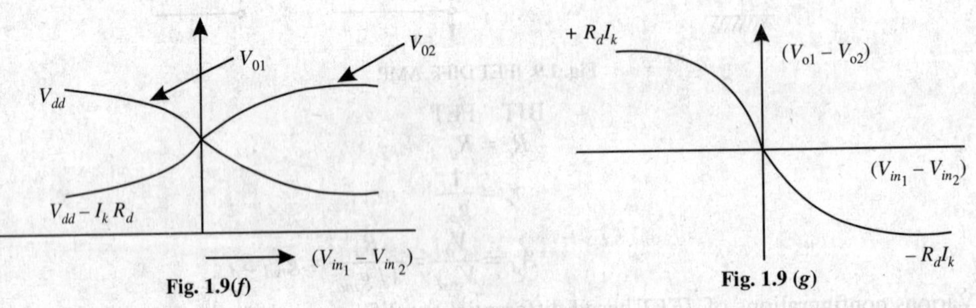

Fig. 1.9(*f*) **Fig. 1.9 (*g*)**

Calculation of differential gain (A_d): [Fig. 1.9 (*d*)].

We apply superposition theorem for calculating the (A_d). by considering V_{in_1} and V_{in_2} two independent signals.

Case *I*: Let $V_{in_2} = 0$ [Fig. 1.9 (*h*)]

If we neglect channel-length modulation and body effect, we can write: R_0 (resistance measured at x) $= \frac{1}{gm_2}$.

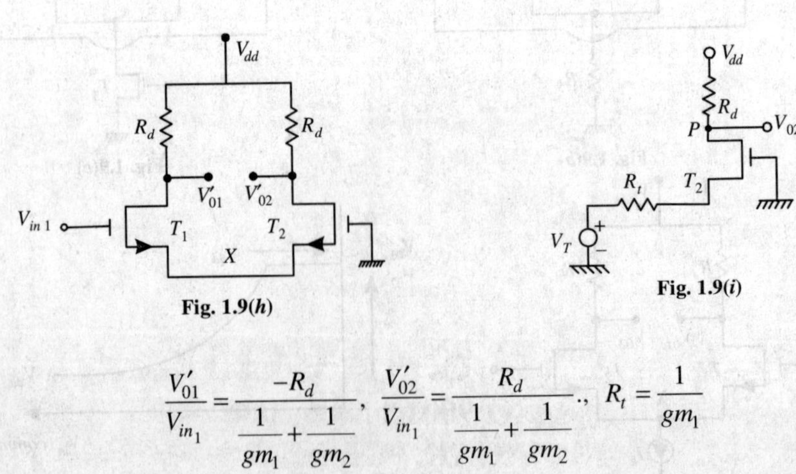

Fig. 1.9(*h*) **Fig. 1.9(*i*)**

$$\frac{V'_{01}}{V_{in_1}} = \frac{-R_d}{\frac{1}{gm_1} + \frac{1}{gm_2}}, \quad \frac{V'_{02}}{V_{in_1}} = \frac{R_d}{\frac{1}{gm_1} + \frac{1}{gm_2}}., \quad R_t = \frac{1}{gm_1}$$

$$V_0' = V_{01}' - V_{02}' = -g_m R_d V_{in_1} . (g_{m1} = g_{m2})$$

Now we make $V_{in_1} = 0$. We will get

$$V_{01}'' - V_{02}'' = g_m R_d V_{in_2}$$

$$\therefore \quad V_0 = (V_{01}' - V_{02}') - (V_{01}'' - V_{02}'') = -g_m R_d . (V_{in_1} - V_{in_2})$$

or

$$\boxed{A_d = \frac{V_0}{V_{in_1} - V_{in_2}} = -g_m R_d}$$

Calculation of common mode gain A_e :
(Ref. Fig. 1.9 *b*, Fig. 1.9 *j* and Fig. 1.9 *k*)

$$A_c = \frac{V_0}{V_{inCom}} = \frac{\frac{R_d}{2}}{\frac{1}{(2g_m)} + R_s}$$

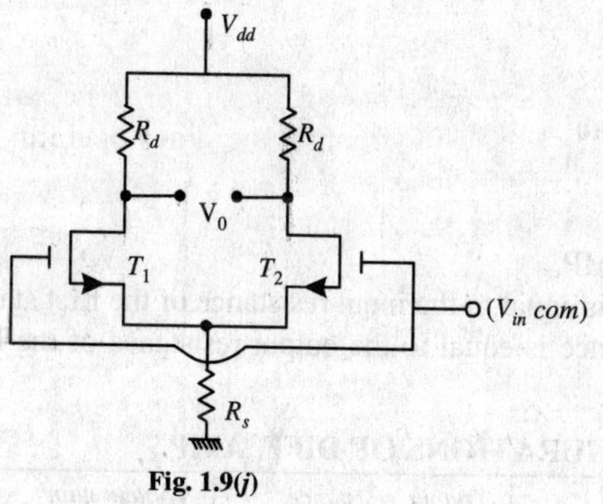

Fig. 1.9(*j*)

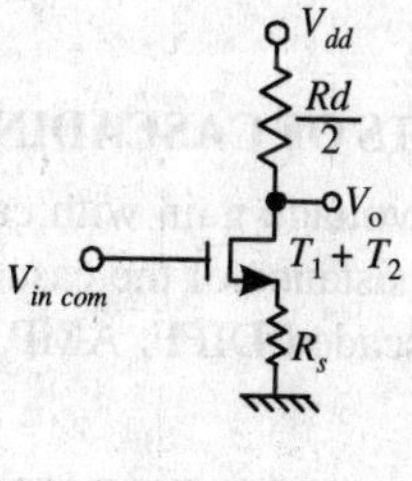

Fig. 1.9(*k*)

CMOS based differential amplifier

The configuration for *CMOS* based differential amplifier is shown in the Fig 1.9 *L*.

The *p mos* transistors provide the opposite inputs, but *n mos* work as the constant current source. Only one output is taken from the common point between V_{in_1}. *n mos* and *p mos* on one side of the circuit. This type of differential amplifier is suitable for battery operation due to the low power dissipation of a *CMOS* circuit.

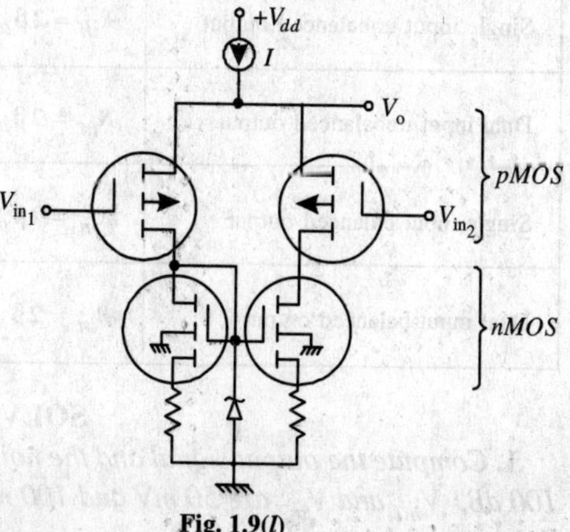

Fig. 1.9(*l*)

1.10. CASCADING OF DIFFERENTIAL AMPLIFIER

It has already been mentioned that differential amplifiers can be cascaded to get higher amplification.

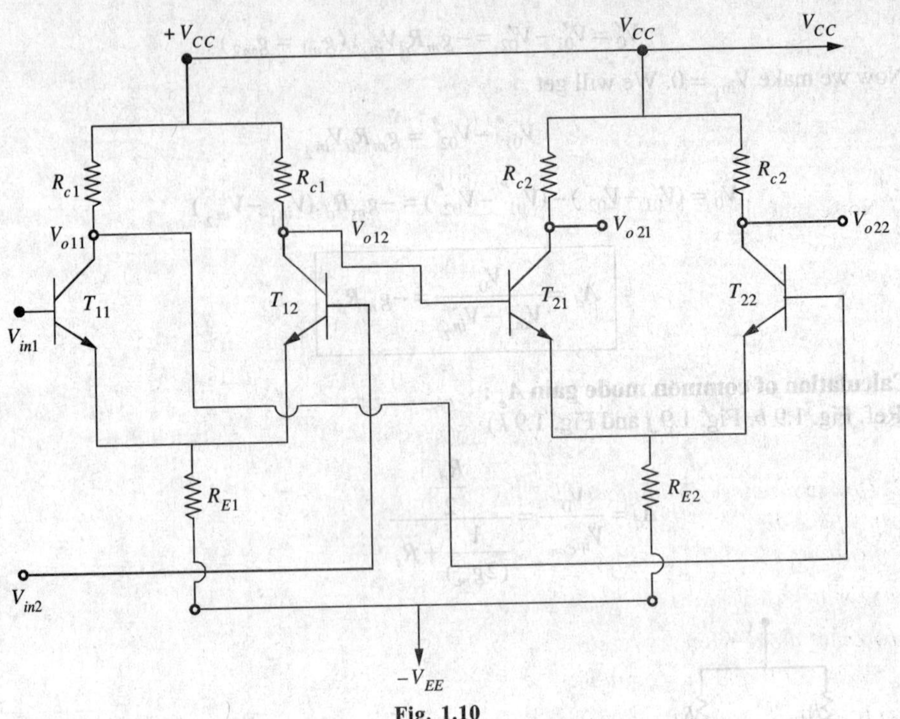

Fig. 1.10

1.11. EFFECTS OF CASCADING

1. Higher voltage gain with cascading DIFF. AMP.
2. Input resistance of the cascaded DIFF. AMP is equal to the input resistance of the first stage.
3. In a cascaded DIFF. AMP the output resistance is equal to the output resistance of the last stage.

1.12. COMPARISON OF DIFFERENT CONFIGURATIONS OF DIFF. AMP.

Configuration	*Input resistance*	*Output resistance*	*Voltage gain*
Single input unbalanced output	$R_{in} = 2\beta_{ae}\, r_e$	$R_o = R_c$	$A_d = \frac{R_c}{2r_e}$
Dual input unbalanced output	$R_{in} = 2\beta_{ae}\, r_e$ (both)	$R_o = R_c$	$A_d = \frac{R_c}{2r_e}$
Single input balanced output	$R_{in} = 2\beta_{ae}\, r_e$	$R_{o1} = R_{o2} = R_c$	$A_d = \frac{R_c}{r_e}$
Dual input balanced output	$R_{in} = 2\beta_{ae}\, r_e$ (both)	$R_{o1} = R_{o2} = R_c$	$A_d = \frac{R_c}{r_e}$

SOLVED PROBLEMS

1. *Compute the output signal and the noise on the output from the following data. $A_d = 100$, ρ = 100 dB. V_{in1} and V_{in2} are 50 mV and 100 mV respectively, with 1mV of noise on each input.*

Solution:

$$\rho = 20 \log_{10} (100 / A_c) = 100 \text{ dB}$$

$$\therefore \quad \log_{10} (100 / A_c) = 5$$

$$\therefore \quad \frac{100}{A_c} = 10^5$$

$$A_c = \frac{1}{1000} = 0 \cdot 001$$

Noise output

$$V_{Os} = A_d V_d + A_c V_c$$

$$= (100 \times 50 + .001 \times 75)\, mV = 5000.075\, mV.$$

$$V_{on} = (V_{\text{in}} \text{ noise})\,(A_c)$$

$$= 10^{-3} \times 0 \cdot 001 = 10^{-6}\,\text{V} = \mathbf{1\mu V.}$$

$$V_{OT} = V_{Os} + V_{On} = (5000.075 + .001)\, mV = \mathbf{5000.076\, mV}$$

2. *Design a zener constant current bias circuit as shown in the Fig. S.1 according to the following specifications.*

(*a*) *Emitter current* $-I_E = 5mA$

(*b*) *Zener diode with* $V_z = 4 \cdot 7\, V$ *and* $I_z = 53\, mA$.

(*c*) $\beta_{ac} = \beta_{dc} = 100$, $V_{BE} = 0 \cdot 715\, V$

(*d*) *Supply voltage* $-V_{EE} = -9\, V$

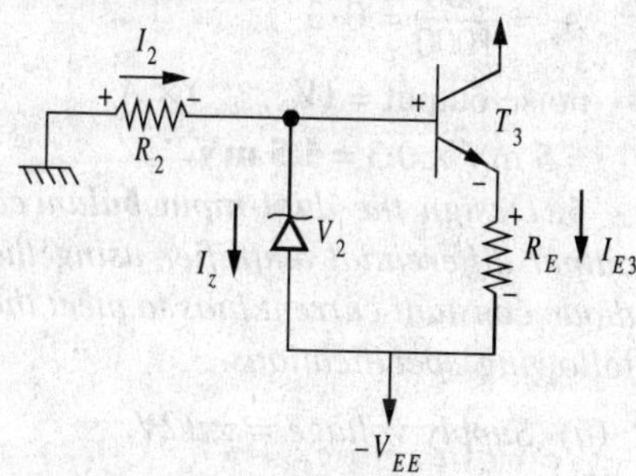

Fig. S.1

Solution:

From the Fig. S.2 using KVL we get

$$V_{BE3} + I_{E3}\, R_E = V_z$$

$$\therefore \quad R_E = \frac{V_z - V_{BE3}}{I_{E3}} = \frac{4 \cdot 7 - 0 \cdot 715}{5}\, \text{k}\Omega$$

$$= 0 \cdot 757\, \text{k}\Omega = 757\, \Omega$$

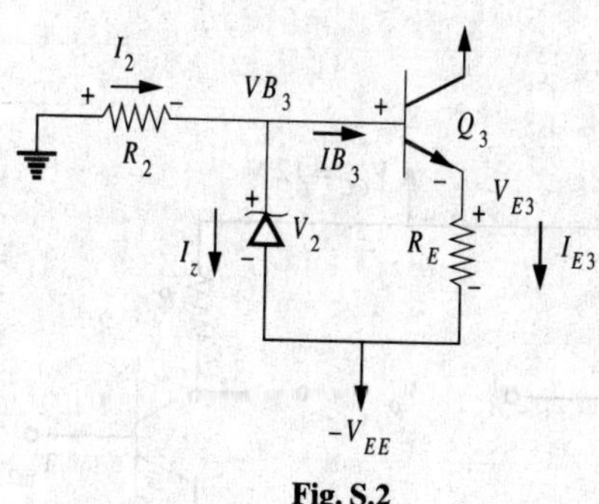

Fig. S.2

Practically we use $R_E = 820\, \Omega$

Again for proper operation

$$I_2 = 1 \cdot 2\, I_z = 1 \cdot 2 \times 53 = 63 \cdot 6\ \text{mA}$$

Again $\quad I_2\, R_2 = V_{EE} - V_z$

$$\therefore \quad R_z = \frac{V_{EE} - V_z}{I_2}$$

$$= \frac{9 - 4 \cdot 7}{63 \cdot 6} \times 10^3\, \Omega = 67 \cdot 6\, \Omega$$

Practically we use $R = 68\Omega$

The designed component values are:

$$R_E = \mathbf{820\Omega}$$

$$R = \mathbf{68\Omega}$$

3. *An amplifier has a differential gain of 300 and a CMRR of 60 dB. V_{in1} = 40 mV, V_{in2} = 60 mV, and V_{noise} = 5 mV, determine the output (noise).*

Solution:

From Fig. S.3,

$$V_o = (V_{in2} - V_{in1})A_d$$
$$= (60 - 40) \times 300 \text{ mV}$$
$$= 6000 \text{ mV} = 6 \text{ V}$$

$$\rho = 20 \log_{10}\left(\frac{300}{A_c}\right) = 60 \text{ dB}$$

$$\frac{300}{A_c} = 10^3$$

$$A_c = \frac{300}{1000} = 0{\cdot}3$$

noise output = $(V_{in\,noise}) \times A_c$

= 5 mV × 0·3 = **1.5 mV.**

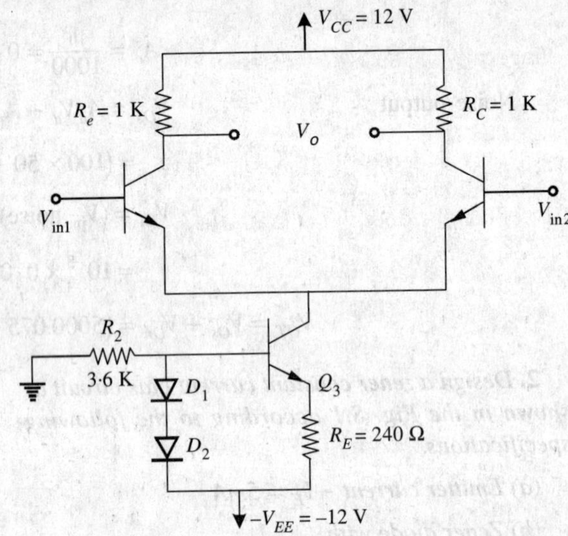

Fig. S.3

4. *Design the dual-input balanced output differential amplifier using the diode constant current bias to meet the following specifications.*

(*a*) *Supply voltage* = ± 12V.

(*b*) *Emitter current I_E in each differential amplifier transistor* = 1·5 mA and $V_{BE} = 0{\cdot}7V$.

(*c*) *Voltage gain* ≤ 60.

Solution:

The voltage at the base of transistor Q_3 is

$$V_{B3} = -V_{EE} + 2V_D$$
$$\therefore V_{E3} = -V_{B3} - V_{BE3}$$
$$= -V_{EE} + 2V_D - V_{BE3}$$
$$\therefore I_{E3} = \frac{V_{E3} - (-V_{EE})}{R_E} = \frac{V_{E3} + V_{EE}}{R_E} = \frac{2V_D - V_{BE3}}{R_E}$$

Assuming that the transistor Q_3 has the same characteristics as diodes D_1 and D_2 that is $V_D = V_{BE3}$, then

$$I_{E3} = \frac{V_D}{R_E}$$

$$\therefore R_E = \frac{V_D}{I_{E3}} = \frac{0{\cdot}7}{1{\cdot}5 \times 2} K\Omega.$$

$$\times 10^3 \; (I_{E3} = 2 \times 1{\cdot}5 = 3\text{mA})$$

$$= 233 \; \Omega$$

Practically we take R_E = **240 Ω**

$$\text{Again } R_1 = \frac{V_{EE} - 1{\cdot}4}{1{\cdot}5 \times 2} \times 10^3 \; \Omega$$

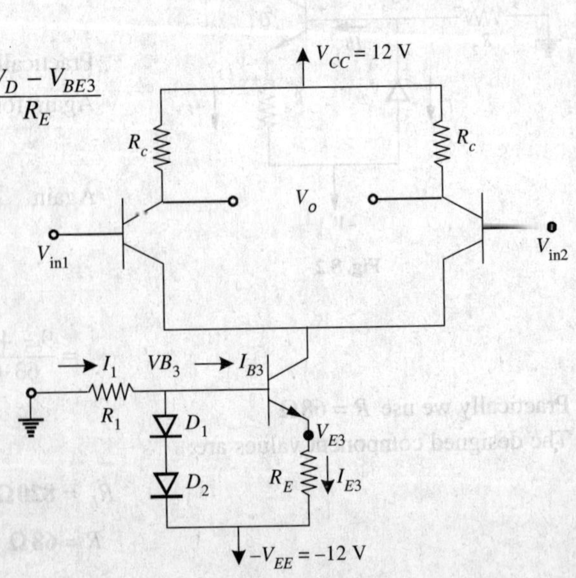

Fig. S.4

$$= \frac{12 - 1 \cdot 4}{1 \cdot 5 \times 2} \times 10^3 \, \Omega$$

$$= 3533 \, \Omega = 3 \cdot 533 \, \text{K}\Omega$$

Practically we take $R_1 = \mathbf{3 \cdot 6 \, k\Omega}$

$$I_{E1} = I_{E2} = 1 \cdot 5 \text{ mA}$$

$$\therefore \quad r_e = \frac{25\,\text{mV}}{\text{I}_{\text{E}_1}} = \frac{25\,\text{mV}}{1 \cdot 5 \text{ mA}} = 16 \cdot 67$$

To obtain the differential gain of 60, the required value of the collector resistor is

$$R_c = A_d \cdot r_e = 60 \times 16 \cdot 67 = 1000 \cdot 2 \, \Omega \quad \left[r_e = \frac{V_T}{I_E} \right]$$

$$= \mathbf{1 \, k\Omega} \quad V_T = 25\,\text{mV}. \; I_E = 1 \cdot 5 \text{ mA}$$

The following figure (Fig. S.4) shows the dual input, balanced output differential amplifier with thc designed component values as $R_c = 1\,\text{K}$, $R_E = 240$, and $R_2 = 3 \cdot 6 \, \text{k}\Omega$

5. *Design a cascaded DIFF. AMP with constant current source. Also calculate the overall gain and maximum output voltage swing.*

Solution:

$$V_{c2} = V_{c1} = 12 - 3 \cdot 9 \, I_{E1} \qquad \therefore (I_{c1} = I_{c2}) \quad \ldots(i)$$

$$\therefore \quad V_{E3} = V_{c2} - 0 \cdot 715 \qquad \ldots(ii)$$

Now,

$$12 + V_{E3} = 0 \cdot 1 \, I_{E3} + (5 \cdot 1 + 5 \cdot 6) \, 2 \, I_{E3}$$

$$\therefore \quad I_{E3} = \frac{12 + V_{c2} - 0 \cdot 715}{21 \cdot 5} \qquad \ldots(iii)$$

$$2 I_{E3} \times 5 \cdot 6 = 0 \cdot 715 + I_{E5} \times 2 \cdot 2$$

or,

$$11 \cdot 2 \times \frac{12 + V_{c2} - 0 \cdot 715}{21 \cdot 5} = 0 \cdot 715 + 2 \, I_{E1} \times 2 \cdot 2$$

or,

$$11 \cdot 2 \times \frac{12 + 12 - 0 \cdot 715 - 3 \cdot 5 \, I_{E1}}{021 \cdot 5}$$

$$= 0 \cdot 715 + 2 \, I_{E1} \times 2 \cdot 2$$

or,

$$12 \cdot 13 - 2 \cdot 03 \, I_{E1} = 0 \cdot 715 + 3 \, I_{E1} \times 2 \cdot 2$$

$$\therefore \quad I_{c1} = \frac{12 \cdot 13 - 0 \cdot 715}{6 \cdot 43} = 1 \cdot 775 \text{ mA} \cong 1 \cdot 78 \text{ mA}$$

$$= I_{c2}$$

$$I_{E3} = \frac{12 + 12 - 3 \cdot 5 \, I_{c1} - 0 \cdot 715}{21 \cdot 5} = 76 \text{ mA}$$

$$= I_{E4}$$

$$V_{c1} = 12 - 3 \cdot 9 \times 1 \cdot 78 = 5 \cdot 06 \text{ V} = V_{c2}$$

$$V_{E1} = -V_{BE1} = -0 \cdot 7 \text{ V}$$

$$V_{E3} = V_{c2} - 0 \cdot 7 = 4 \cdot 36 \text{ V} = V_{E4}$$

$$V_{c4} = 12 - 5 \cdot 6 \times 7 \cdot 6 = 7 \cdot 75 \text{ V}$$

$$V_{CE1} = V_{CE2} = V_{C1} - V_{E1} = 5 \cdot 06 + 0 \cdot 715 = 5 \cdot 775 \text{ V}$$

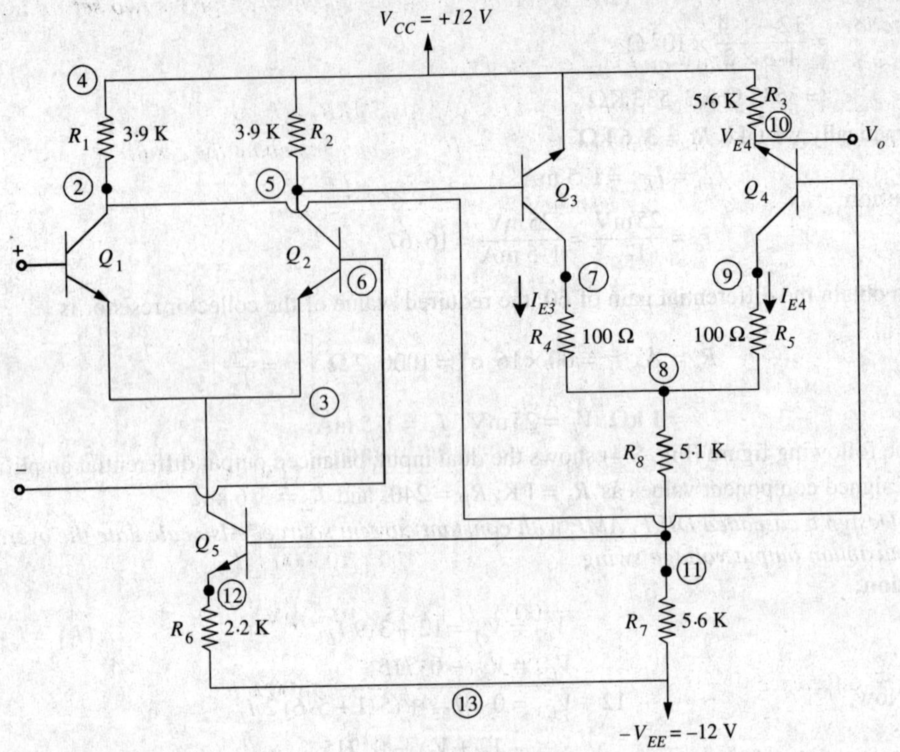

Fig. S.5

$$V_{CE3} = 12 - 4 \cdot 36 = 7 \cdot 64 \text{ V}$$

$$r_{e1} = r_{e2} = \frac{25}{1 \cdot 78} = 14 \cdot 04 \ \Omega$$

$$r_{e3} = r_{e4} = \frac{25}{\cdot 76} = 32 \cdot 9 \Omega$$

$$R_{i3} = 2\beta \left(R_E + r_{c3}\right) = 200 \, (132 \cdot 9)$$

$$= 26 \cdot 08 \, \text{k}\Omega$$

$$A_{v1} = \frac{R_{e1} \parallel R_{i3}}{r_{e1}} = \frac{3 \cdot 9 \parallel 26 \cdot 58}{14 \cdot 04} \times 10^3 = 242$$

$$A_{v2} = \frac{5 \cdot 6 \times 10^3}{2(100 + 32 \cdot 5)} = 21 \cdot 07$$

$$A_v = A_{v1} \cdot A_{v2} = 5098 \cdot 94$$

∴ Gain of the amplifier in d_B is 74·27 dB

Max. output voltage swing

$= \text{Max. voltage drop across } R_{c4}$

$= I_{e4} \cdot R_{c4} = 0 \cdot 76 \times 5 \cdot 6 = 4 \cdot 25 \text{ V (peak)}$

= **8.5 V** (peak to peak)

6. *(a) Compute the percentage difference in output voltage got for the two sets of input signal as follows:*

Set 1: $V_{in1} = +50\ \mu V$ *and* $V_{in2} = -50\ \mu V$

Set 2: $V_{in1} = +1200\ \mu V$ *and* $V_{in2} = 1100\ \mu V$; $\rho(CMRR) = 1000$

(b) Also calculate the same for CMRR = 10^5. Comments about the result.

Solution: (*a*) $$V_d = 100\,\mu\text{V};\ V_c = \frac{V_{in1} + V_{in2}}{2} = 0$$

As $$V_o = A_d\, V_d\left(1 + \frac{1}{\rho}\cdot\frac{V_c}{V_d}\right)$$

$$V_o = A_d\, V_d \text{ as } v_c = 0$$

$$= 100\, A_d\, \mu\text{V}$$

(*b*) $$V_d = 100\,\mu\text{V},\ V_c = \frac{1200 + 1100}{2} = 1150\,\mu\text{V}$$

$$V_o = 100\, A_d\left(1 + \frac{1150}{100}\cdot\frac{1}{100000}\right)$$

$$= 100\, A_d\,(1 + 1{\cdot}15 \times 10^{-4})\,\mu\text{V}$$

% difference $$= \frac{100\, A_d\,(1{\cdot}15\times 10^{-4})}{100\, A_d} \times 100\%$$

$$= 1{\cdot}15 \times 10^{-2}$$

$$= \mathbf{0{\cdot}0115\%}$$

7. *Obtain an expression for the input impedance between the bases of transistors T_{1a} and T_{2a} in Fig. S.6.*

Solution. Let us first consider T_{1a} & T_{1b}.

The input impedance of T_{1b} is $h_{ie(1b)}$ which is connected at the emitter of T_{1a}.

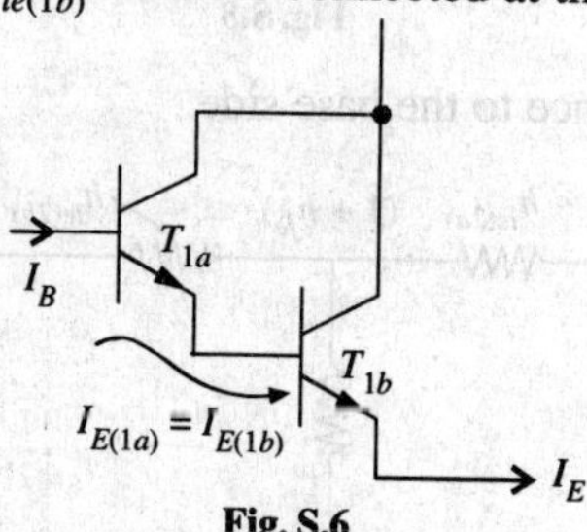

Fig. S.6

If h_{fe} of both transistors are same then $h_{i(1b)}$ reflected to the base of T_{1a} is $(1 + h_{fe})\, h_{ie(1b)}$. So total input impedance seen at the base of T_{1a} (R_i)

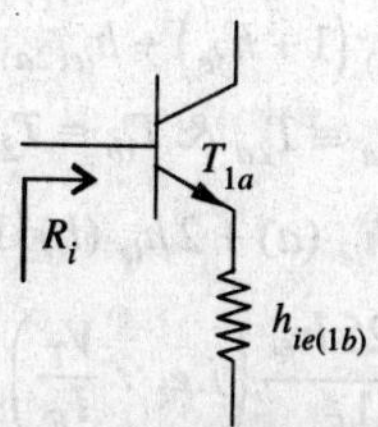

Fig. S.7

$$R_i = h_{ie(1a)} + (1 + h_{fe})\, h_{ie(1b)} \text{ if } h_{fe} >> 1$$

$$R_i = h_{ie(1a)} + h_{fe}\, h_{ie(1b)}.$$

Considering two pairs of transistors. The input impedance between T_{1a} and T_{2a} is $R_i = 2\, h_{ie(1a)} + 2\, h_{fe}\, h_{ie(1b)}$.

Now,
$$I_{E(1a)} = I_{B(1b)} = \frac{I_{E(1b)}}{h_{fe} + 1}.$$

$$h_{ie} = \frac{V_T}{I_E}.$$

$$\therefore \quad h_{ie} = \frac{V_T}{\left(1 + h_{fe}\right) I_{E(1a)}}$$

$$\therefore \quad h_i = 2\, h_{ie(1a)} + 2\left(1 + h_{fe}\right) \frac{V_T}{\left(1 + h_{fe}\right) I_{E(1a)}}.$$

$$= 2\, h_{ie(1a)} + 2\frac{V_T}{I_{E(1a)}} = 2\, h_{ie(1a)} + 2\, h_{ie(1a)}$$

$$= 4\, h_{ie(1a)}.$$

Considering the a_e model of the transistors,

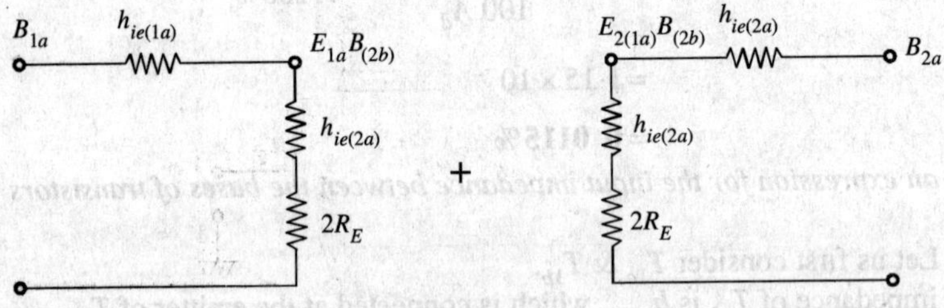

Fig. S.8

Transferring the emitter resistance to the base side.

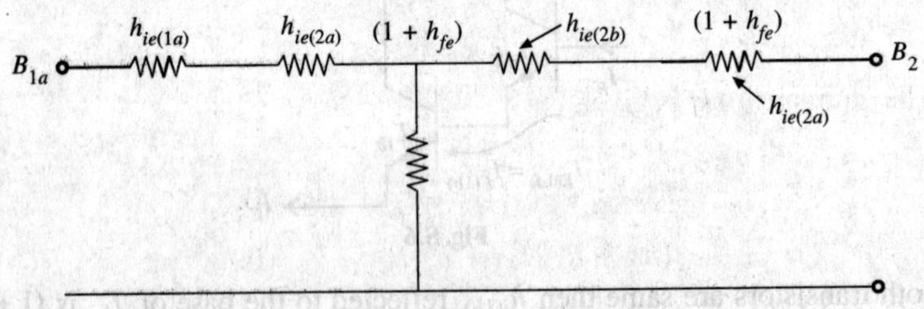

Fig. S.9

Input impedance $\quad R_i = h_{ie(1a)} + h_{ie(1b)}\left(1 + h_{fe}\right) + h_{ie(2a)} + h_{ie(2b)}\left(1 + h_{fe}\right)$

Considering
$$T_{1a} \equiv T_{2a} \;\&\; T_{1b} \equiv T_{2b}.$$

$$R_i = 2\, h_{ie}\,(a) + 2\, h_{ie}\,(b)\left(1 + h_{fe}\right)$$

Now
$$h_{ie} = \frac{\cdot 025\, h_{fe}}{1_E}\left(i.e. \because \frac{V_T}{I_E}\right) R_{ie}\,(1b) = \frac{0 \cdot 025\, h_{fe}}{h_{fe}\, I_{B1b}} = \frac{\cdot 025}{I_{B1b}}.$$

$$I_{B1a} = I_{E1a} \quad h_{ie}\ (1b)\ \frac{0{\cdot}025}{I_{E1a}} = \frac{{\cdot}025}{I_{B1a{\cdot}h_{fe}}} = \frac{1}{h_{fe}} \cdot h_{ie(1a)}$$

or $$h_{fe}\ h_{ie(1b)} = h_{ie(1a)}.$$

$$R_i = 2\,h_{ie}\ (a) + 2\,h_{ie}\ (b)\left(1 + h_{fe}\right)$$
$$= 2\,h_{ie}\ (a) + 2\,h_{ie}\ (b)\ h_{fe},\ \text{if}\ h_{fe} >> 1.$$
$$= 2\,h_{ie}\ (a) + 2\,h_{ie}\ (a) = 4\,h_{ie}\ (a)$$

8. *Consider that the current source in Figure S-11 is a real, not ideal, current source to be represented by an ideal current generator shunted by a resistor R_c. Obtain the small signal equivalent circuit of the difference amplifier. Show that with* $h_{ib} = \frac{h_{ie}}{1 + h_{fe}}$; $\Delta I_{E1} = \frac{1}{2h_{ib}}(\Delta V_1 - \Delta V_2) + \frac{1}{h_{ib} + 2\,R_c}\left(\frac{\Delta V_1 + \Delta V_2}{2}\right) = V_{EE}$ *where* ΔE_1 *responds to the different voltage* $\Delta V_1 - \Delta V_2$ *and also to the common mode voltage* $(\Delta V_1 + \Delta V_2)/2$.

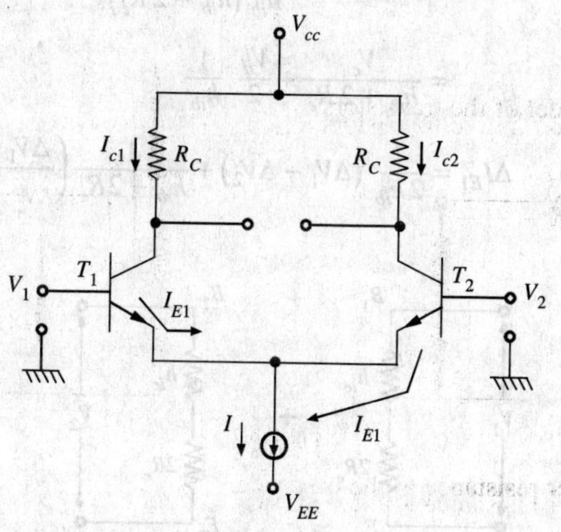

Fig. S.10

Solution. The equivalent *ckf* is given by:

From loop 1.

$$h_{ib}\ I_{E1} + R_e\left(I_{E1} + I_{E2}\right) - V_1 = 0.$$

$\therefore$ $$\left(h_{ib} + R_e\right) I_{E1} + R_c\ I_{E2} - V_1 = 0. \qquad \ldots(1)$$

From loop 2.

$$h_{ib}\ I_{E2} + R_e\left(I_{E1} + I_{E2}\right) - V_2 = 0.$$
$$R_e\ I_{E1} + \left(h_{ib} + R_e\right) I_{E2} - V_2 = 0. \qquad \ldots(2)$$

From 1 & 2

$$\frac{I_{E1}}{-R_e\ V_2 + \left(h_{ib} + R_e\right) V_1} = \frac{1}{\left(h_{ib} + R_e\right)^2 - {R_e}^2}.$$

$\therefore$ $$I_{E1} = \frac{\left(h_{ib} + R_e\right) V_1 - R_e\ V_2}{{h_{ib}}^2 + {R_e}^2 + 2\,h_{ib}\ R_e - {R_e}^2}$$

$$= \frac{(h_{ib} + R_e)V_1 - R_e V_2}{h_{ib}(h_{ib} + 2R_e)}$$

$$\Delta I_{E1} = \frac{(h_{ib} + R_e)\Delta V_1 - R_e \Delta V_2}{h_{ib}(h_{ib} + 2R_e)}$$

Now $$V_d = \Delta V_1 - \Delta V_2,\ V_c = \frac{\Delta V_1 + \Delta V_2}{2}.$$

$\therefore$ $$\Delta V_1 = V_c + \frac{V_d}{2},\ \Delta V_2 = V_c - \frac{V_d}{2}.$$

$$\Delta I_{E1} = \frac{(h_{ib} + R_e)\left(V_c + \frac{V_d}{2}\right) - R_e\left(V_c - \frac{V_d}{2}\right)}{h_{ib}(h_{ib} + 2R_e)}$$

$$= \frac{V_c(h_{ib} + R_e - R_e) + \frac{V_d}{2}(h_{ib} + R_e + R_e)}{h_{ib}(h_{ib} + 2R_e)}$$

$$= \frac{V_c}{h_{ib} + 2R_e} + \frac{V_d}{2}\frac{1}{h_{ib}}$$

$$\Delta I_{E1} = \frac{1}{2h_{ib}}(\Delta V_1 - \Delta V_2) + \frac{1}{h_{ib} + 2R_e}\left(\frac{\Delta V_1 + \Delta V_2}{2}\right).$$

Second Method:

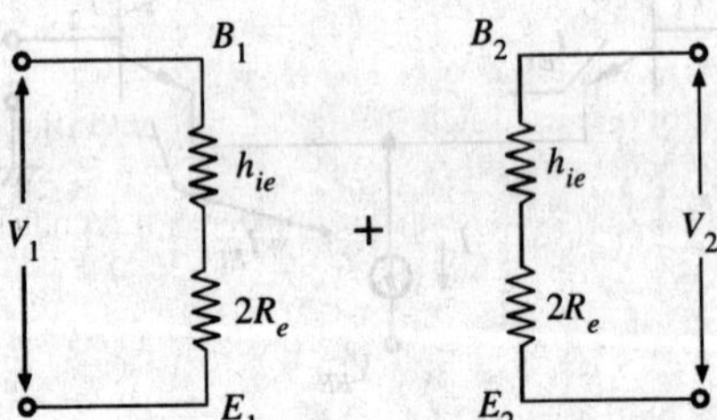

Fig. S.11

Transferring the resistance to the base ckf

$$\Delta V_1 - \Delta V_2 = V_d$$

$$\frac{\Delta V_1 + \Delta V_2}{2} = V_c.$$

$$V_1 = V_c + \frac{V_d}{2},\ V_2 = V_c - \frac{V_d}{2}$$

when $V_d = 0,\ V_1 = V_c,\ V_2 = V_c.$

$$I' = \frac{V_c}{h_{ib} + 2R_e}.$$

when $V_c = 0,\ V_1 = \frac{V_d}{2},\ V_2 = -\frac{V_d}{2}$

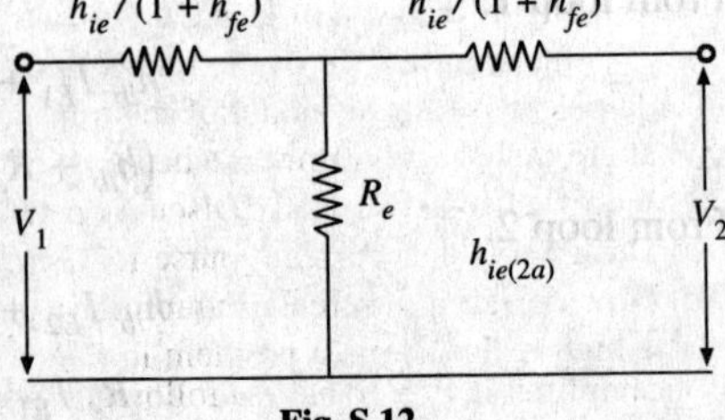

Fig. S.12

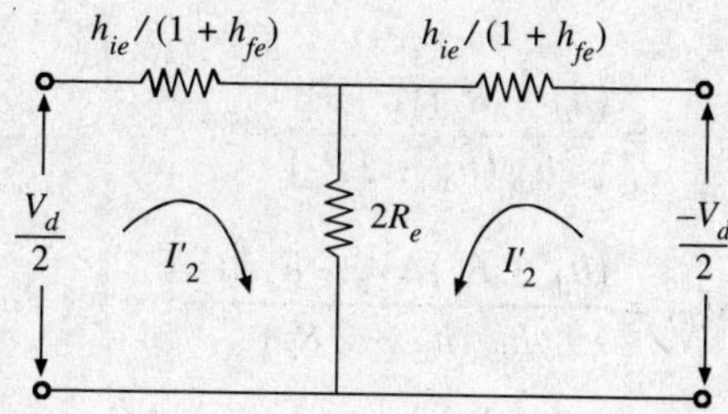

Fig. S.13

Current will flow from $\frac{V_d}{2}$ to $-\frac{V_d}{2}$

$$I'_2 = \frac{\frac{V_d}{2}}{h_{ib}} = \frac{V_d}{2\,h_{ib}};\ \Delta I_{E1} = I'_1 + I'_2 = \frac{V_d}{2\,h_{ib}} + \frac{V_c}{h_{ib} + 2R_e}.$$

$$\therefore \qquad \Delta I_{E1} = \frac{1}{2\,h_{ib}}(\Delta V_1 - \Delta V_2) + \frac{1}{h_{ie} + 2R_e}\left(\frac{\Delta V_1 + \Delta V_2}{2}\right).$$

REVIEW QUESTIONS

1. What is a Differential Amplifier? With a circuit diagram describe how it has got its name?
2. What are the main modes of operation for the Differential Amplifier?
3. Why is CMRR called a figure of merit for the DIFF. AMP? How can we make CMRR as high as possible to make the differential amplifier more ideal one?
4. What do you mean by inverting and non inverting input?
5. What are the advantages of DIF Amp? What type of signal can it amplify? What are the four different configuration of differential Amplifier? Which one is not commonly used and why?
6. Calculate the amplification factor for *ac* signal input in dual input balanced output differential amplifier?
7. What is a cascode amplifier? What is the difference between cascode and cascade?
8. Explain the advantage of constant current bias over emitter bias?
9. What is level transfer circuit? Why it is used with cascaded diff. amplifier.
10. List the characteristics of the cascaded amplifier.
11. Draw the transfer characteristics curve of differential amplifier and comment on
    (a) range of linearity
    (b) transconductance
    (c) action as a limiter.
12. How is noise eliminated in differential amplifier?
13. How is Q point of a differential amplifier, kept constant in temperature variation?
14. How would the CMRR be improved?
15. Determine a procedure to design a DA with prespecified values of Ad and CMRR.
16. Draw a circuit diagram of an FET DA with active load and determine its voltage gain.
17. What is the significance of the output resistance of the current—source circuit.
18. Can a piecewise linear model of the transistor be used to explain the widlar current source? Explain.
19. What are the effects of mismatched transistors on the characteristics of two transistor current source?
20. Why do we use active load? Discuss operation of an active load.
21. (*a*) Design a widlar current course for 1 mA.
    (*b*) Now design a differential amplifier using the current source.
22. "The high resistance is a problem in the current mirror circuit". Explain.
23. The amplifier in Fig. 16 has the following specification: $|V_{CC}| = |-V_{EE}| = 8V$; $R_{c_1} = R_{c_2} = 2.7\ k\Omega$; $R_E = 3.9 K\Omega$; the transistor has $\beta = 100$ and $V_{BE(sat)} = 0.7$ V.
    Calculate the following:-
    (*i*) The operating current and voltage.
    (*ii*) The voltage gain.
    (*iii*) The input resistance of the circuit.

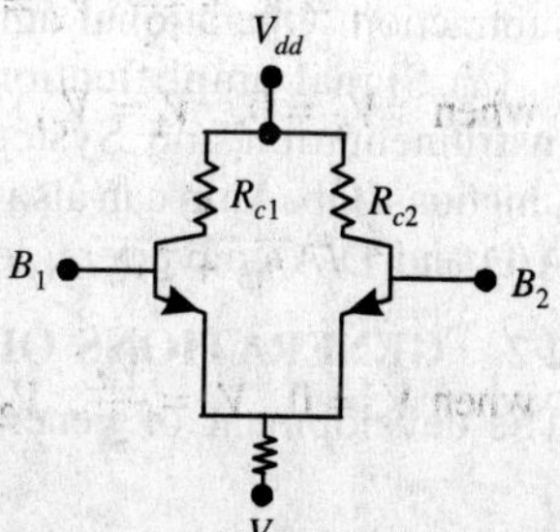

24. Why is emitter resistance in a differential amplifier replaced by a constant current source? Draw such a circuit and explain.

2

OPERATIONAL AMPLIFIER

2·1. Introduction. 2·2. Generations of Operational Amplifier. 2·3. Designations of Operational Amplifiers. 2·4. Pin Configuration and Different Packages of *IC* Operational Amplifier. 2·5. Special Operational Amplifier. 2·6. Ordering Information for *IC* Operational Amplifier. 2·7. Identification of Operational Amplifier. 2·8. Selection of Right Operational Amplifier for the Right Job. 2·9. Block Diagram of a Typical Operational Amplifier. 2·10. Circuit Symbol of Operational Amplifier. 2·11. Need of Power Supplies for Operational Amplifier. 2·12. Characteristics Feature of an Ideal Operational Amplifier. 2·13. Detailed Circuit Description of Operational Amplifier 741. 2·14. Basic Operational Amplifier. 2·15. Virtual Ground. 2·16. Some Important Terms of Operational Amplifier. 2·17. Offset Correcting Resistor. 2·18. Effect of Voltage and Current Drifts. 2·19. Characteristics of Practical or Non-Ideal Operational Amplifier. 2·20. Gain-Bandwidth Product. 2·21. Feedback in Operational Amplifier Circuits. 2·22. Closed-loop Voltage Gain. 2·23. Closed loop Gaen A_d in Terms of Open Loop-Gain (A). 2.24. Input Resistance with Feedback. 2·25. Output Resistance with Feedback. 2·26. Bandwidth with Feedback. 2·27. The Effect of Feedback on Total of Output Offset Voltage. Solved Problems. Review Questions.

2·1. INTRODUCTION

An operational amplifier is basically a direct coupled high gain differential amplifier with high input impedance and low output impedance. The operational amplifier is a versatile device. The IC operational amplifier has become an inexpensive and effective tool for handling circuit design problems. Although the operational amplifier is classified as a linear IC, its range of usefulness extends as well into *non-linear and digital* areas. About *one-third* of all integrated circuits are operational amplifier over 2000 types of which are commercially available. Almost all of these are monolithic ICs with room temperature dissipations of power *under a watt.* Op. Amp. is the short name of "*operational amplifier*" which was originally used to denote an amplifier circuit that performed various mathematical operations like integration, differentiation, summation and subtraction. Operational amplifier has got wide applications like:

(*a*) Signal amplification, (*b*) Wave shaping, (*c*) Servo and process controls, (*d*) Analog instrumentation and System design, (*e*) Impedance transformations, and many other routine functions. Op. Amp can also be used in many non-linear applications such as voltage compensations, A/D and D/A converters, logarithmic amplifiers, and non-linear function generators.

2·2. GENERATIONS OF OPERATIONAL AMPLIFIERS

The development of general purpose operational amplifiers can be traced back to early 1963 when Fairchild Semiconductor introduced the first generally accepted IC Op. Amp. They are utilized in the greatest percentage of applications. General purpose IC op. amps. are loosely defined as having the following characteristics:

(a) Unity-gain bandwidth of approximately 1 MHz.

(b) Operating from power supplies of 5 to 20 volts with no serious degradation of performance.

(c) They may or may not be internally compensated.

709, 101 and 741 types or families are the general purpose IC op. amps.

Generation of Operational Amplifiers

In the development of general-purpose IC op. amp., there are distinct evolutionary steps. Although Fairchild Semiconductor introduced the first generally accepted IC op. amp. in 1963 (μ A 702), but it was not universally accepted for the following reasons. 702 has

(a) very limited common-mode input range

(b) comparatively low voltage gain (only approximately 70 dB)

(c) odd power supply requirement (+ 12 V and –6 V)

(d) no short circuit protection *i.e.,* it may be burnt out if output is temporarily shorted.

All those defects/drawbacks set the stage for improvement of IC op. amp. The commercial 1st generation IC-operational amplifier then came out in 1965 when Fairchild Semiconductor introduced μ A 709. Thereafter Motorola's MC 1709, National Semiconductor's LM 709, Texas Instruments' SN 72709 and others followed μ A 709. All these operational amplifiers have the *same specifications* and as a result they are said to *belong to 709 family.* 709 family is an improved version and has the performance better than 702 in a number of ways. Salient features of 709 family are noted here below (*i.e.,* the features of 1st *generation operational amplifier*). It has

(a) higher gain, (b) a larger input, (c) larger output voltage range, (d) lower input currents, (e) higher output currents and (f) operation from symmetrical power supplies of ± 15V.

Specifications leading to typical Electrical characteristics of μ A 709 operational amplifier are provided in **Appendix A (Table 1).**

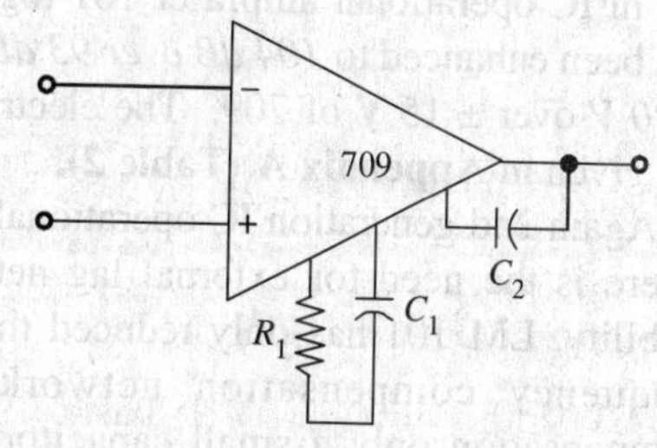

Fig. 2.1. Frequency compensation components.

The available models of 709 family are 709, 709A, 709B and 709C. They have the *same schematic diagrams,* however, tolerances are *larger for later family members.* Moreover, 709C has the *worst* tolerance but cost is *least* whereas 709 is having the *best* tolerance and costs the *most.*

The control of open-loop gain and phase characteristics in the 709 is accomplished by three frequency compensation components (shown in Fig. 2.1) where capacitor C_1 and resistor R_1 are said to be the input compensation components and C_2 is called the output compensation component.

Those three components shape the open-loop responses of the operational amplifier as shown in Fig. 2.2 and Fig. 2.3.

C_2 & C_1 is least for (1) and maximum for (4)

$R_1 = 0$ for (1) and 1·5 K for other cases.

Case 1: C_1 & C_2 least, $R_1 = 0$

Case 4: C_1 & C_2 highest $R_1 = 1·5$ K.

709 operational amplifiers have the following three ingredients.

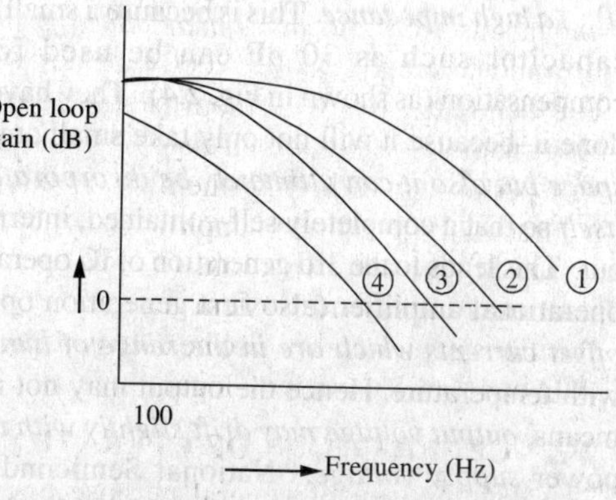

Fig. 2.2. Open-loop frequency response.

(1) Better performance
(2) Versatile
(3) Less costly

Those three ingredients are a hard combination to beat. But family is not free from drawbacks.

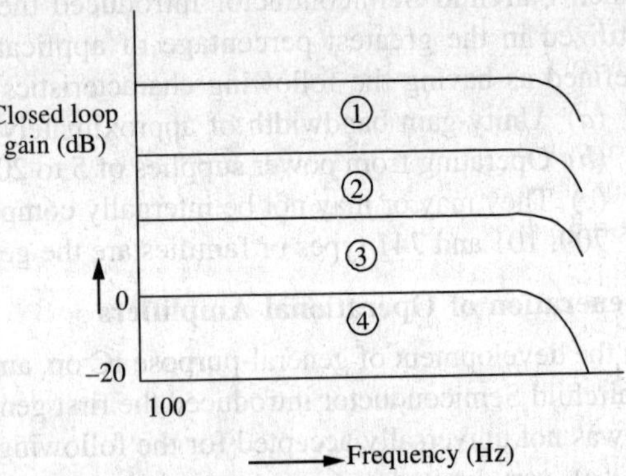

Fig. 2.3. Frequency response for closed loop.

Main drawbacks are (709 and other first generation operational amplifier):–

(*a*) Possible latchup, (*b*) No short-circuit protection, (*c*) Need for external lag networks, (*d*) Too low input difference voltage, (*e*) Excessive power dissipation, (*f*) Sensitivity to capacitive loading, (*g*) Susceptibility to oscillation and (*h*) Limited supply voltage range.

Latchup: It means the output voltage can be latched or stuck at some value, regardless of the input. Certain values of common mode input voltage can create such incident.

Short-circuit protection: It means that accidentally shorting the output terminals can destroy the IC.

Those drawbacks of first generation IC operational amplifier set the stage for 2nd generation of IC operational amplifier.

Second Generation of IC operational amplifiers: It has already been mentioned that the improvements in 709 over 702 produced a new level of *performance and versatility.* Similarly LM 101 is an improvement over the 709. IC *operational amplifier LM 101* introduced by *National Semiconductor in 1967* is a 2nd generation operational amplifier. It is the next evolutionary step in the history of IC operational amplifier technology. All the drawbacks as mentioned have been solved out in IC operational amplifier 101 together with some additional refinements. The voltage gain has been enhanced to *104 dB over 93 dB of 709.* The range of supply voltage has been increased *to ± 20 V* over ± 15 V of 709. The electrical characteristics of the LM 101 IC operational amplifier are given in **Appendix A (Table 2).**

Again 2nd generation IC operational amplifier LM 101 is not also free from all the drawbacks. There is the need for external lag networks to guarantee stability. LM 101 has only reduced the complexity of the frequency compensation networks. For frequency compensation only a small capacitor is to be connected externally as shown in Fig. 2.4.

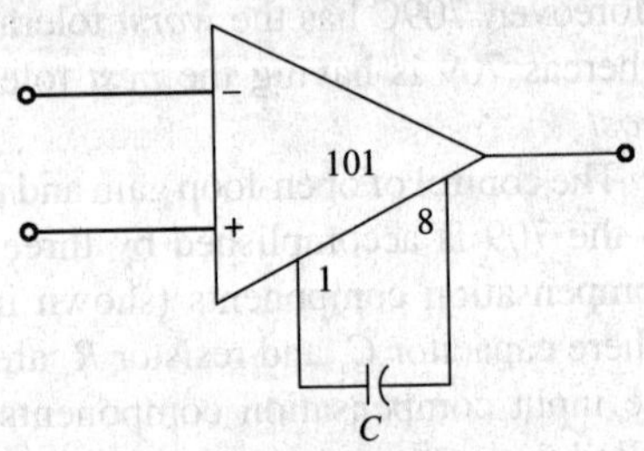

Fig. 2.4. Frequency compensation components.

Designers have given the *input-stage compensation point* (P_{inl}) *a high impedance.* This is because a small compensation capacitor such as 30 pF can be used for frequency compensation (as shown in Fig. 2.4). They have intentionally done it–because it will not only take small amount of *board space but also it can ultimately be incorporated* on *the chip itself* so that a completely self-contained, internally compensated IC operational amplifier may come out. This leads to the 3rd generation of IC operational amplifier. The main drawback of 2nd generation operational amplifier (also first generation operational amplifier) is associated with *input bias and offset currents which are in the range of hundreds of nanoamps.* Moreover these currents change with temperature. Hence the output may not remain balanced when the temperature changes. This means, *output voltage may drift slightly with temperature. Output* may also drift due to variation of power *supply voltage.* National Semiconductor introduced a third generation IC operational amplifier in the middle of 1968 (*LM 101A*). It is an improved version of LM 101 in which the main improvement is the *input bias, offset currents and biasing circuit of the input stage.* It has better control of *input characteristics over the operating temperature* range. Input bias and offset currents for LM 101 A are *30* nA and *1·5* nA respectively, a factor of ten better than that of 709. National Semiconductor also introduced another operational amplifier LM 107 which is having a 30 pF frequency compensation capacitor which is integrated into the chip. Other third generation IC operational amplifiers are:

(1) μ A 741 (Fairchild)

(2) MC 1539 (Motorola)

(3) 2139 (Sprague)

Typical electrical characteristics of μ *A 741* operational amplifier are tabulated in **Table 3 (in Appendix A)**. The difference between 741 and 101 includes: (*i*) means of frequency compensation (*ii*) biasing, (*iii*) method of short circuit protection. 741 has an on-chip *capacitor for frequency compensation*. Certain protective features of 741 enhance the versatility of an operational amplifier. They include output short circuit protection for indefinite time, input *over voltage protection and* protection against supply *voltage reversal.*

Other higher generation of IC Op. Amp.

There is a large and growing list of advanced types of operational amplifier—offering improved specifications. Design of such operational amplifier includes the following point/points:

(*a*) Very low input currents, (*b*) Wide bandwidth, (*c*) Very low drift; (*d*) High slew rate (high speed), (*e*) High output voltage or current, (*f*) Low noise and high CMRR (*i.e.,* high precision, and (*g*) micropower dissipation.

The *fourth generation* operational amplifier improved further on the *low input currents* of the earlier generation. *Offset* and *input bias* currents are *reduced* again by a factor of *from three to ten,* depending upon the device. The next generation (5th generation) operational amplifier then followed, with major improvements in such characteristics as wide bandwidth and high speed. The most recent trends are in favour of the production of operational amplifier with *high precision, high outputs* and *micropower dissipation* (sixth and higher generation).

2·3. DESIGNATIONS FOR OPERATIONAL AMPLIFIERS

Every manufacturer uses a specific code and assigns a specific type number to the operational amplifier (rather ICs) it produces. Some of the well-known manufacturers of linear ICs use initials to specify linear ICs. They are as follos:

(1) Burr-Brown: BB (BB741) (2) Fairchild: μA (μA 741) (3) Intersil ICL (4) Motorola: MC & MFC (MC 1741) (5) National Semiconductor: LM, LH, LF, TBA (LM 101) (6) Signetics S/N (N 5741) (7) Siliconix, Inc. L (8) Sprangue ULN, ULS, ULX (9) RCA CA (CA 3741) (10) Texas Instruments SN (SN 52741).

For digital ICs: Initials used by manufacturers for designating digital ICs generally differ from those used for linear ICs.

National Semiconductor uses the following initials for digital ICs:

(*i*) DM stands for digital monolithic ICs.

(*ii*) CD stands for CMOS digital ICs.

An IC op. amp. say 741 is also available in different classes: like 741, 741A, 741C, 741E, 741S and 741 SC. The alphabet at the end (A, C, E, S, SC) indicates the temperature range and grade of the operational amplifier (*i.e.,* commercial grade or military grade etc.). Table 4 will give such a view.

Table 4: Operating temperature range and grade for operational amplifier.

Operational family	*Designation of operational amplifier*	*Grade*	*Operating temperature range (in °C)*
101	LM 101, LM 101A, L107, LH 101	Military	– 55 to 125
741	741, 741A, 747, 747A, 748, MC 1558	Military	– 55 to 125
101	LM 201, LM 201A, LM 207, LH 201	Industrial	– 25 to 85
741	741C, 741E, 747C, 747E, 748E, MC 1458	Commercial	0 to 70/75
101	LM 301, LM 307	Commercial	0 to 70/75

From the above table it is evident that the higher the beginning number (1̲01, 2̲01, 3̲01) the narrower the specified operating temperature range. Other differences (rather than grade and temperature range of operation) are there such as supply voltages, voltage gains, and offsets.

2·4. PIN CONFIGURATION AND DIFFERENT PACKAGES OF IC OP. AMP.

Several different IC operational amplifier packages are available.

Such as: Flat package, Dual-in-line (DIP) plastic package, Dual-in-line welded-Seal ceramic package, metal can or transistor Pack.

Flat Pack: In such a pack, the chip is enclosed in a rectangular ceramic case with terminal leads extending through the sides and ends as in Fig. 2.5 (*a*). 8, 10, 14 or 16 pin operational amplifiers are available. Those leads are to accommodate the power supplies, inputs, outputs and some other special connections. Pin numbers are counted anticlockwise with number one pin at the dot position or at the left side of notch position as shown in Figure 2.5 (*a*).

Dual-in-line Package (DIP): In such a package, the chip is enclosed in a rectangular ceramic or a plastic case as shown in Figs. 2.5 (*b*) and 2.5 (*c*). DIP IC operational amplifiers are also available with different number of pins (8, 10, 12, 14, 16 etc.). The 8 pin DIPs are called mini DIPs. Pins are numbered anticlockwise with number one at the dot position or notch position.

Metal can or transistor Package: In such a package, the chip is enclosed in a metal or plastic case as shown in Fig. 2.5 (*d*). Metal can operational amplifiers are available in circular as well as DIL package. Pins are numbered in usual ways with last number at the Tab. Transistor Package is indicated by *TO*.

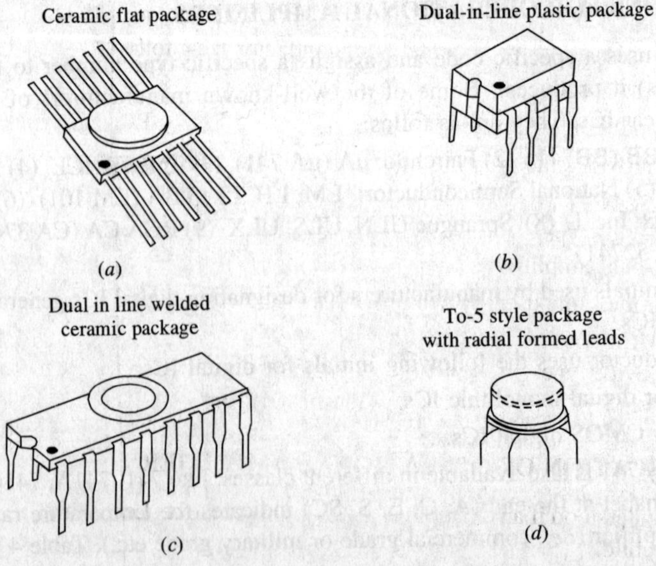

Fig. 2.5

The numbers of pins in the IC basically indicates the density of components integrated inside the chip. More the number of components more is the number of pins in it. Out of all those types dual-in-line package is the most frequently used package. It is easy to mount because of its lead construction and more spacing between the leads. Ceramic DIP is expensive but has more heat dissipating capacity. Flat Package is suited for airborne applications because it is more reliable and lighter than a comparable DIP. However, for power amplifiers, the metal can package is best suited. This is because that metal is a good conductor of heat. Hence it has better dissipation capability than the flat-pack or dual-in-line package. Moreover, external heat sinks can also be used in metal can package.

2·5. SPECIAL OPERATIONAL AMPLIFIERS

Other operational amplifiers: There are several other IC operational amplifiers. They belong to special purpose category. because they have some special feature(s):

(1) *LM 318* (*Operational Amplifier*): It is a high speed operational amplifier. It has 15 MHz. Small signal bandwidth together with the guaranteed 50 V/μs slew rate.

(2) *μA 771*: It is having low input bias current of 200 pA and slew rate of 13 V/μs.

(3) *μA 791*: It is a power amplifier having output current capability of 1 A.

(4) *μA 714*: It is a precision operational amplifier with low offset voltage of 75 μV together with low input offset current of 2.8 nA, low offset voltage drift of 1.3 μV/ºC and low noise.

(5) *μA 776*: It is a multipurpose programmable operational amplifier.

(6) *LM 324*: It is a cost-saving quad operational amplifier.

(7) *LF 351 and LF 353*: They have low input bias and offset currents (200 pA and 100 pA, respectively), a large unity gain bandwidth of 4 MHz, and a slew rate of 13 V/μs.

2·6. ORDERING INFORMATION FOR IC OPERATIONAL AMPLIFIER

It is a matter of regret that manufacturers do not have a common format for the odering information. However they use some method which is of its own. But they specify three different information in different ways. The three information which they specify as ordering information are the following:

(1) Device type, (2) Package type and (3) Grade *i.e.,* the operating temperature range.

The ordering information for National Semiconductor is as follows:

LM 201A	*F*
Device type and temperature range	Package type (*F* for flat package)

But Fairchild provides the ordering information in the following way:

μ*A 741*	*T*	*C*
Device type (operational amplifier)	Package type (DIP mini)	Grade *Commercial type*

The format for the same used by Motorola is as follows:

MC 34001	*P*	0º to 70ºC
Device type	Package (Plastic DIP)	grade

2·7. IDENTIFICATION OF OPERATIONAL AMPLIFIER

It will be better understood if an example is given in this context. Let us take μA 741, an operational amplifier of Fairchild.

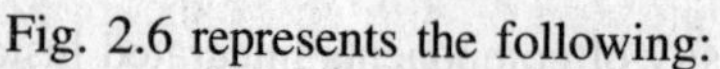

Fig. 2.6 represents the following:

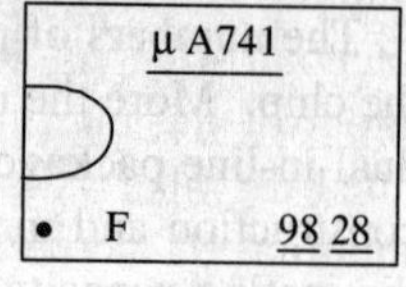

Fig. 2.6

μ A 741 ⟶ It specifies the type of the Device. In the present case it is an operational amplifier.

F ⟶ It gives the manufacturer's initial. Here it is *F* which means *Fairchild*.

98 ⟶ This depicts the year of production. Here it is 98 which means 1998.

28 ⟶ It represents the week of the year (28th week here in the present case).

2·8. SELECTION OF RIGHT OPERATIONAL AMPLIFIER FOR THE RIGHT JOB

Selection of right operational amplifier for the right job includes:

(1) Selection of grade of the operational amplifier.

(2) Package selection depending on ease of mounting.

(3) Cost factor consideration for selection.

Now selection of the right one is done from roughly selected operational amplifiers. In selecting one particular operational amplifier over another, there are some other considerations. Such considerations are:

(1) Easiness of application.

(2) Number of external components required.

(3) Applying overcompensation.

(4) Limits of input currents.

As each situation is to be evaluated on the basis of its own requirements, no one type of operational amplifier is, therefore, overwhelmingly superior in all situations. However, each of 741, 101 and 709 family may fulfil all general purpose applications. But 741 family is favoured in some situations because of its ease of application with a minimum external components.

Out of general purpose area, some special purpose operational amplifiers are recommended. As we have already mentioned that no one operational amplifier is overwhelmingly superior in all situations. In some situations we need one or more of the following where we need some special purpose operational amplifier.

(*i*) High slew rate *i.e.,* high speed.

(*ii*) High output voltage or current.

(*iii*) Extremely low input current.

(*iv*) Very low drifts.

(*v*) Wide bandwidth.

(*vi*) Low noise and CMRR *i.e.,* high precision.

(*vii*) Micro power dissipation.

2·9. BLOCK DIAGRAM OF A TYPICAL OPERATIONAL AMPLIFIER

Operational amplifier is a multistage amplifier. Figure 2.7 presents the block diagram of a typical operational amplifier.

The first stage, also called the input stage is basically a dual input balanced output DIFF. AMP. The function of this stage is to provide most of the voltage gain of the amplifier and also sets up the input resistance of the operational amplifier. The second stage is called intermediate stage which is generally a dual input unbalanced output DIFF. AMP. Next stage following the intermediate stage is a level shifting stage. It is basically an emitter follower with constant current source. As direct coupling is used, the dc voltage at the output of the intermediate stage is well above the ground potential. Hence a level shift stage is used after the intermediate stage to shift the dc level of the output of the intermediate stage down to zero volts with reference to ground. The 4th stage, called the final stage, is also called the output stage. It is a push-pull (class B) complementary amplifier. It increases the output voltage swing and raises the current supplying capability of the operational amplifier. It also establishes the low output resistance.

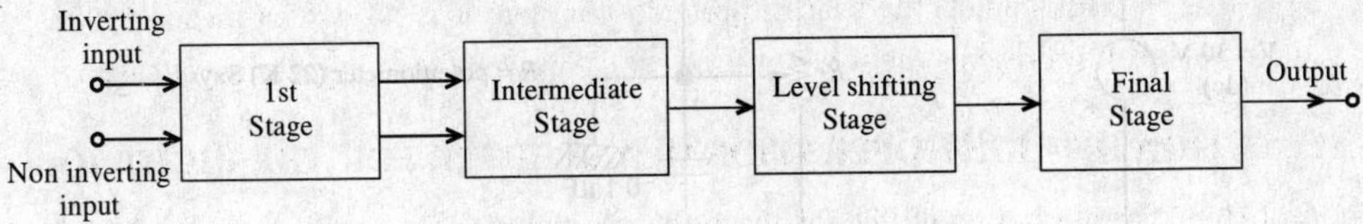

Fig. 2.7. Block diagram representation.

2·10. CIRCUIT SYMBOL OF OPERATIONAL AMPLIFIER

Circuit symbol of operational amplifier is shown in Fig. 2.8.

In the symbol, power supply and other pin connections are omitted for simplicity. As it is known from previous section that 1st stage of an operational amplifier is a DIFF. AMP., the differential inputs are marked by (+) and (–) notations. The input marked positive is called non-inverting input because dc or ac signal applied at this input will produce an inphase signal at the output. The input marked negative is called the inverting input because it produces an 180° out of phase signal at the output.

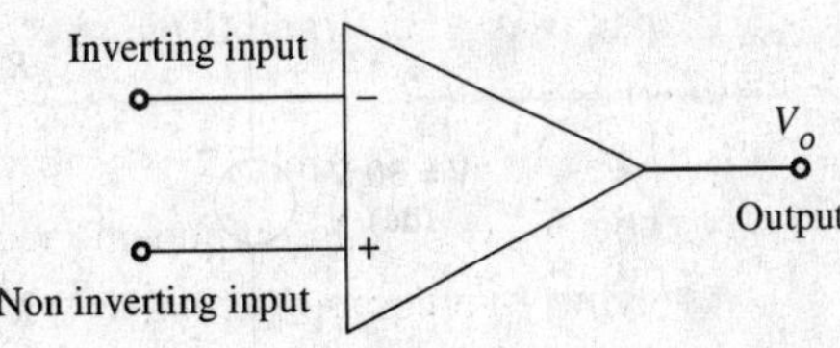

Fig. 2.8. Circuit symbol of operational amplifier.

The model for an operational amplifier is shown in Fig. 2.9.

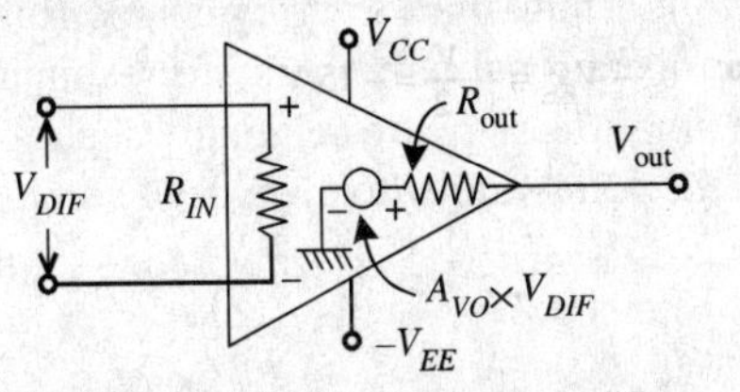

Fig. 2.9. Model of an operational amplifier.

R_{IN} = input resistance

R_{OUT} = output resistance

V_{DIF} = voltage difference between two inputs

A_{VO} = open loop voltage gain of the operational amplifier.

2·11. NEED OF POWER SUPPLIES FOR OPERATIONAL AMPLIFIER

Majority of operational amplifiers will not work properly unless you connect external dc returns. This is because input stage of an operational amplifier is a dual input balanced output DIFF. AMP. This DIFF. AMP. will not work unless dc return path is provided from each base to ground. Hence a connection must be made to both inputs, so that the dc bias currents can flow. Inverting and non-inverting terminal voltages are measured with reference to the ground. DC base currents of both the inputs must flow to ground, either through direct short or through external resistors. From the configuration of DIFF. AMP. it is seen that two [one is + ve (+ V_{CC}) and other is –ve (– V_{EE})] supplies are needed for operational amplifiers. Generally ± 15 volts are recommended for operational amplifiers. But some operational amplifiers are there which can operate with unequal power supplies. As for example, operational amplifier 702 needs unequal power supplies. There are some operational amplifiers which can work with a positive supply only. Example: 324. Moreover, manufacturers do not agree on power supply labelling. Fairchild uses $+V$ for positive and $-V$ for negative supply, whereas, Motorola uses $+V_{CC}$ for positive and $-V_{EE}$ for negative supply.

It has been established that for proper operation of operational amplifier two power supplies are needed. But it is possible to adapt a technique for getting $+V_{CC}$ and $-V_{EE}$ from a single power supply. Any of the following three schemes [Fig. 2.10 (*a*), (*b*) & (*c*)] may be adopted.

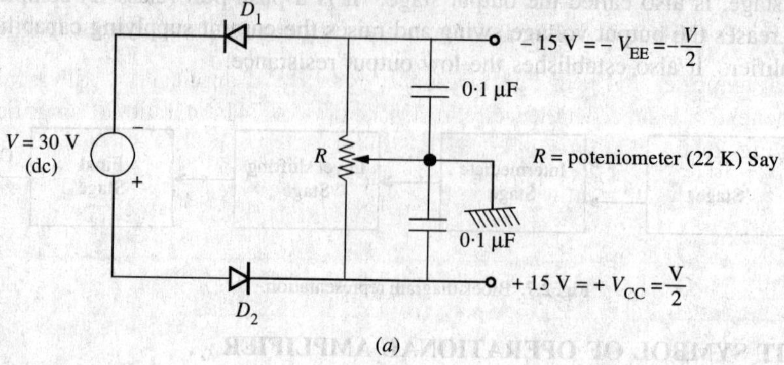

(*a*)

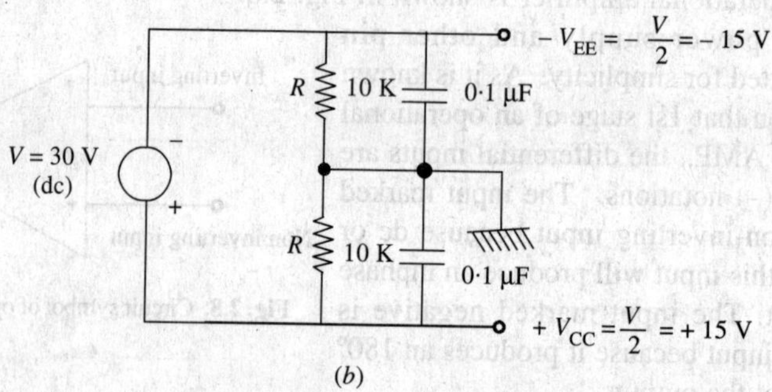

(*b*)

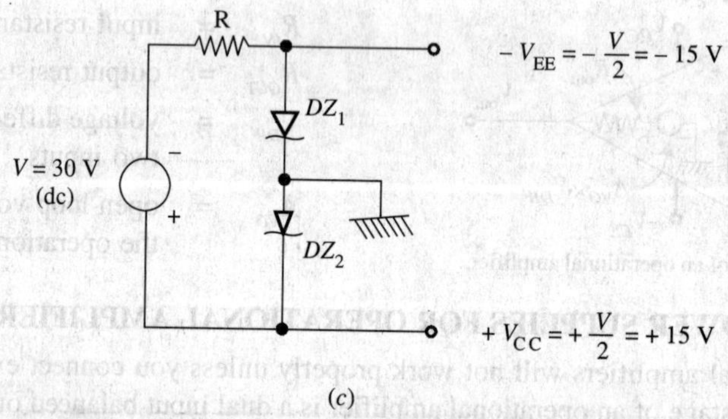

(*c*)

Fig. 2.10. Scheme of getting dual power supplies from a single power supply.

2·12. CHARACTERISTIC FEATURES OF AN IDEAL OPERATIONAL AMPLIFIER

An ideal operational amplifier should have the following characteristics:

1. Infinite input resistance ($R_i = \infty$)
2. Zero output resistance ($R_o = 0$)
3. Infinite voltage gain ($A_v = \infty$)
4. Infinite bandwidth ($B_w = \infty$)
5. Perfect balance ($V_{out} = 0$ when $V_{in1} = V_{in2}$)
6. Zero offset and drift.

7. Infinite common mode rejection.
8. Slew rate is to be infinite so that output voltage changes occur simultaneously with input voltage changes.

2·13. DETAILED CIRCUIT DESCRIPTION OF OPERATIONAL AMPLIFIER 741

The operational amplifier 741 will rate favourably for ease of application, with a minimum of external components. Hence detailed circuit description of 741 operational amplifier is given here below in Fig. 2.11.

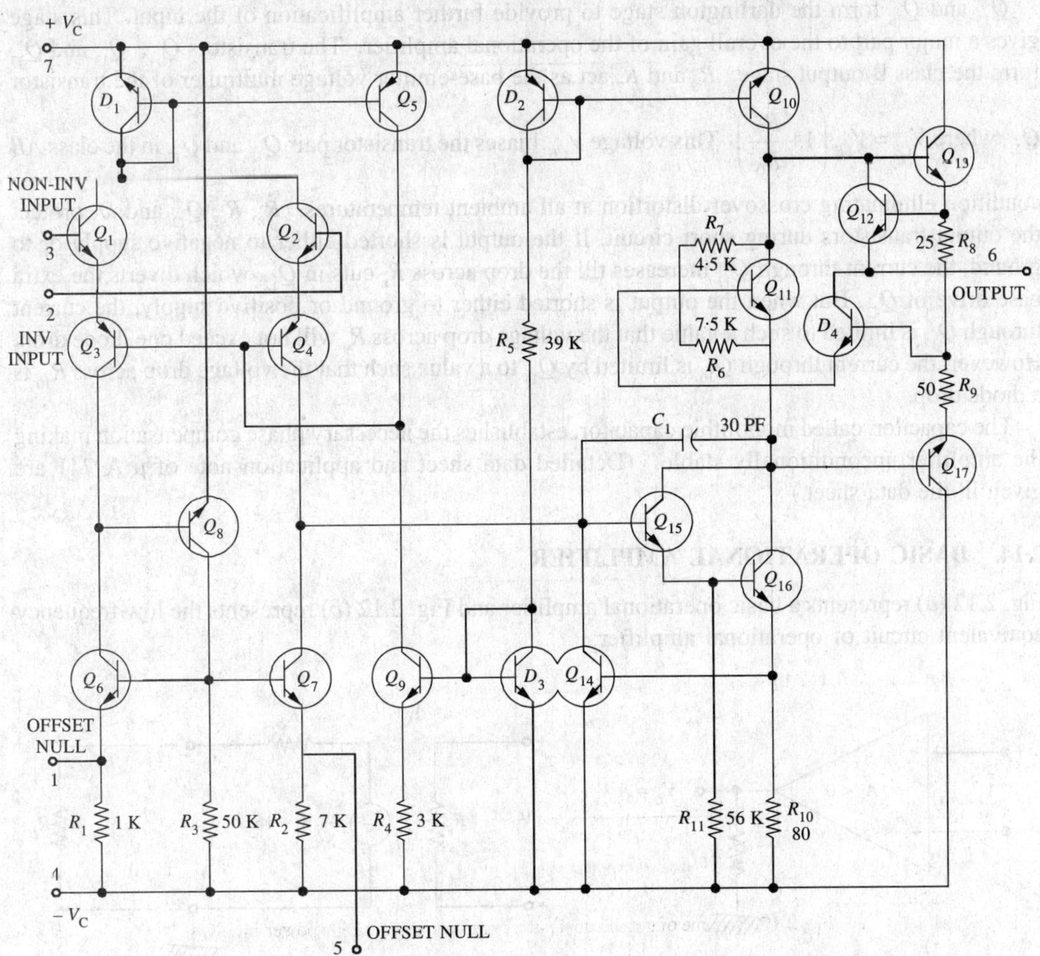

Fig. 2.11. Schematic diagram of CA 741.

Its circuit consists of a differential stage at the input followed by a high gain amplifier and a short circuit protected class B push pull output stage. The complete circuit is shown in Fig. 2.11. The input stage is formed by the transistors Q_1 to Q_9. Transistor Q_5 and diode D_1 act as a current mirror providing the required bias current to transistors Q_1, Q_2, Q_3 and Q_4. Q_1 and Q_2 are starved of quiescent current to obtain high input impedance. These are super beta transistors having common emitter current gains of the order of 1000 event at 2 to 3 microamperes of collector current.

The diode D_1 at collector of Q_1 and Q_2 and the connection of emitters of Q_1 and Q_2 with those of Q_3 and Q_4 respectively allow the common mode signals to swing to almost the supply voltages. Q_4 and Q_3 have high base emitter breakdown voltage at any of the input terminals to go to either of the supply voltages. In addition, Q_4 and Q_3 considerably enhance the input impedance. Q_6 and Q_7 are the current sinks and form the active load. Q_8 establishes the necessary bias for Q_6 and Q_7. In addition, Q_8 enhances the output voltage at the collector of Q_7 by feeling the collector voltage of Q_6 as extra base drive to Q_7. Terminals 1 and 5 are attached with the operational amplifier for rulling the offset by adjusting the emitter resistors of Q_6 and Q_7 externally. Master current source is formed by the diodes D_2, D_3 and resistor R_5. The master current source provides quiescent current to the high gain stage through Q_{10}, and to the input stage through $Q_9 - R_4$ combination.

Q_{15} and Q_{16} form the darlington stage to provide further amplification of the input. This stage gives a major part to the overall gain of the operational amplifier. The transistors Q_{11}, Q_{13} and Q_{17} form the class B output stage. R_6 and R_7 act as the base-emitter voltage multiplier of the transistor Q_{11}, where $V_{CE} = V_{BE}\left(1+\dfrac{R_7}{R_6}\right)$. This voltage V_{CE} biases the transistor pair Q_{13} and Q_{17} in the class AB condition eliminating crossover distortion at all ambient temperatures. R_8, R_9, Q_{12} and D_4 protect the output transistors during short circuit. If the output is shorted either to negative supply or to ground, the current through Q_{13} increases till the drop across R_8 cuts in Q_{12}, which diverts the extra base drive of Q_{13}. But when the output is shorted either to ground or positive supply, the current through Q_{17} is limited to such a value that the voltage drop across R_9 will not exceed one diode drop. However, the current through Q_{16} is limited by Q_{14} to a value such that the voltage drop across R_{10} is a diode drop.

The capacitor, called monolithic capacitor, establishes the necessary phase compensation making the amplifier unconditionally stable. (Detailed data sheet and application note of μ A 741 are given in the data sheet.)

2·14. BASIC OPERATIONAL AMPLIFIER

Fig. 2.12 (*a*) represents a basic operational amplifier and Fig. 2.12 (*b*) represents the low frequency equivalent circuit of operational amplifier.

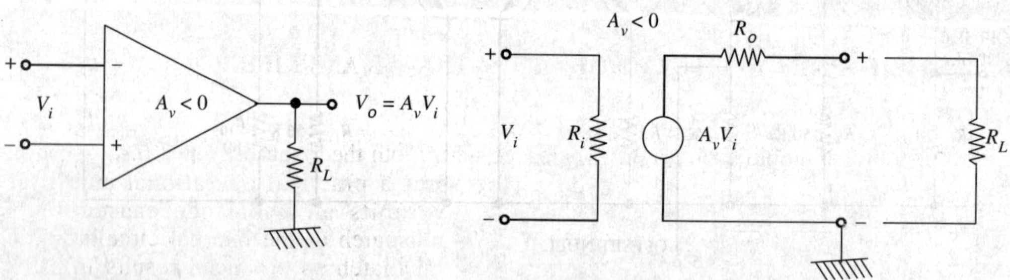

Fig. 2.12 (*a*). Basic Operational Amplifier. **Fig. 2.12 (*b*).** Low Frequency circuit.

Here in the figure, V_i = difference of input voltages, A_v = open circuit voltage gain and A_v (in Fig. 2.12(*b*)) is the gain under load.

2·15. VIRTUAL GROUND

This characteristic plays an important role in explaining the workings of operational amplifier. For an ideal operational amplifier, since the input resistance is infinite there is no current flow into either input terminal. As there is no current through either of the input terminal, the current I

through R_i also passes through R_f shown in Fig. 2.13 (*a*). Further, it is known that $|A_v| \to \infty$ (for an ideal operational amplifier). So $V_i = \frac{V_o}{A_v} \to 0$. This indicates that the input is effectively shorted and hence it can be said that there exists a virtual ground. There is specific reason of employing the term "virtual ground". In this context let the term ordinary ground be explained first. The meaning of the ordinary ground is that it has zero voltage and can sink infinite current. Then a question may come, what is virtual ground? What is its difference with ordinary ground? Why is it so named?

The term virtual ground means any point in a circuit that has zero voltage and draws no current. So as far as voltage is concerned there is no difference between ordinary ground and virtual ground. But for current, ordinary ground can sink infinite current whereas virtual ground draws no current. It is called virtual because it acts like ground as far as voltage, but not current, is concerned. For an operational amplifier the input port appears as a short for voltage, and for current purposes it appears as an open. This is why it is called virtual ground. However there is no physical short circuit between the terminals.

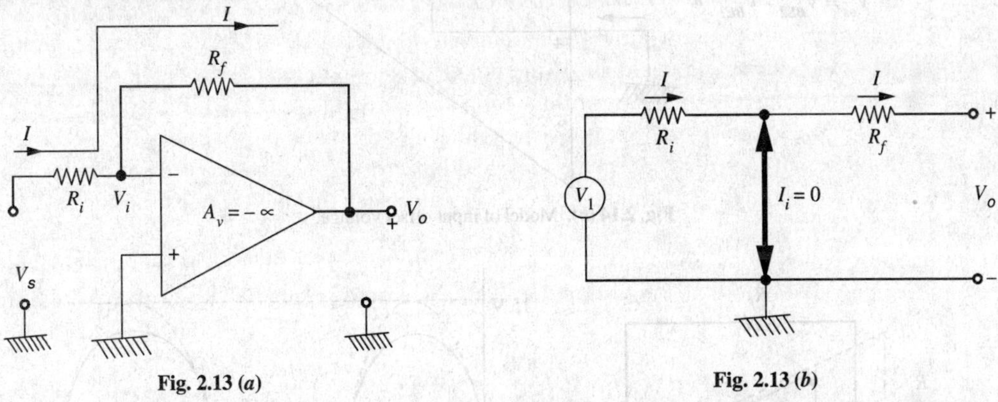

Fig. 2.13 (*a*) Fig. 2.13 (*b*)

Although feedback from output to input through R_f serves to keep the input voltage V_i at zero, no current actually flows into this short as shown in Fig. 2.13 (*b*) where the virtual ground is represented by the thick double-headed arrow. It is not a physical circuit. It is a convenient mnemonic aid.

2·16. SOME IMPORTANT TERMS OF OPERATIONAL AMPLIFIER

Input Offset Voltage

The ideal operational amplifier is perfectly balanced when both the inputs are equal (*i.e.*, $v_1 = v_2$). But a practical operational amplifier exhibits an unbalance caused by a mismatch of the internal circuitry. The mismatch so produced results in error voltage and error currents at the input and output terminals. The input off-set voltage is the voltage that must be applied between the input terminals through two equal resistances to force the output voltage to zero as shown in Fig. 2.14.

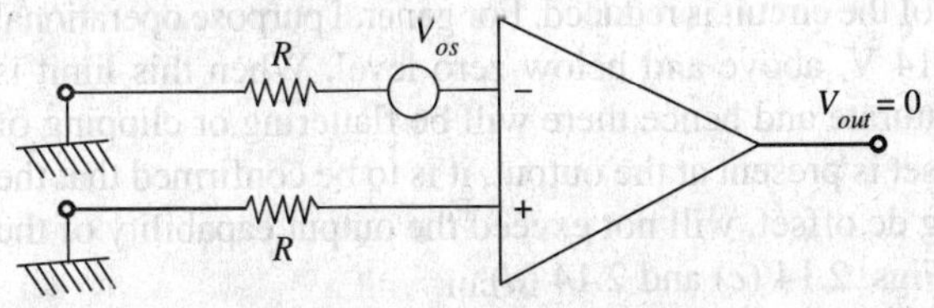

Fig. 2.14 (*a*). Input offset voltage.

Normally V_{os} lies between 0·3 and 7·5 mV. The input offset voltage error is caused by a mismatch in transistor base-emitter voltages in the input DIFF. AMP combined with different unbalances in the other stages. Whereas an output offset error voltage occurs with no signal applied. The output offset voltage is often small enough to be neglected. There are no external resistors to develop an input voltage. Hence the input bias and offset (to be discussed later on) currents will not add any offset in this circuit. Here I_{os} is the input offset current $I_{B1} \sim I_{B2}$

$$E_{os} = V_{os} \times (1 + R_f / R_i)$$

Fig. 2.14 (*b*). Model of input offset voltage.

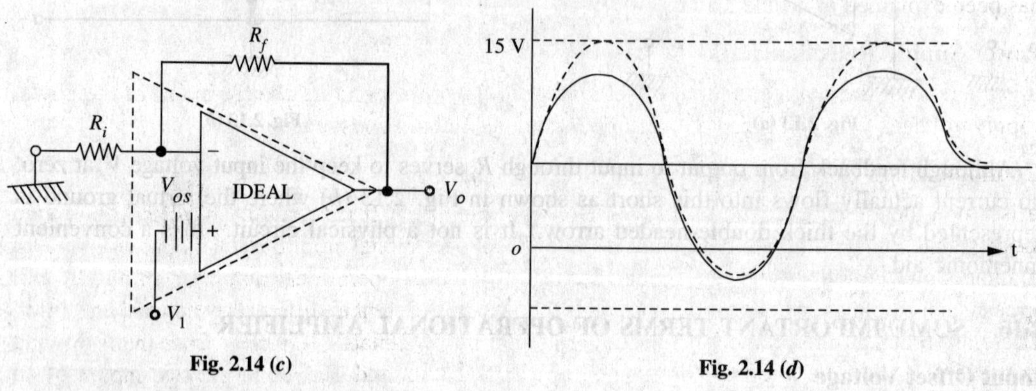

Fig. 2.14 (*c*)

Fig. 2.14 (*d*)

The main problem with this input error is that it gets amplified right along with the input signal. As a consequence the output swing capability of the circuit is reduced. For general purpose operational amplifier, the output can swing upto 13 or 14 V, above and below zero level. When this limit is exceeded, the output-stage transistors will saturate and hence there will be flattering or clipping of the output signal. It concludes that if a dc offset is present at the output, it is to be confirmed that the amplified signal, added on top of the existing dc offset, will not exceed the output capability of the operational amplifier. It is better explained Figs. 2.14 (*c*) and 2.14 (*d*).

Several ways are there to reduce or eliminate the input and output offset. Easiest way is to replace the IC with a higher quality operational amplifier. Many operational amplifiers will have terminals especially for the purpose of offset adjustments. The ratio of the change of input offset voltage to the change in temperature is called input offset voltage drift ($\Delta V_{os} / \Delta T$).

Input Bias and Offset Currents

When the output is at zero voltage the currents I_{B1} and I_{B2} flowing into the input terminals are generally not equal for practical operational amplifier. The difference between the separate currents

(I_{B1} and I_{B2}) entering the input terminals of a balanced amplifier ($V_o = 0$) is called the input offset current I_{os}. The average of I_{B1} and I_{B2} $\left(= \frac{I_{B1} + I_{B2}}{2}\right)$ is called the input bias current I_B. Typical values of I_{os} are in the range of 0.05 to 200 nA and I_B in the range of 0.8 to 500 nA.

It is understood that an operational amplifier has a DIFF. AMP. as its building block. In DIFF. AMP. It has been assumed for its analysis that base currents of the transistors Q_1 and Q_2 (Fig. 2.11) are negligibly small and hence their collector currents are equal to their emitter currents. This means $I_B = (I_{B1} + I_{B2}) / 2 = 0 + 0 = 0$. So there is no bias current. But in practice there is always a base current (whatever may be its value, may be very small but not zero). Hence it is not possible to make the bias current equal to zero in operational amplifier. However, it is possible to make the offset current ($I_{os} = I_{B1} \sim I_{B2}$) equal to zero. It is said in the previous chapter that the parameters of a DIFF. AMP. are such that they give the same quiescent conditions for Q_1 and Q_2. Under this condition $I_{B1} = I_{B2}$ and hence $I_{os} = I_{B1} - I_{B2} = 0$. But it is completely an ideal concept far away from practical. It is not possible because it is very difficult to get two transistors which are identical in all respects. Moreover h_{fe}, V_{BE}, I_{CBO} may vary with temperature. A shift in any of these quantities changes the quiescent points. Also I_{B1} will be different from I_{B2}. However, it is possible to minimize the difference with proper selection of the parameters. An important term is there in connection with the input offset current. The ratio of the change of input offset current to the change of temperature is called the input offset current drift and expressed as

$$\text{Input offset current drift} = \frac{\Delta I_{os}}{\Delta T} \text{ (amp. / C).}$$

Further, even if $V_{os} = 0$, and $I_{B1} = I_{B2} = I_{os} / 2$ (say) in that case there is output offset voltage E_{os}. It has been explained in article 2.17.

Power Supply Rejection Ratio

It is the ratio of the change in input offset voltage to the corresponding change in one of the power supply voltages when all other power supply voltages remain constant.

Common Mode Rejection Ratio

It is a non-ideal characteristic of an IC operational amplifier. It is its ability to reject a common mode signal, one common to both inputs. For an ideal operational amplifier the output will be zero if same signal is fed to both the inputs. But for a practical operational amplifier an output will appear such output as an undesirable one and is found to be different in different operational amplifier. There are practical importance of rejecting common mode signals. It is clear from the following example. Let there be a signal "drowning" in a 50 Hz hum and applied to the two inputs of an operational amplifier. 50 Hz hum common to both inputs will be rejected instead of getting a poor output signal. This leads to an important operational amplifier specification called the common mode rejection ratio.

It is defined as the ratio of the differential mode gain to the common mode gain

$$\text{CMRR} = \frac{\text{Differential mode gain}}{\text{common mode gain}}$$

$$A_d = \text{Differential voltage gain} = \frac{V_o}{V_{\text{in}\,d}}$$

$$A_c = \text{Common mode voltage gain} = \frac{V_o}{V_c}$$

$$V_c = \frac{V_{\text{in}1} + V_{\text{in}2}}{2}, \; V_{\text{in}\,d} = V_{\text{in}\,1} - V_{in\,2}$$

Slew Rate

Slew rate is called the dynamic characteristics of an operational amplifier. It is the time rate of change of the closed loop amplifier output voltage under large-signal conditions. It is also the fastest rate at which the operational amplifier output voltage can change. For an ideal operational amplifier it is infinite. It is expressed as

$$\text{Slew rate} = \left(\frac{dV_o}{dt}\right)_{max} \text{ V/μs} \qquad ...(2.16.1)$$

It changes with change in voltage gain and is normally specified at unity (+1) gain and is measured by a step input dc voltage.

The term unity gain bandwidth indicates the small signal high-frequency limitation on the use of the operational amplifier. But the slew rate is a large signal phenomenon. In case of large-single phenomenon the amplitude of the signal is comparable with the power supply voltages (in the range of volt). Let us drive an expression for slew rate. As it is a large signal phenomenon, let a large signal high frequency sine wave is applied at the input of an operational amplifier as shown in Fig. 2.15.

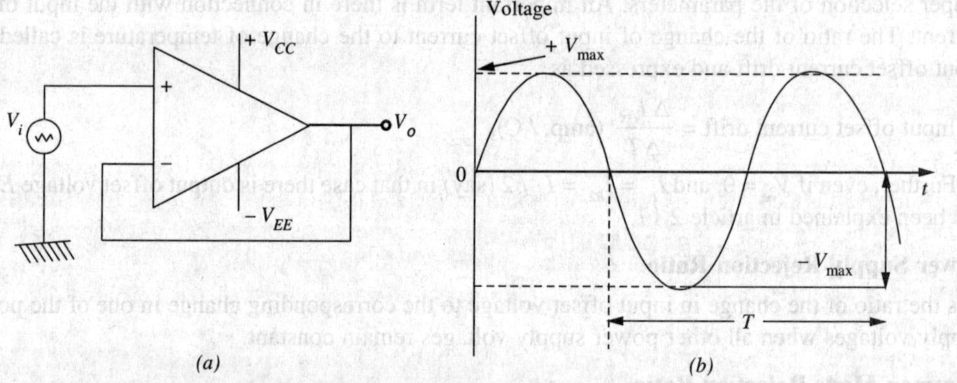

Fig. 2.15. Operational amplifier with large amplitude signal.

Let the applied sine wave is in the form

$$V_i = V_m \sin \omega t \qquad ...(2.16.2)$$

or

$$V_o = V_{max} \sin \omega t \qquad ...(2.16.3)$$

$$\frac{dV_o}{dt} = V_{max}\, \omega \cos \omega t \cdot \cos \omega t \qquad ...(2.16.4)$$

The maximum rate of change of output voltage is

$$\left(\frac{dV_o}{dt}\right)_{max} = V_{max}\, \omega = \text{ slew rate} \qquad ...(2.16.5)$$

$$\text{Slew rate } (SR) = V_{max}\, \omega = 2\,\pi f V_{max} \text{ V/s.}$$

$$= 2\,\pi f V_{max} \times 10^{-6} \text{ V/μ s.} \qquad ...(2.16.6)$$

In practice, slew rate limiting is brought about by *current limiting* and *the saturation of internal stages* of an operational amplifier when a large amplitude, high frequency single is imposed. In case the maximum available current is the current to charge the compensation capacitance network. The capacitor requires a certain amount of time to charge and discharge the compensation capacitors. Hence does not allow the output voltage from responding immediately to a fast changing input. We know that the rise of voltage across a capacitor with time is given by

$$\frac{dV_o}{dt} = \frac{i}{c} \qquad ...(2.16.7)$$

The eqn. (2.16.7) indicates that the slew rate limiting is imposed by such capacitor charging rate where output voltage is the voltage across the capacitor. *Thus the capacitance that limits the slewing ability is most often the frequency compensation capacitance*. However, in some instances, *load capacitance* also limits the slewing ability. The distortion introduced by such phenomenon is shown in Figs. 2.16 (*a*) & 2.16 (*b*).

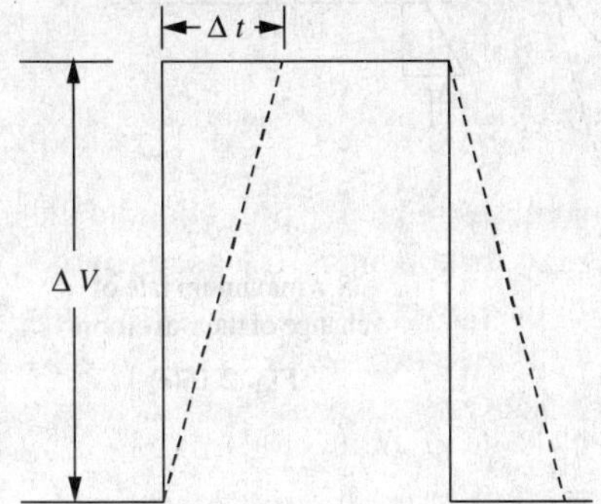

Fig. 2.16 (*a*). Response to square wave (dotted).

$$\text{SR} = \frac{\Delta V}{\Delta t}$$

Fig. 2.16 (*b*). Response to sine wave (dotted).

$$\text{SR} = \frac{\Delta V}{\Delta t}$$

The slew rate can be controlled if the operational amplifier is externally frequency compensated by using smaller capacitors. But this will hamper the stability at unity and low gains. In that case a large value of compensation capacitance is to be selected to get the benefit of improved stability but a lower slew rate. Further slew rate is enhanced with higher closed-loop gains and dc supply voltages. It is a function of temperature with negative temperature coefficient. Wired operational amplifiers with feed-forward compensation have improved slew rate. (Example: LM 108, LM 101]. Operational amplifiers with faster slew rate are sometimes characterised by overshoot and ringing. As a result the output will take longer time to reach steady state. This involves another parameter called settling time. This parameter is important in applications such as D/A or A/D converters using operational amplifiers.

From the equation (2.16.6), it is evident that the slew rate is a function of the *frequency and the amplitude of the input signal.* There will be no distortion at the output waveform unless either the frequency or the amplitude of the input signal exceeds the slew rate of the operational amplifier. Hence it points out that slew rate has important effects in circuits containing operational amplifiers.

Effects of slew rate on the bandwidth and amplitude:

For large output voltage, the upper cutoff frequency is found to be significantly lower than that for small-signal circuits. This is because the slew rate of the op. amp. limits the cutoff frequency. The fastest rate of change of voltage is available at the zero crossing point. Further, for a given distortion. free output signal, the slew rate restricts the maximum operating frequency. The slew rate (S) of the op-amp. should be equal or greater than the maximum rate of change of the waveform to get distortion-free output signal (as shown in Figs. 2.16 (*c*), (*d*) and (*e*).

Effect of slew rate on output pulse rise time:

We have studied that the slew rate effects the cutoff frequency as well as the amplitude of the output waveform. But the rise time of the output waveform is related to the circuit cutoff frequency. The expression for the cutoff frequency limited rise time is written as

$$t_{r(fc)} = \frac{0{\cdot}35}{f_c}.$$

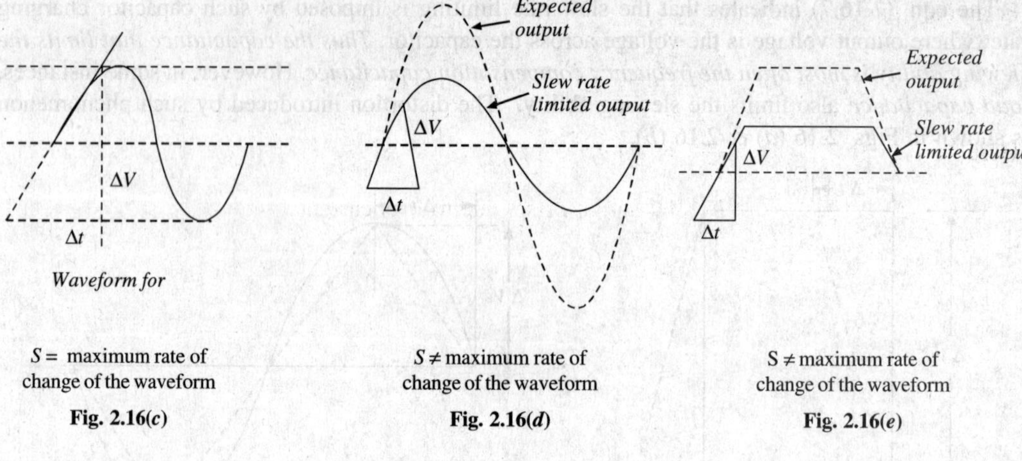

Fig. 2.16(*c*) **Fig. 2.16(*d*)** **Fig. 2.16(*e*)**

Then the slew rate limited rise time is $t_{r(s)} = \dfrac{V_p}{S}$.

This indicates that the slew rate can be said to limit the minimum output rise time for a given output amplitude.

Let us now try to show the distinctions between bandwidth and slew rate:

1. Bandwidth is a small signal phenomenon, whereas slew rate is a large signal phenomenon.
2. Bandwidth is a function of compensating components and closed-loop gain. But slew rate depends on the amplitude and frequency of the input signal. It has increasing tendency with closed loop gain and power supply voltages.
3. Output voltage will be reduced if bandwidth (frequency) is exceeded. But in case of slew rate output is distorted if it is exceeded.

2·17. OFFSET CORRECTING RESISTOR

Let it be explained with Fig. 2.17.

Through R and R_p, the offset current is flowing in opposite direction. As a result an offset voltage is created at the output of the operational amplifier. It is seen from Fig. 2.17 that current from non-inverting input (+) flows through R_p to ground and hence develop a positive voltage at this terminal (V_2) (Polarity is shown in Fig. 2.17). But in the inverting input (–ve input), offset current comes from R and partly from R_f. The offset current which comes from R_p is coming from ground, developing a negative voltage (V_1) at the inverting input. (Polarity is indicated in Fig. 2.17). These two voltages aid mutually and develop a voltage difference (V_D) between the inverting and non-inverting inputs which will be amplified by the operational amplifier. As a result a dc offset voltage will appear at the output (E_{oos}) because of the offset current at the input. The magnitude of this output offset is controlled by the input offset current and the elements of the circuit such as R, R_p and R_f.

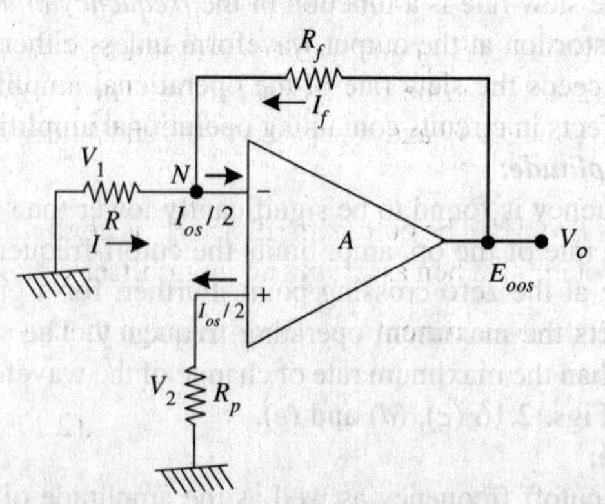

Fig. 2.17. Offset correcting arrangement.

From the figure it is clear that

$$V_2 = \frac{I_{os}}{2} \cdot R_p = -V_1 = E_{oos} - I_f\ R_f \qquad ...(2.17.1)$$

Here
$$\frac{I_{os}}{2} = I + I_f \qquad ...(2.17.2)$$

E_{oos} = output offset due to bias current

$$= \frac{I_{os}}{2} \times R_p + I_f \times R_f = \frac{I_{os}}{2} \times R_p + \left(\frac{I_{os}}{2} - I\right) R_f$$

$$E_{OOS} = \frac{I_{os}}{2} \times R_p + \left(\frac{I_{os}}{2} - \frac{V_1}{R}\right) \times R_f \qquad \left[\because I = \frac{V_1}{R}\right]$$

$$= \frac{I_{os}}{2} \times R_p + \left(\frac{I_{os}}{2} + \frac{I_{os}}{2} \times \frac{R_p}{R}\right) \times R_F \qquad [\because\ V_2 = -V_1]$$

$$= \frac{I_{os}}{2} \times R_p \times \frac{R+R_f}{R} + \frac{I_{os}}{2} \times R_f \qquad \because\ V_2 = \frac{I_{os}}{2} \times R_p$$

$$= \frac{I_{os}}{2}\left[\frac{RP}{R} \cdot (R+R_f) + R_f\right]$$

$$= \frac{I_{os}}{2}\left[\frac{R_f R}{(R+R_f)} \cdot \frac{(R+R_f)}{R} + R_f\right]$$

$$= \frac{I_{os}}{2}\left[R_f + R_f\right] \text{ where } R_P = R \parallel \mathrm{R_f} = \frac{RR_f}{R+R_f}$$

$$\boxed{E_{oos} = I_{os} \cdot R_f} \quad I_B = E_{03}/R_f \qquad ...(2.17.3)$$

In order to eliminate or reduce the output offset voltage (E_{oos}) due to bias current a scheme as shown in Fig. 2.17 is to be adopted so that the voltage V_1 can be made equal to V_2. This simply means that there will be no output voltage (E_{oos}) if the voltages V_1 and V_2 caused by I_{B1} and I_{B2} can be made equal.

The (+ve) terminal (non-inverting) is connected to ground. The output resistance R_o is negligibly small, the right end of R_f is then practically at zero potential. Then assuming no input offset voltage it can be considered that R and R_f are in parallel and the bias current $\frac{I_{os}}{2}$ flows through them:

Hence
$$V_1 = \frac{R R_f}{R+R_f} \cdot \frac{I_{os}}{2} \qquad ...(2.17.4)$$

Applying *KCL* at the node *N*, we get

$$\frac{O-V_1}{R} + \frac{E_{OOS} - V_1}{R_f} = \frac{V_1}{R_{in}} \qquad ...(2.17.5)$$

where R_{in} = input resistance of the operational amplifier.

$$E_{oo3} = R_f \left[\frac{R+R_f}{R_f}\right] \cdot V_1 = R_f .$$

$$R_p = \frac{R\,R_f}{R+R_f} \text{ i.e. } R \parallel R_f$$

$$V_1 = \frac{R\,R_f}{R+R_f} I_{o3}$$

As the non-inverting input terminal is connected to ground, through a resistance R_p through which a current $\frac{I_{os}}{2}$ is flowing.

So $$V_2 = \frac{I_{os}}{2} \cdot R_p \qquad \text{...(2.17.6)}$$

For making $|V_1| = |V_2|$, the value of the resistor R_p is to be adjusted

$$\therefore \quad V_1 = V_2$$

$$\frac{R\,R_f}{R+R_f} \cdot \frac{I_{os}}{2} = \frac{I_{os}}{2} \cdot R_p \qquad \left(\text{Provided both the input currents } I_{B1} = I_{B2} = \frac{I_{os}}{2}\right)$$

$$R_p = \frac{R\,R_f}{R+R_f} \text{ i.e., } R_p = R \parallel R_f \qquad \text{...(2.17.7)}$$

Thus by proper selection of R_p it is possible to eliminate the output offset voltage E_{oos} provided $I_{B1} = I_{B2}$. In that case R_p is the parallel combination of R and R_f. R_p is called the offset correcting resistance. But I_{B1} and I_{B2} are not exactly equal and hence it is not possible to eliminate the output offset voltage completely. But we can reduce it by proper selection of R_p. Hence R_p is also called the offset minimizing resistor.

So the total output offset voltage $E_{oT} = E_{oos} + E_{os}$

$$E_{os} = \text{output offset voltage due to input offset voltage } \left(= \left(1+\frac{R_f}{R}\right) V_{io}\right)$$

and E_{oos} = output offset voltage due to input bias current.

$$E_{oT} = \left(1+\frac{R_f}{R}\right) V_{io} + R_f\, I_{os/2} \qquad \text{...(2.17.8)}$$

2·18. EFFECT OF VOLTAGE AND CURRENT DRIFTS

It has already been discussed that the input offset voltage and input offset current change with temperature. Let us now see what is the effect of voltage and current drifts on the performance of an operational amplifier. It is known from the eqn. (2.17.9) the total output offset voltage is expressed as

$$E_{oT} = \left(1+\frac{R_f}{R}\right) V_{io} + R_f\, I_{os/2}$$

$$\frac{\Delta E_{oT}}{\Delta T} = \left(1+\frac{R_f}{R}\right) \frac{\Delta V_{io}}{\Delta T} + R_f \cdot \frac{\Delta I_{os/2}}{\Delta T} \qquad \text{...(2.18.1)}$$

Where $\frac{\Delta E_{oT}}{\Delta T}$ is the average change in total output offset voltage per unit change in temperature, in μ V/°C. The voltage and current drifts $\left(\frac{\Delta V_{io}}{\Delta T} \;\&\; \frac{\Delta I_{os}}{\Delta T}\right)$ can be negative or positive. In order to get the maximum average drift let both the drifts are +ve. Then the maximum possible change in the total output voltage ΔE_{oT} is

$$\Delta E_{oT} = \left(1+\frac{R_f}{R}\right)\left(\frac{\Delta V_{io}}{\Delta T}\right)\Delta T + R_f\left(\frac{\Delta I_{os/2}}{\Delta T}\right)\Delta T \quad ...(2.18.2)$$

This ΔE_{oT} is called error voltage and is represented as E_r.

$$E_r = \Delta E_{oT} = \left(1+\frac{R_f}{R}\right)\left(\frac{\Delta V_{io}}{\Delta T}\right)\Delta T + R_f\left(\frac{\Delta I_{os/2}}{\Delta T}\right)\Delta T \quad ...(2.18.3)$$

As voltage and current drifts can be either positive or negative, the error voltage E_r can also be either positive or negative.

$$\text{Hence} \quad V_o = \left(-\frac{R_f}{R}\right)V_{IN} \pm E_r \left[\text{ or } \left(1+\frac{R_f}{R}\right)V_{in} \pm E_r \text{ for non-inverting}\right] \quad ...(2.18.4)$$

where V_{IN} is the voltage applied at the inverting input through the resistor R.

It is worthy to mention that voltage and current drifts exhibit a serious problem in ac amplifiers, specially when amplitude of the input voltage is relatively large and the amplifier is operating at its maximum capacity *i.e.,* the amplitude of the output voltage is equal to the saturation voltages, which are slightly lower than the supply voltages (*i.e.,* $+V_{CC}$ and $-V_{EE}$). Further it is observed that the effect of current and voltage drifts is more pronounced in dc amplifiers, particularly if relatively small input voltage is to be amplified by the amplifier.

It has already been discussed about the parameters which force the operational amplifier towards practical operational amplifier from an ideal one. We have discussed the ways of approaching towards ideal one. We have also given some examples at the end of this chapter for different compensation techniques so that we can get approximately ideal operational amplifier.

2·19. CHARACTERISTICS OF PRACTICAL OR NON-IDEAL OPERATIONAL AMPLIFIER

1. The open-loop dc voltage gain is generally in the range of 10^3 to 2×10^5 or more.
2. Input resistance is high, up to hundreds of megohms so that operational amplifier input current can be largely neglected.
3. The output resistance is in the order of 75 ohms, but it can be less than 1 ohm in certain applications.
4. The bandwidth starts at dc and rolls off to unity gain at 1 to 100 MHz (with a slope of 6 to 12 dB per octave, or 10 to 20 dB per decade).
5. Rejection of common-mode signals is of the order of 50,000 to 1.
6. Negative and positive voltage swings over a large dynamic range, usually from $\mp$ 10 to $\mp$ 100 volts.

2·20. GAIN-BANDWIDTH PRODUCT

The bandwidth of an operational amplifier when its voltage gain is unity is called the gain bandwidth product of that operational amplifier. Closed loop bandwidth, unity gain bandwidth, and small-signal bandwidth are the equivalent terms for gain-bandwidth product.

2·21. FEEDBACK IN OPERATIONAL AMPLIFIER CIRCUITS

The open loop gain of an operational amplifier is very large if not infinity. However, many times we want to avoid saturation and hence we will not use the open loop gain. This is done by using what is called feedback. Feedback is taking part or all of the output signal and returning it back to the input. Thus it changes the input and may act to increase or decrease it. If it increases the input, we shall tell it positive feedback. Negative feedback is the opposite feedback. In negative feedback, the returned signal is of opposite polarity or out of phase by 180° (or integer multiple of 180°) with respect to the input signal. Generally negative feedback is employed in *operational amplifier* circuits. This is because a very small *differential input is necessary* to create a *large output*. If we are to take this output and send it back to our input to try and increase the input, we will reach saturation very quickly. This will defeat the purpose of using feedback. An amplifier having negative feedback has self-correcting facility against any change in output voltage caused by changes in environmental conditions. Negative feedback modifies the amplifier characteristics. It provides the following advantages:

(1) Stabilization of gain
(2) Reduction of non-linear distortion
(3) Reduction of output noise
(4) Improvement of bandwidth
(5) Reduction of phase distortion
(6) Effect on input and output impedances.

2·22. CLOSED-LOOP VOLTAGE GAIN

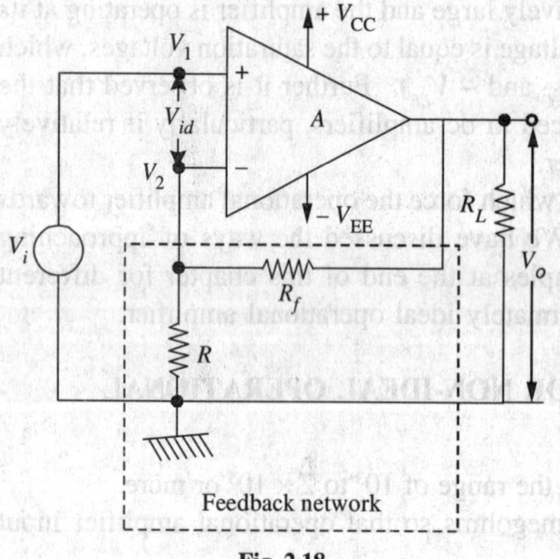

Fig. 2.18.

Fig. 2.18 represents an example of negative feedback, and incorporate the other operational amplifier principles as well.

Open loop voltage gain

$$A_o = \frac{V_o}{V_{id}}$$

Closed loop voltage gain

$$A_{cl} = \frac{V_o}{V_i}$$

$$V_o = A_o(V_1 - V_2) \qquad [\because V_{id} = V_1 - V_2]$$

$$V_2 = V_f = \frac{R V_o}{R + R_f}$$

As R_{in} (input resistance of operational amplifier) is very large compared to R.

$$V_o = A_o\left(V_i - \frac{R V_o}{R + R_f}\right) \qquad [\because V_1 = V_i]$$

$$V_o = \frac{A_o(R + R_f)}{R + R_f + A_o R} \cdot V_i$$

Closed loop voltage gain $$A_{cl} = \frac{V_o}{V_i} = \frac{A_o(R + R_f)}{R + R_f + A_o R} \quad \text{(Practical with feedback)} \quad ...(2.22.1)$$

$$= \frac{A_0}{1 + A_0 \dfrac{R}{R + R_f}} = \frac{A_0}{1 + BA_0}$$

Normally A_o is very high for an operational amplifier.

$$\therefore \quad A_0 R >> (R + R_f) \text{ and } R + (R_f + A_o R) = A_o R$$

Hence
$$A_{cl} = \frac{V_o}{V_i} = \frac{A_o (R+R_f)}{A_o R} = 1 + \frac{R_f}{R} \quad \text{(ideal)} \quad ...(2.22.2)$$

Now we can select the values of R_f and R to get the desired gain. But it is recommended that all external component values should be less than 1 M Ω so that they do not adversely affect the internal circuitry of the operational amplifier. This is to be followed in older generation of operational amplifier like 709 and 741.

The gain of the feedback circuit is $\beta = \frac{V_f}{V_o} = \frac{R}{R+R_f}$ ...(2.22.3)

From the equations (2.22.2) and (2.22.3) we see that

$$A_{cl} = \frac{1}{\beta} \quad \text{(ideal operational amplifier)} \quad ...(2.22.4)$$

Hence Eqn. (2.22.4) indicates that the gain of the feedback circuit is the reciprocal of the closed loop voltage gain.

2·23. CLOSED LOOP GAIN A_{cl} IN TERMS OF OPEN LOOP GAIN (A)

$$A_{cl} = \frac{A_o (R+R_f)}{R+R_f+A_o R} = \frac{A_o \frac{(R+R_f)}{R+R_f}}{\frac{R+R_f}{R+R_f} + \frac{A_o R}{R+R_f}} = \frac{A_o}{1+\frac{A_o R}{R+R_f}}$$

$$A_{cl} = \frac{A_o}{1+\beta A_o} \qquad \left[\because \beta = \frac{R}{R+R_f}\right]$$

This can be represented by the single diagram Fig. 2.19.

Special case

If $V_{id} = 0$ *i.e.*, $V_1 = V_2$

$$V_i = V_1, \quad V_2 = V_f = \frac{R V_o}{R+R_f}$$

$$V_i = V_1 = V_2 = \frac{R V_o}{R+R_f}; \; V_o = \frac{R+R_f}{R} \cdot V_i$$

$$A_{cl} = \frac{V_o}{V_i} = \frac{R+R_f}{R} = 1 + \frac{R_f}{R} \quad ...(2.23.1)$$

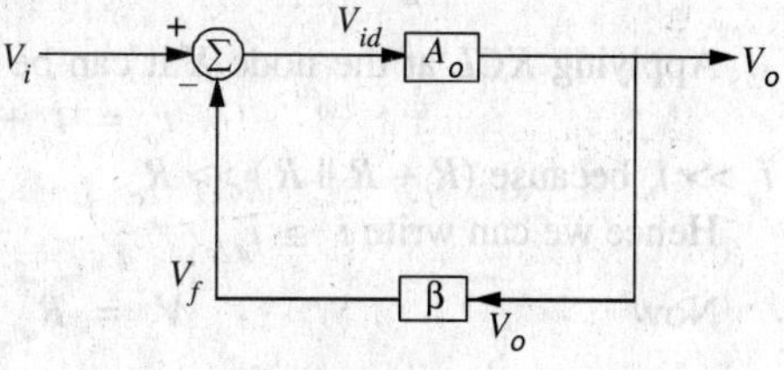

Fig. 2.19.

2·24. INPUT RESISTANCE WITH FEEDBACK

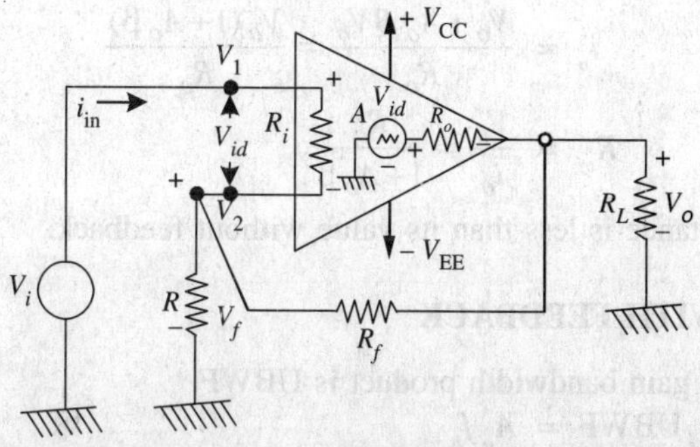

Fig. 2.20. Circuit for the calculation of input resistance with feedback.

R_i = input resistance without feedback.

R_{if} = input resistance with feedback.

$$R_{if} = \frac{V_i}{i_{in}} = \frac{V_i}{V_{id} / R_i}; \; V_{id} = \frac{V_o}{A_o}; \; V_o = \frac{A_o}{1+A_o\,\beta} \cdot V_i$$

$$= \frac{V_i}{\dfrac{V_o}{A_o\,R_i}} = \frac{A_o\,V_i\,R_i}{V_o} = A_o\,R_i\left(\frac{V_i}{V_o}\right) = A_o\,R_i\left(\frac{V_i\,(1+A_o\,\beta)}{A_o\,V_i}\right)$$

$$R_{if} = R_i\,(1 + A_o\,\beta) \qquad \text{...(2.24.1)}$$

The eqn. (2.24.1) indicates that due to feedback the input resistance has been improved.

2·25. OUTPUT RESISTANCE WITH FEEDBACK

Fig. 2.21 shows the circuit for the calculation of output resistance with negative feedback.

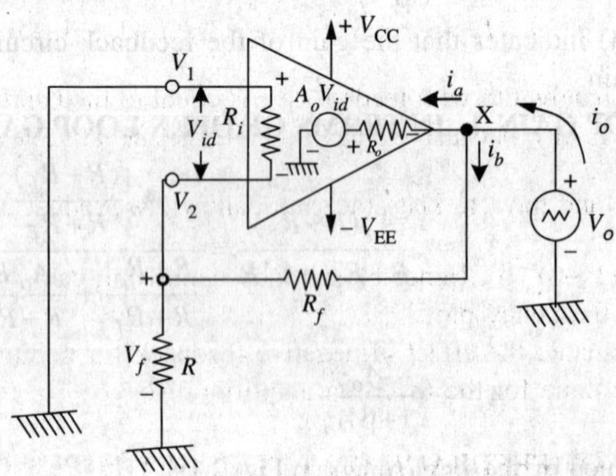

Fig. 2.21. Circuit for the calculation of output resistance with negative feedback.

Applying *KCL* at the node *X* it can be written:

$$i_o = i_a + i_b \qquad \text{...(2.25.1)}$$

$i_a >> i_b$ because $(R_f + R \parallel R_i) >> R_o$

Hence we can write $i_o \cong i_a$

Now $$V_o = R_o\,i_o + A_o\,V_{id} \;\therefore\; i_o = \frac{V_o - A_o\,V_{id}}{R_o} \qquad \text{...(2.25.2)}$$

However $$V_{id} = V_1 - V_2 = 0 - V_f = -\frac{R\,V_o}{R+R_f} = -\beta\,V_o \qquad \text{...(2.25.3)}$$

Then substituting i_o from Eqn. (2.25.2) in Eqn. (2.25.3) we get

$$i_o = \frac{V_o + A_o\,B\,V_o}{R_o} = \frac{V_o\,(1+A_o\,\beta)}{R_o}$$

$$R_{of} = \frac{V_o}{i_o} = \frac{R_o}{1+A_o\,\beta} \qquad \text{...(2.25.4)}$$

Hence the output resistance is less than its value without feedback.

2·26. BANDWIDTH WITH FEEDBACK

It is known that the unity gain bandwidth product is UBWF.

$$\text{UBWF} = A_o\,f_b \qquad \text{...(2.26.1)}$$

where A_o = open loop voltage gain

f_b = break-frequency of an operational amplifier (it is the frequency at which the gain is 3 dB down from its value at 0 Hz.)

Unity gain bandwidth with feedback (UBWF) = $f_F \cdot A_{cl}$

A_{cl} = closed-loop voltage gain.

f_F = bandwidth with feedback.

As gain-bandwidth product is a constant quantity for an operational amplifier,

Hence $$f_F \cdot A_{cl} = A_o f_o$$

$$f_F = \frac{A_o f_o}{A_{cl}} \quad \text{...(2.26.2)}$$

We have seen that $$A_{cl} = \frac{A_o}{1+A_o \beta}$$

$$f_F = \frac{A_o f_o (1+A_o \beta)}{A_o} = f_o (1 + A_o \beta) \quad \text{...(2.26.3)}$$

This shows that the bandwidth with feedback f_F is equal to the bandwidth without feedback f_o, times $(1 + A_o \beta)$. This is also because we have seen that if negative feedback is applied, the gain is reduced by $\frac{1}{1+A_o \beta}$ and have to keep the gain-bandwidth product constant, be the bandwidth should increased to $f_o (1 + A_o \beta)$. Hence closed loop bandwidth can also be determined from the open-loop gain versus frequency plot.

So far we have calculated the effect of negative feedback for noninverting amplifier. Similar calculation can also be done for the inverting amplifier also.

2·27. THE EFFECT OF FEEDBACK ON TOTAL OF OUTPUT OFFSET VOLTAGE

Let us assume that the temperature and power supply voltage are kept fixed. It has been observed that the output voltage is reduced due to the application of negative feed back. Hence it is expected that the output offset voltage with negative feedback will be less than that without negative feedback.

Hence it can be written that the output offset voltage with negative feedback is

$$E_{oTF} = \frac{E_{oT}}{1+A_o\beta} = \frac{\pm E_{sat}}{1+A_o \beta} \quad \text{...(2.27.1)}$$

where A_o = open-loop voltage gain of the operational amplifier.

β = feedback factor *i.e.*, gain of the feedback.

$\pm E_{sat}$ = saturation voltage.

As the voltage gain A_o is very high, the output voltage of the operational amplifier without feedback may be either $+ E_{sat}$ or $- E_{sat}$. It is worthy to mention that the expression of E_{oT} is same for both inverting and non-inverting amplifier. The reason for this is:— when the input signal is absent, both inverting and non-inverting amplifier result in the same circuit. The other effects that negative feedback can introduce are the significant reduction of the effect of (*i*) noise, (*ii*) variations in supply voltages and (*iii*) changes in temperature on the output voltage of the inverting amplifier.

Important parameters are provided in Appendix A vide Tables 4 to 8. Performance curves of 741C (Fairchild) is given in Appendix B. Typical parameters of popular op amps are given in Appendix C.

SOLVED PROBLEMS

1. *A 100 PF capacitor has a maximum charging current of 150 μ A. What is the slew rate?*

Solution:

$$C = 100 \text{ pF} = 100 \times 10^{-12} \text{ F}$$

$$I = 150 \mu \text{ A} = 150 \times 10^{-6} \text{ A}$$

Slew rate $= \dfrac{dV_C}{dt} = \dfrac{I}{C}$

$$= \frac{150\times10^{-6}}{100\times10^{-12}} \text{ V/sec}$$

$$= \frac{150\times10^{-6}}{100\times10^{-12}\times10^{6}} \text{ V/}\mu\text{ s}$$

$$= \mathbf{1{\cdot}5 \text{ V} / \mu \text{ s}}$$

Slew rate is 1.5 V/μ s.

2. *An operational amplifier has a slew rate of 35 V/μs. How long will it take the output to change from 0 to 15 V?*

Solution:

Slew rate = 35 V/μ s

Change in voltage = 15 V

Time taken to change $= \dfrac{15}{35}$

$$= \mathbf{0{\cdot}429 \ \mu \text{ s}}$$

Time needed to change from 0 to 15 V is 0·429 μ s.

3. *An operational amplifier has a slew rate of 2 V/μs. If the peak output is 12 V, what is the power bandwidth?*

Solution:

The slew rate of an Operational Amplifier is

$$SR = 2\pi f \ V_p$$

$$f = \frac{SR}{2\pi V_p}$$

As, for output free of distortion, the slews determine the maximum frequency of operation f_{max} for a desired output swing.

So $f_{max} = \dfrac{1}{12\pi\times10^{-6}} = 26{\cdot}5 \text{ kHz}$

So bandwidth = **26·5 kHz.**

4.

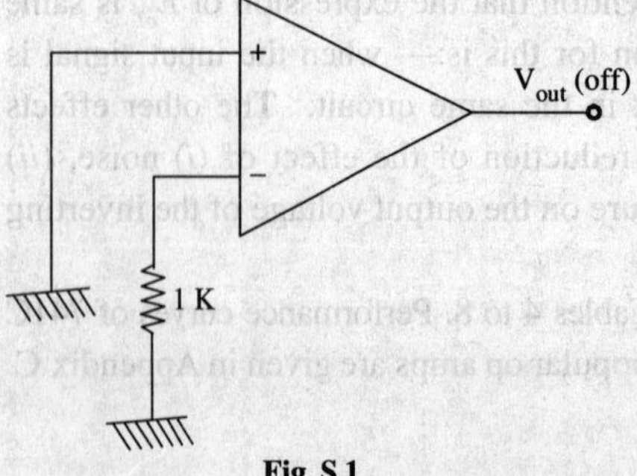

Fig. S.1

I_{in} (off) = 20 nA, If V_{in} (off) = 0, what is the differential input voltage? If A = 10^5, what does the output offset voltage equal?

Solution:

$$I_{in}\ (off) = 20\text{nA}$$
$$V_{in}\ (off) = 0$$

(*i*) The differential input voltage

$$= I_{in}\ (off) \times 1\ \text{K} = 20\ \text{nA} \times 1\ \text{K} = 20\ \mu\ \text{v}$$

The differential input voltage = **20 μV.**

(*ii*) If $A = 10^5$ then the output offset voltage

$$V_{out}\ (off) = 20\ \mu\ \text{V} \times 10^5 = 2\ \text{volts.}$$

Output offset voltage = **2 volts.**

5. *In Figure of the previous problem the input base currents are 90 nA (non-inverter) and 70 nA (inverter). If V_{BE} values are the same, what does the input bias current equal? The input offset current? How much voltage is there at the inverting input? If $A = 10^5$, what does the output offset voltage equal?*

Solution:

Two base current are $I_{B1} = 90$ nA and $I_{B2} = 70$ nA

The input bias current $= \dfrac{1_{B1}+I_{B2}}{2} = \dfrac{90+70}{2} = 80$ nA.

Input offset current $I_{io} = |I_{B1} - I_{B2}| = |90 - 70| = 20$ nA

Voltage at the inverting input = – 20 μV (∵ 2·0 nA × 1K = 20 × 10^{-6} volt)

Now $A = 10^5$

$$V_o\ (off) = -20\ \mu\ \text{V} \times 10^5 = -2\ \text{volt}$$

Output offset voltage = **2 volt.**

6. *The base currents in a differential amplifier are 20 μA & 24 μA. What is the value of input offset current? Input bias current?*

Solution:

The base currents are 20 μA and 24 μA.

Input offset current = (24 – 20) = 4 μA

Input bias current $= \dfrac{20+24}{2} =$ **22μA.**

7. *$R_I = 100\ \Omega$, $R_f = 8{\cdot}2$ K, $R_c = 10K$*

Assume that the amplifier is nulled at 25°C. If V_{in} is 20 mV peak sine wave at 100 Hz.

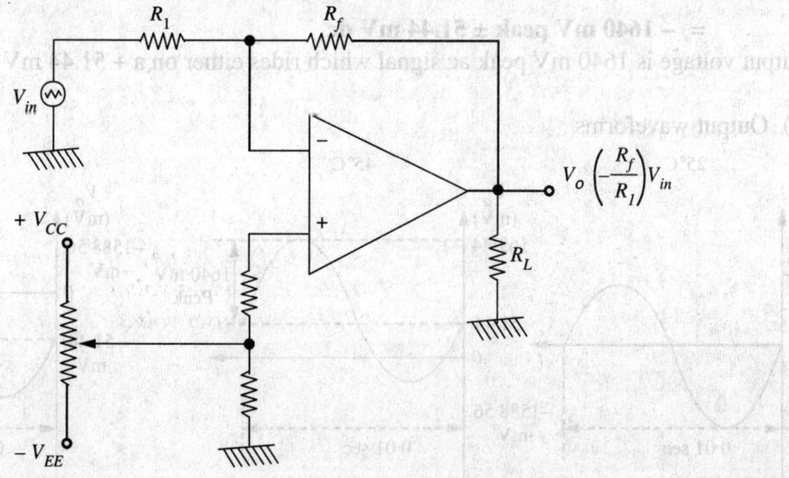

Fig. S.2

(*a*) *Calculate E_r and V_o values at 45ºC.*

(*b*) *Draw the output voltage waveform at 25º and 45ºC.*

Where
$$\frac{\Delta V_{10}}{\Delta T} = 30\ \mu\ V/ºC,$$
$$\frac{\Delta I_{10}}{\Delta T} = 10\ nA\ /\ ºC$$
$$V_o = \left(\frac{-R_f}{R_1}\right)V_{in}$$
$$V_{cc}\ (-V_{EE}) = \pm 15\ V.$$

Solution:

$$R_1 = 100\ \Omega,\ R_f = 8.2\ \text{K},\ R_L = 10\ \text{K},\ \frac{\Delta V_{io}}{\Delta T} = 30\ \mu\ \text{V/ºC}$$
$$\frac{\Delta I_{io}}{\Delta T} = 10\ \text{nA/ºC},\ V_S = \pm 15\ \text{V}$$

The change in temperature $\Delta T = 45 - 25 = 20$ºC.

(*a*) Error voltage E_r

$$= \left(1+\frac{R_f}{R_1}\right)\left(\frac{\Delta V_{io}}{\Delta T}\right)\Delta T + (R_f)\left(\frac{\Delta I_{io}}{\Delta T}\right)\Delta T$$
$$= \left[1+\frac{8\cdot2\times10^3}{100}\right]\left(\frac{30\times10^{-6}}{1^\circ C}\right)(20^\circ\ \text{C}) + (8\cdot2\times10^3)\left(\frac{10\times10^{-9}}{1^\circ C}\right)(20ºC)$$
$$= (1 + 82)\ (30 \times 10^{-3} \times 20)\ \text{mV} + (8\cdot2 \times 10^3)\ (10 \times 10^{-6} \times 20)\ \text{mV}$$
$$= 49\cdot8\ \text{mV} + 1\cdot64\ \text{mV} = 51\cdot44\ \text{mV}$$

Error voltage = 51.44 mV

$$V_o = \left(-\frac{R_f}{R_1}\right)V_{in} \pm E_r = \left(-\frac{8\cdot2\times10^3}{100}\right) \times (20\ \text{mV}) \pm 51.44\ \text{mV}$$
$$= \mathbf{-\ 1640\ mV\ peak \pm 51.44\ mV\ dc}$$

Output voltage is 1640 mV peak ac signal which rides either on a + 51.44 mV or – 51·44 mV dc level.

(*b*) Output waveforms

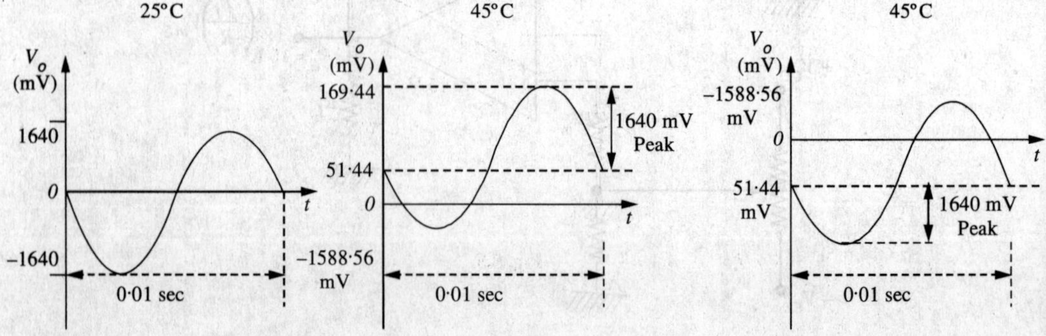

Fig. S.3

8.

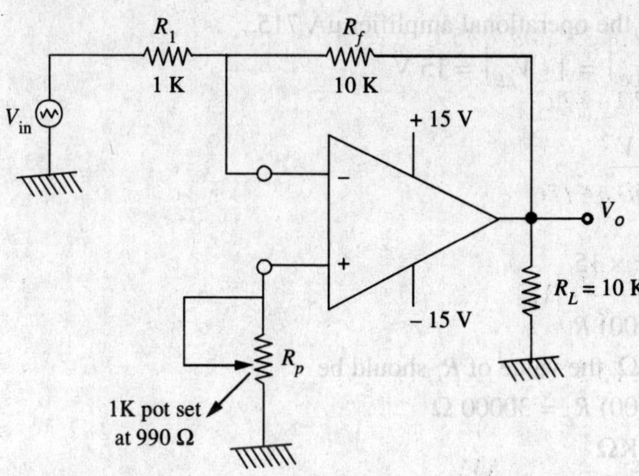

Fig. S.4

Compute the maximum possible total offset voltage in the amplifier shown in Fig. S.4. With supply voltage ± 15 V.

Solution:

Taking the operational amplifier to be LM 307, we get from data sheet

$$V_{io} = 10 \text{ mV}$$

and $$I_{io} = 70 \text{ nA}$$

Total offset voltage $$V_{oT} = \left(1+\frac{R_f}{R_1}\right) V_{io} + (R_f)\,(I_{io})$$

$$= \left(1+\frac{10\text{K}}{1\text{K}}\right) (10 \text{ mV}) + (10 \times 10^3)\,(70 \times 10^{-9}) \times 10^3 \text{ mV}$$

$$= 110 \text{ mV} + 0.7 \text{ mV}$$

$$= \mathbf{110.7 \text{ mV}}$$

Maximum possible total offset voltage is **110.7 mV**.

9. *Design an input offset voltage compensating network for the operational amplifier μA 715 for the circuit shown. Draw the complete circuit diagram.*

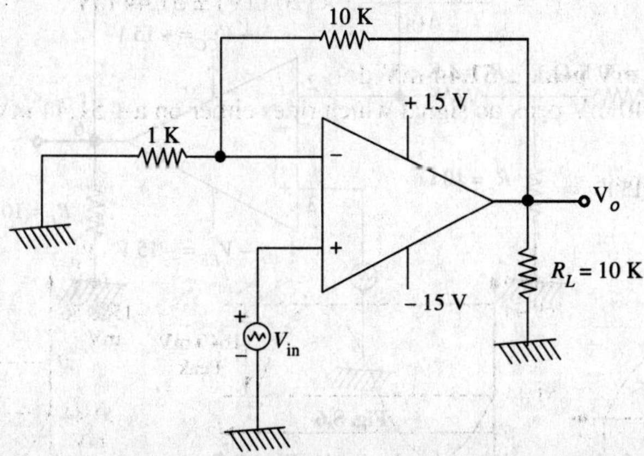

Fig. S.5

Solution:

From data sheet we get $V_{io} = 5$ mV for the operational amplifier μA 715.

$$V = |V_{CC}| = |-V_{EE}| = 15 \text{ V}$$

Now

$$V_{io} = \frac{R_c V}{R_b}$$

$$5 \times 10^{-3} = \frac{R_c}{R_b} \times 15$$

$$R_b = (3000)\, R_c$$

If we select $R_C = 10\ \Omega$, the value of R_b should be

$$R_b = (3000)\, R_C = 30000\ \Omega$$

$$= 30\ \text{K}\Omega$$

Since $R > R_{max}$, let $R_b = 10\, R_{max}$ where $R_{max} = \frac{R_a}{4}$. Therefore

$$R_b = (10)\frac{R_a}{4}$$

or

$$R_a = \frac{R_b}{2 \cdot 5} = \frac{30}{2 \cdot 5} = 12 \text{ k}\Omega \text{ Potentiometer.}$$

If a 124 Ω potentiometer is not available, we may prefer to use to the next lower value available, such as 104 Ω, so that the value of R_a will be larger than R_b by a factor of 10. If we select a 10 kΩ potentiometer as the R_a value, R_b is 12 times larger than R_a. Thus

$$R_a = 10 \text{ k}\Omega \text{ potentiometer}$$

$$R_b = 30 \text{ k}\Omega$$

$$R_c = 10\ \Omega$$

The final circuit, which also includes the pin connections for the μA 715, is shown in the following figure.

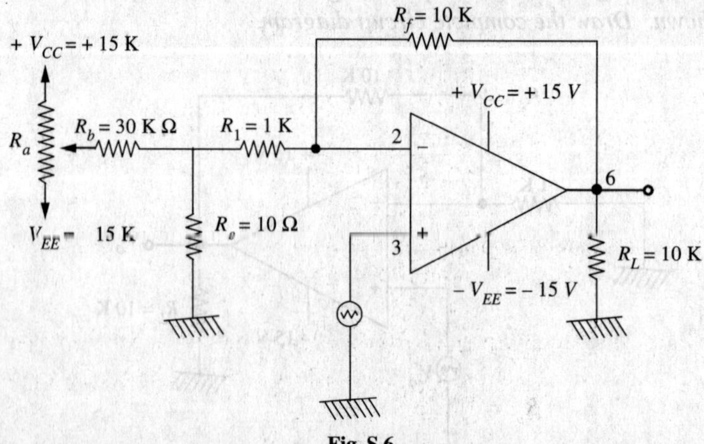

Fig. S.6

10. *For the non-inverting amplifier as shown in Fig. S.7,*

$$R_1 = 100\ \Omega,\ R_f = 10\ K,$$

(i) Determine the maximum possible output offset voltage due to (a) the input offset voltage and (b) input bias current I_B. The operational amplifier has input offset voltage of 10 mV and I_B = 300 nA.

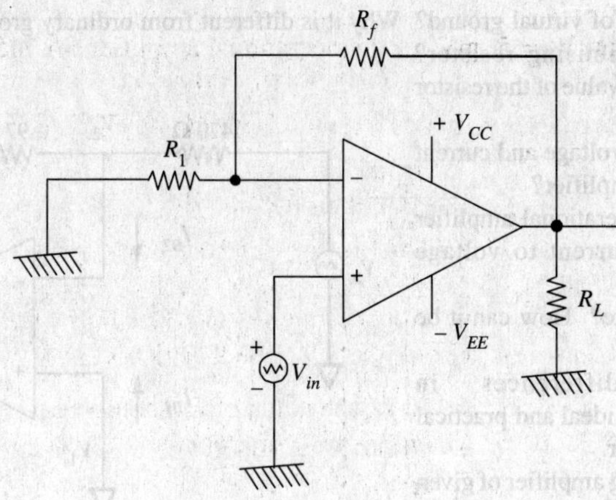

Fig. S.7

(*ii*) *What value of R_p is needed to reduce the effect of input bias current I_B*

Solution:

(*i*)

$$R_1 = 100\ \Omega$$

$$R_f = 10\ \text{K}$$

(*a*) Output offset voltage due to the *i/p* offset voltage

$$= \left(1+\frac{R_f}{R_1}\right) V_{io}$$

$$= \left(1+\frac{10\times 10^3}{100}\right) \times 10$$

$$= 1010\ \text{mV}$$

(*b*) Output offset voltage due to the *i/p* bias current

$$I_B \text{ is } = R_f\ I_B$$

$$= 10 \times 10^3 \times 300 \times 10^{-9}$$

$$= \mathbf{3\ mV.}$$

(*ii*)

$$R_p = R_1 \parallel R_F$$

$$= \frac{R_1\ R_F}{R_1 + R_F}$$

$$= \frac{100\times 10\times 10^3}{100+10\times 10^3}$$

$$= \frac{10^6}{100+10^4} = 99\ \Omega$$

$$R_p = \mathbf{99\ \Omega.}$$

REVIEW QUESTIONS

1. What is slew rate? List the causes of the slew rate. Name the basic parameter which limits the slew rate.
2. Explain the effect of negative feedback on frequency response.
3. Explain the difference between slew rate and bandwidth.
4. Why is it necessary to use an external offset voltage compensating network with practical operational amplifier circuits.

5. What is the concept of virtual ground? Why it is different from ordinary ground?

6. What is error minimising resistor? What is the required value of the resistor and why?

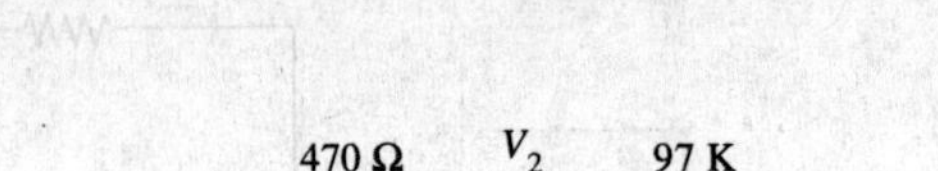

7. What are the offset voltage and current of an operational amplifier?

8. Describe how an operational amplifier can be used for current to voltage conversion.

9. What is error voltage? How can it be reduced?

10. Explain the differences in characteristics of an ideal and practical operational amplifier.

(*i*) For the inverting amplifier of given figure determine the minimum possible output offset voltage due to (*a*) *I/p* offset voltage (*b*) *I/p* bias current I_B.

(*ii*) What value of R_{ON} is needed to reduce the effect of *I/p* bias current I_B?

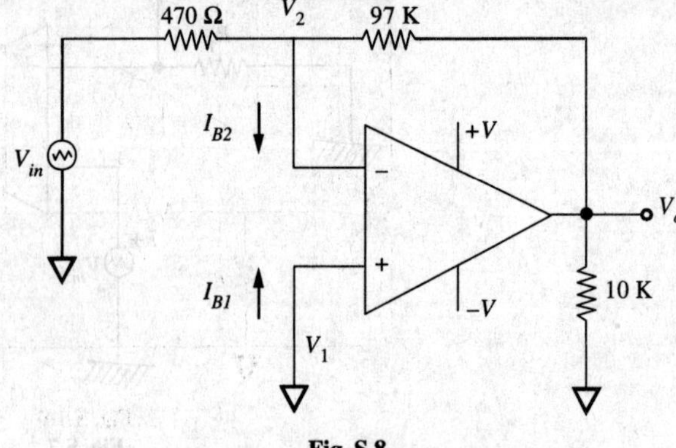

Fig. S.8

11. The above figure operational amplifier has the parameters as: $\Delta V_{io} / \Delta T = 30\ \mu$ V°C (non), $\Delta I_{io} / \Delta T =$ 300 PA / C, $V_f = \pm 15$ V, $R_1 = 1\text{K}\ \Omega$, $R_f = 100$ K, $R_L = 10$K. Assume that the amplifier is nulled at 25°C. Calculate the values of error-voltage E_V and the output voltage at 25°C if (*i*) $V_{in} = 1$ mV dc (*ii*) $V_{in} = 10$ mV dc of draw the o/p voltage of 57°C of $V_{in} = 10$ nv (*p-p*) sin wave 1 kHz.

12. List six characters of an ideal OP AMP and give one example of an OP AMP which is used for audio power application. The 741C op amp having the following parameter is connected as noninverting amplifier with $R_1 = 1$ K and $R_f = 10$ K. Calculate A_f, R_{IF}, R_{oF} and V_{out} · [$A = 2 \times 10^5$, $R_o = 75\ \Omega$, $R_i =$ 2 M Ω, Supply = ± 15 V].

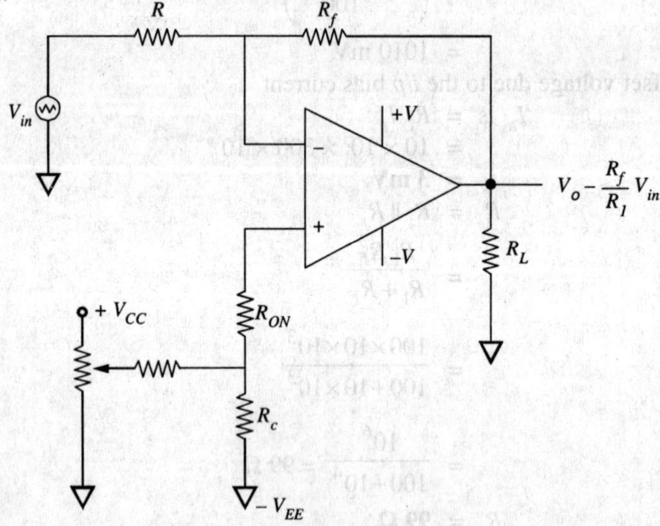

Fig. S.9

13. Define (*i*) input offset voltage (*ii*) input offset current (*iii*) input bias current (*iv*) slew rate.

14. Define the significance of the letters μ A 741 TC.

15. Write disadvantages of first generation OP AMP.

16. Show that negative feedback improves the *I/P* and output resistance and bandwidth of an OP AMP.

17. What are the drawbacks of 709 family?

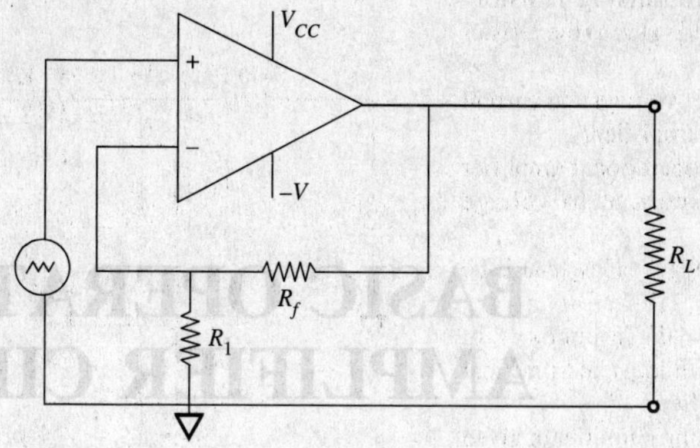

Fig. S.10

18. Draw an equivalent circuit of an OP AMP.

19. Compute the minimum possible output voltage for MC 1536, given that

V_{io} = 75 roman mV

I_{io} = 50 μ A

IB = 250 mA at T = 25ºC

20. Specify four basic building blocks of an OP AMP.

21. Define CMRR.

22. What are the factors that affect above (CMRR) electrical parameter of an OP AMP?

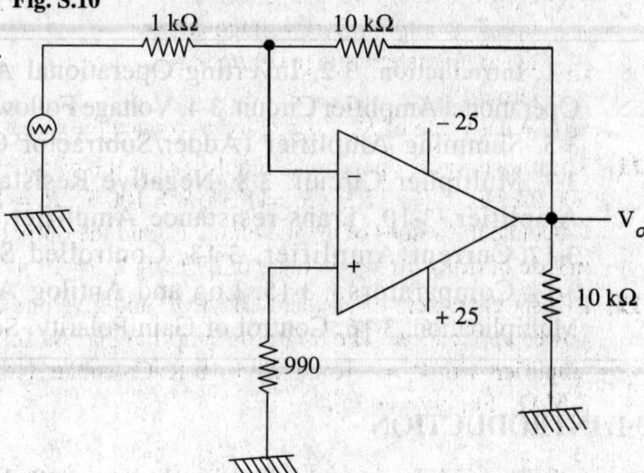

Fig. S.11

3

BASIC OPERATIONAL AMPLIFIER CIRCUITS

3·1. Introduction. 3·2. Inverting Operational Amplifier Circuit. 3·3. Non-Inverting Operational Amplifier Circuit. 3·4. Voltage Follower Circuit Using Operational Amplifier. 3·5. Summing Amplifier (Adder/Subtractor Circuit). 3·6. Difference Amplifier. 3·7. Multiplier Circuit. 3·8. Negative Resistance Converter. 3·9. Instrumentation Amplifier. 3·10. Trans-resistance Amplifier. 3·11. Transconductance Amplifier. 3·12. Current Amplifier. 3·13. Controlled Source Representation of Op. Amp. 3·14. Comparators. 3·15. Log and Antilog Amplifiers. 3·15.a Log Amplifier and Multiplication. 3·16. Control of Gain Polarity. Solved Problems and Review Questions.

3·1. INTRODUCTION

Operational amplifiers are high gain, direct coupled differential linear amplifiers and generally alike. But all dc and ac parameters are not optimized in a particular operational amplifier. Hence, depending upon applications, operational amplifiers are designed to optimize parameters or slew rate. This indicates that for getting best performance it is very vital to select proper operational amplifier. But special purpose operational amplifiers are very expensive. So a compromise is to be made between cost and performance. 741 is a general purpose operational amplifier which can be used in all general applications. But for getting improved circuit performance like large gain bandwidth product, faster slew rate, and higher input impedance, lower noise and offset drift etc we can recommend LF 351 which is a low cost high speed JFET operational amplifier and also pin compatible with 741. But it is surprising that no one operational amplifier has all the dc and ac parameters optimized (not even *LF 351*). Operational amplifier can amplify both dc and ac signals.

In case of dc amplification, the output signal changes in accordance with change in its dc input levels. Such an amplifier can be non-inverting, inverting or differential. In order to get improved accuracy of the dc amplifier the offset null circuitry of the operational amplifier should be used. The dc amplifier can also be used for amplifying the ac signal. However, if the ac input is superimposed on some dc level, in that case an ac amplifier with a coupling capacitor is to be used which not only blocks the dc voltage but also establishes the low frequency cut off limits.

In a cascaded amplifier, because of component tolerances, thermal drift, and variations, dc level may be produced. In order to prevent the amplification of such dc levels, the coupling capacitor is to be used between the stages. Measurement of input resistance input offset voltage and current are given in Chapter 11 under review questions.

3·2. INVERTING OPERATIONAL AMPLIFIER CIRCUIT

Figure 3.1 represents an inverting configuration of an operational amplifier. In order to analyse the circuit of Fig. 3.1, let us apply KCL at the node *A*.

$$\frac{V_o - V_1}{R_f} + \frac{V_i - V_1}{R} = i \qquad ...(3.2.1.)$$

But $\quad$ *A* is virtually grounded and hence $V_1 = 0$ and $i = 0$.

So

$$V_o = -\frac{R_f}{R} V_i \qquad ...(3.2.2)$$

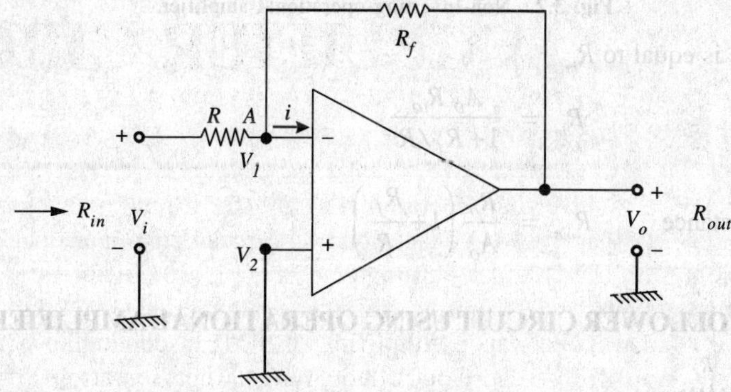

Fig. 3.1. Inverting amplifier.

As the polarity of V_o is always the sposite of V_i, this circuit is called the inverting circuit.

The input resistance of the inverting operational amplifier is equal to R_i. The output resistance is equal to

$$R_{out} = \frac{R_o}{A_o}\left(1 + \frac{R_f}{R}\right)$$

R_o = output resistance without feedback.
A_o = open loop gain of the operational amplifier.

3·3. NON-INVERTING OPERATIONAL AMPLIFIER CIRCUIT

Fig. 3.2 represents a non-inverting operational amplifier. For analysis of the circuit let us apply KCL at the node *A* and apply the condition of virtual ground at *A; i.e.,*

$$V_1 = V_i \text{ and } i = 0$$

Hence

$$\frac{V_1}{R} + \frac{V_1 - V_o}{R_f} = i \qquad ...(3.3.1)$$

$$\therefore \quad V_i\left(\frac{1}{R} + \frac{1}{R_f}\right) = \frac{V_o}{R_f} \qquad ...(3.3.2)$$

(as $V_1 = V_i$ and $i = 0$)

$$\therefore \quad \frac{V_o}{V_1} = \left(1 + \frac{R_f}{R}\right) \qquad ...(3.3.3)$$

This indicates that V_o is always greater than V_i and also that the circuit does not invert the input voltage to give the output voltage.

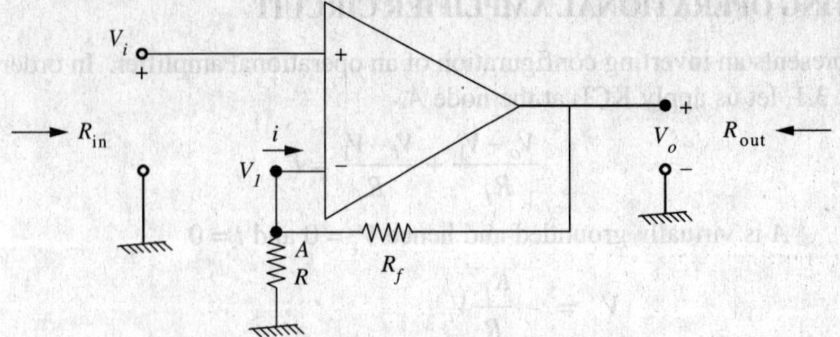

Fig. 3.2. Non-Inverting operational amplifier.

Input resistance is equal to R_{in}

where $$R_{in} = \frac{A_o R_{io}}{1 + R_f/R}$$

The output resistance $$R_{out} = \frac{R_o}{A_o}\left(1 + \frac{R_f}{R}\right)$$

3·4. VOLTAGE FOLLOWER CIRCUIT USING OPERATIONAL AMPLIFIER

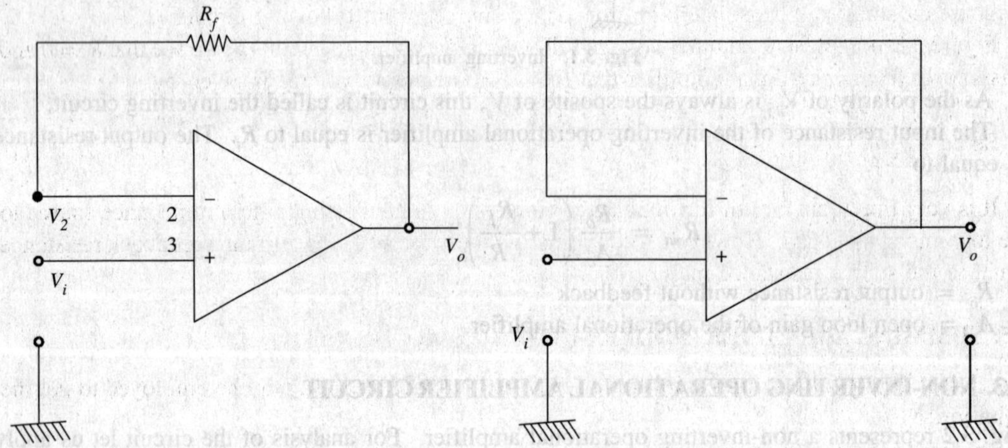

Fig. 3.3 (*a*). Voltage follower circuit. **Fig. 3.3 (*b*).** Voltage follower circuit.

In Fig. 3.3(*a*) V_i is the voltage applied at the non-inverting terminal. R_f is the feedback resistance between the output and the inverting input. Let V_2 be the voltage at the terminal 2 and V_o the voltage at the output.

Application of KCL at terminal 2 gives [Fig. 3.4(*a*)]

$$\frac{V_o - V_2}{R_f} = \frac{V_2}{R_i} \quad \text{...(3.4.1)}$$

where R_i is the input resistance of the operational amplifier.

Again $$V_o = A_o(V_i - V_2) \quad \text{...(3.4.2)}$$

Here A_o = Voltage gain of the operational amplifier.

$$\therefore \quad V_2 = V_i - \frac{V_o}{A_o} \quad \text{...(3.4.3)}$$

Equations (3.4.1) and (3.4.3) give

$$V_o = R_f\left(\frac{1}{R_i}+\frac{1}{R_f}\right)\left(V_i - \frac{V_o}{A_o}\right) \quad ...(3.4.4)$$

$$\therefore \quad V_o = \frac{\left(1+\frac{R_f}{R_i}\right)V_i}{1+\left(1+\frac{R_f}{R_o}\right)\cdot\frac{1}{A_0}} \quad ...(3.4.5)$$

Generally $A_o >> 1$ for an operational amplifier. Hence equation (3.4.5) can be written as

$$V_o = \left(1+\frac{R_f}{R_i}\right)V_i \quad ...(3.4.6)$$

In an operational amplifier R_i is generally much higher than R_f.

So $\boxed{V_o = V_i}$ ...(3.4.7)

The equation (3.4.7) indicates that the gain of the circuit is unity. Hence the output follows the input. The output impedance of the operational amplifier being very low and the input impedance being very high, this circuit is frequently used as a buffer amplifier to reduce voltage error caused by source-loading and to isolate high-impedance sources from following circuitry.

Figure 3.3(*b*) represents another voltage follower. If we compare it with (*a*) we see that $R_f = 0$ and it is known from operational amplifier that $R_i = \infty$. The output voltage is given by

So $$V_o = \left(1+\frac{R_f}{R_i}\right) = 1+\frac{0}{\infty} = 1.$$

It is very important circuit for impedance conversion in connecting a high impedance source to the low impedance load. However, for minimizing the effects of bias current a feedback resistance equal to the source resistance may be connected.

3·5. SUMMING AMPLIFIER (ADDER/SUBTRACTOR CIRCUIT)

Fig. 3.4(*a*) depicts a summing amplifier circuit. At the node *A*, KCL may be employed to get the equation:

$$\frac{V_1-V_i}{R_1}+\frac{V_2-V_i}{R_2}=\frac{V_i-V_o}{R_f} \quad ...(3.5.1)$$

The point *A* is virtually grounded and hence $V_i = 0$ and $i = 0$.

$$\therefore V_o = -\left(\frac{R_f}{R_1}V_1+\frac{R_f}{R_2}V_2\right) \quad ...(3.5.2)$$

If $R_1 = R_2 = R_f$

$$\therefore V_o = -(V_1+V_2) \quad ...(3.5.3)$$

This is equivalent to a controlled source as represented in Fig. 3.4(*b*).

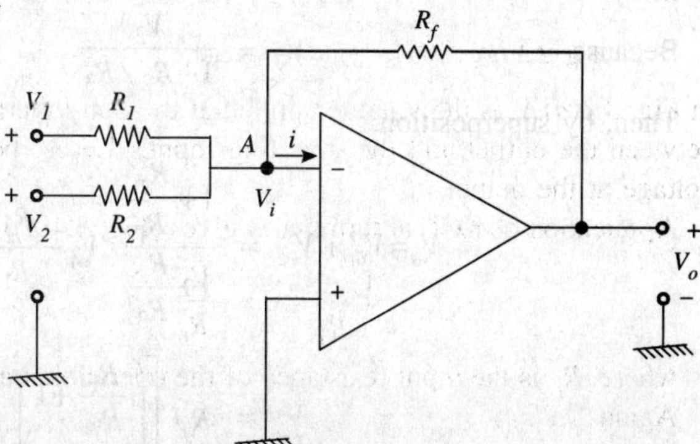

Fig. 3.4(a). Summing amplifier circuit.

It is called summing amplifier because it amplifies the sum of its input. It finds applications in audio mixing, where different sound source signals are combined together with different weights to produce a single sound channel.

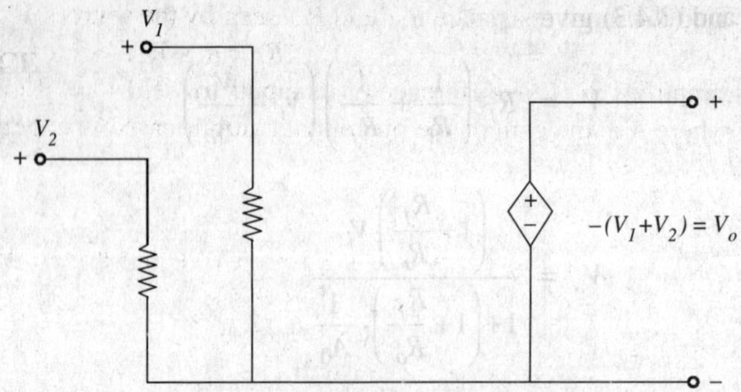

Fig. 3.4(*b*). Controlled source representation.

3·6. DIFFERENCE AMPLIFIER

High input impedance and large open loop voltage gain make operational amplifiers ideally suited for difference amplifier application. The adjoining Fig. 3.5(*a*) represents a difference amplifier.

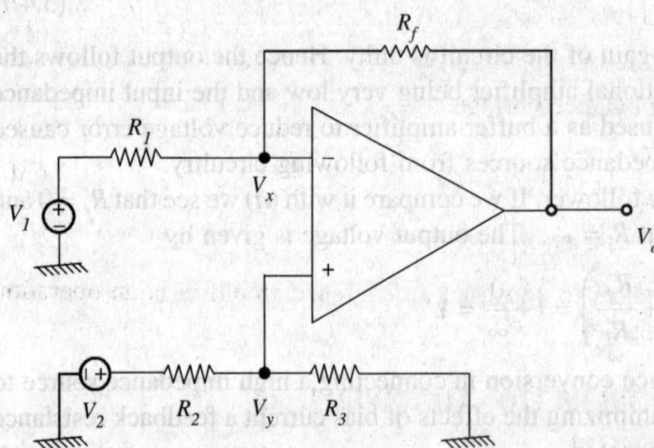

Fig. 3.5(a). Difference Amplifier.

Let us first suppress V_2 and calculate the contribution V_{o1} due to V_1 acting alone. No current can flow in R_2 and R_3, and $V_y = 0$. This is an inverting amplifier, so that

$$V_{o1} = -\frac{R_f}{R_1} \cdot V_1 \quad \text{...(3.6.1)}$$

Next, we set $V_1 = 0$ and calculate the contribution V_{o2} due to V_2 acting alone. This is a non-inverting amplifier.

So $$V_{o2} = \left(1+\frac{R_f}{R_1}\right)V_y = \frac{1+R_f/R_1}{1+R_2/R_3} \cdot V_2 \quad \text{...(3.6.2)}$$

Because $$V_y = \frac{V_2}{1+R_2/R_3}$$ (using voltage divider formula)

Then, by superposition,

$$V_o = V_{o1} + V_{o2} = \frac{1+\dfrac{R_f}{R_1}}{1+\dfrac{R_2}{R_3}} \cdot V_2 - \frac{R_f}{R_1} \cdot V_1 \quad \text{...(3.6.3)}$$

$$\therefore \quad V_o = \frac{R_f}{R_1}\left[\left(\frac{\dfrac{R_1}{R_f}+1}{\dfrac{R_2}{R_3}+1}\right)V_2 - V_1\right] \quad \text{...(3.6.4)}$$

This shows that the circuit yields a weighted difference between its inputs.

Let us now try to find the input resistance R_{i1} and R_{i2} seen by the sources V_1 and V_2.

$$R_{i1} = R_1 \qquad R_{i2} = R_2 + R_3$$

An amplifier that amplifies the true difference of its inputs to yield $V_o = A\,(V_2 - V_1)$ is called a difference amplifier where A is the gain of the operational amplifier. Now to get this function with the circuit Fig. 6.5 (*b*).

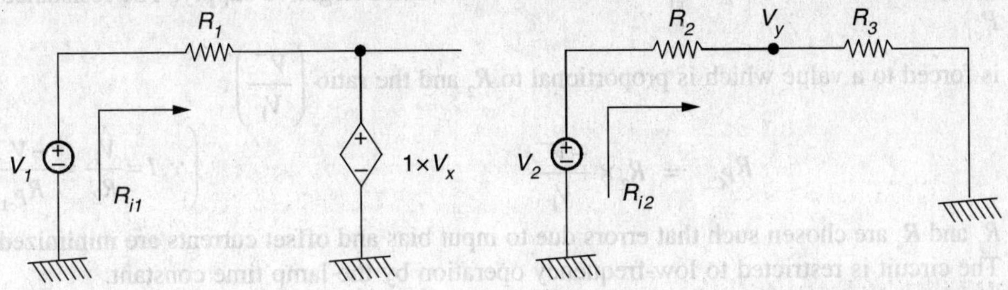

Fig. 3.5(*b*)

$$1 + \frac{R_1}{R_f} = 1 + \frac{R_2}{R_3} \;\therefore\; \frac{R_f}{R_1} = \frac{R_3}{R_2} \qquad \text{...(3.6.5)}$$

It requires that the resistances form a balanced bridge.

Hence
$$V_o = \frac{R_f}{R_1}(V_2 - V_1) \qquad \text{...(3.6.6)}$$

$$V_o = (V_2 - V_1) \text{ if } R_f = R_1$$

So it is thus fair to say that what it takes to construct a difference amplifier is an operational amplifier and a balanced resistance bridge.

3·7. MULTIPLIER CIRCUIT USING OPERATIONAL AMPLIFIER

Fig. 3.6 represents an analog multiplier circuit. In the figure V_1 and V_2 represent the voltage representing the multiplier and multiplicand (or vice versa), respectively. (Example: 3·5 × 6·5 V_1 = 3·5 V, V_2 = 6·5 V. etc.)

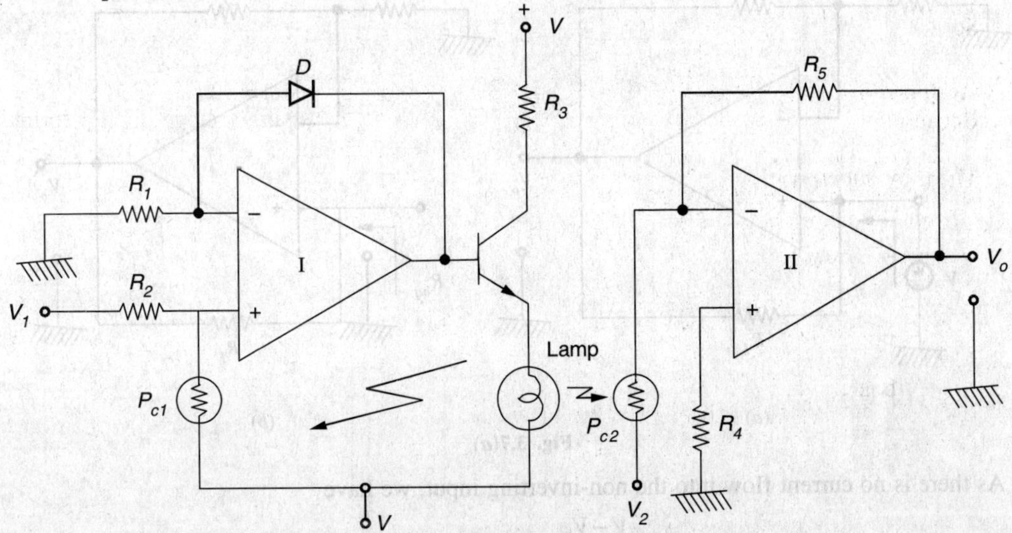

Fig. 3.6. Multiplier circuit.

Conditions for satisfactory results are:

(1) V_1 must be positive while V_2 may be positive or negative. The maximum values of V_1 and V_2 should be such that V_o does not exceed the output voltage capability of the II operational amplifier. V_1 causes I operational amplifier to drive the lamp until the current through the photoconductive cell P_{c1} equates that through R_2.

(2) The photoconductive cell P_{c1} is connected to the fixed negative supply. The resistance of P_{c1}

is forced to a value which is proportional to R_2 and the ratio $\left(\frac{V^-}{V_1}\right)$.

$$R_{P_{C1}} = R_2 \times \frac{-V^-}{V_1} \qquad \left(\because I = \frac{V_1}{R_2} = \frac{-V^-}{R_{P_{c1}}}\right)$$

(3) R_1 and R_4 are chosen such that errors due to input bias and offset currents are minimized.

(4) The circuit is restricted to low-frequency operation by the lamp time constant.

The resistor R_3 is included to reduce the such current when first turning on the (cold) lamp. The photoconductive cells P_{c1} and P_{c2} are mounted on an aluminium block with the lamp mid way between them to get equal illumination.

Hence the resistance of P_{c1} = that of P_{c2} as they are equally illuminated.

$$R_{P_{c1}} = R_{P_{c2}} = -R_2 \times \frac{V^-}{V_1}$$

$$V_o = -\frac{R_5}{R_{P_{c2}}} \times V_2 \qquad \text{[as it is in inverting mode]}$$

$$= -\frac{R_5 . V_2}{-R_2 \dfrac{V^-}{V_1}} = \frac{R_5 / R_2}{V^-} (V_1 \times V_2)$$

If

$$R_5 / R_2 = V^- \text{ i.e., } R_5 = R_2 \times V^-$$

$$V_o = V_1 \times V_2$$

3·8. NEGATIVE RESISTANCE CONVERTER

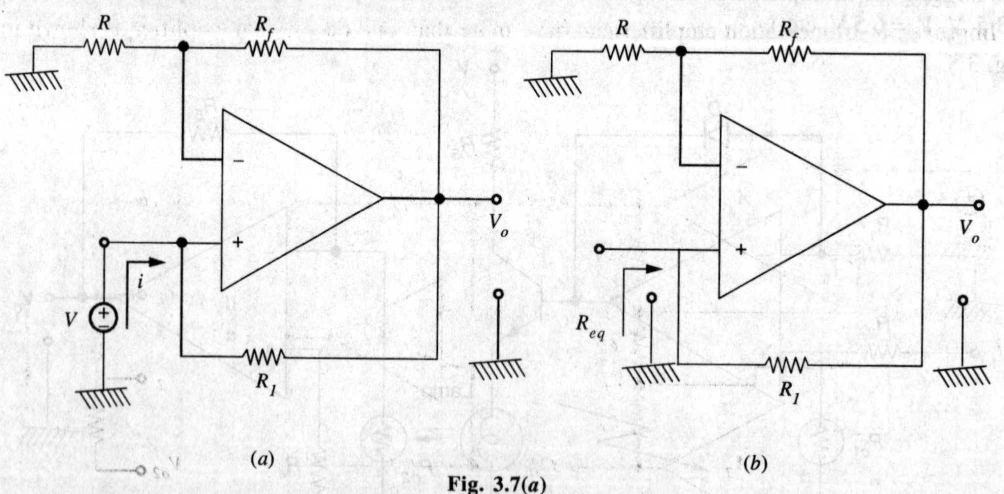

Fig. 3.7(a)

As there is no current flow into the non-inverting input, we have

$$i = \frac{V - V_o}{R_1} \qquad ...(3.8.1)$$

For a non-inverting amplifier.

$$V_o = \left(1+\frac{R_f}{R}\right)V \qquad ...(3.8.2)$$

From Eqns. (3.8.1) and (3.8.2), we get

$$i = -\left(\frac{R_f}{R}\right)\left(\frac{V}{R_1}\right) \qquad ...(3.8.3)$$

Finally we can write

$$R_{eq} = \frac{V}{i} = -\frac{R}{R_f} \cdot R_1$$

$$\therefore \qquad R_{eq} = -(R/R_f) \,.\, R_1 \qquad ...(3.8.4)$$

As we apply V, the circuit causes i to flow into the positive terminal of the test source rather than out, thus providing negative resistance behaviour.

3.9. INSTRUMENTATION AMPLIFIER

There is frequently a need for an amplifier with the following key features in many instrumentation applications:

(*a*) High input impedance
(*b*) High common mode rejection
(*c*) Differential input
(*d*) Single ended output
(*e*) High gain, without large output offset errors.

They are used with pressure sensors, temperature sensors, strain gauges etc. However, there are drawbacks with the circuit as well.

Drawbacks are:

(*a*) Each input lead presents a different input impedance.
(*b*) Loading effect is there.
(*c*) High gain leads to large output offset errors due to input bias currents and offset voltage.
(*d*) Slight mismatches between the resistors can create large reduction in common-mode rejection.

Improved instrumentation amplifier can have more than one operational amplifier as shown in Fig. 3.8.

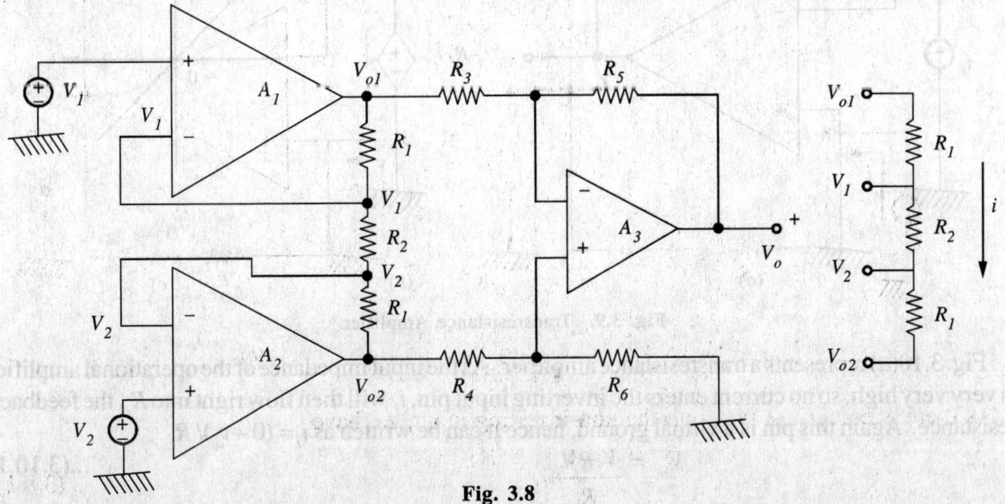

Fig. 3.8

Let us find out an expression for V_o in terms of V_1 and V_2. The operational amplifier A_3 is basically a difference amplifier.

Hence
$$V_o = \frac{R_5}{R_3}(V_{o2} - V_{o1}) \quad ...(3.9.1)$$

where V_{o2} and V_{o1} are, respectively, the output of A_2 and A_1. As the inverting inputs of A_1 and A_2 draw no currents, we can write (using ohm's law)

$$V_{o1} - V_{o2} = (R_1 + R_2 + R_1)\,i$$

or
$$V_{o1} - V_{o2} = (2\,R_1 + R_2)\,i \quad ...(3.9.2)$$

Where i is the current through the series $R_1 \to R_2 \to R_1$ as shown separately. The voltage across R_2 is $V_1 - V_2$. Now using ohm's law we get.

$$i = \frac{V_1 - V_2}{R_2} \quad ...(3.9.3)$$

Then from the equations (3.9.3), (3.9.2) and (3.9.1) we can get

$$V_o = \left(1 + \frac{2R_1}{R_2}\right)\frac{R_5}{R_3}(V_2 - V_1) \quad ...(3.9.4)$$

The equation (3.9.4) indicates that the gain with which the circuit amplifies the difference ($V_2 - V_1$) consists of two terms, (*a*) the term $\left(1 + \frac{2R_1}{R_2}\right)$ indicates the gain of the circuit made up of A_1 and A_2 and the corresponding resistors and (*b*) the terms $\left(\frac{R_5}{R_3}\right)$ representing the gain of the difference amplifier based on A_3.

3·10. TRANSRESISTANCE AMPLIFIER

It is known that the operational amplifier is a voltage amplifier. However, with the help of suitable external components it can also be configured to operate as a transresistance amplifier.

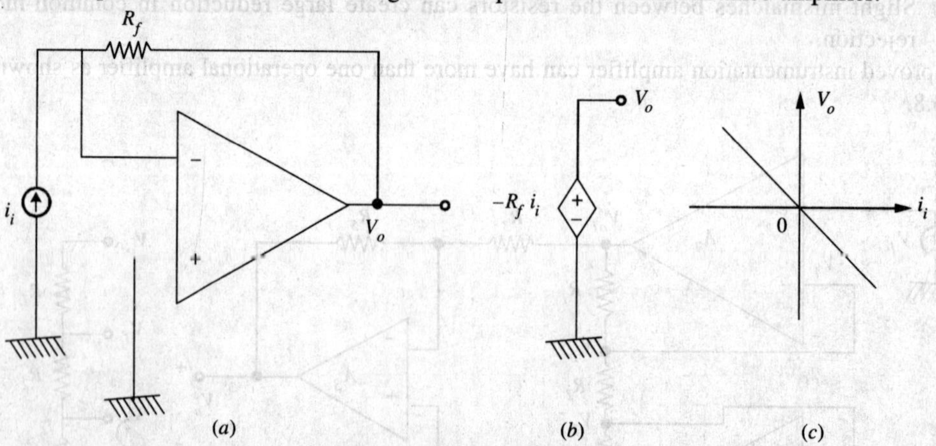

Fig. 3.9. Transresistance Amplifier.

Fig. 3.10(*a*) represents a transresistance amplifier. As the input impedance of the operational amplifier is very very high, so no current enters the inverting input pin, i_i will then flow right into R_f, the feedback resistance. Again this pin is a virtual ground, hence it can be written as $i_i = (0 - v_o)/R_f$

$$\therefore \quad V_o = -R_f i_i \quad ...(3.10.1)$$

"$-R_f$" is the transresistance gain and is expressed in V/A. The reason of negative sign is that i_i is assumed to flow into the circuit. The gain will be positive if the reference direction of i_i is inverted. It is also called an $I - V$ converter because of the relation (3.9.1). Its output behaves as a current controlled voltage source [shown in Fig. 3.10(*b*)].

The relationship (3.10.1) can be had by feeding i_i directly to a grounded resistance R_f without the need for any operational amplifier. But, with the operational amplifier in place the input source sees $R_i = \infty$ because it is connected to a virtual ground, and an output load sees $R_o = 0$ because V_o comes from the ideal **internal** source.

3·11. TRANSCONDUCTANCE AMPLIFIER

Fig. 3.10(*a*) depicts a transconductance amplifier. It is called a $V - I$ converter. Its function is to convert an input voltage V_i to an output current i_L which is independent of the load added at the output. Hence, the load will see an output residence $R_o = \infty$. The above CKT is called the Howland circuit after the name of the inventor. Let us see what is the relation between i_L and V_i?

Assuming the existence of virtual ground at the non-inverting pin of the operational amplifier we can write with the help of KCL at non-inverting pin:

$$i_L = \frac{V_i - V_L}{R_2} + \frac{V_o - V_L}{R_3} \qquad \text{...(3.11.1)}$$

where V_L is the voltage developed across the load.

It is also known that (as it is working in non-inverting mode).

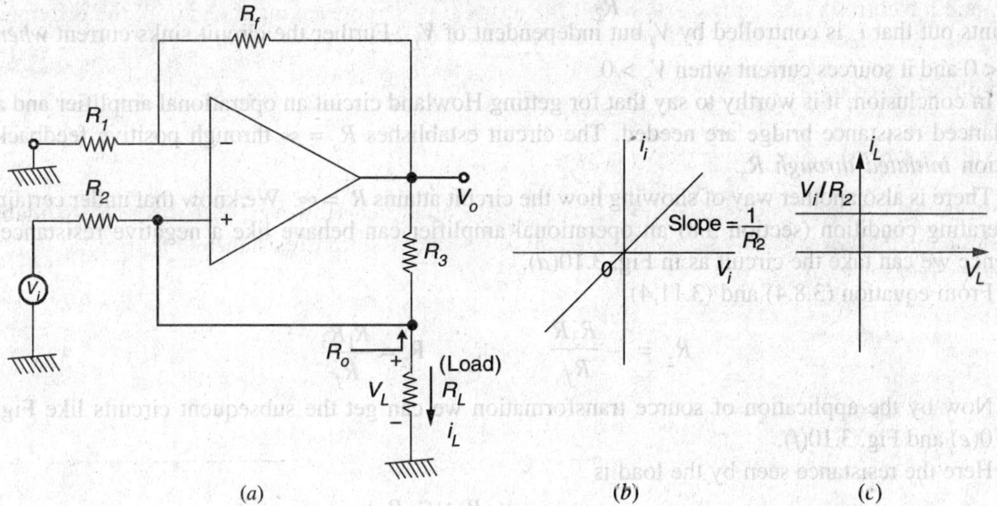

Fig. 3.10. Transconductance Amplifier (*a*) circuit (*b*) transfer characteristic (*c*) output characteristic.

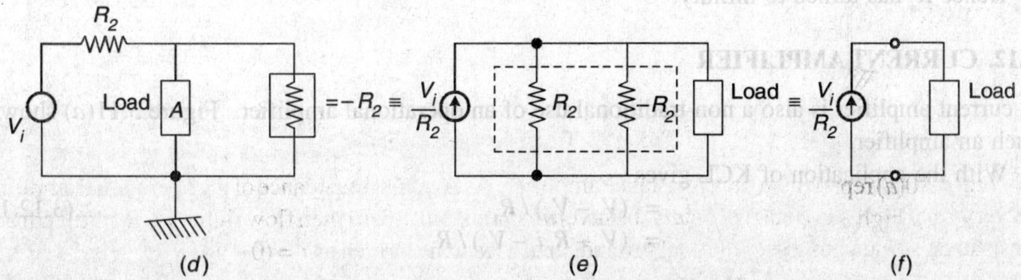

Fig. 3.10. (*d*) circuit (*e* and *f*) subsequent circuits.

$$V_o = \left(1+\frac{R_f}{R_1}\right)V_L \qquad ...(3.11.2)$$

This expression can be had with the subcircuit made up of R_1, R_f and the operational amplifier which formed a non-inverting amplifier.

In inserting V_o from equation (3.11.2) into (3.11.1) we can get

$$i_L = \frac{V_i}{R_2} - \frac{V_L}{R_3}\left(\frac{R_3}{R_2} - \frac{R_f}{R_1}\right) = \frac{V_i}{R_2} - \frac{V_L}{R_o} \qquad ...(3.11.3)$$

where $$R_o = \frac{R_3}{R_3 / R_2 - R_f / R_1}$$

From the features of transconductance amplifier it is said that i_L is independent of particular load appearing at the output. Hence to make i_L independent of load we are to make

$$\frac{R_3}{R_2} = \frac{R_f}{R_1} \qquad ...(3.11.4)$$

This indicates that $R_o = \infty$.

Then the equation (3.11.3) reduces to

$$i_L = \frac{1}{R_2} \cdot V_i \qquad ...(3.11.5)$$

The gain of the transconductance is $\frac{1}{R_2}$ and it is expressed in Ampere/Voltage. Equation (3.11.5) points out that i_L is controlled by V_i but independent of V_L. Further the circuit sinks current *when* $V_i < 0$ and it sources current when $V_i > 0$.

In conclusion, it is worthy to say that for getting Howland circuit an operational amplifier and a balanced resistance bridge are needed. The circuit establishes $R_o = \infty$ through positive feedback action *initiated through* R_3.

There is also another way of showing how the circuit attains $R_o = \infty$. We know that under certain operating condition (section 3.8) an operational amplifier can behave like a negative resistance. Hence we can take the circuit as in Fig. 3.10(*d*).

From equation (3.8.4) and (3.11.4)

$$R_2 = -\frac{R_3 R}{R_f} \quad \therefore \quad R_2 = \frac{R_1 R_3}{R_f}$$

Now by the application of source transformation we can get the subsequent circuits like Fig. 3.10(*e*) and Fig. 3.10(*f*).

Here the resistance seen by the load is

$$R_o = R_2 \,||\, (-R_2) = \frac{R_2 \times (-R_2)}{R_2 - R_2} = \infty$$

Hence R_o has turned to infinity.

3.12. CURRENT AMPLIFIER

A current amplifier is also a non-traditional use of an operational amplifier. Figure 3.11(*a*) shows such an amplifier.

With the application of KCL gives

$$\begin{aligned} i_L &= (V_o - V_N) / R_1 \qquad ...(3.12.1) \\ &= (V_1 - R_f i_i - V_N) / R_1 \end{aligned}$$

as $$\frac{V_1 - V_0}{R_f} = i_i$$

But as $V_I = V_N$ for an operational amplifier.

$$i_L = \left(-\frac{R_f}{R_1}\right)i_i \qquad ...(3.12.2)$$

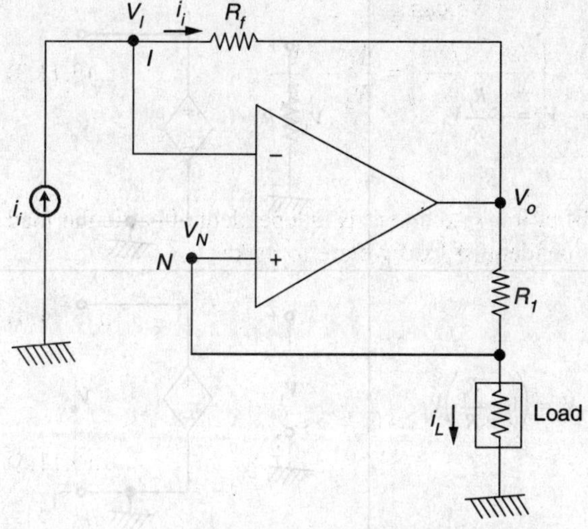

Fig. 3.11 (*a*). Current Amplifier.

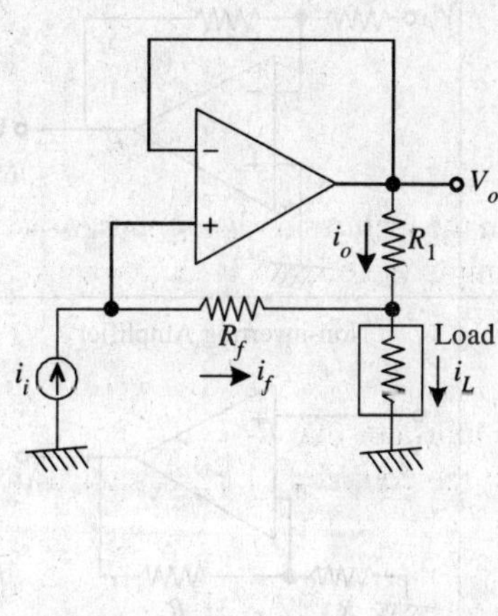

Fig. 3.11 (*b*). Current Amplifier circuit.

If $\qquad R_f = R_1$

Then $\qquad i_L = -i_i \qquad ...(3.12.3)$

The circuit is then said to be a ***current reverser or a current mirror***. The negative sign indicates that if we sink (source) current from the circuit, it will in turn source (sink) current to the load.

There is yet another elegant way of getting current amplification using operational amplifier. Such a circuit is shown in Fig. 3.11(*b*).

For an operational amplifier inputs appear virtually shorted, hence resistances R_1 and R_f in Fig. 3.11(*b*) experience the same voltage drop.

Hence $\qquad R_f i_f = i_o R_1 \qquad ...(3.11.4)$

Application of KCL at *X* gives

$$i_L = i_o + i_f = i_o + \left(\frac{R_1}{R_f}\right)i_o$$

$$\therefore \qquad i_L = \left(1+\frac{R_1}{R_f}\right)i_o \qquad ...(3.11.5)$$

Sinking (or sourcing) current from the circuit causes it to sink (or source) a current $(1 + R_1 / R_f)$ times as large as the load.

3·13. CONTROLLED SOURCE REPRESENTATION OF DIFFERENT OPERATIONAL AMPLIFIER CONFIGURATIONS

We have already observed that different configurations of operational amplifier can have different controlled source representation. They are given here in tabular form together with the expression for the output voltage.

Sl. No.	*Circuit Configuration*	*Expression for output voltage* V_o	*Controlled Source Representation*
1.	Inverting Amplifier	$V_o = -\frac{R_f}{R} V_1$	
2.	Non-inverting Amplifier	$V_o = \left(1 + \frac{R_f}{R}\right) V_1$	
3.	Voltage follower	$V_o = V_1$	
4.	Summing Amplifier	$V_o = -R_f \left(\frac{V_1}{R_1} + \frac{V_2}{R_2}\right)$	
5.	Difference Amplifier	$V_o = \frac{R_f}{R_1}(V_2 - V_1)$	

Fig. 3.12

3·14. COMPARATORS

A comparator is a circuit consisting of two input voltages (inverting and non-inverting) and one output voltage. The purpose of a comparator circuit is to compare one voltage with another to check which is larger and it provides yes or no answer accordingly. The comparator produces a high output voltage, when the *non-inverting voltage* is larger than the inverting voltage. This high output voltage corresponds to "yes" answer. But when the non-inverting input is less than the inverting input, the output is low and it corresponds to "no" answer. ***High input impedance and large open loop voltage gain make an operational amplifier perfectly suitable for comparator applications***. Fig. 3.13(*a*) represents a simple comparator circuit and Fig. 3.13(*b*) depicts the transfer characteristic of comparator.

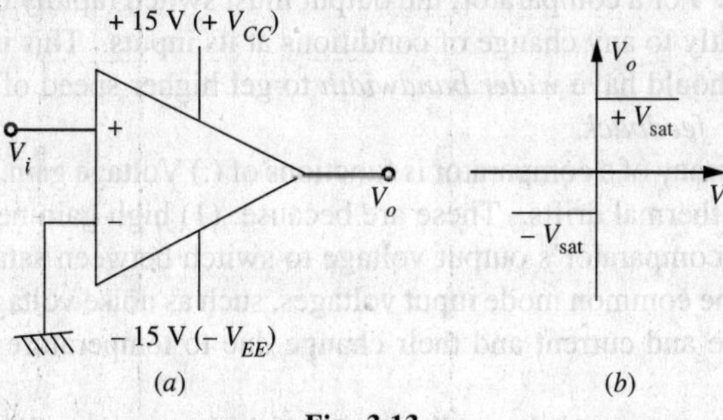

Fig. 3.13

The inverting input is grounded. The slightest input voltage will saturate the operational amplifier.

Fig. 3.13(*c*) and Fig. 3.13(*d*) show two other comparator circuits.

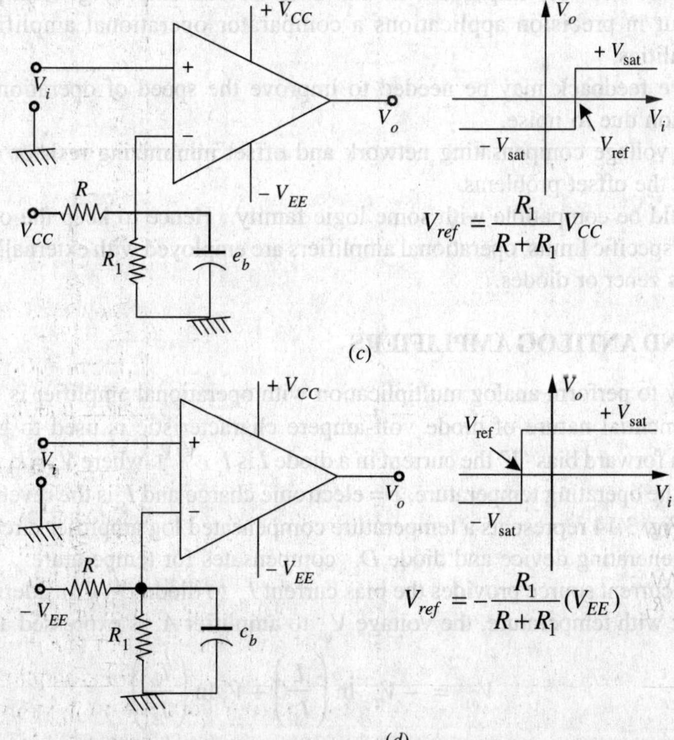

Fig. 3.13

Here $V_{ref} = \frac{R_1}{R+R_1} \cdot V_{CC}$ [for Fig. 3.11 (*c*)]

$V_{ref} = -\frac{R_1}{R_1+R} \cdot V_{EE}$ [for Fig. 3.11 (*d*)]

$\pm V_{sat}$ are the ± saturation voltages of the op. amp.

Comparator Characteristics and Limitations of Operational Amplifier as Comparators

Following are the characteristics of a comparator: (*a*) Speed of operation, (*b*) Accuracy and (*c*) Compatibility of output.

Speed of operation: For a comparator, the output must switch rapidly between saturation levels and also respond instantly to any change of conditions at its inputs. This indicates that operational amplifier comparator should have *wider bandwidth* to get higher speed of operation which *can be improved with positive feedback.*

Accuracy: The accuracy of a comparator is functions of (:) Voltage gain, common mode rejection ratio, input offsets and thermal drifts. These are because: (1) high gain needs a smaller difference voltage to produce the comparator's output voltage to switch between saturation levels, (2) a high CMRR helps to reject the common mode input voltages, such as noise voltage, at the input terminals. (3) input offset voltage and current and their change due to temperature variations must be very small.

Compatibility: A comparator is basically a form of A/D converter. Hence it is expected that its output must swing between two logic levels suitable for a certain logic family like DTL, TTL CMOS etc.

Limitations of operational amplifier comparators: In some applications speed of operation, and accuracy are not very important, in that case we can employ general purpose operational amplifier. But in precision applications a comparator operational amplifier should have the following qualities:

(*i*) Positive feedback may be needed to improve the speed of operation and to avoid false transition due to noise.

(*ii*) Offset voltage compensating network and offset minimizing resistor can be employed to reduce the offset problems.

(*iii*) It should be compatible with some logic family. Hence to keep the output voltage swing within specific limits, operational amplifiers are employed with externally wired components such as zener or diodes.

3·15. LOG AND ANTILOG AMPLIFIERS

A popular way to perform analog multiplication with operational amplifier is with log and antilog circuits. Exponential nature of diode volt-ampere characteristic is used to generate logarithmic function. For a forward bias '*V*' the current in a diode *I* is $I_s e^{V/V_T}$ where $V_T = k_B T/e$, k_B = Boltzmann constant, *T* is the operating temperature, *e* = electronic charge and I_s is the reverse saturation current of the diode. Fig. 3.14 represents a temperature compensated log amplifier circuit. Diode D_1 is the log function generating device and diode D_2 compensates for temperature.

A constant current source provides the bias current I_B to diode D_2. Considering this current to be fairly constant with temperature, the voltage V_{o1} to amplifier A_2 is expressed as

$$V_{o1} = -V_T \ln\left(\frac{I}{I_s}\right) + V_T \ln\left(\frac{I_b}{I_s}\right) \quad ...(3.15.1)$$

Here the reverse saturation currents for both the diodes are taken equal,

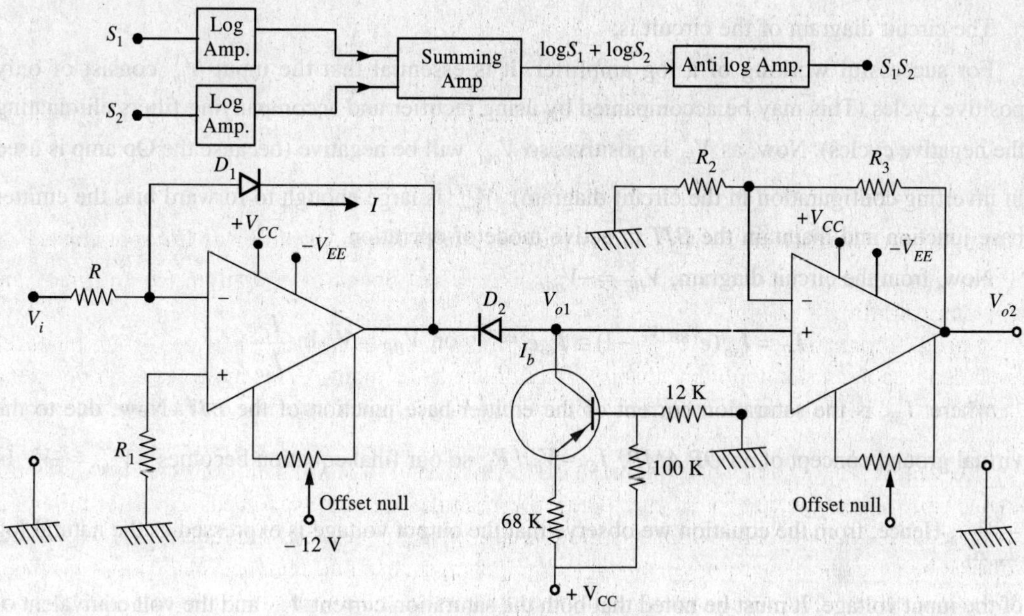

Fig. 3.14. Logarithmic Amplifier.

$$V_{o1} = -V_T \ln \left(\frac{I}{I_s} \bigg/ \frac{I_b}{I_s} \right) \quad \text{...(3.15.2)}$$

$$= -V_T \ln \left(\frac{I}{I_b} \right) \quad \text{...(3.15.3)}$$

$$= -V_T \ln \left(\frac{V_i}{R I_b} \right) \quad \text{...(3.15.4)}$$

Hence the output voltage

$$V_{o2} = -\left(1 + \frac{R_3}{R_2} \right) V_T \ln \left(\frac{V_i}{R I_b} \right) \quad \text{...(3.15.5)}$$

Antilog function can easily be realised by simply interchanging the diode D_1 and resistor R in the above circuit.

3·15*a*. LOG AMPLIFIER AND MULTIPLICATION

The log amplifier is an amplifier in which the output voltage V_{out} is the product of the amplifier gain K and the natural logarithm of the ratio V_{in}/V_{ref}., where V_{in} is the input voltage and V_{ref} is a fixed reference voltage. Thus the equation depicting the operation of the circuit is:

$$V_{out} = K \, In \frac{V_{in}}{V_{ref}}$$

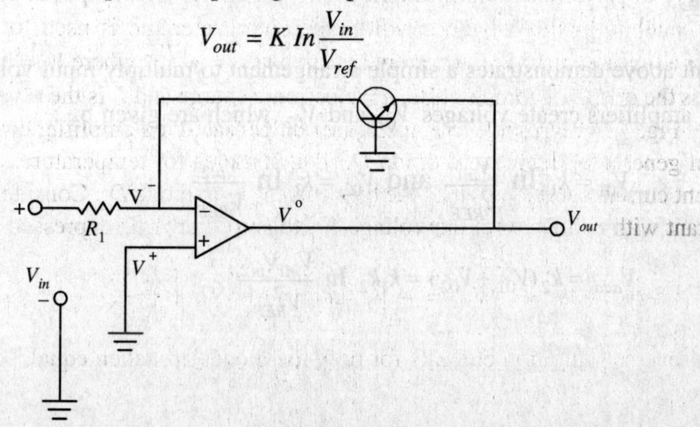

The circuit diagram of the circuit is:

For successful working of a log amplifier, it is essential that the input V_{in} consist of only positive cycles (This may be accompanied by using rectifier and accompanying filters eliminating the negative cycles). Now, as V_{in} is positive, so V_{out} will be negative (because the Op amp is used in inverting configuration in the circuit diagram). V_{out} is large enough to forward bias the emitter base junction and maintain the *BJT* in active mode of operation.

Now, from the circuit diagram, $V_{BE} = -V_{out}$

$$I_C = I_{so}(e^{V_{BE}/V_r} - 1) \cong I_{so}e^{V_{BE}/V_r} \text{ or, } V_{BE} = V_r \text{ In } \frac{I_C}{I_{so}}$$

where I_{so} is the saturation current of the emitter-base junction of the *BJT*. Now, due to the virtual ground concept of an *OP AMP*, $I_C = V_{in}/R_1$, so our final equation becomes : $V_{out} = -V_r$ In $\frac{V_{in}}{I_{so}R_1}$. Hence, from the equation we observe that the output voltage is expressed as the natural log of the input voltage. It must be noted that both the saturation current I_{so} and the volt equivalent of temperature V_r are temperature dependent. Hence, proper compensating circuits should be employed to minimize the effect of temperature change. Compensating feedback circuits may be employed.

Now we know that to construct an analog multiplier using log amplifiers, we can simply sum the logarithms of the input voltages and add them by a simple *OP AMP* summer circuit.

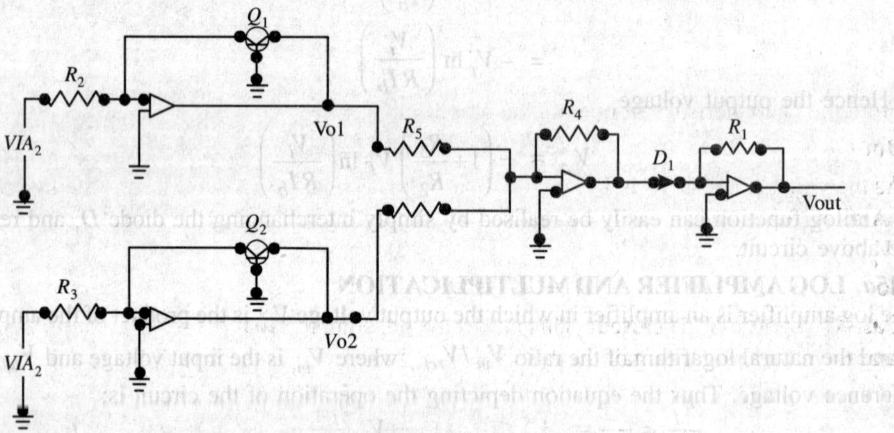

The circuit above demonstrates a simple arrangement to multiply input voltages V_{in1} and V_{in2}. The two log amplifiers create voltages V_{01} and V_{02} which are given by :

$$V_{01} = k_1 \text{ In } \frac{V_{in1}}{V_{REF}} \text{ and } V_{02} = k_1 \text{ In } \frac{V_{in2}}{V_{REF}}$$

Also, $$V_{add} = k_2(V_{01} + V_{02}) = k_1 k_2 \text{ In } \frac{V_{in1}V_{in2}}{V_{REF}^2}$$

$$\Rightarrow \quad V_{out} = ke^{vadd} = ke^{k_1k_2 \ln \frac{V_{in1}V_{in2}}{V_{REF}^2}} = kc + k\frac{V_{in1}V_{in2}}{V_{REF}^2}, \text{ where } c = e^{k_1k_2}$$

Hence, the output voltage is related to the product of the two input voltages as given by the above equation. In this way an analog multiplier can be realized from a log amplifier.

3·16. CONTROL OF GAIN POLARITY

The Fig. 3.15 shows a circuit for gain polarity control. It has two distinct conditions.

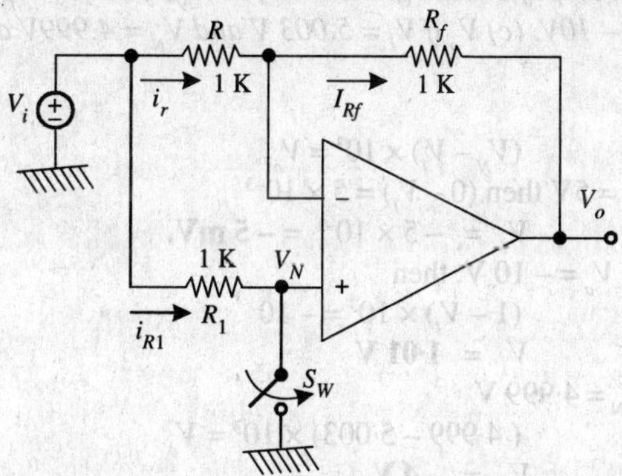

Fig. 3.15. Circuit for gain polarity control.

(1) Case I. Switch S_w is open:

Under this situation the non-inverting input draws no current. We must have

$$i_{R1} = 0, \text{ so } V_{R_1} = 0. \text{ Application of KVL}$$

gives
$$V_N = V_i - V_{R_1} = V_i \qquad I_{R_1} = \frac{V_i - V_N}{R_1} \qquad \text{...(3.16.1)}$$

From the characteristics of operational amplifier $V_I = V_N$

But
$$V_N = V_i \text{ so } V_N = V_I = V_i \qquad \text{...(3.16.2)}$$

As the voltage across R is $V_i - V_I = 0$, it indicates that $i_R = 0$. Further as the inverting input draws no current, hence $i_{R_f} = i_R = 0$. So $V_{R_f} = 0$, indicating that $V_o = V_I - V_{R_f} = V_I = V_i$ and the gain $A = V_o / V_i$

So
$$A = +1 \text{ V/V} \qquad \text{...(3.16.3)}$$

Case II. Switch S_w is closed: This makes the op. amp. to act as inverting amplifer as it grounds the non-inverting pin. The gain in this case

$$A = -\frac{R_f}{R} = -\frac{1}{1} = -1 \text{ V/V} \qquad \frac{V_0 - V_I}{R_f} = \frac{V_I - V_i}{R} \qquad V_I = V_N = 0 \qquad \text{...(3.16.4)}$$

We can now summarize the function of the circuit by saying that, depending on the position of the switch, the circuit behaves, respectively, as a unity gain non-inverting or inverting amplifier.

SOLVED PROBLEMS

1. *An operational amplifier with $R_i = 1\ M\,\Omega$, $A = 10^5$ V/V, $R_o = 100\ \Omega$ and an output load $R_L = 2\ K$ is part of a circuit where $V_N = 0$ and $V_I = 10$ V. Find the voltages across and the currents through R_I and R_o.*

Solution: $R_o = 100\Omega$

$$A = 10^5$$

Voltage across 100 Ω (R_o) = 10 V

Current through 100 Ω (R_o) is

$$I = \frac{10 \text{ V}}{100\Omega} = \cdot 1 \text{ amplifier}$$

$$\therefore \quad \text{Current through } R_i = \frac{100\times10^{-6}}{10^6} = \mathbf{10\ Amp.}$$

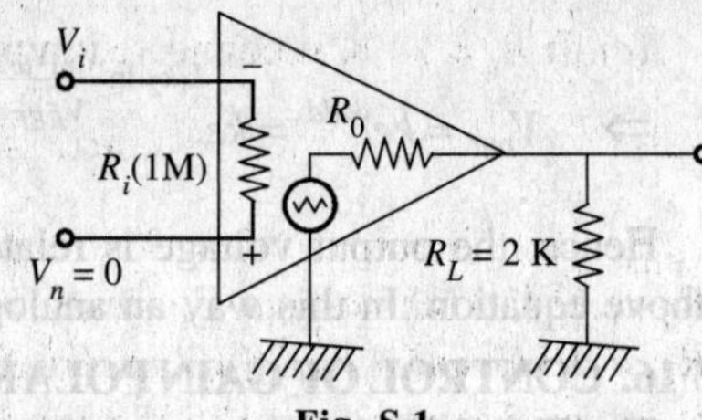

Fig. S.1

2. *For an operational amplifier with gain A = 1000 V/V, find (a) V_I if V_N = 0 and V_o = 5V and (b) V_N if V_I = IV and V_o = – 10V. (c) V_o if V_I = 5.003 V and V_N = 4.999V and (d) V_N if V_I = 3.0 V and V_o = 3.0 V.*

Solution:

$$(V_N - V_I) \times 10^3 = V_o$$

(*a*) When V_N = 0, V_o = 5V then $(0 - V_I) = 5 \times 10^{-3}$

$$\therefore \quad V_I = -5 \times 10^{-3} = \mathbf{-5\ mV.}$$

(*b*) When V_N = 1 V V_o = – 10 V, then

$$(1 - V_I) \times 10^3 = -10$$
$$V_I = \mathbf{1{\cdot}01\ V}$$

(*c*) V_I = 5·003 V, V_N = 4·999 V

$$(4{\cdot}999 - 5{\cdot}003) \times 10^3 = V_o$$
$$V_o = \mathbf{-4\ V}$$

(*d*) When V_I = 3·0 V and V_o = 3·0 V then

$$10^3 \times (V_N - V_I = 3{\cdot}0 \Rightarrow (V_N - 3{\cdot}0) \times 10^3 = 3.0\text{ V}$$
$$\Rightarrow \quad V_N = 3 + 3 \times 10^{-3}$$
$$V_N = \mathbf{3{\cdot}003\ V}$$

3. (*a*) *Find A for an inverting amplifier with R = 10 Ω and R_f = 20 kΩ.* (*b*) *How does A change if a third resistance R_2 = 10 K is connected in series with R? In parallel with R ?*

Solution: (*a*) $A = -\frac{R_f}{R} = -\frac{20}{10} = -2$

(*b*) When R_2 is in series with *R*

$$A = -\frac{R_f}{R_L + R} = -\frac{20}{10+10} = -1$$

When R_2 is in parallel with *R*

$$A = -R_f / \left(\frac{R_2 R}{R + R_2}\right) = -\frac{20\times20}{10\times10} = \mathbf{-4}$$

4. *Find A for a non-inverting amplifier with R = 10 K and R_f = 20 K.* (*b*) *How does A change if a third resistance R_1 = 10 K is connected in series with R?* (*c*) *In parallel with R?*

Solution: (*a*) For a non-inverting amplifier, given that

$$R = 10\text{ K}, R_f = 20\text{ K}$$

The gain of the amplifier

$$A_F = 1 + \frac{R_f}{R} = 1 + \frac{20}{10}$$
$$= \mathbf{3}$$

(*b*) If a 3rd resistance, R_1 = 10 K, is connected in series with *R*, then new gain

$$A_F = 1 + \frac{20\text{ K}}{(10+10)\text{ K}} = 1 + 1 = \mathbf{2}$$

Thus gain is reduced.

(*c*) If R_1 = 10 K is connected in parallel, then gain

$$A_{F''} = 1+\frac{R_f}{R_1 \| R} = 1+\frac{20\,\text{K}}{10\,\text{K} \| 10\,\text{K}} = 1+\frac{20}{5} = \mathbf{5}$$

5. *(a) A source V_s = 1 V is fed to a voltage divider implemented with R_A = 10 K and R_B = 30 K. The voltage V_B developed by R_B is fed, in turn, to a non -inverting amplifier having R_1 = 10 K and R_2 = 30 K, so that A = 4 V/V. Sketch the current and find V_B and V_o. (b) Repeat it for an inverting amplifier with R_1 = 10 K and R_2 = 40. Comment on the differences.*

Solution: Now $$V_B = \frac{30\times 1}{30+10} = \frac{3}{4}\text{ V}$$

$$\therefore \quad V_o = \left(1+\frac{R_f}{R_1}\right)\times V_B = \left(1+\frac{30}{10}\right)\times\frac{3}{4} = 4\times\frac{3}{4} = 4\text{ V}.$$

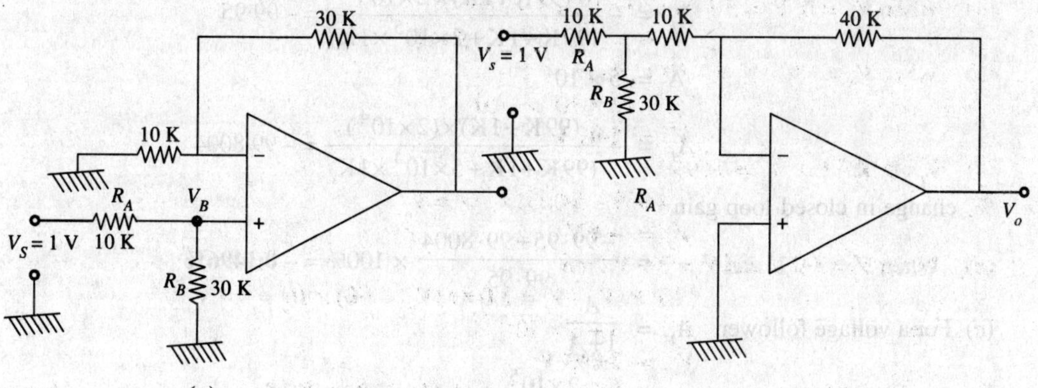

(*a*) (*b*)

Fig. S.2

Here $$V_B = \frac{1\text{V}}{R_A+R_B}\times R_B = \frac{1\text{V}}{40k}\times 30\,k$$

$$A_{inv} = \frac{-40\text{ V}}{10\text{ V}} = -4$$

$$V_B = \frac{3}{4}\text{ V}$$

$$\therefore \quad V_o = -\frac{40\,K}{10\,K}\,.\,V_B = -4\times\frac{3}{4} = \mathbf{-3V.}$$

6. *(a) An inverting amplifier is implemented with R_1 = 1K and R_f = 100K. Find the % change in the closed-loop gain A if the open loop gain a changes from 2 × 10^5 V/V to 5 × 10^4 V/V. (b) Repeat, but for a non-inverting amplifier with R_1 = 1K at R_f = 99K. (c) Repeat, but for a voltage follow ($R_1 = \infty$, F_f = 0).*

Solution: (*a*) Inverting amplifier

$$A_F = \frac{-R_F\cdot A}{(R_1+R_F+AR_1)}$$

Here $$R_F = 100\text{ K}$$
$$R_1 = 1\text{ K}$$

When $A = 2\times 10^5$ $$A_F = \frac{-100\,\text{K}\times 2\times 10^5}{(101\,\text{K}+2\times 10^5\times 1\,\text{K})} = -99{\cdot}9995$$

$A = 5 \times 10^5$ $\quad A_F = \dfrac{-100\,\text{K}\times 5\times 10^4}{(101\,\text{K}+5\times 10^4\times 1\,\text{K})} = -99{\cdot}7984$

Thus the % change $= \dfrac{-99\cdot 9445+99\cdot 7984}{99\cdot 9495}\times 100\% =$ **– 0·15%**

(*b*) Non-inverting amplifier

$$A_F = \frac{(R_1+R_F)A}{R_1+R_F+AR_1}$$

Here $\quad R_1 = 1\,\text{K}$

$R_f = 99\,\text{K}$

$A = 2\times 10^5$

$$A_F = -\frac{(99\,\text{K}+1\,\text{K})\times 2\times 10^5}{(99\,\text{K}+1\,\text{K}+2\times 10^5\times 1\,\text{K})} = -99{\cdot}95$$

$A = 5\times 10^4$

$$A_F = -\frac{(99\,\text{K}+1\,\text{K})\times(2\times 10^4)}{(99\,\text{K}+1\,\text{K}+5\times 10^4\times 1\,\text{K})} = -99{\cdot}8004$$

% change in closed loop gain

$= \dfrac{-99\cdot 95+99\cdot 8004}{99\cdot 95}\times 100\% =$ **– 0·1496%**

(*c*) For a voltage follower $\quad A_F = \dfrac{A}{1+A}$

When A = 2×10^5 V/V $\quad A_F = -\dfrac{2\times 10^5}{2\times 10^5+1} = -0{\cdot}999995$

When A = 5×10^4 V, $\quad A_F = -\dfrac{5\times 10^4}{5\times 10^4+1} = -0{\cdot}99998$

% change = **– 0·0015 %**

7. *An inverting amplifier with R_1 = 10 K Ω and R_2 = 1 M Ω is driven by a source V_I = 0.1 V. Find the closed loop gain A, the percentage deviation of A from the ideal value – R_2/R_1, and the inverting input voltage V_N for the cases A = 1000 V/V, 10^5 V/V, and 10^5 V/V.*

Solution: We have $A_F = \dfrac{-AR_F}{R_1+R_F+AR_1}$

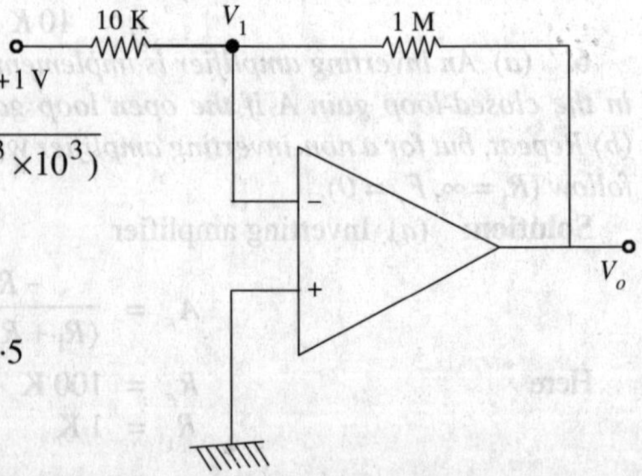

when $A = 10^3$, $A_F = -\dfrac{10^3\times 1\times 10^6}{(10\times 10^3)+(1\times 10^6)+(10^3\times 10^3)}$

$$= -\frac{10^9}{10^4+10^6+10^6}$$

$$= -\frac{10^9}{10^4\,(1+100+100)} = -497{\cdot}5$$

Now A_F (*ideal*) $= -\dfrac{R_F}{R_1} = 10^3$

$\therefore$ Deviation $= \dfrac{A_F\,(ideal) - A_F\,(actual)}{A_F\,(ideal)}\times 100\%$

Fig. S.3

$$= \frac{502\cdot5\times100\%}{1000}$$
$$= 50\cdot25\ \%$$
$$V_o = \cdot1\text{V}\times497\cdot5$$
$$= 49\cdot75\ \text{V}$$

$$\therefore \quad \frac{\cdot1-V_i}{10\times10^3} = \frac{V_1-49\cdot75}{10^6}$$
$$\therefore \quad (\cdot1-V_1)\,100 = V_1-49\cdot75$$
or $$10-100\,V_1 = V_1-49\cdot75$$
or $$V_1 = \frac{59\cdot75}{101}\text{V}$$
$$= \cdot5915\ \text{V}\approx\cdot6\text{V}$$
$$\therefore \quad V_1 = \mathbf{\cdot6V}$$

8. *Find V_I, V_N and V_o from the given circuit*

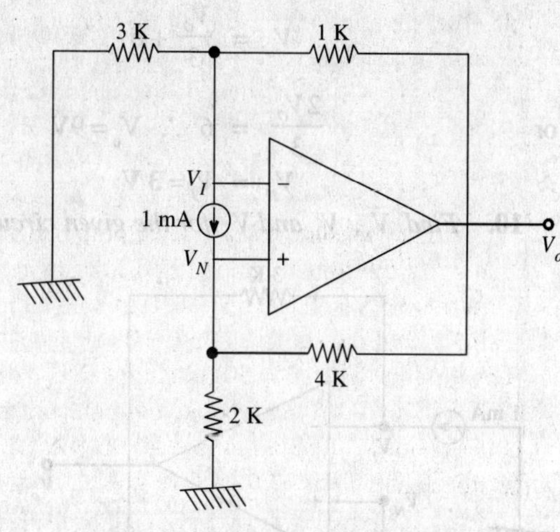

Fig. S.4

Solution: Redrawing the ckt,

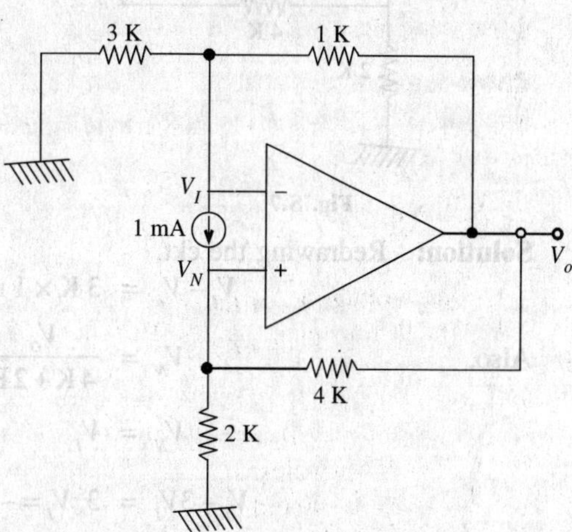

Fig. S.5

Applying KCL to the inverting node,

$$\frac{0-V_I}{3K}+\frac{V_o-V_I}{1K} = 1\text{ mA} \qquad ...(1)$$

Applying *KCL* to the non-inverting node

$$\frac{V_N}{2K}+\frac{V_N-V_o}{4K} = 1\text{ mA} \qquad ...(2)$$

By the property of the operational amplifier

$$V_N = V_I$$
$$-4V_I+3\,V_o = 3 \qquad ...(3)$$
$$2\,V_N+V_N-V_o = 4 \qquad ...(4)$$

Putting $V_I = V_N$ in (3) & (4) we get,

$$-4\,V_I+3\,V_0 = 3$$
$$3\,V_I-V_o = 4$$
$$9\,V_I-3\,V_o = \text{R}$$
$$5\,V_I = 15\,V_I = 3\,V,\ V_N = 3\text{ V}$$
$$V_o = 3\,V_I-4 = \mathbf{5\ V.}$$

9. *Find V_N, V_I and V_o of the CKT of Fig. S.6.*

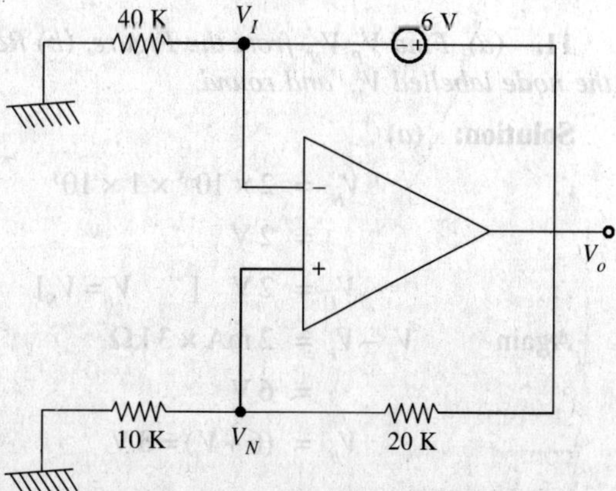

Fig. S.6

Solution:

Applying KCL at *N*

$$\frac{V_N}{10}+\frac{V_N-V_o}{20} = 0$$

or $$2\,V_N+V_N = V_o$$

$$\therefore \quad V_N = \frac{V_o}{3}$$

Now $$V_o-V_I = 6$$

as point *I* and *N* are virtually shorted.

$$V_o - V_N = 6\text{V}$$

$$\therefore \quad V_o = V_N + 6$$

$$\therefore \quad V_o = \frac{V_o}{3} + 6$$

$$\text{or} \quad \frac{2V_o}{3} = 6 \;\therefore\; V_o = 9\text{V}$$

$$\therefore \quad V_N = V_I = \mathbf{3\ V}$$

10. *Find V_N, V_I and V_o for the given circuit.*

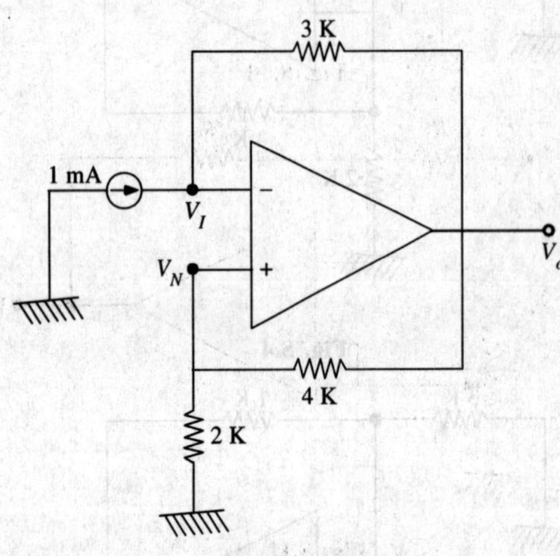

Fig. S.7

Fig. S.8

Solution: Redrawing the ckt,

$$V_I - V_o = 3\text{ K} \times 1\text{ mA} = 3\text{ V} \qquad ...(1)$$

Also,

$$V_N = \frac{V_o}{4\text{K}+2\text{K}} \times 2\text{ K} = \frac{V_o}{3} \qquad ...(2)$$

$$V_N = V_I \qquad ...(3)$$

$$V_I - 3V_I = 3,\; V_I = -\frac{3}{2}\text{ V}$$

and finally

$$V_o = -\frac{3}{2} - 3 = \frac{9}{2}\text{ V} = \mathbf{-4{\cdot}5\ V}$$

11. *(a) Find V_I, V_N from the Figure, (b) Repeat, but with a 5K resistance converted between the node labelled V_N and round.*

Solution: (*a*)

$$\therefore \quad V_N = 2 \times 10^{-3} \times 1 \times 10^3$$

$$= 2\text{ V}$$

$$\therefore \quad V_I = 2\text{ V} \quad [\because\; V_I = V_N]$$

Again $\quad V_o - V_I = 2\text{ mA} \times 3\text{ k}\Omega$

$$= 6\text{ V}$$

$$\therefore \quad V_o = (6 + V_i) = \mathbf{8\ V}$$

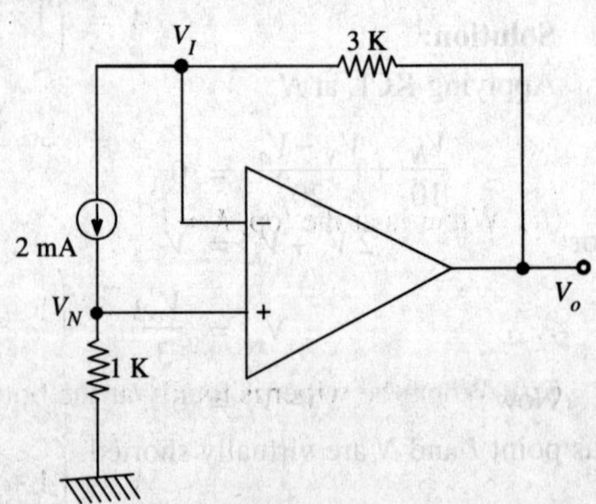

Fig. S.9

(*b*) Using KCL at inverting node we get (Fig. S.10)

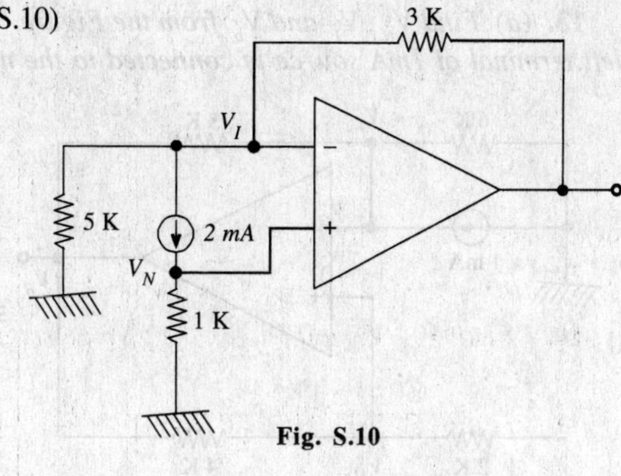

Fig. S.10

$$\frac{V_O - V_I}{3K} = 2\,\text{mA} + \frac{2\,\text{V}}{5\,\text{K}}$$

$$V_o - V_I = 6 + \frac{6}{5}$$

$$\therefore \quad V_o = V_I + 6 + \frac{6}{5}$$

$$= 2 + 6 + 1{\cdot}2$$

$$= 9{\cdot}2\text{ V}$$

$$\therefore \quad V_o = \mathbf{9{\cdot}2\ V}$$

12. *Let $R_1 = R_2 = 10$ K. Find an expression for the gain* $A = V_o/V_i$ in terms of the parameters *k, with $0 \le k \le 1$. What is the value of A with the wiper half way between the top and the bottom? All the way to the top? All the way to the bottom?*

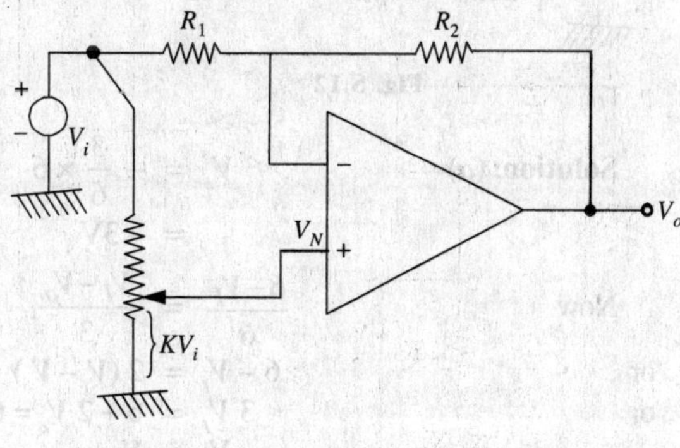

Fig. S.11

Solution: Redrawing the ckt,

O/P due to source V_1 (assume $K V_1 = 0$)

$$V_{o1} = -\frac{R_2}{R_1} V_i \qquad \text{...(1)}$$

O/P due to K V_i is (assume $V_i = 0$)

$$V_{o2} = \left(1 + \frac{R_2}{R_1}\right) K V_i \qquad \text{...(2)}$$

Total o/p $\quad V_o = V_{o1} + V_{o2}$

$$= \left[\left(1 + \frac{R_2}{R_1}\right) K - \frac{R_2}{R_1}\right] V_i$$

$$\frac{V_o}{V_i} = A = \left(1 + \frac{R_2}{R_1}\right) K - \frac{R_2}{R_1} \qquad \text{...(3)}$$

(*i*) Wiper is midway, then $K = 1/2$

$$A = \left(1 + \frac{R_2}{R_1}\right)\frac{1}{2} - \frac{R_2}{R_1}$$

$$= \frac{1}{2} - \frac{1}{2}\frac{R_2}{R_1} = \frac{1}{2}\left(\frac{R_1 - R_2}{R_1}\right)$$

(*ii*) Wiper is at the top, $K = 1$

$$A = \left(1 + \frac{R_2}{R_1}\right)1 - \frac{R_2}{R_1} = 1$$

(*iii*) When the wiper is totally at the bottom $K = 0$.

$$A = \left(1 + \frac{R_2}{R_1}\right)(0) - \frac{R_2}{R_1} = -\frac{R_2}{R_1}$$

13. (*a*) *Find V_N, V_I and V_o from the Figure,* (*b*) *Repeat the problem if 6 K resistance and the left terminal of 1mA source is connected to the node labelled Ground and V_N, respectively.*

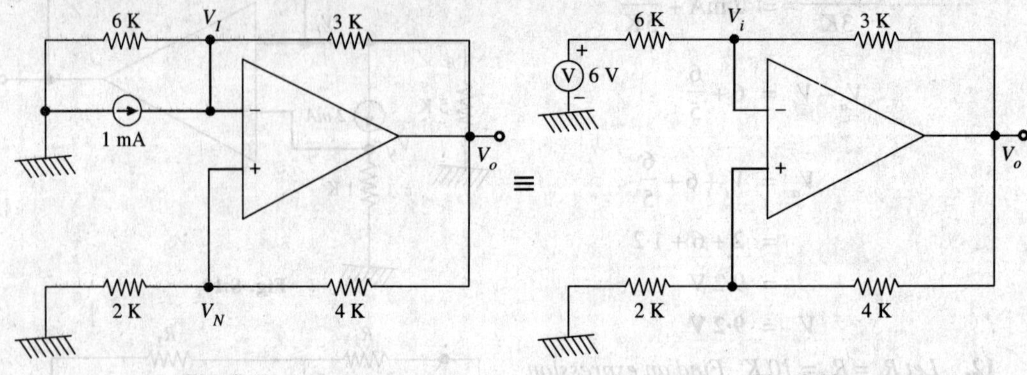

Fig. S.12 Fig. S.13

Solution: (*a*)

$$V_o = -\frac{3}{6} \times 6$$
$$= -3\text{V}$$

Now
$$\frac{6 - V_I}{6} = \frac{V_I - V_o}{3}$$

or $$6 - V_I = 2(V_i - V_o)$$

or $$3\,V_I = 6 + 2\,V_o = 6 + 2\,(-3) = 6 - 6 = 0$$

∴ $$V_I = \text{V}$$

$$V_N = \frac{V_0}{4+2} \times 2 = -\frac{3}{\not{6}_3} \times \not{2} = \mathbf{-1\,V.}$$

(*b*) When 6 K resistance is removed

$$V_o = 3 + V_I \;\therefore\; V_o - V_I = 3$$

$$\frac{V_N}{2\text{K}} = \frac{V_o - V_N}{4\text{K}}$$

∴ $$V_N = \frac{V_o}{3} = V_i$$

or $$V_o - V_I = \frac{2\,V_o}{3} \;\therefore\; V_o = 4.5\text{V}$$

∴ $$V_N = V_1 = \frac{4.5V}{3} = 1.5\,V_i$$

Here $$\frac{V_N}{2\text{K}} + 1\text{ mA} = \frac{V_o - V_N}{4\text{K}}$$

or $$2\,V_N + 4 = V_o - V_n$$

or $$3\,V_n = V_o - 4$$

∴ $$V_N = \frac{V_o - 4}{3} = V_i$$

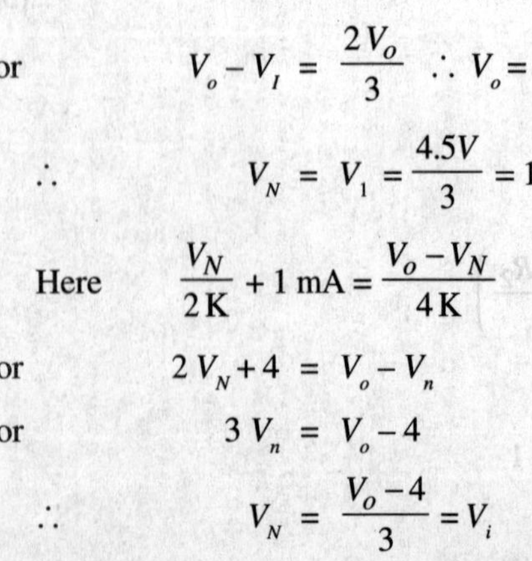

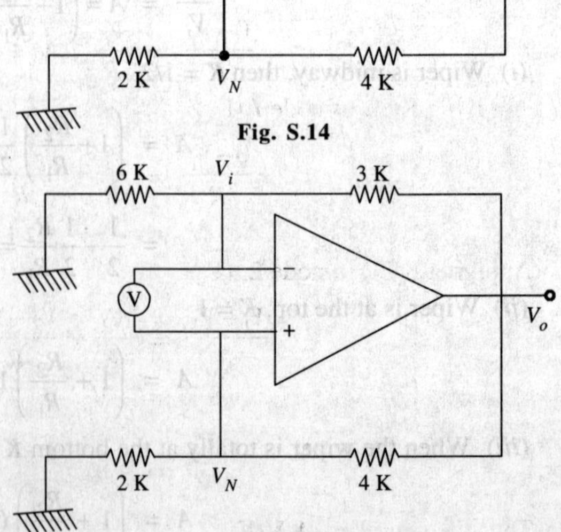

Fig. S.14

Fig. S.15

Again

$$-\frac{V_o+V_i}{3}+\frac{V_i}{6} = 1\text{ mA}$$

or $$\frac{V_o+V_i}{3} = \frac{V_i}{6}-1$$

or, $$2V_o - 2V_i = V_i - 6$$

or, $$3V_i = 2V_o + 6$$

$$\therefore \quad V_i = \frac{2V_o+6}{3}$$

$$\therefore \quad \frac{V_o-4}{3} = \frac{2V_o+6}{3}$$

or, $$V_o - 4 = 2V_o + 6$$

or, $$V_o = -10\text{ V}$$

$$\therefore \quad V_i = N_N = \frac{-10-4}{3} = -\frac{\mathbf{14}}{\mathbf{3}}\ \textbf{volt.}$$

14. *Find the gain V_o / V_i of the circuit of Figure.*

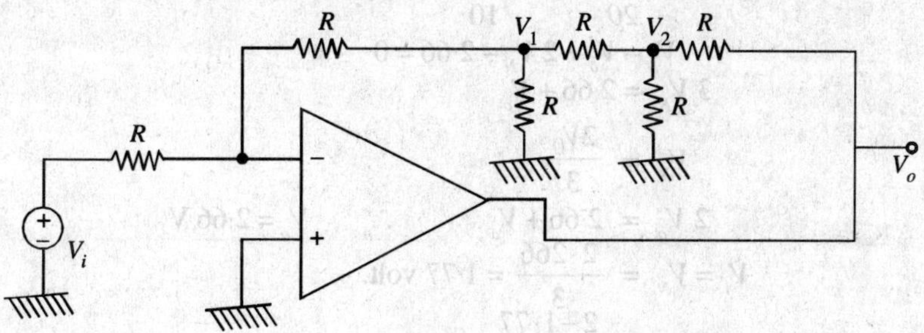

Fig. S.16

Solution: Current entering at the inverting terminal = $\frac{V_i}{R}$ ...(1)

$$\therefore \quad \frac{0-V_1}{R} = \frac{V_i}{R} \qquad V_1 = -V_i$$

Applying KCL to node I/1

$$\frac{0-V_1}{R} = \frac{V_1}{R}+\frac{V_1-V_2}{R}$$

$$V_2 = -3V_i \qquad [\because \; V_1 = -V_i]$$

Applying KCL to node 2, (V_2)

$$\frac{V_1-V_2}{R} = \frac{V_2}{R}+\frac{V_2-V_o}{R}$$

$$8V_i = -V_o$$

or, $$\frac{V_o}{V_i} = -8$$

Thus the gain A = **– 8 V/V.**

15. *From Figure find V_o and R_i*

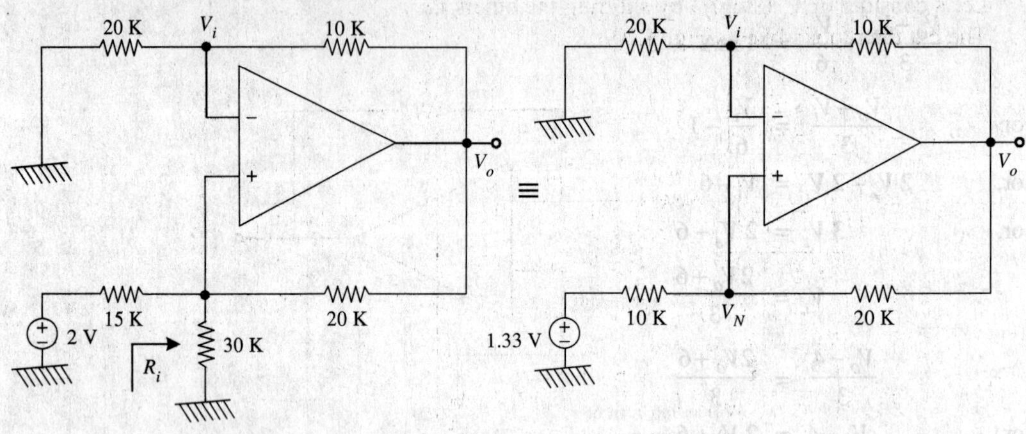

Fig. S.17 Fig. S.18

Solution:

$$\therefore \quad V_i = \frac{20}{20+10} V_o = \frac{2V_o}{3} = V_N$$

$$\therefore \quad \frac{V_N - V_o}{20} + \frac{V_N - 1\cdot 33}{10} = 0$$

or, $\quad V_N - V_o + 2\,V_N - 2\cdot 66 = 0$

or, $\quad 3\,V_N = 2\cdot 66 + V_o$

As, $\quad V_N = \dfrac{2V_0}{3}$

or, $\quad 2\,V_o = 2\cdot 66 + V_o \qquad \therefore \quad V_o = 2\cdot 66 \text{ V}$

$$\therefore \quad V_i = V_N = \frac{2\cdot 266}{3} = 1\cdot 77 \text{ volt.}$$

$$\therefore \quad I = \frac{2 - 1\cdot 77}{15\text{K}} = 15.3\ \mu\text{A}$$

$$R_i = \frac{2\text{V}}{15\cdot 3\mu\text{A}} = \mathbf{130\cdot 7\ k\,\Omega}$$

16. *Find a relationship between V_0 and V_1 through V_6 in the circuit of Fig. S.19.*

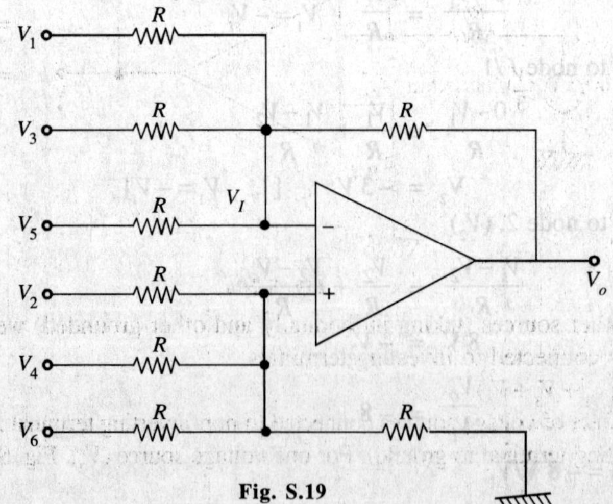

Fig. S.19

Solution:

Let's consider of V_1 (singly) by shorting the others *i.e.*

The ckt then looks like as Fig. S.20.

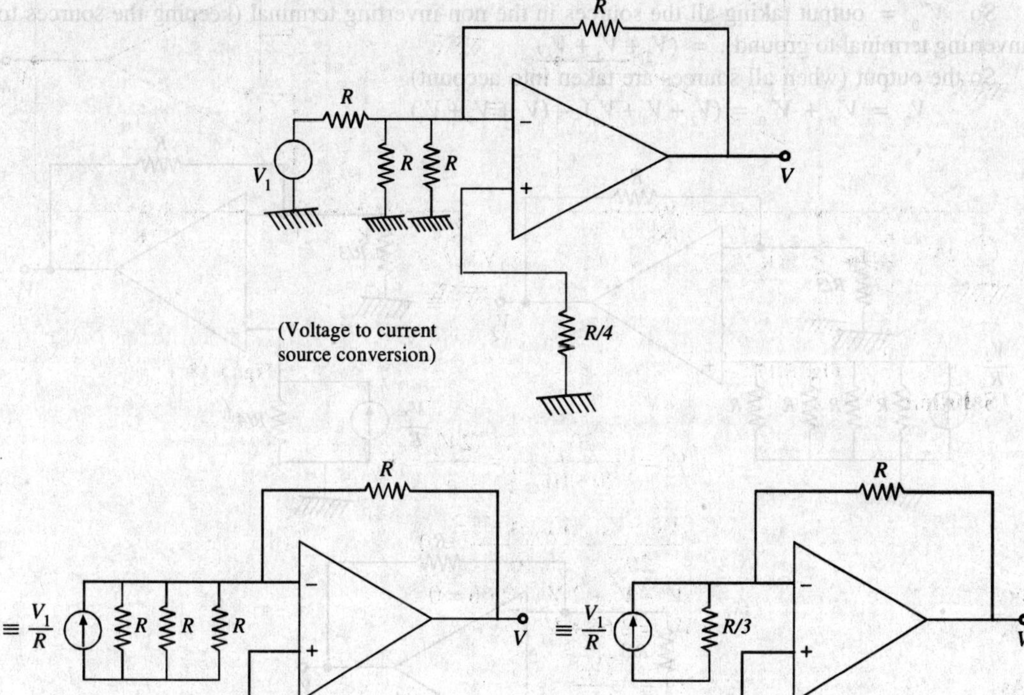

Fig. S.20

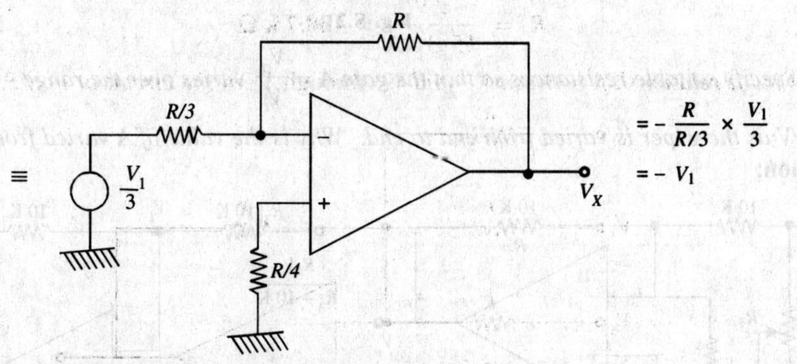

Fig. S.20a

Similarly for other sources (taking individually and other grounded) we get the output voltage for all the sources connected to investing terminals

$\therefore \quad V'_0 = -(V_1 + V_3 + V_5).$

Now take the effect of voltage sources connected to non-inverting terminal : (keeping all the sources connected to inverting terminal to ground). For one voltage source (V_2). Fig. S.21 can be modified as

$$V_y = \left(1 + \frac{R}{R/3}\right) \cdot \frac{V_2}{4} = \left(1 + \frac{3R}{R}\right) \cdot \frac{V_2}{4} = 4 \times \frac{V_2}{4} = V_2.$$

Similarly for other sources.

So V''_0 = output taking all the sources in the non-inverting terminal (keeping the sources to inverting terminal to ground). $= (V_2 + V_4 + V_6)$

So the output (when all sources are taken into account)

$$V_0 = V'_0 + V''_0 = (V_2 + V_4 + V_6) - (V_1 + V_3 + V_5)$$

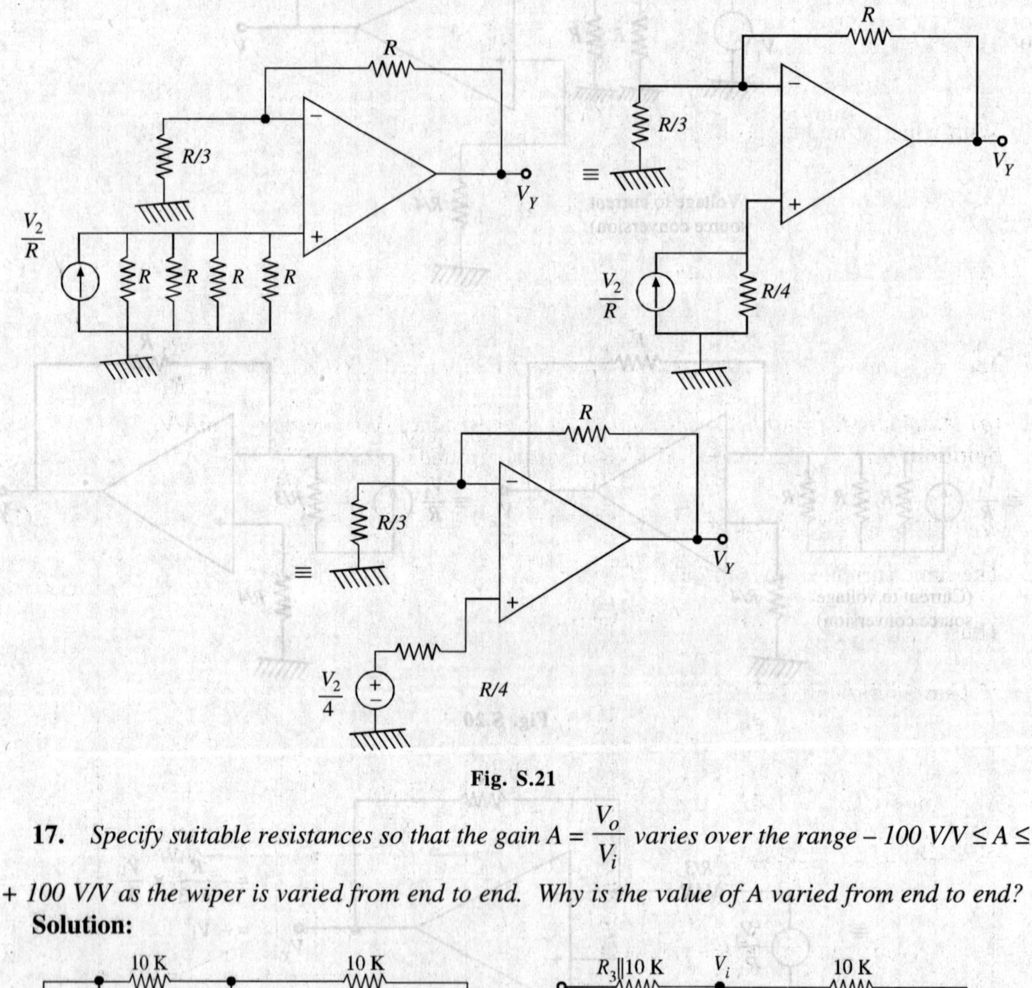

Fig. S.21

17. *Specify suitable resistances so that the gain* $A = \dfrac{V_o}{V_i}$ *varies over the range* -100 *V/V* $\leq A \leq$ $+100$ *V/V as the wiper is varied from end to end. Why is the value of A varied from end to end?*

Solution:

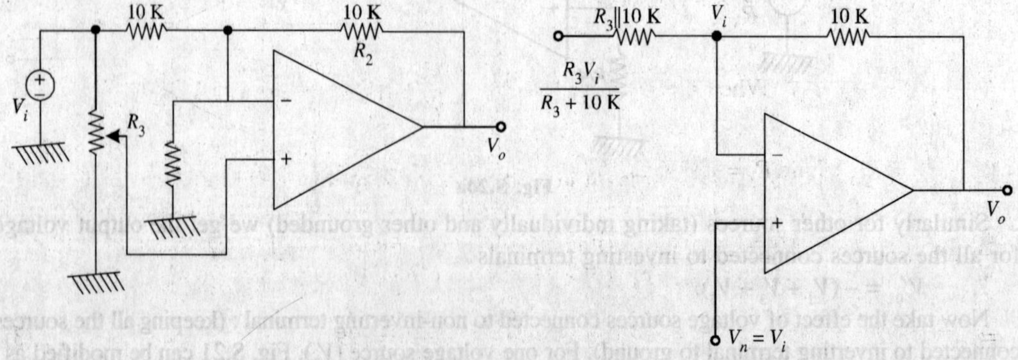

Fig. S.22 Fig. S.23

$$A = \frac{V_o}{V_i}$$

$$-100 \le A \le 100$$

With the wiper at the top:–

$$\therefore \quad \frac{10\times(10\,\text{K}+R_3)}{10\,\text{K}\times R_3}\left(\frac{R_3}{R_3+10\,\text{K}}-1\right)V_i = V_o = -100\,V_i$$

or

$$-\frac{10\,\text{K}\cdot 1\text{K}}{\text{K}\cdot R_3} = -100$$

$$\therefore \quad R_3 = 100\,\Omega$$

With wiper at middle position.

$$\therefore \quad \frac{10\,\text{K}}{99}\left(V_i - \frac{V_i}{2}\right) = V_o$$

$$\therefore \quad \frac{V_o}{V_i} = \frac{10\,\text{K}}{2\times 99} = \mathbf{55{\cdot}5}$$

18. (*a*) *Show that the circuit is a V-I converter with* $i_L = V_i/R_i/K)$, $K = 1 + \frac{R_2}{R_3}$

(*b*) *Assuming* R_I *= 100K, specify standard 5% resistances for a gain of 1 mA/V.*

Solution: (*a*) V_N is grounded so V_I is at virtual ground.

$$\therefore \quad i = \frac{V_i - V_I}{R_1} = \frac{V_i}{R_1} \qquad [\because V_I = 0] \qquad ...(1)$$

The same current i flows through R_2

Thus $$V_1 = -\frac{V_i}{R_1}\cdot R_2$$

$\therefore$ Current through

$$I_{R_3} = \frac{V_1}{R_3} = -\frac{V_i R_2}{R_1 R_3} \qquad ...(2)$$

Applying KCL, $i = i_i + i_L$

$$\Rightarrow \quad \frac{V_i}{R_1} = -\frac{V_i\,R_2}{R_1\,R_3} + i_L$$

$$i_L = \frac{V_i}{R_1} + \frac{V_i\,R_2}{R_1\,R_3} = \frac{V_i}{R_1}\left(1+\frac{R_2}{R_3}\right)$$

$$= \frac{V_i}{R_1/K} \quad \text{When } K = \mathbf{1 + R_2/R_3}$$

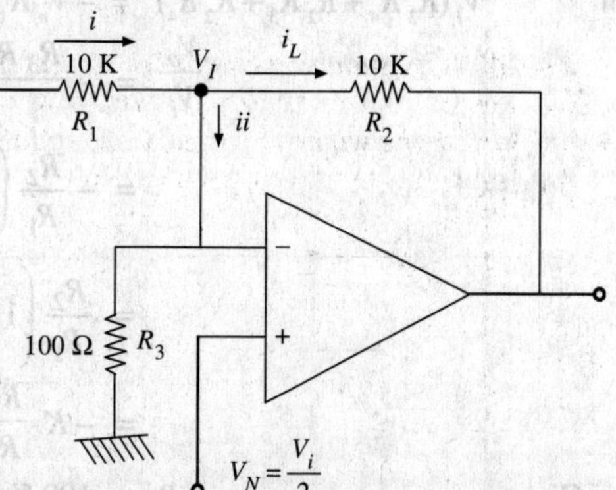

Fig. S.24

(*b*) $\frac{i_L}{V_i} = K_{k_1}$ given $R_1 = 100\,\text{K}\,\Omega$

$$\frac{i_L}{V_i} = 1\,\text{mA/V} \;\therefore\; \frac{1\,\text{mA}}{V} = \frac{K}{100\,\text{k}\Omega}$$

$$\Rightarrow \quad K = 100 = 1 + \frac{R_2}{R_3} \qquad \frac{R_2}{R_3} = \mathbf{99} \qquad ...(3)$$

Any resistor values which satisfy constant K of Eq. (3) will serve the purpose.

19. *(a) Show that the ckt of Figure has* $A = V_o / V_i = -K(R_2/R_1)$ *with* $K = 1 + R_4/R_2 + R_4/R_3$ *and* $R_i = R_1$. *(b) Specify resistance not larger than 100 K to achieve* $A = -200$ *V/V and* $R_i = 100\ k\Omega$.

Solution: $$\frac{V_i - V_I}{R_1} = \frac{V_I - V_2}{R_2} = \frac{V_2 - V_o}{R_4} + \frac{V_2 - 0}{R_3}$$

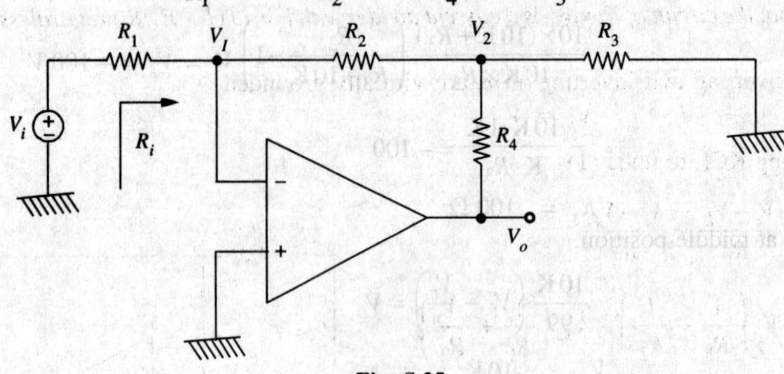

Fig. S.25

$$\Rightarrow \quad \frac{V_i}{R_1} = -\frac{V_2}{R_2} = \frac{V_2 - V_0}{R_4} + \frac{V_2}{R_3}$$

$$\therefore \quad V_2 = -V_i \frac{R_2}{R_1}$$

$$\frac{V_i}{R_1} = \frac{V_2 - V_o}{R_4} + \frac{V_2}{R_3}$$

$$\therefore \quad \frac{V_i}{R_1} = \frac{-V_i \dfrac{R_2}{R_1} - V_o}{R_4} - \frac{V_i \dfrac{R_2}{R_1}}{R_3}$$

$$\therefore \quad \frac{V_i}{R_1} = -\frac{V_i R_2 - V_o R_1}{R_1 R_4} - \frac{V_i R_2}{R_1 R_3}$$

or $$V_i R_4 R_3 = -V_i R_2 R_3 - V_o R_1 R_3 - V_i R_2 R_4$$

or $$V_i (R_3 R_4 + R_2 R_3 + R_2 R_4) = -V_o R_1 R_3$$

$$\therefore \quad \frac{V_o}{V_i} = -\frac{R_3 R_4 + R_2 R_3 + R_2 R_4}{R_1 R_3}$$

$$= -\frac{R_2}{R_1}\left(\frac{R_4}{R_2} + 1 + \frac{R_4}{R_3}\right)$$

$$= \frac{R_2}{R_1}\left(1 + R_4\left(\frac{R_2 + R_3}{R_2 R_3}\right)\right)$$

$$= -K \frac{R_2}{R_1} \quad \text{where } K = 1 + R_4\left(\frac{R_2 + R_3}{R_2 R_3}\right)$$

Given $R_i = 100$ K

$\therefore$ $R_1 = 100$ K

Assuming $R_2 = R_4 = 100$ K

$$\left|\frac{V_o}{V_i}\right| = \frac{R_2}{R_1}\left(1 + R_4\left\{\frac{R_2 + R_3}{R_2 + R_3}\right\}\right) = 200$$

or $$1 + 100\text{ K}\left(\frac{100\,K + R_3}{100\,k + R_3}\right) = 200$$

$$\therefore \quad R_3 = \mathbf{505\ \Omega}$$

20. *Show that the circuit of Figure is a current divider with $i_o = i_i / (1 + R_2/R_1)$ regardless of the load.*

Solution:

Since non-inverting and inverting 11ps are virtually grounded.

$$\therefore \quad V_I = V_L$$

Now applying KCL to node (1)

$$i_i = \frac{V_i - V_L}{R_1} + \frac{V_i - V_L}{R_2}$$

$$\Rightarrow \quad i_i = V_i\left(\frac{1}{R_1} + \frac{1}{R_2}\right) - V_L\left(\frac{1}{R_1} + \frac{1}{R_2}\right)$$

$$\Rightarrow \quad \frac{i_i + V_L\left(\frac{1}{R_1} + \frac{1}{R_2}\right)}{\left(\frac{1}{R_1} + \frac{1}{R_2}\right)} = V_i$$

$$\Rightarrow \quad V_i = \frac{i_i}{\left(\frac{1}{R_1} + \frac{1}{R_2}\right)} + V_L$$

Fig. S.26

Now Current is $$i_0 = \frac{V_i - V_L}{R_2} = \frac{i_i}{\left(\frac{1}{R_1} + \frac{1}{R_2}\right)R_2} = \frac{i_i}{1 + \frac{R_2}{R_1}}$$

So proved that the circuit acts like a current divider.

21. *(a) From circuit of Figure show that $A = V_o / V_i = -R_2 / R_1$ and $R_i = R_3 R_1 / (R_3 - R_1)$.*

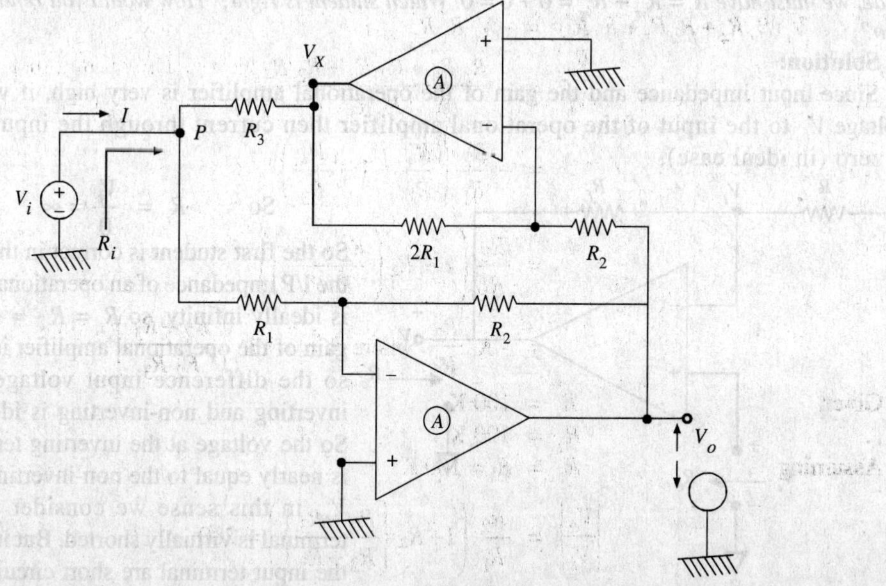

Fig. S.27

Solution:

Now
$$A = -\frac{R_2}{R_1}$$

$$V_x = -\frac{2R_1}{R_2}V_o$$

$$= \frac{2R_1}{R_2}\frac{R_2}{R_1}V_i$$

$$= 2V_i$$

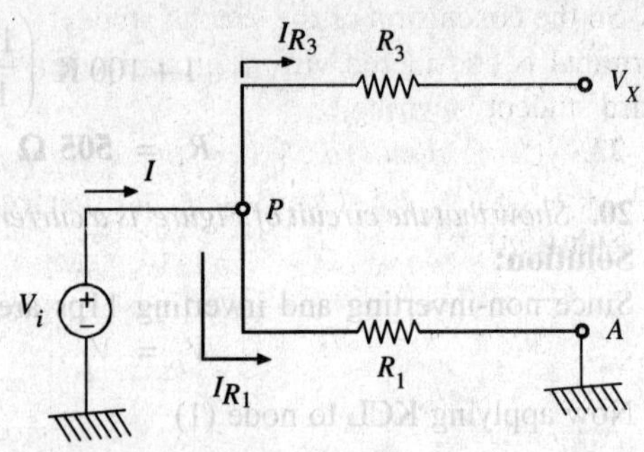

As B is grounded and A is virtually shorted so A is also at ground potential.

Fig. S.28

Applying *KCL* at node *P*.

$$I = I_{R_3} + I_{R_1}$$

$$= \frac{V_i - V_x}{R_3} + \frac{V_i}{R_1}$$

$$= \frac{V_i - 2V_x}{R_3} + \frac{V_i}{R_1}$$

$$= \frac{V_i}{R_3} + \frac{V_i}{R_1}$$

$$= V_i\left(\frac{1}{R_1} - \frac{1}{R_3}\right)$$

$$= V_i\left(\frac{R_3 - R_1}{R_1R_3}\right) \qquad \therefore \quad \boxed{R_i = \frac{V_i}{I} = \frac{R_1R_3}{R_3 - R_1}}$$

22. *Three students are discussing an input resistance R_i of the non-inverting amplifier of Fig. S.29. The first student says that since we are looking into the non-inverting input, which is open circuit (OC), we must have $R_i = R_{oc} = \infty$. The second student claims that since the input terminals appear virtually shorted (vs), we must have $R_i = R_{vs} + (R \parallel R_f) = 0 + (R \parallel R_f) = R \parallel R_f$. The third student claims that since the non inverting input is virtually shorted to the inverting input, which is in turn a virtual ground (v_g) node, we must have $R_i = R_{vs} + R_{vg} = 0 + 0 = 0$. Which student is right? How would you refute the other two?*

Solution:

Since Input impedance and the gain of the operational amplifier is very high, if we apply a voltage V_i to the input of the operational amplifier then current through the input terminal is zero (in ideal case),

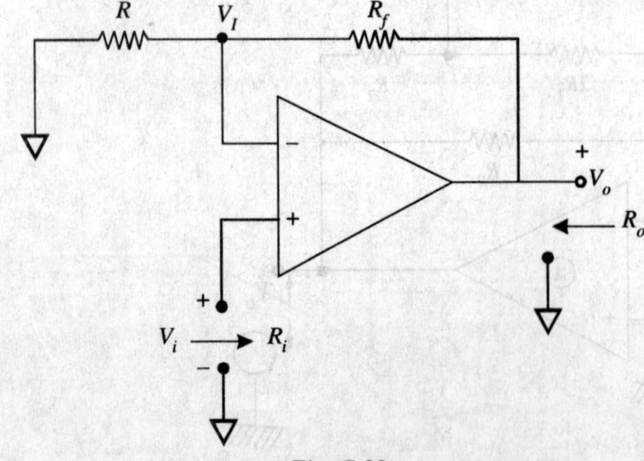

Fig. S.29

So $\quad R_i = \frac{V_i}{0} = \infty$

So the first student is correct in this sense as the I/P impedance of an operational amplifier is ideally infinity, so $R_i = R_{oc} = \infty$. As the gain of the operational amplifier is ideally ∞ so the difference input voltage between inverting and non-inverting is ideally zero. So the voltage at the inverting terminal (V_I) is nearly equal to the non-inverting terminal V_N, in this sense we consider that input terminal is virtually shorted. But it is not that the input terminal are short circuited.

So the conclusion of the second student $R_i = R_{vs} + (R \parallel R_f) = 0 + (R \parallel R_f)$ is wrong. Inverting I/P terminal is considered virtual ground when the non-inverting input is grounded. So the claim of third student is wrong.

23. *Using standard 5% resistance in the k Ω range, design a circuit to yield $V_o = -10\,(V_1 + 2V_2 + 3V_3 + 4V_4)$. Let us assume an expected circuit as shown.*

Solution:

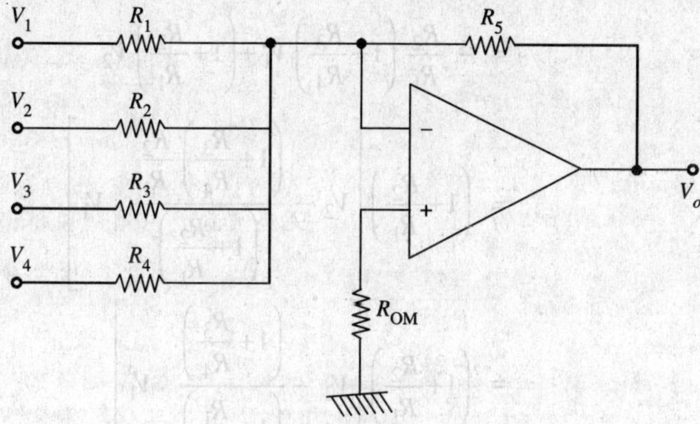

Fig. S.30

$$V_o = R_5\left(\frac{V_1}{R_1}+\frac{V_2}{R_2}+\frac{V_3}{R_3}+\frac{V_4}{R_4}\right)$$

Choosing $R_1 = 2R_2 = 3R_3 = 4R_4$, we have

$$V_o = -R_f\left(\frac{V_1}{R_1}+\frac{2V_2}{R_1}+\frac{3V_3}{R_1}+\frac{4V_4}{R_1}\right)$$

$$= -\frac{R_f}{R_1}(V_1 + 2V_2 + 3V_3 + 4V_4)$$

$$= -10\,(V_1 + 2V_2 + 3V_3 + 4V_4)$$

If $\frac{R_f}{R_1} = 10 \quad \therefore \; R_f = 10R_1$

Taking $R_1 =$ **10 K,** we get

$R_2 =$ **5 K**, $R_3 =$ **3·3 K,** $R_4 =$ **2·5 K** and $R_f =$ **100 K.**

24. (*a*) *Show that* $$v_o = \left(1+\frac{R_2}{R_1}\right)\left(V_2 - \frac{1+R_3/R_4}{1+R_1/R_2}\right)$$

(*b*) *Verify that if $R_3/R_4 = R_1/R_2$, the circuit is an instrumentation amplifier with gain $A = 1 + R_2/R_1$.*

Solution: (*a*)

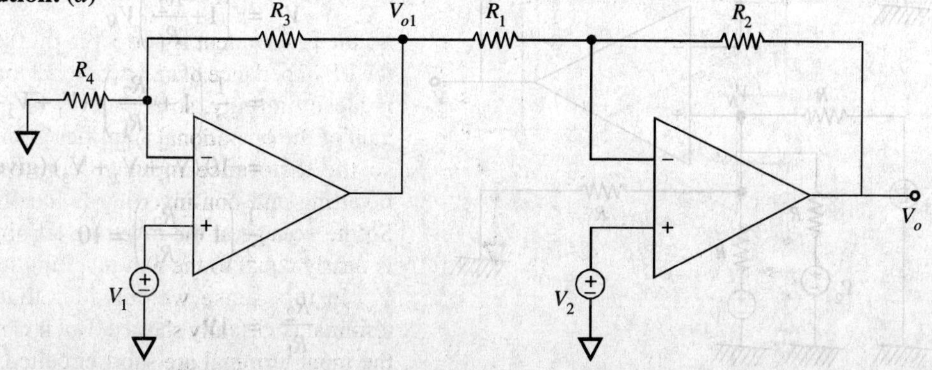

Fig. S.31

Here $$V_{o1} = \left(1+\frac{R_3}{R_4}\right)V_1$$

$$V_o = -\frac{R_2}{R_1}V_{o1} + \left(1+\frac{R_2}{R_1}\right)V_2$$

$$= -\frac{R_2}{R_1}\left(1+\frac{R_3}{R_4}\right)V_1 + \left(1+\frac{R_2}{R_1}\right)V_2$$

$$= \left(1+\frac{R_2}{R_1}\right)\left[V_2 - \frac{\left(1+\frac{R_3}{R_4}\right)\frac{R_2}{R_1}}{\left(1+\frac{R_2}{R_1}\right)}\cdot V_1\right]$$

$$= \left(1+\frac{R_2}{R_1}\right)\left[V_2 - \frac{\left(1+\frac{R_3}{R_4}\right)}{\left(1+\frac{R_1}{R_2}\right)}\cdot V_1\right]$$

(*b*) If $$\frac{R_3}{R_4} = \frac{R_1}{R_2}$$

then $$V_o = \left(1+\frac{R_2}{R_1}\right)\left[V_2 - \frac{1+R_1/R_2}{1+R_1/R_2}\cdot V_1\right]$$

$$= \left(1+\frac{R_2}{R_1}\right)(V_2 - V_1)$$

So in this condition ckt acts as an instrument amplifier with gain $\left(1+\frac{R_2}{R_1}\right)$.

25. *Using Standard 5% resistances in the KΩ range, design a circuit to achieve $V_o = 10\,(V_1 + V_2 + V_3)$. Show the circuit with components.*

Solution:

$$\frac{V_N - V_1}{R} + \frac{V_N - V_2}{R} + \frac{V_N - V_3}{R} + \frac{V_N}{R} = 0 \qquad (KCL\ at\ V_N)$$

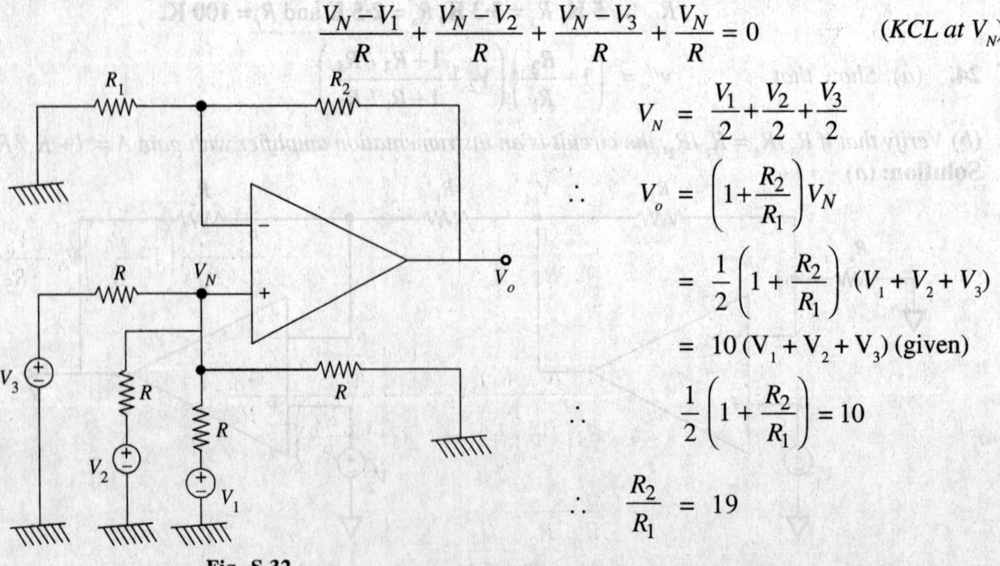

Fig. S.32

$$V_N = \frac{V_1}{2} + \frac{V_2}{2} + \frac{V_3}{2}$$

$$\therefore \quad V_o = \left(1+\frac{R_2}{R_1}\right)V_N$$

$$= \frac{1}{2}\left(1+\frac{R_2}{R_1}\right)(V_1 + V_2 + V_3)$$

$$= 10\,(V_1 + V_2 + V_3) \text{ (given)}$$

$$\therefore \quad \frac{1}{2}\left(1+\frac{R_2}{R_1}\right) = 10$$

$$\therefore \quad \frac{R_2}{R_1} = 19$$

∴ $R_2 = 19\,R_1$

If $R_1 = 1\text{ K}$

then $R_2 = 19\text{ K}$

26. *Obtain an expression of the type $i_o = V_i / R - V_o / R_o$. Hence verify that if $R_4/R_3 = R_2/R_1$ the circuit is a V-I converter with $R_o = \infty$ and $R = R_1 R_5 / R_2$.*

Solution:

Here
$$V_x = V_o + \frac{V_i - V_o}{R_3 + R_4} \cdot R_4$$

$$= V_o + \frac{V_i + R_4}{R_3 + R_4} - \frac{V_o R_4}{R_3 + R_4}$$

$$= \frac{V_i + R_4}{R_3 + R_4} + \frac{V_0 R_3}{R_3 + R_4}$$

$$V_{o1} = \left(1 + \frac{R_2}{R_1}\right) V_x = \frac{R_4}{R_3 + R_4}\left(1 + \frac{R_2}{R_1}\right) V_i + \frac{R_3}{R_3 + R_4}\left(1 + \frac{R_2}{R_1}\right) V_o$$

i_o = current through the load.

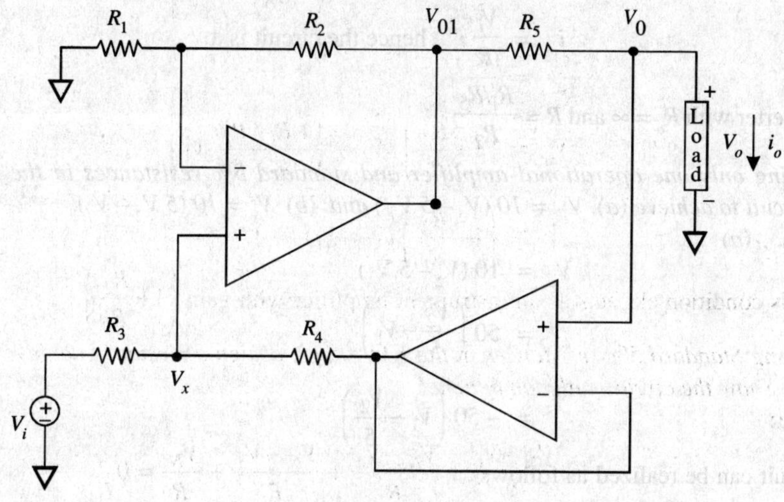

Fig. S.33

$$= \frac{V_{o1} - V_o}{R_5}$$

$$= \frac{R_4}{R_5(R_3 + R_4)}\left(1 + \frac{R_2}{R_1}\right) V_i + \frac{R_3}{R_5(R_3 + R_4)}\left(1 + \frac{R_2}{R_1}\right) V_o - \frac{V_o}{R_5}$$

$$= \frac{(1 + R_2 / R_1)}{R_5\left(1 + \dfrac{R_3}{R_4}\right)} V_i + \frac{\left(1 + \dfrac{R_2}{R_1}\right) V_o}{R_5\left(1 + \dfrac{R_4}{R_3}\right)} - \frac{V_o}{R_5}$$

$$= \frac{V_i}{R} - \frac{V_o}{R_o}$$

where $$R = \frac{R_5\left(1+\dfrac{R_3}{R_4}\right)}{1+\dfrac{R_2}{R_1}}$$

$$R_o = \frac{R_5}{\dfrac{1+R_2/R_1}{1+R_4/R_3}-1}$$

So when $$\frac{R_4}{R_3} = \frac{R_2}{R_1}$$

then $$R = \frac{R_5\left(1+\dfrac{R_3}{R_4}\right)}{\dfrac{R_2}{R_1}\left(1+\dfrac{R_1}{R_2}\right)} = \frac{R_5 \cdot R_1}{R_2}$$

$$R_o = \frac{R_5}{\dfrac{1+R_2/R_1}{1+R_4/R_3}-1} = \frac{R_5}{1-1} \to \infty$$

$$i_o = \frac{V_i}{R},$$ hence the circuit is a

V-I converter with $R_o = \infty$ and $R = \dfrac{R_1 R_5}{R_2}$.

27. *Using only one operational amplifier and standard 5% resistances in the KΩ range, design a circuit to achieve (a) $V_o = 10\,(V_2 - 5\,V_1)$ and (b) $V_o = 10\,(5\,V_2 - V_1)$.*

Solution. (*a*)

$$V_o = 10\,(V_2 - 5\,V_1)$$

$$= 50\left(\frac{V_2}{5} - V_1\right)$$

$$= -\,50\left(V_1 - \frac{V_2}{5}\right)$$

The circuit can be realized as follows

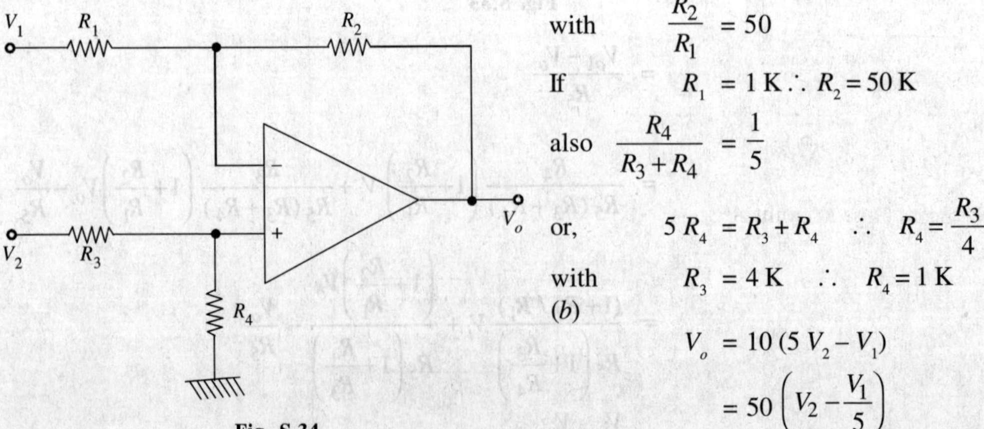

Fig. S.34

with $$\frac{R_2}{R_1} = 50$$

If $R_1 = 1\text{ K} \therefore R_2 = 50\text{ K}$

also $$\frac{R_4}{R_3+R_4} = \frac{1}{5}$$

or, $5\,R_4 = R_3 + R_4 \quad \therefore \quad R_4 = \dfrac{R_3}{4}$

with $R_3 = 4\text{ K} \quad \therefore \quad R_4 = 1\text{ K}$

(*b*)

$$V_o = 10\,(5\,V_2 - V_1)$$

$$= 50\left(V_2 - \frac{V_1}{5}\right)$$

$$= -50\left(\frac{V_1}{5} - V_2\right)$$

$$\frac{R_2}{R_1+R_2} = \frac{1}{5} \quad \therefore \quad R_2 = \frac{R_1}{4}$$

with $\quad R_2 = 1\text{ K}$

$\therefore \quad R_1 = 4\text{ K}$

$\therefore \quad R_1 \,\|\, R_2 = \frac{4}{5}\text{ K}$

$\therefore \quad \frac{R_3}{R_1 \,\|\, R_2} = 50 \quad \therefore \; R_3 = \frac{4}{5} \times 50 = 40\text{ K}$

$\therefore \quad R_4 = 40\text{ K} \,\|\, \frac{4}{5} = \mathbf{800\ \Omega}$

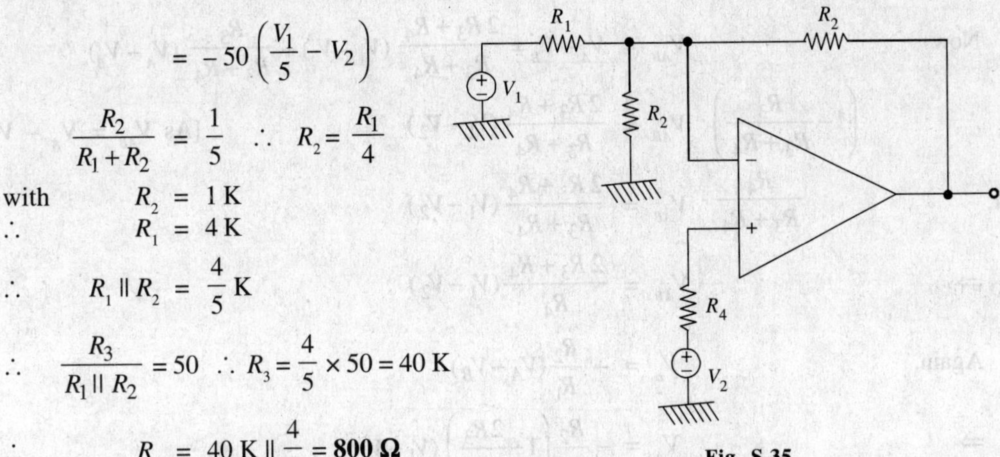

Fig. S.35

28. *Obtain an expression for V_o of the circuit of Figure.*

Solution: Now the voltage at point A

$$V_A = \left(1 + \frac{R_3}{R_3+R_4}\right)V_1 - \frac{R_3}{R_3+R_4}\cdot V_B$$

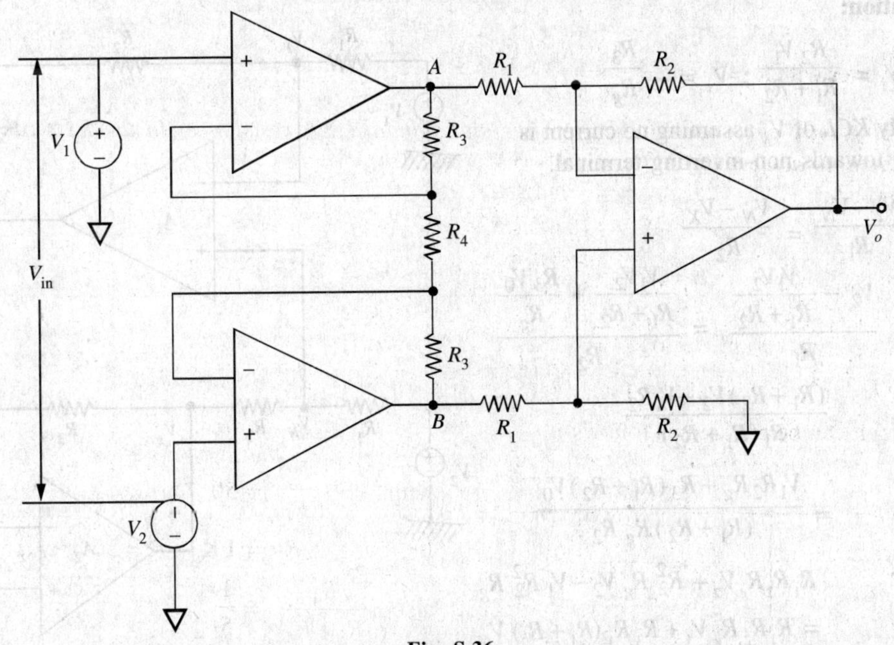

Fig. S.36

Now the voltage at point A

$$V_A = \left(1 + \frac{R_3}{R_3+R_4}\right)V_1 - \frac{R_3}{R_3+R_4}\cdot V_B$$

$$= \frac{2R_3+R_4}{R_3+R_4}\cdot V_1 - \frac{R_3}{R_3+R_4}\cdot V_B$$

and

$$V_B = \left(1 + \frac{R_3}{R_3+R_4}\right)\cdot V_2 - \frac{R_3}{R_3+R_4}\cdot V_A$$

Now $$V_{AB} = V_A - V_B = \frac{2R_3 + R_4}{R_3 + R_4}(V_1 - V_2) + \frac{R_3}{R_3 + R_4}(V_A - V_B)$$

$\therefore$ $$\left(1 - \frac{R_3}{R_3 + R_4}\right) \cdot V_{AB} = \frac{2R_3 + R_4}{R_3 + R_4}(V_1 - V_2) \qquad [\text{As } V_{AB} = V_A - V_B]$$

or, $$\frac{R_4}{R_3 + R_4} \cdot V_{AB} = \frac{2R_3 + R_4}{R_3 + R_4}(V_1 - V_2)$$

$\Rightarrow$ $$V_{AB} = \frac{2R_3 + R_4}{R_4}(V_1 - V_2)$$

Again, $$V_o = -\frac{R_2}{R_1}(V_A - V_B)$$

$\Rightarrow$ $$V_o = -\frac{R_2}{R_1}\left(1 + \frac{2R_3}{R_4}\right)(V_1 - V_2)$$
$$= \frac{R_2}{R_1}\left(1 + \frac{2R_3}{R_4}\right)(V_2 - V_1)$$

29. *Show that the difference amplifier of Figure yields* $V_o = \left(\frac{R_2}{R_1}\right)\left(\frac{R_g}{R_3}\right)(V_2 - V_1)$ *so its gain can be made variable by varying the single resistance* R_g.

Solution:

$$V_I = \frac{R_2 V_1}{R_1 + R_2}\ ;\ V_x = -\frac{R_3}{R_g}$$

Apply *KCL* of V_N assuming no current is flowing towards non-inverting terminal.

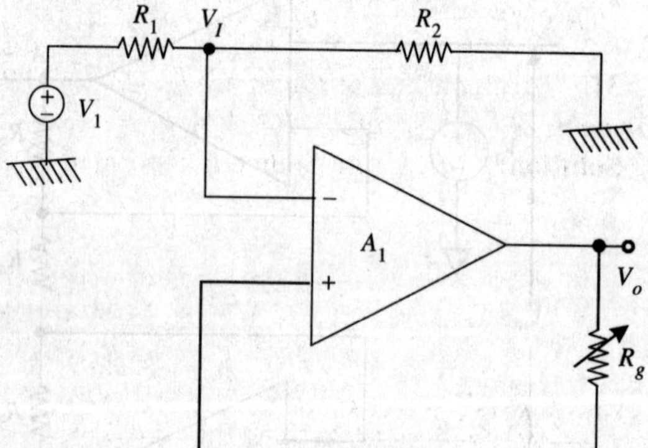

$$\frac{V_2 - V_N}{R_1} = \frac{V_N - V_X}{R_2}$$

$$\frac{V_2 - \frac{V_1 V_2}{R_1 + R_2}}{R_1} = \frac{\frac{V_1 V_2}{R_1 + R_2} + \frac{R_3 V_0}{R_g}}{R_2}$$

or, $$\frac{(R_1 + R_2)V_2 - V_1 R_2}{R_1(R_1 + R_2)}$$
$$= \frac{V_1 R_2 R_g + R_3(R_1 + R_2)V_0}{(R_1 + R_2)R_g R_2}$$

or, $$R_1 R_2 R_g V_2 + R_2^2 R_g V_2 - V_1 R_2^2 R_g$$
$$= R_1 R_2 R_g V_1 + R_3 R_1 (R_1 + R_2) V_0$$

or, $V_0 [R_1 + R_2] R_1 R_3 = R_1 R_2 R_g (V_2 - V_1) + R_2 R_g (V_2 - V_1)$

or $V_0 (R_1 + R_2) R_1 R_3 = (V_2 - V_1)(R_1 R_2 R_g + R_2^2 R_g)$

or $$V_0 = \frac{R_2 R_g (R_1 + R_2)}{R_1 R_3 (R_1 + R_2)}(V_2 - V_1)$$

or $$V_0 = \frac{R_2 R_g}{R_1 R_3}(V_2 - V_1)$$

Hence $V_0 \propto R_g$ if $R_1, R_2 R_3 (V_2 - V_1)$ are all constant.

Fig. S.37

30. *Find R_{eq} in the circuit of Figure.*

Solution:

Let V_i is applied as in the adjoining Figure.

As in between I and N there is an infinite impedance. So $i_{IN} = 0$.

Applying KCL at N.

$$\frac{V_i - V_N}{40\,K} = \frac{V_N}{30\,K}$$

or, $V_N = \frac{3}{7} V_i \quad \because \quad V_N = V_I$

Now current

$$I = \frac{V_i - V_N}{10\,\text{K}} + \frac{V_i - V_N}{40\,\text{K}}$$

$$= (V_i - V_N)\left(\frac{1}{8\,\text{K}}\right)$$

$$\therefore \quad I = \left(V_i - \frac{3}{7}V_i\right)\left(\frac{1}{\mathbf{8k}}\right) = \frac{4}{7}V_i \times \frac{1}{\mathbf{8K}} = \frac{1}{\mathbf{14\,K}} \cdot V_i$$

$$R_{eq} = \frac{V_i}{I} = \frac{14\,\text{K}}{1} = \mathbf{14\,K}$$

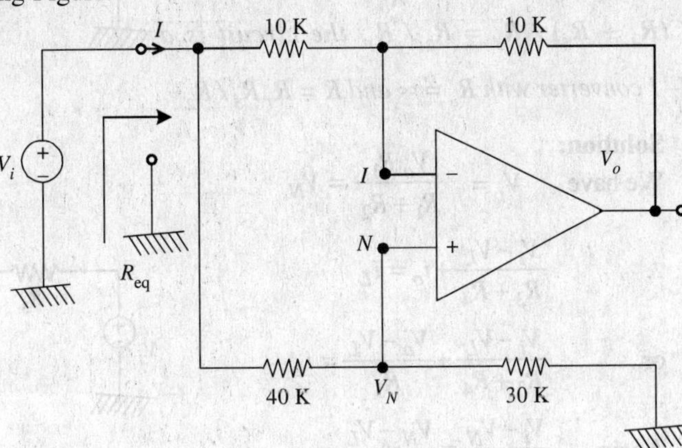

Fig. S.38

31. *(a) Show that in Figure we have $V_o = -(R_2 / R_1) \times V_i - R_2 I_i$, (b) Specify suitable resistance for gains of – 100 $^V/_V$ and – 10^6 V/A.*

Solution: (*a*) Using Source transformation technique

$$\therefore \quad V_o = -\frac{R_2}{R_1}(V_i + I_1 R_1)$$

$$= -\frac{R_2}{R_1}V_i - R_2 I_i$$

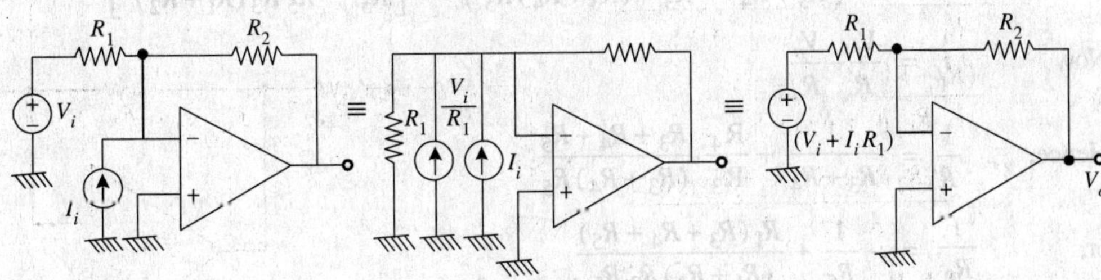

Fig. S.39

(*b*)

$$1 = -\frac{R_2}{R_1} \cdot \frac{1}{\frac{V_o}{V_i}} - R_2 \cdot \frac{1}{\frac{V_o}{I_i}} = -\frac{R_2}{R_1}\left(-\frac{1}{10^2}\right) - R_2 \frac{1}{-10^6}$$

If $\quad R_1 = 1$ K, then $R_2 = \frac{10^6}{11} = 91$ k Ω

$$\because \quad \frac{V_o}{V_i} = -100, \quad \frac{V_o}{V_i} = \mathbf{10^6.}$$

32. *For the given circuit obtain an expression of the type* $i_o = V_i / R - \dfrac{V_L}{R_o}$. *Hence, verify that if* $(R_4 + R_5) / R_3 = R_2 / R_1$, *the circuit is a V– I converter with* $R_o = \infty$ *and* $R = R_1 R_5 / R_2$.

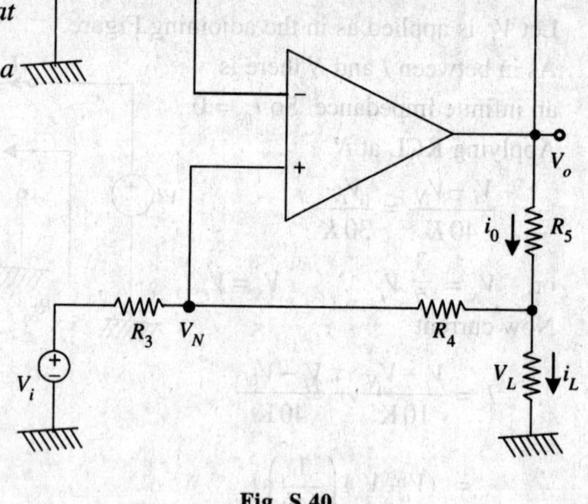

Fig. S.40

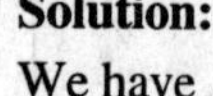

Solution:

We have $\quad V_I = \dfrac{V_o R_1}{R_1 + R_2} = V_N$

$$\therefore \quad \frac{V_i - V_L}{R_3 + R_4} + i_o = i_L$$

$$\text{or,} \quad \frac{V_i - V_L}{R_3 + R_4} + \frac{V_o - V_L}{R_5} = i_L$$

$$\text{Again} \quad \frac{V_i - V_N}{R_3} = \frac{V_N - V_L}{R_4}$$

$$\text{or,} \quad \frac{V_i}{R_3} + \frac{V_L}{R_4} = V_N\left(\frac{1}{R_3} + \frac{1}{R_4}\right)$$

$$= \frac{V_o R_1}{R_1 + R_2} \cdot \frac{R_3 R_4}{R_3 + R_4}$$

$$\therefore \; i_L = \frac{V_i}{R_3 + R_4} + \frac{V_o}{R_5} - \left(\frac{1}{R_3 + R_4} + \frac{1}{R_5}\right)$$

$$\left[\frac{V_o R_1}{R_1 + R_2} \cdot \frac{R_3 + R_4}{R_3 R_4} - \frac{V_i}{R_3}\right] R_4$$

$$\text{or,} \quad i_L = V_i\left(\frac{1}{R_3 + R_4} + \frac{R_4}{R_3} \cdot \frac{R_3 + R_4 + R_5}{(R_3 + R_4) R_5}\right) + V_o\left[\frac{1}{R_5} - \frac{(R_3 + R_4 + R_5) R_1}{R_5 R_3 (R_1 + R_2)}\right]$$

$$\text{Now} \quad i_L = \frac{V_i}{R} - \frac{V_o}{R_o}$$

$$\text{Hence,} \quad \frac{1}{R} = \frac{1}{R_3 + R_4} + \frac{R_4}{R_3} \cdot \frac{R_3 + R_4 + R_5}{(R_3 + R_4) R_5}$$

$$\text{or,} \quad \frac{1}{R_0} = -\frac{1}{R_5} + \frac{R_1 (R_3 + R_4 + R_5)}{(R_1 + R_2) R_3 R_5}$$

with $\quad R_o \to \infty$

i.e., $\quad \dfrac{1}{R_o} \to 0$

$$\therefore \quad \frac{1}{R_5} = \frac{R_1 (R_3 + R_4 + R_5)}{(R_1 + R_2) R_3 R_5}$$

$$\therefore \quad (R_1 + R_2) R_3 = R_1 (R_3 + R_4 + R_5)$$

$$\therefore \quad R_2 R_3 = R_1 R_4 + R_1 R_5 = R_1 (R_4 + R_5)$$

$$\therefore \quad \frac{R_4 + R_5}{R_3} = \frac{R_2}{R_1} \quad \text{(Proved).}$$

and $$\frac{1}{R} = \frac{1}{R_3+R_4}+\frac{R_4}{R_3}\cdot\frac{R_3+\frac{R_2 R_3}{R_1}}{(R_3+R_4)R_5}$$

$$= \frac{1}{R_3+R_4}+\frac{R_4(R_1+R_2)}{R_1 R_5(R_3+R_4)} = \frac{1}{R_3+R_4}\left[1+\frac{R_1 R_4+R_2 R_4}{R_1 R_5}\right]$$

$$= \frac{1}{R_3+R_4}\left[\frac{R_1 R_5+R_1 R_4+R_2 R_4}{R_1 R_5}\right]$$

$$= \frac{R_1(R_4+R_5)+R_2 R_4}{R_1 R_5(R_3+R_4)} = \frac{R_2 R_3+R_2 R_4}{R_1 R_5(R_3+R_4)} = \frac{R_2}{R_1 R_5}$$

$$\therefore \quad R = \frac{R_2}{R_1 R_5} \quad \text{(Proved)}$$

33. *From the given Fig. S.41, obtain an expression of the type $i_o = v_i / R_L - V_L / R_o$. Hence verify that if $R_1 + R_2 = R_3$, the circuit is a V-I converter with $R_o = \infty$ and $R = R_2 / 2$.*

Solution:

$$V_x = -\frac{R_3}{R_1}V_L$$

$$\therefore \quad V_o = -(V_x - V_1) = V_1 - V_x = V_1 + \frac{R_3 V_L}{R_1}$$

$$\therefore \quad I_o = -\frac{V_L}{R_1}+\frac{V_o - V_L}{R_2}$$

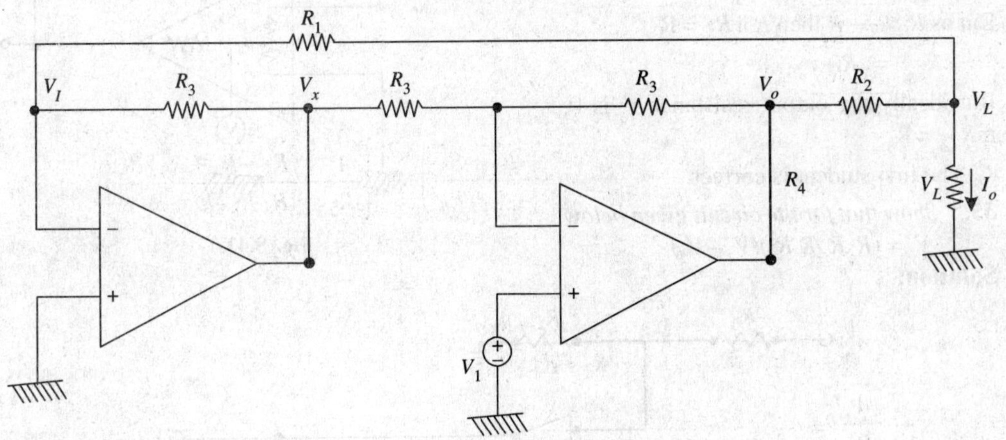

Fig. S.41

$$\therefore \quad I_o = -\frac{V_L}{R_1}+\frac{V_1+\frac{R_3-R_1}{R_1}\cdot V_L}{R_2}$$

$$= V_L\left[-\frac{1}{R_1}-\frac{R_1-R_3}{R_1 R_2}\right]+\frac{V_1}{R_2} = \frac{V_1}{R} - \frac{V_L}{R_o}$$

$$R = R_2 \text{ and}$$

$$\frac{1}{R_o} = \frac{1}{R_1}+\frac{R_1-R_3}{R_1 R_2}$$

when $$R_o \to \infty \quad \frac{1}{R_o} \to 0$$

$$\therefore \quad 0 = \frac{1}{R_1} + \frac{R_1 - R_3}{R_1 R_2}$$

or, $$R_2 = R_3 - R_1$$

$$\therefore \quad R_3 = R_1 + R_2 \text{ (Proved).}$$

34. *Three students are discussing the resistance R_0 seen by the load in the V-I converter of the given figure. The 1st student notes that at the bottom the load sees the output resistance r_o of the operational amplifier, which is assumed zero, whereas at the top it sees R; consequently $R_o = R + r_o = R + 0 = R$. The 2nd student observes that at the top the load sees not R but a virtual ground (V_g). So $R_o = R_{vg} + r_o = 0 + 0 = 0$. The 3rd student reports rumours that $R_o = \infty$. Which student is right? How do you refute the other two?*

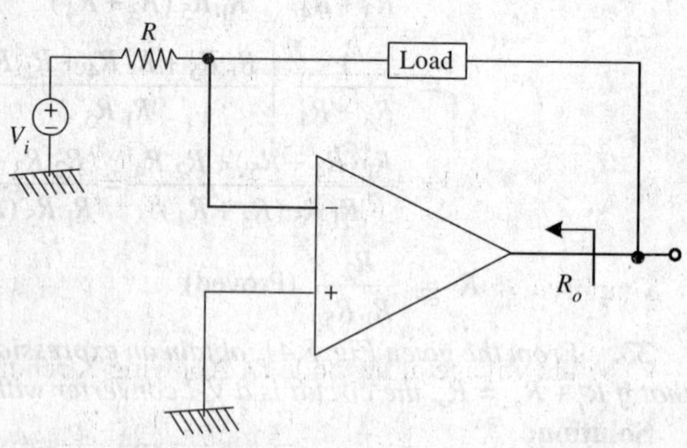

Fig. S.42

Solution:

So the equivalent resistance seen from the load is

$$R_{equ} = (R \parallel R_{in}) + r_o$$

But as $R_{in} \to \infty$ then $R \parallel R_{in} = R$

$$\therefore \quad R_{equ} = R + r_o$$

But ideally the output resistance r_o is 0, then $R_{equ} = R$

∴ The first student is correct.

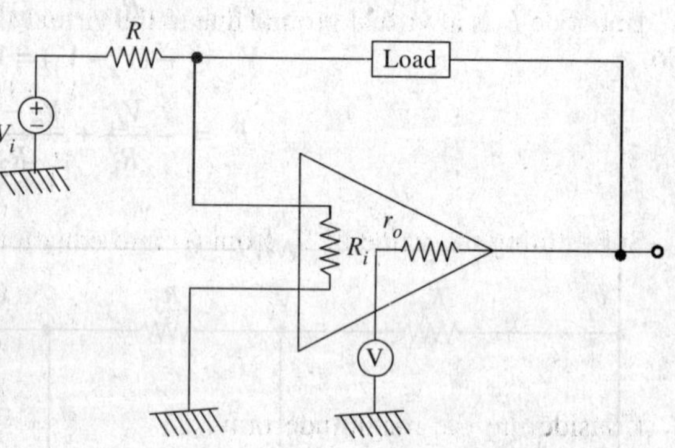

Fig. S.43

35. *Show that for the circuit given below $V_0 = (R_G R_2/R_1 R_3)(V_1 - V_2)$*

Solution:

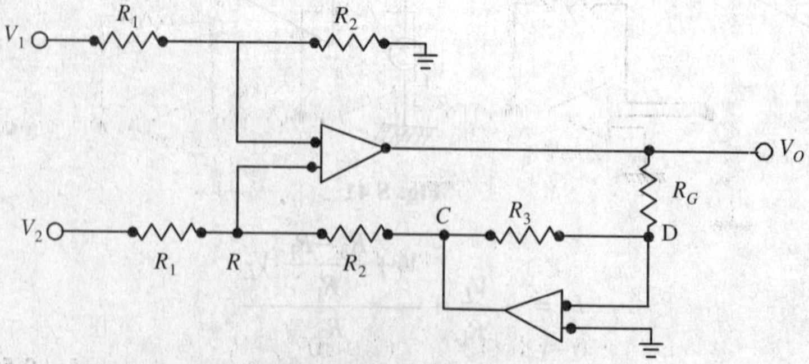

Fig. S.44

Voltage at the node *A* is given by:

$$V_A = \frac{V_1 R_2}{R_1 + R_2}$$

The nodes A and B are virtually short circuited. Therefore, the voltage appearing at the node B is given by:

$$V_B = \frac{V_1 R_2}{R_1 + R_2}$$

Let V_C be the voltage at node C. Applying Kirchoff's current law at node B,

$$\frac{V_2 - \frac{V_1 R_2}{R_1 + R_2}}{R_1} + \frac{V_C - \frac{V_1 R_2}{R_1 + R_2}}{R_2} = 0$$

or $$R_2 V_2 - \frac{V_1 R_2}{R_1 + R_2} + R_1 V_C - \frac{V_1 R_1 R_2}{R_1 + R_2} = 0$$

Simplifying, we get, $$V_c = (V_1 - V_2)\frac{R_2}{R_1} \quad \ldots (i)$$

V_D be the voltage at the node D. Applying Kirchoff's current law at node D,

$$\frac{V_C - V_D}{R_3} + \frac{V_0 - V_D}{R_G} = 0$$

But node D is at virtual ground due to the virtual short circuit at the input terminal of the op amp. So,

$$V_D = 0;$$

$\therefore$ $$V_0 = \frac{R_G}{R_3} V_C \quad \ldots (ii)$$

Substituting the value of V_C from (*i*) into equation (*ii*), we get,

$$V_0 = \frac{R_G R_2}{R_1 R_3}(V_2 - V_1)$$

Considering the magnitude only, $$V_0 = \frac{R_G R_2}{R_1 R_3}(V_1 - V_2)$$

36. *Find V_0 for the circuit :*

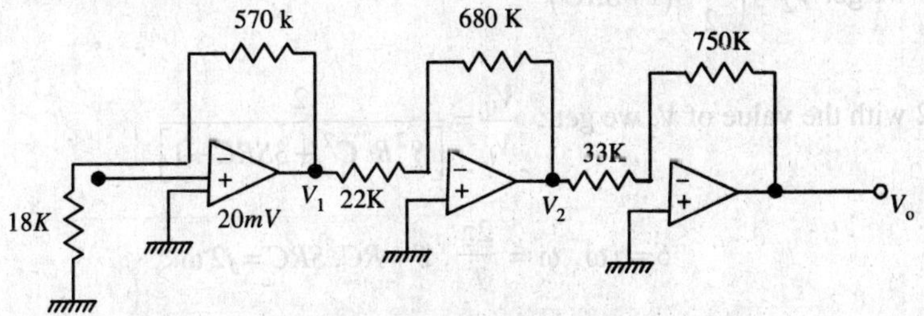

Fig. S.45

Solution:

$$\frac{0 - (20\times10^{-3})}{18\times10^3} = \frac{(20\times10^{-3}) - V_1}{510\times10^3} \; \ldots . (1) \text{ or } V_1 = 0.587 \, mV.$$

Again : $$\frac{V_1 - 0}{22\times10^3} = \frac{0 - V_2}{680\times10^3} \text{ or } V_2 = -18.133 \, mV.$$

Now : $$\frac{V_2 - 0}{33\times10^3} = \frac{0 - V_0}{750\times10^3} \text{ or } V_0 = 412.121 \, mV.$$

37. *Find V_0 for the circuit :*

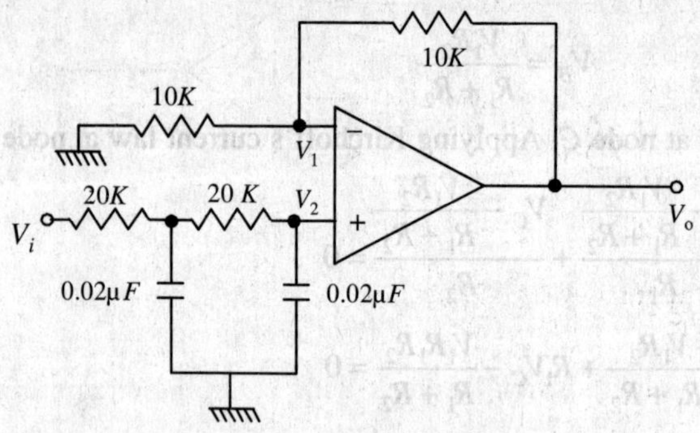

Fig. S.46

Solution.

$$\frac{0-V_1}{10\times10^3}=\frac{V_1-V_0}{10\times10^3}$$

or $$\boxed{V_1=\frac{V_0}{2}} \quad \dots (1)$$

Again : $$\frac{V_i-V_2}{R}=\frac{V_2}{\frac{1}{sc}}+\frac{V_2-\frac{V_0}{2}}{R} \quad \dots (2)$$

And, $$\frac{V_2-V_{0/2}}{R}=\frac{\left(\frac{V_0}{2}\right)}{\frac{1}{sc}} \quad \dots (3)$$

From Eq. 3 we get $V_2=\left(\frac{V_0}{2}\right)(1+SRC)$ ... (4)

From Eq. 2 with the value of V_2 we get : $\frac{V_0}{V_i}=\frac{2}{\left[S^2R^2C^2+3SRC+1\right]}$ ... (5)

$$S=j\omega,\ \omega=\frac{2\pi}{T},\ T=RC,\ SRC=j2\omega$$

$$\frac{V_0}{V_i}=\frac{2}{(-4\omega^2+6j\omega+1)}$$

or $$\left|\frac{V_0}{V_i}\right|=\left|\frac{2}{-4\omega^2+6j\omega+1}\right|=0.04.$$

$$\boxed{V_0=0.04\ V_i}$$

38. *What is the condition for which the circuit should have maximum CMRR?*

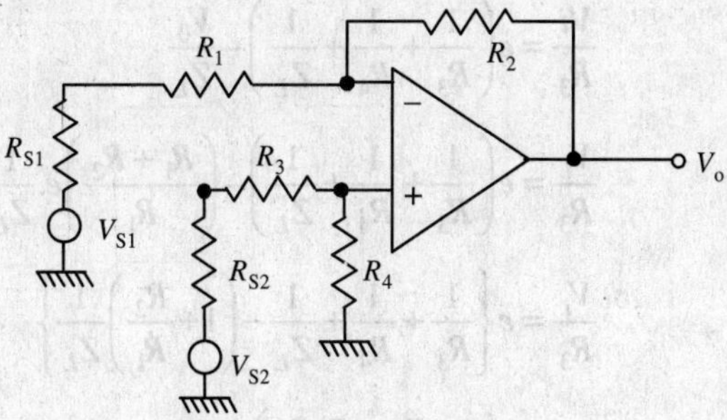

Fig. S.47

Solution. We apply superposition theorem: with V_{s1} in the circuit, output voltage (V_{01}) is

$$V_{01} = -\frac{R_2}{R_{s_1}} Vs_1$$

With V_{s_2} in the circuit, output voltage

$$(V_{02}) = \left(\frac{R_{s_1} + R_1 + R_2}{R_{s_1} + R_1}\right)\left(\frac{R_4}{R_{s_2} + R_3 + R_4}\right)^{V_{s2}}$$

So, $$V_o = V_{0_1} + V_{0_2} = \left(\frac{R_{s_1} + R_1 + R_2}{R_{s_1} + R_1}\right)\left(\frac{R_4}{R_{s_2} + R_3 + R_4}\right)^{V_{S2}} - \left(\frac{R_2}{R_{s_1} + R_2}\right)^{V_{S1}}$$

In order the circuit has maximum *CMRR*, the common mode output should be minimum, ideally it should be zero. Equating $V_0 = 0$ with

$$V_{s_1} = V_{s_2}, \text{ we get. } \left(\frac{R_{s_1} + R_1 + R_2}{R_{s_1} + R_1}\right)\left(\frac{R_4}{R_{s_2} + R_3 + R_4}\right) = \frac{R_2}{R_{s_1} + R_2}$$

or $$\boxed{\frac{Rs_1 + R_1}{R_2} = \frac{R_{s_2} + R_3}{R_4}}$$

This is the required condition.

39. *Find V_o and analyse it.*

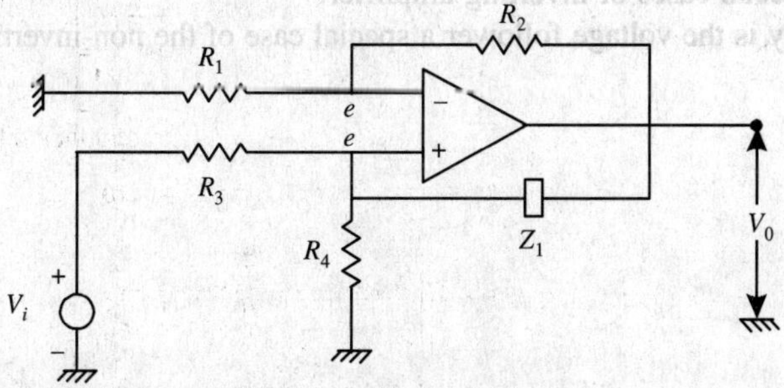

Fig. S.48

Here, $$e = \frac{V_0 \times R_1}{R_1 + R_2}$$

$$\frac{v_i - e}{R_3} = \frac{e}{R_4} + \frac{e - V_0}{Z_L}$$

or
$$\frac{Vi}{R_3} = e\left(\frac{1}{R_3} + \frac{1}{R_4} + \frac{1}{Z_L}\right) - \frac{V_0}{Z_L}$$

or
$$\frac{V_i}{R_3} = e\left(\frac{1}{R_3} + \frac{1}{R_4} + \frac{1}{Z_L}\right) - \left(\frac{R_1 + R_2}{R_1}\right) e.\frac{1}{Z_L}$$

or
$$\frac{V_i}{R_3} = e\left\{\frac{1}{R_3} + \frac{1}{R_4} + \frac{1}{Z_L} - \left(1 + \frac{R_2}{R_1}\right)\frac{1}{Z_L}\right\}$$

or
$$V_i = e\left(1 + \frac{R_3}{R_4} - \frac{R_2 R_3}{R_1 Z_L}\right)$$

or
$$V_i = \frac{V_0 R_1}{R_1 + R_2}\left(1 + \frac{R_3}{R_4} - \frac{R_2 R_3}{R_1 Z_L}\right)$$

$$V_0 = \left(\frac{R_1 + R_2}{R_1}\right)\frac{V_i}{1 + \frac{R_3}{R_4} - \frac{R_2 R_3}{R_i Z_L}}$$

Now, Z_L being a reactive component, the denominator of the above expression can be rationalized. It can be observed that Z_L can be of the form $Z_L = jX_L$ or $Z_L = -jX_L$. If $Z_L = -jX_L$, then only V_0 will have a leading phase at the output of the circuit.

QUESTIONS

1. State two terms that are used to describe the inverting I/P of an operational amplifier.
2. What effect will increasing the number of inputs have on the performance of a summing amplifier?
3. Why high CMRR is important in instrumentation amplifier applications?
4. What is an instrumentation amplifier? List three applications of the instrumentation amplifier besides those discussed in this chapter.
5. How can we get the negative resistance using op. amp.?
6. What term is given to the inverting terminal of an op. amp. configured as an inverting amplifier?
7. List two special cases of inverting amplifier.
8. In what way is the voltage follower a special case of the non-inverting amplifier?

4

FREQUENCY RESPONSE AND COMPENSATION OF OPERATIONAL AMPLIFIER

4·1. Introduction. 4·2. Stability in Op. Amp. Circuit. 4·3. Frequency Response. 4·4. Frequency and Phase Response of Operational Amplifier. 4·5. Oscillation and Precaution. 4·6. Stability of Amplifiers. 4·7. Methods of Frequency Compensation. 4·8. Miller Effect Compensation. 4·9. Feedforward Compensation. 4·10. Effects of Stray Capacitance on Circuit Instability. 4·11. More about the Compensation for Stray Capacitance. 4·12. Effect of Load Capacitance on Circuit Instability. 4·13. How to Improve Stability with Capacitive Load. 4·14. Frequency Compensation using Input Impedance Modification Technique. 4·15. Some Important Terms of Compensation Recommended by Manufacturers. 4.16 Precautions to be taken for Better stability.

Objectives

After studying this chapter, the student will be able to:

- Understand the effects of feedback in op.amp. circuits and also the conditions under which oscillation occurs.
- Define some important terms like loop phase shift, loop gain, open loop gain, close loop gain related to op. amps.
- Draw the typical open loop gain vs. frequency and phase vs frequency response curves for an op.amp.
- Construct lag/lead compensation and Miller-effect compensation circuits and to study their effects on op. amp. frequency.
- Describe how to select compensating components for inverting and non-inverting modes.
- And some other important terms like gain bandwidth product, stray capacitance, load capacitance etc.

4·1. INTRODUCTION

There are phase shifts from input to output for op. amps. It is more prominent at high frequencies. However, there is a particular frequency at which this phase shift to adds up 2π when instability occurs and finally leads to oscillation. At the oscillation condition, the loop voltage gain from the inverting input terminal to the output and back to the input via the feedback network must be equal to or greater than unity. In order to avoid instability some compensating components like capacitors and resistors are employed for reducing either voltage gain or minimizing the phase shift. The compensating components and the particular op.amp. are used (combinedly) to determine the upper cutoff frequency of the op.amp circuit.

4·2. STABILITY IN OP. AMP. CIRCUIT

In inverting amplifier $|\text{gain}| = \dfrac{R_f}{R}$ and there is a phase shift of 180° between input and output [Fig. 4.1(*a*)]. But if we redraw the same circuit like [Fig. 4.1(*b*)] it is seen that the output voltage V_o is divided by the feedback circuit and produces a feedback voltage V_f. If G be the gain, then

$$V_o = G\,V_f \text{ and } V_f = \beta V_o$$

$$\beta = \frac{R}{R+R_f} \text{ if } R_g = 0$$

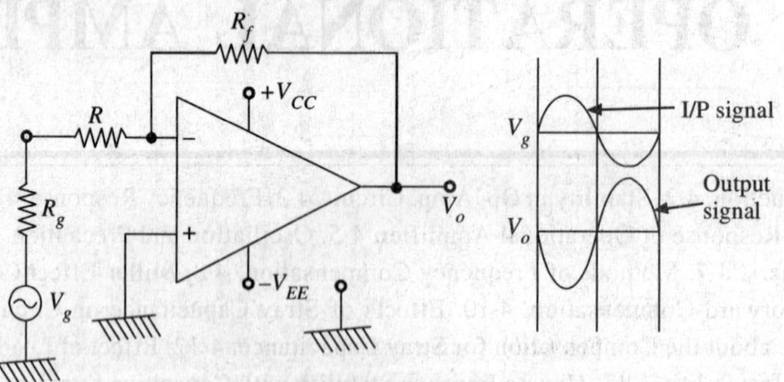

Fig. 4.1(*a*). Inverting amplifier.

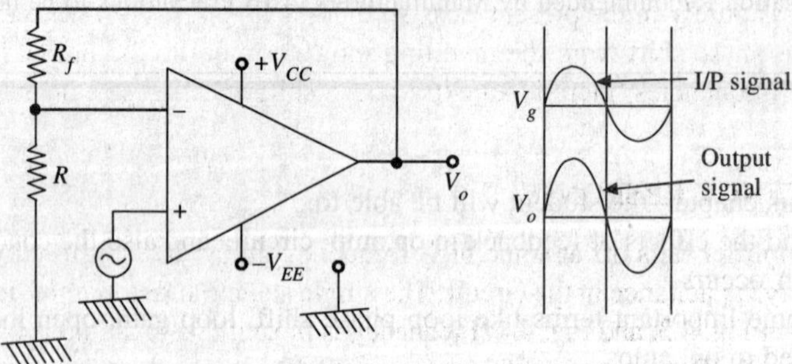

Fig. 4.1(*b*). Oscillating inverting amplifier.

When βV_o is exactly equal to and also in phase with the original V_g, the network is now providing its own ac input leading to a state of continuous oscillation. Figure 4.2 shows the similar situation for non-inverting mode of operation.

Due to feedback circuit, every op.amp. circuit is a potential oscillator. To combat or avoid oscillation some measures are adopted which are called frequency compensation. However, some op. amps. (like 741) are internally compensated and hence have limited frequency response leading to restrictions in some special applications. But for oscillation to occur Barkhausen conditions are to be satisfied. Those conditions are: (*i*) for a circuit to oscillate the loop gain should be equal to or greater than one and (*ii*) the loop phase shift should be equal to 360°. The loop gain here is the gain around the loop from the inverting input terminal to the amplifier output and back to the inverting input via the feedback circuit. Loop gain is then expressed as

$$\text{loop gain} = (\text{gain of the amplifier}) \times \text{attenuation in feedback circuit} = G\beta.$$

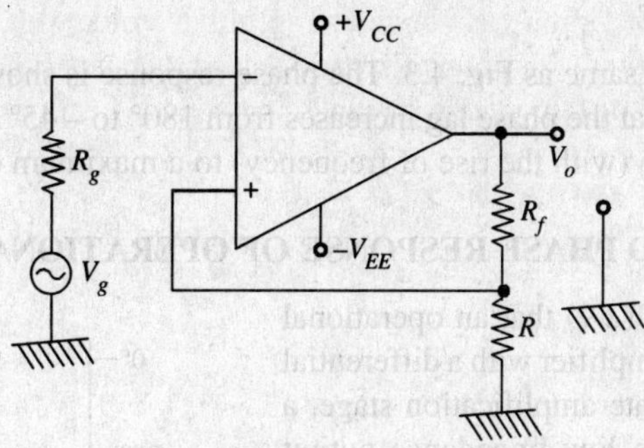

Fig. 4.2(*a*). Noninverting amplifier.

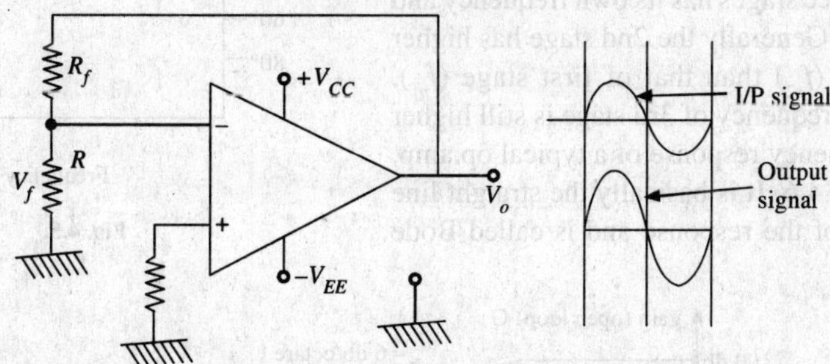

Fig. 4.2(*b*). Oscillating noninverting amplifier

Similarly, the loop phase shift is the total phase shift around the loop from the inverting input terminal to the amplifier output and back to the inverting input via the feedback network. As the feedback network is purely in the present case, so there is no phase shift produced by the feedback network hence the phase shift from the inverting input terminal to the output is normally – 180°. However, at high frequencies, there is an extra phase shift and the total phase shift can approach – 360°.

4·3. (a) FREQUENCY RESPONSE

The gain of an amplifier falls off at some high frequency due to the construction of the individual transistor or to stray capacitance in the circuit. The single stage transistor amplifier and its frequency response is shown in Fig. 4.3. and Fig. 4.4 (Frequency is plotted to a logarithmic base). The rate of fall of voltage gain is (–) 6 dB per octave of frequency or 20 dB per decade increase of frequency. f_p is the pole frequency at which the gain falls down by 3dB from the mid band gain G.

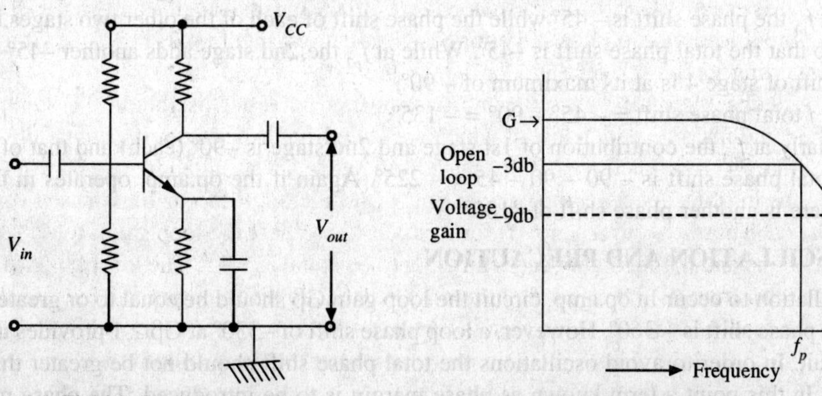

Fig. 4.3. Transistor amplifier. **Fig. 4.4.** Frequency response.

(*b*) PHASE RESPONSE

The referred circuit is the same as Fig. 4.3. The phase response is shown in Fig. 4.5. It is observed from continues Fig. 4.4 that the phase lag increases from 180° to – 45° at the pole frequency and the lag continuous to increase (with the rise of frequency) to a maximum of – 90°.

4·4. FREQUENCY AND PHASE RESPONSE OF OPERATIONAL AMPLIFIER

We know from chapter 2 (2.9) that an operational amplifier is a multistage amplifier with a differential input stage, an intermediate amplification stage, a level shifting stage and a low impedance output stage (Fig. 2.7). Excluding the level shifting stage each of these three stages has its own frequency and phase response. Generally the 2nd stage has higher pole frequency (f_{p2}) than that of first stage (f_{p1}). Again the pole frequency of 3rd stage is still higher ($f_{p3} > f_{p2}$). Frequency response of a typical op.amp. is shown in Fig. 4.6. It is basically the straight line approximation of the response and is called Bode Plot.

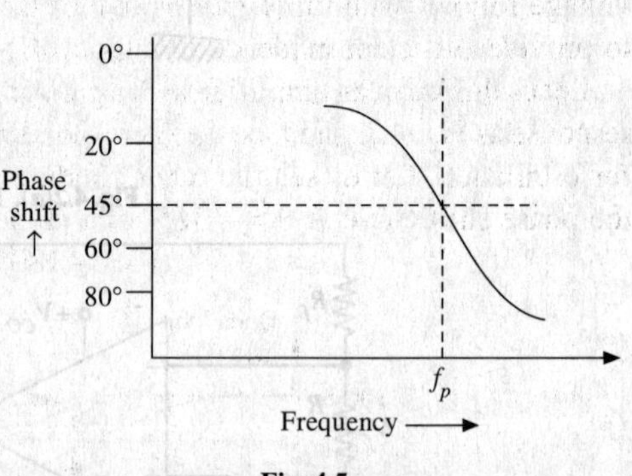

Fig. 4.5.

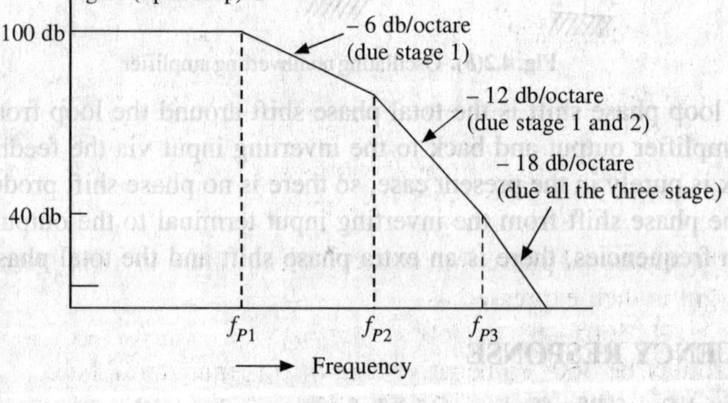

Fig. 4.6

From the figure it is revealed that between f_{p1} to f_{p2} the fall of the gain is only – 6dB/octave as only stage 1 is in operation. But between f_{p2} to f_{p3} fall rate is (–6 – 6) = –12 dB/octave due to stage 1 and stage 2. Above f_{p3} the fall rate is (–6–6–6) = – 18dB/octave due to all the three stages. For phase response it is seen that the phase shift of each stage is added together to get the total phase shift. At f_{p1} the phase shift is – 45° while the phase shift of each of the other two stages is negligibly small, so that the total phase shift is –45°. While at f_{p2} the 2nd stage adds another –45° but at f_{p2} the phase shift of stage 4 is at its maximum of – 90°.

So at f total phase shift = – 45° – 90° = – 135°.

Similarly at f_{p3} the contribution of 1st stage and 2nd stage is –90° (each) and that of 3rd stage is –45°. Total phase shift is – 90 – 90 – 45 = – 225°. Again if the op.amp. operates in the inverting mode there is another phase shift of –180°.

4·5. OSCILLATION AND PRECAUTION

For oscillation to occur in op.amp. circuit the loop gain Gβ should be equal to or greater than 1 and the loop phase shift is – 360°. However, a loop phase shift of –330° at Gβ ≥ 1 provides unstability in the circuit. In order to avoid oscillations the total phase shift should not be greater than – 315° at Gβ = 1. In this point a term known as phase margin is to be introduced. The phase margin is the difference between 360° and the actual phase shift at $G\beta = 1$. Hence to get stability the phase margin is 360 – 315 = 45°.

4·6. STABILITY OF AMPLIFIERS

Let us discuss the stability issue in amplifier (with op.amp.). It is said that op.-amp. circuit with a low closed-loop gain is more difficult to stabilize than with a high closed-loop gain. Further, the voltage follows with unity gain is one of the most difficult circuits to stabilize. Now we proceed to provide sufficient evidence of supporting such remarks.

Let us think that an amplifier with a gain of 50 dβ which is an op.amp. amplifier with the frequency response as Fig. 4.7. and f_2 be the corresponding frequency (f_2) at which $G\beta = 1$. This is one condition for oscillation. Let us see the other condition for oscillation. A vertical line drawn at f_2 intersects the phase shift curve at $\theta = -165°$ and the loop phase shift is given by

$$\theta = -180° - 165 = -345°$$

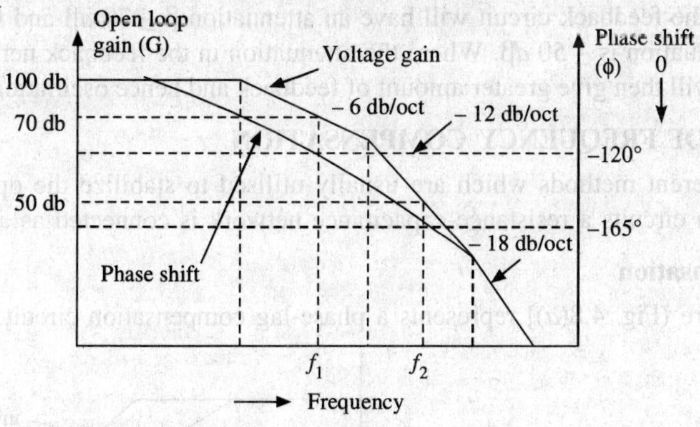

Fig. 4.7.

[where, – 180° is the additional phase shift between the op. amp. inverting terminal and the output.]

The phase margin is then expressed as

$$360° - \theta° = 360° - 345° = 15°.$$

as total phase shift may be 360° so negative sign of θ is immaterial here.

So the phase margin is 15° with $A_v = 50\ d\beta$ at $\beta G = 1$.

So the other condition for oscillation is also satisfied and hence the circuit is likely to oscillate. So phase margin is to be increased to stabilize the circuit. Otherwise, frequency may be changed so that $G\beta = 1$ to some other stable point on the phase response may be employed.

Let us focus our attention on high gain amplifier which uses an op.amp. with the frequency response curve as shown in Fig. 4.7.

The maximum gain is 100 dβ which is equivalent to a voltage gain of 10^5. The overall voltage gain with negative feedback is then

$$A_v = \frac{1}{\beta} \text{ and } G\beta = G/A_v.$$

Let with feedback the amplifier has a closed loop gain of 70dβ occurs at frequency f_1. A horizontal line drawn on the frequency response graph at $A_v = 70d\beta$ intersects the open-loop gain/frequency graph at frequency f_1. At this point $A_v = 70\ d\beta$ and $G = 70\ d\beta$.

Loop gain is then $\quad G\beta \simeq G/A_v = \dfrac{70\,d\beta}{70\,d\beta} = 1.$

This indicates that at a frequency f_1, the closed loop gain A_v equals the open-loop gain G is the frequency when $G\beta = 1$. This is one of the conditions required for oscillation.

A vertical line from f_1 intersects the phase response curve at $\phi = -120°$, giving a loop phase shift $\theta = -180 - 120 = -300°$.

The phase margin = $360° - \theta = 360° - 300° = 60°$ with $A_v = 70\ d\beta$ at $G\beta = 1$, the phase margin is 60°. But the minimum value for the phase margin is 45°. Thus this circuit with $A_v = 70$ dβ is unlikely to oscillate because out of two conditions for oscillation, only one condition is satisfied. However, at frequencies higher than f_1, the open-loop phase-shift increases to a phase angle greater than – 1 whereas gain G becomes progressively smaller beyond f_1 thereby making Gβ smaller than unity. This indicates that θ remains between – 330° and – 360° when the frequency is beyond f_1 but the other condition for oscillation $G\beta = 1$ is not satisfied. Hence oscillation is unlikely beyond f_1.

At frequencies lower than f_1, although Gβ is more than unity the open loop phase shift is smaller than – 120° and hence the closed loop phase shift θ is smaller than – 300°. This means only one condition for oscillation is satisfied so the circuit is likely to be stable.

In view of the above analysis it is clear that the amplifier with $A_v = 70$ dβ is likely to be stable and the amplifier with $A_v = 50$ dβ is unstable. This can be attributed in the following way.

For $A_v = 70\ d\beta$ the feedback circuit will have an attenuation $\beta \simeq 70\ d\beta$ and for $A_v = 50\ d\beta$ the corresponding attenuation is $\simeq 50\ d\beta$. Where the attenuation in the feedback network is lower, the feedback network will then give greater amount of feedback and hence oscillations are more likely.

4·7. METHODS OF FREQUENCY COMPENSATION

There are two different methods which are usually utilised to stabilize the op.amp. circuits. In those compensation circuits a resistance-capacitance network is connected as a part of the loop.

Phase-lag Compensation

The following figure (Fig. 4.8(*a*)] represents a phase-lag compensation circuit.

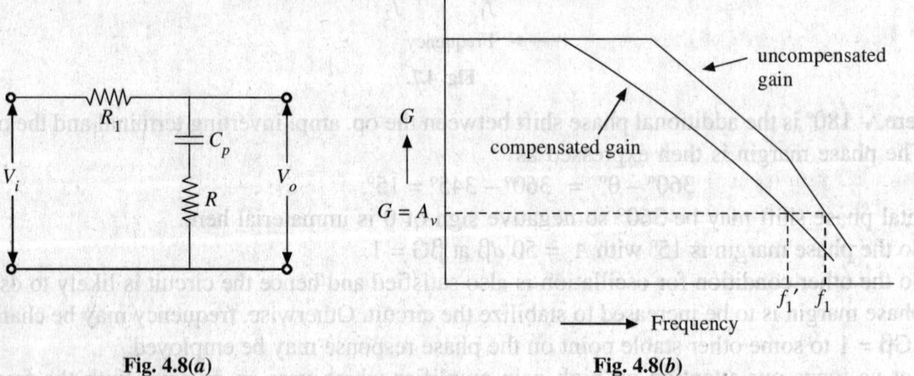

Fig. 4.8(*a*) **Fig. 4.8(*b*)**

If we look into Fig. 4.8(*a*), it can be realised that at frequencies where $X_C >> R$, the output voltage V_o lags the input voltage V_i. A maximum phase lag that can be introduced by this network is – 90°. But at higher frequencies when $X_C << R$ the network is now largly resistive and no significant phase lag occurs thereby it merely provides some attenuation.

The elements of the compensation network is selected so that at lower frequencies where the op.amp. open-loop phase-shift is still so small that additional phase shift has no effect on the circuit stability. Again at higher frequencies there is no additional phase lag other than the attenuation. However the response curve is altered due to compensation circuit as depicted in Fig. 4.8(*b*). The effect of lag network is to introduce attenuation and f_0 moves the frequency f_1 at which $G\beta = 1$ for a given closed-loop gain A_v, to a lower frequency f_1'. As f_1' is less than f_1, the open-loop phase shift at f_1' is less than that at f_1, and hence the circuit is likely to be stable. This indicates that lag compensation network is used to reduce the loop gain, so that $G\beta = 1$ takes place at a frequency at which the amplifier phase shift is inadequate to cause oscillation.

Phase-Lead compensation

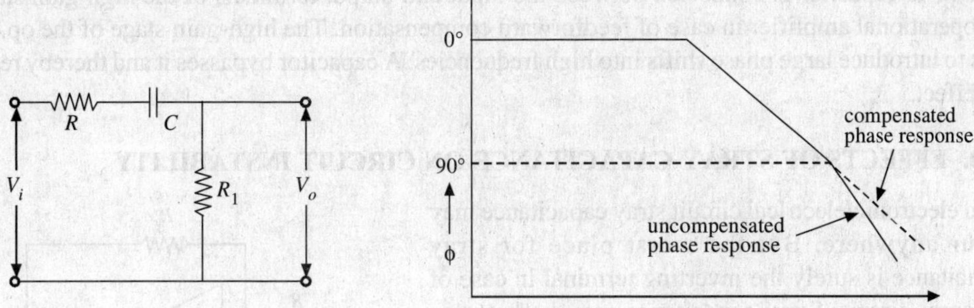

Fig. 4.9(*a*). Phase-lead compensation network. **Fig. 4.9(*b*).** Frequency.

The figures [Fig. 4.9(*a*) & 4.9 (*b*)] represent the phase-lead network and its phase response curve, respectively, when $X_c >> R$ V_o leads V_i. This circuit introduces a phase-lead.

The phase-lead compensation network cancels some of the unwanted phase lag in the op-amp. Thereby improves the phase margin at Gβ = 1, and provides better circuit stability.

4·8. MILLER EFFECT COMPENSATION

The adjoining figure represents a common emitter transistor amplifier having a capacitor connected between base and the collector terminal (Fig. 4.10). In the amplifier both amplification and phase inversion takes place. Hence

$$V_o = -A_v V_i$$

This means that the collector voltage goes down by an amount $A_v V_i$ when the voltage change across the base goes up by an amount V_i. So the change of voltage acros the capacitor is given by

$$\Delta V_c = V_i + A_v V_i = V_i (1 + A_v)$$

And the charge given to the capacitor is

$$q = C \times \Delta V_c = CV_i (1 + A_v)$$

This indicates that when there is change in the base voltage V_i, the capacitor is charged to $q = c(1 + A_v) V_i$ but not by CV_i. It seems that the capacitor is amplified by a factor of $(1 + A_v)$. This phenomena is called miller effect. The similar reasoning may be given to the op.-amp. inverting amplifier circuit as shown in Figure 4.11.

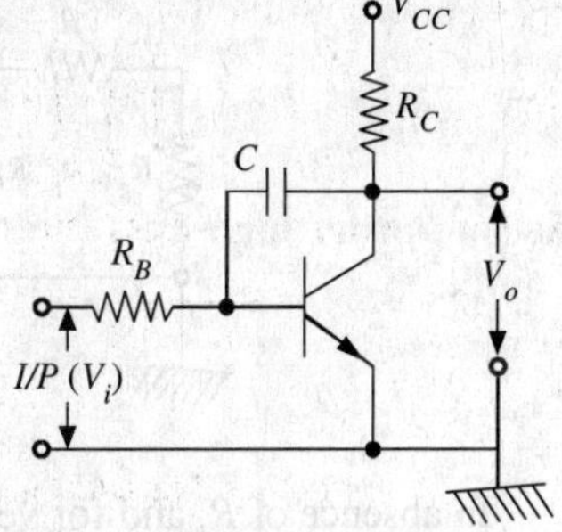

Fig. 4.10. Frequency.

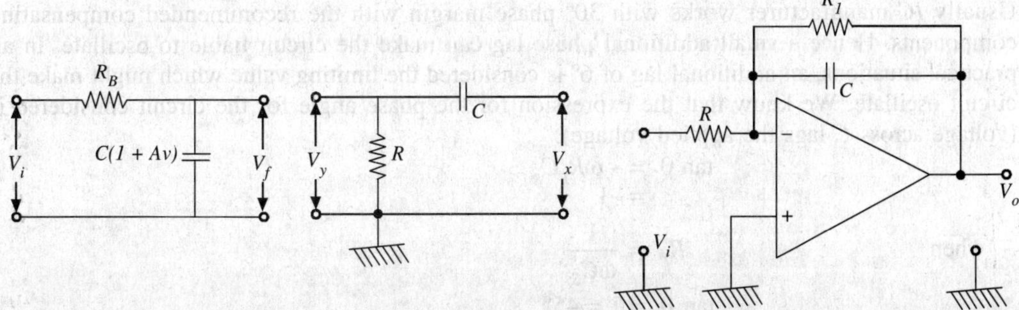

Fig. 4.11(*a*). Equivalent of which forms a lag network. **Fig. 4.11(*b*).** Equivalent of which forms a lead network.

In case of transistor circuit it is equivalent to a phase lag network for signal voltages and the op.amp. circuit is a lead network for feedback voltages.

4·9. FEEDFORWARD COMPENSATION

A suitable capacitor is connected between the input and output terminals of the high-gain stage of the operational amplifier in case of feedforward compensation. The high-gain stage of the op.-amp. tries to introduce large phase shifts into high frequencies. A capacitor bypasses it and thereby reduces the effect.

4·10. EFFECTS OF STRAY CAPACITANCE ON CIRCUIT INSTABILITY

In an electronic/electrical circuit stray capacitance may occur anywhere. But the worst place for stray capacitance is surely the inverting terminal in case of op.-amp. circuit. Stray capacitance may be between either inverting/non-inverting terminal and the ground or in both the terminals. But the compensating methods are more or less same in all the cases. The adjoining figure depicts a compensating network where the stray capacitance is shown between the inverting and non-inverting terminals of the op.-amp. [Fig. 4.12(*a*)]. Now if we look back into the resistor network from the capacitance we get equivalent resistor (R_E)

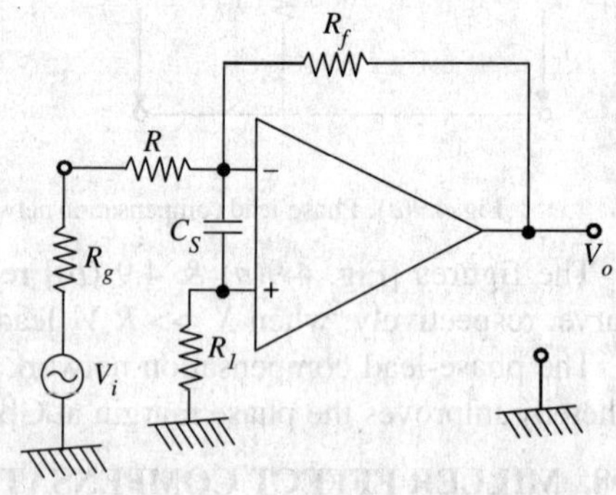

Fig. 4.12(a). Stray capacitance and circuit instability.

$$R_E = R_1 + R_f \parallel (R + R_g)$$

Fig. 4.12(*b*)

In absence of R_1 and for very small value of R_g compared to R ($R_g << R$), $R_E \simeq R_f \parallel R$.

Now if we look to this modified circuit, we feel that the stray capacitance and the equivalent network resistance R_E make a *phase-lag network* which produces an additional phase lag in the feedback loop thereby makes the circuit suspectable to oscillate. Now we shall discuss about the limit of tolerance of stray capacitance for safe operation of the circuit so that there is no oscillation. Usually *IC* manufacturer works with 30° phase margin with the recommended compensating components. Hence a small additional phase lag can make the circuit liable to oscillate. In all practical situations, an additional lag of 6° is considered the limiting value which might make the circuit oscillate. We know that the expression for the phase angle for the circuit considered is (voltage across C lags the applied voltage).

$$\tan\theta = -\omega R_E C_S$$
$$= -1$$

when
$$R_E = \frac{1}{\omega C_S}$$
$$\tan\theta = 1 = 45°$$

So the voltage across C_s lags the applied voltage by 45°, when θ = 6° (lag) this gives capacitive reactance = 10 R_E.

$$\tan\theta = \frac{1}{10} \text{ if } \theta = 6°. = \omega R_E C_S.$$

$$\boxed{\frac{1}{\omega C_S} = 10\,R_E}$$

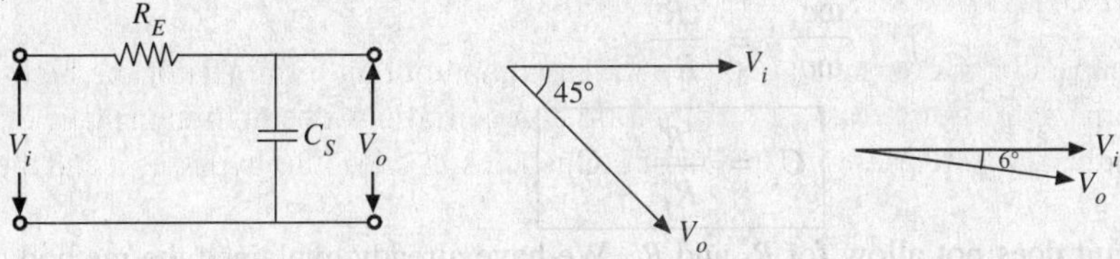

Fig. 4.12(c). Phase lag circuit. **Fig. 4.12(d).** $X_C = R_E$. **Fig. 4.12(e).** $X_C = 10R_E$.

So for stability of the circuit, the stray capacitance should be very much less than,

$$C_S = \frac{1}{20\pi f R_E} \quad \text{...(1)}$$

where 'f' is the frequency at which $G\beta = 1$. (The frequency at which the circuit is likely to oscillate).

Analysis of the Circuit: If the resistors are of high values, R_E will also be very large thereby reducing the calculated value of C_S [as per Eq. (1)]. This indicates that for larger resistor values in an op.-amp. circuit, the stray capacitance is very small thereby the circuit is liable to oscillate.

But for small resistor values, R_E is also small and hence calculated value of C_S is quite higher and the possibility of oscillation is unlikely. Hence the conclusion is the smallest possible resistor values ensure the greatest circuit stability. But this actually goes against the conventional circuit designing methods. In conventional circuit design method, largest possible resistor values are selected for minimization of current demand on the supply and for maximising the input resistance of the circuit.

For further better stability the resistor R_1 may be eliminated from the circuit. If such option is not feasible, a capacitor having an impedance much smaller than R_1 at the frequency at which $G\beta = 1$, is employed across the capacitor.

Again if the signal source (V_i) is open-circuited, the network resistance will be

$$R_E = R_f + R_1 \text{ [Fig. 4.12(a)]}$$

R_E is now very large and hence the stray capacitance (C_S) will be extremely small thereby making the op.-amp. circuit prone to oscillation (likely to oscillate) when the signal source is open circuited.

4·11. MORE ABOUT THE COMPENSATION FOR STRAY CAPACITANCE

In the previous article it is seen that for greatest circuit stability the smallest possible resistor values should be selected. There are also other ways of precautions for removing oscillation in the circuit by keeping the stray capacitance as low as possible. The possible way of keeping stray capacitance low is to keep the component leads to their minimum lengths (at the op.-amp. input terminals).

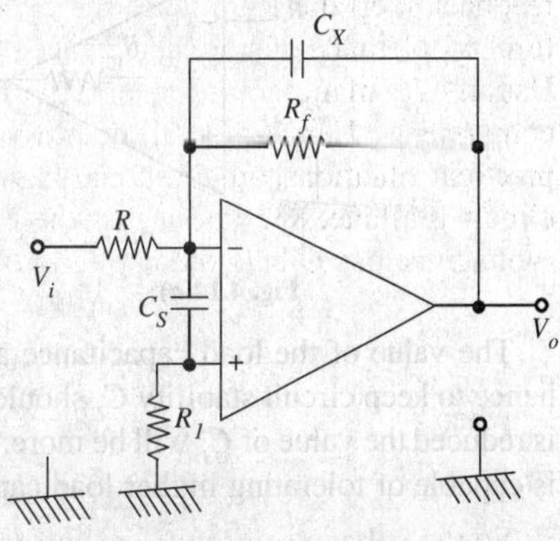

Fig. 4.13 (*a*)

A capacitor (C_x) can be connected across the feedback resistor (R_f) for getting compensation for stray capacitance (as shown in Fig. 4.13). The question may arise that how is compensation obtained. The phase-shift produced by the stray capacitance is eliminated by dividing the output voltage developed by C_s and C_x in series and making equal to that produced by resistors R and R_f. Thus we get:

$$\frac{X_{cs}}{X_{cx}} = \frac{R}{R_f}$$

$$\frac{\omega c_x}{\omega c_s} = \frac{R}{R_f}$$

$$\therefore \qquad \boxed{C_x = \frac{R}{R_f} \cdot C_s} \qquad ...(2)$$

This circuit does not allow for R_1 and R_g. We have already explained the method of by passing R_1 if it is there in the circuit. Again if R_g is not very small then R is to be replaced by $(R + R_g)$. Eq. (2) indicates that $(C_x R_f = RC_s)$ the time constant $R_f\, C_x$ should be equal to or greater than the time constant $C_s R$.

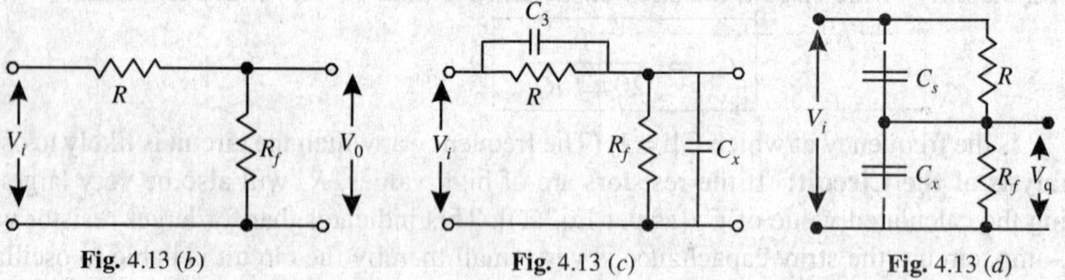

Fig. 4.13 (*b*) **Fig.** 4.13 (*c*) **Fig.** 4.13 (*d*)

4·12. EFFECT OF LOAD CAPACITANCE ON CIRCUIT INSTABILITY

Load capacitance of an op.-amp. circuit is the capacitance connected at its output terminal. Such capacitance can provide an additional phase lag in the feedback network thereby creating instability in the circuit. Actually the load capacitance together with the output impedance (R_o) of the op.-amp. constitutes a phase-lag network. Thus the value of R_o will basically determine the extents of load capacitance that will not cause oscillation in the circuit. We have already discussed that an additional 6° of phase lag in the feedback network is undesirable. 6° phase lag occurs for $X_{CL} = 10\, R_o$.

$$\therefore \qquad \boxed{C_L = \frac{1}{10\,\omega\, R_o}} \qquad ...(3)$$

Fig. 4.14(*a*) **Fig. 4.14(*b*)**

The value of the load capacitance available from Eq. (3) is the base minimum value of C_L and hence to keep circuit stability C_L should be smaller than this. If the output impedance of an op.-amp. is reduced the value of C_L will be more. This indicates that an op.-amp. having low output impedance is capable of tolerating higher load capacitance than one with a higher output impedance.

4·13. HOW TO IMPROVE STABILITY WITH CAPACITIVE LOAD

Figs. 4.15(*a*) & (*b*) give the idea how to improve the circuit stability with capacitive load. Here an additional resistance (R_x) is connected in series with C_L and the feedback resistor R_f is connected at the junction of R_o and R_x. Under this situation, the function of R_x is to reduce the phase lag generated by R_o and C_L. If a phase lag of 6° occurs because of R_o and C_L, then including $R_x = R_o$, reduces the phase lag to approximately 3°. Higher the value of R_x greater will be the reduction in the phase lag by nearly 3°. A further reduction is also possible using further larger values of R_x. However, this technique has a majordraw back of increasing the output impedance of the op.-amp. As output impedance of an op.-amp. is usually very small, hence this enhancement of output impedance may be unacceptable in some circumstances. But this technique may be adopted in the circuits where this enhanced impedance is acceptable.

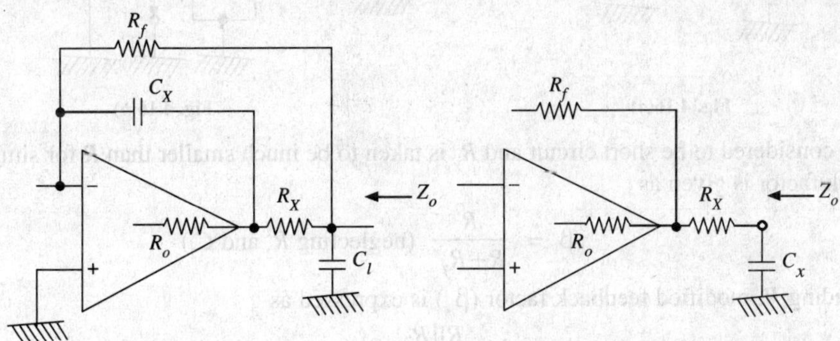

Fig. 4.15(*a*) **Fig. 4.15(*b*)**

Figure 4.15(*b*) represents a method of using a feedback capacitor (C_x) for providing a phase lead which will counter the phase lag generated by C_L and R_o. The expression for feedback capacitor can be had in the same way as done in the case of stray capacitance at the op.-amp. input.

$$\boxed{C_x = \frac{R_o}{R_x} C_l}$$

There is another way of improving the technique [as shown in Fig. 4.15(*a*)]. This provides a larger feedback capacitor where an additional resistor R_x is connected in series with the load capacitance and it forms a part of the feedback network. Now the feedback capacitor value is given as

$$C_x = \left(\frac{R_o + R_x}{R_f}\right) C_l$$

As the feedback resistor R_f is connected at the node where R_x and C_l are connected, the output impedance remains more or less unaffected. Z_{om} = modified output impedance = $(R_o + R_x)/(1 + G\beta)$. It is expected that low value resistors are to be used for better result.

4·14. FREQUENCY COMPENSATION USING INPUT IMPEDANCE MODIFICATION TECHNIQUE

The following figure represents such a method of frequency compensation technique [Fig. 4.16(*a*)]. The capacitor C_2 acts as ac coupling for R_2. That is why the value the capacitor C_2 so that its impedance will be much smaller than the resistance R_2 at the frequency at which $G\beta = 1$. So R_2 falls in parallel with R to give the feedback network [as in Fig. 4.16(*b*)] at the possible oscillation frequency or higher than that frequency.

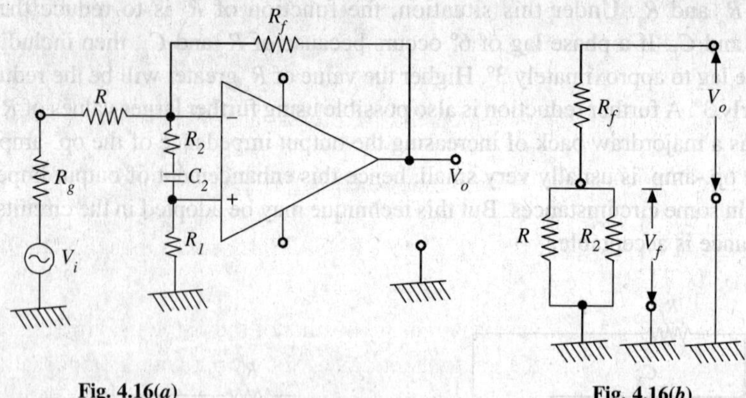

Fig. 4.16(*a*) Fig. 4.16(*b*)

R_1 is considered to be short circuit and R_g is taken to be much smaller than R for simplicity. The feedback factor is given as

$$\beta = \frac{R}{R+R_f} \text{ (neglecting } R_2 \text{ and } C_2\text{)}$$

Including R_2 modified feedback factor (β_m) is expressed as

$$\beta_m = \frac{R \| R_2}{(R \| R_f)+R_f}.$$

This indicates that feedback signal is reduced in the presence of R_2.
Then for the circuit stability we get ($G\beta_m = 1$).

The voltage gain is then $A_v = \dfrac{R_f}{R}$.

$R \| R_2 < R$ so $\dfrac{1}{\beta_m}$ is greater than A_v and hence we can select the compensating components for higher gain *i.e.* higher $\left(\dfrac{1}{\beta_m}\right)$. This technique is basically used as a method of increasing the bandwidth of an op.-amp. circuit. It will be better understood by an example. Before going to the example let us explain why this technique is so named. The presence of R_2 and C_2 will positively modify the input impedance of the op.-amp. C_2 provides short circuit for ac and open-circuit for dc thereby ensuring that R_2 will not change the dc conditions of the circuit. We know that for an inverting amplifier, the non-inverting terminal is grounded and the inverting terminal is at virtual ground. Hence the input impedance is equal to R despite the presence of components used for input impedance modification technique. But for non-inverting amplifier the resistor R_2 appears in parallel with input impedance of the op. amp. (Z_i) thereby input impedance is modified and expressed as

$$Z_{im} = (1 + G\beta)\,(Z_i \| R_2)$$

It is still sufficiently high. It is to be noted that in both the modes a small value of the signal current will be directed through R_L which will generate a very small differential voltage across the op.-amp. input terminals ($V_d = V_o/G$). The current diversion is minute and hence will not generate D significant change in the amplifier gain.

Let $A_v = 100$ (i.e. $4d\beta$)

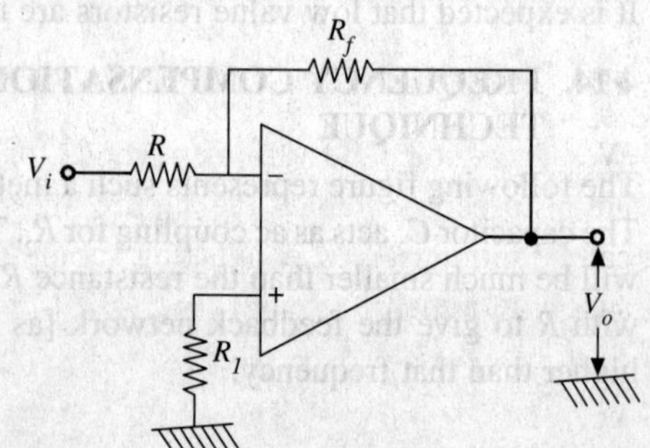

Fig. 4.17

Suppose the upper cut off frequency for the circuit be f_{vc} = 600 k Hz (at a gain of 40 $d\beta$). Now let us consider the compensation circuit so that

$\frac{1}{\beta_m}$ = 1000 for the compensation components used for a gain of 60$d\beta$. But A_v = 40 $d\beta$ and f_u = 2MHz. So the bandwidth has increased from 600 KHz to 2MHz.

4·15. SOME IMPORTANT TERMS OF COMPENSATION RECOMMENDED BY MANUFACTURERS

From the analysis of the discussions we have made in some of the previous, articles it is clear that it is a tedious process to calculate the component values for an op. amp. compensation network. Moreover, frequency response curve is essential for the particular op. amp. under consideration. To get rid of such hazards and to make the compensation technique simpler it is better to use the manufacturer's specified compensation components available in the datasheet (amplifier closed loop gain and the component values for the compensation).

Over-Compensation

It may happen that in some occasions the voltage gain of an amplifier may fall between the gain values for which compensating components are recommended in the datasheet. In such cases components should be taken for the next lower gain. Such a provision of larger components than actually required, is called over-compensation which ensures better stability in the amplifier. Over-compensation also produces an upper cutoff frequency which is not as high as could be obtained with smaller compensating components.

For the similar component values the non-inverting gain is larger than the inverting gain. So when compensating components are taken for an inverting amplifier from those recommended for non-inverting amplifier, the circuit is obviously being over-compensated.

Cut-off Frequencies

Internally operational amplifiers are directly coupled. The lower cutoff frequency is zero when the signal and load are direct-coupled. For a capacitor-coupled circuits, the lower cutoff frequency is determined by the selection of capacitors. However, the upper cutoff frequency is dependent upon the frequency response of the op. amp., the compensating components, and the circuit voltage gain.

Gain Bandwidth Product

The gain bandwidth product of an operational amplifier is defined as the product of the closed loop gain and the cutoff frequency for that gain. The unity gain bandwidth of an op.-amp. is also called the gain bandwidth product.

4·16. PRECAUTIONS TO BE TAKEN FOR BETTER STABILITY

We have studied the various methods for compensation leading to better stability. However, these are also feedback along the supply lines which provides instability in the circuit. This instability can be minimised by connecting supply decoupling capacitors (each equal to 0.01 μF) from each supply terminal to ground (Fig. 4.18).

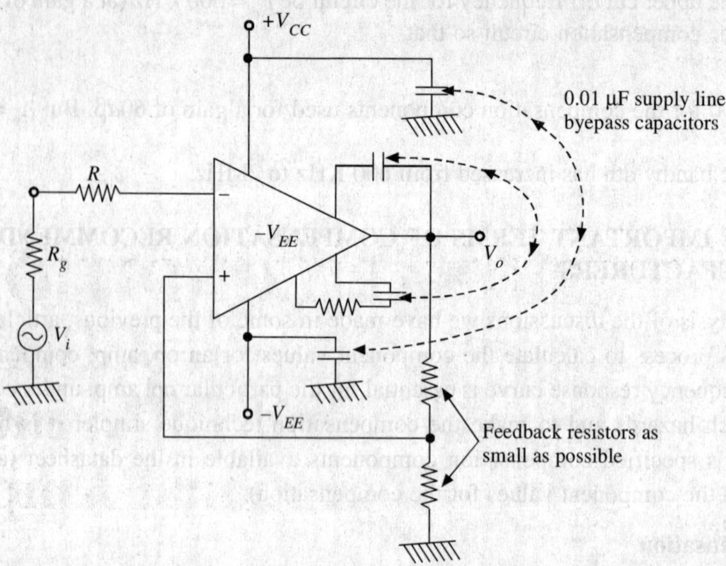

Fig. 4.18

In some cases capacitor values may be 0.1 μF.

There are some recommended precautions for getting better stability in the circuit. The precautions are:

(1) For low frequency applications, internally compensated op.-amp. like 741 is recommended.

(2) For op.-amp. circuit it is better to use manufacturer's recommended technique and components for compensation.

(3) Components leads are to be kept as small as possible and proper care should be taken for their (components) placement in the circuit. As for example for the connection of resistors to the input terminals of the op.-amp., the body of the resistor should be placed close to the input terminal.

(4) Supply line byepass capacitors (either 0.01 μF or 0.1 μF depending upon the need) are to be connected close to the IC terminals.

(5) Oscilloscopes or other instruments should not be connected at the op.-amp. input terminals (inverting or noninverting).

(6) If the circuit is found unstable even after satisfying the above precautions, all circuit resistors excluding compensating resistors are to be reduced (including signal source resistors if possible). The compensation techniques for stray and load capacitance should be done if necessary.

(7) Frequency compensation technique using input impedance modification method is to be done with the recommended compensating components if the circuit bandwidth is not adequate.

5

SIGNAL CONDITIONING CIRCUITS (Integrators and Differentiators using Operational Amplifier)

5·1. Introduction. 5·2. Integrator Circuit. 5·3. Non-inverting Integrator. 5·4. Setting of Initial Condition 5·5. Other Practical Considerations 5·6. Integrator with bias Current Compensation. 5·7. Integrator with Feed Forward Frequency Compensation. 5·8. Integrator with two Operational Amplifier. 5·9. Double-integrator Circuit Using Single Operational Amplifier. 5·10. Some Specific Integrator Circuits. 5·11. Differentiator Circuits. 5·12. Practical Differentiator. 5·13. Some Specilised Differentiator.

5·1. INTRODUCTION

Operational amplifiers have been employed to a wide range of signal *conditioning circuits.* These circuits change the relationships of signals to time, other signals, and frequency. Some of these circuits include the differentiators, integrators, and active filters. In this chapter basic integrators and differentiator circuits together with their specialised circuits are discribed at first and then active filter circuits are explained in next chapter.

5·2. INTEGRATOR CIRCUIT

A circuit is said to be an integrator circuit if its output voltage waveform is the integral of the input voltage waveform. The Fig. 5.1 shows such an integrator circuit.

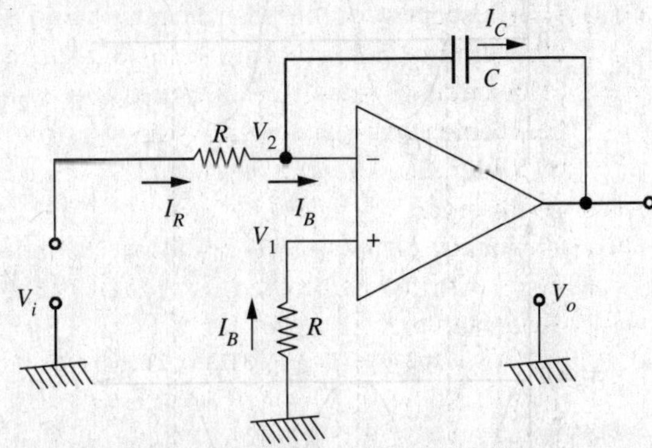

Fig. 5.1. Integrator circuit using operational amplifier.

Application of KCL at node V_2 gives

$I_R = I_B + I_C$. Where I_B is negligibly small

Hence $\qquad I_R = I_C$

For a capacitor $\qquad I_C = C\,\dfrac{dV_C}{dt}$

V_c = voltage across the capacitor

$$= V_2 - V_0$$

Here $$I_R = \frac{V_i - V_2}{R} = C \cdot \frac{d}{dt}(V_2 - V_o)$$

As $V_1 = V_2 = 0$ (As they are virtually grounded)

Hence $$\frac{V_i}{R} = C\frac{d}{dt}(-V_o)$$

On integration with respect to t we get

$$\int_0^t \frac{V_i}{R}\,dt = \int_0^t C\frac{d}{dt}(-V_o)\,dt = C\left[-V_0\right]_0^t = C[-V_0]_{t=t} + C[-V_0]_{t=0}$$

$$= -C\,V_o + K_1$$

So $$V_o = -\frac{1}{RC}\int_0^t V_i\,dt + K, \text{ where } K = \frac{K_1}{C} \qquad ...(5.2.1)$$

where K is the integration constant and is proportional to the value of the output voltage V_o at time $t = 0$ second. If K is zero then Eq. (5.2.1) can be written as:

$$V_o = -\frac{1}{RC}\int_0^t V_i\,dt \qquad ...(5.2.2)$$

In addition if $$RC = 1,\; V_o = -\int_0^t V_i\,dt \qquad ...(5.2.3)$$

This indicates that if

(*i*) a sine wave is applied at the input, the output will be a cosine wave [shown in Fig. 5.2(*a*)].

(*ii*) a square wave is applied at the input, the output will be a triangular wave [shown in Fig. 5.2(*b*)]

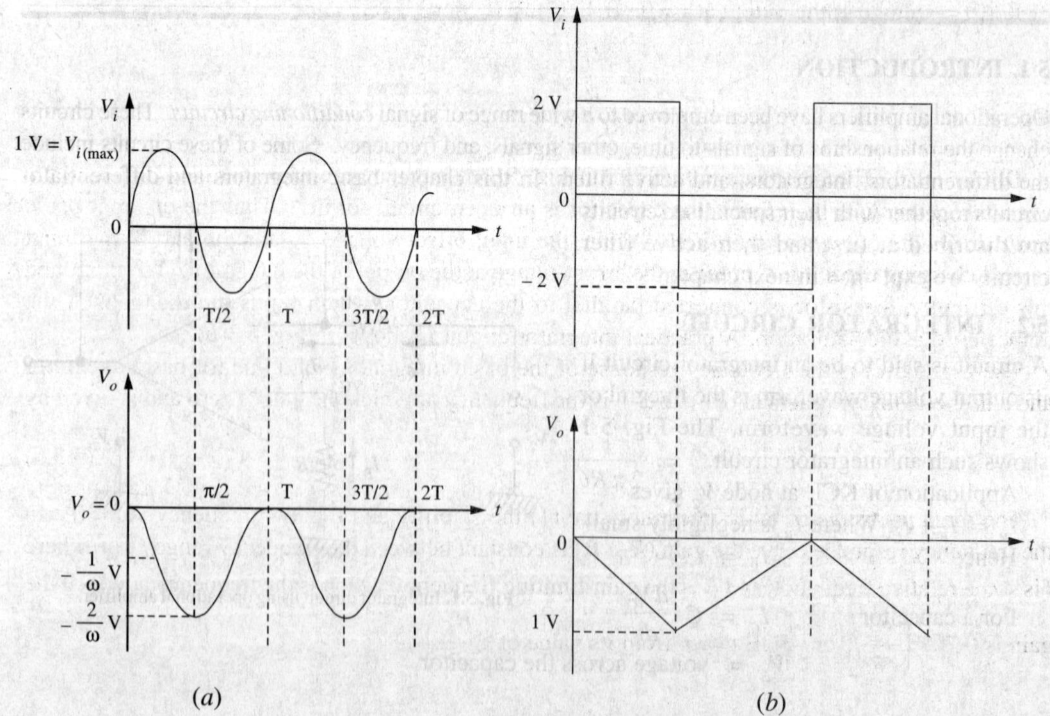

Fig. 5.2.

5·3. NONINVERTING INTEGRATOR

Figure 5.3(*a*) represents a noninverting integrator. Capacitor current

[In an integrator time constant is very high so the current in the circuit ($V_i - R - C$) is controlled by the resistance only. The current in the circuit is

$$i_R = i_C = \frac{V_i}{R} \qquad \text{...(5.3.1)}$$

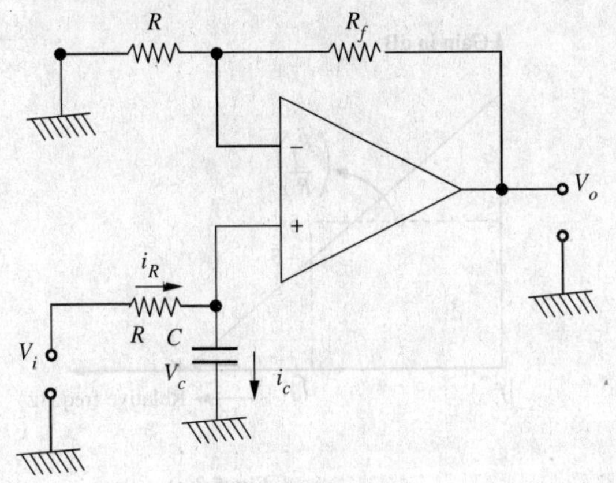

Fig. 5.3(*a*). Non-inverting Integrator.

The operational amplifier in the figure acts as a non-inverting amplifier with respect to V_c

$$V_o = \left(1 + \frac{R_f}{R}\right) V_c \qquad \text{...(5.3.2)}$$

But $$i_c = \frac{V_i}{R} = C\frac{dV_c}{dt}$$

$$\therefore \quad \frac{V_i}{R} = \left[C \Big/ \left(1 + \frac{R_f}{R}\right)\right] \frac{dV_o}{dt},$$

or $$dV_o = \left[\left(1 + \frac{R_f}{R}\right) \Big/ (RC)\right] \times V_i\, dt$$

Integrating both sides with respect to t we get

$$V_o = \frac{1 + (R_f / R)}{RC} \int_0^t V_i\,(t)\,\mathrm{dt} + V_o\,(0) \qquad \text{...(5.3.3)}$$

V_o (0) = voltage at the output at $t = 0$. If V_o (0) = 0 then

$$V_o = \frac{1 + \dfrac{R_f}{R}}{RC} \int_0^t V_i\,(t)\,dt \qquad \text{...(5.3.4)}$$

Discussions: The basic integration circuit Fig. 5.3(*a*) has the drawback that the *dc gain of the operational amplifier is infinite* (the capacitor is an open circuit for dc). Thus the dc input *offset error drives the output to saturation*. Again, the input offset voltage V_{io} and the part of the input current charging capacitor *C* produce the error voltage at the output of the integrator. To get around this difficulty, a resistor is connected parallel to the capacitor, which limits the d.c. gain of the amplifier to avoid saturation. A practical integrator circuit is shown in Fig. 5.3(*b*).

The Fig. 5.3(*c*) is the frequency response of the basic integrator (solid line for basic integrator and a dashed line for practical one). Let f_b is the frequency at which the gain is zero and is given by

$$f_b = \frac{1}{2\pi RC} \qquad \text{...(5.3.5)}$$

The main problems of basic integrators are (1) the stability and the low frequency volt-off: In the frequency response curve the gain (R_f / R) is constant between the frequency range f to f_a where f is some relative frequency and f_a is the gain-limiting frequency which is the frequency at which the gain is 0·707 $\left(\frac{R_f}{R}\right)$ or –3 dB down from its value of $\left(\frac{R_f}{R}\right)$

$$f_a = \frac{1}{2\pi R_f C_f} \qquad \text{...(5.3.6)}$$

Resistors and capacitor values are selected such that $f_a < f_b \rightarrow$ generally $f_b = 10 f_a$. It has also been observed that for getting proper integration of the input signal the time period (T) of the signal should satisfy the condition $T \geq R_f\ C_f$.

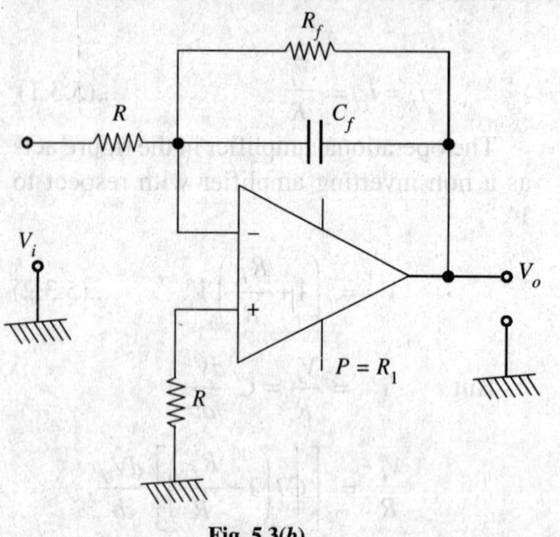

Fig. 5.3(*b*).

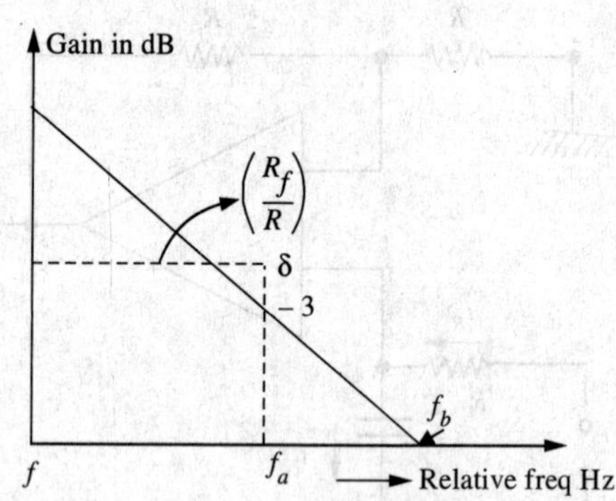

Fig. 5.3(*c*).

Between f_a and f_b it acts as an integrator.

5·4. SETTING OF INITIAL CONDITION

The Fig. 5.4 shows an arrangement for setting an initial condition.

It is essential for an integrator to have an external method of setting an initial condition. In most of the applications this amounts to a means for resetting the output to zero volts, (shown in Fig. 5.4). The switches S_{w1} and S_{w2} are ganged so that they are switched together. When the switch S_{w1} is grounded, S_{w2} is closed, the capacitor is discharged and output is reset to zero. When switch S_{w2} is open, S_{w1} is connected to the signal source and the integrator starts functioning.

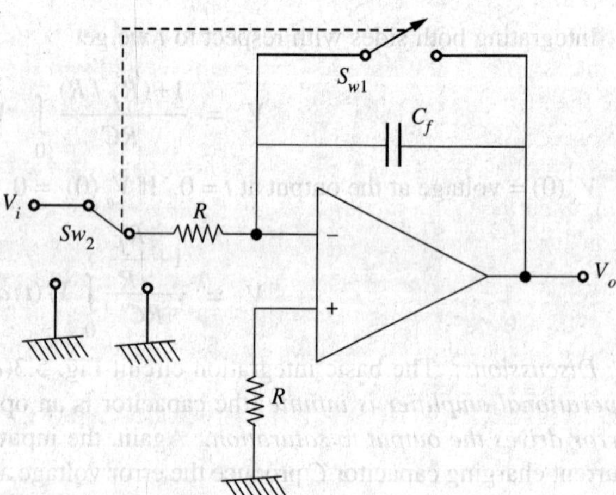

Fig. 5.4. Circuit arrangement for setting zero initial condition.

5·5. OTHER PRACTICAL CONSIDERATIONS

In order to get a reliable integrator, the operational amplifier used should have large differential mode and common-mode range. The input voltage limits can be inadvertently crossed in a number of ways. Out of those, the most evident way is from fleetings at the output which are coupled back to the input through the integrating capacitor C_f. Differential-mode or common-mode voltage limits can be exceeded under such condition.

When the operational amplifier is driven from fast rising or falling inputs, another evident problem may arise. The output of the *operational amplifier can not respond instantly*. As a result, *during a short interval, the inverting input may not hold at ground potential*. The voltage at the inverting input can crossed the safe limits for the operational amplifier *in case the input signal is large enough.*

5·6. INTEGRATOR WITH BIAS CURRENT COMPENSATION

The Fig. 5.5 depicts a circuit for an integrator with bias current compensation.

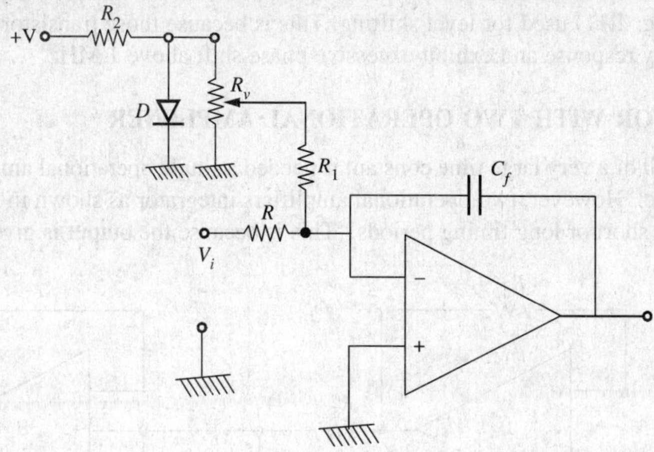

Fig. 5.5. Integrator with bias current compensation.

Generally a compensation resistance is connected to the noninverting input of an operational amplifier to minimize error due to input bias currents. Inspite of that the integrating capacitor will accumulate any residual error voltage. Such an error voltage may create some problem in precision applications, especially when long integration times are involved because then resulting drift may be intolerable. The figure 5.5 represents a circuit arrangement for compensating the bias current so that the drift rate is reduced to zero. A current is feed into the inverting input through R_1 to supply the bias current, so no current needs to flow through *R*. The variable resistor, R_v, is adjusted for the exact bias current needed, thereby reducing the drift rate to zero. There are two specific reasons of using the diode *D* in the circuit. (1) It behaves like a regulator to create the bias-current adjustment insensitive to power supply variations. (2) It makes the bias current adjustment less sensitive to temperature changes, because the temperature drift of the diode voltage is about the same as that of the bias current. If the operational amplifier used is not frequency compeniated, in that case an adequate capacitor can be employed for frequency compensation.

5·7. INTEGRATOR WITH FEED FORWARD FREQUENCY COMPENSATION

The slew rate of the operational amplifier limits the speed of an operational amplifier integrator. However, the integrator can be made faster using feed-forward frequency compensation technique. The Fig. 5.6 shows such an arrangement.

Generally, the μA741 is frequency compensated by a single 30pF capacitor. From its data sheet it has been observed that it is having a unity-gain bandwidth of 1 MHz and a slew rate of 0·5 V/μ sec. But with feed forward frequency compensation, the unity-gain bandwidth can be extended to about

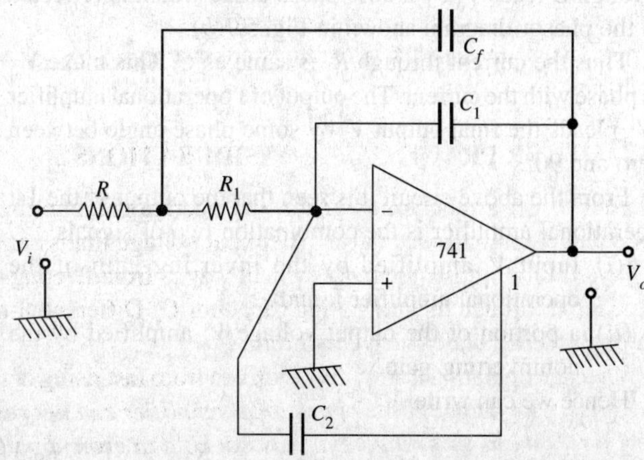

Fig. 5.6. Integrator circuit with feed-forward frequency compensation.

3.5 MHz and the slew rate to 10 V/μ sec. In the circuit the resistor R_1 incorporated for isolating the compensation capacitor C_1 from integrating capacitor C_f. The compensation capacitor C_2 is not connected to pin 5. It is connected to the inverting input (as shown in Fig. 5.6) to bypass the internal PNP transistors (Fig. 2.11) used for level shifting. This is because those transistor are having very poor high-frequency response and exhibit excessive phase shift above 1 MHz.

5·8. INTEGRATOR WITH TWO OPERATIONAL AMPLIFIER

If either a very small or a very large time constant is needed a single operational amplifier integrator may be troublesome. However, two operational amplifiers integrator as shown in Fig. 5.7(*a*) finds it easy to get either short or long timing periods. This is because the output is given by

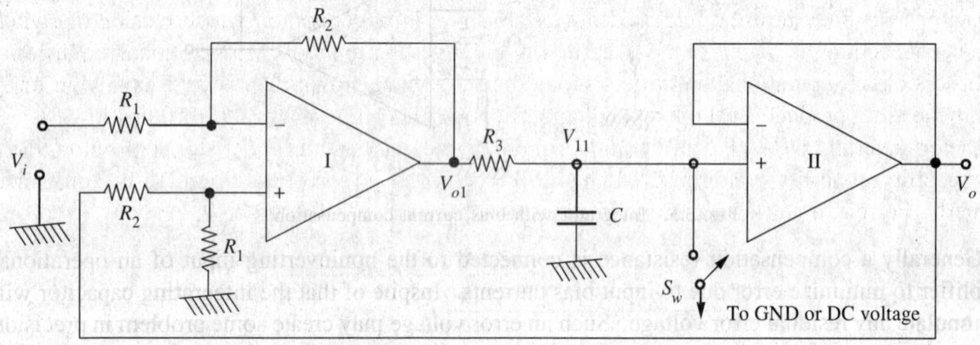

Fig. 5.7(*a*). Integrator with two operational amplifier.

$$V_o = -\frac{1}{RC}\int V_i\, dt \qquad \text{...(5.8.1)}$$

where RC = integrator time constant

$$= \frac{R_1}{R_2} \times (R_3 \times C) \qquad \text{...(5.8.2)}$$

If precision resistors are used for R_1 and R_2, the circuit gives very good linearity. Let us explain how the circuit operates. The II operational amplifier is a voltage follower. Hence the output V_o is also the voltage across C. The 2nd operational amplifier practically does not draw any current from C. The current through C leads V_o by a 90% phase angle which is reflected in the phasor diagram shown in Fig. 5.7(*b*).

Thus the current through R_3 is same as C. This make V_{o1} in phase with the current. The output of I operational amplifier (V_{o1}) leads the final output V_o by some phase angle between zero and 90º.

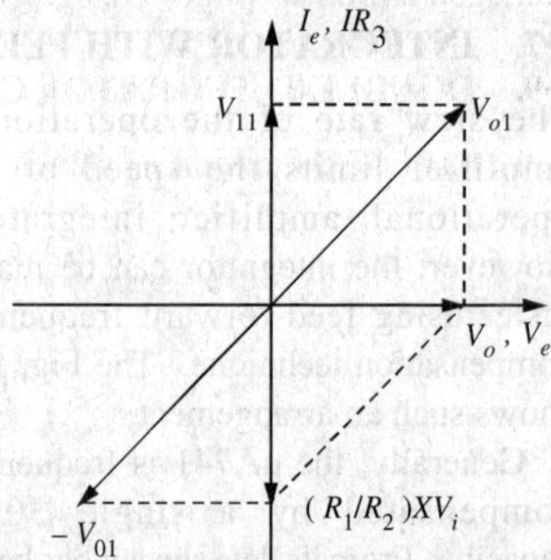

Fig. 5.7(*b*). Phasor diagram of two operational amplifier.

From the above circuit it is seen that the output of the 1st operational amplifier is the combination two of signals.

(*i*) Input V_i amplified by the inverting gain of the operational amplifier I, and

(*ii*) a portion of the output voltage V_o amplified by the noninverting gain.

Hence we can write

$$V_{o1} = -\frac{R_2}{R_1}\times V_i + \left(1+\frac{R_2}{R_1}\right)\left(\frac{R_1}{R_1+R_2}\right) V_o$$

$$\therefore \qquad V_{o1} = -\frac{R_2}{R_1} V_i + V_o \qquad ...(5.8.3)$$

Hence
$$\frac{R_2}{R_1} V_i = V_o - V_{o1} \qquad ....(5.8.4)$$

Again from the phasor diagram and from the equation 5.8.4 it appears that the phasor for V_o must be added to the phasor for $-V_{o1}$ to present the formula of the said equation (5.8.4). From the phasor diagram, once again it reveals that the result is a phasor which is proportional to V_i and always lags V_o by exactly 90°. Further, if V_o leads V_i by 90°, then V_o lags-V_i by 90°, and hence V_o is proportional to the negative integral of V_i. The function of the switch S_w is to establish initial condition. It may be connected to ground or to any DC voltage. Here the switch is not placed across the integrating capacitor as is done in usual integrator for establishing initial condition where closing of switch means connecting the output of the integrator to the inverting input of the operational amplifier.

In this circuit operational amplifiers should be selected such that they should have high unity gain bandwidth product. Best operational amplifiers for this purpose are CA 3100 or LM 318.

In non-inverting *OPAMP* configuration, for use in integrator and differentiator application, there are specific reliability conditions that has to be achieved in order the circuit to be functional properly. For e.g. a non-inverting integrator is as following:

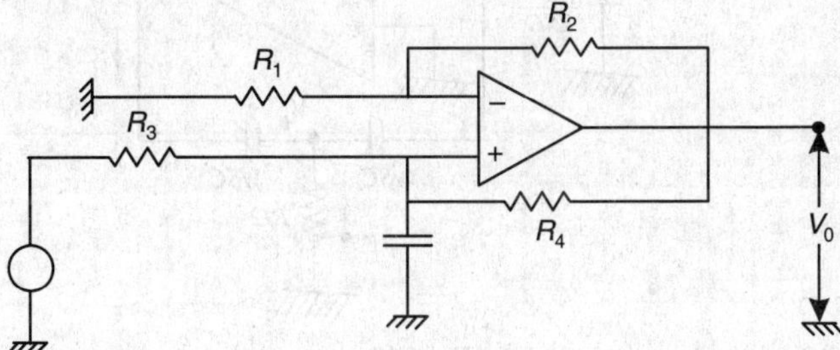

Realisability condition for the above non-inverting integrator circuit is $\frac{R_1}{R_2} = \frac{R_3}{R_4}$. This has to be realised in order the circuit to function as integrator. But it is not always possible to have resistors that fulfil the above condition. Even if initially resistors satisfy it, with time they get damaged and their values change, so no longer the condition is satisfied.

5·9. DOUBLE-INTEGRATOR CIRCUIT USING SINGLE OPERATIONAL AMPLIFIER

Let us take the circuit as shown to get double integration using single operational amplifier.

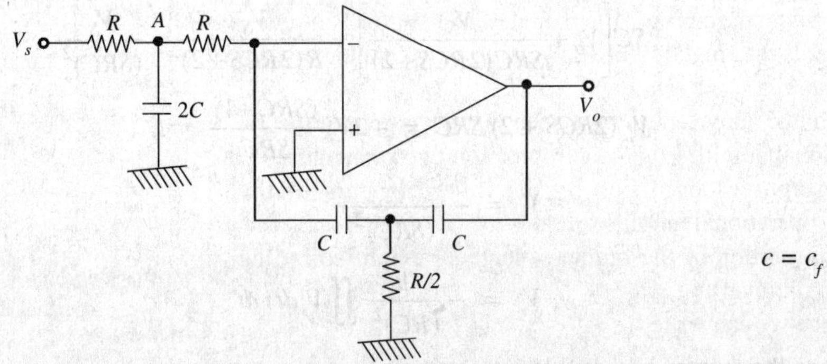

Fig. 5.8.

The input circuit in Laplace transform domain is

$$V_A = \frac{V}{R + \dfrac{(1/2SC)\times R}{R + \dfrac{1}{2SC}}} \times \frac{R \times \dfrac{1}{2SC}}{R + \dfrac{1}{2SC}}$$

Fig. 5.9. Time domain angles.

$$\therefore \quad V_A = \frac{V \times R \times \dfrac{1}{2SC}}{R\left(\dfrac{1}{2SC} + R\right) + \dfrac{1}{2SC} \times R} = \frac{V}{2(SCR+1)}$$

$$I = \frac{V_A}{R} = \frac{V_S}{R(2RSC+2)}$$

(as noninverting input is grounded)

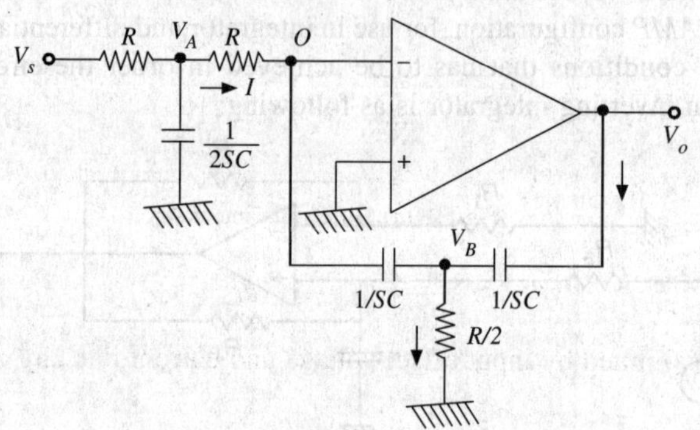

Fig. 5.10.

$$I_{(1/SC)} = I$$

Again $$\frac{0 - V_B}{1/SC} = \frac{V_S}{R(2RCS+2)}$$

$$\therefore \quad V_B = -\frac{V_S}{SRC(2SRC+2)}$$

Again $I_{1/SC} + I_{1/SC} = I_{1/2}$ $$\frac{V_O - V_B}{1/SC} + \frac{V_S}{R(2RCS+2)} = \frac{2V_B}{R}$$

or $$SC\left[V_o + \frac{V_S}{SRC(2RCS+2)}\right] + \frac{V_S}{R(2RCS+2)} = \frac{V_S}{(SRC)^2}$$

or $$V_o\,(2RCS + 2)\;SRC = -2V_s\,\frac{(SRC+1)}{SRC}$$

or $$V_o = -\frac{V_S}{(SRC)^2}$$

$$\therefore \quad V_o = -\frac{1}{(RC)^2}\iint (V_s dt)\,dt$$

Hence the system is a double integration.

5·10. SOME SPECIALISED INTEGRATOR CIRCUITS

Modification of feedback network of an integrator gives rise to several variations on the basic function. Some of such different integrators are explained here below.

Differential integrator

The Fig. 5.11 (*a*) represents a differential integrator.

It takes the difference between two input signals and integrates the result. The output is given by

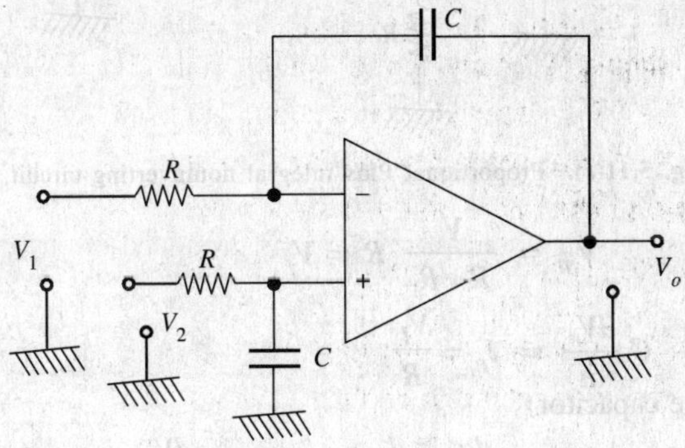

Fig. 5.11(*a*). Differential integrator.

$$V_o = \frac{1}{RC}\int (v_2 - v_1)\,dt \qquad \text{...(5.10.1)}$$

Its performance is limited by input offset voltage and current like any other standard integrator circuits.

Proportional plus integral inverting circuit

The Fig. 5.11 (*b*) is a proportional plus internal inverting circuits. The resistor R_1 is connected in series with the integrating capacitor. The output is expressed as

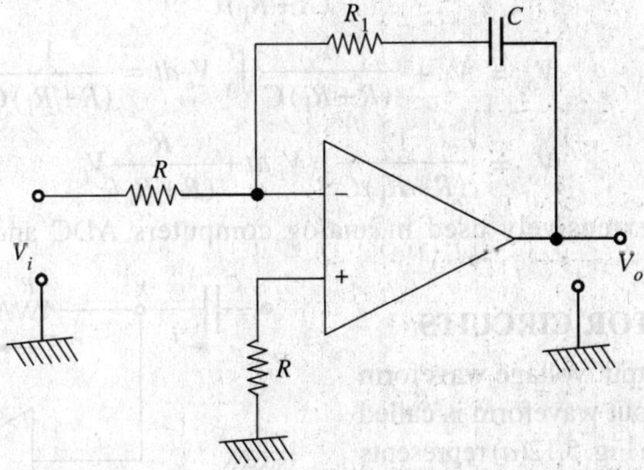

Fig. 5.11(*b*). Proportional Plus integral inverting circuit.

$$V_o = -\frac{1}{RC}\int V_i\,dt - \frac{R_1}{R}\cdot V_i$$

This type of signal is needed in many control system applications. The Fig. 5.11(*c*) shows a similar circuit excepting that the signal is applied to the noninverting input. The output is expressed in noninverting case like:

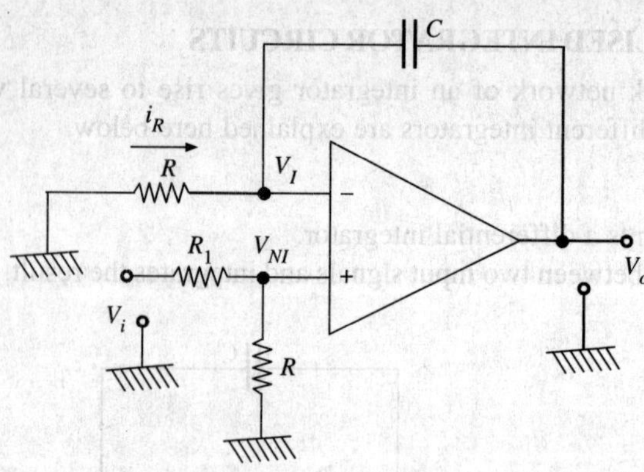

Fig. 5.11(c). Proportional Plus integral noninverting circuit.

$$V_{NI} = \frac{V_i}{R+R_1} R = V_I$$

$$\therefore \quad C\frac{dV_e}{dt} = i_c = \frac{V_I}{R} \qquad (\because \; i_e = i_R)$$

i_C (current through the capacitor)

$$= \frac{dq}{dt} = \frac{d}{dt}(V_c \cdot C) = C\frac{dV_e}{dt}$$

$$dV_c = \frac{V_i}{(R+R_1)C} dt$$

$$V_C = \int_0^t \frac{V_i}{(R+R_1)C} dt + V_C(0)$$

As at $t = 0$ capacitor is uncharged so $V_C(0) = 0$

$$\therefore \quad V_C = \frac{1}{(R+R_1)C}\int_0^t V_i \, dt$$

$$V_C = V_0 - V_I = \frac{1}{(R+R_1)C}\int_0^t V_i \, dt$$

$$V_0 = V_I + \frac{1}{(R+R_1)C}\int_0^t V_i \, dt = \frac{1}{(R+R_1)C}\int_0^t V_i \, dt = \frac{RV_i}{R+R_1}$$

$$V_o = \frac{1}{(R+R_1)C}\int V_i \, dt + \frac{R}{(R+R_1)} V_i \qquad (5.10.2)$$

The integrators are extensively used in analog computers ADC and signal waveshaping circuits.

5·11. DIFFERENTIATOR CIRCUITS

A circuit in which the output voltage waveform is the derivative of the input waveform is called a differentiator circuit. The Fig. 5.12(a) represents a simple differentiator circuit. It is known that the operational amplifier, via the feed back path provided by the resistance, sets its inverting input at virtual ground potential.

Hence capacitor current

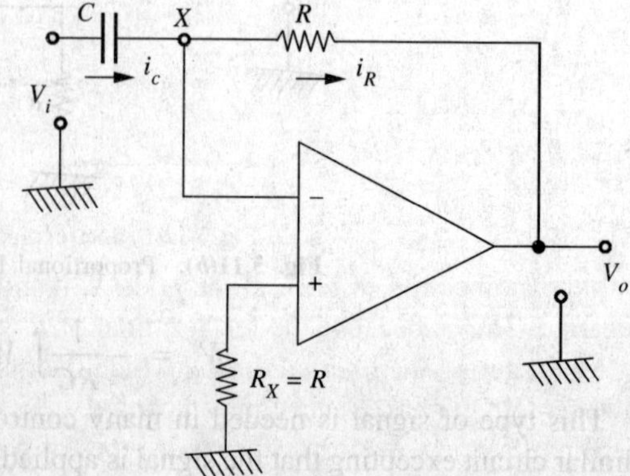

Fig. 5.12(a). Differentiator Circuit.

$$i_C = \frac{dq}{dt} = \frac{d}{dt}(CV) = C\frac{d}{dt}(v_i - 0)$$

$$i_c = C\frac{d}{dt}V_i \qquad \text{...(5.11.1)}$$

The current through the resistor R is i_R

$$i_R = \frac{0 - V_o}{R} = -\frac{V_o}{R} \qquad \text{...(5.11.2)}$$

As no current flows into or out of the inverting input pin, hence $i_c = i_R$.

Hence $$V_o = -RC\frac{d}{dt}V_i \qquad \text{...(5.11.3)}$$

Hence the output is proportional to the time derivative of the input and the constant of proportionality is negative and equal to RC (dimension is time).

Let us try to explain it with some input signals.

For triangular input waveform

During the interval over which V_i increases (A to B), the capacitor current i_C flows towards right

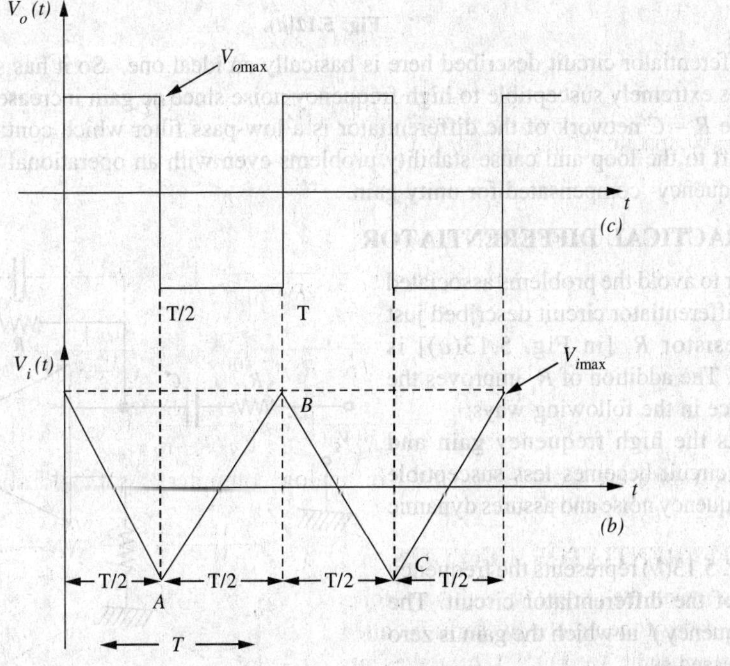

Fig. 5.12(b) and (c). Input and Output waveform.

with the application of KCL at the node X, it shows that i_R flows towards the right and hence V_o is negative. This is because the left terminal of R is at virtual ground potential.

Again during the interval during which the input voltage decreases (B to C), both i_c and i_R flows towards left and have V_o becomes positive.

Slopes of the waveforms for other types of waveforms are given in the Fig. 5.12(d).

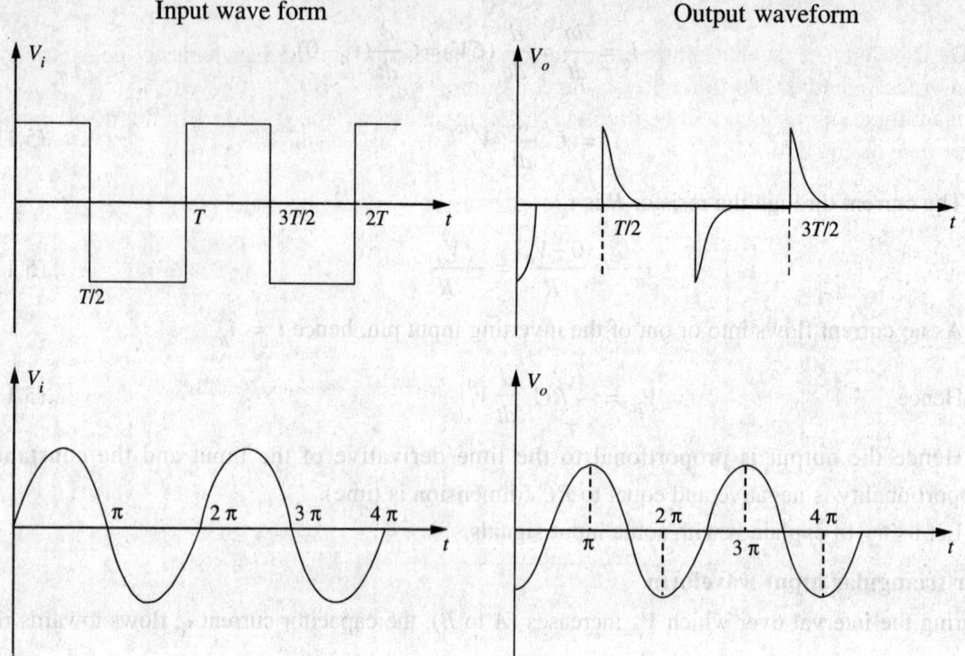

Fig. 5.12(*d*).

The differentiator circuit described here is basically an ideal one. So it has some drawbacks.

(*i*) It is extremely susceptible to high frequency noise since ac gain increases.

(*ii*) The $R - C$ network of the differentiator is a low-pass filter which contributes a 90º phase shift to the loop and cause stability problems even with an operational amplifier which is frequency- compensated for unity gain.

5·12. PRACTICAL DIFFERENTIATOR

In order to avoid the problems associated with the differentiator circuit described just now, a resistor R_1 [in Fig. 5.13(*a*)] is connected. The addition of R_1 improves the performance in the following ways:

It limits the high frequency gain and hence the circuit becomes less susceptible to high-frequency noise and assures dynamic stability

The Fig. 5.13(*b*) represents the frequency response of the differentiator circuit. The corner frequency f_a at which the gain is zero *dB* is expressed as

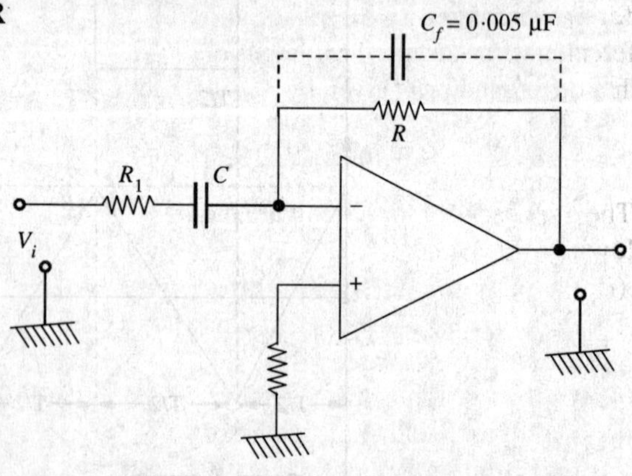

Fig. 5.13(*a*). Practical differentiator circuit.

$$f_a = \frac{1}{2\pi RC} \quad ...(5.12.1)$$

The frequency at which the gain of the practical differentiator starts decreasing at 20 *dB* per decade (f_b) is expressed as

$$f_b = \frac{1}{2\pi R_1 C} \quad ...(5.12.2)$$

f_c = Unity gain-bandwidth

The capacitor C_f is having influence on reducing the unstability and the high frequency noise problems.

In order to get better differentiation the condition $f_a < f_b < f_c$ is to be obeyed.

In addition input signal will be properly differentiated if the time period T of the input signal is larger than or equal to RC.

Hence $$T \geq RC \quad ...(5.12.3)$$

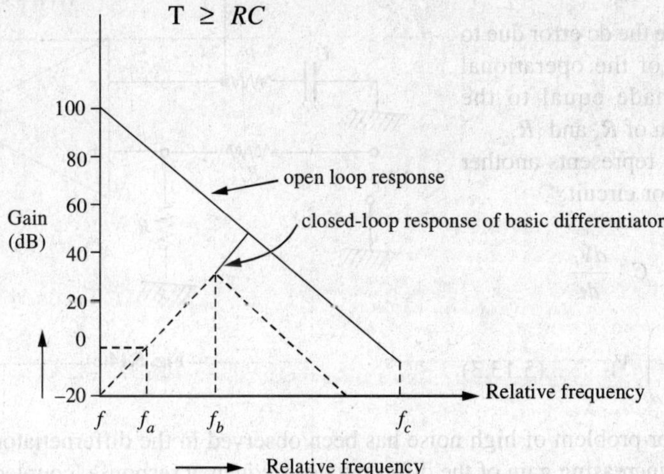

Fig. 5.13(*b*). Frequency response.

5·13. SOME SPECIALISED DIFFERENTIATOR

(*a*) Differential differentiator circuit

The Fig. 5.14(*a*) represents a differentialdifferentiator. It takes the difference between two signals and differentiates the result. The output of such a differentiator is given by

$$V_o = -R_f\, C \frac{d}{dt}(V_1 - V_2) \quad ...(5.13.1)$$

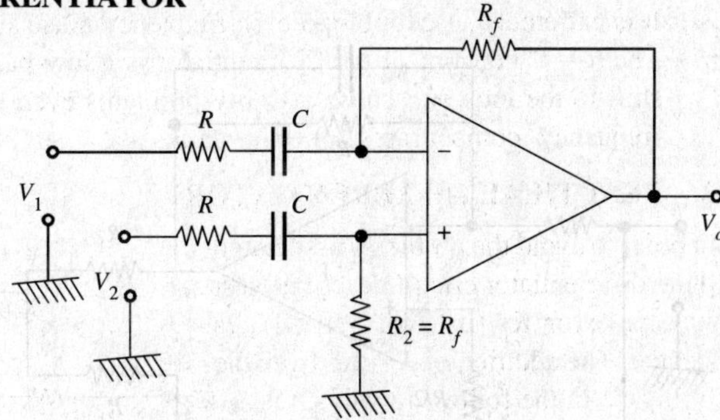

Fig. 5.14(*a*). Differential differentiator.

The drawbacks of this circuit are the following:

(*i*) Common-mode signals introduce one of the errors of this circuit.

(*ii*) Gain error limits the accuracy.

(*iii*) Gain-bandwidth limitations of the operational amplifier greatly limit the circuit response.

(*iv*) DC errors in the input of the operational amplifier create an error by creating an output offset.

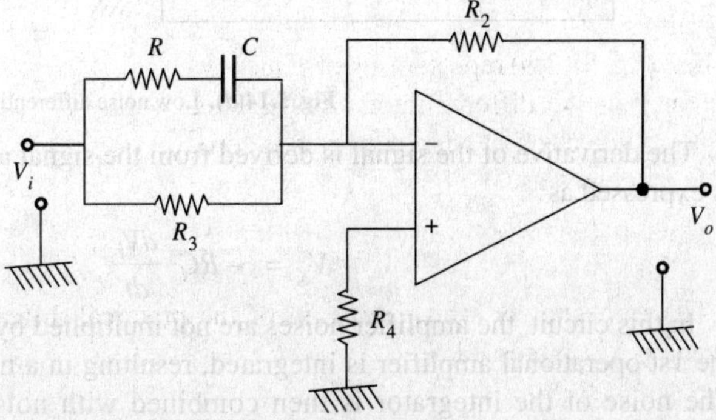

Fig. 5.14(*b*).

A better differentiator circuit is shown in the Fig. 5.14(*b*). Where an additional circuit element R_3 is connected. This element alone would give the operation of an inverting amplifier, while R and C alone would provide differentiator operation.

$$V_o = -R_2 C \frac{dv_i}{dt} - \frac{R_2}{R_3} V_i \quad ...(5.13.2)$$

In order to reduce the dc error due to input bias current of the operational amplifier, R_4 is made equal to the parallel combination of R_2 and R_3.

The Fig. 5.14(*c*) represents another form of differentiator circuit.

$$V_o = \left(\frac{R_f R_1}{R_f + R_1}\right) \cdot C \cdot \frac{dV_i}{dt} + \left(\frac{R_1}{R_f + R_1}\right) V_1 \quad ...(5.13.3)$$

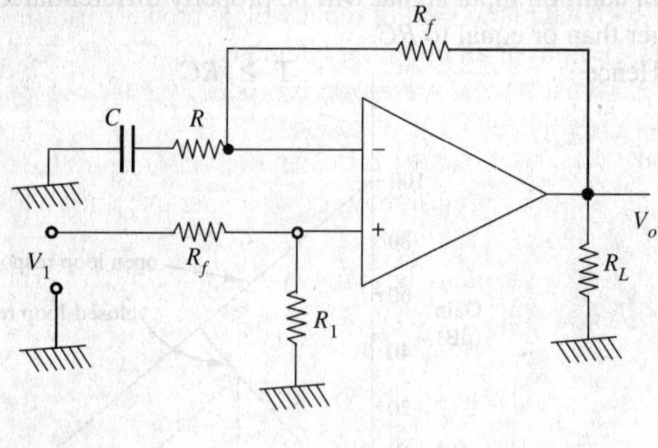

Fig. 5.14(*c*).

However, a major problem of high noise has been observed in the differnetiator just discussed. This is because the increasing gain of the differentiator frequency response, coupled with high gain amplification of the amplifier noise.

(*c*) In order to reduce this noise a special differentiator is used called low-noise differentiator circuit [as shown in Fig. 5.14(*d*)].

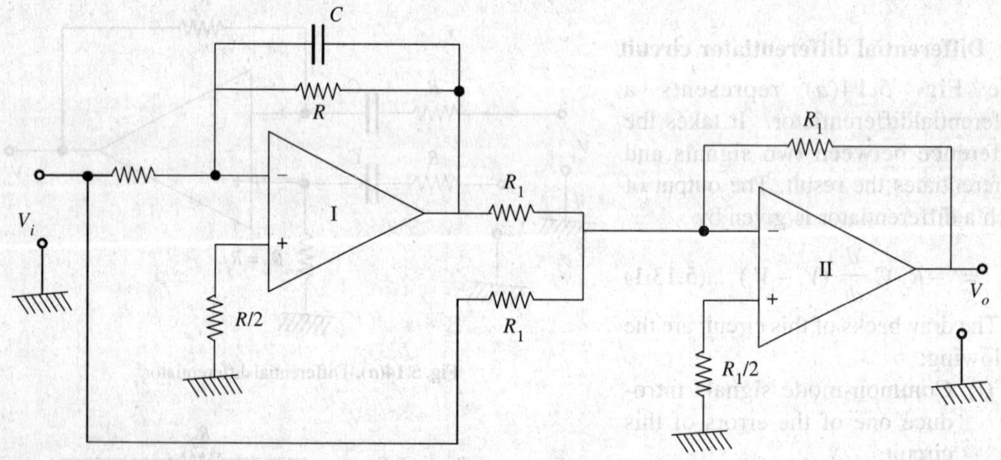

Fig. 5.14(*d*). Low noise differentiator circuit.

The derivative of the signal is derived from the signal and its integral. The output of this circuit is expressed as

$$V_o = -RC \frac{dV_i}{dt} \quad ...(5.13.4)$$

In this circuit, the amplifier noises are not multiplied by the differentiator gain. But the noise of the 1st operational amplifier is integrated, resulting in a noise that decreases with increasing gain. The noise of the integrator is then combined with noise which is much less than that of the conventional differentiator.

QUESTIONS

1. How do the outputs of op.amp. based integrations and differentiations differ from their mathematically derived counter parts?
2. What phase shift of input will be produced at the output of an op.amp. differentiator? At the output of an op.-amp. integrator?
3. What type of waveform is produced at the output of an integrator when a square wave input is applied?
4. Why are input off-set voltages a serious problem in the realization of op.-amp. integrations?
5. Explain the difference between the integrator and differentiator and give one application of each.
6. Draw the ckt diagram of double integrator ckt and explain the operation using mathematical relations.

6

ACTIVE FILTER CIRCUIT

6·1. Filters. 6·2. Advantages of Active Filters. 6·3. Applications of Active Filters. 6·4. Filter Classification. 6·5. Butter Worth, Chebyshev and Cauer Filters. 6·6. Low Pass Filter Butter-Worth. 6·7. Frequency Scaling. 6·8. Advantages of Higher Order Filters. 6·9. High Pass Filter (Butterworth) 6·10. Band Pass Filter (BPF). 6·11. Band Stop Filter. 6·12. Notch Filters. 6·13. All Pass Filter. 6·14. Characteristic Impedance of Active Filters.

6·1. FILTERS

It is a network which allows through it signals of certain frequencies but suppresses signals of other frequencies. Filters find wide range of applications in communication systems. An ideal filter allow undistorted transmission of signals and suppresses noise. But practical filters deviate from ideal filters. The extent of deviation from ideal behaviour depends upon the amount of reflection due to unequal terminal impedances and also due to losses in the networks. This indicates that an ideal filter is a pure reactive network. A classical method to filter synthesis is by means of inductances, capacitances, and resistances. Such filters are called passive filters because of those passive elements. But the inductor is the least ideal among the three elements mentioned above. Hence it is desirable to avoid it whenever possible. Moreover inductors can be large and physically awkward to use, especially at low frequencies. However, active filters meet this goal by using resistances, capacitance and amplifiers, but no inductances. The active element (operational amplifier) in active filter permits the simulation of an LCR filter with only capacitors and resistors.

6·2. ADVANTAGES OF ACTIVE FILTERS

The main advantages of active filters are their small size and weight for low frequency applications and their ruggedness. Advantages of active filters are given here below.

(1) Active filters provide excellent isolation because of its high input imepedances (ranging from few kilohms to serval thousand megaohms).

(2) Filter designs are possible in the vicinity of 1 MHz.

(3) The active filter permits the use of reasonably valued resistors and capacitors at low frequencies like 0.001 Hz. Hence frequencies as low as 0.001 Hz are possible with active filters.

(4) In low frequency low Q active filters, they (active filters) can have voltage gain as much as 40 dB.

(5) Q can be extended upto a few hundred in active filters.

(6) All types of filter responses are possible with active filters.

Active and passive filters are referred to as analog filters. This is because they operate directly on physical signals, which are by nature analog or continuous.

However they are not without some disadvantages. A drawback is the tolerance and drift of their physical components, which limit the degree of accuracy.

Drawback of active filters

(1) It requires extra power supply that can generate noise and can oscillate due to thermal drift and component aging.

(2) Active filters usually have single-ended inputs and outputs. They do not float with respect to supply or common as can a passive RLC network.

(3) The input and output voltages are limited to a few volts (± 10 volts generally). The output current of an operational amplifier is usually limited to a few milliamperes.

(4) High Q stable active filters need more expensive, usually large size capacitors and resistors (some times more number of operational amplifiers).

6·3. APPLICATIONS OF ACTIVE FILTERS

Active filters are most extensively employed in the field of communication and signal processing. But they are used in almost all sophisticated electronic systems. It is very difficult to give the names of all such systems. However, some of the applications of active filters are in: biomedical equipments, space satellite, radar, television, radio telephone etc. The operational amplifier μA 741 has satisfactory performance as an active component in active filter. But for higher speed of operation and higher unity gain-bandwidths operational amplifiers like LM 318 or ICL 8017 are preferred.

6·4. FILTER CLASSIFICATION

Filters are classified according to the function they perform. There are several types of filter network. They are (*i*) Active filter (*ii*) Passive (*iii*) Digital (*iv*) switched capacitor (*v*) Microwave (*vi*) Mechanical.

Each of the above six filter types has the following filter function.

(*i*) Low pass filter (*ii*) High pass (*iii*) Band pass (*iv*) Band rejection (or elimination)

(*v*) All pass filter.

(1) *Low pass filter*: This filter is characterized by a frequency f_c, called the cutoff frequency such that it transmits signals from a frequency $f = 0$ to a frequency $f = f_{CL}$. $(f_{CL} - 0)$ range of frequency is called the pass band as over this frequency range unattenuated transmission takes place. The frequency range over which transmission does not take place is called stop band. Fig. 6.1(*a*) shows the response curve of an ideal low pass filter. The response of a practical low pass filter is shown in the same figure in dotted lines. At f_c the gain falls to 0.707 of its maximum value.

(2) *High pass filter*: The frequency response curve of high pass filter is shown in the Fig. 5.1(*b*). The dotted curve represents the response curve of a practical filter whereas solid curve is for an ideal high pass filter. It has a stop band $0 < f < f_{CH}$ and a pass band $f > f_{CH}$. Here f_{CH} is the cut off frequency of the high pass filter at which the gain rises to 0.707 of its maximum value.

(3) *Band pass filter*: A band pass filter transmits all frequencies being in a certain range. Signal lying outside this range are attenuated. It has two cutoff frequencies f_L and f_H (as shown in Fig. 6.1(*c*). The solid curve depicts the frequency response of an ideal band pass filter but the dashed curve is for a practical one. It is basically the cascaded version of one low pass and one high pass filter. The cutoff frequency of low pass filter is f_L and that of high pass filter is f_H (*i.e.*, $f_H > f_L$).

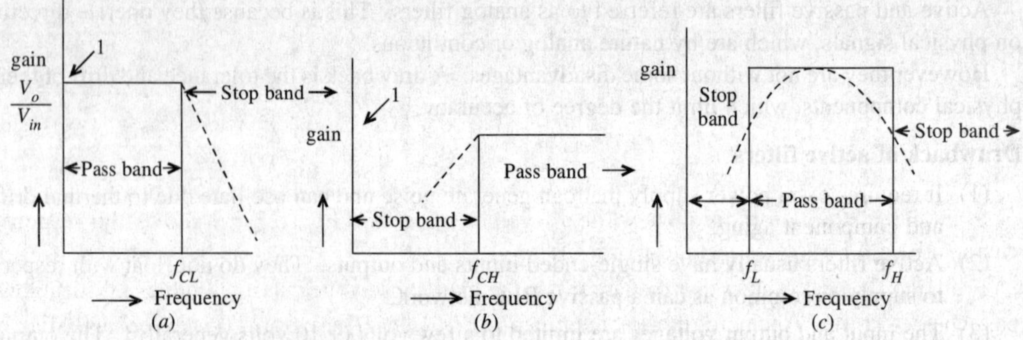

Fig. 6.1 (*a*), (*b*) and (*c*). Frequency response of active filters.

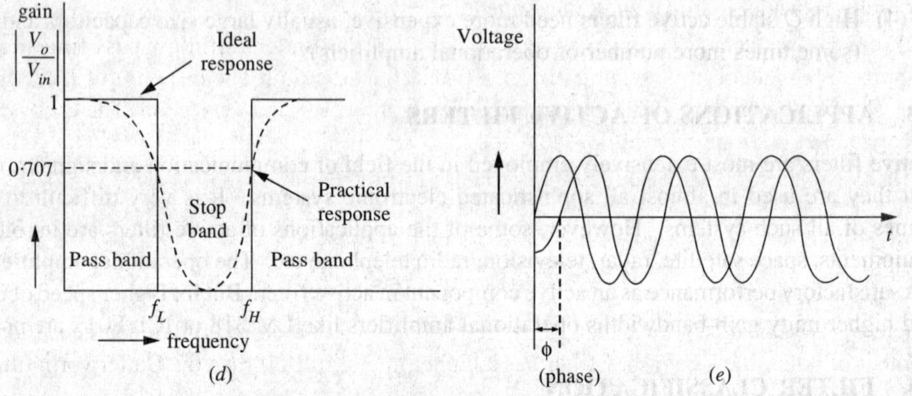

Fig. 6.1 (*d*) and (*e*). Frequency of active filters.

(4) *Band elimination filter*: A band elimination filter passes all frequencies lying outside a certain range. While signals lying inside that range are attenuated. The frequency response curve of a band elimination filter is shown in the Fig. 6.1(*d*). The solid curve is for an ideal band elimination filter, where as dashed curve is for a practical one. It has two cutoff frequencies (f_L and f_H as shown in the figure).
The band elimination filter is also the combination of two filters (one low pass and one high pass). The cutoff frequency of the high pass filter (f_H) should be greater than the cutoff frequency (f_L) of the low pass filter.

(5) *All pass filter:* This filter, is also called a delay filter, passes all frequencies equally well. The input and output voltages are equal in amplitude for all frequencies, but the phase shift between the two is a function of frequency. The frequency upto which the input and output remain equal is dependent on the operational amplifier unity gain bandwidth [Fig. 6.1(*e*)].

6·5. BUTTERWORTH, CHEBYSHEV AND CAUER FILTERS

Cauer, Butterworth and Chebyshev filters are some of the most commonly used practical filters that approximate the ideal response. Let us explain the function of those categories taking a typical case of low pass filter.

The voltage transfer function is in the form

$$T(s) = \frac{1}{P_n(s)} \qquad \text{...(6.5.1)}$$

where $P_n(s)$ is a polynomial in s having zeros in the left half of the s-plane. The polynomial P_n (s) is expressed in the form of Butterworth polynomial $B_n(S)$, so that

$$T(s) = \frac{H_o}{B_n(S)} \qquad \text{...(6.5.2)}$$

where $s = j\omega$ and $|B_n(j\omega)| = \sqrt{1 + \left(\frac{\omega}{\omega_c}\right)^{2n}}$

ω_c is called the cutoff frequency for all values of n. The Fig. 6.2 (a) shows the response characteristics of a low pass Butterworth filter.

From the figure it is clear that the larger is n the more closely the curve resembles the ideal low-pass characteristics. Again, for large n, the function $|T(j\omega)/H_o|$ near $\omega \cong 0$ is exceedingly flat, or maximally flat as is defined in the literature. Taking $\omega_C = 1$ rad/sec, the Butterworth polynomials for a few values of n are given in the Appendix.

From the frequency response curve it is clear that the Butterworth low pass filter's amplitude response is excellent in the vicinity of $\omega \cong 0$ and for $\omega >> \omega_c$. The responsc of Butterworth low pass filter in the vicinity of the cut off frequency is, however, not very good. The chebyshev filter, discussed below is superior in this respect.

The response of Chebyshev low pass filter is given by

$$\left|\frac{T(j\omega)}{H_o}\right| = \frac{1}{\sqrt{1+\varepsilon^2 C_n^2(\omega)}}$$

where ε is a constant $C_n(\omega)$ is the Chebyshev polynomial of the first kind of degree n. For an equal number of poles, the Chebyshev filter has a higher rate of roll-off than the Butterworth filter. A list of Chebyshev polynomials for $n = 0, 1, 2...6$ is given in appendix.

The Chebyshev filter is more often called an equiripple filter since it posses ripples in the passband which are equal in magnitude. The Chebyshev low pass filter response for different values of n but for constant value of ε is shown in the Fig. 6.2(b).

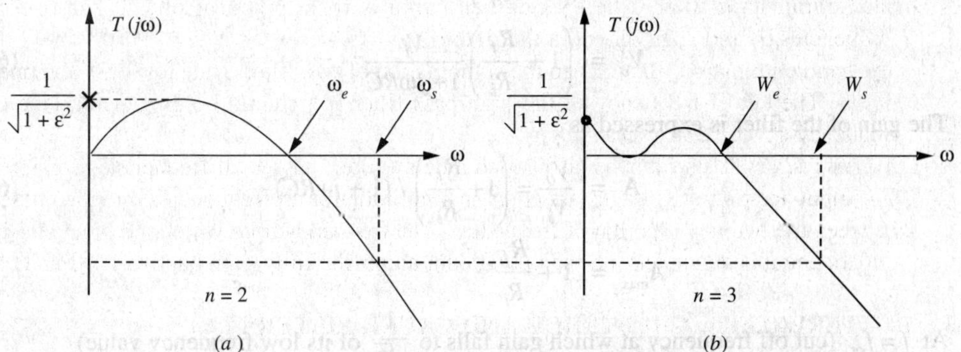

Fig. 6.2. Low pass filter response.

The key characteristic of the Butterworth filter is that it has a flat passband as well as stopband. For this reason, it is sometimes called a flat filter. The Chebyshev filter has a ripple passband and flat stopband, while the Cauer filter has a ripple passband and a ripple stopband. Among the three Cauer filter gives the best stopband response. However, because of their simplicity of design, Butterworth filters are most popularly used. Chebyshev polynomials and Butterworth *LP* filter transfer function for different values of n are given in *Appendix D.*

6·6. LOW PASS FILTER (BUTTERWORTH)

(*a*) **First order:** Butterworth 1st order low pass filter circuit and its frequency response are shown in the adjoining figure (Fig. 6.3). As *RC* network is connected at the noninverting terminal hence operational amplifier will not load it. The purpose of R_i and R_f are to control the gain to the desired level.

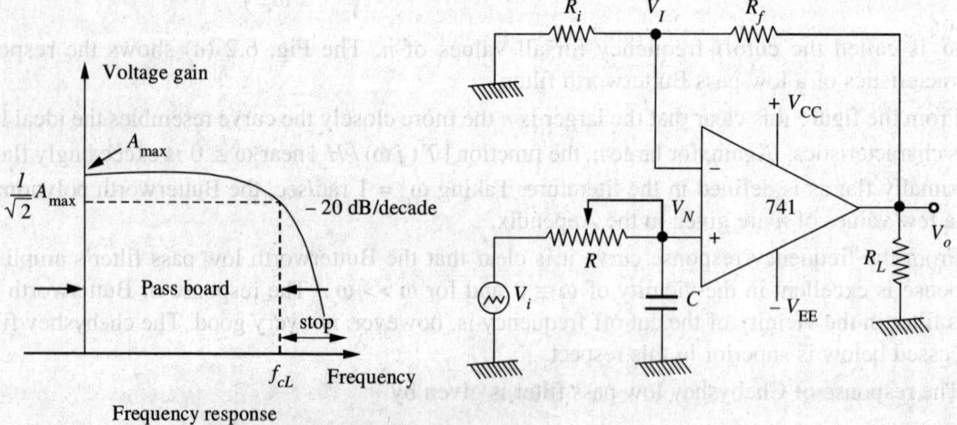

Fig. 6.3. Low pass filter circuit Frequency response.

The voltage at the non-inverting terminal is

$$V_N = \frac{-j/\omega c}{R - j/\omega c} V_i \quad ...(6.6.1)$$

$$= \frac{V_i}{1 + j\omega RC} \quad ...(6.6.2)$$

The output voltage $$V_o = \left(1 + \frac{R_f}{R_i}\right) V_N$$

$$\therefore \quad V_o = \left(1 + \frac{R_f}{R_i}\right) \frac{V_i}{1 + j\omega RC} \quad ...(6.6.3)$$

The gain of the filter is expressed as

$$A = \frac{V_o}{V_i} = \left(1 + \frac{R_f}{R_i}\right) / (1 + jwRC) \quad ...(6.6.4)$$

$$A_{max} = 1 + \frac{R_f}{R_i}$$

At $f = f_{CL}$ (cut off frequency at which gain falls to $\frac{1}{\sqrt{2}}$ of its low frequency value)

$$A = \frac{1}{\sqrt{2}} A_{max}$$

$$\therefore \quad \frac{1}{\sqrt{2}} A_{max} = \frac{A_{max}}{1 + j\omega_{CL} RC}$$

or, $$\sqrt{2} = \sqrt{1^2 + (\omega_{CL} RC)^2}$$

or, $$2 = 1 + (w_{CL} RC)^2$$

$$\text{or} \quad (\omega_{CL}RC)^2 = 1$$

$$\text{or} \quad \omega_{CL}RC = 1$$

$$\text{or} \quad \omega_{CL} = \frac{1}{RC}$$

$$\text{or} \quad 2\pi f_{CL} = \frac{1}{RC}$$

$$\text{or} \quad f_{CL} = \frac{1}{2\pi RC}$$

$$\text{or} \quad f_{CL} = \frac{1}{2\pi RC} \quad \text{...(6.6.5)}$$

$$\text{Hence} \quad |A| = \frac{A_{\max}}{\sqrt{1+(f/f_{CL})^2}} \quad \text{...(6.6.6)}$$

$$\delta = -\arctan(f/f_{CL}) \quad \text{...(6.6.7)}$$

If the frequency is made double or increased by 10 times the gain decreases by 6dB or 20 dB, respectively.

$$A = \frac{V_0}{V_i} = \frac{A_f}{1+\dfrac{jf}{f_{CL}}} \qquad \left[\because A_f = 1+\frac{R_f}{R}\right]$$

$$|A| = \frac{A_f}{\sqrt{1+\left(\dfrac{f}{f_{CL}}\right)^2}}, \quad 20\log_{10}|A| = 20\log_{10}A_f - 10\log_{10}\left(1+\left(\frac{f}{f_{CL}}\right)^2\right)$$

At $f = 10f_{eL}$, $\left(\dfrac{f}{f_{CL}}\right)^2 >> 1$. Hence $20\log_{10}|A| = 20\log_{10}A_f - 20$

$$20\log_{10}|A| - 20\log_{10}A_f = -20$$

So the slope of the curve is 20 *dB*/decade.

(*b*) Design parameters:

(1) Cutoff frequency f_{CL} (2) Capacitor, resistors (3) Maximum gain $A_{\max} = 1 + \dfrac{R_f}{R_i}$

Problem: $R_i = 10$ K, $R_f = 10$ K, $V_{CC}, -V_{EE} = \pm 15$ V
$R = 15{\cdot}9$ K, $C = 0{\cdot}01\ \mu$F $R_L = 10$ K

Calculate f_{CL}, $A_{\max}$ and δ at f_{CL}. Also draw the frequency response and calculate the drop of gain after f_{CL} per octave or decade.

2nd order low pass filter

An addition of a *RC* network converts the first order low pass filter to a 2nd order low pass filter as shown in Fig. 6.4. The response of 2nd order filter is more nears to the ideal frequency response. The fall of gain beyond the cut off frequency is –40 dB per decade *i.e.,* much sharper than that of 1st order which is –20 dB per decade.

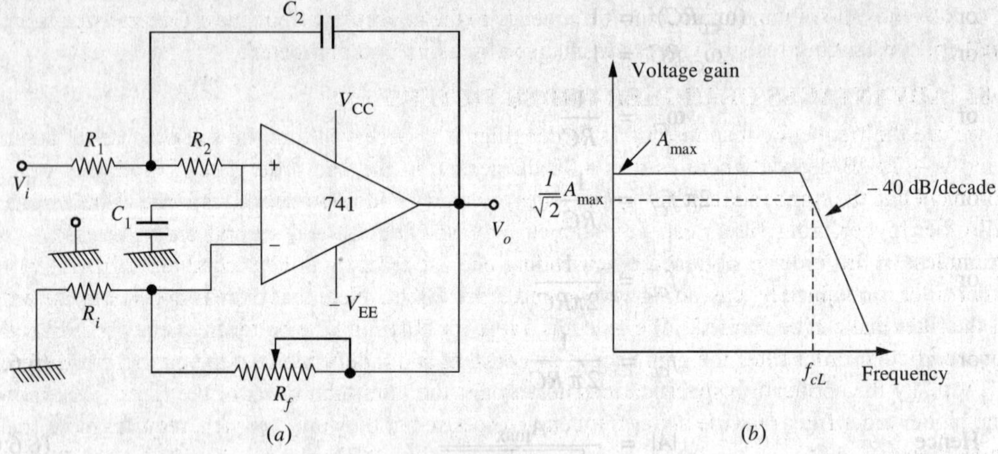

Fig. 6.4. 2nd order Butterworth low pass filter circuit (*a*) and its frequency response (*b*).

The cut off frequency $$f_{CL} = \frac{1}{2\pi\sqrt{R_1 R_2 C_1 C_2}} \quad ...(5.6.8)$$

Maximum gain $A_{max} = 1 + \frac{R_f}{R_i}$. It is called the pass gain of the filter.

The gain of the filter is

$$A = \frac{A_{max}}{\sqrt{1+(f/f_{CL})^2}}$$

f = frequency of the input signal. (Hz)

Design procedure: Several approaches are given in the literature for designing this circuit.

Steps for design

Step I: Select a value of cutoff frequency f_{CL}

Step II: Select the values of *C* which are available

$$[C_1 = C_2 = C]$$

Step III: Then determine the value of R ($R_1 = R_2 = R$) using the relation

$$R = \frac{1}{2\pi f_{CL} C}$$

Step IV: The pass band gain A_{max} is usually kept at 1·586.

So $$1{\cdot}586 = 1 + \frac{R_f}{R_i}$$

Hence $R_f = 0{\cdot}586\ R_i$. Then choose a value of R_i and calculate R_f.

Problem: Calculate the cutoff frequency and stop band roll off rate for the following parameter values with reference to the Fig. 6.4. $A_{max} = 1{\cdot}586$, $R_i = 27$ K.

$R_1 = R_2 = 33$ K, $C_1 = C_2 = 0{\cdot}0047$ µF. Supply voltage is ± 15 V (V_{CC} & $-V_{EE}$). Also draw the frequency response curve.

6·7. FREQUENCY SCALING

Once a filter has been designed it has a fixed cutoff frequency. But there may sometimes be a need to change its cutoff frequency. This procedure of converting an original cutoff frequency f_{CL} to a new cutoff frequency f_{CL} is called the frequency scaling. This scaling is done by multiplying either

C or *R* by the ratio of the original cutoff frequency to the new cutoff frequency. Generally capacitors are kept constant but resistor values are changed by using potentiometer.

6·8. ADVANTAGES OF HIGHER ORDER FILTERS

If we see the frequency response of 1st order filter it is observed that the roll-off rate in the stop band is – 20 dB/decade where as it is – 40 dB/decade in the 2nd order filter. From this we can comment that the stopband response approaches towards the ideal stopband response characteristics. All other higher order filters can be obtained by cascading 1st and second order filters. As for examples: (*i*) 3rd order is obtained by cascading one 1st order and one second order filter, (*ii*) 4th order filter is obtained by cascading two second order filters. Note that there is no limit to the order of the filter that can be formed. The gain has a role for obtaining the better frequency response and for a particular order filter the gain should be constant and independent of the cut off frequency.

Actually the application specifications determines the minimum order of the filter. It is known that higher order filter provide better frequency response but they are complex, requires more space and expensive.

6·9. HIGH PASS FILTER (BUTTERWORTH)

1st order filter

If we interchange the positions of the filtering resistor and capacitor we can get high pass filter. Fig. 6.5 shows a high-pass Butterworth filter.

$$V_N = \frac{V_i}{R+\dfrac{1}{j\omega c}}\,R = \frac{j\omega CR}{1+j\omega RC}\,V_i$$

$$V_o = \left(1+\frac{R_f}{R_i}\right)V_N = \left(1+\frac{R_f}{R_i}\right)\left(\frac{j\omega CR}{1+j\omega CR}\right)V_i$$

Fig. 6.5. Circuit (*a*) and frequency response.

Gain $$A = \frac{V_o}{V_i} = A_{\max}\left(\frac{j\omega CR}{1+j\omega CR}\right) = A_{\max}\left(\frac{1}{1-\dfrac{j}{\omega CR}}\right)$$

where, $$A_{\max} = \text{maximum gain} = \left(1+\frac{R_f}{R_i}\right)$$

Cutoff frequency is the frequency at which the gain is $\frac{1}{\sqrt{2}}$ times the maximum gain ($A_{\max}$).

$$\therefore \quad \frac{1}{\sqrt{2}} A_{max} = \left(\frac{A_{max}}{1 - j/2\pi f_{CH} 4CR} \right)$$

$$\therefore \quad f_{CH} = \frac{1}{2\pi CR}$$

Hence $$|A| = \frac{A_{max}}{\sqrt{1 + \left(\frac{f_{CH}}{f}\right)^2}} \quad \text{as,} \quad CR = \frac{1}{2\pi f_{CH}}$$

$$\delta = \text{arc tan} \left(\frac{f_{CH}}{f} \right).$$

The gain of the high-pass filter increases at a constant rate of 20 dB/decade with an increase of frequency starting from zero frequency. When frequency exceeds a certain limit the gain attains a constant value (A_{max}). At cutoff frequency (f_{CH}) the gain is $\frac{1}{\sqrt{2}}$ times A_{max}.

Problem: Design a High pass filter (1st order) to meet the following:

(*i*) f_{CH} = 1 KHz (*ii*) A_{max} = 2 (*iii*) rise rate is 20 dB/decade.

Problem: Calculate A_{max}, f_{CH}, and rate of increase of gain in the stopband in dB per decade and per octave with the following data:

$$R = 15{\cdot}9 \text{ K}\,\Omega, \quad C = 0{\cdot}01\ \mu\text{F}, \quad R_i = 10 \text{ K}\,\Omega, \quad R_f = 10 \text{ K}\Omega$$

$$R_L = 10 \text{ K}\,\Omega \text{ and supply voltages are} \pm 15 \text{ V}.$$

Second-order high-pass filter (Butterworth)

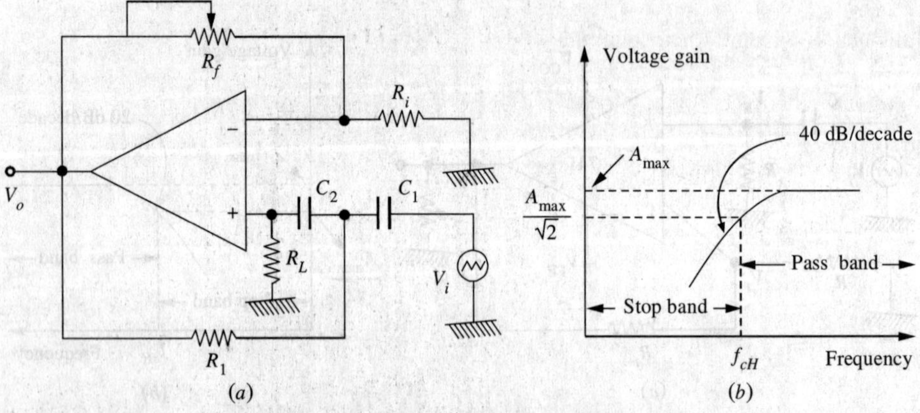

Fig. 6.6. Circuit and response of 2nd order high-pass filter.

Similar procedure of interchange of capacitors and resistors of 1st order LPF can be done to get the 2nd order High pass filter as shown in the adjoining figure.

The gain of the filters is expressed

as $$|A| = \left|\frac{V_o}{V_i}\right| = \frac{A_{max}}{\sqrt{1 + \left(\frac{f_{CH}}{f}\right)^4}}$$

where A_{max} = maximum gain in the passband.

f_{CH} = high pass filter cutoff frequency

f = Frequency of the input signal.

Problem: Calculate the following A_{max}, f_{CH}, δ of a 2nd order HPF using the following data and with reference to the Fig. 6.6.

R_i = 27 K, R_f = 15·8 K, $R_1 = R_2$ = 33 K, $C_1 = C_2$ = 0·0047 μF

R_L = 10 K and supply is ± 15 V.

6·10. BAND PASS FILTER (BPF)

As we have already mentioned that a band pass filter is a combination of one HPF and one LPF provided the cutoff frequency of the LPF is greater than that of HPF (*i.e.*, $f_{CL} > f_{CH}$). Fig. 6.7 depicts a bandpass filter which is a combination of LPF and HPF (as marked in the figure).

$$f_{CH} = \frac{1}{2\pi R_x C_x}, f_{CL} = \frac{1}{2\pi R_y C_y}, f_{CL} > f_{CH}$$

$f_{CL} - f_{CH}$ = Pass band (*PB*) and rest regions are stopband. Quality factor is given by

$$Q = \frac{f_o}{f_{CL} - f_{CH}}$$ where f_o is called the central frequency. f_o is normally the geometric mean of f_{CH} and f_{CL}.

So $f_o = \sqrt{f_{CL} f_{CH}}$.

Problem: Design BPF to meet the following

$$Q = 10,\ f_o = 1\text{KHz}$$

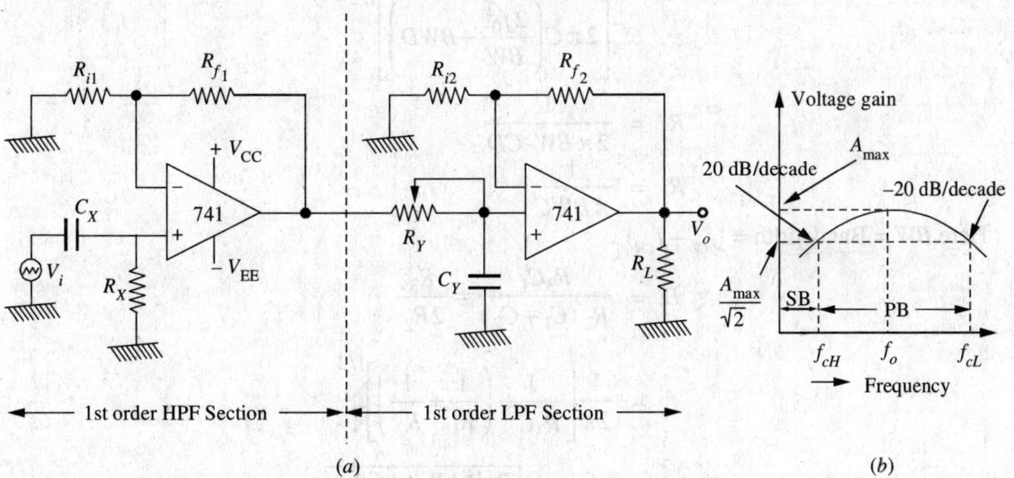

Fig. 6.7. Circuit (*a*) and frequency response (*b*) for BPF.

Problem: Calculate $Q, f_o, A_{max}, f_{CH}, f_{CL}$ from the following data with reference to the figure 6.7.

$C_x = 0\cdot05\,\mu F$ | $R_{i1} = R_{i2} = R_i = 10\,K$ | $R_x = R_y = 15\cdot9\,K$

$C_y = 0\cdot01\,\mu F$ | $R_{f1} = R_{f2} = R_f = 10\,K$ | Supply = ±15 V

Band Pass filter with single operational amplifier

There is no lack of BPF circuits in the literature. Now it is the task of the circuit designer to determine which of those numerous circuits will do the following:

(*i*) Allow a BPF to be designed in a shot span of time without going through many difficult equations.

(*ii*) Gives a filter with good feed back stability.

(*iii*) Need not require a large circuit.

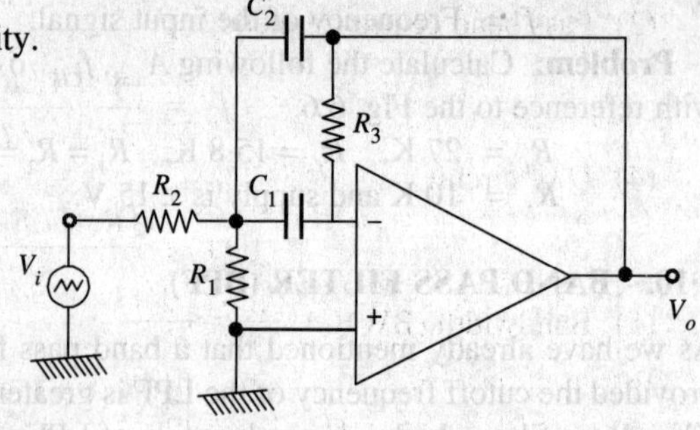

Fig. 6.8. Single operational amplifier BPF.

Here in this article we will give logically organized design information. It is very economic circuit because of the following:

(*a*) It uses only one operational amplifier.

(*b*) Central frequency to change the Q can be obtained with the adjustment of only one resistor (R_o).

(*c*) The circuit is more or less insensitive (with respect to Q and f_o) to the variation of component values provided Q is less than 10.

The operational amplifier is working in the inverting circuit with a transfer function or gain

$$A = \frac{V_o}{V_i} = \frac{-HS}{S^2 + As + B}$$

where $H = \dfrac{1}{R_2 C_2}$, $A = \dfrac{1/C_1 + 1/C_2}{R_3}$ and $B = \dfrac{1/R_1 + 1/R_2}{R_3 C_1 C_2}$

It is difficult to trim the capacitors, hence we asume $C_1 = C_2 = C$ where C is some practically available value.

Then
$$R_1 = \frac{1}{\left[2\pi C\left(\dfrac{2f_0^2}{BW} - BWD\right)\right]^{1/2}}$$

$$R_2 = \frac{1}{2\pi\, BW \cdot CD}$$

$$R_3 = \frac{1}{\pi\, BWC}$$

Here BW = Bandwidth = $(f_{CL} - f_{CH})$

$$D = \frac{R_3 C_1}{R_2 (C_1 + C_2)} = \frac{R_3}{2R_2}$$

$$f_o = \frac{1}{2\pi}\left[\frac{1}{R_3 C^2}\left(\frac{1}{R_1} + \frac{1}{R_2}\right)\right]^{1/2}$$

$$Q = \frac{f_o}{BW} = \sqrt{\frac{R_3 (1/R_1 + 1/R_2)}{2}}$$

where D is the voltage gain at central frequency ($= A_{max}$)

Design Equations

(1) Voltage gain of the circuit

$$A_v = \frac{V_o}{V_i} = \frac{-HS}{S^2 + As + B}$$

where $H = \dfrac{1}{R_2 C_2}$, $A = \dfrac{2}{R_3 C}$, $B = \dfrac{1/R_1 + 1/R_2}{R_3 C^2}$, $S = 2\pi fc$ where $C_1 = C_2 = C$

(2) Voltage gain at $f_o = D = R_3 / 2\,R_2$.

(3) Pass band centre frequency

$$f_o = \frac{1}{2\pi}\left(\frac{1/R_1 + 1/R_2}{R_3\,C^2}\right)^{1/2}$$

(4) Q of circuit

$$Q = \frac{[R_3\,(1/R_1 + 1/R_2)]^{1/2}}{\sqrt{2}}$$

(5) Bandwidth (BW) $= \dfrac{f_o}{Q} = \dfrac{1}{R_3 C}$

(6) $R_1 = \left[\dfrac{1}{2\pi C\left(\dfrac{2f_o^2}{BW} - BWD\right)}\right]^{1/2}$

(7) $R_2 = \dfrac{1}{2\pi\,BW \cdot CD}$

(8) $R_3 = \dfrac{1}{\pi\,BWC}$.

6·11. BAND STOP FILTER

It has other names like Notch filter, band elimination filter, parasitic suppressor, hum-reduction circuit, and band-rejection filter. It can also be designed using a low-pass filter and a high pass filter provided the cut off frequency of high pass filter should be higher than that of the low pass filter and the pass band gain will be the same for both of them. The circuit (*a*) and the frequency response (*b*) of the Band stop filter is shown in the Fig. 6.9.

Problem: Calculate the width of the stopband, f_{CL}, f_{CH}, A_{max} and central frequency (f_o) with reference to the Fig. 6.9. The circuit parameters are:

$$R_i = R_f = 10\text{ K},\quad C = 0{\cdot}05\ \mu\text{F},\quad C_1 = 0{\cdot}01\ \mu\text{F},\quad R = 15{\cdot}9\text{ K} = R_1\ R_x = 3{\cdot}3\text{ K}.$$

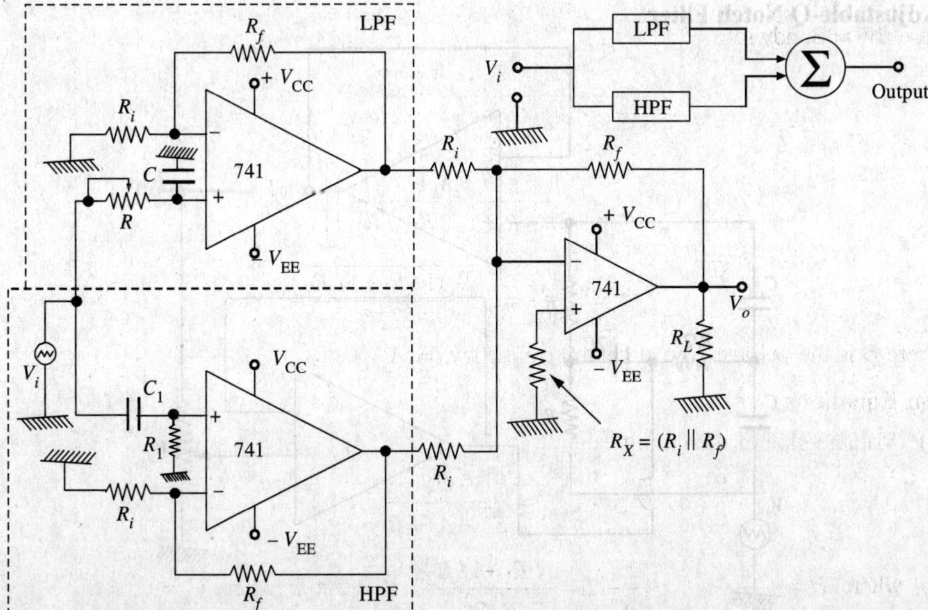

Fig. 6.9(*a*). Circuit and frequency response of band stop filter.

6·12. NOTCH FILTERS

Notch filter is a narrow bandstop filter which can passes all frequencies except those near its centre frequency these types of filters are used to reject undesirable signal frequency. It can be used to reject the supply frequency noise. There are different types of notch filters. They are explain below.

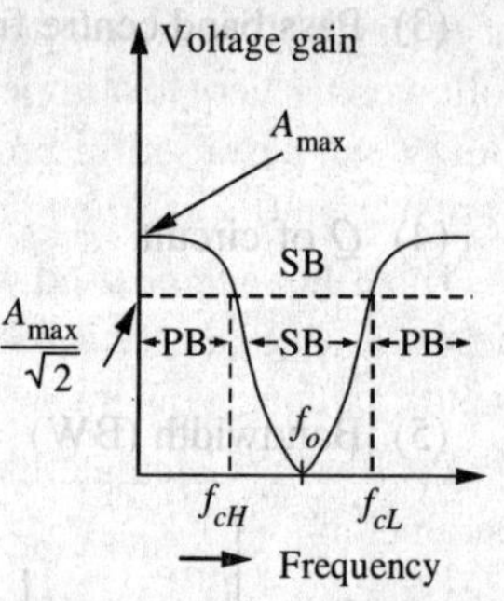

Fig. 6.9(*b*). Circuit and frequency response of band stop filter.

(*a*) Twin-T Notch Filter

The Fig. 6.10 shows a Twin-T-Notch filter. It has two *T* networks and hence so named.

The centre frequency

$$f_o = \frac{1}{2\pi RC}$$

Problem: Find out the value of the frequency the circuit will reject when the parameter values are

C = 0·027 μF, R = 100 K, R_1 = 3·3 M

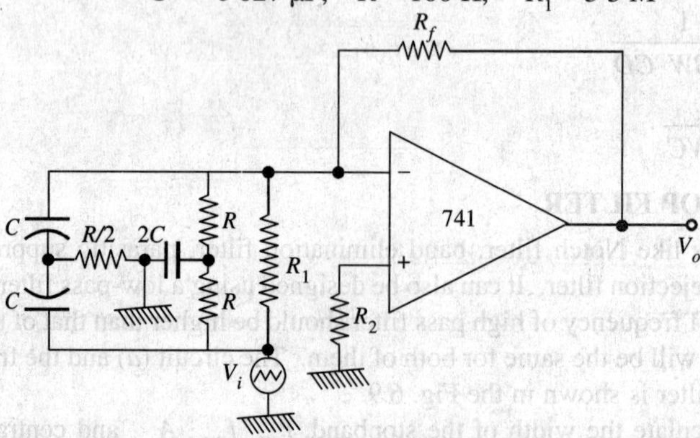

Fig. 6.10. Circuit for Twin-T Notch Filter.

R_f = 330 K, R_2 = 120 K.

(*b*) Adjustable-Q Notch Filter

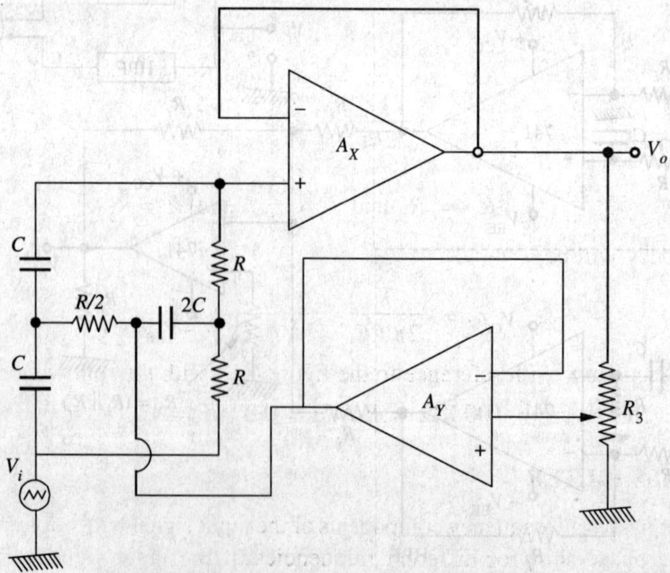

Fig. 6.11. Circuit for adjustable-*Q* Notch filter.

The Twin-T Notch Filter can be converted to a adjustable-Q notch filter by bootstrapping the junction of $R/2$ and $2C$ to the output of voltage followers A_x and A_y. It is known that the output of a voltage follower has very low impedance, hence neither the depth nor the frequency of the notch will change. But Q can be raised in proportion to the amount of the signal fed back to $R/2$ and $2C$. Q can be varied from 0·3 to 50 by adjusting R_3.

This filter can be used where the rejected signal might deviate slightly from the null of the notch network. In that case it is better to lower the Q of the network. Thus rejection over a wider angle of input frequencies is insured.

Problem: Calculate the centre frequency for the circuit of Fig. 6.11 with the following circuit parameters

$$R = 10\ \text{M}\Omega,\ C = 270\ \text{pF},\ R_3 = 50\ \text{K}\Omega\ \text{(potentiometer)}$$

Wien-Bridge Notch Filter

A wien-Bridge type Notch Filter is shown in the Fig. 6.12. The notch frequency is given by

$$f_o = \frac{1}{2\pi\sqrt{R R_1 C C_1}}$$

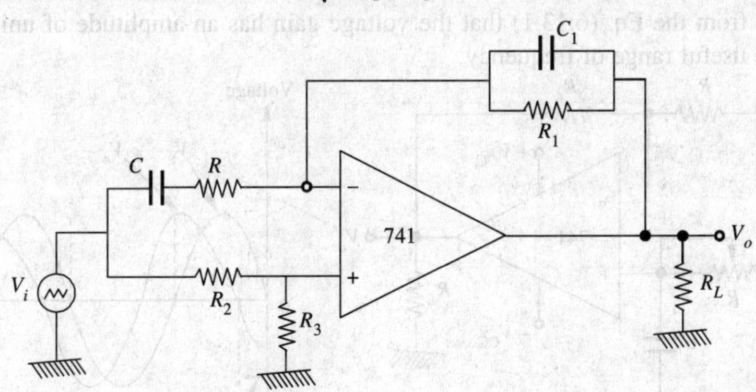

Fig. 6.12. Wien Bridge Notch filter circuit.

However, due to the balanced condition of the bridge $R = R_1$ and $C = C_1$ an effective notch occurs at the f_{01}, if $R_3 = \frac{R_2}{2}$,

$$f_o = \frac{1}{2\pi RC}$$

But if $R_1 = R_2$ and $C = \frac{C_1}{2}$, and $R_3 = R_2$

the notch frequency will be

$$f_o = \frac{1}{2\pi RC} = \frac{1}{2\pi R_1 C_1}$$

Problem: Calculate f_o with reference to the figure 6.12 with the following circuit parameters.

$$R = 100\ \text{K}\Omega = R_2,\ C_1 = 0{\cdot}27\ \mu\text{F} = C_2,\ R_2 = 300\ \text{K}\Omega,\ R_3 = 150\ \text{K}\Omega.$$

6·13. ALL PASS FILTER

The all pass filter passes all frequency components of the input signal with no attenuation but provides prognosticatable phase shift for different frequencies of the input signal. The most important applications of all pass filter are telephone wires. When signals are transmitted over telephone wires, they will get their phases changed.

In order to compensate such change of phase all pass filters are essential we have already mentioned in the beginning of the chapter that all pass filter are also called phase correctors or delay equalizers. Fig. 6.13 shows an all pass filter.

Where R_f is equal to R_i. By applying superposition theorem, the ouptut V_0 of the filter can be obtained as:

$$V_o = -V_i + \frac{\frac{-j}{\omega C}}{R - \frac{1}{\omega C}} V_i$$

$$= V_i \left(-1 + \frac{2}{j\omega RC + 1} \right) \quad \text{as } -i > \frac{1}{j}$$

$$= \left(\frac{1 - j\omega RC}{1 + j\omega RC} \right) V_i$$

It is evident from the Eq. (6.13.1) that the voltage gain has an amplitude of unity *i.e.*, $V_o = V_i$ through out the useful range of frequency.

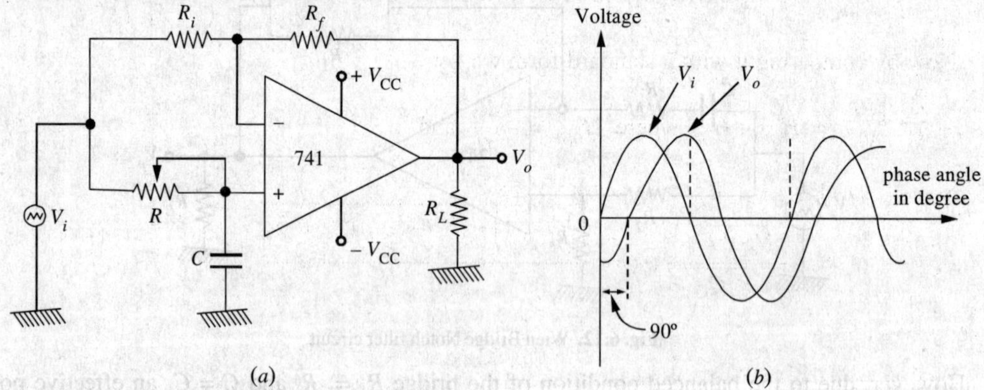

Fig. 6.13. (*a*) Circuit for all pass filter and (*b*) phase relation between input and output signal.

The phase angle is $\delta = -2 \text{ arc tan} \left(\frac{\omega RC}{1} \right)$.

State variable filters (SVFs): It is compound circuit consisting of two integrators and a summing amplifier to provide the second order low-pass, band pass, and high pass responses. It can realize a second-order differtial equation and hence it is so named. A state-variable filter is depicted in the Fig. 6.14.

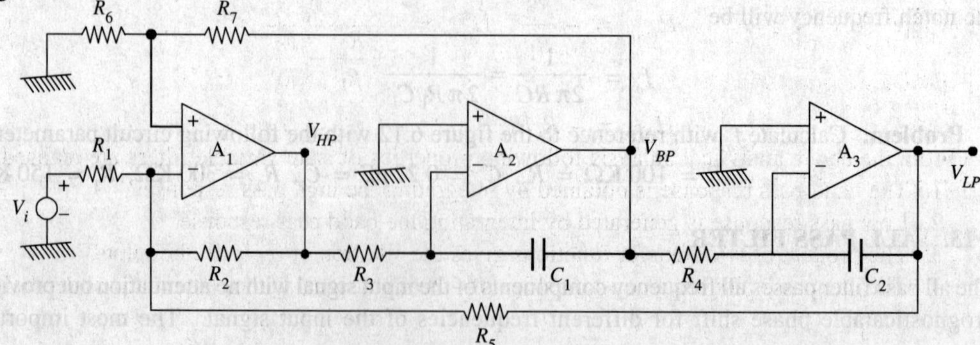

Fig. 6.14. State-variable filter.

Using superposition principle, we can write

$$V_{HP} = -\frac{R_2}{R_1}V_i - \frac{R_2}{R_5}V_{LP} + \left(1+\frac{R_2}{R_1 \| R_5}\right)\frac{R_6}{R_6+R_7}V_{BP}$$

$$= -\frac{R_2}{R_1}V_i - \frac{R_2}{R_5}V_{LP} + \frac{1+\frac{R_2}{R_1}+\frac{R_2}{R_5}}{1+R_7/R_6}V_{BP}.$$

As A_2 and A_3 form two integrator circuits, we have

$$V_{BP} = \frac{-1}{R_3 C_1 S}V_{HP} \text{ and } V_{LP} = \frac{-1}{R_4 C_2 S}V_{BP}$$

Hence $$V_{LP} = \left(\frac{1}{R_3 R_4 C_1 C_2 S^2}\right)V_{HP}.$$

Putting the values of V_{BP} and V_{LP} into Eq. (A) we get.

$$\frac{V_{HP}}{V_i} = -\frac{R_2}{R_1}\times\frac{R_5 R_3 R_4 C_1 C_2 S^2/R_2}{R_1 R_5 R_3 R_4 C_1 C_2 S^2/R_2 + R_5(1+R_2/R_1+R_2/R_5)S/\left(1+\frac{R_7}{R_6}\right)R_2+1}$$

Now by comparing it with a standard form we get

$$\frac{V_{HP}}{V_i} = H_{OHP}\,.\,H_{HP} \text{ where } H_{OHP} = -\frac{R_2}{R_1} \text{ and}$$

$$\omega_o = \frac{\sqrt{R_2/R_5}}{\sqrt{R_3 R_4 C_1 C_2}},\; Q = \frac{\left(1+\frac{R_7}{R_6}\right)\sqrt{R_2 R_3 C_1/R_5 R_4 C_2}}{1+\frac{R_2}{R_1}+\frac{R_2}{R_5}}$$

Utilizing $$\frac{V_{BP}}{V_i} = \left(-\frac{1}{R_3 C_1 S}\right)V_{HP}/V_i \text{ indicates that}$$

$$V_{BP}/V_i = H_{OBP}\,.\,H_{BP}, \text{ we can similarly get}$$

$$\frac{V_{LP}}{V_i} = \left(-\frac{1}{R_4 C_2 S}\right)V_{BP}/V_i = H_{OLP}\,.\,H_{LP}$$

where $$H_{OHP} = -\frac{R_2}{R_1},\; H_{OBP} = \frac{1+\frac{R_7}{R_6}}{1+\frac{R_2}{R_1}+\frac{R_2}{R_5}}$$

$$H_{OLP} = -R_5/R_1$$

From the above analytical anlaysis following properties of state variable filters are realised.

1. The band pass response is obtained by integrating the high pass response.
2. Low pass response is generated by integrating the band pass response.
3. The product of two transfer functions gives the addition of their decibel plots.
4. The integrator plot has a constant slope of – 20-dB/decade. Hence the bandpass decibel plot

is got by rotating the high pass decibel plot clockwise by 20dB/decade. The low pass plot is obtained by similar rotation of the band pass plot.

In SV filters, normally we choose, $R_2 = R_5 = R_1$,
$R_3 = R_4 = R$ and $C_1 = C_2 = C$.

Then $\omega_o = \dfrac{1}{RC}$, $Q = \dfrac{1}{3}\left(1 + \dfrac{R_7}{R_6}\right)$, $H_{OHP} = -1$,

$H_{OBP} = Q$, and $H_{OLP} = -1$.

This filter is also called KHN filter after the names of the inventors (W.J. kerwin, L.P. Huelsman, and R.W. Newcomb). Whatever analysis is give above is for investing SV filter. The circuit of noninverting SV filter is shown in the Fig. 6.15 operation can be explained in a similar manner.

Now $\omega_o = \dfrac{1}{R_4 C}$ $\quad Q = 1 + \dfrac{R_2}{2R_1}$, $\quad H_{OHP} = \dfrac{1}{Q}$,

$H_{OBP} = -1$, $\quad H_{OLP} = \dfrac{1}{Q}$.

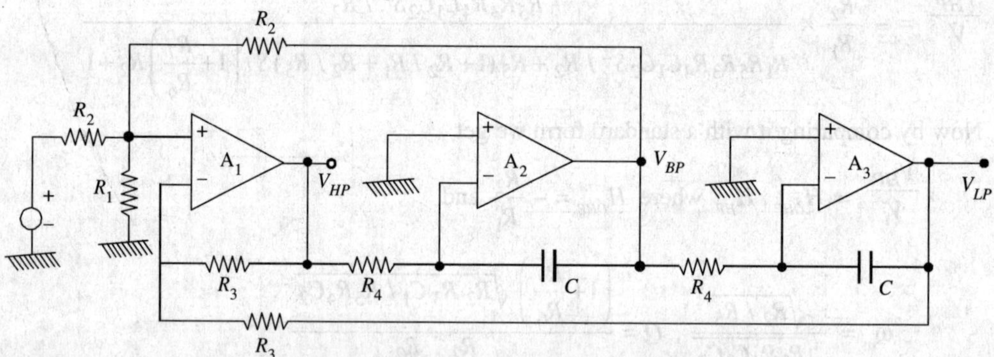

Fig. 6.15. Noninverting state variable filter circuit.

6·14 CHARACTERISTIC IMPEDANCE OF ACTIVE FILTERS

If a symmetrical network is terminated by a suitable impedance such that the impedance measured at the input is equal to the terminating impedance, such an impedance is called the characteristic impedance of the network. So the characteristic impedance of a symmetrical network is equal to its input as well as output impedance.

$$Z_{in} = Z_{out} = Z_o$$

In case of active filters which incredibly contain operational amplifiers, the term characteristic impedance has absolutely no meaning. Consider an operational amplifier with feedback and without feedback.

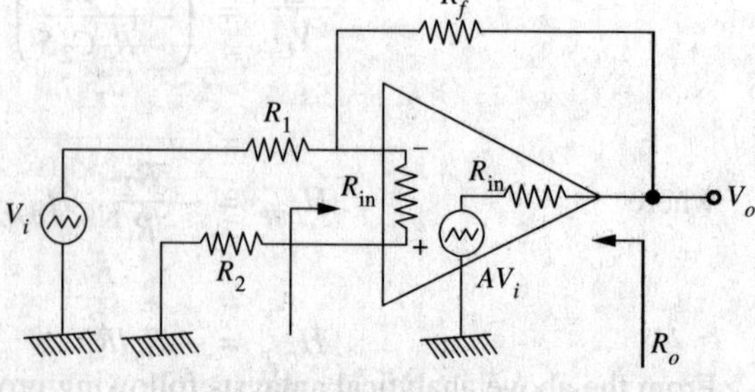

Fig. 6.16.

In this case with feedback $R_{if} = R_i(1 + AB)$

$$R_{of} = \frac{R_o}{1 + AB}$$

Without feedback they become

R_{in} and R_o

In case of an operational amplifier R_{in} is very large, as the input stage is basically a dual input balanced output differential amplifier, and the output impedance R_o is very low.

Hence under no circumstances we can have $R_o = R_{in}$ = characteristic impedance.

Due to the above reason the term characteristic impedance has no meaning in connection with active filters.

SOLVED PROBLEMS

1. *Design a 1st-order low-pass filter so that it has a cutoff frequency of 2 KHz and pass-band gain is 1.*

Solution. For this ckt we have, cut off frequency,

$$f_c = \frac{1}{2\pi RC}$$

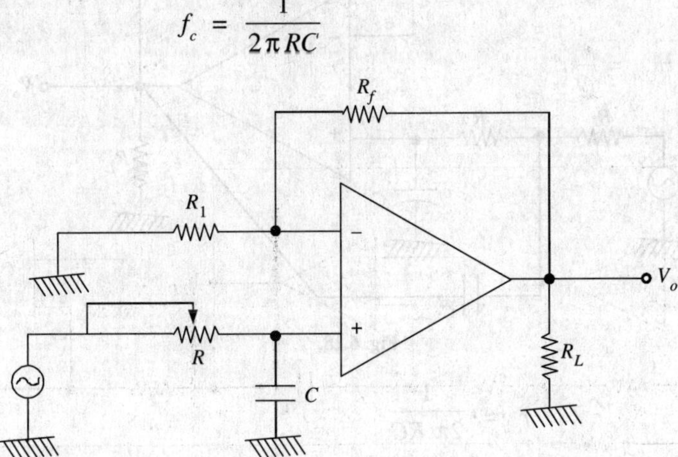

Fig. 6.17.

Pass band gain $\qquad A_F = 1 + \frac{R_F}{R_1}$

Now, given $\qquad f_c = 2$ KHz, $A_F = 1$.

Let $\qquad C = 0.01\ \mu$F, $\quad \therefore \quad f_c = \frac{1}{2\pi RC}$

$$\Rightarrow \qquad R - \frac{1}{2\pi f_c C}$$

$$= \frac{1}{2\pi\times2\times10^3\times0.01\times10^{-6}} \text{ Hz}$$

$$\Rightarrow \qquad R = 7.96\ \text{K}\Omega\ (8.2\ \text{K}\Omega)$$

Also, $\qquad A_F = 1 + \frac{R_F}{R_1} = 1$

$\Rightarrow \qquad R_1 >> R_F$

Let, $\qquad R_1 = 10$ K

$R_F = 150\ \Omega$

$\therefore \qquad R_1 = 10\ \text{K}\Omega$

$C = 0.01\ \mu$F

$R_F = 150\ \Omega$ $R = 7.96\ \text{K}\Omega$ (10 K pot)

2. *Design a second order low pass filter at cutoff frequency of 1.2 KHz.*

Solution. For this ckt

$$f_c = \frac{1}{2\pi \sqrt{R_1 C_1 R_2 C_3}}$$

We assume,

$$R_1 = R_2 = R$$
$$C_1 = C_2 = C$$

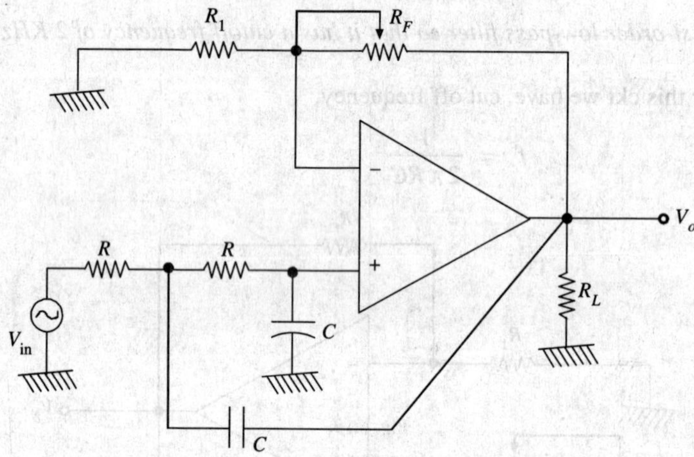

Fig. 6.18.

$$\therefore \quad f_c = \frac{1}{2\pi RC}$$

$$A_F = 1.586.$$

Given $\quad f_c = 1.2$ KHz

Let, $\quad C = 0.1\ \mu F$

$$\Rightarrow \quad R = \frac{1}{2\pi f_c C}$$

$$= \frac{1}{2\pi \times 1.2 \times 10^3 \times 0.1 \times 10^{-6}}\ \Omega$$

$$= 1.32\ K\Omega\ (1.2\ K\Omega)$$

Also, $\quad A_F = 1 + \dfrac{R_F}{R_1} = 1.586$

$\Rightarrow \quad R_F = 0.586\ R_1$

Let, $\quad R_1 = 10\ K\Omega$

$\therefore \quad R_F = 5.86\ K\Omega$ (10 K pot)

$\therefore \quad R = 1.2\ K\Omega, \quad C = 0.1\ \mu F$

$R_1 = 10\ K\Omega, \quad R_F = 5.86\ K\Omega$ (10 K pot).

3. *Design a 1st order highpass filter at a cut-off frequency of 1 KHz.*

Solution. We use a voltage follower ckt as the pass band gain is given to be 1. $[R_1 = R_F]$

We have, $\quad f_c = \dfrac{1}{2\pi RC}$

We assume, $\quad C = 0.01\ \mu F$

given, $f_c = 1\,\text{KHz}$

$$\therefore \quad R = \frac{1}{2\pi f_c C}$$

$$= \frac{1}{2\pi \times 10^3 \times 0.01 \times 10^{-6}}\ \Omega$$

$$= 10.9\ \text{K}\Omega\ (20\ \text{K pot})$$

$$\therefore \quad R = 15.9\ \text{K}\Omega \text{ set at } 20\ \text{K pot}$$

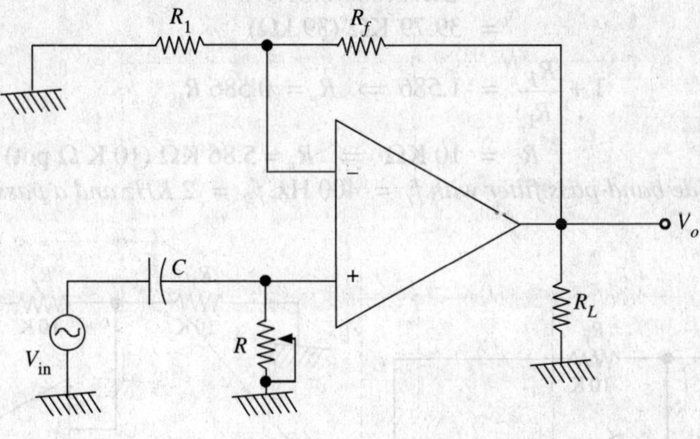

Fig. 6.19

$$C = 0.01\ \mu\text{F}.$$

4. *Design a second-order high-pass filter at a cut-off frequency of 400 KHz.*

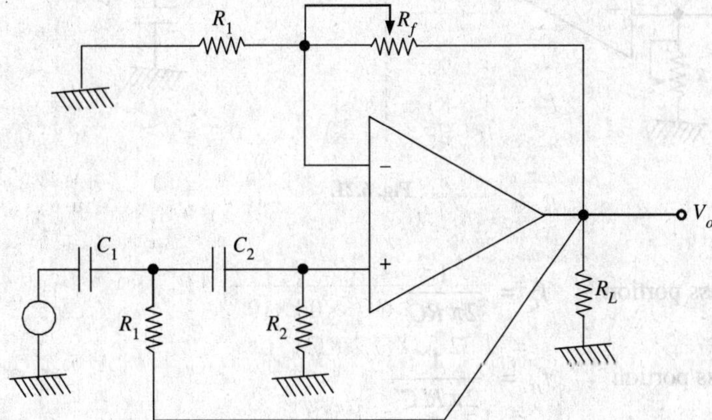

Fig. 6.20.

Solution. For this ckt,

$$f_c = \frac{1}{2\pi\sqrt{R_1 C_1 R_2 C_2}}$$

$$= \frac{1}{2\pi RC}$$

if we assume, $\begin{cases} R_1 = R_2 = R \\ C_1 = C_2 = C \end{cases}$

Also, we have the passband gain

$$A_F = 1 + \frac{R_F}{R_1} = 1.586$$

We assume, $C = 0.01\ \mu F$

$$\therefore \quad R = \frac{1}{2\pi R_c C}$$

$$= \frac{1}{2\pi \times 400 \times 0.01 \times 10^{-6}}\ \Omega$$

$$= 39.79\ K\Omega\ (39\ k\Omega)$$

Also, $1 + \frac{R_F}{R_1} = 1.586 \Rightarrow R_F = 0.586\,R_1$

Let, $R_1 = 10\ K\Omega \Rightarrow R_F = 5.86\ K\Omega$ (10 K Ω pot)

5. *Design a wide band-pass filter with f_L = 400 Hz, f_H = 2 KHz and a pass band gain = 4.*

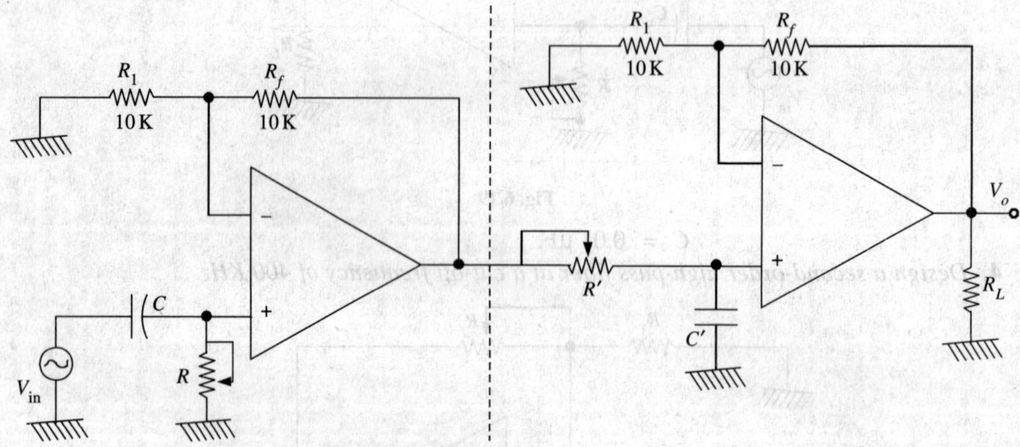

Fig. 6.21.

Solution.

For the highpass portion $f_L = \frac{1}{2\pi RC}$

For the lowpass portion $f_H = \frac{1}{2\pi R'C'}$

Also, total voltage gain

$$A_{FT} = 1 + \frac{R_F}{R_1} \quad [\because \text{ second part has a voltage follower, } \therefore A_{F2} = 1]$$

Let, $C = 0.1\ \mu F \quad f_L = 400$ Hz

$$\therefore \quad R = \frac{1}{2\pi \times 400 \times 0.1 \times 10^{-6}}\ \Omega$$

$$= 3.98\ K\Omega\ (5\ K\ \text{pot})$$

Let, $C' = 0.01\ \mu F \therefore$

$$R' = \frac{1}{2\pi \times 2 \times 10^{3} \times 0.01 \times 10^{-6}}\ \Omega$$

$$= 7.96\ \text{K}\Omega\ (10\ \text{K pot})$$

Also, $1 + \dfrac{R_F}{R_1} = 4 \Rightarrow R_F = 3R_1$

Let, $R_1 = 1.5\ \text{K}\Omega$

$\therefore$ $R_F = 4.5\ \text{K}\Omega (4.7\ \text{K}\Omega)$

$\therefore$ $R = 3.988\ \text{K}\Omega\ (5\ \text{k pot})$

$R' = 7.96\ \text{K}\Omega\ (10\ \text{K pot})$ $R_1 = 1.5\ \text{K}\Omega$

$C = 0.1\ \mu\text{F}$ $R_F = 4.5\ \text{K}\Omega$

$C' = 0.01\ \mu\text{F}.$

6. *Design a narrow bandpass filter so that, $f_c = 2$ KHz, $Q = 20$, $A_F = 10$.*

Solution. We assume

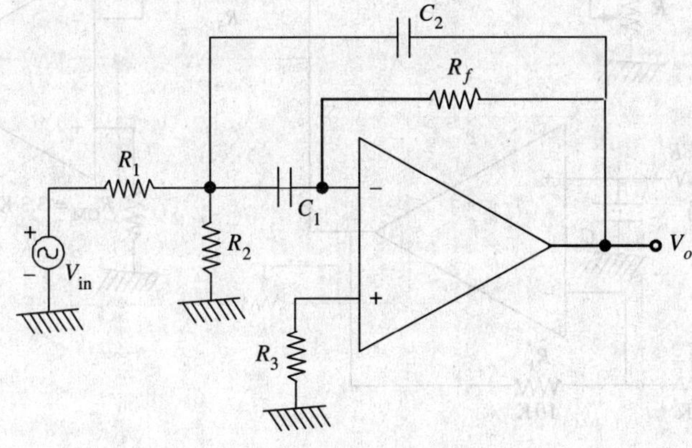

Fig. 6.22.

$$C_1 = C_2 = C$$

$\therefore$ $R_1 = \dfrac{Q}{2\pi f_c C A_F}$

$$R_f = \frac{Q}{\pi f_c C}$$

and, $A_F = \dfrac{R_3}{2R_1}$

We assume, $C_1 = C_2 = C = 0.1\ \mu\text{F}$

$$Q = 20,$$

$$f_c = 2\ \text{KHz},\quad A_F = 10$$

$\therefore$ $R_1 = \dfrac{Q}{2\pi f_c C A_F} = \dfrac{20}{2\pi \times 2\times 10^3 \times 0.1\times 10^{-6} \times 10}\ \Omega = 1.59\ \text{K}\Omega\ (1.5\text{K})$

$$R_2 = \frac{Q}{2\pi f_c (2Q^2 - A_F)}$$

$$= \frac{20}{2\pi \times 2\times 10^3 (800-10) \times 0.1\times 10^{-6}}\ \Omega = 20\ \Omega = (22\ \Omega)$$

$$R_f = \frac{Q}{\pi f_c C} = \frac{20}{\pi \times 2 \times 10^3 \times 0.1 \times 10^{-6}} \Omega = 31.8 \text{ K}\Omega \text{ (33 K}\Omega)$$

$$\therefore \quad R_1 = 1.5 \text{ K}\Omega,\ R_2 = 22\Omega,\ R_f = 33 \text{ K}\Omega,\ C_1 = C_2 = 0.1\ \mu\text{F}.$$

7. *Design a wide band reject filter using 1st order high-pass & low-pass filters having $f_L = 2$ KHz, $f_H = 400$ Hz.*

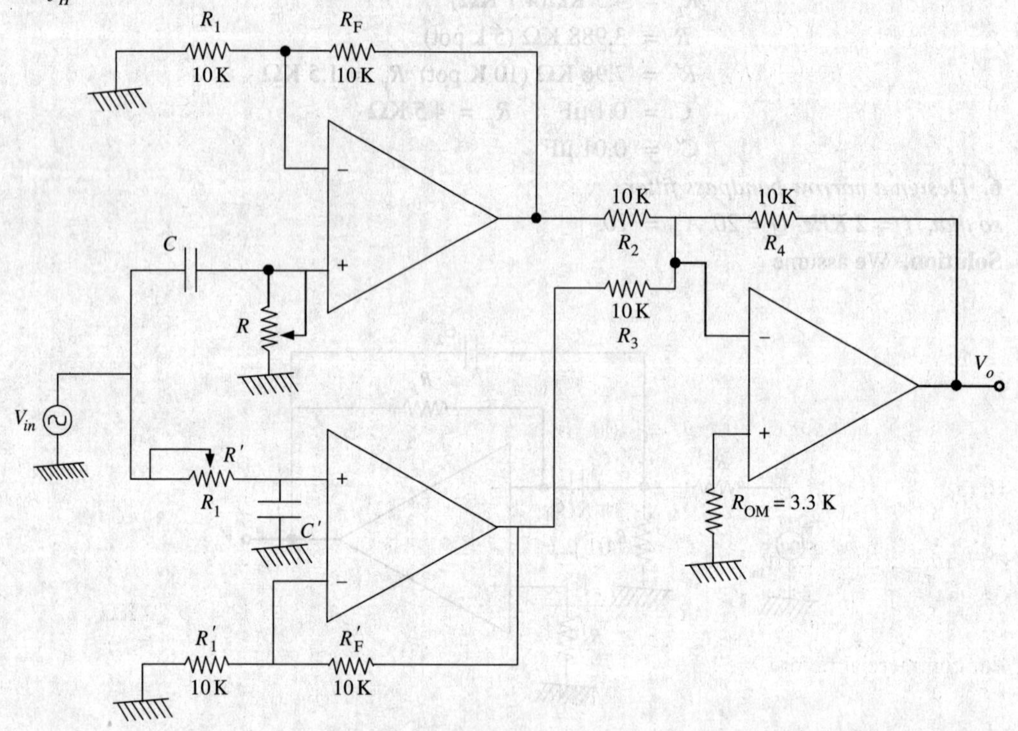

Fig. 6.23.

Solution. We have,

$$f_L = \frac{1}{2\pi RC}$$

$$f_H = \frac{1}{2\pi R'C'}$$

$$R_4 = R_2 = R_3,$$

$$R_{OM} = R_4 \parallel R_2 \parallel R_3$$

$$\text{Gain of each section} = 1 + \frac{R_F}{R_1} \ \&\ 1 + \frac{R'_F}{R'_1}$$

Let $\quad C = 0.01\ \mu\text{F},\ R = \dfrac{1}{2\pi f_L C} = \dfrac{1}{2\pi \times 2 \times 10^3 \times 0.01 \times 10^{-6}}\ \Omega$

$\Rightarrow \quad R = 7.96\ \text{K}\Omega$

Let, $\quad C¢ = 0.1\ \mu\text{F},\ R' = \dfrac{1}{2\pi f_H C} = \dfrac{1}{2\pi \times 2 \times 10^3 \times 0.01 \times 10^{-6}}\ \Omega$

$\Rightarrow \quad R' = 3.98\ \text{K}\Omega$

Let, $\quad R_4 = R_2 = R_3 = 10\ \text{K}\Omega$

$$R_{OM} = R_4 \parallel R_2 \parallel R_3 = 3.3\ \text{K}\,\Omega$$

There is no restriction for gain; we take it 2 for each section.

$$\therefore \quad R_1 = R_F = R'_1 = R'_F = 10\text{ K}.$$

8. *Design a narrow band reject notch filter for the frequency 400 Hz.*

Solution.

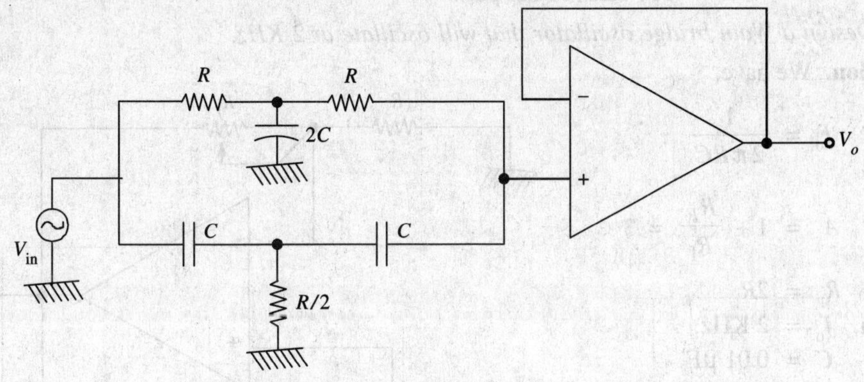

Fig. 6.24.

$$f_L = 400\text{ Hz}$$

Here, $$f_C = \frac{1}{2\pi RC}$$

Let, $$C = 0.01\,\mu\text{F};\; f_C = 400\text{ Hz}$$

$$\therefore \quad R = \frac{1}{2\pi f_C C} = \frac{1}{2\pi\times 400\times 0.01\times 10^{-6}}\,\Omega = 39.79\text{ K}\Omega$$

For commercial before, we take

$$R = 39\text{ K}\Omega$$

$$\therefore \quad \begin{cases} R = 39\,K\Omega \\ C = 0.01\mu F \end{cases}$$

9. *Design a phase-shift oscillation*

$$f_0 = 1\text{ KHz}.$$

Solution. Here, we have

$$f_0 = \frac{1}{2\pi\sqrt{6}\,RC}$$

$$\& \quad \left|\frac{R_F}{R_1}\right| = 29$$

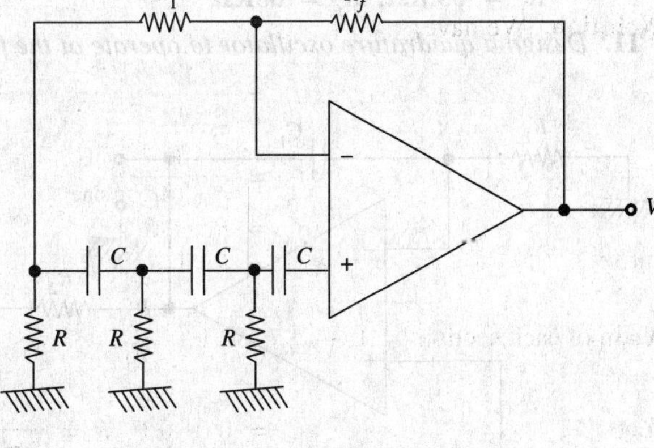

Fig. 6.25.

We have, $f_0 = 1$ KHz

Let, $C = 0.1\,\mu$F

$$\therefore \quad R = \frac{1}{2\pi f_0\sqrt{6}\,C}$$

$$= \frac{1}{2\pi\times 10^3\sqrt{6}\times 10^{-7}}\,\Omega$$

$$= 649.7\Omega$$

$$\therefore \quad R = 680\,\Omega$$

Also, $R_F = 29\ R_1$

Let, $R_1 = 33\ \text{K}\ \Omega$

$\therefore$ $R_F = 33 \times 29\ \text{K}\ \Omega$

$= 957\ \text{K}\Omega\ (1\ \text{M}\ \Omega\ \text{pot}).$

10. *Design a Wain bridge oscillator that will oscillate at 2 KHz.*

Solution. We have,

$$f_0 = \frac{1}{2\pi RC}$$

$$A_v = 1 + \frac{R_F}{R_1} = 3$$

$\Rightarrow$ $R_F = 2R_1$

Given, $f_0 = 2\ \text{KHz},$

Let, $C = 0.01\ \mu\text{F}$

$$\therefore \quad R = \frac{1}{2\pi f_0 C}$$

$$= \frac{1}{2\pi \times 2 \times 10^3 \times 10^{-8}}\ \Omega$$

$$= 7.96\ \text{K}\Omega$$

$\therefore$ $R = 82\ \text{K}\Omega$

Also, $R_F = 2R_1$ Let $R_1 = 33\ \text{K}\Omega$

$\therefore$ $R_F = 68\ \text{K}\Omega$

$\therefore$ $R = 8.2\ \text{K}\Omega,\ C = 0.01\ \mu\text{F}$

$R_1 = 33\ \text{K}\Omega,\ R_F = 68\text{K}\Omega$

Fig. 6.26.

11. *Design a quadrature oscillator to operate at the frequency of 1.5 KHz.*

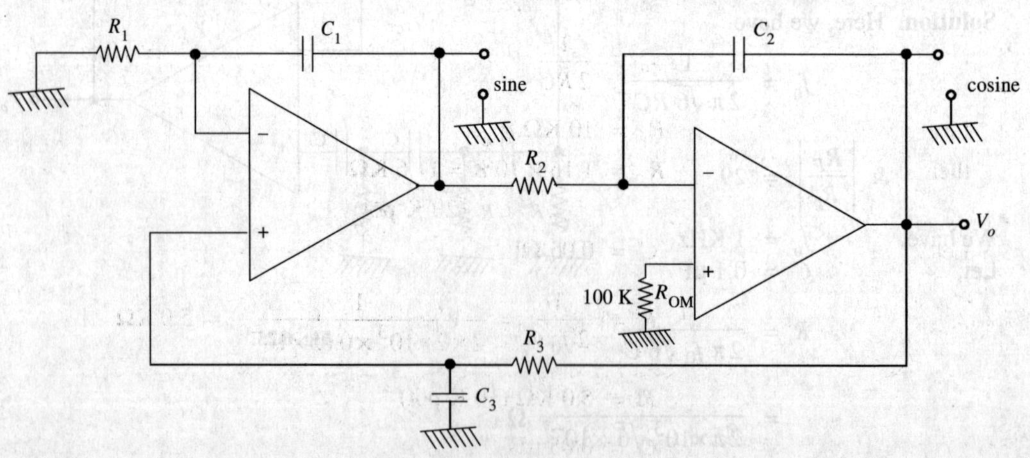

Fig. 6.27.

Solution. Here, we have, $R_1 = R_2 = R_3 = R$ (say)

$C_1 = C_2 = C_3 = C$ (say)

$$\therefore \quad f_0 = \frac{1}{2\pi RC}$$

Let, $C = 0.1\ \mu\text{F},\ f_0 = 1.5$ KHz

$$\therefore \quad R = \frac{1}{2\pi f_0 C} = \frac{1}{2\pi \times 1.5 \times 10^3 \times 10^{-7}}\ \Omega = 1.06\ \text{K}\Omega$$

$$\therefore \quad R = 1\ \text{K}\Omega$$

12. *Design a square wave generator to operate at the frequency of 2 KHz.*

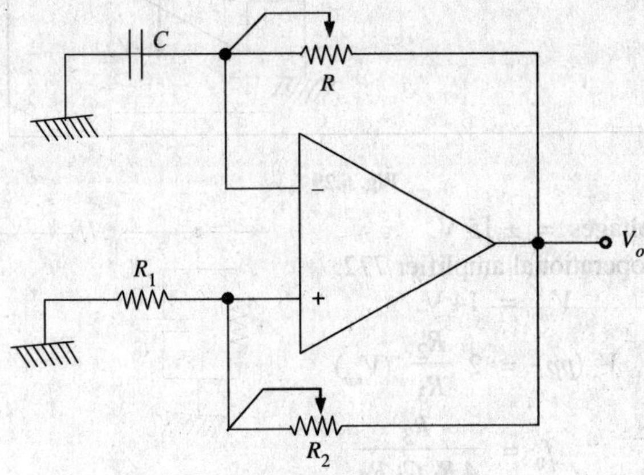

Fig. 6.28.

Solution. The operating frequency is given by

$$f_0 = \frac{1}{2RC \ln (2R_1 + R_2)/R_2]}$$

when, $R_2 = 1.16\ R_1$ we get

$$f_0 = \frac{1}{2RC}$$

Lct, $R_1 = 10\ \text{K}\Omega$,

then $R_2 = 1.16 \times 10\ \text{K} = 11.6\ \text{K}\Omega$

(20 K pot)

Let $C = 0.05\ \Omega\text{F}$

$$\therefore \quad R = \frac{1}{2 f_0 C} = \frac{1}{2 \times 2 \times 10^3 \times 0.05 \times 10^{-6}} = 5.0\ \text{K}\Omega$$

$\therefore \quad R = 5.0\ \text{K}\Omega$ (10 K pot)

$C = 0.05\ \mu\text{F}$

$R_1 = 10\ \text{K}\Omega,\ R_2 = 11.6\ \text{K}\Omega$ (20 K pot).

13. *Design a triangular wave generator with f_0 = 1.5 KHz and V_0 (p – p) = 5V.*
Solution.

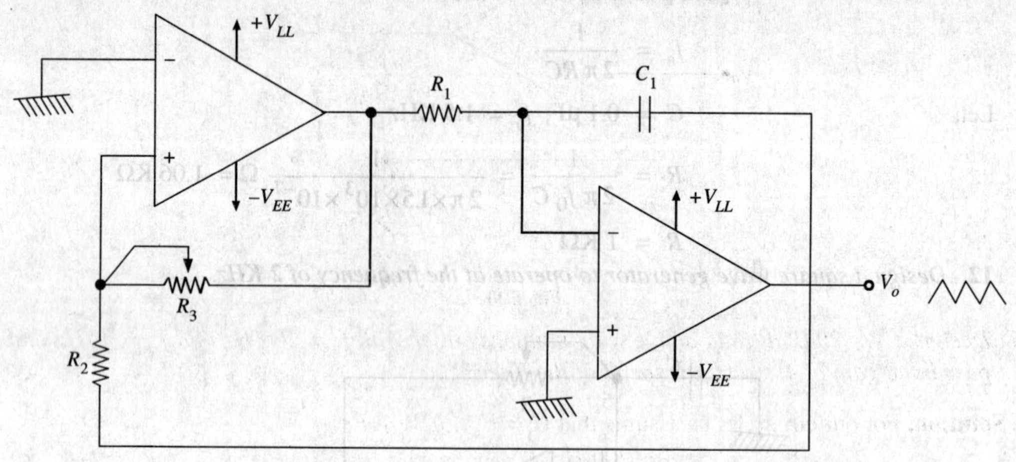

Fig. 6.29

Considering supply voltages = ± 15 V.
Here, we have used a operational amplifier 772.

So, V_{sat} = 14 V.

$$\therefore \quad V_o(pp) = 2\frac{R_2}{R_3}(V_{sat})$$

$$f_0 = \frac{R_3}{4R_1C_1R_2}$$

As, V_{sat} = + 14 V

$$\therefore \quad \frac{R_2}{R_3} = \frac{5}{2\times 14} = 0.1786$$

Let, R_3 = 10K, ∴ R_2 = 1.78 KΩ (1.8 KΩ)

Let, C_1 = 0.05 μF

$$\therefore \quad 1.5\times 10^3 = \frac{10\times 10^3}{4(R_1C_1)\times 1.8}$$

$$\Rightarrow \quad R_1C_1 = 0.926$$

$$\therefore \quad R_1 = \frac{0.926}{0.05\times 10^{-6}}\ \Omega = 18.5\ \text{M}\Omega\ (18\ \text{H}\Omega)$$

∴ R_1 = 18 HΩ, R_2 = 1.8 KΩ, R_3 = 10 KΩ, C_1 = 0.05 μF.

14. *Design an op-amp inverting Schmitt trigger with UTP = 4V, LTP = 2V, supply voltage = +/– 15V and Vsat = +/– 13V. Draw the circuit diagram and incorporate the designed values.*

Solution, UPT = $V1 = 4V$, LTP = $V2 = 2V$

Now, $V1 = Vr*R2(R1 + R2) + Va*R1/(R1 + R2)$

Hence, Vr = 0V and Va = 13V

So, $4R1 + 4R2 = Vr*R2 + 13R1$

⇒ $9R1 = (4 - Vr)*R2$

For designing purpose $R1 = 1\ k\Omega$

So, $R2 = 2.25\ k\Omega$

So the circuit diagram will be.

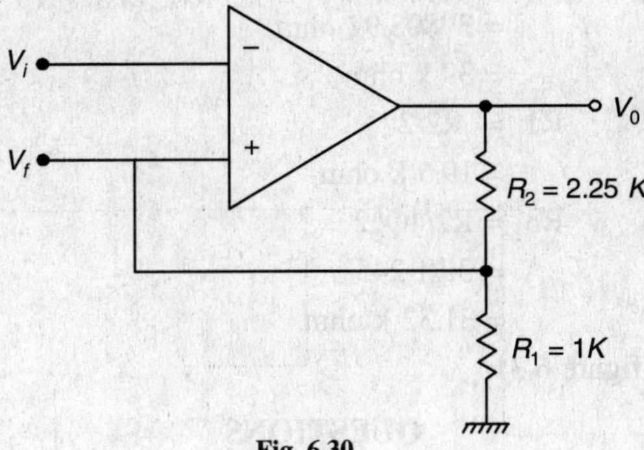

Fig. 6.30.

15. *Design a +/– 20dB/decade active wide bandpass filter with f_L = 200 Hz and f_H = 1 kHz and pass band gain of 4. Calculate the Q of the filter.*

Solution. For our circuit let us assume that $C_1 = C_2 = 0.01\ \mu F$.

$$f_L = 200\ Hz$$
$$W_L = 2*3.14*f_L \text{ rad/sec}$$
$$= 1256 \text{ rad/sec}$$
$$f_N = 1000\ Hz$$
$$W_N = 6282 \text{ rad/sec}$$

So, bandwidth $(B) = W_N - W_L$

$$= 5024 \text{ rad/sec}$$

$$fr = (f_L * f_N)^{\wedge}½$$
$$= 447.21$$
$$WN = 2808 \text{ rad/sec}$$

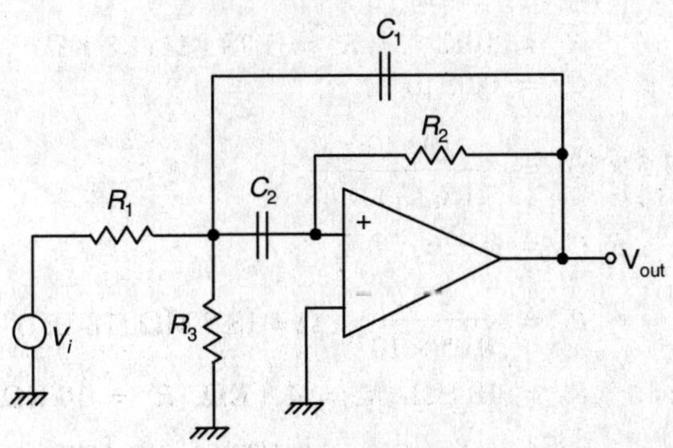

Fig. 6.31.

So, Q = WN/B

$$= 2808/5024$$
$$= 0.558$$

Now, R2 $= 2/(B*C)$

$$= 2/(5024*0.001*10 \wedge -6)$$

= 20*10 ∧ 6/502.4

= 39808.92 ohm

= 39 k ohm

R1 = R2/2

= 19.5 k ohm

R3 = R2/4Q^2

= 39/1.245

= 31.32 k ohm

So the ckt will be like figure 6.31.

QUESTIONS

1. What filter parameter determines the shape of an HPF or LPF response?
2. For a given BPF, if *fo* is increased and BW is held constant, will the *Q* increase or decrease?
3. What term is given to the maximum attenuation obtained from a band stop filter?
4. Define the term "Corner frequency" as applied to a filter that exhibits a chebyshev response.
5. What is the Butter worth response?
6. What are the advantages of active filters over passive ones?
7. What are the advantages of higher order filters?
8. Why characteristic impedence has no meaning in connection with active filters?
9. What are the characteristics of Butterworth filters?
10. A bandpass filter has a resisant frequency of 2 KHz and a bandwidth of 5 KHz. Find the lower and the upper cutoff frequencies.
11. Write the names of the following filters:

    (*a*) It has a constant output voltage from dc upto the cutoff frequency.

    (*b*) It passes a band of frequencies while attenuate are the other frequencies.

7

NOISE CONTROL IN OPERATIONAL AMPLIFIER

7·1. Introduction. 7·2. Noises Associated with Differential Amplifier (Operational Amplifier). 7·3. Equivalent Input Noise for BJT Differential Amplifier. 7·4. Noise Characteristics of a BJT Differential Stage. 7·5. Equivalent Input Noise for FET Differential Amplifier. 7·6. Optimum Noise Performance Conditions. 7·7. Noise in Cascaded Operational Amplifiers.

7·1. INTRODUCTION

In an electrical sense, noise is an unwanted form of energy which tend to interfere with the proper and easy reception and reproduction of wanted signals. In electronics and telecommunications it is probably the only topic with which every one must be acquainted irrespective of his or her specialization. Noise is everpresent. It limits the performance of virtually every system. Its measurement is contentious. Noise may produce hiss, snow or confetti, unwanted pulses or perhaps cancel out the wanted pulses. Noise sometimes even forces a reduction in the bandwidth. Noise is the combine effects of many sources and hence it is random in nature. It may come from external sources as well as self induced *i.e.,* internal noise. External noise may be caused by (*i*) switching of rotating machinery, (*ii*) ignition systems, and (*iii*) various control circuits. Fluorescent lights are another powerful source of external noise. The probable sources of internal noises are:

(*i*) Production of ac random voltages and currents within conductors and semiconductors of one circuit due to the switching of another circuit.

(*ii*) The speed of operation of the circuit.

(*iii*) Time rate of change of current voltage in the circuit.

(*iv*) Type of coupling with other circuit (s).

Several types of noises are available with operational amplifiers. As differential amplifier is the basic building block of an operational amplifier, we should study the noises associated with differential amplifier.

7·2. NOISES ASSOCIATED WITH DIFFERENTIAL AMPLIFIER (OPERATIONAL AMPLIFIER)

Different types of noise phenomena are associated with a differential amplifier stage, as are the cases with all amplifying devices. They are

(1) Schottky or shot noise.

(2) Johnson or thermal noise, and
(3) Flicks or $1/f$ noise.

Schottky or Shot noise

Schotty noise or shot noise is attributed to the discrete particle nature of current carriers in semiconductors. This type of noise basically exists in all amplifying devices and virtually in all active devices. It is assumed that the current in BJT or FET (which form the differential amplifier) under dc condition from the emitter to the collector consists of a stream of individual electrons or holes. Although a current of average value I_{dc} governed by the various bias voltages may be flowing, at any instant of time there may be more or fewer electrons arriving at the output electrode. In case of BJT, this is because of the random drift of the discrete current carriers across the junctions as the paths taken by the carriers are random and hence unequal. Such fluctuations in the number of current carriers is said to be shot or schottky noise. The mean-square schottky-noise current in any device is expressed as

$$I_{sh} = \sqrt{2\,e\,I_{dc}\,\Delta f} \quad \text{...(7.2.1)}$$

where I_{dc} = dc current
e = electronic charge
Δf = Bandwidth of the system

The I_{sh} is a nondeterministic time-varying noise current due to the random arrival times of the current carriers. The spectral density ($S_{i(f)}$) associated with this shot noise current is related by

$$I_{sh}^2 = \int_{f}^{f+\Delta f} S_i(f)\,df \quad \text{...(7.2.2)}$$

The spectral density for semiconductor is written as

$$S_i(f) = 2\,e\,I_{dc} \quad \text{...(7.2.3)}$$

The most convenient way of studying the schottky noise is to find out the value or formula for an equivalent input noise resistor (which is generally quoted in the manufacturer's specifications). With this equivalent noise resistance (shown separately in the circuit) the system is said to be noiseless, and has a value such that the same amount of noise is present at the output of the equivalent system as in the practical amplifier.

Johnson Noise or Thermal Noise or White noise

The noise produced in a resistance or the resistive component of any impedance is referred to as the thermal noise. As it is random in nature hence it is called the agitation, thermal, white or Johnson noise. The cause of such noise is the rapid and random motion of the molecules, atoms and electrons of which any such resistor is made up but independent of their mean or average motion.

It is learnt from thermodynamics, that the "temperature" of a body is the statistical root mean square value of the velocity of motion of the particles in the body. Hence the noise power generated by a resistor is proportional to its absolute temperature. If a resistance is ohmic in nature and is at thermal equilibrium the white noise has an associated constant spectral density. It is given by

$$S_i(f) = 4\,kTR \quad \text{...(7.2.4)}$$

where k = Boltzmann's constant.
T = temperature in degree kelvin.

The mean-square thermal noise voltage of a resistor (R) is obtained by integrating the spectral density over the system band width and is expressed as

$$\bar{e}_{th}^2 = 4\,kTR\,\Delta f \quad \text{...(6.2.5)}$$

where Δf = Bandwidth of the system.

The mean square thermal noise current is obtained from noise voltage by applying a Norton theorem.

$$\bar{i}_{th}^2 = \frac{\bar{e}_{th}^2}{R^2} + \frac{4KT\Delta fR}{R^2} = \frac{4KT\Delta f}{R} \quad ...(7.2.6)$$

Flicker or 1/f Noise or modulation noise

In transistors, at low audio frequencies, a poorly understood form of noise is found. This noise is called Flicker or modulation noise or 1/*f* noise. It is inversely proportional to frequency, but directly proportional to emitter current and junction temperature. As it is inversely proportional to the frequency hence its effect can be ignored beyond about 500 Hz. Above 500 Hz it is not very serious.

7·3. EQUIVALENT INPUT NOISE FOR BJT DIFFERENTIAL AMPLIFIER

The dc input error signals are generated due to input offset voltage, input current and their drifts. But equivalent input noise voltage and current constitute ac input error signals in a differential stage. It is well known that any amplified signal must be of sufficient magnitude to be detectable over the inherent noise level of the amplifier. Hence the noise generated within a differential stage imposes a limit on the signal sensitivity of the circuit.

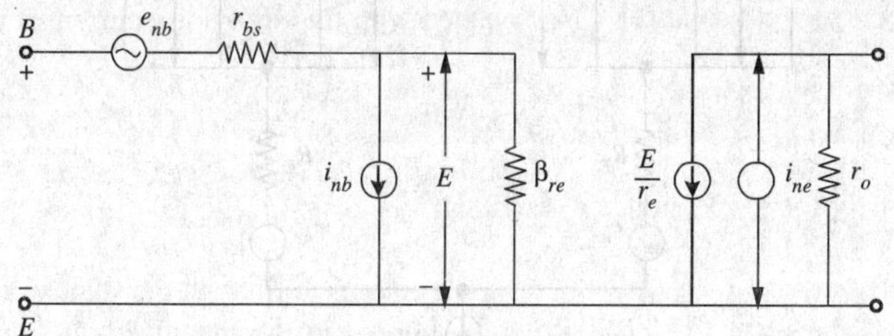

Fig. 7.1(*a*). Equivalent noise representation of a bipolar transistor.

The overall noise performance will be significantly affected by the source resistances as noise currents from the inputs flow in these resistances.

In order to get the overall noise behaviour of an amplifier, many noise sources, both internal and external to the amplifier, are to be taken into account. Noise theory states that a set of mean-square noise voltages or currents may be added to obtain the cumulative mean-square value, provided the noise sources are uncorrected. (*i.e.*, statistically independent).

Fig. 7.1(*a*) and (*b*) represent noise equivalent representation of transistor and ohmic resistor respectively.

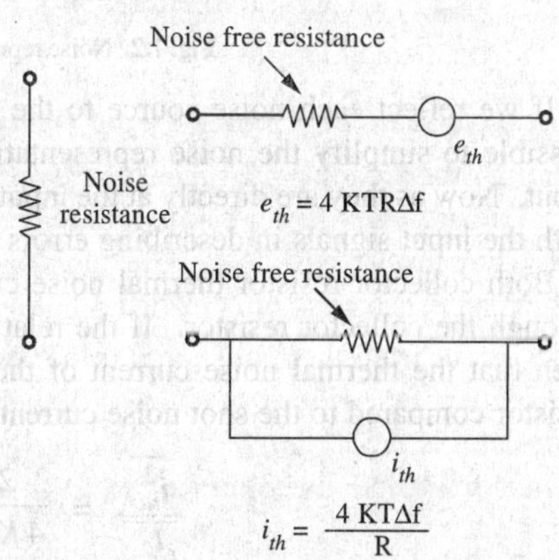

Fig. 7.1(*b*). Equivalent Noise representation of a ohmic resistance

where
$$\overline{i_{nb}^2} = 2\,e\,I_B\,\Delta f \text{ (shot noise)} \quad ...(7.3.1)$$

$$\overline{i_{nc}^2} = 2\,e\,I_c\,\Delta f \text{ (shot noise)} \quad ...(7.3.2)$$

r_b = base spreading resistance

$$\overline{e_{th}^2} = 4\,K\,T\,r_b\,\Delta f \text{ (thermal)} \quad ...(7.3.3)$$

On applications of this model to the basic differential stage leads to the result in Fig. 7.2.

This figure can be employed to develop equivalent noise sources at the stage inputs. Identical characteristics have been assumed for both the BJTs. However, typical unbalances will result in only minor noise differences. Output resistance r_o is not considered in the complete diagram because of $R_c << r_e(1 - \alpha)$. In the figure:

i_{thrc} = thermal noise of R_C

e_{ne} = thermal noise of R_E

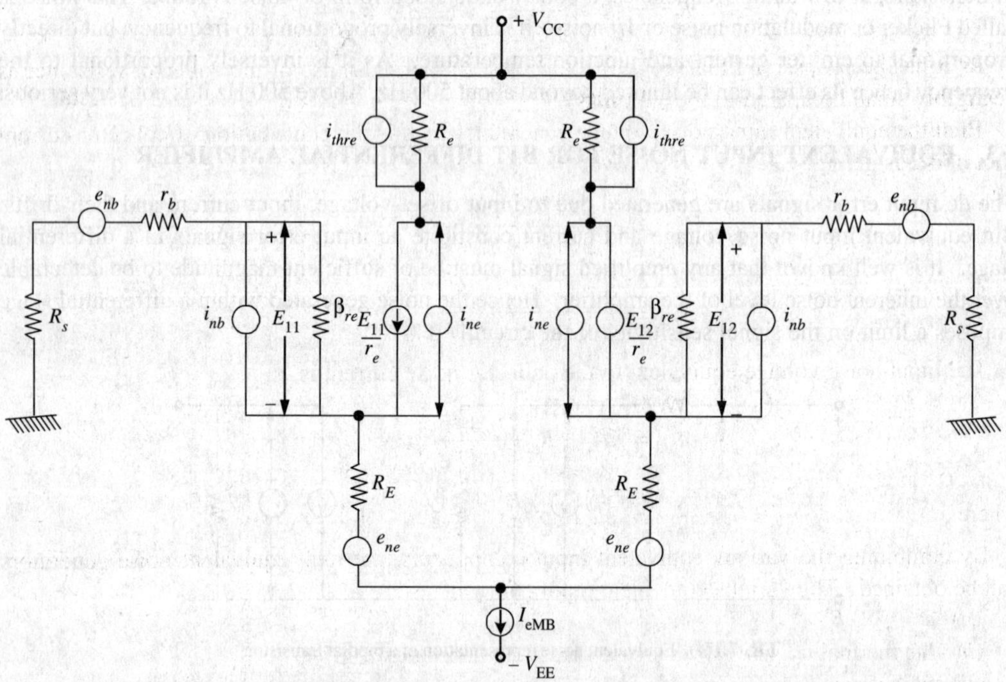

Fig. 7.2. Noise representation of a BJT differential stage.

If we reflect each noise source to the stage input as an equivalent noise generator, it is then possible to simplify the noise representation of one noise voltage and one noise current at each input. Now as they are directly at the inputs, these net equivalent noise generators can be compared with the input signals in describing errors contributed by noise.

Both collector resistor thermal noise current and the collector current shot noise current flow through the collector resistor. If the relative magnitude of them are checked by taking ratio it is seen that the thermal noise current of the collector resistance results in negligible noise on the resistor compared to the shot noise current and hence it can be omitted.

$$\frac{\overline{i_{nc}^2}}{i_{thre}^L} = \frac{2\,e\,I_c\,\Delta f}{4\,KT\,\Delta f\,/\,R_c} = \frac{I_C\,R_e}{2\,KT\,/\,e}$$

At room temperature KT/e = 25 mV and for normal operation $I_c\,R_c$ (collector resistor drop) = 2·5V

$$\frac{\overline{i_{nc}^2}}{i_{thre}^L} = 500$$

I_{CMB} = Common-mode biasing current. Generally I_{CMB} divides equally between the two sides of the stage and hence develop equal noise signals on the collector resistors. As a result no differential output noise due to this noise source, unless the small resulting base noise currents flow in very high source resistances (R_s). Hence to avoid complieacy the noise associated with I_{CMB} can be neglected.

In order to reflect the collector noise current generators to the stage input as equivalent noise generation(s), the circuit is separated at the junction of the emitter resistors. The equivalent resistance (R_{eq}) presented by the differential stage to the emitter of the left of the stage is the output resistance of an emitter follower made by the right side of the stage provided I_{CMB} is neglected.

$$R_{eq} = R_e + \frac{R_s + r_b}{\beta} \quad \text{where } R_e = R_E + r_e$$

As it has been observed that (for collector resistor) thermal noise of the collector resistance is negligibly small compared to the shot noise.

Then the equivalent input noise voltage generator which is the contribution of collector current shot noise, is given by

$$E_{11} = \frac{e_{nc}(2\beta R_e + R_s + r_b)}{2(\beta R_e + R_s + r_b)}$$

$$i_{nc} = \frac{E_{11}}{2R_e + (R_s + r_b)/\beta}$$

The input noise voltage equivalent to the collector noise current is

$$e_{nc} = 2\, i_{nc}\left(R_e + \frac{r_b + R_s}{\beta}\right)$$

where $\overline{i_{nc}^2} = 2\, e\, I_c\, \Delta f$

By combining the various equivalent input components, the total equivalent noise generators can be obtained. The various equivalent input components are

(*i*) e_{nc}

(*ii*) the thermal noise e_{nb} of the base spreading resistance, and

(*iii*) the reflected thermal noise of the emitter resistor.

The noise generator associated with the emitter resistance may be transferred directly to the input because it will contribute the same emitter current in either position.

The equivalent input noise voltage e_{ni1} (measured in one sides) can be expressed in terms of the three noise sources

$$\overline{e_{ni1}^2} = \overline{e_{nc}^2} + \overline{e_{ne}^2} + \overline{e_{nb}^2}$$

where $\overline{e_{nc}^2} = 4\, e\, I_c\, \Delta f\left(R_e + \frac{r_b + R_s}{\beta}\right)^2$

$$\overline{e_{ne}^2} = 4\, kT\, R_E\, \Delta f$$

$$\overline{e_{nb}^2} = 4\, kT\, r_b\, \Delta f$$

$$\therefore \quad \overline{e_{ni1}^2} = 4\, e\, I_c\, \Delta f\left(R_e + \frac{r_b + R_s}{\beta}\right)^2 + 4\, KT\, \Delta f\,(r_b + R_E)$$

Similar expression can be had from the other side of the differential amplifier

$$\overline{e_{ni2}^2} = \overline{e_{ni1}^2} \quad \text{(provided both sides are identical)}$$

Hence the total equivalent differential input noise of the differential amplifier e_{ni} is given by

$$\overline{e_{ni}^2} = \overline{e_{ni1}^2} + \overline{e_{ni2}^2} = 2\,\overline{e_{ni1}^2}$$

$$e_{ni} = 2\sqrt{\overline{e_{ni1}^2}} = \sqrt{2\,\overline{e_{ni1}^2}}$$

$$e_{ni} = 2\sqrt{2\,e\,I_c\,\Delta f\left(R_e + \frac{r_b + R_s}{\beta}\right)^2 + 2\,KT\,\Delta f\,(r_b + R_E)}$$

Equivalent input noise current calculation:– The input noise currents are

$$i_{ni1} = i_{nb1} = \sqrt{2\,e\,I_{B_1}\,\Delta f}$$

$$i_{ni2} = i_{nb2} = i_{nb} = \sqrt{2\,e\,I_{B_2}\,\Delta f}$$

From the Fig. 7.2 it is seen that in addition to flowing in the source resistance (R_s), the input noise currents flow through the emitter resistors. It is already know that

$$\overline{i_{nb}^2} = 2\,e\,I_B\,\Delta f$$

and $\overline{i_{nc}^2} = 2\,\text{e}\,I_c\,\Delta f$ where $I_c = \beta\,I_B$

It is evident from the above three relations that the effect of the base current shot noise in the emitter resistors is small compared with that generated by the collector noise current. Hence the base current noise producer may be returned to common instead of to the emitters. Moreover, the base current noise in the small r_b will provide some noise voltage which is negligible in comparison with the preceding equivalent input noise voltage. So, the base current noise generators can be returned to the base terminal (*i.e.*, to the opposite side of r_b). Thus by reflecting all noise sources to the inputs of a differential stage, it can be represented by a noise free stage preceded by the equivalent input noise generators as depicted in the Fig. 7.3(*a*), Fig. 7.3(*b*) and Fig. 7.3(*c*) represent the equivalent circuits of a differential stage referred to one input with (*i*) equivalent input noise voltage generator and (*ii*) the collector current noise generator, respectively.

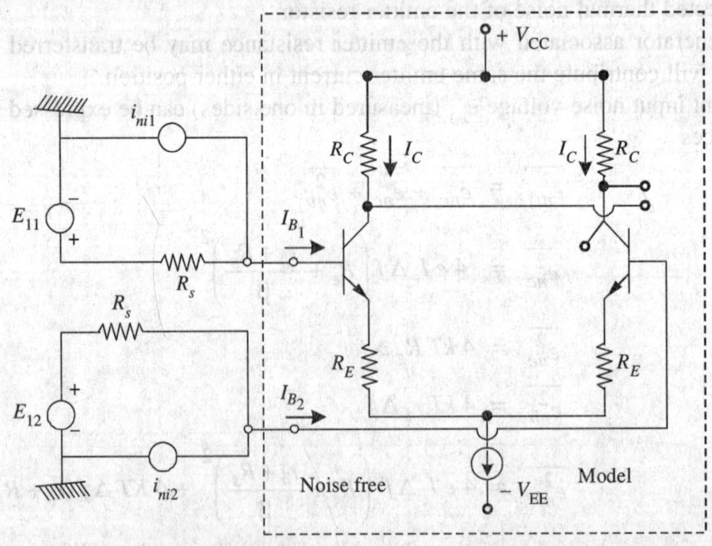

Fig. 7.3(*a*). Equivalent input noise model of BJT differential amplifier.

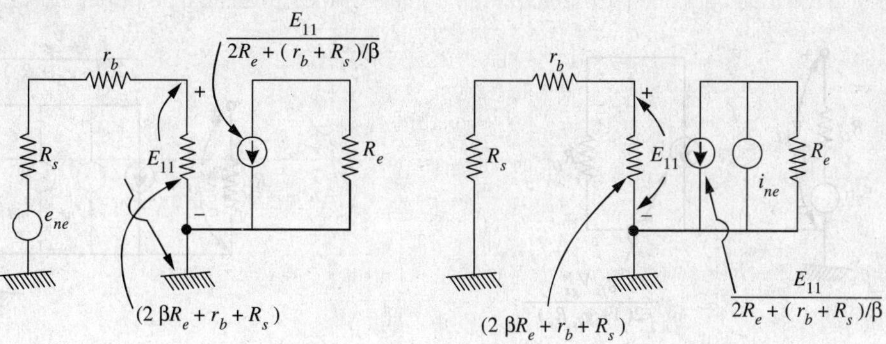

Fig. 7.3(*b*) and (*c*). Equivalent input noise model of BJT differential amplifier.

7·4. NOISE CHARACTERISTICS OF A BJT DIFFERENTIAL STAGE

Several comments can be made on the noise characteristics of BJT differential stage

(*i*) The input noise currents and input noise voltage are proportional to the square root of the bandwidth of the system.

(*ii*) Input noise voltage can be minimised by lowering collector current.

(*iii*) Shot noise currents can be reduced by lowing the collector current and with BJT having high β.

(*iv*) If the thermal noise of the source resistance are excluded, it is seen that the equivalent input noise voltage has a slight dependence upon source resistances.

7·5. EQUIVALENT INPUT NOISE FOR FET DIFFERENTIAL AMPLIFIER

Equivalent input noise model of an FET differential stage is shown in Fig. 7.4. The equivalent circuit of an FET differential stage referred to one input with (Fig. 7.5) the equivalent input noise voltage generator and (Fig. 7.6) channel drain resistance noise current generators are shown in Fig. 7.4 and Fig. 7.5, respectively.

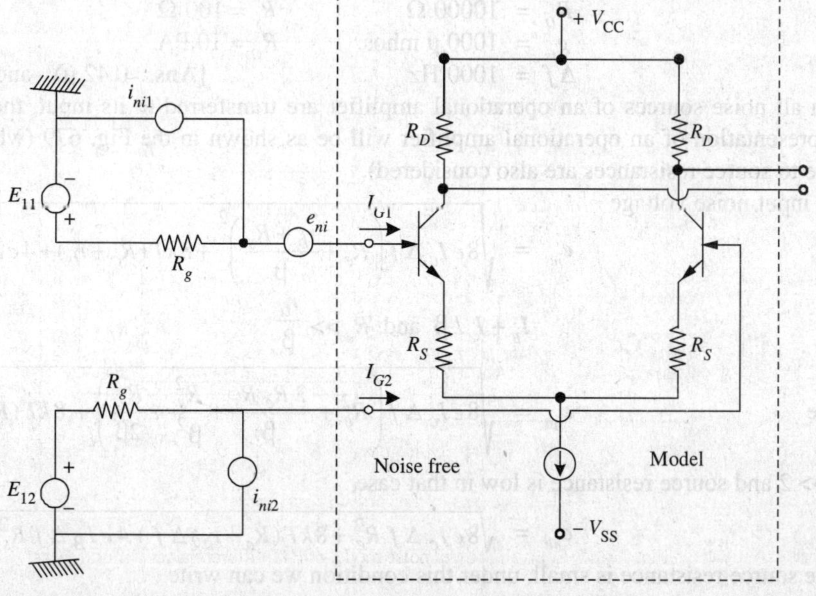

Fig. 7.4. Equivalent input noise model.

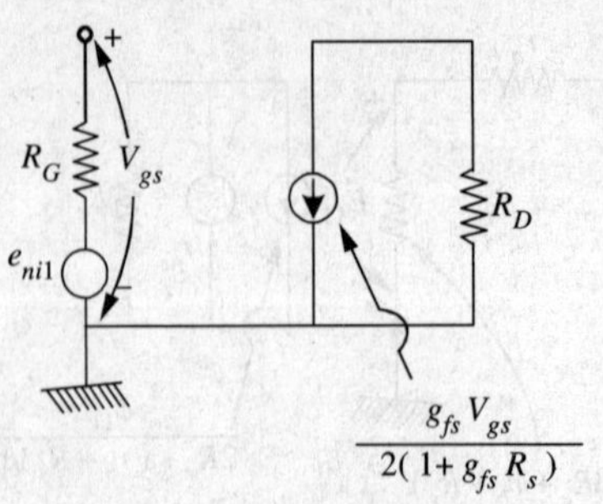

Fig. 7.5.

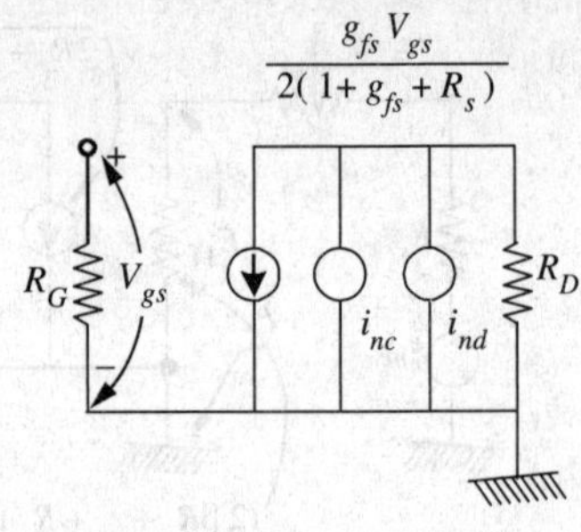

Fig. 7.6.

$$e_{ni} = \left(4\left(\frac{1}{(g_{fs}+R_s)}\right)\right)\sqrt{2\,KT\,\Delta f\,(g_{fs}+1/R_0)}$$

$$i_{ni1} = \sqrt{2\,e\,I_{G1}\,\Delta f} \;\&\; i_{ni2} = \sqrt{2\,e\,I_{G2}\,\Delta f}$$

Where channel noise is generated that is approximated by the thermal noise of a resistor equal to $\frac{1}{g_{fs}}$.

Calculate the noise levels with the following parameters:

(1) For BJT:

$I_c = 25\ \mu A$ $\quad R_s = 1000\ \Omega$

$\beta = 200$ $\quad \Delta f = 1000$ Hz

$R_E = 500\ \Omega$

$r_b = 50\ \Omega$

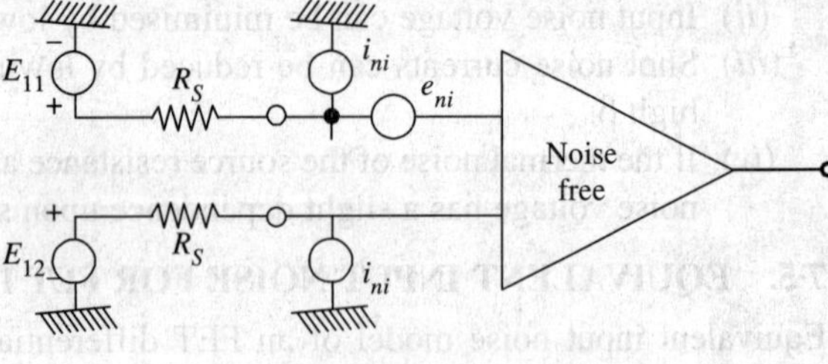

Fig. 7.7. Equivalent noise model.

[**Ans.** 0·3 μV & 6·3 PA rms]

(2) For JFET

$R_D = 10000\ \Omega$ $\quad R_s = 100\ \Omega$

$g_{fs} = 1000\ \mu$ mhos. $\quad R_G = 10$ PA.

$\Delta f = 1000$ Hz

[**Ans.** 0.42 μV and 0.056 PA]

When all noise sources of an operational amplifier are transferred to its input, the equivalent noise representation of an operational amplifier will be as shown in the Fig. 679 (where thermal noise due to source resistances are also considered).

Total input noise voltage

$$e_{nit} = \sqrt{8\,e\,I_c\,\Delta f\left(R_e+\frac{r_b+R_s}{\beta}\right)^2+8kT(R_c+r_b)+4\,e\,I_B\,\Delta f\,R_s^2}$$

$$I_B + I_c/\beta \text{ and } R_e >> \frac{r_b}{\beta}$$

Hence

$$e_{nit} = \sqrt{8\,e\,I_c\,\Delta f\left(R_e^2+\frac{2\,R_e\,R_s}{\beta}+\frac{R_s^2}{\beta^2}+\frac{R_2^2}{2\beta}\right)+8\,kT\,(R_e+r_b)\,\Delta f}$$

If $\beta >> 2$ and source resistance is low in that case

$$e_{nit} = \sqrt{8\,e\,I_c\,\Delta f\,R_e^2+8\,kT\,(R_e+r_b)\,\Delta f+4\,e\,I_B\,\Delta f\,R_s^2}$$

As the source resistance is small, under this condition we can write

$$e_{nit} + \sqrt{2\,e\,I_e\,\Delta f\,R_c^2+2\,kT\,(R_e+r_b)\,\Delta f}$$

The Fig. 7.8 shows the representative curves of total input noise voltage versus source resistance for various types of operational amplifiers.

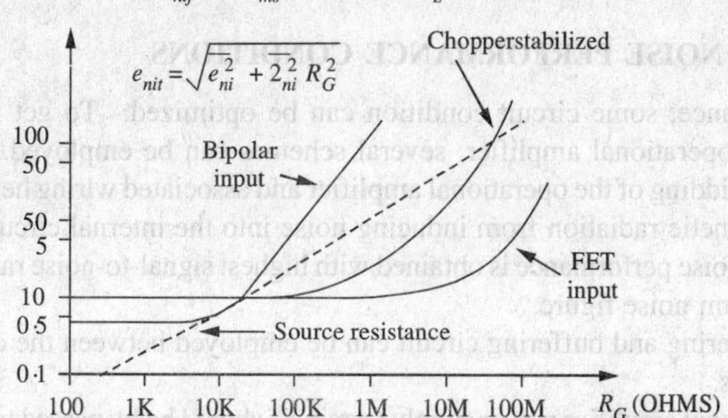

Fig. 7.8. Representative curves of total input noise voltage versus source resistance for various types of operational amplifiers. (Empirical results from Burr-Broun Models 3050/01, 3071/25 and 3307/12C)

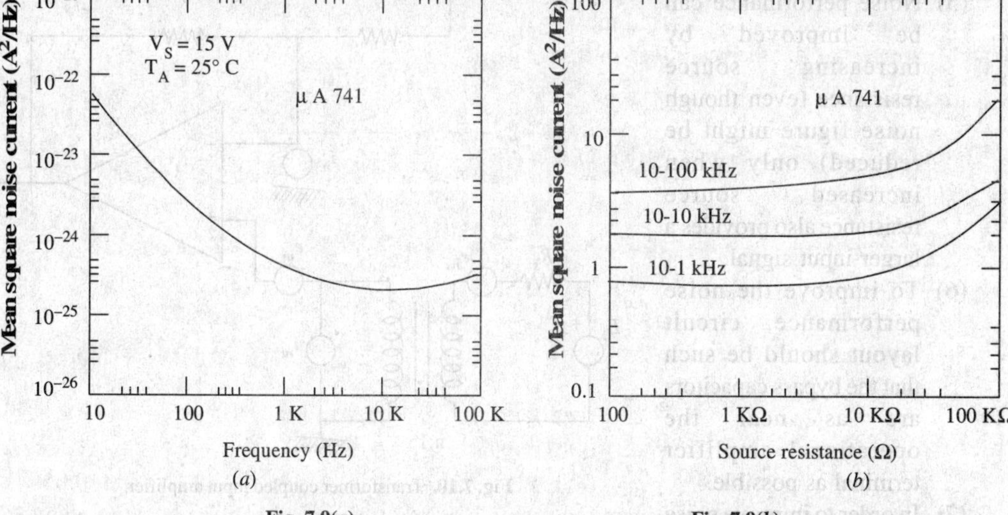

Fig. 7.9(*a*) **Fig. 7.9(*b*)**

From our calculations on thermal shot and flicker noises following observations have been made.

(1) Thermal noise increases with the increase of temperature and also wider for wider bandwidth.

(2) Shot noise is greater with wider bandwidths and larger resistances.

(3) Flicker noise increases with a decrease in frequency provided frequency is below 500 Hz.

Fig. 7.9(*a*), (*b*) and (*c*) represent the (*i*) input noise voltage versus frequency, (*ii*) Input noise current versus frequency and (*iii*) broadband noise for various bandwidths, respectively (Fairchild semiconductor corporation).

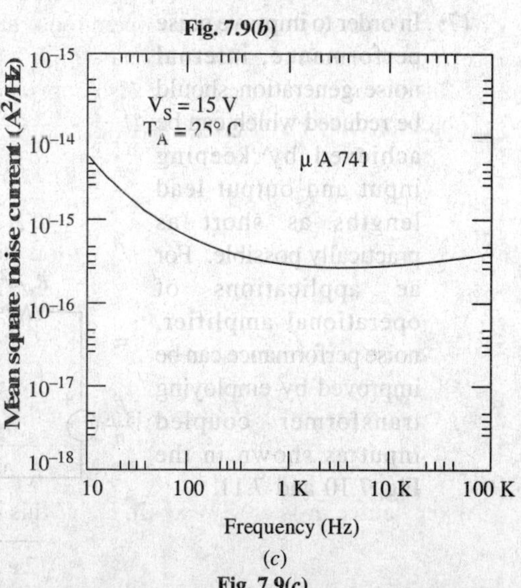

Fig. 7.9(*c*)

From the figures it is clear that for a given value of source resistance, noise is more for wider bandwidths. Further, the noise is higher at larger source resistances for a given bandwidth. It is also evident that noise is lower at higher frequencies.

7·6. OPTIMUM NOISE PERFORMANCE CONDITIONS

For noise performance, some circuit condition can be optimized. To get the reduced effect of electrical noise in operational amplifier, several schemes can be employed.

(1) Physical skidding of the operational amplifier and associated wiring helps to prevent external electromagnetic radiation from inducing noise into the internal circuitry.

(2) Optimum noise performance is obtained with highest signal-to-noise ratio and not necessarily the minimum noise figure.

(3) Special filtering and buffering circuit can be employed between the electronic circuits and signal leads.

(4) All operational amplifier power supply terminals should be by passed to ground for providing a path for any radio frequency (*RF*).

(5) Noise performance can be improved by increasing source resistance (even though noise figure might be reduced) only when increased source resistance also provides a larger input signal.

(6) To improve the noise performance, circuit layout should be such that the bypass capacitors are as near the operational amplifier terminal as possible.

(7) In order to improve noise performance, internal noise generation should be reduced which can be achieved by keeping input and output lead lengths as short as practically possible. For ac applications of operational amplifier, noise performance can be improved by employing transformer coupled input as shown in the Fig. 7.10 and 7.11.

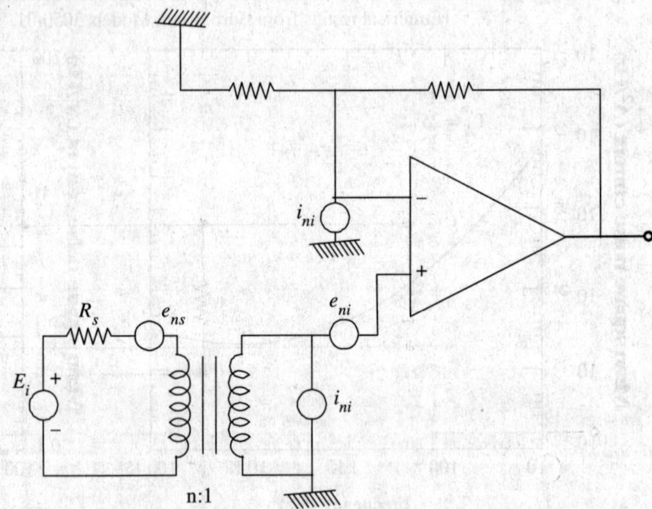

Fig. 7.10. Transformer coupled input amplifier.

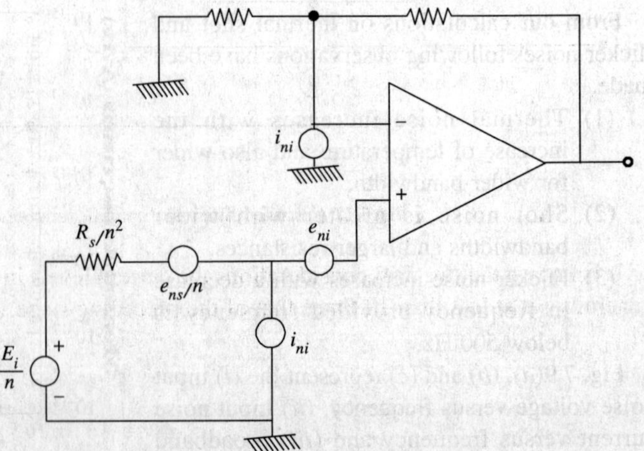

Fig. 7.11. Equivalent of Fig. 7.10.

7·7. NOISE IN CASCADED OPERATIONAL AMPLIFIERS

When a several operational amplifier are cascaded, equivalent input noise voltage and input noise currents of an operational amplifier are derived from the individual stage noise components. In order to reflect the input noise components of the second stage to the first stage input the noise currents that would be induced in the first stage outputs by these noise components are considered. Input noise currents of the loading stage add directly to the collector (for BJT) or drain current (for FET) of the first stage such additional collector current/drain currents reflecting the input noise voltage of the following stage are produced and equal that noise voltage divided by the load resistors. The mean-square noise currents reflected to a differential-stage output from a loading stage results in

$$\overline{i_{nr}^2} = \overline{i_{ni2}^2} + \frac{\overline{e_{ni}^2}}{(2R_L)^2}$$

(mean square noise component i'_{ni}) $$\overline{i_{ni}^2} = \overline{i_{ni1}^2} + \frac{\overline{i_{nr}^2}}{\beta^2}$$

$$\overline{i_{ni}^2} = \overline{i_{ni1}^2} + \frac{\overline{i_{ni2}^2}}{\beta^2} + \frac{\overline{e_{ni2}^2}}{4\beta^2 R_c^2}.$$

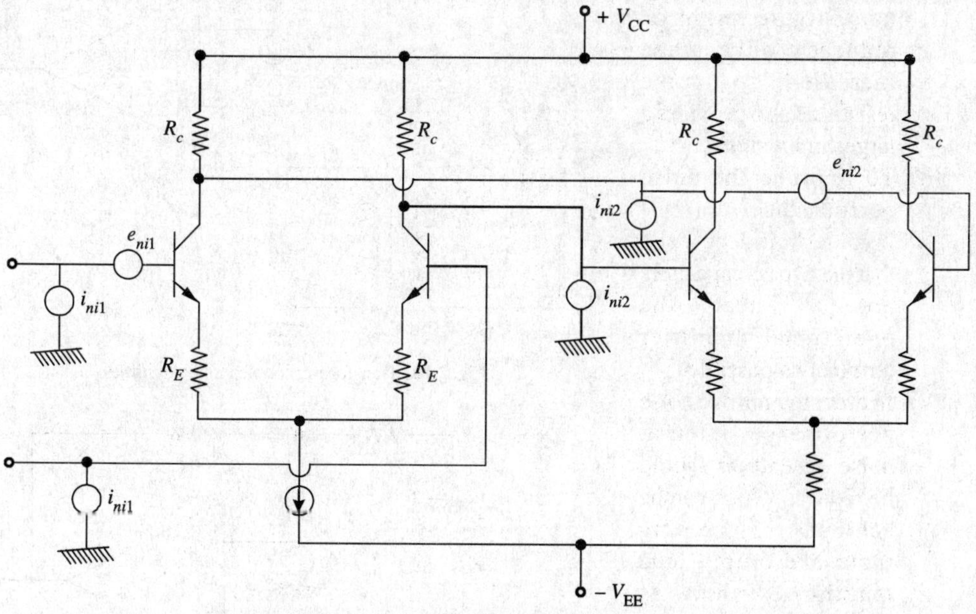

Fig. 7.12. Cascaded differential amplifier and noise representation.

It is known that for drift considerations the current levels in a loading bipolar transistor stage are generally set at less than 10 times that of the preceding stage.

Then $$\overline{i_{ni2}^2} = \frac{I_{B2}}{I_{B1}} \cdot \overline{i_{ni1}^2} \le 10\,\overline{i_{ni1}^2}$$

Similarly the equivalent noise at one input of a BJT input stage due to loading by a second stage will be

$$\overline{e_{nil2}^2} = 2\,\overline{i_{nr}^2}\left(R_c + \frac{R_s + r_b}{\beta}\right)^2$$

Adding this input noise to a similar noise at the other input and to the input noise voltage of the first stage itself results in a net equivalent input noise voltage of

$$\overline{e_{nieq}^2} = \overline{e_{ni1}^2} + 2\,\overline{e_{ni2}^2}$$

$$\therefore \quad \overline{e_{nieq}^2} = \overline{e_{ni1}^2} + 4\left(\overline{i_{ni2}^2} + \frac{\overline{e_{ni2}^2}}{4R_c^2}\right)\left(R_c + \frac{R_s + r_b}{\beta}\right)^2$$

8

OPERATIONAL AMPLIFIER APPLICATIONS

8·1. Introduction. 8·2. Audio Mixer using operational amplifier. 8·3. Active Voltage Divider. 8·4. Equializers using operational amplifier. 8·5. Audio tone control using operational amplifier. 8·6. Operational amplifier operated photo electric relay. 8·7. Photovoltaic Light sensors using operational amplifier. 8·8. High-precision voltage sources using operational amplifier. 8·9. Resistance temperature sensor. 8·10. Signal rectification using operational amplifier. 8·11. Variable voltage power supply. 8·12. High voltage power supply using operational amplifier. 8·13. Operational amplifier as a phase detector. 8·14. Operational amplifier electronic thermometers. 8·15. Operational amplifier in medical electronic monitoring system. 8·16. Operational Amplifier as a power amplifier.

8.1. INTRODUCTION

Operational amplifier has attained wide acceptance as a versatile, predictable, and economic system building block. Operational amplifier provides all the advantages of monolithic *IC* namely, small size, reduced weight, high reliability, reduced cost, temperature traking and low offset voltage and current. Practically you will find operational amplifier at work everywhere.

8·2. AUDIO MIXER USING OPERATIONAL AMPLIFIER

The adjoining Fig. 8.1 represents an audio mixer using operational amplifier. An *IC* operational amplifier can be used as an audio mixer. It is an inputs audio mixer.

The gain in each channel is determined by the ratio $\frac{R_f}{R_i}$ $(i = 1, 2, N)$.

But increased gain will increase distortion and noise. If operational amplifier is selected such that it should have high open loop gain to reduce the crosstalk. Further to get minimum cross talk we should

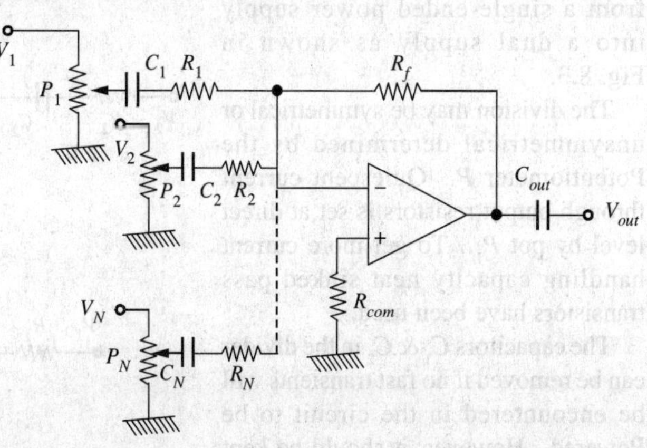

Fig. 8.1. Audio mixer with gain adjustment facilities.

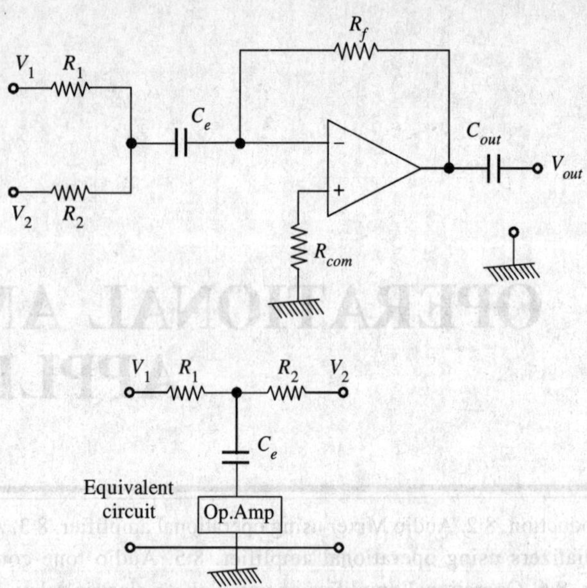

Fig. 8.2(*a*). Common capacitor

provide the lowest source impedance and highest input series resistor. From the figure it is evident that each channel has its own capacitor for increasing the isolation from input to input at low frequencies. If a single common capacitor is used for the inputs, the shunting action of the operational amplifier is reduced at low frequencies as explained by separate Fig. 8.2(*a*) and (*b*).

Fig. 8.2(*c*) depicts another audio mixer which can accept up to seven audio inputs from either of the following (*i*) phone-stereo preamps, (*ii*) microphone preamps. (*iii*) tapehead preamps, (*iv*) tone controls or (*v*) the like.

In this circuit pots are replaced by sealed pots which are noise reliable and practically noise free. The output is about five times the sum of the input voltages μA 741 has been used in this circuit.

8.3. ACTIVE VOLTAGE DIVIDER

An operational amplifier voltage follower can easily be transformed from a single-ended power supply into a dual supply as shown in Fig. 8.3.

The division may be symmetrical or unsymmetrical determined by the Potentiometer *P*. Quiescent current through output resistors is set at direct level by pot P_1. To get more current handling capacity heat sinked pass transistors have been used.

The capacitors C_1 & C_2 in the divider can be removed if no fast transients will be encountered in the circuit to be Powered. However, it should be kept in mind that the single ended supply voltage should not exceed the

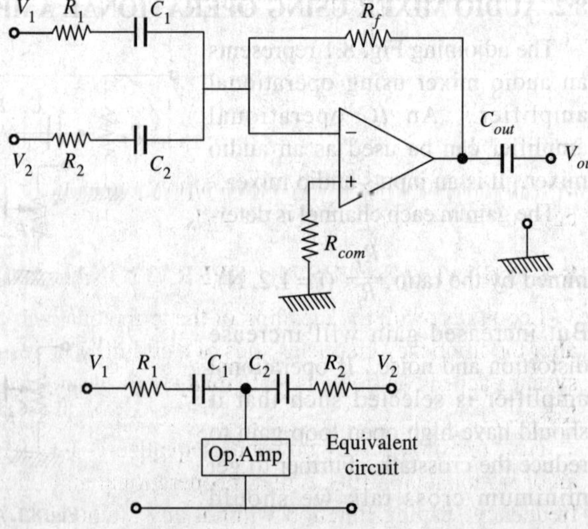

Fig. 8.2(*b*). Individual capacitors.

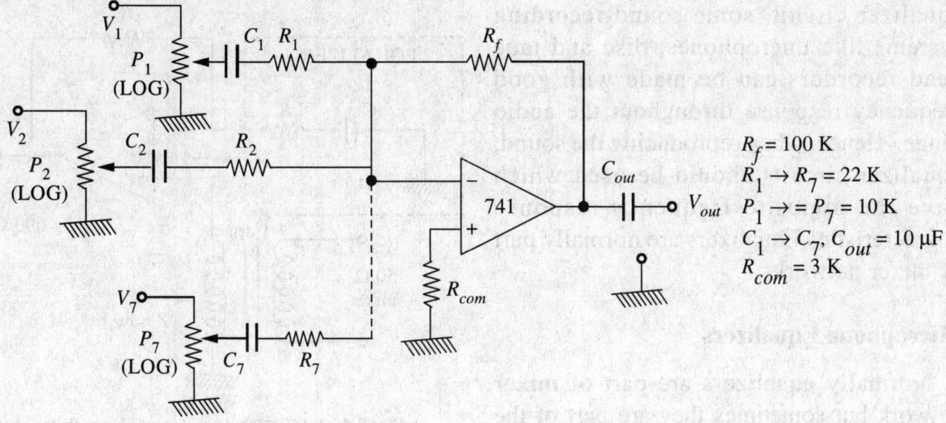

Fig. 8.2(*c*). Audio mixer with sever inputs.

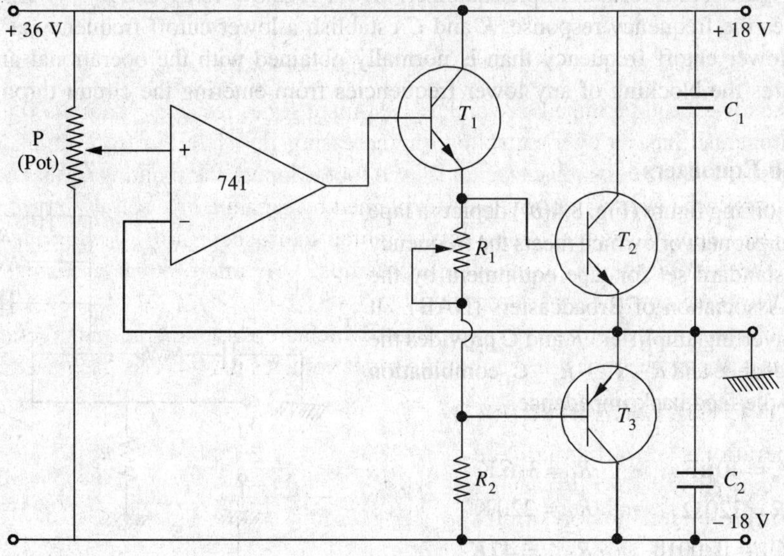

Fig. 8.3. Active voltage divider.

operational amplifier's 36V input supply range. ($C_1 = C_2 = 0{\cdot}1$ μF is the usual value). For practical circuit $P = 100$K, $P_1 = 5$K, $R_2 = 4{\cdot}7$K, T_1 is BC 108, T_2 is 2N5293 and T_3 is 2N6106.

8·4. EQUALIZERS USING OPERATIONAL AMPLIFIER

Let us start with the meaning of the term equalizer. It is a collection of reactive elements used to alter the frequency characteristics of a circuit. The response of all sound recording and reproducing systems depend on frequency. In many such systems, equalizers are used to compensate for frequency losses.

Now question is why do we use equalizer? The main attracting point of using an equalizer with an operational amplifier is that it (operational amplifier) isolates the equalizer, so it can perform its frequency shaping function without any attenuation of the frequencies of interest. Incorporating equalizer circuit, some sound-recording systems like microphones, disc and tape head recorders can be made with good frequency response throughout the audio range. Hence, when reproducing the sound, equalizer circuits should be used which have the opposite frequency-response characteristics Equalizers are normally part of mixer networks.

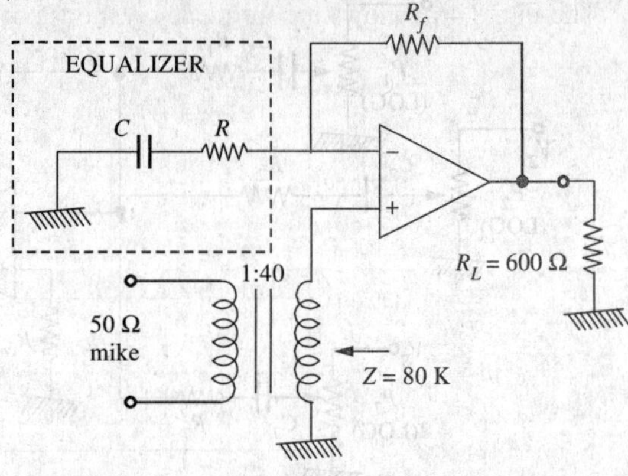

Fig. 8.4(*a*). Microphone prcamplifier with equalizer.

Microphone Equalizers

Normally equalizers are part of mixer network but sometimes they are part of the input amplifier. In microphone, equalizers are used in audio systems a head of the mixer control (in normal situation). The Fig. 8.4(*a*) depicts a simple equalizer circuit for microphone.

In the figure R & C form a simple equalizer. ($R = 1$ K & $C = 15$ μF and $R_f = 47$ K). The capacitor C improves the frequency response. R and C establish a lower cutoff frequency at 10Hz, thereby giving a lower cutoff frequency than is normally obtained with the operational amplifier alone. This ensures the blocking of any lower frequencies from entering the circuit through the ground line.

Tape head Equalizers

The adjoining figure (Fig. 8.4(*b*)) depicts a tape head equalizer network which meets the frequency response standard set for tape equipment by the National Association of Broadcasters (NAB). It is a non-inverting amplifier. R and C provides the input impedance and $R_f - C_f - R_1 - C_1$ combination constitute the feed back impedance.

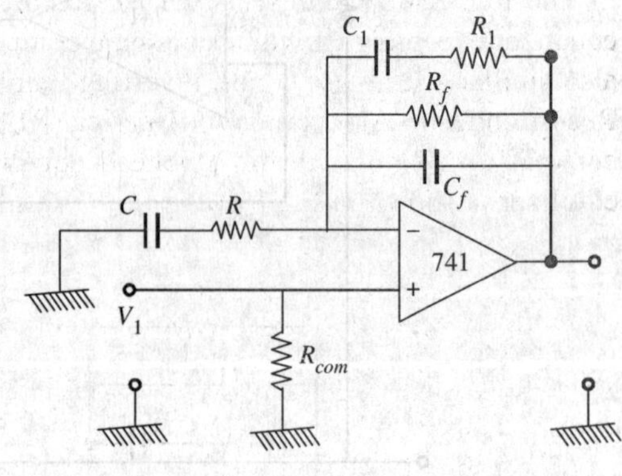

$C = 40\,\mu F$	$R_1 = 3\cdot6$ K
$R = 220\,\Omega$	$R_f = 220$ K
$C_f = 0\cdot0018$	$R_{com} = 47$ K
$C_1 = 0\cdot015\,\mu F$	

Fig. 8.4(b). Tape head equalizer.

Both the impedances (input and feed back) of the equalizer vary in magnitude with signal frequency. Moreover, the gain of the equalizer varies with the change of the ratio of the feedback to input impedance. A lower cutoff frequency of 20 Hz is established by R and C. Hence at frequencies below 20 Hz, C provides a very large reactance and thereby makes the input impedance (R — C) very large, and accordingly the equalizer gain is very low. Therefore, it effectively blocks all signal frequencies below the audio range (20 Hz to 20 KHz). The input impedance is nearly equal to R above 20 Hz. As a result of the change of signal frequency, the feedback impedance also changes. This is because the reactances of C_f and C_1 are inversely proportional to signal frequency C_1 will come into play at a lower frequency than C_f because of its large value.

The Fig. 8.4(c) shows the frequency response of the tape head equalizer.

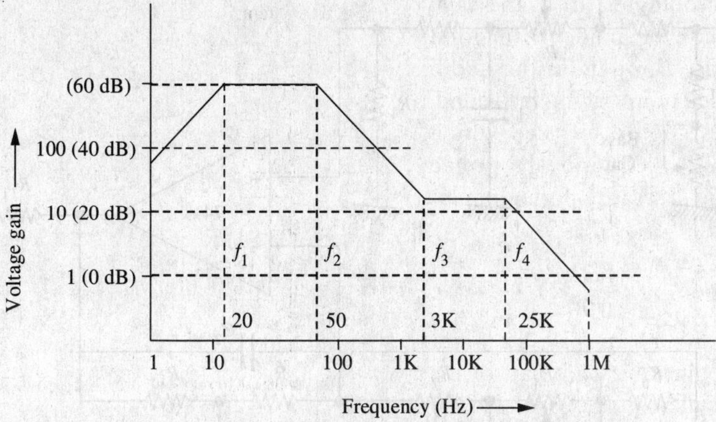

Fig. 8.4(c). Frequency response curve of type head equalizer.

The low frequency cutoff (f_1 = 20 Hz) is established by $R - C$ combination. The second break frequency (f_2 = 50 Hz) is determined by R_f and C_f. The fall of gain between 50 Hz to and 3 kHz is due to the change in the ratio of the feedback to input impedance. C_1 comes into play during 3 k to 25 kHz. Above 25 kHz the gain again starts falling due to the combined effects of R_1 and C_f.

Disc Record Equalizers

The Fig. 8.4(d) represents a Disc Record equalization preamp. It is similar to tape head equalizer excepting the values of some components. Frequency-response (Fig. 8.4(c)) curve is also similar. It is also a non-inverting amplifier which meets the frequency standard set for Record Industry Association of America (RIAA). Explanation of the circuit as well as response curve is also similar to the tapehead equalizers. Frequency response curve of Disc Record equilizer is shown in Fig.8.4(e).

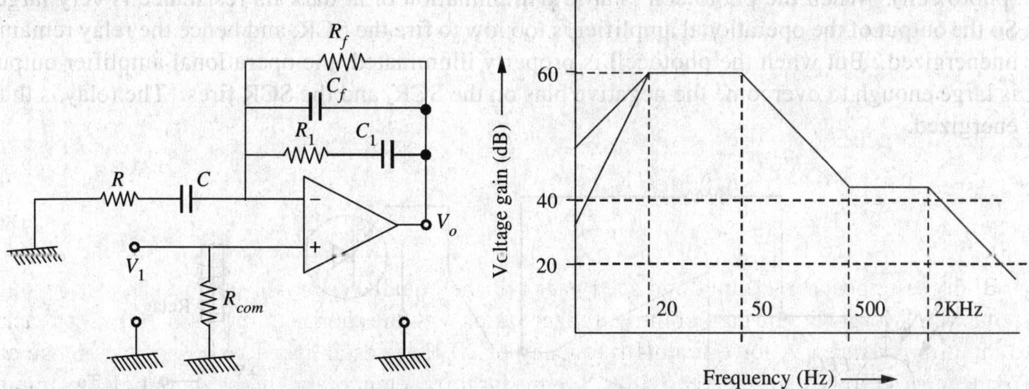

Fig. 8.4(d). Disc Record equalization preamplifier. **Fig. 8.4(e).** Frequency response curve of Disc Record equalizer.

8·5. AUDIO TONE CONTROL USING OPERATIONAL AMPLIFIER

A most popular tone control for high quality audio system is depicted in the Fig. 8.5. It is normally placed between the input stage and the mixer and line-output stages. The input signal strength in the range of 10 to 30 mV, which is well above the noise level. It is having unity gain because adequate gain can be obtained from the mixer and output line stages. It has four separate tone controls: bass cut, bas boost, treble cut, and treble boost. In this circuit, the bass and treble cut

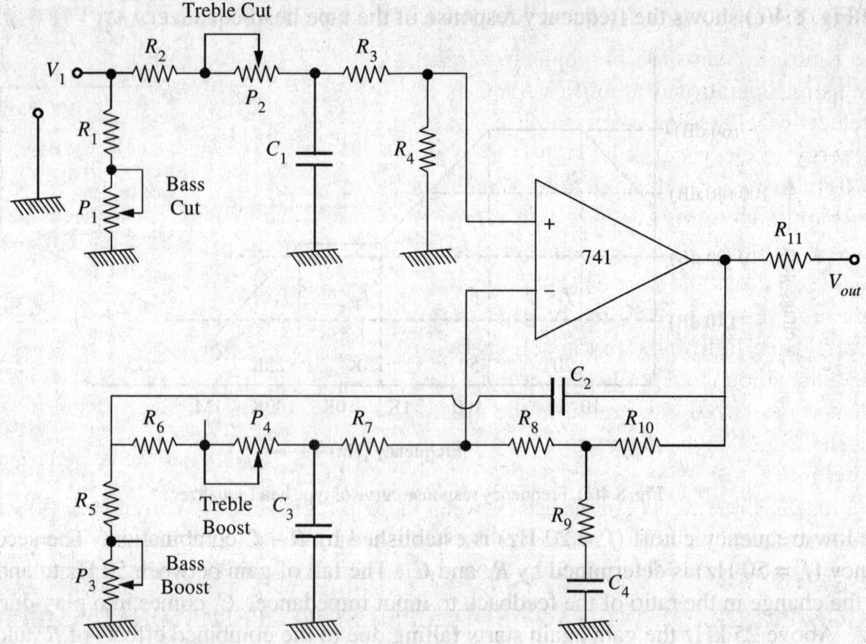

Fig. 8.5. Audio tone control circuit.

and boost are separate, so there is control not only of how much boost or cut, but also the turnover (cut off) frequency can be adjusted. It boosts only the low frequencies below the point at which the speaker falls off.

8·6. OPERATIONAL AMPLIFIER OPERATED PHOTO ELECTRIC RELAY

The Fig. 8.6 shows a operational amplifier operated photo electric relay. PEC is a CdS cell (photo cell). When the photo cell is at low illumination or at dark its resistance is very large. So the output of the operational amplifier is too low to fire the SCR, and hence the relay remains unenergized. But when the photocell is properly illuminated, the operational amplifier output is large enough to overcome the negative bias on the SCR, and the SCR fires. The relay is thus energized.

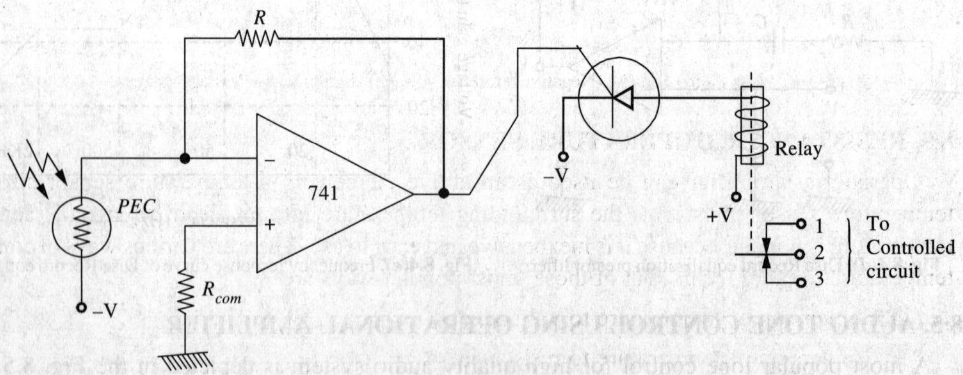

Fig. 8.6. Photoelectric Relay.

8·7. PHOTOVOLTAIC LIGHT SENSORS USING OPERATIONAL AMPLIFIER

The figure 8.7 shows a photoelectric light sensor using operational amplifier. PVC is a photoelectric cell (solar cell) which convert light energy to electrical power. It is used to detect light that passes through holes punched in cards or tapes employed in data-control devices. When the cell is dark, current carrier are unable to cross the barrier separating the N-type and P-type regions of the cell. However, when light falls on the cell carriers get adequate amount of energy to overcome the barrier and pass from one region to the other. When electrons leave one region they leave holes behind.

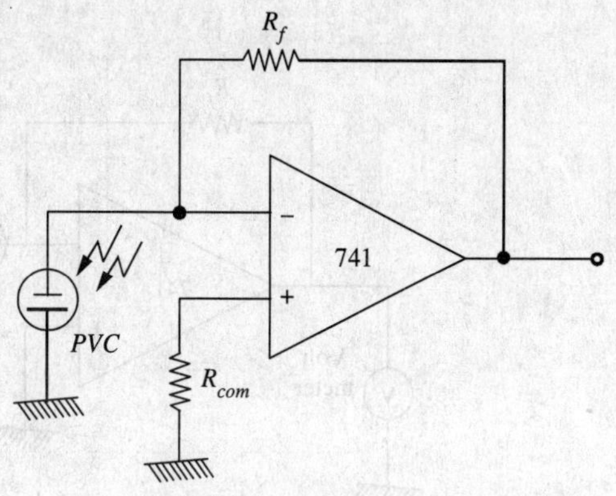

Fig. 8.7. Photovoltaic Light sensor.

As a result a potential is established between the two regions. Now current will flow in a circuit if it is connected to the cell. The flow of current is proportional to the intensity of the light falling on the cell. In this way, light intensity can be determined by measuring the current.

8·8. HIGH-PRECISION VOLTAGE SOURCES USING OPERATIONAL AMPLIFIER

These two circuits find several areas of applications. Fig. 8.8(*a*) and (*b*) are such high precision voltage sources.

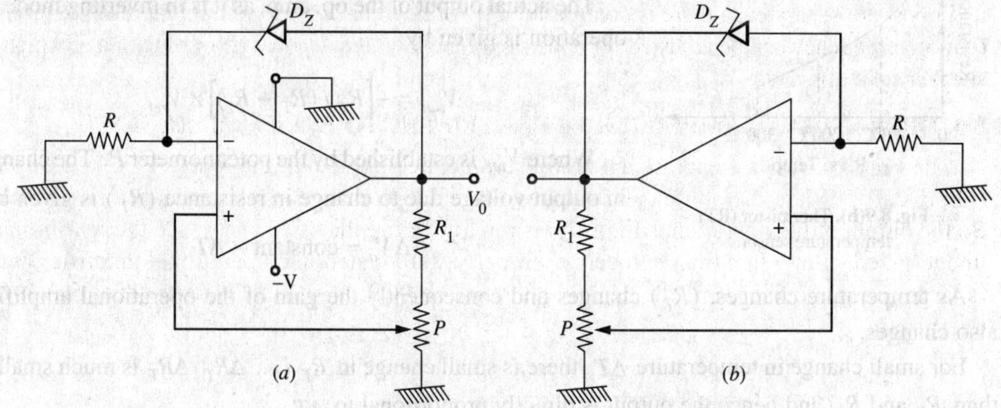

Fig. 8.8(*a*) and (*b*). (Negative reference voltage) High precision voltage sources.

8·9. RESISTANCE TEMPERATURE SENSOR

Operational amplifier can be used as an active element in a temperature sensor circuit. A temperature sensor transforms the surrounding temperature into an electrical signal. Sensing of temperature is popular because it is inexpensive and easy to use. There are various ways of converting temperature to other form. Out of those, most popular ways are

(1) Conversion of temperature to voltage, and

(2) Conversion of temperature to resistance.

Here in the present application, sensor converts temperature changes into resistance changes. The resistance of a semiconductor goes down as temperature raises and it goes up as temperature falls. Thus we can measure a temperature change by measuring a resistance change. But this change of resistance with temperature is non-linear and also supply only very small output signals (only a

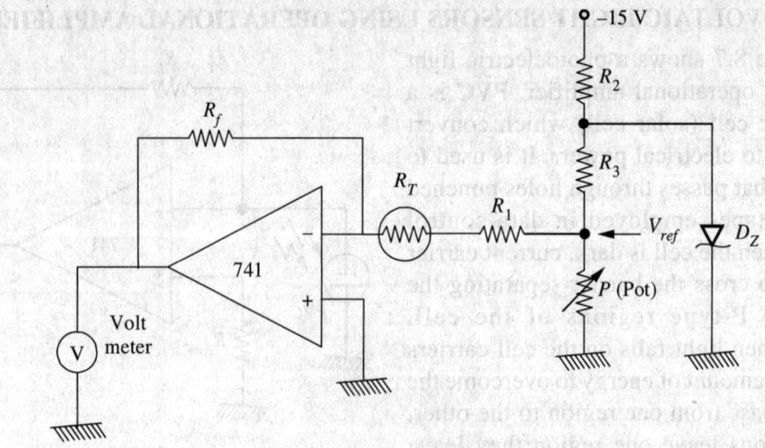

Fig. 8.9(*a*). R.V.S.T. Curve.

few microwatts). Hence these sensors are rarely used by themself. However, operational amplifier converts a change in sensor resistance to an useful output voltage (as shown in the Fig. 8.9(*b*)).

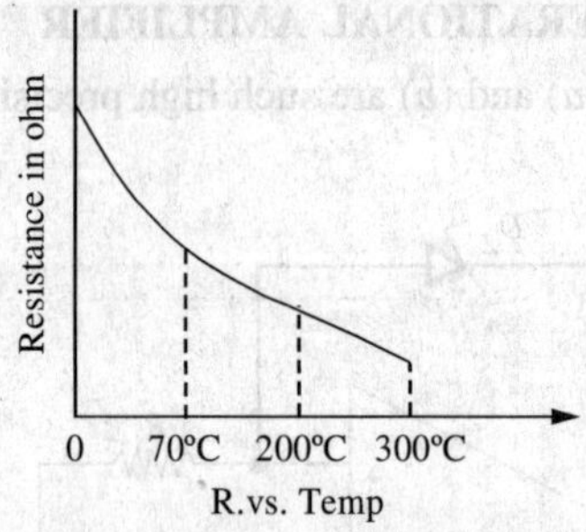

Fig. 8.9(b). Thermistor (RT) temperature sensor.

From the temperature versus resistance curve of a typical thermistor, it is clear that curve is more or less linear over the temperature range of 0°C to 70°C.

The actual output of the op. amp. as it is in inverting mode of operation is given by

$$V_{out} = -\left[R_f / (R_T + R_1)\right] \times V_{ref}$$

Where V_{ref} is established by the potentiometer P. The change in output voltage due to change in resistance (R_T) is given by

$$\Delta V_o = \text{constant} \times \Delta T$$

As temperature changes, (R_T) changes and consequently the gain of the operational amplifier also changes.

For small change in temperature ΔT, there is small change in R_T *i.e.*, $\Delta R_T \cdot \Delta R_T$ is much smaller than R_T and R_1, and hence the output is directly proportional to ΔT.

8.10. SIGNAL RECTIFICATION USING OPERATIONAL AMPLIFIER

Both types of rectifications *i.e.*, half wave and full wave rectification can be done with the circuit as shown in Fig. 8.10. To get full wave rectification the switch S_w is kept open where as for half wave rectification the switch S_w is closed.

The output of the operational amplifier will be an amplified and inverted replica of the negative portion of the input waveform. The output will be clamped to zero during the positive portion of the input as shown in the figure. This is the waveform for the halfwave rectification because only one-half of the input gets through. The circuit can be easily changed to get only the positive portions of the input get through by simply reversing both diodes.

In case of full wave rectification, the entire input signal gets through, but the output will be a series of pulses of one polarity as depicted in the figure.

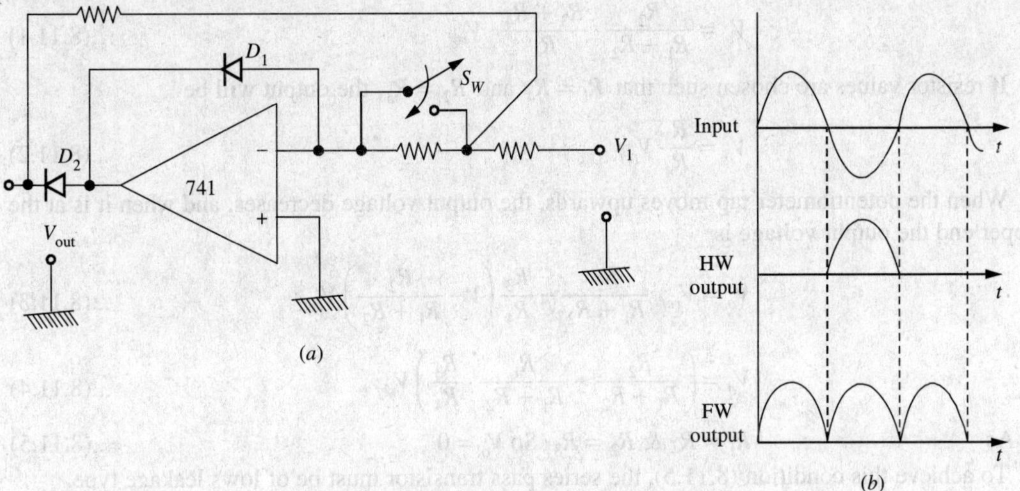

Fig. 8.10. Rectifier circuit using operational amplifier.

8·11. VARIABLE VOLTAGE POWER SUPPLY

The Fig. 8.11 depicts a variable voltage power supply together with a maximum load current capacity of 1 amp. The transistor T_1 provides a constant current source to the zener D_1 which provides the main reference voltage. A part of this reference voltage, determined by R_1 and R_2 is

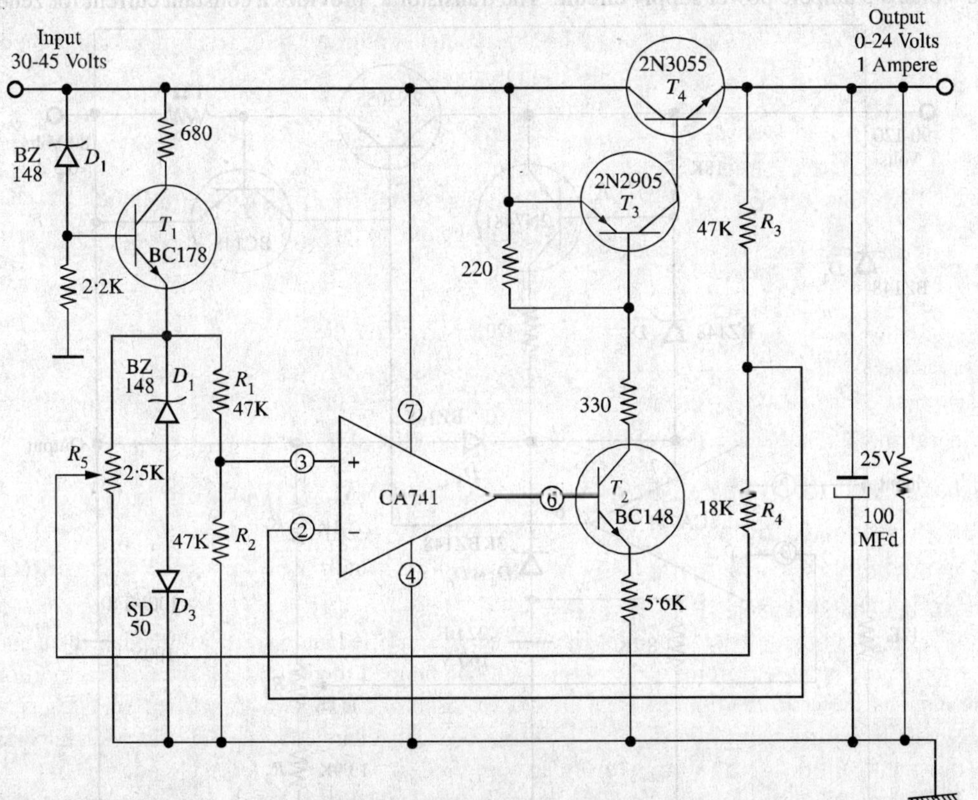

Fig. 8.11. Variable voltage power supply.

feed to the non inverting input of operational amplifier 741. A voltage determined by the resistors combination (R_3, R_4 and R_5) is feed to the inverting terminal of the operational amplifier. For the potentiometer at the lower end of R_5, the output voltage is given by

$$V_o = \frac{R_2}{R_1 + R_2} \cdot \frac{R_3 + R_4}{R_4} \cdot V_{ref} \qquad \text{...(8.11.1)}$$

If resistor values are chosen such that $R_1 = R_4$ and $R_2 = R_3$, the output will be

$$V_o = \frac{R_3}{R_4} V_{ref} \qquad \text{...(8.11.2)}$$

When the potentiometer tap moves upwards, the output voltage decreases, and when it is at the upper end the output voltage is

$$V_o = V_{ref} \frac{R_2}{R_1 + R_2} - \frac{R_3}{R_4}\left(1 - \frac{R_2}{R_1 + R_2}\right) V_{ref} \qquad \text{...(8.11.3)}$$

$$V_o = \left(\frac{R_2}{R_1 + R_2} - \frac{R_1}{R_1 + R_2} \cdot \frac{R_3}{R_4}\right) V_{ref} \qquad \text{...(8.11.4)}$$

As $R_1 = R_4$ & $R_2 = R_3$ So $V_o = 0$ ...(8.11.5)

To achieve this condition (8.11.5), the series pass transistor must be of lows leakage type.

Speciality of this circuit is that it is having the load regulation of 0·1%.

Precaution: Suitable heat sinks have to be provided for T_3 and T_4.

8·12. HIGH VOLTAGE POWER SUPPLY USING OPERATIONAL AMPLIFIER

The adjoining Fig. 8.12 represents a high voltage power supply using operational amplifier. It is a 80 Volts, 0·5 ampere power supply circuit. The transistor T_3 provides a constant current for zeners

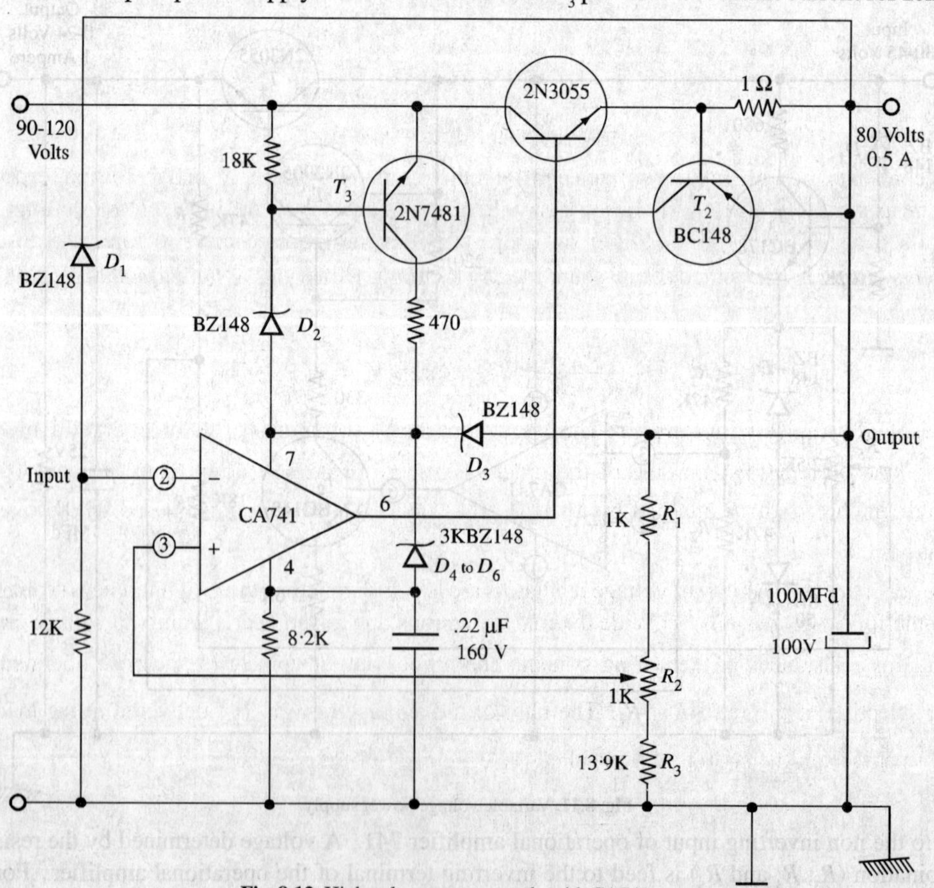

Fig. 8.12. High voltage power supply with CA741.

D_4 to D_6. The operational amplifier is floated above the ground. The zeners D_4 to D_6 provide the supply to the operational amplifier. The output variation is directly fed to inverting input through D_1 and a sample of the output is fed to the non-inverting input through R_1, R_2 and R_3. The series pass transistor T_1 is driven by the operational amplifier. The load current is limited (to 500 mA) by the transistor T_2. The starting excitation of the circuit is provided by the zener D_3.

Series voltage regulator using op-amp:

The adjoining Figure depicts a series voltage regulator using op-amp.

In the figure transistors T_1 and T_2 basically form a Darlington pair. They are also called series pass element.

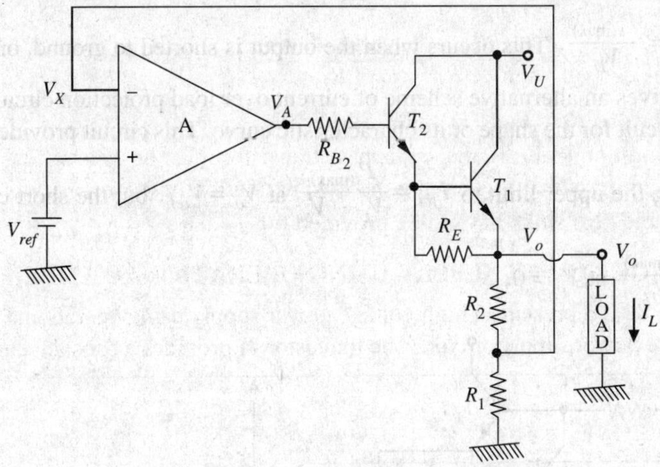

Fig. 8.13. Series voltage regulator.

V_u represents the unregulated voltage and V_o is the regulated voltage. R_1 and R_2 form a feedback path and provides a portion of the output voltage V_o to the inverting input of the op-amp for comparison against V_{ref}. The amplifier (op-amp) provides the required drive to force V_A close to zero. This circuit is also called series-shunt feedback circuit. Under this assumption that $V_A \cong 0$, we can write

$$|V_X| = V_{ref} = \left(\frac{V_o}{R_1 + R_2}\right) \times R_1 \quad \text{or,} \quad V_o = \left(1 + \frac{R_2}{R_1}\right) V_{ref}.$$

Reason of using Darlington pair: The output current of an op-amp is of the order of milliamperes and the load current (I_L) may be of the order of ampere. Hence a current gain of about 10^3 is required which cannot be attained by a single BJT. Hence Darlington pair is used whose overall current gain $\beta = \beta_{T_1} \times \beta_{T_2}$.

The accuracy and stability of voltage regulators are less stringent than those of references (voltages) due to the following reasons. (*i*) Wide thermal excursions due to self heating, and (*ii*) voltage errors due to stray resistances in the wiring system. The proper output voltage (V_o) can be obtained by proper selection of the ratio R_2 / R_1. The ratio of the average power (P_o) delivered to the load to that absorbed from the source (P_i) is called the efficiency of the regulator.

$$\text{Efficiency } (\eta) = \frac{P_o}{P_i} \times 100\% = \frac{V_o \cdot I_L}{V_u \cdot I_L} \times 100\%$$

$$\therefore \ \eta = \frac{V_o}{V_u} \times 100\%$$

Here we considered that the currents drawn by the reference, amplifier, and feedback network are insignificant compared to I_L.

Output overload protection for regulators

Generally special protection circuits are provided with regulator circuits for the protection of the power stage against thermal overload, current overload and second breakdown. Maximum power-rating considerations determine the current overload protection. The power dissipated by the series pass transistor is given by $P_s = (V_U - V_o) \times I_L$. Now for safe operation the relation to be satisfied is $I_o \leq P_{s(\max)} / (V_U - V_o)$. In the figure given below utilizes a brute-force approach to maintain I_L below the limit $I_{sL} = \frac{P_{s(\max)}}{V_U}$. This occurs when the output is shorted to ground, or $V_o = 0$.

The next figure gives an alternative scheme of current over load protection circuit. This is called current fold-back circuit for the shape of its characteristic curve. This circuit provides more efficient protection by raising the upper limit to $I_{fbl} = \frac{P_{s(\max)}}{V_U - V_o}$ at $V_o = V_{ref}$, but the short circuit current is retained at $I_{sL} = \frac{P_{s(\max)}}{V_U}$ at $V_o = 0$.

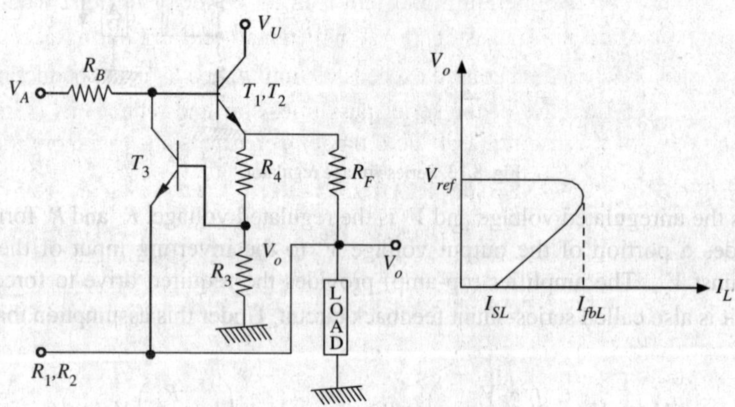

Fig. 8.15. Fold-back protection circuit.

Then we can write: $\frac{1}{R_{se}} \frac{I_{fbL} - I_{SL}}{V_{ref}} = \frac{1}{R_F}$ and

$$\frac{R_4}{R_3} = \frac{R_F}{R_{sc}} - 1$$

Overload, *SOA*, and thermal protection in positive series regulator:

For proper protection, the series pass BJT must operate within its safe operating area (SOA). To assure it, the collector current must be diminished when the collector-emitter voltage rises above a safety level. This may occur when high-voltage transients are present on the unregulated input line. Such a protection is attained by adding a zener diode (as shown in the figure).

The added zener diode remains at cut off but it turns on when V_u rises above a safety level. The current supplied by the zener will make T_3 to conduct and divert away the current from the base of the series pass transistor. The resistor R_4 is used to limit the current through zener, specially when

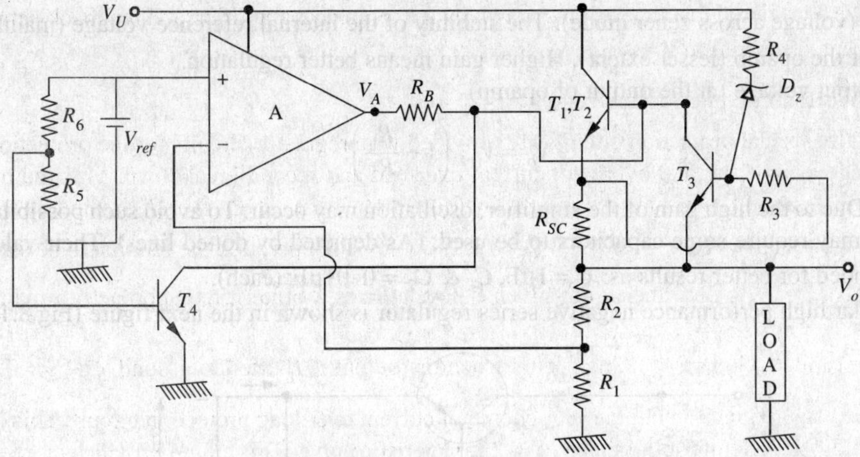

Fig. 8.16. SOA, overload and thermal protection circuit.

a large noise spike comes on the input line. R_3 is used to decouple the base of T_3 from the low-impedance emitter of the power BJT. There is the possibility of permanent damage to $BJTs$ due to excessive self-heating. However, in case of thermal over load, the series-pass transistor is protected by sensing its instantaneous temperature and reducing its collector current. This protection is established by incorporating the transistor T_4. T_4 will remain cut off during acceptable thermal conditions, but to turn on when temperature exceeds its limit, when T_4 is in conduction state, it will divert away current from the base of the series-pass transistor and reduces its (series-pass BJT) conduction to the point of even shutting off until the temperature drops to a more tolerable level.

8·13. HIGH PERFORMANCE SERIES REGULATOR

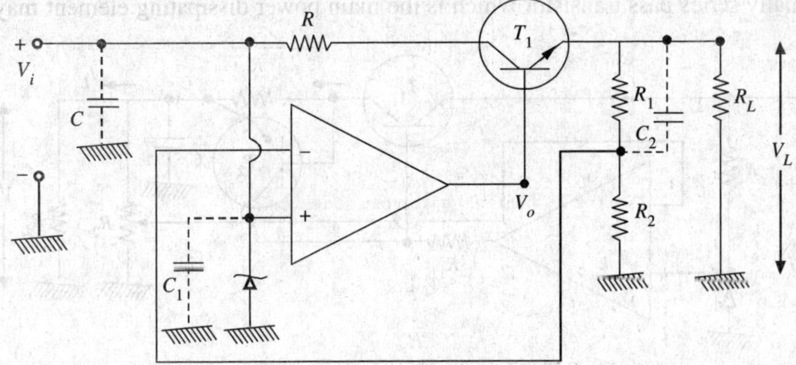

Fig. 8.17. High performance series regulator.

The performance of a series regulator can be improved exceptionally by using an operational amplifier having high gain which senses the changes in the load voltage (V_L) as depicted in the adjoining figure. The zener diode is used as a stable reference to which the sampled voltage across R_2 is compared. The load voltage (V_L) starts decreasing when a load is applied. This causes a subsequent decrease of voltage across R_2. When voltage across R_2 becomes less than V_{ref}, the opamp output becomes positive, turning transistor T_1 on harder. As a result V_{CE} decreases and hence V_L increases to its original level. Thus, the load voltage is held such that voltage across

$R_2 = V_{ref}$ (voltage across zener diode). The stability of the internal reference voltage (mainly) and the gain of the opamp (lesser extent). Higher gain means better regulation.

The output voltage (at the output of opamp)

$$V_o = V_{ref}\left(1 + \frac{R_1}{R_2}\right).$$

Note: Due to the high gain of the amplifier, oscillation may occur. To avoid such possibility, the regulator may require some capacitors to be used. (As depicted by dotted lines). Their values are recommended for better results as: $C = 1\mu F$, C_1 & $C_2 = 0{\cdot}01\mu F$ (each).

A similar high performance negative series regulator is shown in the next figure (Fig.8.18).

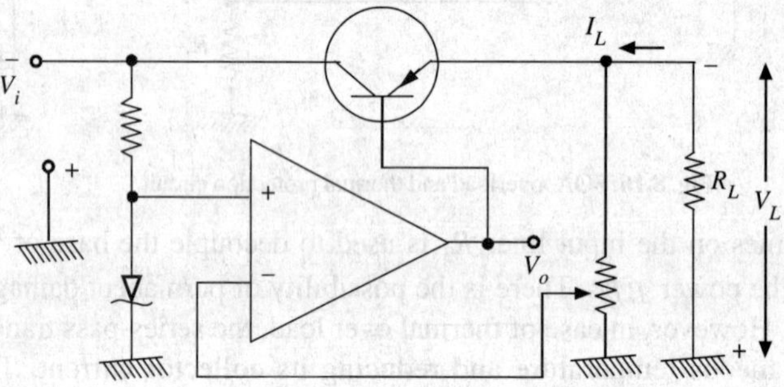

Fig. 8.18. Negative regulator.

Note: Points of differences are: 1. NPN is replaced by PNP series pass transistor. A potentiometer is used here for the adjustment of output voltage.

8·14. OPAMPIN OVERCURRENT PROTECTION CIRCUIT

A short circuit at the output of a power supply can cause the destruction of the circuit. In that condition normally series pass transistor which is the main power dissipating element may exceed

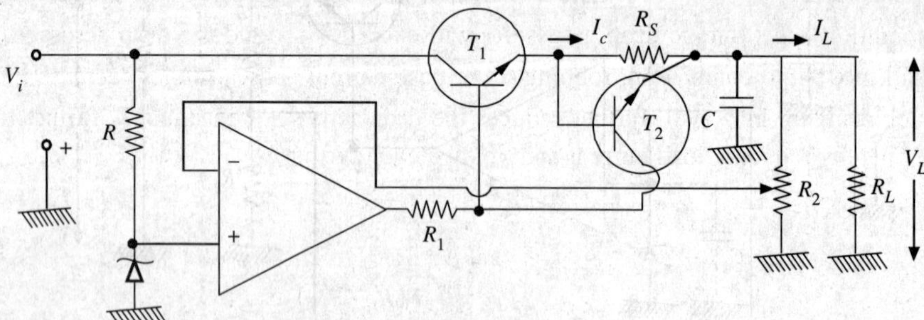

Fig. 8.19. Current limiting in series regulator.

its power dissipating limit. If this overload condition persists for long periods of time, other components in the circuit like rectifier, even the power transformer may be destroyed. To overcome this problem and to prevent the regulator current limiters are used. In the present circuit a current sensing resistor R_s and a second transistor T_2 are incorporated to implement over current protection.

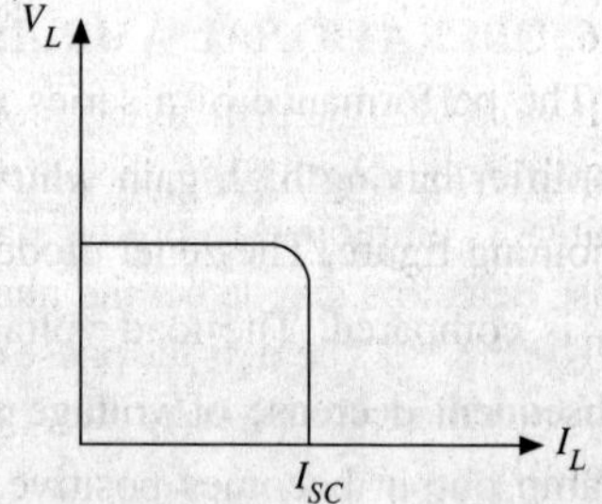

Fig. 8.20. $V_L \cdot V_S \cdot I_L$ curve.

Under normal condition R_s and T_2 are not having any effect on the circuit. But when a short circuit is placed across the output circuit, I_C and I_L both will increase and hence voltage drop across

R_s will also increases. When I_L becomes sufficient to make a drop across R_s equal to 0·7V then T_2 will starts conducting diverting base current from T_1. As a result T_1 will move to cutoff resulting a constant short-circuit current I_{sc} being drawn from the supply.

I_{sc} is given by

$$I_{sc} = \frac{0 \cdot 7V}{R_s}$$

8·15. FOLDBACK CURRENT LIMITING IN A SERIES REGULATOR

By foldback current limiting circuit it is possible to reduce the load current and the load voltage once overload conditions occur. Such a circuit together with its $V - I$ characteristics are represented in the Fig. 8.21(a) & (b).

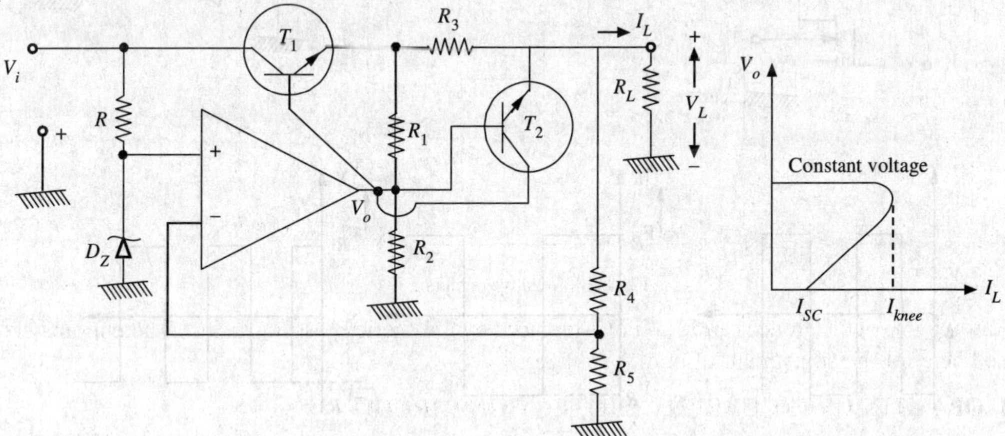

Fig. 8.21. (a) Series regulator with fold back current limiting. **Fig. 8.21.** (b) V-I characteristic

For normal circuit operation, R_1, R_2 and T_2 will have no effect on circuit performance. But during overload conditions, the voltage drop across R_3 will exceed V_{BE2} and the drop across R_1. As a result T_2 will move into conduction, robbing T_1 of base current and causing a decrease in output voltage. Such decrease in v_o will further reduces the drop across R_1, pushing T_2 further towards saturation. Thereby reducing load current and voltage even further.

$$I_{sc} \text{ (short circuit current)} = \frac{0 \cdot 7}{R_3}\left(\frac{R_1 + R_2}{R_2}\right)$$

$$I_{Kne} = \frac{V_o R_1}{R_2 R_3} + \frac{0 \cdot 7(R_1 + R_2)}{R_3 R_2}.$$

8·16. OPERATIONAL AMPLIFIER AS A PHASE DETECTOR

It works on the principle of comparison of the signal against a reference signal having the same frequency. Actually the zero-crosing times of the signals are compared and the difference in the timings is employed to produce a dc voltage which is proportional to the phase difference. Such phase detectors can detect the phase of square-wave signals or signals of arbitray waveform.

The Fig. 8.22 depicts the phase detection of a square-wave signal. The circuit contains an amplifier A_x for getting signal controlled gain polarity and another operational amplifier A_y as a low-pass filter.

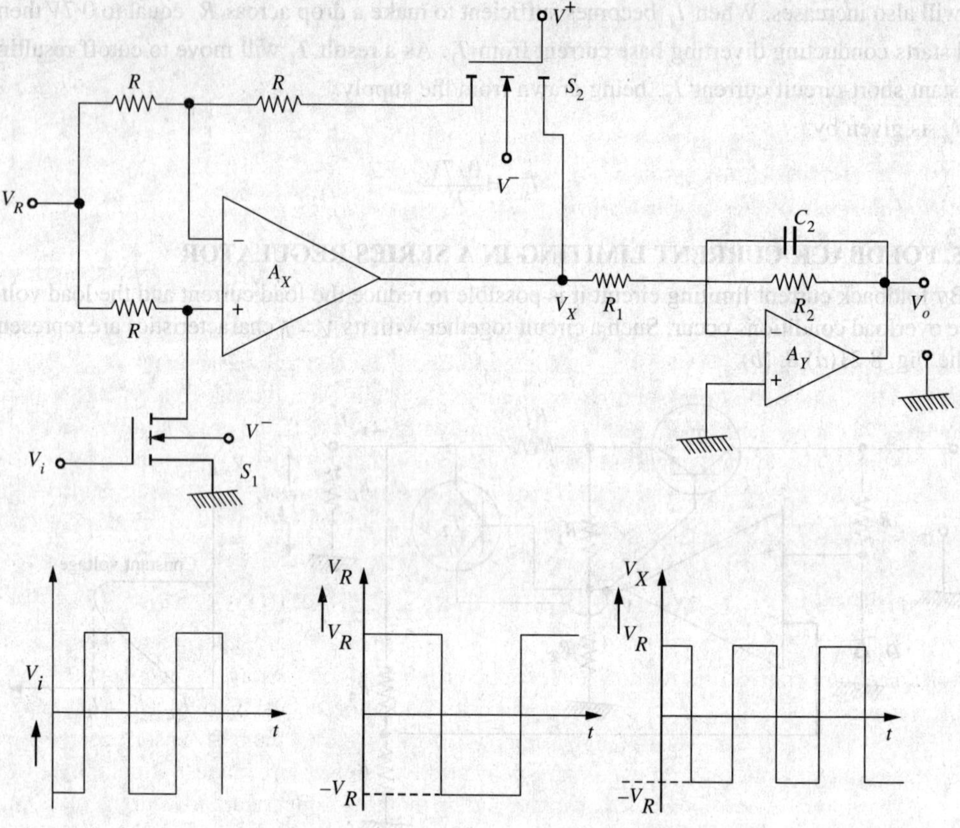

Fig. 8·22. Phase detection circuit with different wave forms.

The signal V_X which is switched gain polarity controlled by A_X is an average signal determined by the time difference between the two input signal zero crossings.

The gain polarity of A_X is reversed by the polarity switching of input signal V_i by changing it from an invertor to a voltage follower. S_1 is on and grounds the inverting input of A_X when V_i is positive. A_X then behaves like a unity-gain inverter to the reference signal V_R. The ON resistance of the switch S_1 produces an input error voltage, which is compensated by connecting a matching ON resistance in the amplifier feed back path. When V_i is negative, S_1 is off, the reference signal reaches the noninverting input of A_X direct. There is no feed back current around A_X as there is no voltage (then) across the R_1 summing resistor. As there is no feedback current, there is no feed back voltage drop. Hence the output of A_X follows the signal V_R. In other words, A_X has been switched to a voltage follower from an inventor to reverse the polarity of the gain it provides to V_R.

Because of this gain polarity switching A_X produces an output signal of nonzero average value from the zero average value signal V_R. When V_i and V_R are in phase, the gain polarity will always be opposite the amplitude polarity of V_R *i.e.*, $V_X = -V_R$. But when V_i and V_R are out of phase, the polarity of the gain provided by A_X will always' be the same as the amplitude polarity of V_R. V_X will equal V_R then. If V_R and V_i differ in phase by 90°, V_X is a square wave of zero average value. Similarly, for other values of phase shift between 0 and 180°, other average values at the output of A_X will be produced. A low pass filter is used to detect and invert this average value. The output of the filter will give a phase related dc output as given below.

$$V_o = \left(1 - \frac{\Delta\phi}{90°}\right)\frac{R_2}{R_1} \cdot V_R \text{ for } 0° \le \Delta\phi \le 180° \qquad ...(8.13.1)$$

Limitation of the circuit

In accuracy to this phase detector response result primarily from

(*i*) The amplitude error or V_R,

(*ii*) The ripple of the low-pass filter, and

(*iii*) The slew-rate limit of A_X.

How to overcome these limitations

In order to reduce the output ripple, a large filter time constant is desirable, but the associated longer settling time must also be considered to avoid excessive measurement times. For lower frequency signals, this ripple-settling compromise is really significant. But for higher frequency signals inaccuracy arises from the slew-rate limiting of A_X. By virtue of this finite slewing time of this amplifier, its output signal is not truely rectangular; so its average value deviates from that anticipated. If the positive and negative slewing times are equal, compensating deviations result. However, at some point slew-rate limiting will prevent complete output swing during short signal periods.

8·17. OPERATIONAL AMPLIFIER ELECTRONIC THERMOMETERS

If electrical measurement of temperature is concerned, we use thermocouples, thermistors, resistance temperature devices and semiconductor junctions as sensors. Semiconductor junction is a low-cost sensor with a linear response and error on the order of 1°C over its useful temperature range of –55 to 125°C in which range semiconductor function is the best sensor choice. However, lower sensing error can be achieved for more restrictive temperature ranges. Bipolar transistors can be used as temperature sensors for absolute and differential temperature measurements.

Measurement of absolute temperature

Fig. 8.23(*a*) represents a circuit for the measurement of absolute temperature with the help of a differential transistor pair biased with unbalanced currents which result in an emitter-base voltage difference. The voltage difference is given by

$$\Delta V_{BE} = \frac{kT}{e} \log_{e}, \frac{I_{b2}}{I_{b1}} \qquad ...(8.14.1)$$

Here *K*/*e* = 0·086mV/K and it is considered that the two transistors are matched. Hence ΔV_{BE} is a linear function of temperature with a sensitivity determined by the ratio of the transistor currents and by physical constants. The purpose of the operational amplifier in the circuit is to establish the current ratio and to provide a buffered output.

The amplifier A provides feed back which forces the voltage between its inputs to zero so that the voltage on R_1 and R_2 are equal such that

$$\Delta V_{BE} = \frac{kT}{e} \log_e \frac{R_{c1}}{R_{c2}} \qquad ...8.14.2$$

This voltage and the scaling voltages are actually amplified by the gain established by the resistance pair R_x and R_y. The output of the amplifier is

$$V_o = \left(1 + \frac{R_y}{R_x}\right)\left(V_s + \frac{kT}{e} \log_e, \frac{R_{c1}}{R_{c2}}\right)$$

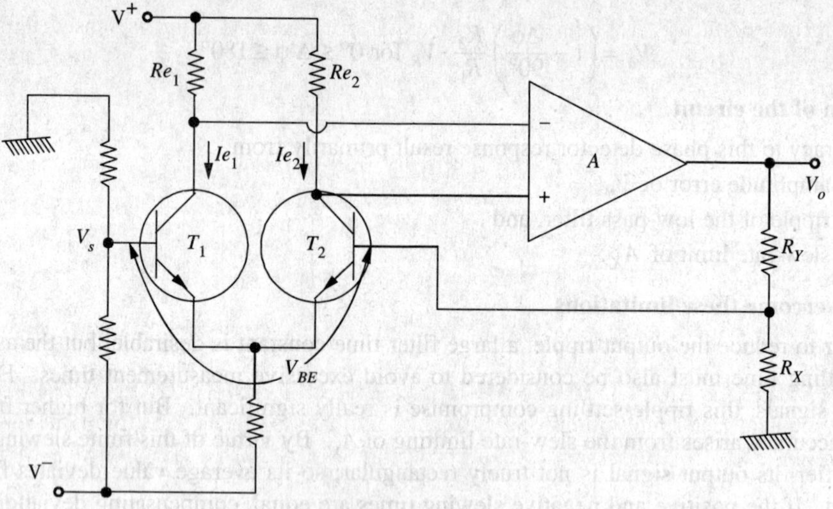

Fig. 8.23(*a*). Circuit for absolute temperature measurement.

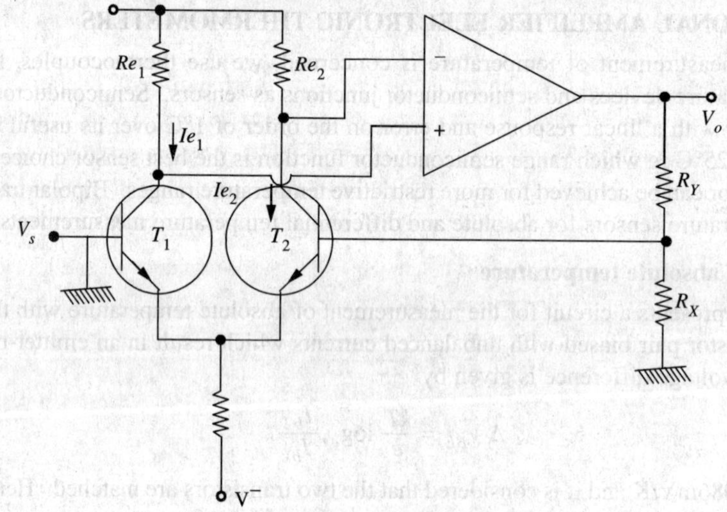

Fig. 8.23(*b*). Circuit for the measurement of difference.

The scaling voltage V_s actually sets zero output corresponding to 0°F or 0°C and expressed as

$$V_s = -\frac{kT}{e} \log_e, \frac{R_{c1}}{R_{c2}} \qquad \text{...(8.14.3)}$$

Parameters which control accuracy

Accuracy is primarily determined by the followings:

(1) transistor matching and the ratio control of the resistor values.

(2) amplifier's input offset voltage drift.

(3) large transistor current ratios (which can induce non linearity).

(b) Application of operational amplifier for the measurement of temperature difference:

In this arrangement a zero scaling bias is not needed but equal transistor currents are used Fig. 8.23(*b*). Two transistors one used to sense the temperatures T_1 and T_2 at different points.

Assuming one point as a reference, the temperature of a second point is sensed through the approximately linear thermal relation

$$\frac{dV_{BE}}{dT} = \frac{V_{BE} - E_g / e}{T} - \frac{3K}{e} \qquad ...(8.14.4)$$

$$= -2{\cdot}2 \text{ mV/°K for } S_i \text{ transistors}$$

So
$$V_{BE_2} - V_{BE_1} = -(T_2 - T_1) * 2\cdot 2 \text{ mV/° K} \qquad ...(8.14.5)$$

and
$$V_o = 2\cdot 2\left(1 + \frac{R_y}{R_x}\right)(T_1 - T_2) \text{ mV/° K} \qquad ...(8.14.6)$$

Accuracy is affected as we have seen in case of absolute temperature measurement.

8·18. OPERATIONAL AMPLIFIER IN MEDICAL ELECTRONIC MONITORING SYSTEM

In many medical electronic monitoring system operational amplifier are effectively used. One such use (in case of stroke patients) is monitoring the ELECTRO MYO GRAM (EMG) of the muscle.

In human body when a muscle contracts, a very small voltage appears on the surface of the skin covering the muscle. The voltage waveform is called the EMG of the muscle. The strength of EMG signal is usually less than 1mV in amplitude and a differential amplifier with good CMRR is required to amplify it a useful amplitude, in isolation from the relatively noisy electronic environment. Such a function can be suitably done by operational amplifiers.

Fig. 8.24 depicts a schematic diagram for audio EMG monitoring circuit. The input is obtained from the two electrodes taped to the skin over the muscle being examined. The differential amplifier *ckt* gain can be varied adjusting R_X. V_1 acts as a half wave rectifier by amplifying only half section of the output from the operational amplifier. The bias of V_1 is controlled by R_Y. C_1 averages the rectified output of V_1. Hence, the averaged amplified EMG signal controls the base current of V_2. V_2 controlls the charging current of C_2 and hence the oscillation frequency of the UJT (Q_3), which in turn controls the pitch of the tone produced by the speaker.

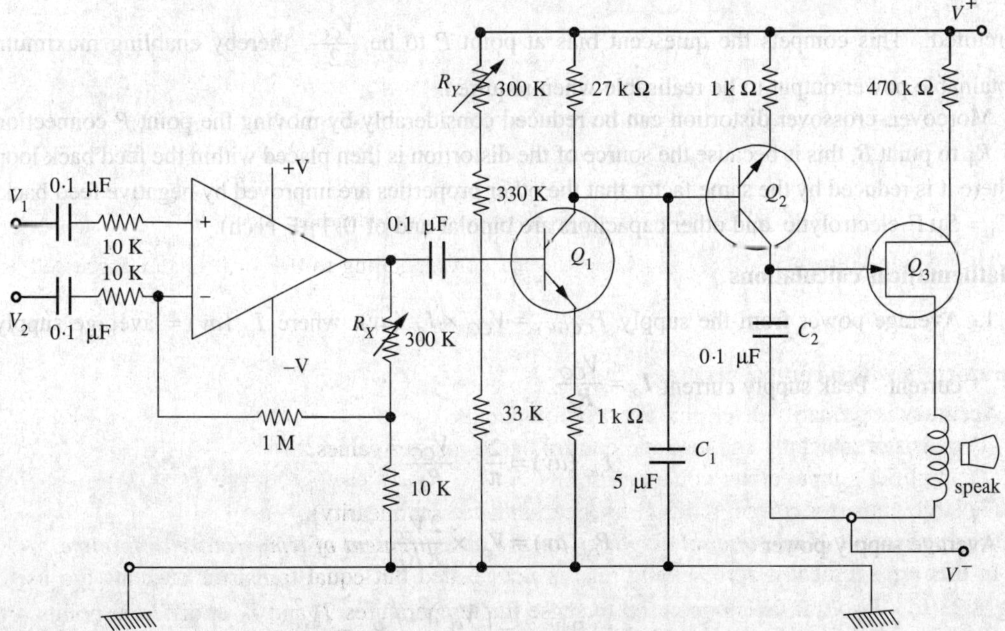

Fig. 8.24. EMG monitoring circuit.

8·19. OPERATIONAL AMPLIFIER AS A POWER AMPLIFIER

Fig. 8.16 represents a power amplifier circuit. hence power capability has been enhanced by the addition of the complementary symmetry output stage composed of T_1 and T_2. When R_1 and R_2 are equal, the quiescent voltage at the inverting terminal of A will be $\frac{V_{CC}}{2}$. Here earthing is done through R_3 via C_2 rather than directly to ground to get the following benefit.

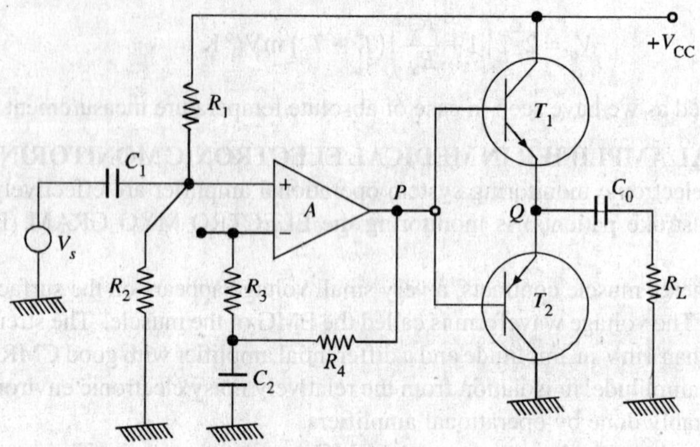

Fig. 8.25. Operational amplifier power amplifier.

(*a*) The gain of the ckt at medium frequencies is $1 + R_4 / R_3$. This lowers in value at low frequencies, as the increasing reactance of C_2 increases the impedance of the R_3 branch of the circuit. This is useful in audio ckts where undesirable signals may be present at much lower frequencies than the desired signal.

(*b*) At dc, the operational amplifier becomes a voltage follower because C_2 becomes open circuited. This compels the quiescent bias at point *P* to be $\frac{V_{CC}}{2}$, thereby enabling maximum obtainable power output to be realisable when required.

Moreover, crossover distortion can be reduced considerably by moving the point *P* connection of R_4 to point *B*, this is because the source of the distortion is then placed within the feed back loop where it is reduced by the same factor that the other properties are improved by negative feed back. ($C_1 = 5\,\mu$F electrolytic and other capacitors are bipolar and of $0{\cdot}1\,\mu$F each).

Mathematical calculations

1. Average power from the supply $P_{CC(ac)} = V_{CC} \times I_{dc}\,(av)$, where $I_{dc}\,(av) =$ average supply current. Peak supply current $I_o = \frac{V_{CC}}{R_L}$

$$I_{dc}\,(av) = \frac{2}{\pi} \cdot \frac{V_{CC}}{R_L}$$

Average supply power $$P_{cc}\,(av) = V_{cc} \times \frac{2\,V_{cc}}{\pi\,R_L}$$

$$P_{o(\max)} = \left(\frac{V_{cc}}{V_2}\right)^2 \Big/ R_L = \frac{V_{cc}^2}{2\,R_L}$$

The peak sinusoidal voltage swing across the load is V_{cc},

Efficiency
$$\eta = \frac{P_{o(\max)}}{P_{cc}\,(av)} = \frac{\dfrac{V_{cc}^2}{2\,R_L}}{\dfrac{2V_{cc}^2}{\pi\,R_L}} = \frac{\pi}{4}$$

$$\eta 9 = 78 \cdot 5\%$$

REVIEW QUESTIONS

1. Why will you find opamp at work everywhere?
2. What will you do to get minimum cross-talk?
3. Explain the functioning of a microphone equalizer.
4. How can a opamp be used to get audio tone control circuit?
5. Draw the circuit diagram of an opamp based rectifier and explain its operation with suitable input output waveform.
6. Why do we use Darlington pair in series voltage regulator using opamp?
7. Explain with circuit diagram a Fold-back protection circuit.
8. Give an application of opamp in medical electronic monitoring system.
9. Show that the efficiency of an opamp based power amplifier is 78.5%.

9

MORE OPERATIONAL AMPLIFIER APPLICATIONS

9·1. Introduction. 9·2. Quadrature Oscillator. 9·3. Wien bridge oscillator. 9·4. Zero crossing detector. 9·5. Phase shift oscillator. 9·6. Wave form generation. 9·7. Sawtooth wave generation using operational amplifier. 9·8. Generation of sine wave from square wave using operational amplifier. 9·9. Schmitt Trigger circuit. 9·10. Applications of operational amplifier as A/D and D/A converts. 9·11. Multiplication of capacitance using operational amplifier. 9·12. Simulation of Inductance using operational amplifier. 9·13. Special operational amplifier circuit for capacitance multiplier.

9·1. INTRODUCTION

In this chapter we will continue to study further more applications of operational amplifiers. Many circuit functions which are generally performed with digital microcircuits can also be performed with operational amplifier circuits. Such circuits can be implemented much more easily and need less space with digital microcircuits. But operational amplifier circuits have a much wider selectable range of circuit parameters. The extreme signal levels are usually fixed at +5V and ground or –12V and ground etc. However operational amplifier circuits provide the possibility of using any upper and lower amplitude which falls within the range ± 20 V. Further, longer time constants are also possible using operational amplifier with high input impedance.

9·2. QUADRATURE OSCILLATOR

The amplifier A_y is an inverting *i.e.,* plus it is an integrator. Thus it introduces a phase shift of –90°–180° = 270° phase shift.

The additional phase shift of 90° is introduced by the feedback network consisting of R_3 & C_3 and the operational amplifier A_x.

Thus we see that the feedback signal is 360° out of phase or totally in phase with the input.

More over if the feedback fraction β is taken such that $A\beta = 1$, then Berkhousen criteria is satisfied and the circuit bursts into oscillation. Where A is the gain of the system.

The 360° phase shift is achieved only at one frequency, f_{OSC} which is called the frequency of oscillation. The mathematical expression for oscillation frequency is given by

$$f_{OSC} = \frac{1}{2\pi RC} = \frac{0\cdot159}{RC}$$

Which is based on the assumption that

$$R_1 C_1 = R_2 C_2 = R_3 C_3 = RC.$$

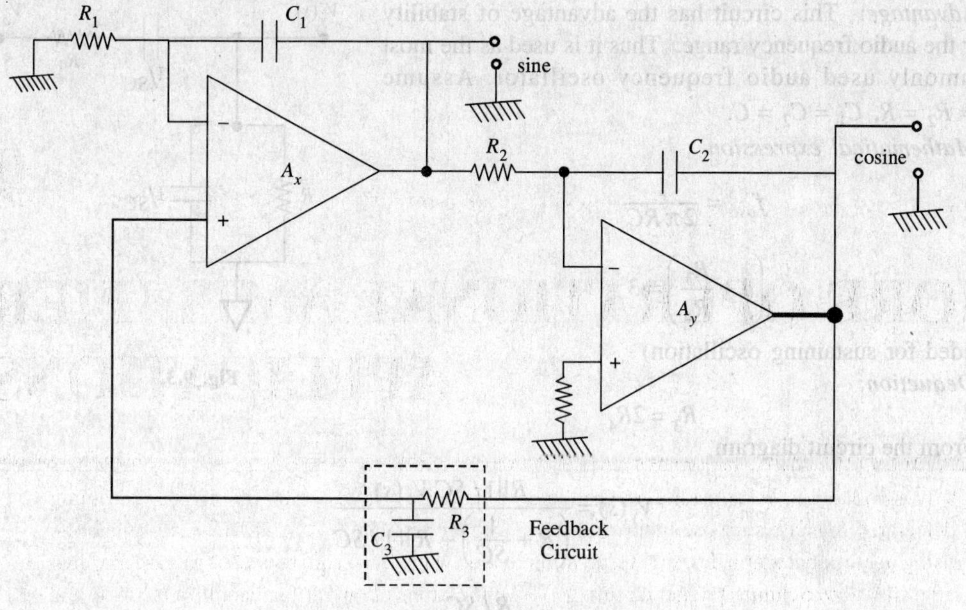

Fig. 9.1.

Problem: Design a quaduture oscillator with oscillation frequency of 50 Hz (use 741 or 747 operational amplifier).

9·3. WIEN BRIDGE OSCILLATOR

The operational amplifier is fitted in a circuit which looks like a Wien bridge.

Two arms of wien bridge form the "feedback-part" of the oscillator & the other two arms act as the amplifier part. Together these two parts are made to satisfy the Berkhousen's criteria and the circuit oscillates.

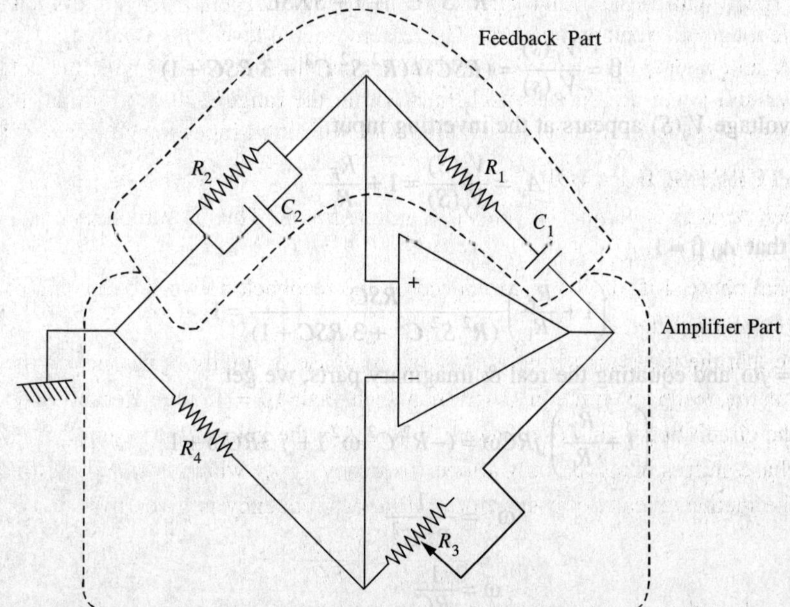

Fig. 9-2.

Advantage: This circuit has the advantage of stability over the audio frequency range. Thus it is used as the most commonly used audio frequency oscillator. Assume $R_1 = R_2 = R$, $C_1 = C_2 = C$.

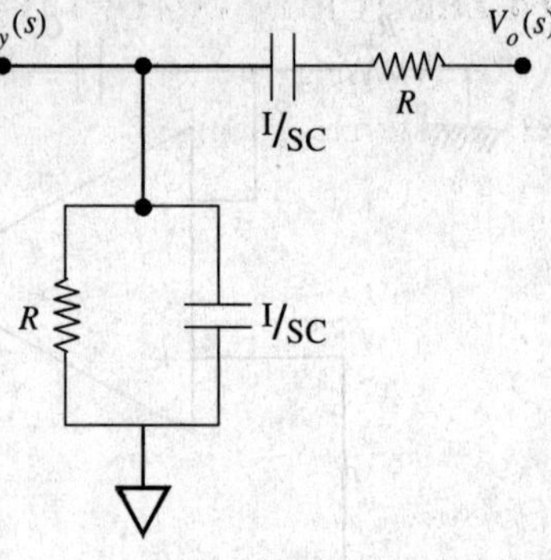

Fig. 9.3.

Mathematical expression

$$f_{osc} = \frac{1}{2\pi RC}$$

$$\left(1 + \frac{R_3}{R_4}\right) = 3$$

(needed for sustaining oscillation)

Deduction:

$$R_3 = 2R_4$$

From the circuit diagram

$$V_y(s) = \frac{R \| 1/SC\, V_o(s)}{\left(R + \frac{1}{SC}\right) + R \| 1/SC}$$

$$= \frac{\frac{R/SC}{R + 1/SC} V_o(s)}{R + 1/SC + \frac{R/SC}{R + 1/SC}}$$

or

$$V_y(s) = \frac{R/SC\, V_o(s)}{R^2 + \left(\frac{1}{SC}\right)^2 + \frac{2R}{SC} + R/SC}$$

$$= \frac{RSC\, V_o(s)}{R^2 S^2 C^2 + 1 + 3RSC}$$

$$\therefore \qquad \beta = \frac{V_f(s)}{V_o(s)} = (RSC)/(R^2 S^2 C^2 + 3RSC + 1) \qquad \text{...(9.3.1)}$$

Also, the voltage $V_y(S)$ appears at the inverting input.

$$A_v = \frac{V_o(S)}{V_y(S)} = 1 + \frac{R_F}{R_1} \qquad \text{...(9.3.2)}$$

We know that $A_v\, \beta = 1$

or

$$\left(1 + \frac{R_F}{R_1}\right) \frac{RSC}{(R^2 S^2 C^2 + 3RSC + 1)} = 1$$

Putting $s = j\omega$ and equating the real & imaginary parts, we get

$$\left(1 + \frac{R_f}{R_1}\right) jRC\omega = (-R^2 C^2 \omega^2) + j\,3RC\omega + 1$$

or

$$\omega^2 = \frac{1}{R^2 C^2}$$

$$\therefore \qquad \omega = \frac{1}{RC}$$

$$f_{osc} = \frac{1}{2\pi RC}$$

9·4. ZERO CROSSING DETECTOR

Zero crossing detector is an example of comparator circuit. Here is a reference voltage which is the reference level of comparison. Now if V_{ref} is set to zero, then the comparison acts as zero crossing detector.

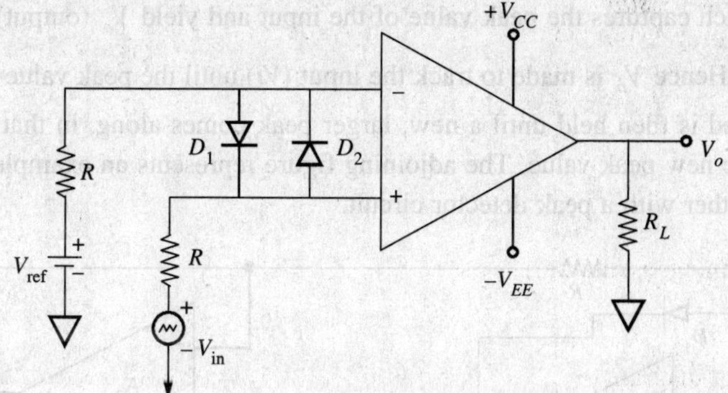

Fig. 9.4.

Importance of zero crossing

A zero crossing detector has a single analog *i/p* and the other *i/p* is grounded and at the *o/p* we get a digital signal with $+ V_{sat}$ as its 1 level & $-V_{sat}$ as logic low.

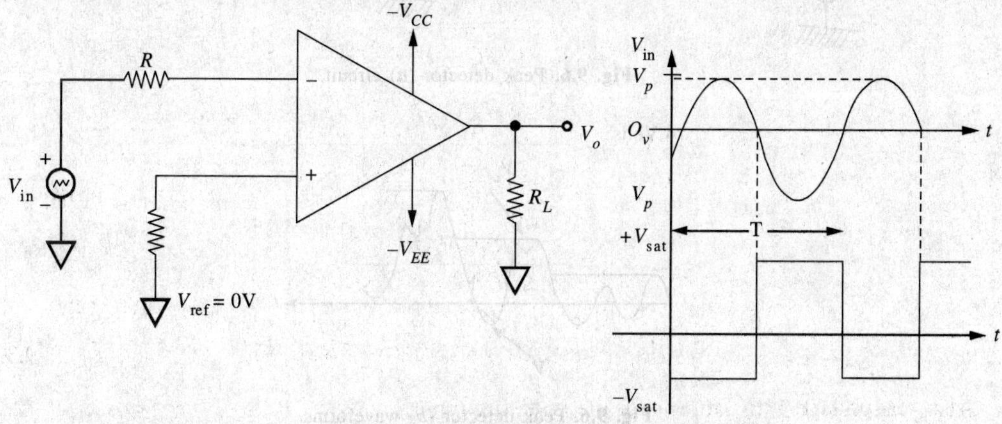

Fig. 9.5(*a*) & (*b*) Input and output waveforms under different conditions.

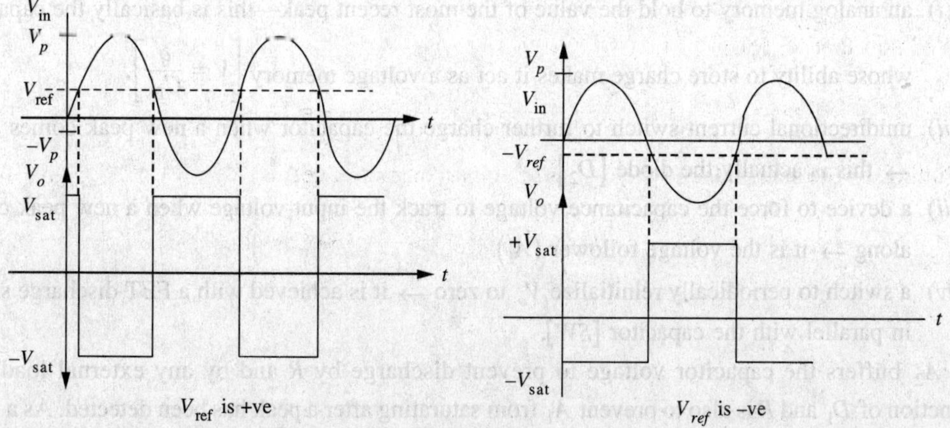

Fig. 9.5(*c*) and (*d*) Input and output waveforms under different conditions.

Operation: Zero crossing detector is amplifier without any type of feedback. Thus even a small *i/p* voltage swing appears at the *o/p* as a swing from $-V_{sat}$ to $+V_{sat}$.

Peak detector

A circuit which captures the peak value of the input and yield V_o (output) = peak value of the input $\left(V_{i(peak)}\right)$. Hence V_o is made to track the input (*Vi*) until the peak value is reached. The peak value so obtained is then held until a new, larger peak comes along, in that case the circuit will update V_o to the new peak value. The adjoining figure represents an example of input and output waveforms together with a peak detector circuit.

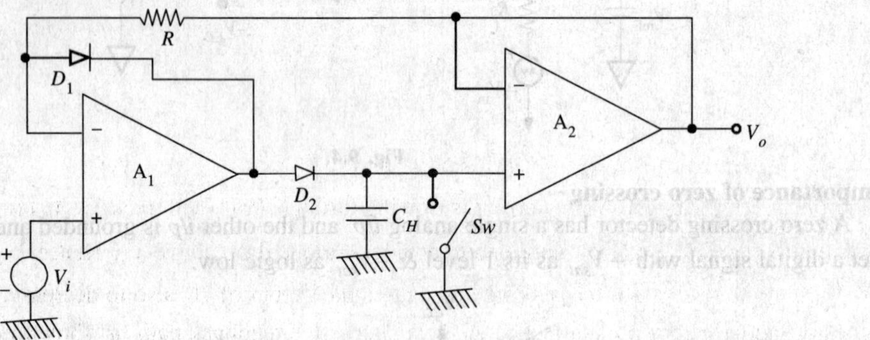

Fig. 9.6. Peak detector (*a*) circuit.

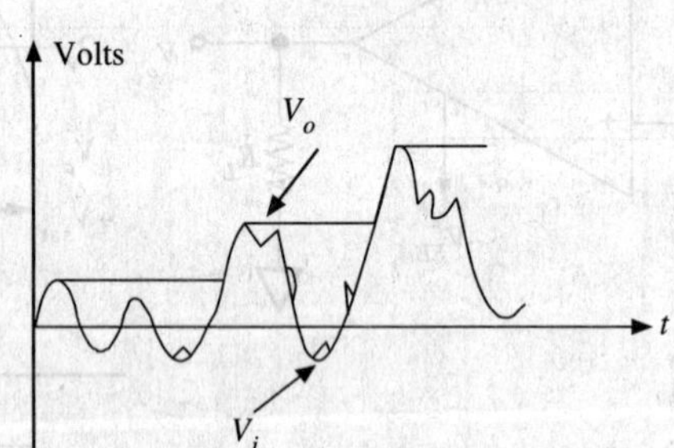

Fig. 9.6. Peak detector (*b*) waveforms.

From the above figure it appears that there are four blocks having distinct separate activities.

(*i*) an analog memory to hold the value of the most recent peak—this is basically the capacitor, whose ability to store charge makes it act as a voltage memory $\left[V = \dfrac{q}{C_H}\right]$.

(*ii*) unidirectional current switch to further charge the capacitor when a new peak comes along $\rightarrow$ this is actually the diode $[D_2]$.

(*iii*) a device to force the capacitance voltage to track the input voltage when a new peak comes along $\rightarrow$ it is the voltage follower (A_1).

(*iv*) a switch to periodically reinitialize V_o to zero $\rightarrow$ it is achieved with a FET discharge switch in parallel with the capacitor $[SW]$.

A_2 buffers the capacitor voltage to prevent discharge by R and by any external load. The function of D_1 and R is also to prevent A_1 from saturating after a peak has been detected. As a result they $(R \& D_1)$ speed up recovery when a new peak comes along. The circuits works in the following way: when a new peak comes, A_1 swings its output V_i positive, making D_1 off and D_2 on as observed from the figure 9.6(*c*). A_1 utilizes the feedback path $D_2 - OA_2 - R$ to maintain a virtual

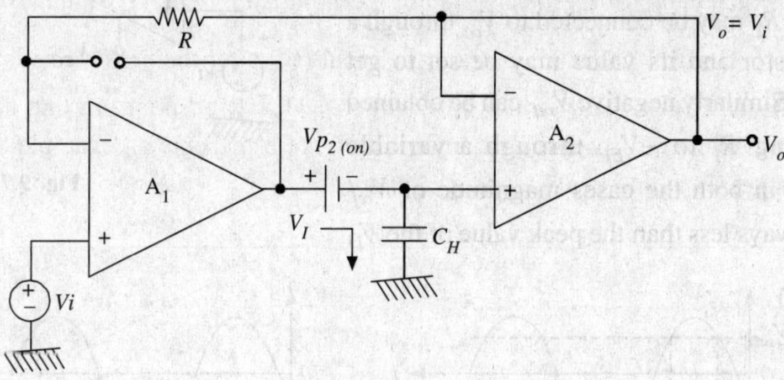

Fig. 9.6 (*c*).

short between its inputs. As no current is flowing through *R*, V_o will track V_i. A_1 provides necessary current to charge C_H via D_2 and its output rides a diode drop above V_o. Hence $V_1 = V_o + V_{D2(\text{on})}$.

V_i starts to decrease after peaking and causes the output of A_1 also to decrease. As a result D_2 goes off and D_1 goes on, and hence A_1 gets alternative feedback path (as shown in Figure 9.6(*d*).

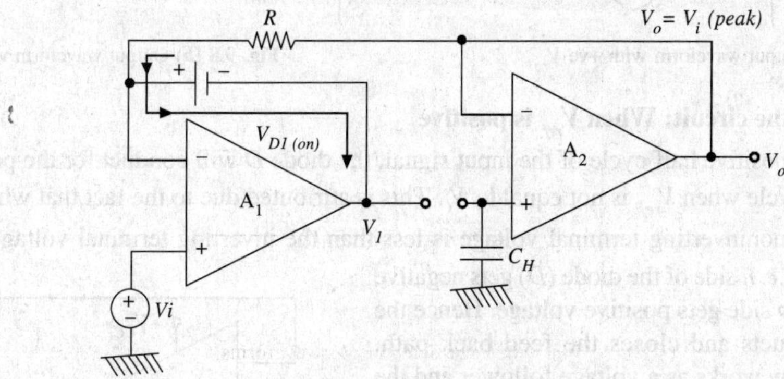

Fig. 9.6 (*d*).

By the concept of virtual short, the output of A_1 rides a diode drop below V_i. Hence we can write $V_1 = V_i - V_{D1(\text{on})}$. [This is called hold mode]. Then the capacitor voltage remains constant and *R* provides a current path for D_1. It is clear from the above circuit that if the direction of the diodes is just reversed we can use it for the detection of negative peak. The speed of the peak detector is limited by the slew rates of A_1 and A_2 as well as the maximum rate at which A_1 can charge or discharge C_H.

Clipper and clamper circuit using opamps

Clipping and clamping circuits are waveshaping circuit which are commonly used in digital computers and communications such as TV and FM receivers. A clipping circuit basically clips off a portion of the input waveform and a clamper circuits does not deform the shape of the input waveform but shift the waveform below or above a reference level which may be zero or any positive or negative value.

Clipping circuit

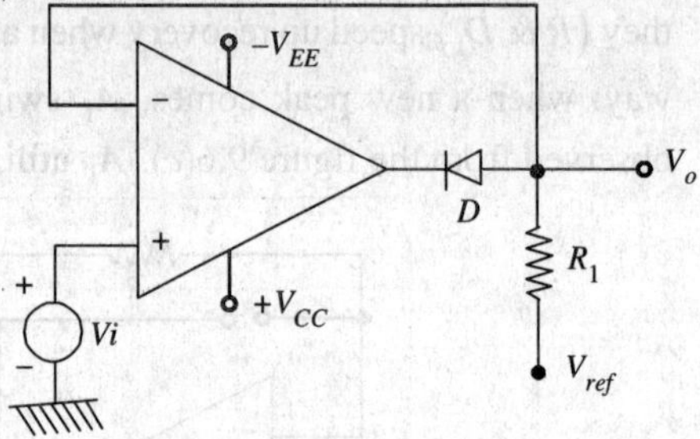

Fig. 9.7.

The adjoining Fig. 9.7 & 9.8(*a*) & (*b*) gives a positive clipper circuit.

Here V_{ref} may be separately supplied or for positive V_{ref} R_1 may be connected to V_{cc} through a variable resistor and its value may be set to get desired V_{ref}. Similarly negative V_{ref} can be obtained by connecting R_1 to $-V_{EE}$ through a variable resistor. But in both the cases magnitude of V_{ref} should be always less than the peak value of the V_i.

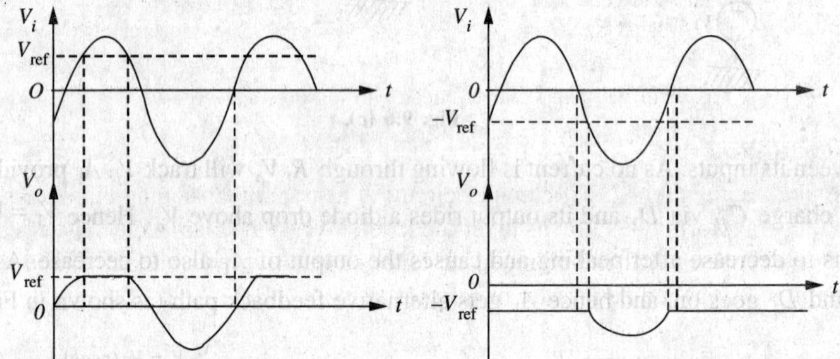

Fig. 9.8 (*a*) Output waveform with +ve V_{ref}. **Fig. 9.8** (*b*) Output waveform with –ve V_{ref}

Operation of the circuit: When V_{ref} is positive

During the positive half cycle of the input signal, the diode *D* will conduct for the portion of the positive half cycle when V_{ref} is not equal to V_i. This is attributed due to the fact that when V_i is less than V_{ref}, the noninverting terminal voltage is less than the inverting terminal voltage and hence opamp output *i.e. n* side of the diode (*D*) gets negative voltage while *p* side gets positive voltage. Hence the diode *D* conducts and closes the feed back path. The opamp now works as a voltage follower and the output will be the same as input so long $V_i \neq V_{ref}$. However, when V_i is higher than V_{ref} the noninverting terminal voltage is now higher than that of the inverting terminal and hence the *n* side of the diode *D* will get positive voltage which is more than the positive voltage existing at its *p* side. As a result the diode *D* stops conducting and the output voltage (V_o)

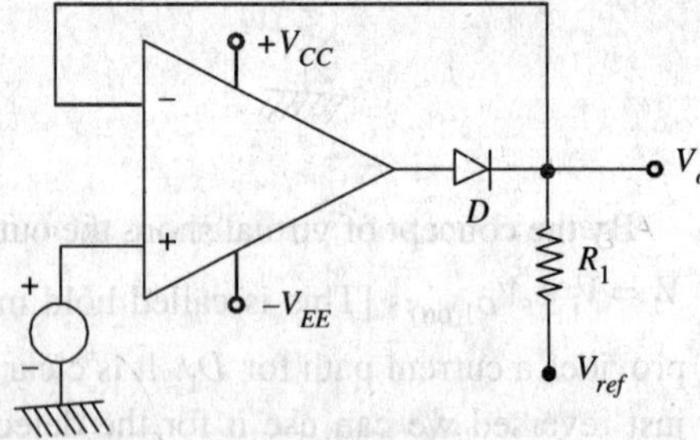

Fig. 9.9(*a*).

becomes equal to V_{ref}. This circuit can be used as a half wave rectifier also. In that case the V_{ref} is to be made positive half cycles will be clipped off to get negative dc voltage. We can get positive dc voltage also in that case the polarity of the diode *D* is to be reversed and then all negative half cycles will be clipped off.

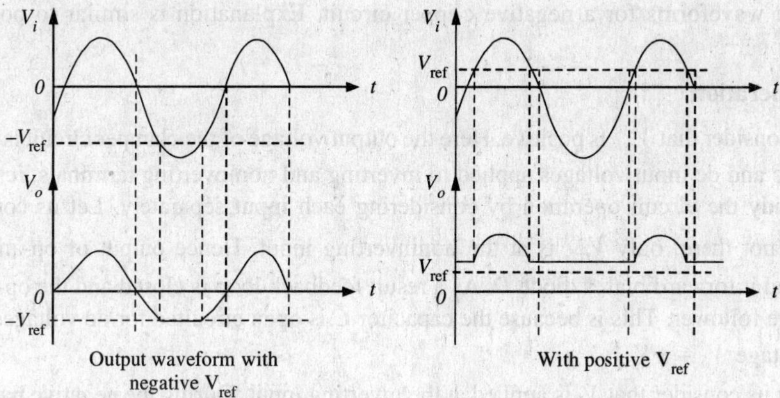

Fig. 9.9(*b*). Negative clipper circuit with positive and negative V_{ref}.

CLAMPER CIRCUIT

We have already mentioned that clamper circuit is also a wave shaping circuit but it does not distort the input waveform but shifts its level (dc level). When the clamped dc level is positive it is called positive clamper but if the clamped dc level is negative it is called negative clamper. A clamper circuit is also called dc inserter or restorer.

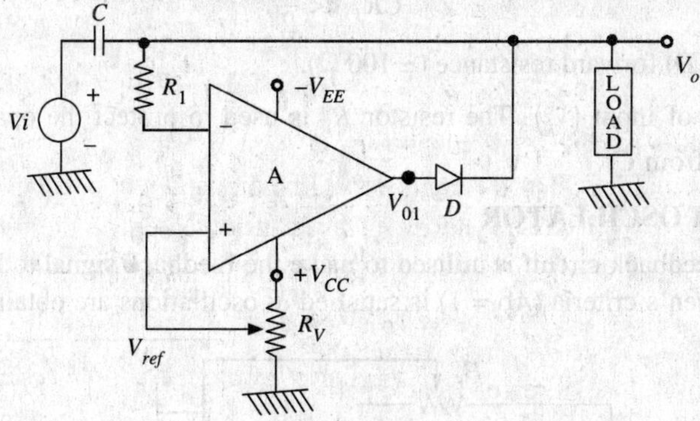

Fig. 9.10(*a*).

A generalised clamper circuit is shown in the Fig. 9.10 (*a,b,c*).

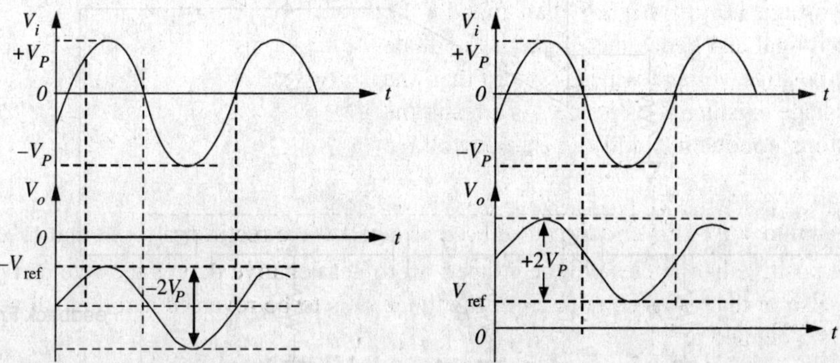

Fig. 9.10(*b*). V_{ref} is negative. **Fig. 9.10(*c*)** V_{ref} is positive.

Similarly explanation can be given when V_{ref} is kept negative. The Fig. 9.9(*a*) & (*b*) gives the circuit and waveforms for a negative clipper circuit. Explanation is similar to positive clipper circuit.

Circuit Operation

Let us consider that V_{ref} is positive. Here the output voltage of the clamper circuit is the combined effect of ac and dc input voltages applied to inverting and noninverting terminals, respectively. So we can study the circuit operation by considering each input separately. Let us consider that ac voltage is not there, only V_{ref} is at the noninverting input. Hence output of op-amp (*A*) V_{o1} is positive and it forward biases diode *D*. As a result feedback loop is closed and the op-amp operates as a voltage follower. This is because the capacitor *C* is open circuited for dc voltages. So the final output voltage $V_o = +V_{ref}$.

Now let us consider that V_i is applied at the inverting input. During the negative half cycle of the input $V_i\,(ac)$, the diode *D* conducts and the capacitor *C* is charged to the negative peak value of V_p. But, during the positive half-cycle of V_i, the diode D_1 is reversed biased; hence the voltage V_p across the capacitor established during the negative half cycle is retained. As this voltage V_p is in series with the positive peak Voltage V_p, the output voltage $V_o = 2\,V_p$. Thus the total output is V_{ref} plus $2\,V_p$ (just like superposition principle), hence the negative peak $2\,V_p$ is at V_{ref} (as shown in Fig. 9.10(*c*)). For precision clamping, the following condition is to be satisfied.

$$CR_f << \frac{T}{2}.$$

where R_f = diode (*D*) forward resistance ($\simeq 100\ \Omega$).

T = time period of input (V_i). The resistor R_1 is used to protect the opamp against excessive discharge currents from *C*.

9·5. PHASE SHIFT OSCILLATOR

Here also, the feedback circuit is utilised to make the feedback signal to be in phase with the *i/p* so that Berkhousen's criteria (Aβ = 1) is satisfied & oscillations are obtained.

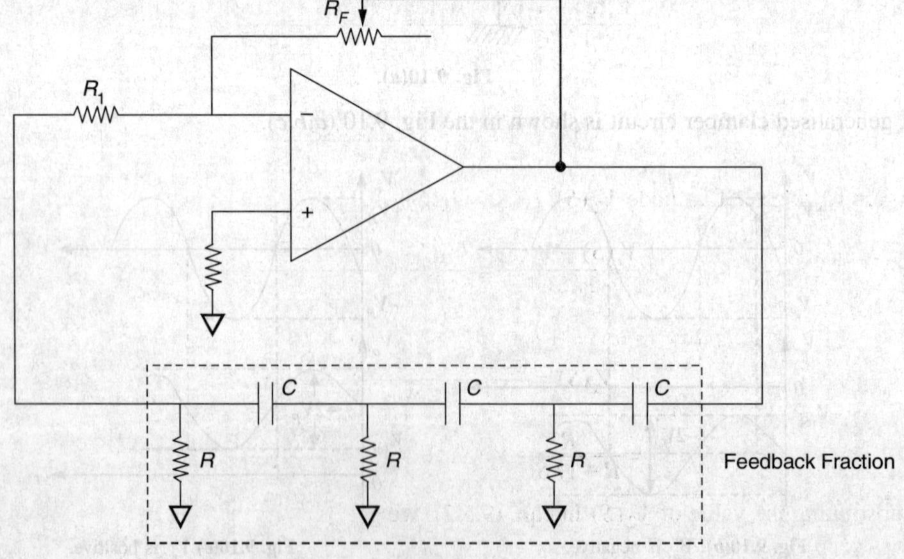

Fig. 9.11.

The potentiometer in place of R_F is provided so that it can be adjusted to get a perfectly distortionless *o/p*.

From the figure it is seen that the operational amplifier is used in the inverting mode. hence, any signal that appears at the inverting terminal is shifted by 180° at the output. An additional 180° phase shift required for sustained oscillation is obtained from the cascaded *RC* networks. Hence the total phase shift around the loop is 360°(0°). This condition is satisfied only at a particular frequency which is called the frequency of oscillation and is expressed as

$$f_{osc} = \frac{1}{2\pi\sqrt{6}\,RC} = \frac{0{\cdot}065}{RC}$$

The minimum value of the gain is 29 *i.e.*, $\left|\frac{R_f}{R_1}\right| = 29.$

Derivation of formula for oscillation frequency

$$f_{osc} = \frac{1}{2\,\pi\sqrt{6}\,RC}$$

First consider the feedback ckt consisting of *RC* sections of the phase shift oscillator. For simplicity we use the Laplace transform again. Thus the ckt is represented in the *S* domain as shown in the figure below. Let us consider to determine $\frac{V_f(S)}{V_o(S)}$ for the circuit.

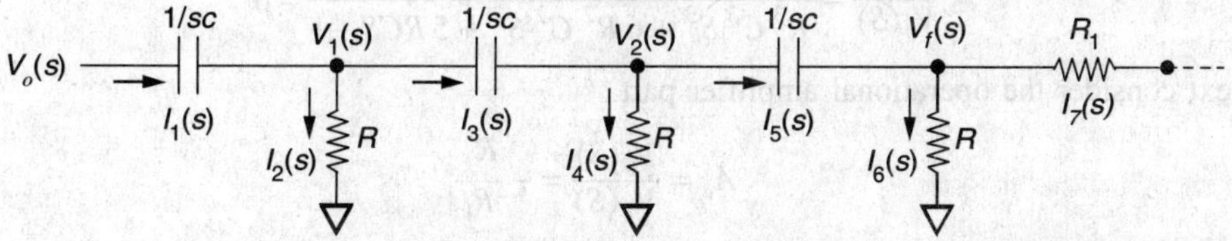

Fig. 9.12.

Writing KCL at node $V_1(S)$, we get $I_1(S) = I_2(S) + I_3(S)$

$$\frac{V_o(S) - V_1(S)}{1/SC} = \frac{V_1(S)}{R} + \frac{V_1(S) - V_2(S)}{\frac{1}{SC}}$$

$$V_1(S) - \frac{[V_o(S) + V_2(S)]\,RCS}{2\,RCS + 1} \qquad \text{...(9.5.1)}$$

Again writing KCL at node $V_2(S)$, $I_3(S) = I_4(S) + I_5(S)$

$$\frac{V_1(S) - V_2(S)}{1/SC} = \frac{V_2(S)}{R} + \frac{V_2(S) - V_f(S)}{\frac{1}{SC}}$$

$$V_1(S) = \frac{(2RCS+1)/V_2(S)}{RCS} - V_f(S) \qquad \text{...(9.5.2)}$$

$$V_f(S) = \frac{R}{R + 1/SC}\,V_2(S) \qquad V_2(S) = \frac{(RSC+1)}{RCS}\,V_f(S) \qquad \text{...(9.5.3)}$$

Substituting the value of $V_2(S)$ in eqn. (9.5.2) we get

$$V_1(S) = \frac{(2\,RCS+1)\,(RCS+1)\,V_f(S)}{(RCS)\,(RCS)} - V_f(S) \qquad ...(9.5.4)$$

Substituting the value of $V_2(S)$ in eqn. (9.5.1) we get

$$V_1(S) = \frac{(RCS)\,V_o(S)}{(2\,RCS+1)\,RCS} + \frac{(RCS+1)\,V_f(S)}{(2\,RCS+1)\,RCS} \qquad ...(9.5.5)$$

Equating (9.5.4) & (9.5.5) and simplifying for $V_f(S)/V_o(S)$, we get

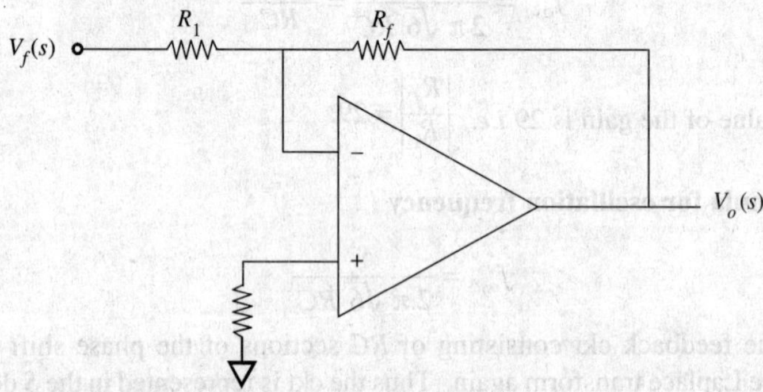

Fig. 9.13.

$$\frac{V_f(S)}{V_o(S)} = \frac{R^3\,C^3\,S^3}{R^3\,C^3\,S^3 + 6\,R^2\,C^2\,S^2 + 5\,RCS + 1} = \beta \qquad ...(9.5.6)$$

Next consider the operational amplifier part.

$$A_v = \frac{V_o(S)}{V_f(S)} = -\frac{R_f}{R_1} \qquad ...(9.5.7)$$

For an oscillator $A_v\,\beta = 1$ using eqn. (9.5.6) and (9.5.7) we get

$$= \frac{R_f}{R_1} \cdot \frac{R^3\,C^3\,S^3}{R^3\,C^3\,S^3 + 6\,R^2\,C^2\,S^2 + 5\,RCS + 1} = 1$$

Substituting $s = j\omega$ and equating real and imaginary part, respectively, we get

$$-\frac{R_f}{R_1}\left(-i\,R^3\,C^3\,\omega^3\right) = \left(-i\,R^3\,C^3\,\omega^3\right) - \left(6\,R^2\,C^2\,\omega^2 + i\,5\,RC\omega\right) + 1$$

$$0 = -6\,R^2\,C^2\,\omega^2 + 1$$

$$\therefore \qquad f_{osc} = \frac{1}{2\pi\sqrt{6}\,RC}$$

9·6. WAVE FORM GENERATION

(*a*) Triangular and square waveforms generation

Explanation: Let us consider that the voltage across the capacitor C is zero at the moment when the dc supply voltages V_{CC} and $-V_{EE}$ are applied. So the voltage at the inverting terminal is zero at t = 0. But the voltage at the non inverting terminal (V_N) is very small but finite which is determinal by the output offset voltage and values of R_1 and R_2 resistors.

$\therefore\ V_N$ = the differential input voltage

V_N will start to drive the operational amplifier into saturation. If the output offset is positive V_N is also positive. As the capacitor acts as a short circuit, V_N drives the output of the operational amplifier (A_1) into its positive saturation $(+V_{sat})$. The capacitor C then starts charging through resistor R towards $+V_{sat}$. But when the voltage V_C across the capacitor C is slightly more positive than V_N, the output of the operational amplifier is compelled to switch to a negative saturation, $-V_{sat}$. Under that condition V_N also becomes negative.

Hence $$V_N = \frac{R_1}{R_1 + R_2}(-V_{sat}) \qquad ...(9.6.1)$$

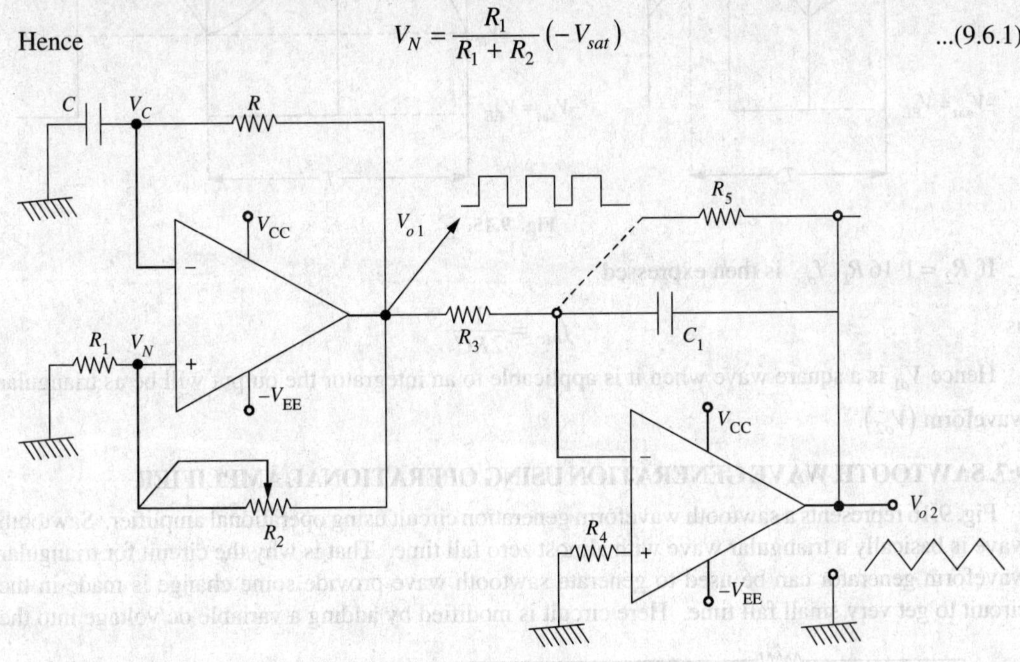

Fig. 9.14.

As differential voltage = $V_N - V_C$ is negative, which forces the operational amplifier into negative saturation and the operational amplifier output will remain in the negative saturation until capacitor C discharges and then recharges to a negative voltage slightly higher than $-V_N$. When the capacitor voltage V_C is more negative than $-V_N$, the differential voltage becomes positive which drives the output of the operational amplifier (A_1) back to $+V_{sat}$. This cycle is repeated. When the operational amplifier output is $+V_{sat}$, V_N is then

$$V_N = \frac{R_1}{R_1 + R_2}(+V_{sat}) \qquad ...(9.6.2)$$

The output wave form is thus having the time period

$$T = 2RC \ln\left(\frac{2R_1 + R_2}{R_2}\right) \qquad ...(9.6.3)$$

The frequency of the square (V_{o1}) waveform is thus given by

$$f_{osc} = \frac{1}{2RC \ln\left[(2R_1 + R_2)/R_2\right]} \qquad ...(9.6.4)$$

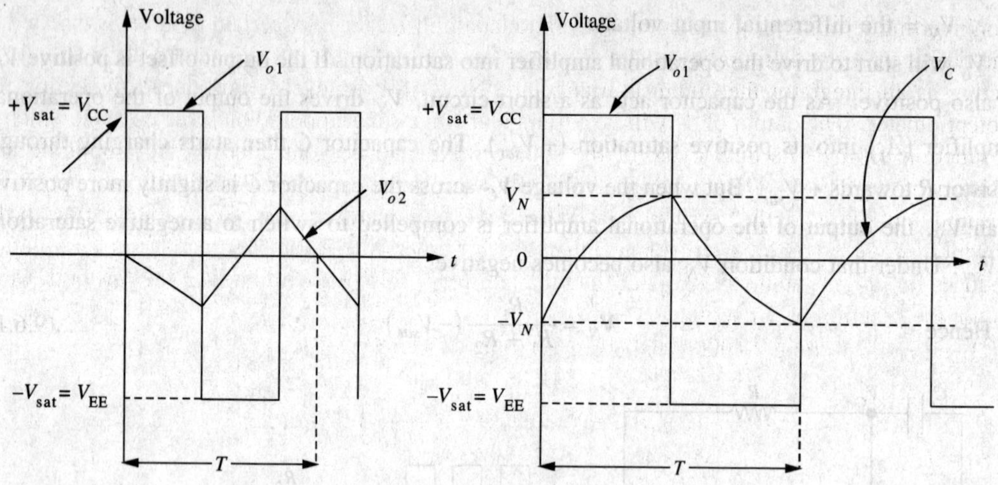

Fig. 9.15.

If $R_2 = 1{\cdot}16\,R_1$, f_{osc} is then expressed

as
$$f_{osc} = \frac{1}{2RC}$$

Hence V_{o1} is a square wave when it is applicable to an integrator the output will be as triangular waveform (V_{o2}).

9·7. SAWTOOTH WAVE GENERATION USING OPERATIONAL AMPLIFIER

Fig. 9.16 represents a sawtooth waveform generation circuit using operational amplifier. Sawtooth wave is basically a triangular wave with almost zero fall time. That is why the circuit for triangular waveform generator can be used to generate sawtooth wave provide some change is made in the circuit to get very small fall time. Here circuit is modified by adding a variable dc voltage into the

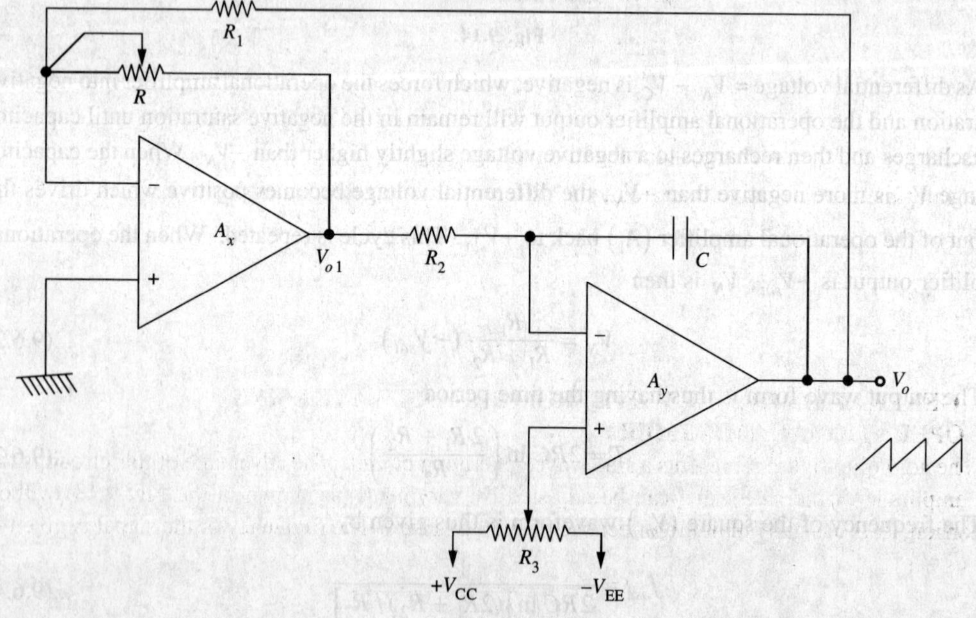

Fig. 9.16.

noninverting terminal of the integrator operational amplifier (A_y). A certain dc level is inserted in the output of A_y by setting the resistor R_3 properly. As the out of A_x is a square wave and A_y is acting as an integrator the output is triangular. Now, if a dc level is introduced by setting the potentiometer. The output of A_y will be a triangular wave superimposed on some dc level which is a function of R_3. The duty cycle of the square wave will be controlled by the amplitude and polarity of the dc level. Output will be a swatooth wave if the duty cycle is less than 50% except for the midpoint setting of the resistance R_3. When R_3 is set towards V_{cc} (or $-V_{EE}$) the rise time of the sawtooth wave becomes shorts (longer) than the fall time. Moreover, the frequency of oscillation reduces for R_3 sets at any other place than the mid point. But the amplitude of the sawtooth wave is not the function of R_3 setting.

Waveform: In time T_x the signal changes from $-V$ to $+V$.

$$V_o(pp)\text{ [Peak to peak]} = -\frac{1}{R_2C}\int_0^{T_x} V_{o1}\, dt$$

$$= -\frac{1}{R_2C}\int_0^{T_x}(-V_{sat})\, dt = \frac{V_{sat}\, T_x}{R_2C}$$

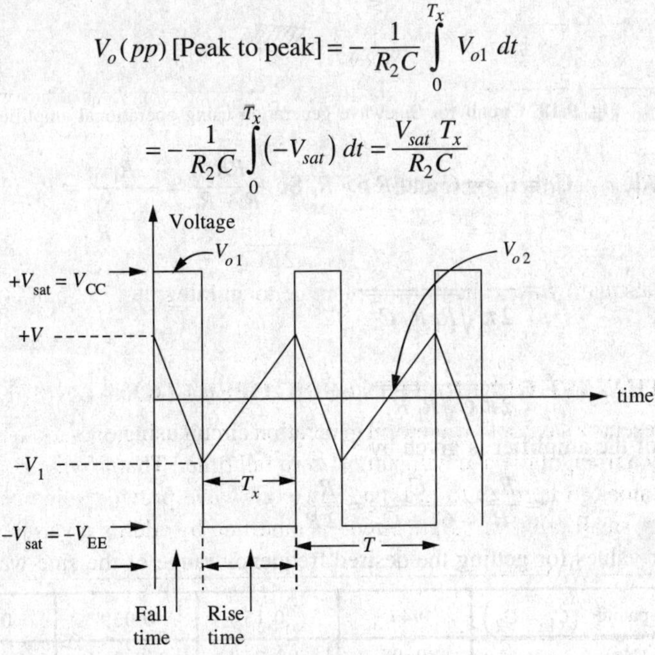

Fig. 9.17.

$\because$ At $t = T_x$, $V_{o1} = -V_{sat} = V_i$ for the integration.

If fall time is very small compared to T_x (rise time). T = total time period = T_x

$$T_x = T = \frac{V_o(PP)\, R_2C}{V_{sat}}$$

$$f_{osc} = \left(\frac{V_{sat}}{2V}\right)\cdot\frac{1}{R_2C}$$

9·8. GENERATION OF SINE WAVE FROM SQUARE WAVE USING OPERATIONAL AMPLIFIER

The adjoining figure represents a sine wave generating circuit. The advantage of this circuit is that the amplitude of the sine wave can be adjusted by varying R (as shown in the Fig. 9.18) without distortion. It is basically a multiple-feedback bandpass filter. The frequency of the signal is given by

$$f = \frac{1}{2\pi\sqrt{\dfrac{RR_1}{R_1+R}\cdot R_2\, C_1\, C_2}}$$

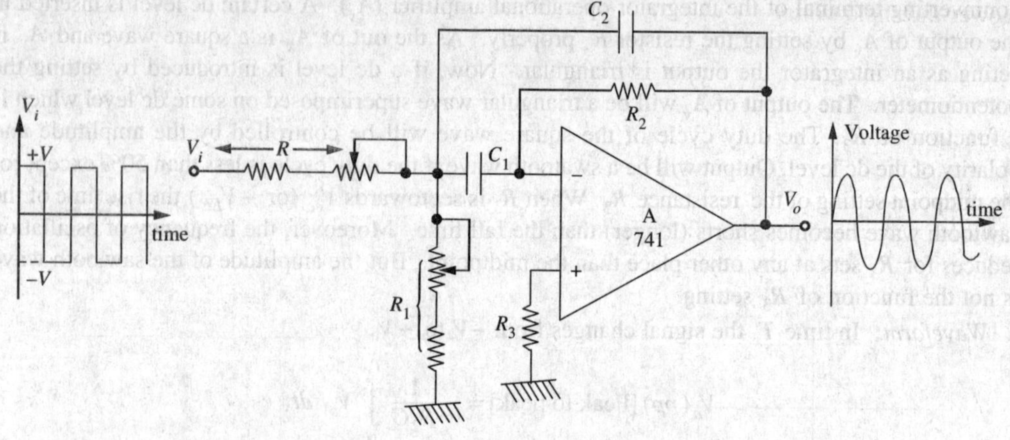

Fig. 9.18. Circuit for Sinewave generation using operational amplifier.

If $\quad C_1 = C_2 = C$ and $R >> R_1$ So $\dfrac{RR_1}{R+R_1} = \dfrac{R_1}{1+\dfrac{R_1}{R}} = R_1$

So $$f = \frac{1}{2\pi\sqrt{R_1 R_2 C^2}}$$

$\therefore$ $$f = \frac{1}{2\pi C\sqrt{R_1 R_2}}$$

The gain (A) of the amplifier is given by

$$A = \frac{R_2}{R} \times \frac{C_1}{C_1 + C_2} = \frac{R_2}{2R} \qquad [\because C_1 = C_2]$$

The capacitor values for getting the desired frequency range of the sine-wave are given below.

Value of (μ F) capacitor $(C_1 = C_2)$	0·47	0·15	0·039	0·01	0·0022
Frequency range (Hz)	20–90	90-250	250–1 K	1K–4·3 K	4·3 K–20 K

9·9. SCHMITT TRIGGER CIRCUIT

The adjacent figure depicts a circuit popularly known as Schmitt Trigger circuit or a squaring circuit. The input voltage V_i changes the stage of the output V_o every time it exceeds certain voltage levels which are known as the upper threshold voltage V_u and lower threshold V_L (shown in the Fig. 9.19).

Upper threshold voltage

$$V_u = \frac{R}{R+R_f}(+V_{sat}) \qquad ...(8.9.1)$$

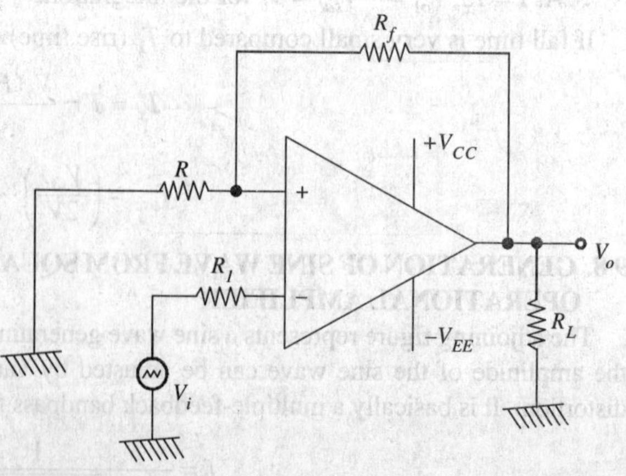

Fig. 9.19(*a*).

Lower threshold voltage

$$V_L = \frac{R}{R + R_f}(-V_{sat}) \qquad ...(8.9.2)$$

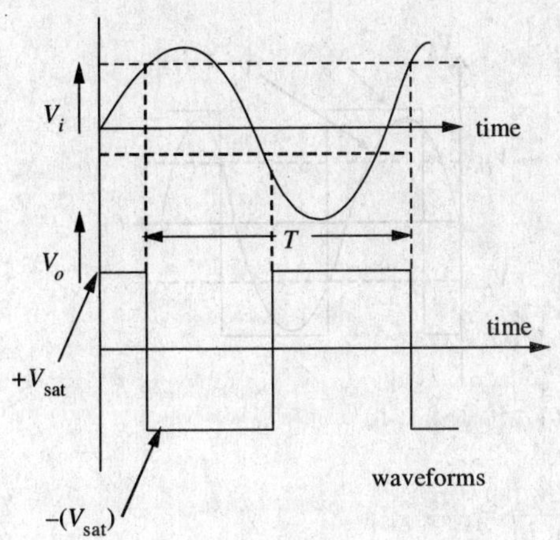

Fig. 9.19(*b*).

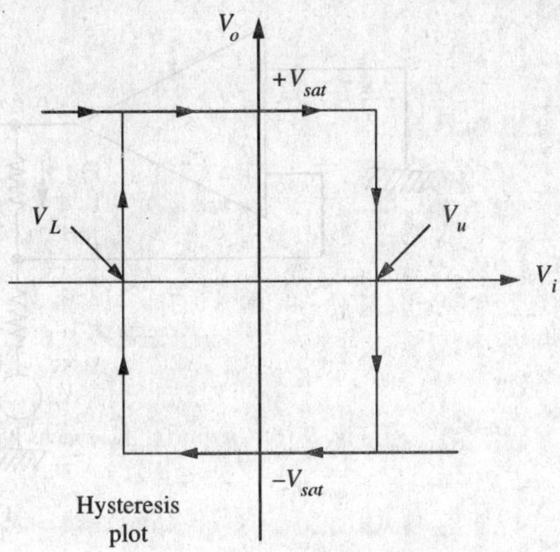

Fig. 9.19(*c*).

$V_u - V_L = V_{hy}$ is called the hysterias voltage.

$$V_{hy} = V_u - V_L$$

$$= \frac{R}{R + R_f}\left[+V_{sat} - (-V_{sat})\right]$$

$$= \frac{2R}{R + R_f} V_{sat} \qquad ...(9.9.3)$$

It is basically a regeneration comparator, using positive feedback to greatly increase switching speed. The switching time can be reduced to a limiting value set by the operational amplifier slew rate.

Inverting and noninverting Schmitt Trigger Circuit

1. Inverting Circuit

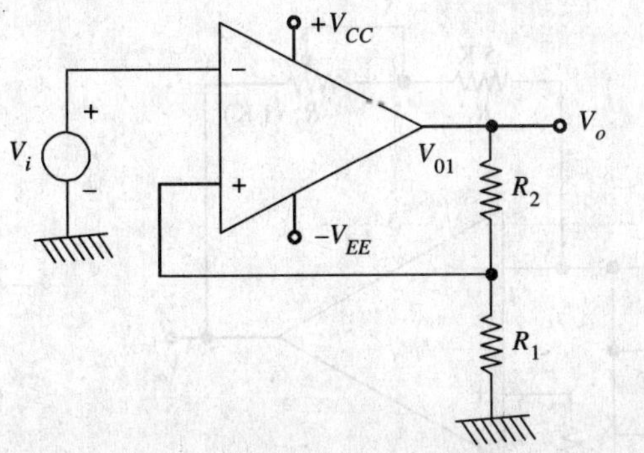

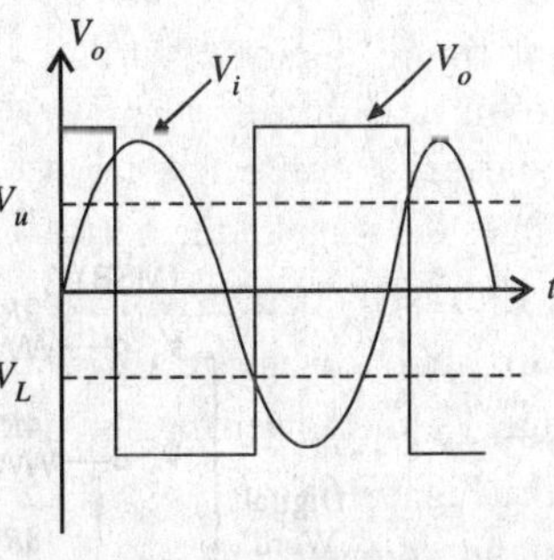

Fig. 9.20.

$$V_L = \frac{R_1}{R_1 + R_2}(-V_{sat}),\ V_u = \frac{R_1}{R_1 + R_2} V_{sat}$$

$$V_{hy} = V_u - V_L = \frac{2R_1}{R_1 + R_2} V_{sat}.$$

2. Non-inverting circuit

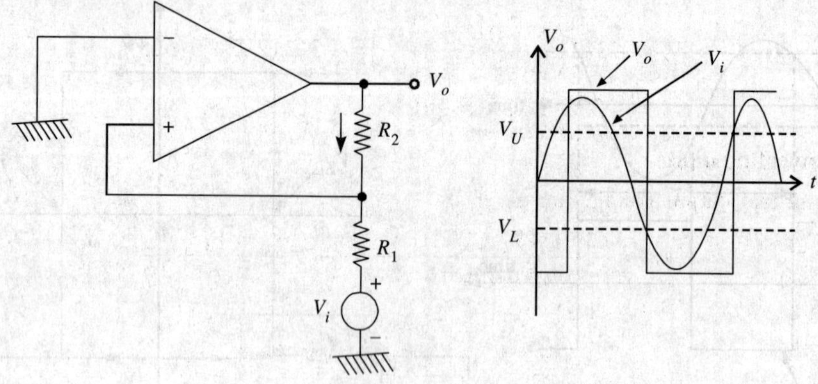

Fig. 9.21.

$$V_L = -\frac{R_1}{R_2}(+V_{sat})$$

$$V_U = -\frac{R_1}{R_2}(-V_{sat})$$

$$V_{hy} = \frac{2R_1}{R_2}(V_{sat})$$

9·10. APPLICATIONS OF OPERATIONAL AMPLIFIER AS A/D AND D/A CONVERTERS

(*a*) 4 bit D/A converter (Digital to Analog)

Figure 9.22(*a*) depicts D/A converters.

For inverting amplifier the output V_o is expressed as:

$$V_o = -\frac{R_f}{R}\left(\frac{V_1}{2} + \frac{V_2}{4} + \frac{V_3}{8} + \frac{V_4}{16}\right)$$

where $R_f = R_1 +$ portion of R_2 included in the feedback path.

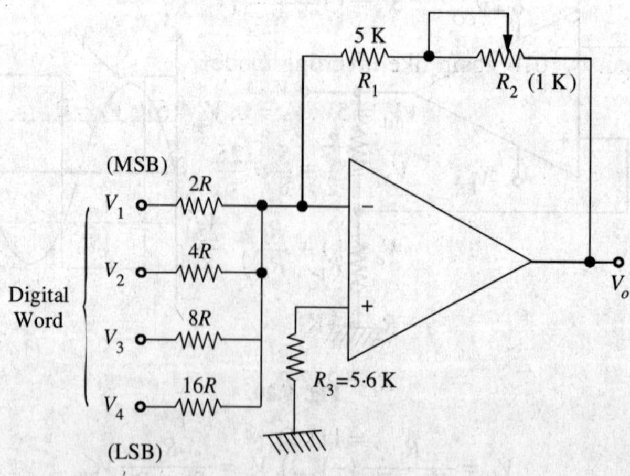

Fig. 9.22(*a*). Inverting Amplifier D/A converter.

Example: For an input of say 1010 = analog 10 V(Say)

$$V_1 = 1,\ V_2 = 0,\ V_3 = 1,\ V_4 = 0$$

1 means logic high level = 5 V (for TTL)

$$R_f = 3\cdot 2R = 32\,\text{k}\Omega \text{ (assume)} \qquad [R = 10\,\text{k}\Omega]$$

$$V_o = -3\cdot 2\left(\frac{5}{2}+\frac{0}{4}+\frac{5}{8}+\frac{0}{16}\right) = -3\cdot 2\,(2\cdot 5 + 0\cdot 625)$$

$$= -3\cdot 2\,(3\cdot 125) = -10\,\text{V}$$

For non-inverting mode

The input and output voltage are given by

$$V_{NI} = \frac{8V_1 + 4V_2 + 2V_3 + V_4}{1+2+4+8} = \frac{V_1}{2} + \frac{V_2}{4} + \frac{V_3}{8} + \frac{V_4}{16}.$$

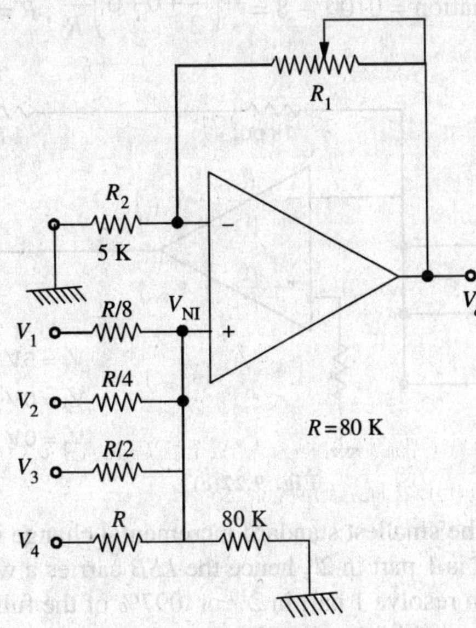

Fig. 9.22(*b*). Non-Inverting Amplifier D/A converter.

$$V_o = \left(1 + \frac{R_1}{R_2}\right)(V_{NI})$$

Example: If input is 1010 again like inverting mode

$$V_1 = 5V,\ V_2 = 0,\ V_3 = 5V,\ V_4 = 0$$

So

$$V_{NI} = \frac{5}{2} + \frac{5}{8} = \frac{25}{8}$$

$$V_o = \left(1 + \frac{R_1}{R_2}\right)\cdot\frac{25}{8}$$

$$R_2 = 5\text{K}$$

$$R_1 = 2\cdot 2\,R_2$$

$$= 11\,\text{k}\Omega$$

$$V_o = \left(1+\frac{R_1}{R_2}\right)\cdot\frac{25}{8}$$

$$= (1+2\cdot 2)\frac{25}{8} = 3\cdot 2\times\frac{25}{8}$$

$$= 10.$$

Example: For a binary weighted type 4 bit *DAC*, the *o/p* is to be 8*V* for an *i/p* combination of 0100, suggest a suitable ckt with component values and ref. voltage. For the suggested circuit, estimate the resolution: (Take $R_f = 10\ K\Omega$).

Sol: Let us assume $V_{in} = 5\ V$, $\quad V_{out} = -\left(\frac{V_1}{2}+\frac{V_2}{4}+\frac{V_3}{8}\right)\frac{R_f}{R}$, $V_{out} = 8\ V$ (given)

$$i/p \text{ combination} = 0100,\ -8 = -\left(\frac{5}{2}+0+0\right)\frac{10}{R},\ R = \frac{25}{8}k\Omega$$

The circuit will be:

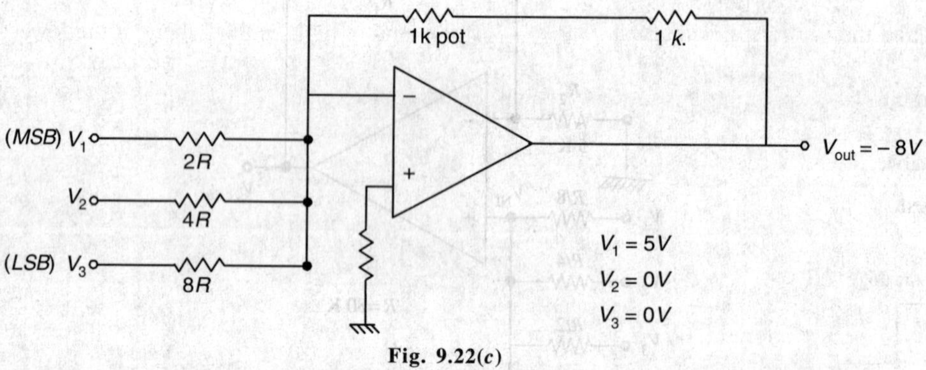

Fig. 9.22(c)

Resolution: It is basically the smallest standard incremental change in output voltage of a *DAC*. The decoding for a *n*-bit DAC is 1 part in 2^n, hence the *LSB* carries a weight of 2^n. For example, a *DAC* with 10 bit resolution can resolve 1 part in 2^{10} or .097% of the full scale output voltage when the binary input code is incremented by one *LSB*.

$$\therefore \quad \text{Resolution} = \frac{\text{Full scale reading}}{2^n} = \frac{-\left(1+\frac{1}{2}+\frac{1}{4}+\frac{1}{8}\right)*5*\frac{R_f}{R}}{2^4} = 1.875\,V.$$

(*d*) A 4 bit digital ramp *ADC* has an *i/p* range of 0 to 7.5 V. Estimate (*i*) resolution and (*ii*) conversion time if the clock frequency is 1*MHz* .

Sol: (*i*) For resolution, maximum *i/p* voltage = 7.5 *V*.

$$\text{Resolution} = \frac{7.5}{2^4} = 0.46875mV.$$

(*ii*) Conversion time = $(2^n - 1)*(1 \text{ clock cycle}) = (2^4 - 1)\left(\frac{1}{\text{clock frequency}}\right)$

$$= 15*\frac{1}{10^6} = 15 \text{ microsecond.}$$

Example: Draw the ckt diagram of a 4-bit *D/A* convertor with binary weighed registors. In this *D/A* converter find the size of each step if $R_f = 1.2\ k$ and $R = 10\ k$. *What* is the output voltage when (*i*) b_0 through b_3 are at 5_V, (*ii*) $b_0 = b_2 = 0V$, and $b_1 = b_3 = 5\ V$.

Sol: The circuit for 4-bit D/A convertor is

(*i*) $b_0 = b_1 = b_2 = b_3 = 5\text{V}$. *i.e.*, input is 1111.

$$V_{out} = -(b_3 + b_{2/2} + b_{1/4} + b_{0/8}) * 5R_f / R$$

$$= -\left(1 + \frac{1}{2} + \frac{1}{4} + \frac{1}{8}\right) * 5 \times 1.2/10 = -1.125V$$

(*ii*) When input sequence is 1010.

$$V_{out} = -\left(1 + 0 + \frac{1}{4} + 0\right) * 5 * 1.2/10 = -0.75\text{ V}.$$

Fig. 9.22(*d*)

(*b*) *A/D* convertor

(*i*) A parallel comparator type A/D convertor. Fig. 9.23 represents a 3 bit A/D convertor. The table 1 gives the relationship of the digital output to the analog input which is divided into eight ranges out of eight ranges six ranges encompass an interval $I = V_o/7$. The rest two ranges are the first and the last range of interval $I/2 = \frac{V_o}{14}$. If the analog input is any where in the lowest range from 0 to $\frac{V_o}{14}$, the output of the converts will be 000. The other digital output will be as given in the table. It is worthy to mention that if any signal is below $\frac{V_o}{14}$ the output is 000 hence error is $\frac{V_o}{14}$ at best.

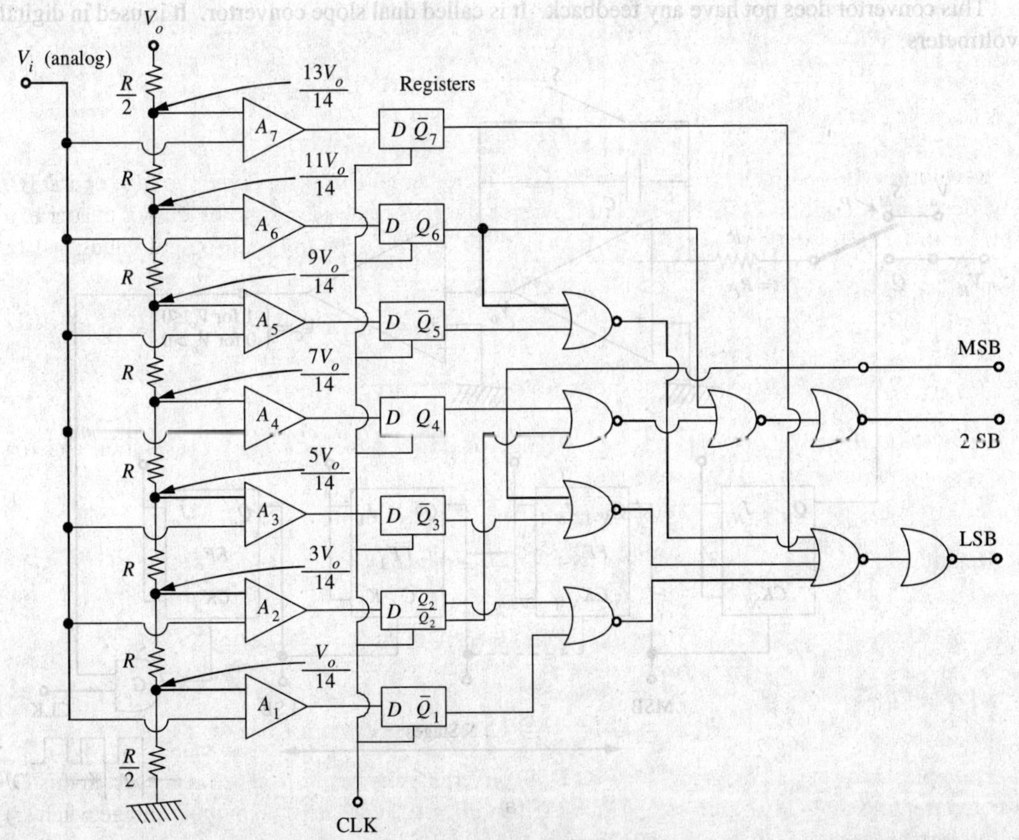

Fig. 9.23. A/D convertor.

Table 8.1

Analog voltage (V_O)	Digital output	Equivalent analog voltage
$V_O = 0$ to $\frac{V_O}{14}$	000	0
$\frac{V_O}{14}$ to $\frac{3V_O}{14}$	001	$\frac{V_O}{7}$
$\frac{3V_O}{14}$ to $\frac{5V_O}{14}$	010	$\frac{2}{7}V_O$
$\frac{5V_O}{14}$ to $\frac{7V_O}{14}$	011	$\frac{3}{7}V_O$
$\frac{7V_O}{14}$ to $\frac{9V_O}{14}$	100	$\frac{4}{7}V_O$
$\frac{9V_O}{14}$ to $\frac{11}{14}V_O$	101	$\frac{5}{7}V_o$
$\frac{11}{14}V_O$ to $\frac{13}{14}V_O$	110	$\frac{6}{7}V_O$
$\frac{13}{14}V_O$ to V_O	110	V_O

(*ii*) Dual slope A/D convertor

This convertor does not have any feedback. It is called dual slope convertor. It is used in digital voltmeters.

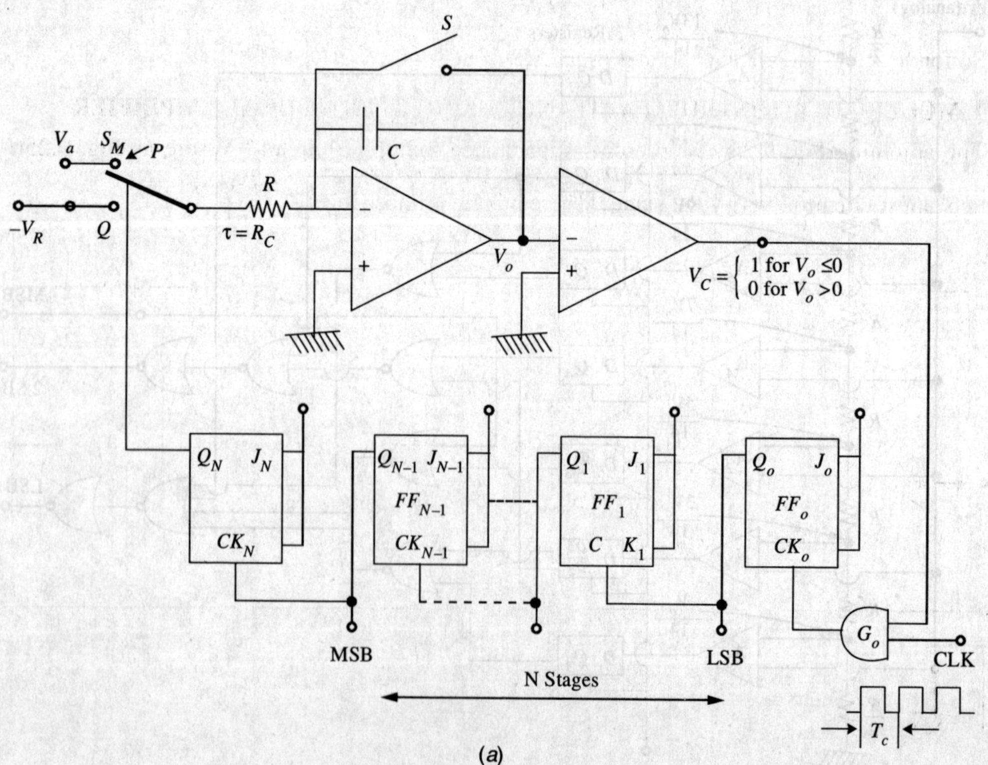

(*a*)

Fig. 9.24(*a*). Dual slope A/D convertor.

At $t = 0$, the switch S_M is connected to point P and the analog voltage is applied to the analog integrator of time constant $\tau = RC$. The integrator output is $V_o = -(t/\tau)V_a$. The output waveform is shown in fig. (b). At $t = 0$, a clock waveform is applied to a counter which was clear at the beginning when $Q_0 = Q_1 = \cdot = Q_{N-1} = 0$, the counter FF_N is set *i.e.*, $Q_N = 1$. This output of Q_N actually controls the state of S_M and when $Q_N = 1$ the switch is moved to point Q. The integrator output then starts to move in the positive direction as the applied reference voltage is negative. The counter continues counting till the output V_o becomes just barely positive and the output of the comparator goes to zero state. Then the gate G_o is disabled and the counter stops counting. As its output waveform has two slopes hence it is so named. $(N + 1)$ flip-flops need T_x time to go from 00 .... 00 to 10.....00 and is given by $T_x = 2^N T_C$. Here T_C is the clock time period. The output voltages then

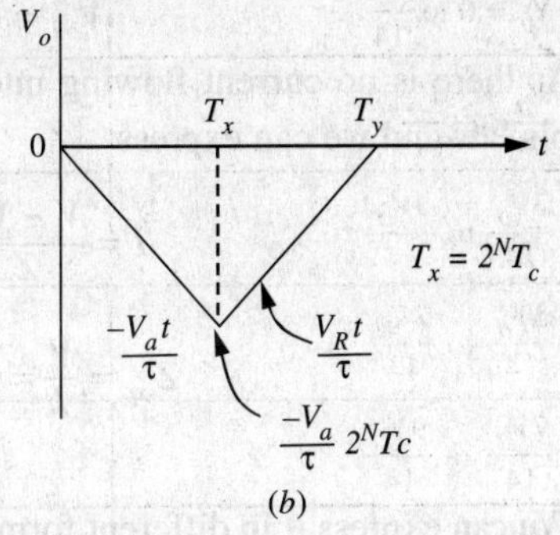

Fig. 9.24(b). Dual slope A/D convertor.

$$V_o = -\frac{V_a}{\tau} T_x = -\frac{V_a}{\tau} 2^N T_C \text{ if } t = T_y,\ V_o = 0 \text{ again.}$$

Hence
$$\frac{V_R\left(T_y - T_x\right)}{\tau} = \frac{V_o}{\tau} T_x$$

where
$$T_y - T_x = \frac{V_a}{V_R} 2^N T_C$$

So for $V_a < V_R$, the system operates as an A/D convertor.

9·11. MULTIPLICATION OF CAPACITANCE USING OPERATIONAL AMPLIFIER

The adjoining Fig. 9.25(*a*) represents capacitance multiplier circuit. Where as Fig. 9.25(*b*) depicts a test circuit to verify the same. The equivalent impedance $Z_{eq} = \frac{V}{I}$.

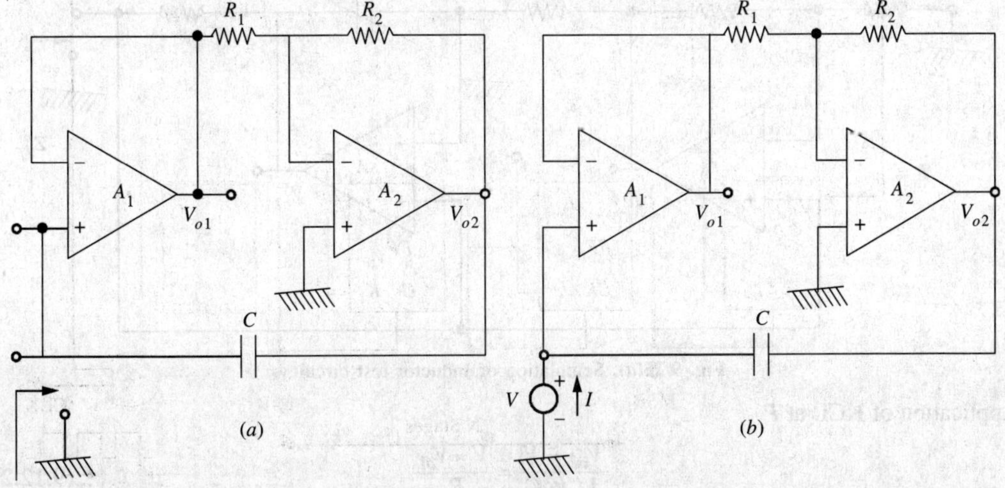

Fig. 9.25 (*a*) and (*b*). Capacitance Multiplier ckt.

From the figure it is clear that the operational amplifier A_1 operates as a voltage follower, hence we can write $V_{o1} = V$. The 2nd operational amplifier acts as an inverting amplifier and gives output as

$$V_{o2} = -(R_2 / R_1)\, V_{o1} = -(R_2 / R_1)\, V$$

As there is no current flowing into or out of the noninverting input of A_1, we can then apply ohm's law and we can express

$$I = \frac{V - V_{o2}}{Z_c} = \frac{V + (R_2 / R_1)V}{Z_c} = \frac{(1 + R_2 / R_1)}{Z_c} V$$

$$Z_{eq} = \frac{V}{I} = \frac{Z_c}{\left(1 + \dfrac{R_2}{R_1}\right)} = 1/[j\omega C\,(1 + R_2 / R_1)]$$

We can express it in different form as

$$Z_{eq} = \frac{1}{j\omega\, C_{eq}} \quad \text{where } C_{eq} = \left(1 + \frac{R_2}{R_1}\right) C$$

This is why the circuit is said to as a capacitance multiplier. The most important applications of the above principle is in integrated circuit technology where, for reasons of miniaturization, only very small capacitors can practically be fabricated. In case of larger capacitance requirement, a multiplier is used. This capacitance multiplication effect is referred to as the miller effect for capacitances.

9·12. SIMULATION OF INDUCTANCE USING OPERATIONAL AMPLIFIER

It is possible to simulate the inductance using operational amplifier. Fig. 9.26 (*a*) represents one such circuit and (b) provides a test circuit. In order to simulate a test voltage V is applied (Fig. 9.26(*b*)). Since no current flows into or out of the noninverting input of A_1 we can apply ohm's law and write.

$$I = \frac{V - V_{o2}}{R_4} \qquad \text{...(9.12.1)}$$

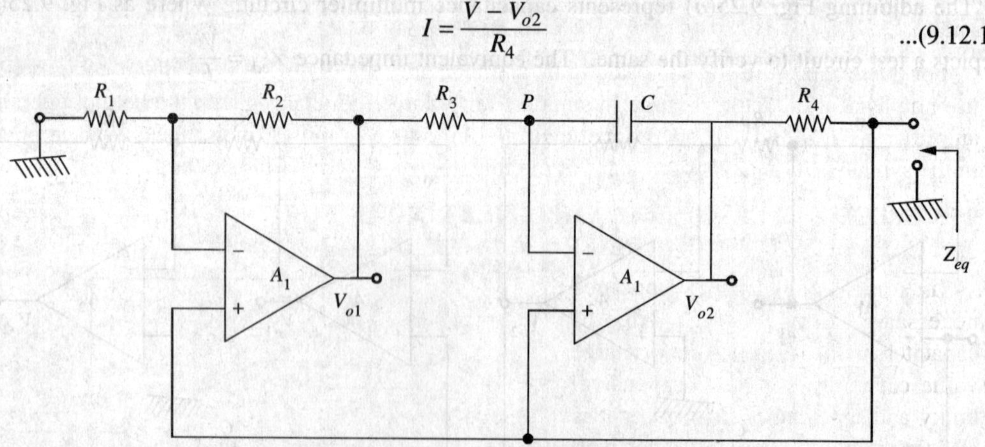

Fig. 9·26(*a*). Semulation of Inductor test circuit.

Application of KCL at P.

$$\frac{V_{o2} - V}{1/\,j\omega C} = \frac{V - V_{o1}}{R_3} \qquad \text{...(9.12.2)}$$

As A_1 operates as a noninverting amplifier, we can write

$$V_{o1} = \left(1 + \frac{R_2}{R_1}\right) V \qquad \text{...(9.12.3)}$$

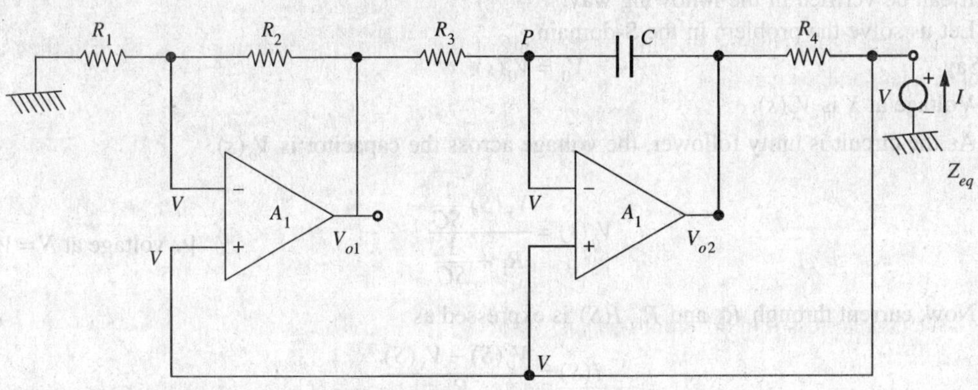

Fig. 9.26(*b*). Semulation of Inductor test circuit.

Inserting Eq. 9.12.3 into Eq. (9.12.2), solving for the difference $V_{o2} - V$, and then substituting it into Eq. (9.12.1), we get

$$I = \frac{V}{j\omega R_1\, R_3\, R_4\, C / R_2} \qquad \text{...(9.12.4)}$$

$$Z_{eq} = \frac{V}{I} = j\omega R_1\, R_3\, R_4\, C / R_2$$

which can be put in the form:

$$Z_{eq} = j\omega L_{eq} \qquad \text{...(9.12.5)}$$

$$L_{eq} = \frac{R_1\, R_3\, R_4}{R_2} C \qquad \text{...(9.12.6)}$$

For this reasons the circuit is said to be an inductance simulator. It is seen that not only does it use no physical inductor, it can also simulate fairly large inductances with the help of operational amplifier. This ability of operational amplifier circuits to simulate inductances finds application in the synthesis of an important class of circuits known as active filters.

9·13. SPECIAL OPERATIONAL AMPLIFIER CIRCUIT FOR CAPACITANCE MULTIPLIER

In some occasions it becomes necessary to connect large value of capacitors in the circuit. But very large value capacitors are very expensive, bulky and unrealistic. Moreover it is also unsuitable to incorporate such high values of capacitance in the integrated circuit (*IC*). However, such high value of capacitor can be realised using operational amplifier. Such a circuit is shown in the Fig. 9.27.

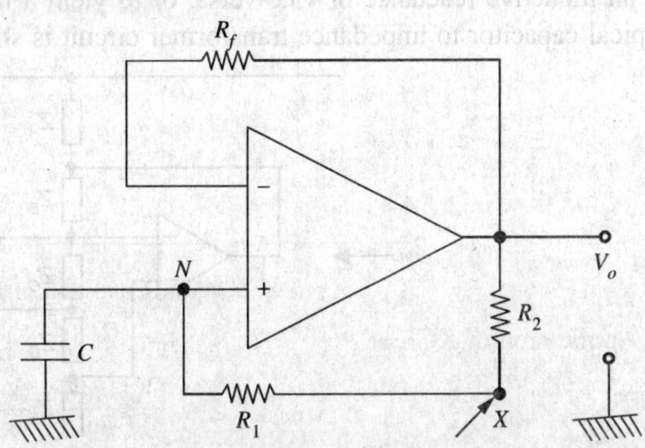

Fig. 9.27. Capacitor Multiplier circuit.

The effective value of capacitance at X is

$$C_x = \frac{R_1}{R_2} C \qquad ...9.13.1$$

It can be verified in the following way.

Let us solve the problem in the S-domain.

Say $\qquad V_0 = V_0(s).$

Voltage at X is $V_x(s)$.

As the circuit is unity follower, the voltage across the capacitor is $V_o(s)$.

$$V_o(s) = \frac{V_x(S)\dfrac{1}{SC}}{R_1 + \dfrac{1}{SC}} \qquad [\because \text{voltage at } N = V_o]$$

Now, current through R_2 and R_1, $I(S)$ is expressed as

$$I(S) = \frac{V_o(S) - V_x(S)}{R_2}$$

$$= V_x(S)\left[\frac{\dfrac{1}{SC}}{R_1 + \dfrac{1}{SC}} - 1\right]\frac{1}{R_2}$$

$$= V_x(S)\left[\frac{-R_1}{R_2\left(R_1 + \dfrac{1}{SC}\right)}\right]$$

So impedance (effective) at X is $\qquad = \dfrac{V_x(S)}{I(S)} = \dfrac{R_2\left(R_1 + \dfrac{1}{SC}\right)}{R_1}$

$$= R_2 + \frac{R_2}{R_1}\cdot\frac{1}{SC} = R_2 + \frac{1}{S\left(\dfrac{R_1}{R_2}\right)C}$$

So effective capacitance $\qquad = C_x = \dfrac{R_1}{R_2} C$

(*a*) A **generalized impedance converter** is a circuit which can transform a capacitive reactance to an inductive reactance or vice-versa, or to yield a frequency dependant negative resistance. A typical capacitor to impedance transformer circuit is shown in the following figure.

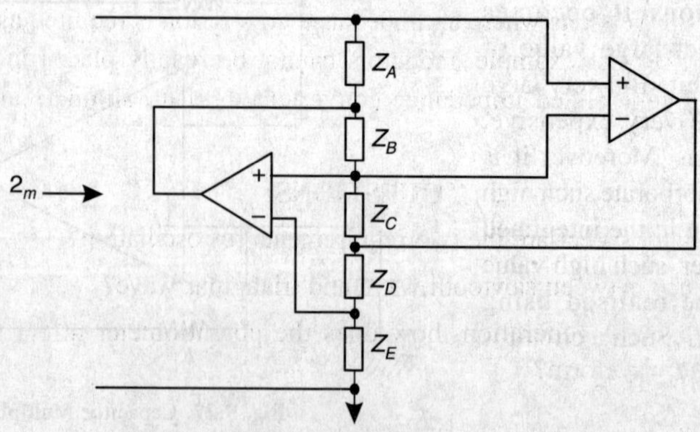

Fig. 9.28 Generalized impedance converter.

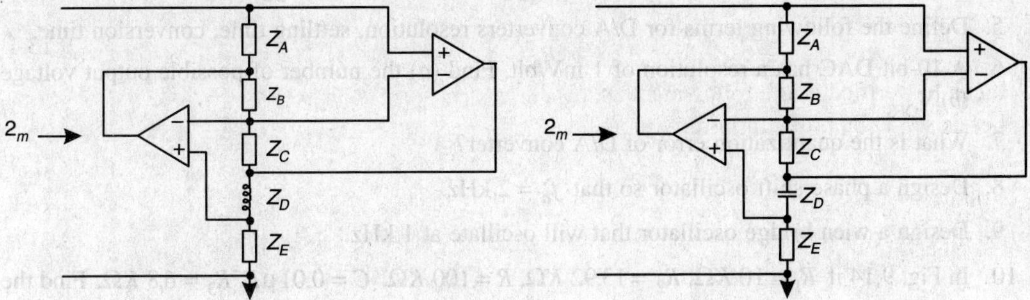

Fig. 9.29. Inductance to capacitance convertor **Fig. 9.30.** Capacitance to inductance convertor

The input impedance of this circuit is given by: $Z_{in} = \dfrac{Z_A Z_C Z_E}{Z_B Z_D}$

If we take $Z_D = \dfrac{1}{j\omega C_D}$ and the remaining impedance as simple resistances R_A, R_B, R_C, R_E, the input impedance is given by:

$$Z_{in} = j\omega \frac{R_A R_C R_E C_D}{R_B}$$

This is impedance of an inductor with inductance = $(R_A R_C C_D R_E)/R_B$.

We thus see that the circuit can easily convert a capacitance into an inductance.

If we take $Z_D = j\omega L_D$ and the remaining impedances again as simple resistances R_A, R_B, R_C, R_E, the input impedance is given by:

$$Z_{in} = \frac{R_A R_C R_E}{R_B \, j\omega L_D}$$

This is impedance of a capacitor with capacitance = $\dfrac{R_B L_D}{R_A R_C R_E}$

We thus see that the circuit can easily convert an inductance into a capacitance. It can be similarly shown that an impedance converter can also convert a resistance into a negative resistance by shifting phase of a signal by 180°.

Such circuits find applications where an impedance conversion is required as a substitute of the actual impedance device. For example, inductors cannot be readily placed in integrated circuits and so we can use a generalized impedance converter circuit to simulate an inductor in such circumstances.

QUESTIONS

1. Define an oscillator. What are the two requirements for oscillation?
2. What is difference between sawtooth wave and triangular wave?
3. In the sawtooth wave generation, how does the potentiometer affect the frequency and amplitude of the waveform?

4. What is the basic difference between comparator and Schmitt trigger?
5. Define the following terms for D/A converters resolution, settling time, conversion time.
6. A 10-bit DAC has a resolution of 1 mV/bit. Find (*a*) the number of possible output voltage (*b*) V_{OFS}.
7. What is the quantization error of D/A converter?
8. Design a phase shift oscillator so that $f_o = 2$ kHz.
9. Design a wien bridge oscillator that will oscillate at 1 kHz.
10. In Fig. 9.14 if $R_1 = 10\ K\Omega$, $R_2 = 13.92\ K\Omega$, $R = 100\ K\Omega$. $C = 0.01\ \mu F$. $R_3 = 6.8\ K\Omega$. Find the frequency of oscillation of square and triangular waveform.

10

APPLICATION OF SPICE & PSPICE IN THE ANALYSIS OF OPERATIONAL AMPLIFIER CIRCUITS

10·1. Introduction. 10·2. SPICE/PSPICE General Description 10·3. Working Principle of SPICE/PSPICE. 10·4. Rules Regarding SPICE/PSPICE. 10·5. Some Special Statements. 10·6. Spice Analysis for Purly Resistive Circuit.10·7. SPICE Analysis to Find the Thevenin and Norton Equivalents Across the Terminal (*a, b*). Solved Problems.

10·1. INTRODUCTION

We have learnt about four different circuit analysis techniques: viz (i) mesh analysis (ii) node analysis (iii) superposition principle and (iv) source transformation. But when the circuit complexity increases, the calculations leading to circuit analysis also become complex. Moreover, it becomes time consuming even to analyse the circuit, which motivates us to move towards computer method of circuit analysis. Its name is Simulation Program with Integrated Circuit Emphasis and in short SPICE, which can be used as a means for checking the results of hand calculations.

10·2. SPICE/PSPICE GENERAL DESCRIPTION

SPICE is capable of performing the dc, ac and transient analysis of circuits having dependent and independent sources, resistors, capacitors, inductors, mutual inductances, and transmission lines. Also it can analyse the circuits having common semiconductor devices viz, diodes BJTs, JFETs, and MOSFETs and operational amplifier (OC). SPICE program is available at most of the colleges and Universities now a days.

Recently it is also used in personal computer. PSPICE is one such widely used computer program for circuit analysis. (*P* for personal computer).

Computer-aided circuit analysis made its first appearance in the mid 1960 when Electric Circuit Analysis Program (ECAP) was developed and made available. Several similar program for computer aided circuit analysis came after ECAP. They are SPECTRE, NET, CIRCUS and TRAC. But here we will use SPICE/PSPICE for circuit analysis.

10·3. WORKING PRINCIPLE OF SPICE/PSPICE

Now a question comes into our mind. How does SPICE/PSPICE work? To run the SPICE we are to do the following:

(1) Create an input file and figures out all the circuit elements connected to each node.

(2) Control commands or statements defining the type of analysis and print out desired.

Thereafter a SPICE/PSPICE utilizes KCL to create a system of equations for the circuit, where the voltages at each node are the unknowns, and the admittance of each branch having two nodes are the known quantities. This group of equations is made into an admittance matrix.

Newton-Raphson technique is then used to solve this matrix. To analyse circuit it is not essential to understand the mathematical techniques and the algorithms that are necessary by SPICE/PSPICE. But it is very much essential to be competent in electronic circuit analysis in order to verify results of SPICE.

10·4. RULES REGARDING SPICE/PSPICE

We have already mentioned that for running a SPICE, it is necessary to create an input file containing element statements and control statements. SPICE then analyses the circuit utilizing numerical technique and presents the results in an output file. For the level of this book, the coverage of SPICE is adequate. However, you can own either of the following for a comprehensive and more systematic description of the program.

(1) SPICE User's Guide and

(2) Student SPICE Manual by James S. Kang (Saunders College Publishing, Philadelphia, PA, 1994).

1. Labelling of nodes

First, all the nodes of the circuit to be analysed are labelled as 0, 1, 2, 3 ...... *n*, with the reference node being node *O* by definition. It is depicted in the Fig. 10.1.

Step 2: Next step is to create an input file containing element statements and control statements. The first statement in the input file is a title statement and the last statement is "END" statement. Some times a statement called comment statement is put just before the last (END) statement with an asterisk at the beginning.

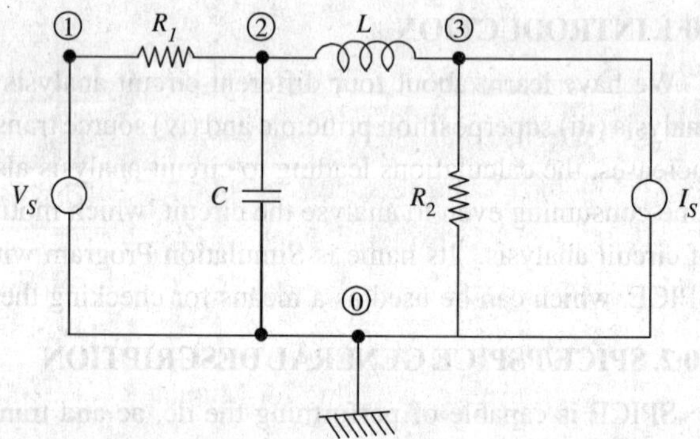

Fig. 10.1. Preparing a circuit for analysis using SPICE program.

(*a*) Now it is the time to specify the type of elements forming the circuit, the manner in which they are interconnected, and their values.

(*b*) General form of the element statements:

For Resistors:

RXXX N_1 N_2 value.

(*i*) Here, RXXX is an alphanumeric string up to eight characters. The beginning letter must be *R*. XXX indicates an arbitrary alphanumeric string up to seven characters uniquely identifying the particular resistance. We can write R_1, R_2, R_{IN}, R_{OUT}, R_{EQ} etc.

(*ii*) N_1 and N_2 are the nodes between which the resistance is connected. It is worthy to mention that their order is unimportant.

(*iii*) The Value of the resistance is expressed in ohms.

For Capacitor:

CXXXX N_1 N_2 value.

XXXX and N_1, N_2 are having the same meaning like resistors. If value is in μF then it is to be suffixed as *U* and for *nF* it is *N*. If nothing is mentioned then it means that the value of *C* is in Farad.

For Inductor:

LXXX N_1 N_2 Value.

Meaning and significances of *L, XXX*, N_1 and N_2 are the same as Resistor. Value is expressed in Henry.

Voltage Source

Current source IXXXX or V_{XXX} $N+$ $N-$ *DC* Value.

V, XXX are having the same significance as that in case of a Resistor. $N+$ and $N-$ are the nodes between which the source is connected. For a voltage source $N+$ and $N-$ are the positive and negative terminals. In case of a current, $N+$ is the terminal from which the source sinks current and $N-$ the terminal from which it sources current. The current through a voltage source is represented as I(VXXX), the voltage across a current source as $V(N+, N-)$. The value is expressed in volts or amperes.

DC indicates the nature of the source *i.e.*, it is dc type.

Elements are generally recognizes by the first letter of the element name on the element line. In SPICE there are 15 such letter for element names. They are as follows:

Letter	Element name
C	Capacitor
D	Diode
E	Voltage-controlled Voltage Source
F	Current-controlled current source
G	Voltage-controlled current source
H	Current-controlled voltage source
I	Independent current source
J	JFET
K	Coefficient of coupling for Mutual Inductance
L	Inductor
M	MOSFET
Q	BJT
T	Transmission line
V	Independent Voltage Source

Value	Symbolic form	Exponential form
10^{-15}	F	1E-15
10^{-12}	P	1E-12
10^{-9}	N	1E-9
10^{-6}	U	1E-6
10^{-3}	M	1E-3
10^{3}	K	1E3
10^{6}	MEG	1E6
10^{9}	G	1E9
10^{12}	T	1E12

Scale Factors

We can use either exponential form or symbolic form when expressing element values in interms of powers of ten. The above figure gives a table containing symbolic and exponential forms with the value.

Spice Representation of Operational Amplifier (Op. Amp.)

It is known that for an ideal operational amplifier (*i*) Gain = ∞. (*ii*) Input resistance $R_1 = \infty$ (*iii*) Output resistance $R_o = 0$ (no current flows into or out either input pin). An ideal operational amplifier model is shown in Fig. 10.2.

Step 3

Automatic dc analysis

When the description of the circuit is completed, control statements are then to be given for indicating the type of analysis and print out we require. However, if those statements are omitted,

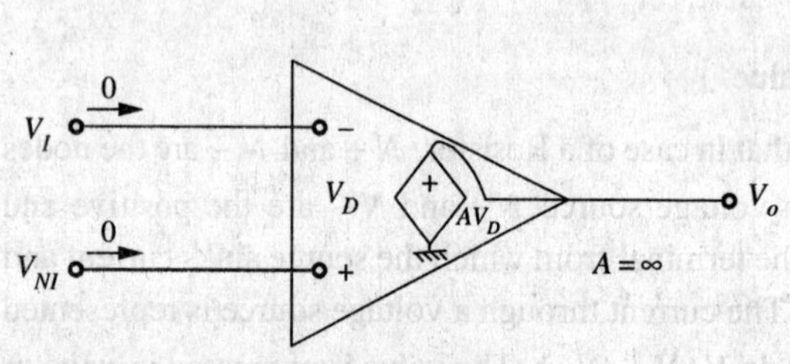

Fig. 10.2.

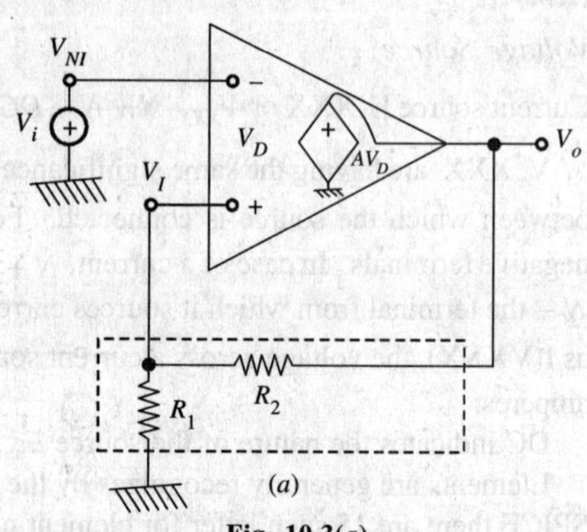

Fig. 10.3(*a*)

$$\underset{A \to \alpha}{\text{Lt}} \text{ Gain} = 1 + \frac{R_2}{R_1}$$

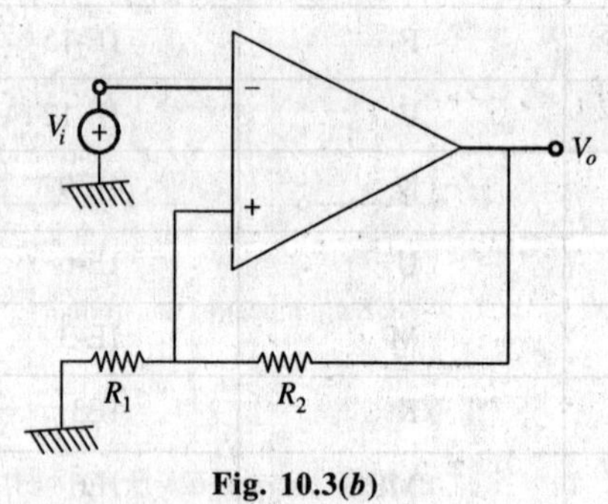

Fig. 10.3(*b*)

Fig. 10.3(*c*)

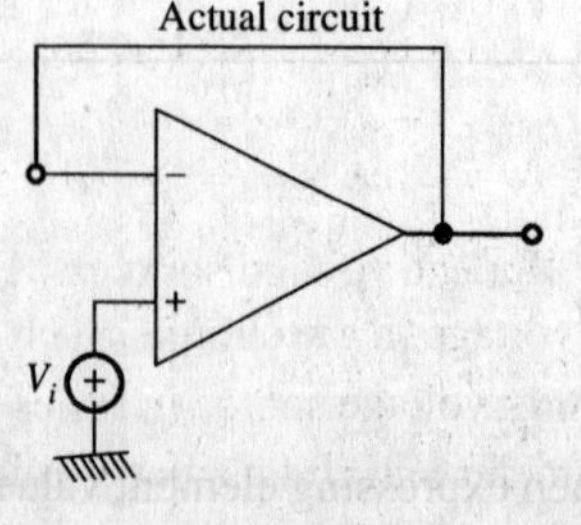

Equivalent circuit

(*b*)

Fig. 10.4 (*a*) and (*b*). Voltage.

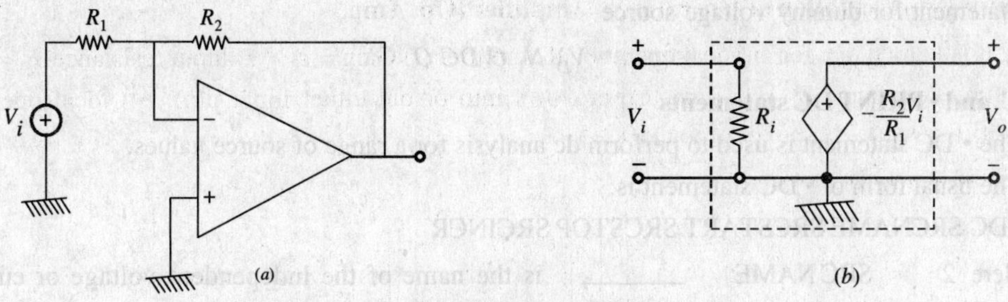

Fig. 10.5 (*a*) and (*b*). Inverting configuration.

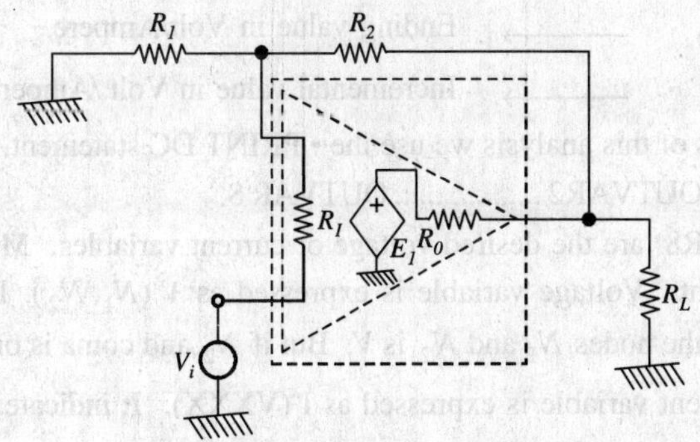

Fig. 10.6. Practical operational amplifier (Non-inverting).

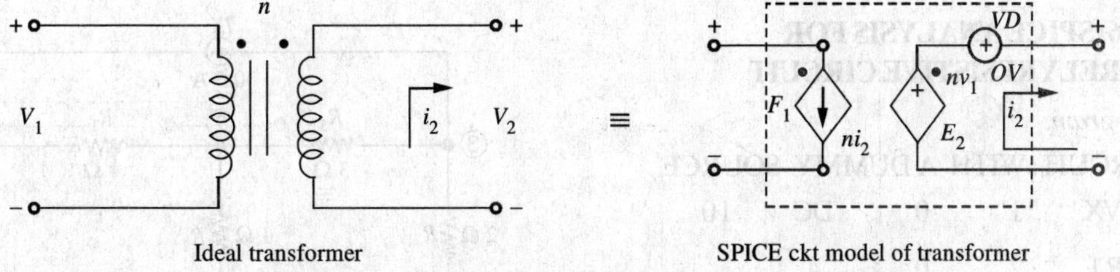

Fig. 10.7(*a*). Ideal transformer and (*b*) SPICE ckt model of transformer.

then SPICE program will automatically do the dc analysis and gives out all node voltages in tabular form. In PSPICE version currents through the voltage sources as well as the total energy supplied by these sources and the power dissipated in the circuit are also come out in the output file.

10·5. SOME SPECIAL STATEMENTS

(*i*) Dummy Voltage Source

SPICE program gives only the currents through independent voltage sources. But sometimes we want to know the value of a particular branch current/voltage in the circuit. Such a limitation of SPICE is overcome by the grace of inserting a $O-V$ dummy voltage source in series with the given branch. The inserted dummy source acts as an ideal ammeter and it does not perturb the existing conditions in the circuit. But on the other hand it allows us to monitor the current in the given branch.

Statement for dummy voltage source

$$V_D\ N_1\ O\ DC\ O$$

• DC and • PRINT DC statements

The • DC statement is used to perform dc analysis for a range of source values.

The usual form of • DC statement is:

• DC SRCNAME SRCSTART SRCSTOP SRCINCR

Here 2	SRC NAME	⟶	is the name of the independent voltage or current source to be varied.
	SRC START	⟶	starting value in volt/ampere.
	SRC STOP	⟶	Ending value in Volt/Ampere.
	SRC INCR	⟶	Incremental value in Volt./Ampere.

In order to get the results of this analysis we use the • PRINT DC statement. Its usual form is:

• PRINT DC OUTVAR1 OUTVAR2 .... OUTVAR 8.

OUTVAR 1 to OUTVAR8 are the desired voltage or current variables. Maximum number of permitted variables are eight. Voltage variable is expressed as $V(N_1, N_2)$. It indicates that the voltage difference between the nodes N_1 and N_2 is V. But if N_2 and coma is omitted, then ground $(N_2 = 0)$ is assumed. Current variable is expressed as I (VXXX). It indicates that the current is flowing through the independent voltage source named VXXX.

Let us introduce SPICE/PSPICE gradeually, by discussing only the capabilities needed at the time so that we can avoid cramming too many information at a time.

10·6. SPICE ANALYSIS FOR PURELYRESISTIVE CIRCUIT

Program:

```
CIRCUIT WITH A DUMMY SOURCE
  VX    1    0    DC    10
  R1    2    0     4
  R2    2    1     1
  R3    2    3     3
  R4    3    4     2
  IX    0    3    0.5
  * DUMMY SOURCE
  VD   40         DC   0
  • END
```

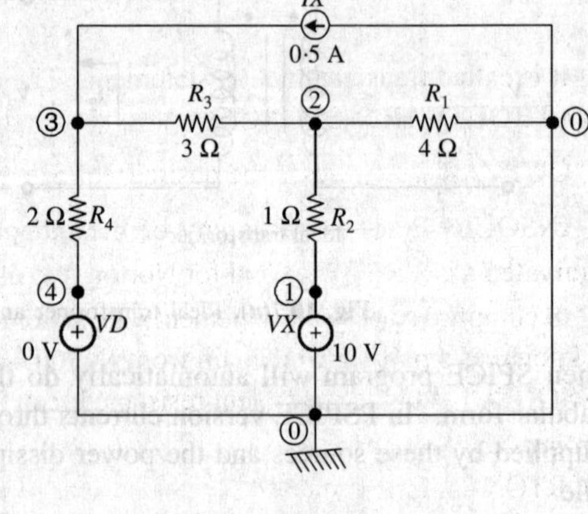

Fig. 10.8.

Output after SPICE is run:

DC ANALYSIS:

NODE VOLTAGE	NODE VOLTAGE	NODE VOLTAGE	NODE VOLTAGE
(1) 10·0000	(2) 7·0345	(3) 3·4138	(4) 0·0000

10·7. SPICE ANALYSIS TO FIND THE THEVENIN AND NORTON EQUIVALENTS ACROSS THE TERMINAL (*a, b*)

Program:

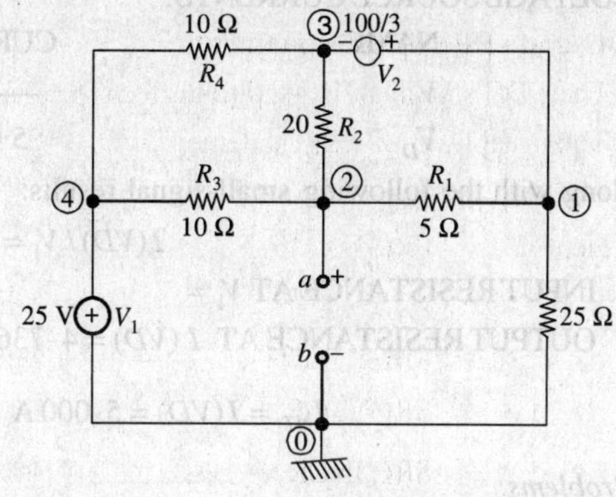

Fig. 10.9.

```
THEVENIN CKT
      V1   4   0    DC   25
      V2   1   3    DC   33·34
      R1   1   2    5
      R2   2   3    20
      R3   2   4    10
      R4   3   4    10
      • TF V(2,0) V1
      • END
```

Output after SPICE Program is run:

NODE VOLTAGE	NODE VOLTAGE	NODE VOLTAGE	NODE VOLTAGE
(1)————	(2) 23·6842	(3)————	(4)————

along with the following small-signal results,

$$V(2)/V_1 = 23\cdot 6842$$

INPUT RESISTANCE AT V_1 =————————

OUTPUT RESISTANCE AT $V(2) = 4\cdot 7368$

So $$V_{Th} = 23\cdot 6842 \text{ and } R_{Th} = 4\cdot 7368\ \Omega$$

We have given the printout of the required values. Some other values are not provided. You can try to get them. Here we have use one unknown statement

• *TF V*(2, 0) V_1

It is called transfer function statement. The usual form of it is:

• TF OUTVAR INSOURCE

OUTVAR ———→ is the desired voltage or current variable.

INSOURCE ———→ is any of the independent source in the ckt. OUTVAR for thevenin equivalents is $V(N_1, N_2)$ and for Norton it is of the form I (VXXX).

In compliance with the statement • TF statement, SPICE does the dc analysis and also gives what is known as small signal dc gain from INSOURCE to OUTVAR, the equivalent resistance seen by INSOURCE and the equivalent resistance seen by OUTVAR.

Program:

```
NORTON CKT
          V1     4    0     DC    25
          V2     1    3     DC    33.34
          R1     1    2     5
          R2     2    3     20
          R3     2    4     10
          R4     3    4     10
          • TF I (VD) V1
          • END
```

Result after SPICE is run

VOLTAGE SOURCE CURRENTS:

NAME	CURRENT
V_1	________
V_D	5·0000

along with the following small-signal results:

$$I(VD)/V_1 = \ldots\ldots\ldots\ldots\ldots\ldots$$

INPUT RESISTANCE AT V_1 =

OUTPUT RESISTANCE AT $I(VD) = 4\cdot7368$

$$I_{NT} = I(VD) = 5\cdot000\text{ A} \text{ and } Y_{NT} = \frac{1}{R_{eq}} = 0\cdot2111U$$

Problems:

Use SPICE to solve the following.

(1) Find the magnitude and polarity of the voltage across the 12A current source

(Ans. 33V + @ top)

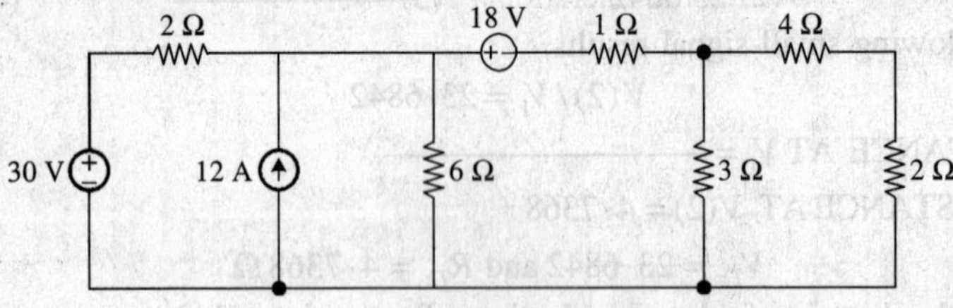

Fig. 10.10.

(2) Find Thevenin and Norton equivalents of the circuit problem 2 across (a, b)

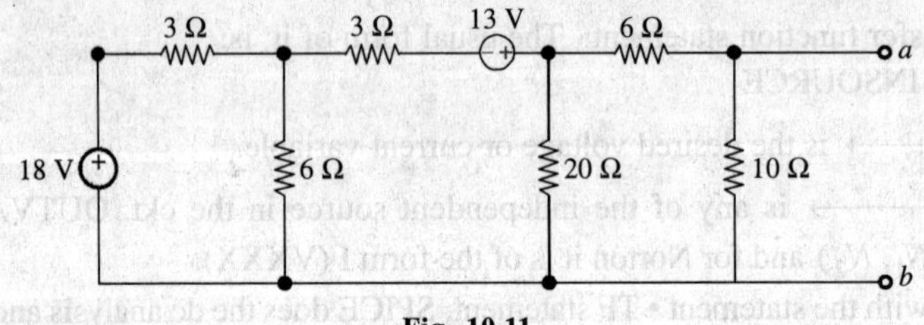

Fig. 10.11.

(3) Use SPICE to final R_{eq}.

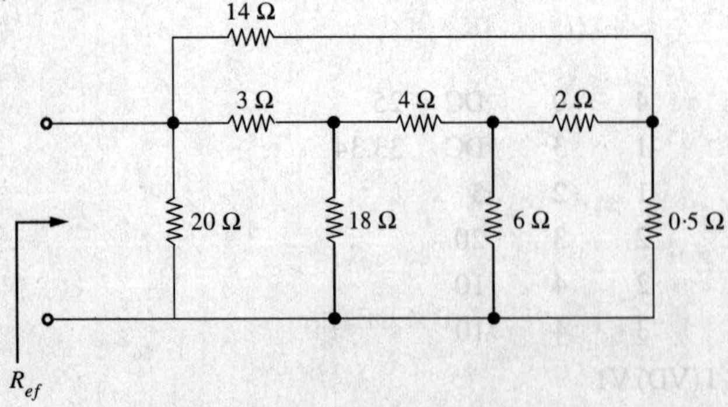

Fig. 10.12.

(4) Use SPICE to find R_{eq}.

(5) USE SPICE to find Thevenin and Norton equivalent ckts. across (a, b)

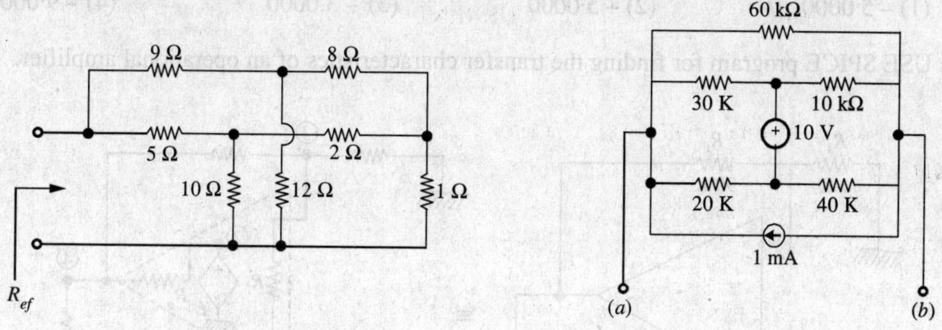

Fig. 10.13.

Fig. 10.14.

10·8. SOLVED PROBLEMS

1. Find all the node voltages using SPICE for analysis of circuit having operational amplifier.

Solution: Usually SPICE is unable to accept infinite gain $(A = \infty)$. However, we take a fairly high gain $A = 10^2\,\text{V}/\text{V}$. The input file is

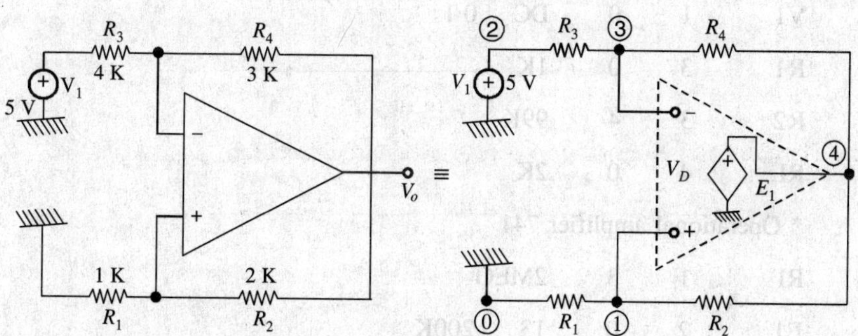

Fig. 10.15.

```
SPICE PROB WITH OPERATIONAL AMPLIFIER
        V1      2   0   DC  5
        R1      1   0   1K
        R2      1   4   2K
        R3      2   3   4K
        R4      3   4   3K
        • OP. AMP.
        E1      4   0   13  1.OE12
        • END
```

when SPICE file is run the output file will have:

NODE VOLTAGE	NODE VOLTAGE	NODE VOLTAGE	NODE VOLTAGE
(1) – 5·0000	(2) + 5·0000	(3) – 3.0000	(4) – 9·0000

2. USE SPICE program for finding the transfer characteristics of an operational amplifier.

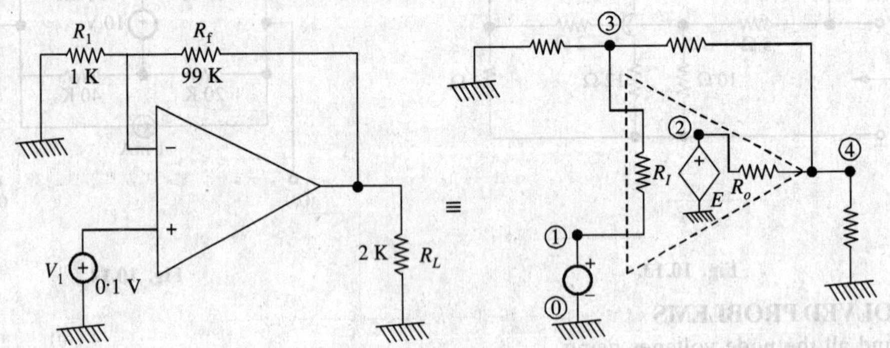

Fig. 10.16.

Solution:

NONINVERTING AMPLIFIER

```
V1      1   0   DC   0·1
R1      3   0   1K
R2      3   4   99K
RL      4   0   2K
* Operational amplifier 741
RI      1   3   2MEG
E1      2   0   13   200K
R0      4   0   75
• TF    V(4)   VI
• END
```

Output file after SPICE is run

NODE VOLTAGE	NODE VOLTAGE	NODE VOLTAGE	NODE VOLTAGE
(1) 0·1000	(2) 10· 3770	(3) 0·0999	(4) 9·9948

along with the small-signal results:

$$V(4)/V_1 = 9\cdot 995E+01$$

INPUT RESISTENCE AT $V_1 = 3\cdot 855E+09$

OUTPUT RESISTANCE AT $V(4) = 3\cdot 750-02$

3. Design an instrument amplifier using operational amplifier μA 741 with gain $A = 10^2$ V / V. Now find V_o, if $V_1 = 5\text{V}$ $V_2 = 5{\cdot}01\,V$ and it drives a 2K Ω load (use SPICE program).

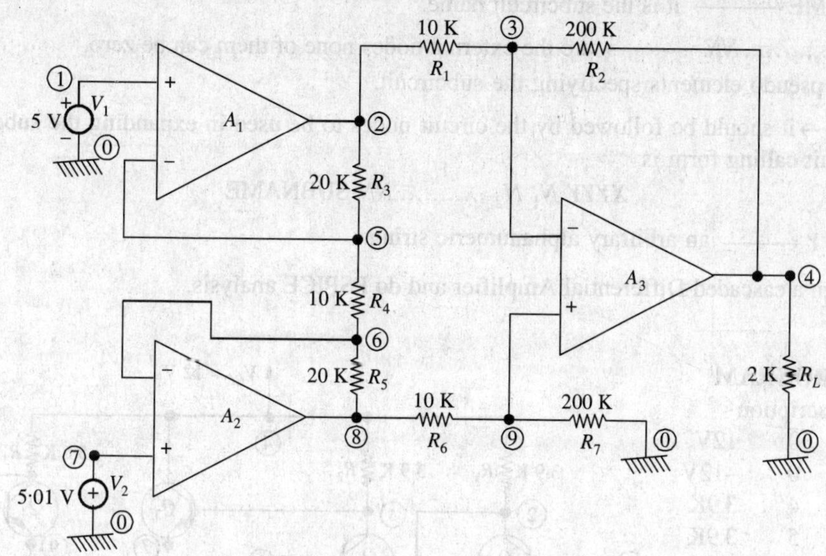

Fig. 10.17. SPICE model for instrumentation Amp.

Solution:

```
INSTRUMENTATION AMPLIFIER
* OPERATIONAL AMPLIFIER SUBCIRCUIT
* CONNECTION: INVERTING INPUT
* NON INVERTING INPUT
* OUTPUT
• SUB CKT OP AMP   2   3   6
RI    7   2   2MEG
E1    1   0   27    200K
RO    1   8   75
• ENDS OP AMP
* MAIN CKT
V1    1   0   DC   5·0000
V2    7   0   DC   5·0100
R3    2   5   20K
R4    5   6   10Ke
R5    6   8   20Ke

* THIRD OPERATIONAL AMPLIFIER
XOA3  3   9   4    OPAMP
RL    4   0   2K
• END
```

```
* OPERATIONAL AMPLIFIER ONE AND TWO
XOA 1   5   1   2   Operational Amplifier
XOA 2   6   7   8   Operational Amplifier
R   1   2   3   10K
R   2   3   4   200K
R   6   8   9   10K
R   7   9   0   200K
```

Results after the program execution

NODE VOLTAGE	NODE VOLTAGE	NODE VOLTAGE
(1) 5·0000	(2) 4·9800	(3) 4·7904
(4) 0·9999	(5) 5·0000	(6) 5·0100
(7) 5·0100	(8) 5·0300	(9) 4·7905

- SUB CKT SUBNAME N_1 N_2 .... NN and it must be followed by
- ENDS SUBNAME

SUBNAME ⟶ it is the subcircuit name.

N_1, N_2 .... NN ⟶ are the external nodes none of them can be zero.

X is the pseudo elements specifying the subcircuit.

X ⟶ it should be followed by the circuit nodes to be used in expanding the subcircuit.

Subcircuit calling form is

$$XYYY\ N_1\ N_2\ \dots\dots\ NN\ \text{SUBNAME}$$

Y .... Y ⟵ an arbitrary alphanumeric string.

4. Design a cascaded Differential Amplifier and do PSPICE analysis.

Solution:

PSPICE PROGRAM

Circuit Description

```
VCC  4   0   12V
VEE  13  0   -12V
R1   2   4   3.9K
R2   4   5   3.9K
R3   4   10  5.6K
R4   7   8   100
R5   8   9   100
V1   1   0   AC  10mV
V2   6   0   AC  5mV
R6   12  13  2.2K
R7   11  13  5.6K
R8   8   11  5.1K
Q1   2   1   3 TRAN
Q2   5   6   3 TRAN
Q5   3   11  12 TRAN
Q3   4   5   7 TRAN
Q4   10  2   9 TRAN
```

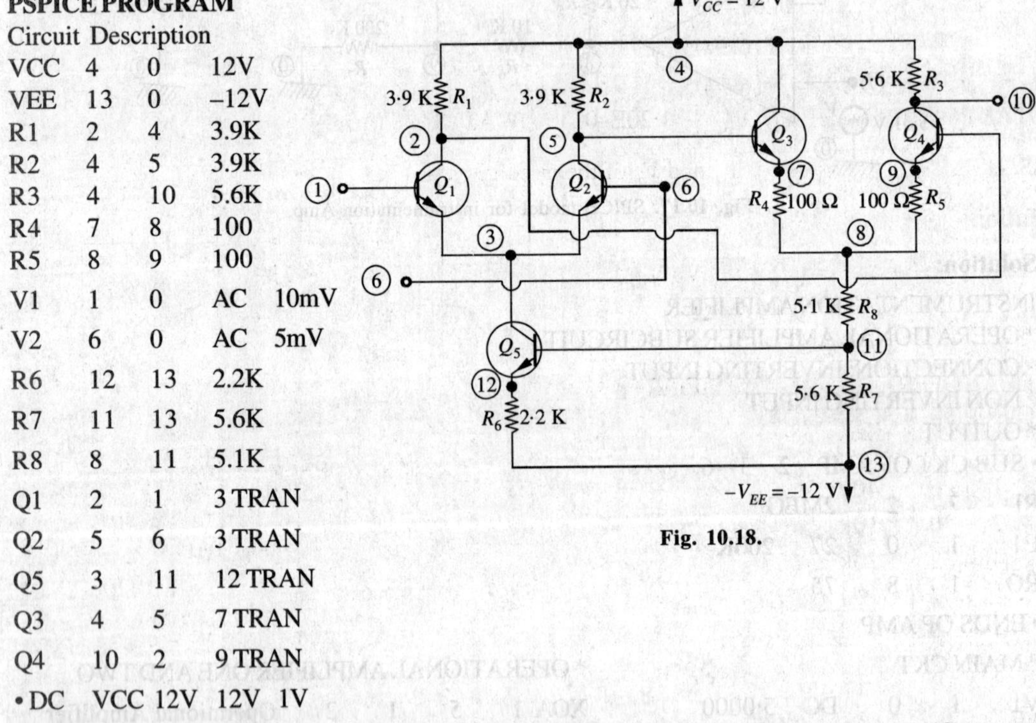

Fig. 10.18.

```
• DC  VCC 12V  12V  1V
• PRINT DC V(1) V(2) V(3) V(4) V(5) V(6) V(7) V(8) V(9) V(10) V(11) V(12) V(13)
• MODEL TRAN NPN
• OPTION
• END
DIFFERENTIAL AMPLIFIER
BJT MODEL PARAMETERS
TRAN
NPN
IS    100.000000E-18
BF    100
```

NF 1
BR 1
NR 1

DIFFERENTIAL AMPLIFIER

NODE	VOLTAGE	NODE	VOLTAGE	NODE	VOLTAGE	NODE	VOLTAGE
(1)	0·0000	(2)	5·2881	(3)	–·7882	(4)	12·0000
(5)	5·2781	(6)	0·0000	(7)	4·5107	(8)	4·4330
(9)	4·5107	(10)	7·6921	(11)	–3·4921	(12)	– 4·2984
(13)	–12·0000						

VOLTAGE SOURCE CURRENTS

NAME	CURRENT
VCC	–4·986E–03
VEE	5·020E–03
V1	–1·716E–05
V2	–1·716E–05

TOTAL POWER DISSIPATION 1·20E–01 WATTS

5. USE PSPICE to find V_1, V_{NI} and V_o of the circuit given.

Solution:

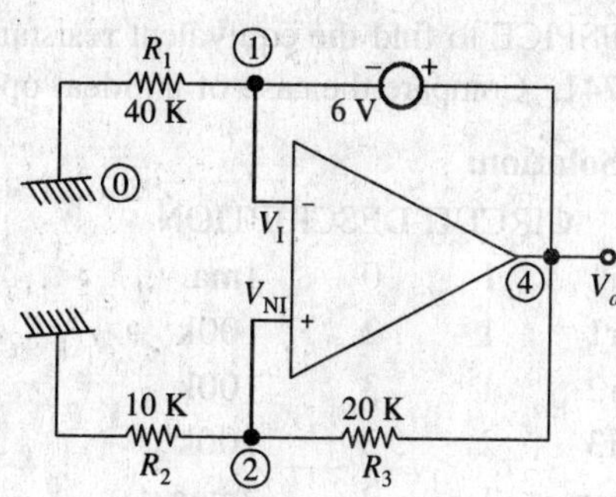

Fig. 10.19.

Take gain $A = 2 \times 10^9$ V / V

$R_{in} = 100$ MΩ

$R_o = 1$Ω.

```
DEAL OPERATIONAL AMPLIFIER
CIRCUIT DESCRIPTION
v1   4   1   6v
r1   1   0   40k
r2   2   0   10k
r3   4   2   20k
rin  1   2   100 meg
ro   4   3   1
e1   3   0   2   1   200e7
¢end
```

IDEAL OPERATIONAL AMPLIFIER
SMALL SIGNAL BIAS SOLUTION TEMPERATURE = 27.000 DEG C

NODE VOLTAGE	NODE VOLTAGE	NODE VOLTAGE	NODE VOLTAGE
(1) 3·0000	(2) 3·0000	(3) 9·0004	(4) 9·0000

VOLTAGE SOURCE CURRENTS (TOTAL POWER DISSIPATION –4·50E –04 WATTS)

NAME	CURRENT
v1	7·500E–05

TOTAL JOB TIME 2.86

6. USE PSPICE program to investigate the departure from the ideal of a voltage follower implemented with an operational amplifier having $r_i = 250$ K Ω, $R_o = 1$k, and $A = 10^4$ V/V. Assume the circuit is driven by a 10·0 V source with a 10 k Ω internal resistance, and drives a 2k Ω load. Comment on the result.

Solution:

```
    CIRCUIT DESCRIPTION
v1   1   0   10V
r1   3   1   10K
ri   2   3   250K
e    4   0   3   2   1e4
rl   2   0   2K
¢ print dc v(1,2)
¢end
    SMALL SIGNAL BIAS SOLUTION            TEMPERATURE = 27.000 DEG C
    NODE VOLTAGE     NODE VOLTAGE      NODE VOLTAGE     NODE VOLTAGE
      (1) 10·0000      (2) 9·9984        (3) 9·9999       (4) 14·9980
    VOLTAGE SOURCE CURRENTS
    NAME          CURRENT
    v1            – 5·999E – 09
    (TOTAL POWER DISSIPATION   –6·00E–08 WATTS)
    JOB CONCLUDED      TOTAL JOB TIME         2.86
```

7. In the I-V converter of Fig given below let $R = 100K$, $R_1 = 100\,\Omega$ and $R_2 = 100\text{ K }\Omega$. USE PSPICE to find the equivalent resistance seen by the source i_I if the operational amplifier is μA 741. Compare the case of an ideal operational amplifier.

Solution:

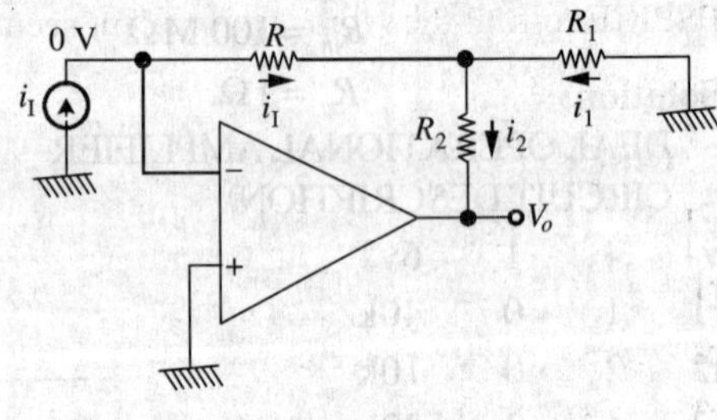

Fig. 10.20.

```
    CIRCUIT DESCRIPTION
i1   1   0   1ma
r1   1   2   100k
r2   1   3   100k
r3   2   3   100k
rin  1   2   2meg
ro   4   3   75
e    4   0   2   1   2e5
¢end
    SMALL SIGNAL     BIAS SOLUTION        TEMPERATURE = 27.000 DEG C
    NODE VOLTAGE     NODE VOLTAGE         NODE VOLTAGE      NODE VOLTAGE
    (1) 99·49E + 03  (2) 99·49E + 03      (3) 99·59E + 03   (4) 99·66E + 03
```

8. Do the PSPICE analysis of the instrumentation amplifier using "SUBCIRCUIT" statement.

Solution:

```
    INSTRUMENTATION AMPLIFIER
    CIRCUIT DESCRIPTION
v1   1   0   2V
v2   6   0   2.004V
r1   5   7   50K
r2   3   5   1K
r3   2   3   20K
r4   2   0   1K
```

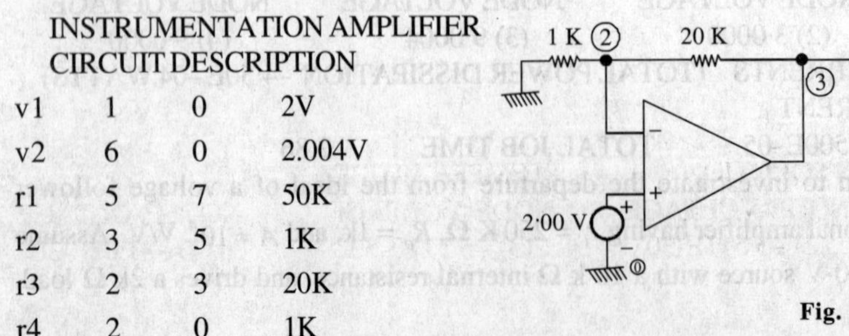
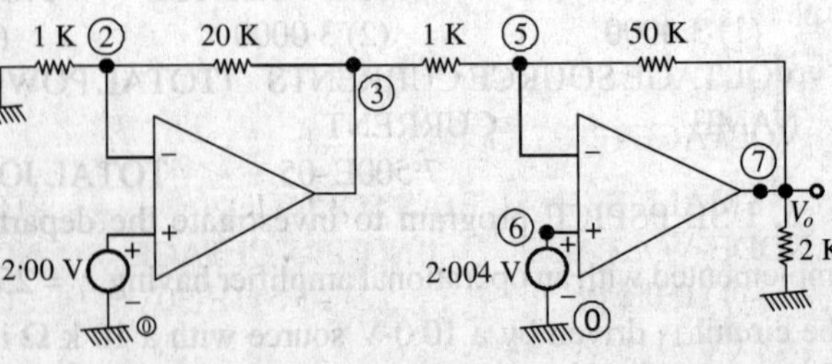

Fig. 10.21.

```
r1   7   0   2K
x1   1   2   3 op amp
x2   6   5   7 op amp
¢ sub ckt operational amplifier x y z
ri   x   y 1meg
ro   w   z   100
e    w   o   x   y   1e5
¢ends
¢end
```

INSTRUMENTATION AMPLIFIER (SMALL SIGNAL BIAS SOLUTION-TEMPERATURE = 27·000 DEG C)

NODE VOLTAGE	NODE VOLTAGE	NODE VOLTAGE	NODE VOLTAGE
(1) 2·0000	(2) 1·9995	(3) 41·9900	(5) 2·0250
(6) 2·0040	(7) –1996·2000	(xl·w) 46·1870	(x2·w) –2100·0000

VOLTAGE SOURCE CURRENTS

NAME	CURRENT
v1	– 4·619E–10
v2	2·000E–08

TOTAL POWER DISSIPATION – 4·12E–08 WATTS

9. In the V-I converter of Fig. 10.22 given below Assume the operational amplifier is ideal, use PSPICE to find the Norton equivalent seen by the load [DO PSPICE analysis first].

Solution:

CIRCUIT DESCRIPTION

```
v1    1    0    ac     10v
r1    1    2    10k
r2    3    0    10k
r3    3    4    10k
rf    2    4    10k
rl    4    0    10k
ri    2    3    100meg
ro    5    4    1
e1    5    0    3      2     200e5
¢ac   lin  16   1      1k
¢plot ac   i(rl) i(rl)
¢end
```

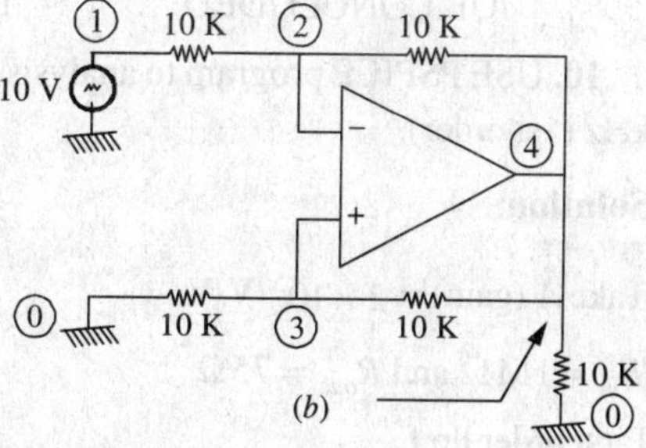

Fig. 10.22 (*a*) **and** (*b*).

VOLTAGE TO CT. CONV.

SMALL SIGNAL BIAS SOLUTION TEMPERATURE = 27·000 DEG C

NODE VOLTAGE	NODE VOLTAGE	NODE VOLTAGE	NODE VOLTAGE
(1) 0·0000	(2) –5·511E-30	(3) –5·511E-30	(4) –81·02E-30
(5) –11·02E-30			

```
VOLTAGE SOURCE CURRENTS
NAME          CURRENT
v1            0·000E+00
TOTAL POWER DISSIPATION      0·00E+00      WATTS
AC ANALYSIS             TEMPERATURE = 27·000 DEG C
LEGEND:
* : I(r1)
+ : I(r1)
FREQ                 I(r1)
(*+) ———————— 1·0000E+03  1·0000E+04   1·0000E+05   1·0000E+06   1·0000E+07
1·000E+00    9·997E+03     ′         + *          ′            ′            ′
6·760E+01    9·997E+03     ′         + *          ′            ′            ′
1·342E+02    9·997E+03     ′         + *          ′            ′            ′
2·008E+02    9·997E+03     ′         + *          ′            ′            ′
2·674E+02    9·997E+03     ′         + *          ′            ′            ′
3·340E+02    9·997E+03     ′         + *          ′            ′            ′
4·006E+02    9·997E+03     ′         + *          ′            ′            ′
4·672E+02    9·997E+03     ′         + *          ′            ′            ′
5·338E+02    9·997E+03     ′         + *          ′            ′            ′
6·004E+02    9·997E+03     ′         + *          ′            ′            ′
6·670E+02    9·997E+03     ′         + *          ′            ′            ′
7·336E+02    9·997E+03     ′         + *          ′            ′            ′
8·002E+02    9·997E+03     ′         + *          ′            ′            ′
8·668E+02    9·997E+03     ′         + *          ′            ′            ′
9·334E+02    9·997E+03     ′         + *          ′            ′            ′
1·000E+03    9·997E+03     ′         + *          ′            ′            ′
     JOB CONCLUDED          TOTAL JOB TIME          3·79
```

10. USE PSPICE program to analysis the active low pass filter having cut off frequency $f_e = 1 \cdot 25$ kHz (1st order).

Solution:

Take A (gain) = 2×10^5 V/V

$R_{in} = 1\,\text{M}\Omega$ and $R_{out} = 75\Omega$

```
First order l.p.f.
V1    1    0    AC    1V
E     4    0    3     2     200E3
RI    3    2    1000K
RO    6    4    75
R     1    3    15.8K
C     3    0    0.008UF
R1    0    2    10K
RF    6    2    10K
RL    6    0    10K
′AC   LIN   1000   100   100kHZ
′OPTION NOPAGE
′END
```

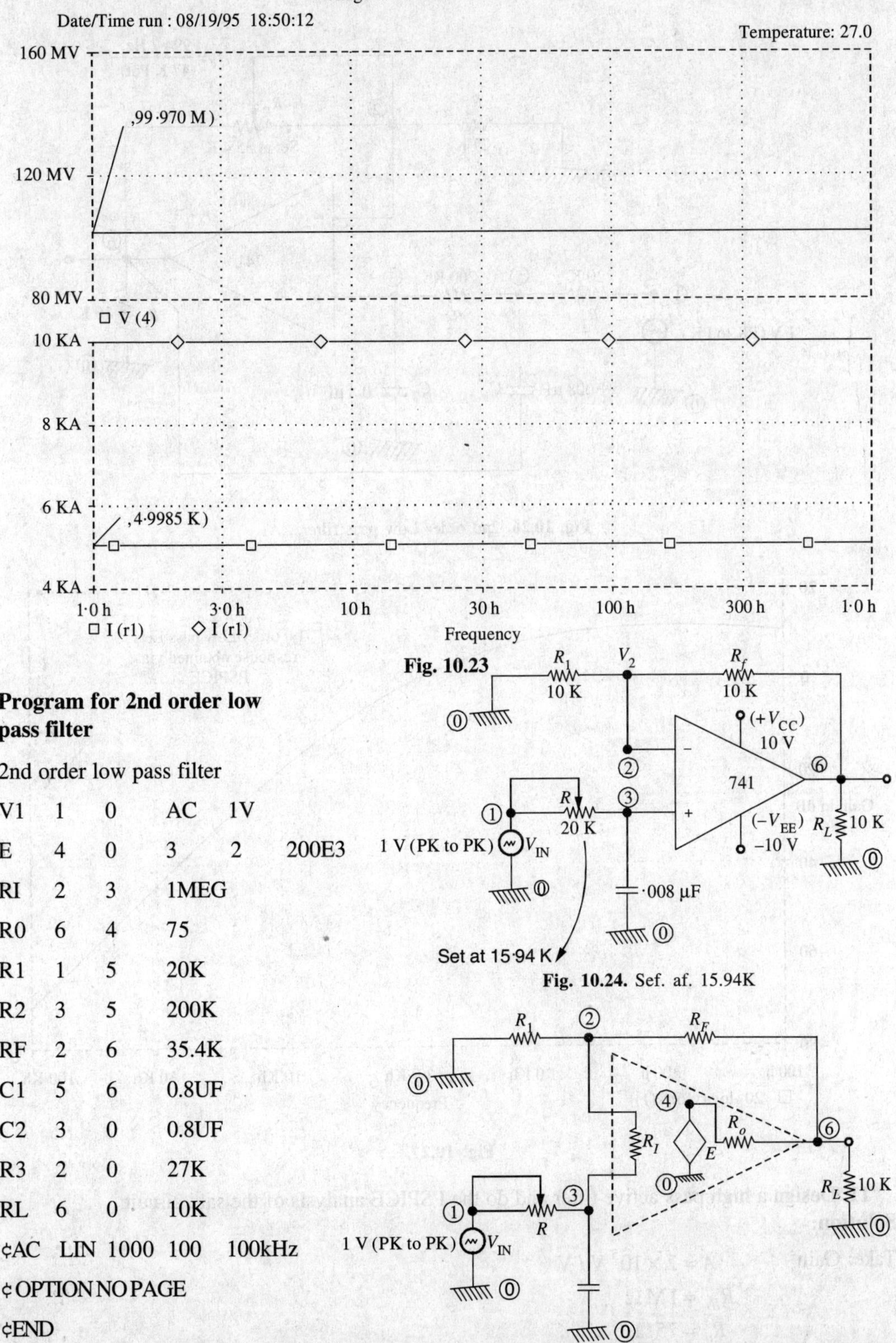

Fig. 10.23

Fig. 10.24. Sef. af. 15.94K

Fig. 10.25. PSPICE equivalent circuit.

Program for 2nd order low pass filter

```
2nd order low pass filter
V1   1   0   AC    1V
E    4   0   3     2     200E3
RI   2   3   1MEG
R0   6   4   75
R1   1   5   20K
R2   3   5   200K
RF   2   6   35.4K
C1   5   6   0.8UF
C2   3   0   0.8UF
R3   2   0   27K
RL   6   0   10K
¢AC  LIN 1000 100   100kHz
¢OPTION NOPAGE
¢END
```

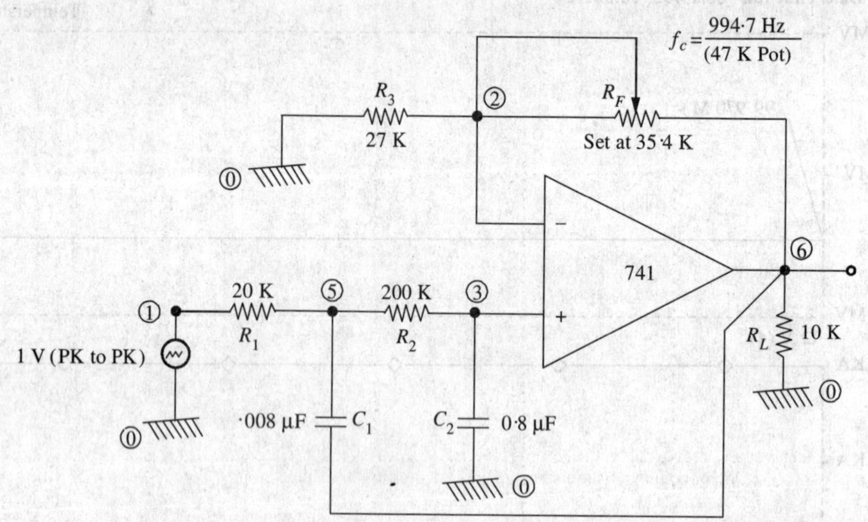

Fig. 10.26. 2nd order Low pass filter.

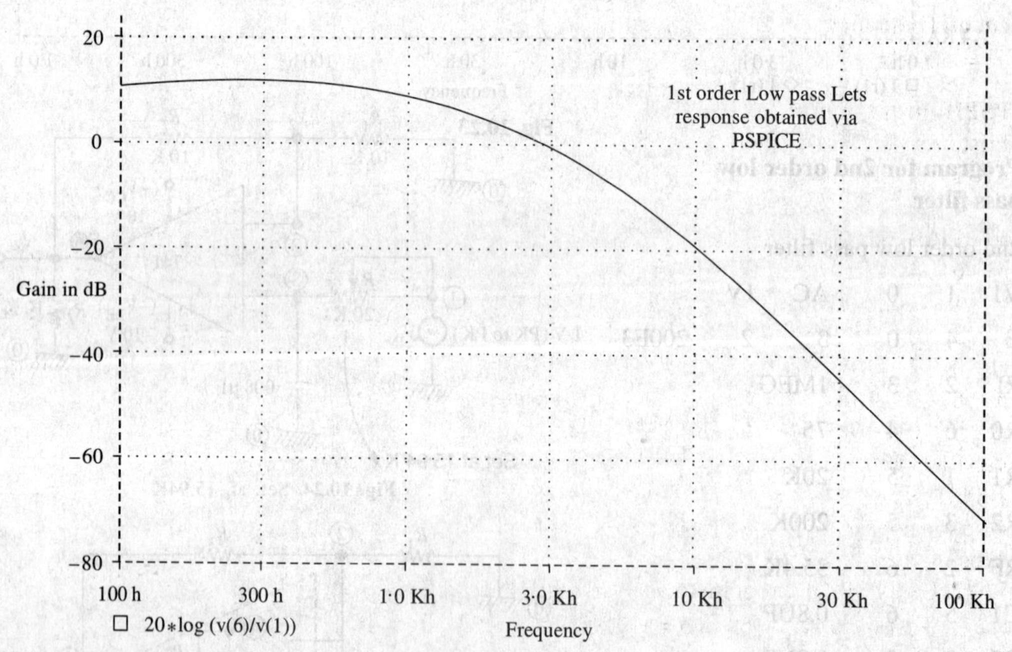

Fig. 10.27.

11. Design a high pass active filter and do the PSPICE analysis of the said circuit.

Solution:

Take: Gain $A = 2 \times 10^5 \text{ V/V}$

$R_{IN} = 1\text{M}\Omega$

$R_o = 75\Omega$

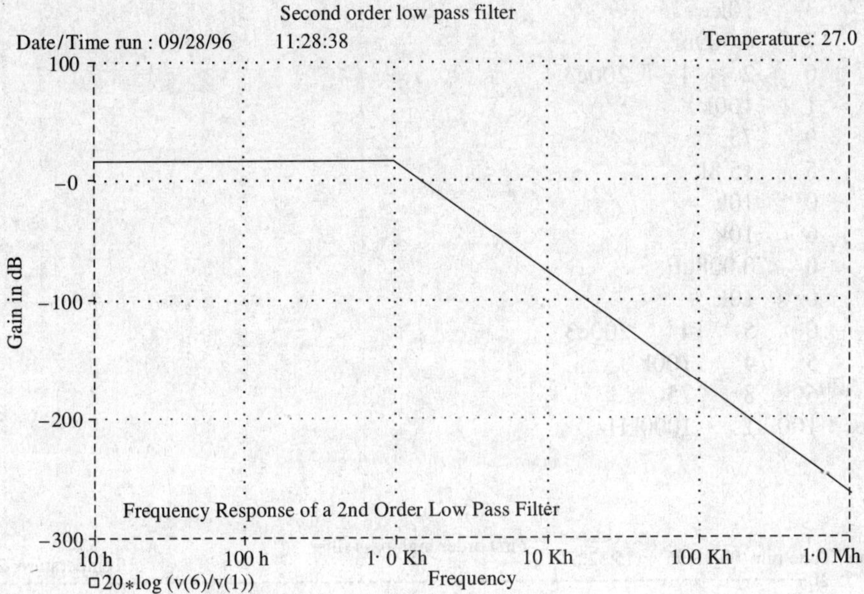

Fig. 10.28.

cut off frequency

$f_c = 500$ Hz

PSPIC program for.

First order high pass filter

```
v1  1  0  ac  1V
e   4  0  3  2  200e3
ri  3  2  1000K
ro  6  4  75
c   1  3  0.009μF
r   3  0  35.3K
r1  0  2  10K
rf  6  2  10K
rl  6  0  10K
¢ac lin 1000   100
100kHz
¢ option nopage
¢end
```

Fig. 10.29.

12. USE PSPICE program to analysis a band pass filter.

Pass band $\Delta B = 1 \cdot 3\,\text{kHZ}$

Solution:

Take: Gain $A_1 = A_2 = 2 \times 10^5\ \text{V/V}$

$$R_{IN_1} = R_{IN_2}\ 1\,\text{M}\Omega$$

$$R_{o_1} = R_{o_2} = 75\,\Omega$$

band pass filter

```
vin  7  0  ac  1v
r1   2  0  35.3k
r2   1  0  10k
```

```
r3   1   3   10k
c1   2   7   0.009uf
e1   9   0   2   1   200e3
ril  2   1   100k
rol  3   9   75
r4   3   5   15.8k
r5   4   0   10k
r6   4   6   10k
c2   5   0   0.008μF
r1   6   0   10k
e2   8   0   5   4   200e3
ri   2   5   4   100k
ro2  2   6   8   75
¢ac  dec 100 1   1000kHz
¢probe
¢end
```

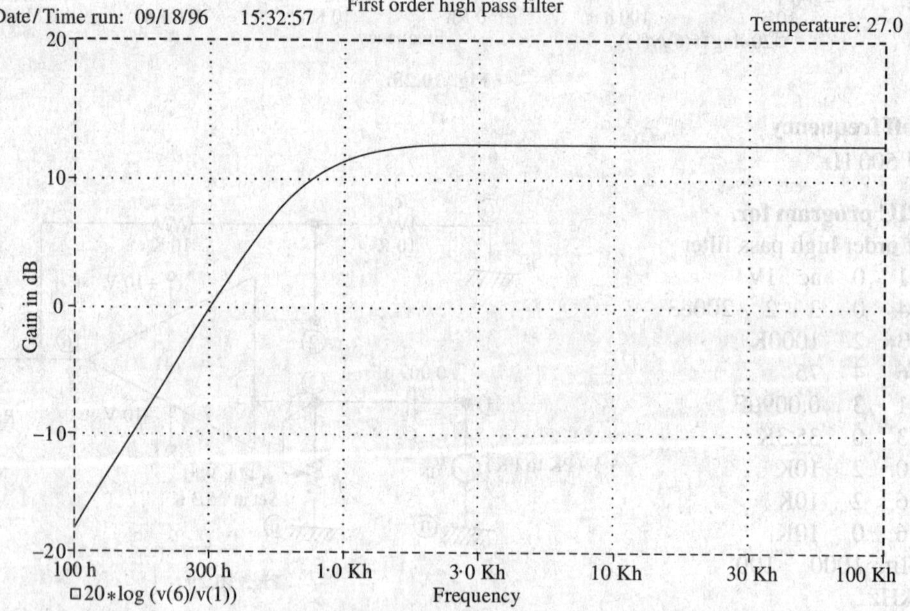

Fig. 10.30.

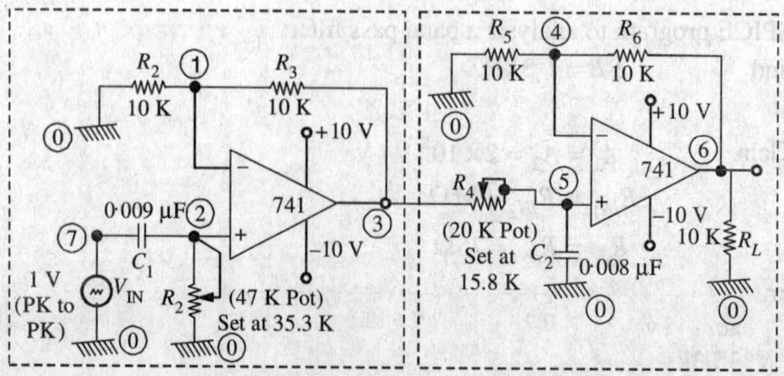

Fig. 10.31.

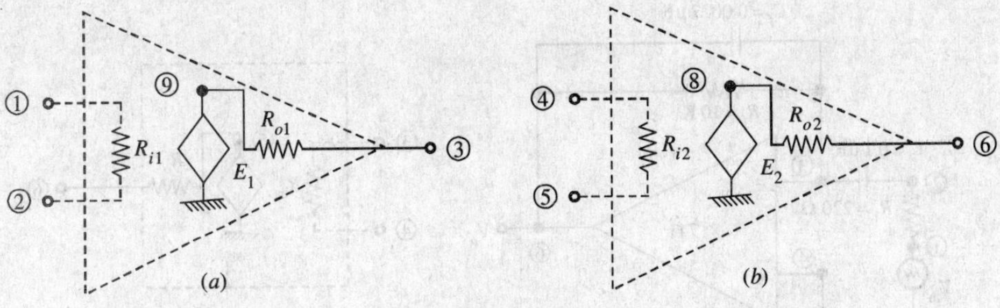

Fig. 10.32. (*a*) and (*b*)

13. USE PSPICE program to analysis the differentiator circuit given below.

Solution:

Take: Gain $A = 2 \times 10^5$ V / V

$R_{IN} = 1\,\text{M}\Omega$

$R_o = 75\,\Omega$

```
study of differentiator circuit
v1    1    0    ac    5v
e     5    0    4     3     200e3
ri    4    3    1000k
ro    6    5    75
r1    1    2    220
r2    4    0    10k
rf    3    6    10k
c1    2    3    0.1uf
cf    6    3    0.0027µF
¢ac   lin  40   1     1000kHz
¢probe
¢end
```

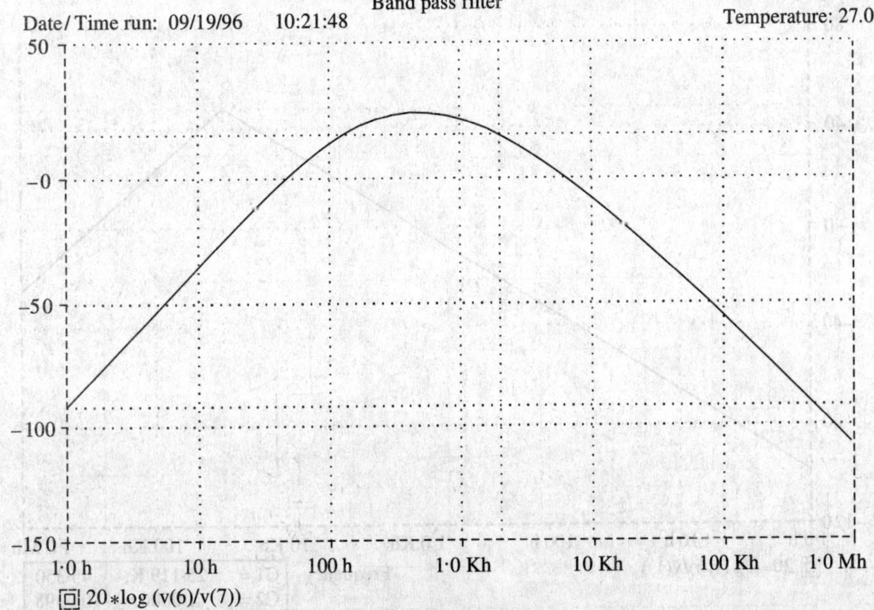

Fig. 10.33.

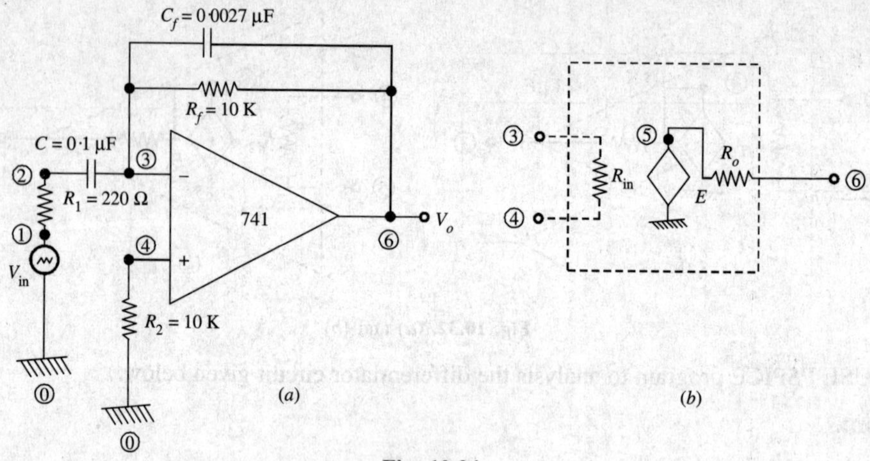

Fig. 10.34.

14. USE PSPICE program to study the integrator circuit given below with the operational amplifier 741 having non ideal parameters same as in problem 12.

Solution:

```
Study of integrator circuit
v1    1    0    ac    1v
e     5    0    3     2     200e3
ri    3    2    1000k
ro    6    5    75
r1    1    2    10k
r     3    0    10k
c     6    2    0.1µF
r2    6    2    100k
¢ac   lin  6000 10Hz 100kHz
¢ option no page
```

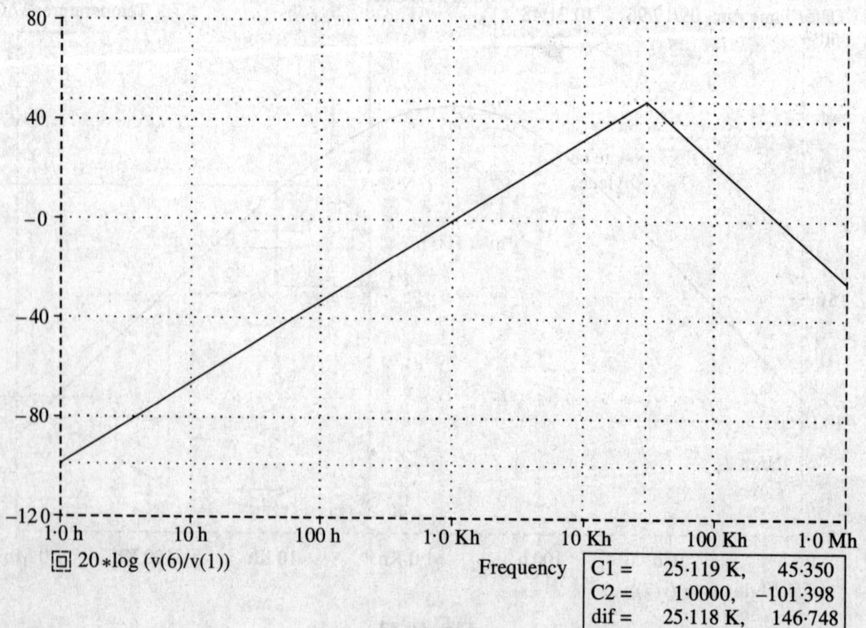

Fig. 10.35.

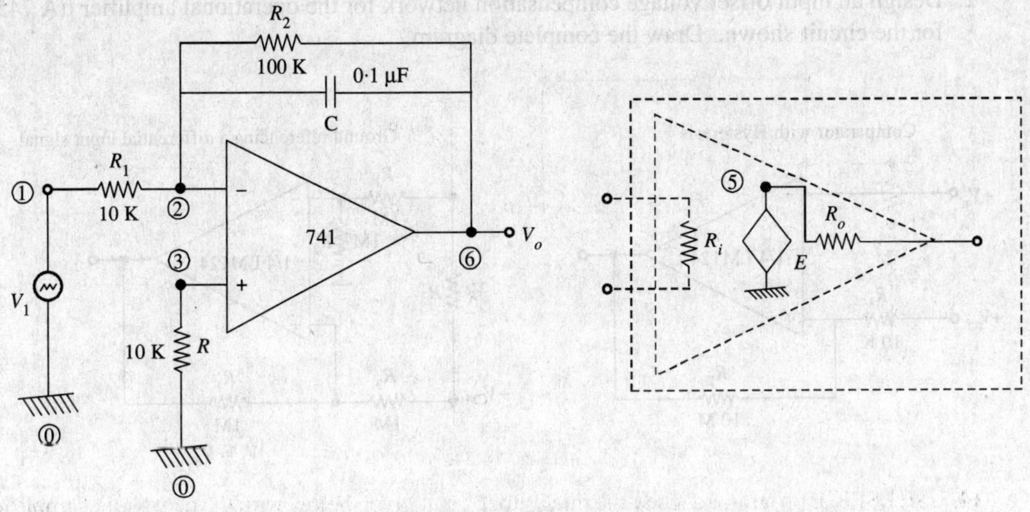

Fig. 10.36. **Fig. 10.37.**

REVIEW QUESTIONS

Use PSPICE/SPICE program to solve the following problems.

1. Compute the maximum possible total offset voltage in the amplifier shown with supply voltage ± 15V.

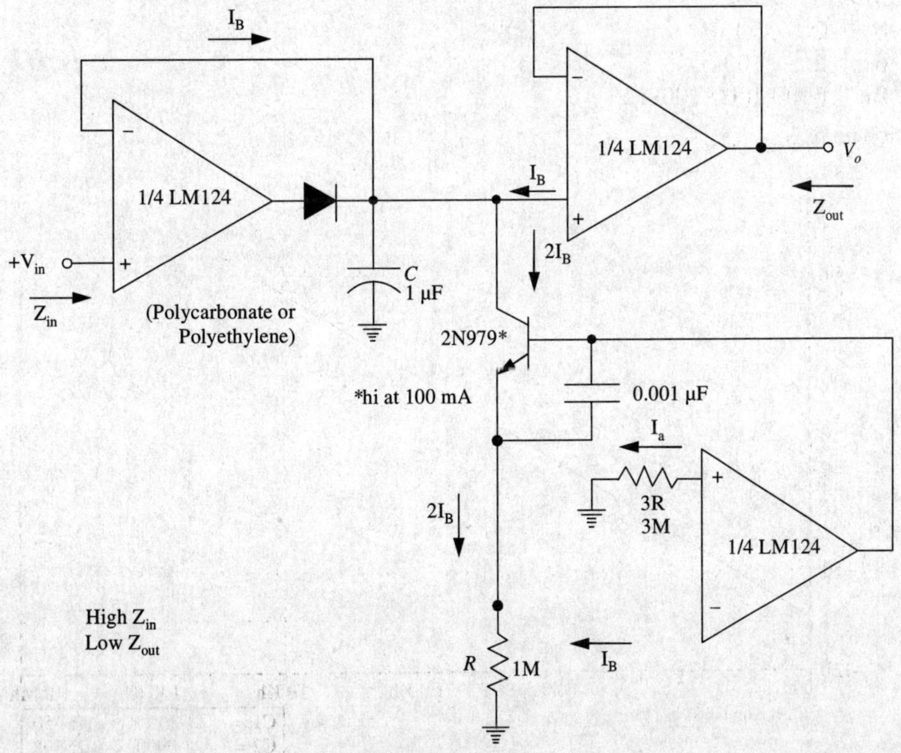

Fig. S.1

2. Design an input offset voltage compensation network for the operational amplifier μA 745 for the circuit shown. Draw the complete diagram.

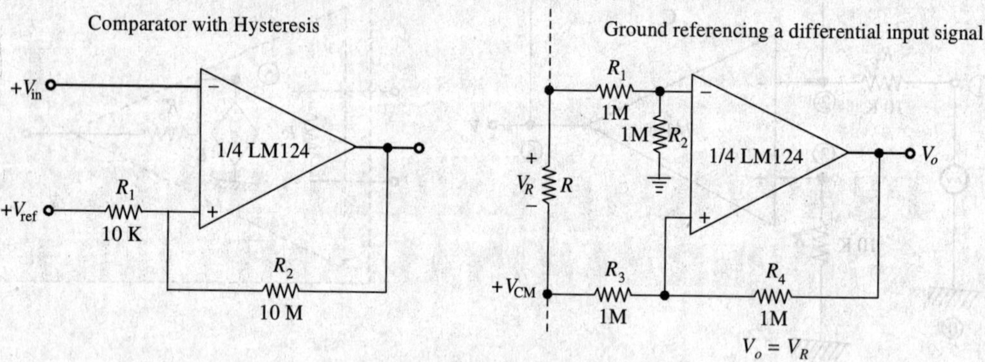

Fig. S.2.

3. Repeat the problem X, but for the case of a non ideal operational amplifier having $R_I = 100\text{K}$, $R_o = 100\Omega$, and gain $A = 1000\text{V/V}$.

11

PRACTICAL EXPERIMENTS ON OPERATIONAL AMPLIFIERS

(*i*) To study of unity gain buffer using operational amplifier (*ii*) To measure input resistance (R_i) of operational amplifier. (*iii*) To measure the output resistance (R_o) of operational amplifier. (*iv*) To study the frequency response of an operational amplifier and calculation of gain bandwidth product.

EXPERIMENT 11·1

Title

(*i*) To study of unity gain buffer using operational amplifier (*ii*) To measure input resistance (R_i) of operational amplifier. (*iii*) To measure the output resistance (R_o) of operational amplifier. (*iv*) To study the frequency response of an operational amplifier and calculation of gain bandwidth product.

Objective

(*i*) The main object of the experiment is to study the functioning of an operational amplifier (IC 741) as a voltage follower.

(*ii*) To study the variation of V_{out} with V_{in} for different values of R_f.

(*iii*) To study the variation of the ratio $\left(\dfrac{V_{out} \text{ with no } R_L}{V_{out} \text{ with } R_L}\right)$ with $1/R_L$ and thus find the output resistance of the operational amplifier.

(*iv*) To find the frequency response and thus the bandwidth of IC 741.

Components/Equipments Required

Power supply (±15 V)	–	One
IC 741	–	One (AN 1741A·710)
Digital multimeter/analog meter	–	One
Bread-board	–	One
Resistors		1K, 10K, 1M, 100K All 1/2 or 1/4 watt.
CRO	–	One
Potentiometer 10K	–	One
Function generator. (0–1 MHz)	–	One

Use of the Potentiometer

The potentiometer was used to supply different voltages to the pin number three.

By keeping one end terminal of the potentiometer intact and moving the other end terminal between A and B gives both positive and negative variation to the pin 3.

Theory and Circuits

Ideal Operational Amplifier

The ideal operational amplifier has the following characteristics.

(*i*) Input resistance $R_i = \infty$

(*ii*) Output resistance $R_o = 0$

(*iii*) Voltage gain $A_V = -\infty$

(*iv*) Band width (B.W.) $= \infty$

(*v*) $V_o = 0$ when $V_{in1} = V_{in\,2}$ and independent of input voltage.

(*vi*) Characteristics are independent of temperature.

Fig. 11.1

OPERATIONAL AMPLIFIER

Operational amplifier performs the operation like differentiation, integration, addition, subtraction etc.

CALCULATION OF UNITY GAIN

At node 2 applying KCL we get $I_1 + I_2 = 0$

$$I_1 = \frac{V_2 - V_{out}}{R_f} \text{ and } I_2 = \frac{V_2}{R_i}$$

So $$\frac{V_2 - V_{out}}{R_f} + \frac{V_2}{R_i} = 0 \quad [\text{As } I_1 = -I_2]$$

$$\frac{V_{out}}{R_f} = \frac{V_2}{R_f} + \frac{V_2}{R_i}$$

$$= \frac{V_2}{R_f}\left(1 + \frac{R_f}{R_i}\right)$$

$$\Rightarrow \quad V_{out} = V_2\left(1 + \frac{R_f}{R_i}\right) \quad ...(1)$$

Again we know that

$$V_{out} = A\,(V_2 - V_{in})$$

$$\Rightarrow \quad \frac{V_{out}}{A} + V_{in} = V_2$$

So from Eqn. (1)

$$V_{out} = \left(\frac{V_{out}}{A} + V_{in}\right)\left(1 + \frac{R_f}{R_i}\right)$$

$$V_{out} - \frac{V_{out}}{A}\left(1 + \frac{R_f}{R_i}\right) = V_{in}\left(1 + \frac{R_f}{R_i}\right)$$

$$\frac{V_{out}}{A}\left\{A - \left(1 + \frac{R_f}{R_i}\right)\right\} = V_{in}\left(1 + \frac{R_f}{R_i}\right)$$

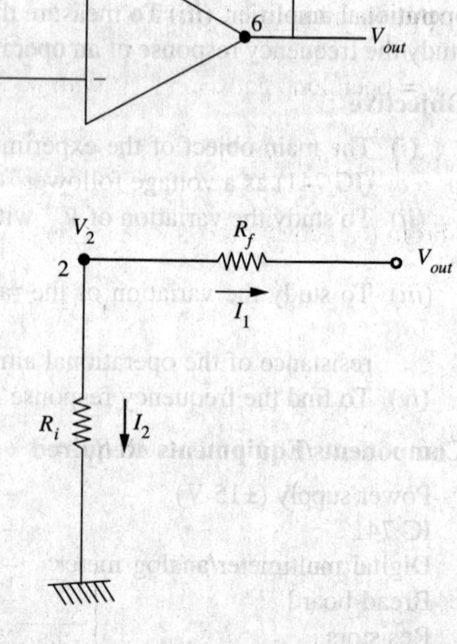

Fig. 11.2

Now as $$A >> \left(1+\frac{R_f}{R_i}\right)$$

$$\Rightarrow \quad \frac{V_{\text{out}}}{A}.A = V_{\text{in}}\left(1+\frac{R_f}{R_i}\right)$$

$$V_{\text{out}} = V_{\text{in}}\left(1+\frac{R_f}{R_i}\right) \quad ...(2)$$

$$\frac{V_{\text{out}}}{V_{\text{in}}} = 1+\frac{R_f}{R_i} = \text{gain}$$

$$\frac{dV_{\text{out}}}{dV_{\text{in}}} = 1+\frac{R_f}{R_i}$$

So slope of the curve (V_{out} · Versus · V_{in})

will givc $$1+\frac{R_f}{R_i} = m \text{ (say)}$$

So $$\frac{R_f}{R_i} = m-1$$

$$R_i = \frac{R_f}{m-1}$$

Again if we draw a graph for different values of R_f keeping input voltage fixed (gain . vs. R_f curve). Gain vs. R_f will a straight line cutting the gain axis at unity. The inverse of the slope of the curve will give R_i.

as $R_i >> R_f$ then $R_f/R_i << 1$, then from Eq. (2) we get

$V_{out} = V_{in} \Rightarrow$ unity gain differential amplifier *i.e.*, voltage follower.

Output Resistant Calculation: (R_o)

A_o = open loop gain = $\left(\frac{V_o}{V_i}\right)$ with no R_L

$A = \left(\frac{V_o}{V_i}\right)$ with R_L

From the above circuit

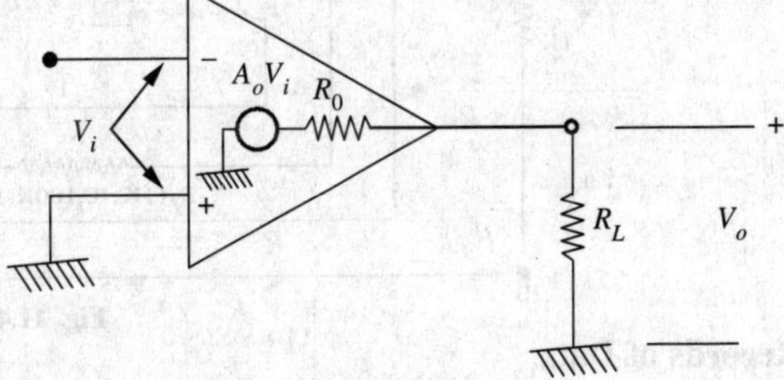

Fig. 11.3

$$V_0 = \frac{A_o V_i}{R_o+R_L} . R_L$$

$$\left(\frac{V_o}{V_i}\right) \text{with } R_L = \frac{\left(\frac{V_o}{V_i}\right)\text{with no } R_L}{1+\frac{R_o}{R_L}} \left(\begin{array}{l}\text{measure voltage}\\ \text{at PIN 6 with no}\\ \text{R}_\text{L} \text{ with a multimeter}\end{array}\right)$$

$$\left(\frac{\left(\frac{V_o}{V_i}\right)\text{with no } R_L}{\left(\frac{V_o}{V_i}\right)\text{with } R_L}\right) = 1+\frac{R_o}{R_L}$$

$$Y = 1+\frac{R_o}{R_L}\text{; where } Y = \frac{\left(\frac{V_o}{V_i}\right)\text{with no } R_L}{\left(\frac{V_o}{V_i}\right)\text{with } R_L}$$

If we draw a graph with Y vs. $\frac{1}{R_L}$ we will get a straight line graph with unity intercept with the Y axis. The slope of the curve will give R_o.

Procedure

Unity Gain Buffer

(*i*) Assemble the circuit on the breadboard by making connection according the given pin out diagram.

(*ii*) Next we connect the power supply to the pin No 7 & 4 and set the power supply out about ± 10 V.

(*iii*) We have used the resistance R_f as 10K, 100K & 1M Ω between the 2 & 6 pins.

(*iv*) For each value of R_f we vary the input voltage from – 10V to 10V and plot the output V_o versus V_{in} and calculate gain.

(*v*) After this connect a load resistance R_L across the 6 & ground and measure the output with varying R_L.

(*vi*) For fixed R_L, R_f & V_{in} change the frequency of signal input to plot the gain vs frequency curve.

Circuit Diagram

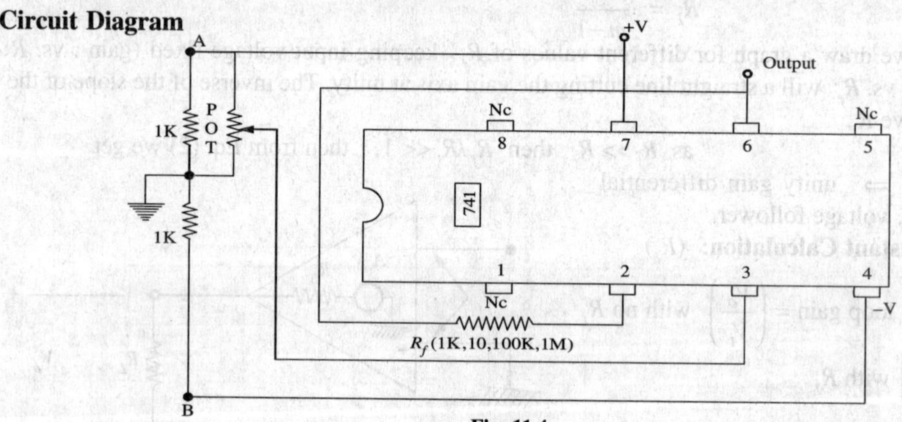

Fig. 11.4

Records of Data

Table 11.1: (DC analysis)

R_f →	1K Ω		10K Ω		100K Ω		1M Ω	
Sl. No.	V_{in} (V)	V_{out} (V)	V_{in} (V)	V_{out} (V)	V_{in} (V)	V_{out} (V)	V_{in} (V)	V_{out} (V)
1	– 9·74	– 8·08	– 9·00	– 8·78	– 9·10	– 7·98	– 8·33	– 7·94
2	– 8·30	– 8·08	– 8·92	– 8·98	– 8·54	– 7·98	– 8·02	– 7·94
3	– 7·37	– 7·37	– 7·56	– 7·56	– 7·54	– 7·54	– 7·02	– 6·97
4	– 5·49	– 5·49	– 5·14	– 5·14	– 5·01	– 5·00	– 5·31	– 5·25
5	– 2·84	– 2·84	– 2·50	– 2·50	– 2·81	– 2·81	– 2·65	– 2·58
6	2·58	2·58	2·69	2·69	2·39	2·40	2·15	2·22
7	5·15	5·15	5·32	5·32	5·28	5·29	5·84	5·91
8	7·60	7·60	7·55	7·55	7·19	7·20	7·56	7·63
9	9·00	8·75	8·86	8·72	8·78	8·78	9·48	9·44
10	9·56	8·75	9·48	8·72	9·64	9·44	9·76	9·44

Table 11.2: Observation (Taking R_f = 1 K V_{in} = 2·7 V) DC analysis

$(V_{out})\ R_L = \infty$	$(V_{out})\ R_L \neq 0$	$(V_{out})\ R_L = \infty\ /\ (V_{out})\ R_L \neq 0$	R_L	$1/\ R_L$
2·7 V	0·18 V	1·5	10Ω	0·1
2·7 V	0·72 V	3·75	47 Ω	0·021
2·7 V	1·32 V	2·045	120 Ω	$8{\cdot}33 \times 10^{-3}$
2·7 V	2·12 V	1·27	470 Ω	$2{\cdot}127 \times 10^{-3}$
2·7 V	2·66 V	1·015	10 K	10^{-4}
2·7 V	2·70 V	1	100 K	10^{-5}
2·7 V	2·70 V	1	1 M	10^{-6}

$V_{in} = 2{\cdot}2$ V

$R_f = 1$ K

AC Analysis

f_{in} (V)	V_{out} (V)	Gain in (dB)	f_{in} (kHz)	V_{out} (V)	Gain in (dB)
80 Hz	2·2	0	110 kHz	2·1	– 0·40
120	2·2	0	115	2·1	– 0·40
200	2·3	0·45	125	2·1	– 0·40
400	2·1	– 0·40	130	2·0	– 0·83
800	2	– 0·83	135	2·0	– 0·83
1 kHz	2·1	– 0·40	140	1·9	– 1·27
5 kHz	2·2	0	150	1·8	– 1·74
15 kHz	2·2	0	170	1·7	– 2·34
40 kHz	2·15	– 0·41	180	1·7	– 2·34
60 KHz	2·1	– 0·40	200	1·6	– 2·77
90 kHz	2·2	0	250	1·4	– 3·93
			280	1·2	– 5·26
			320	1·0	– 6·85

Results

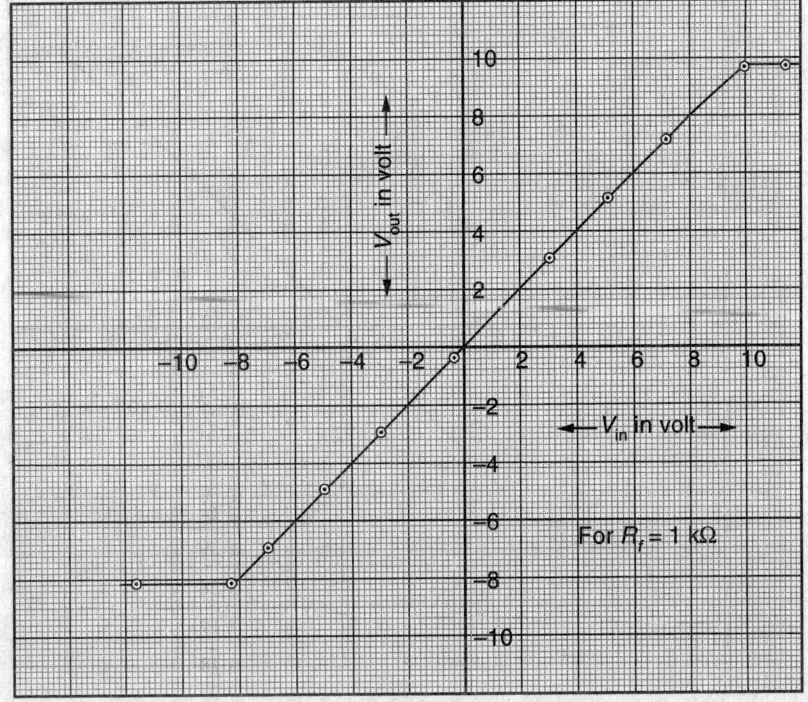

G. 1

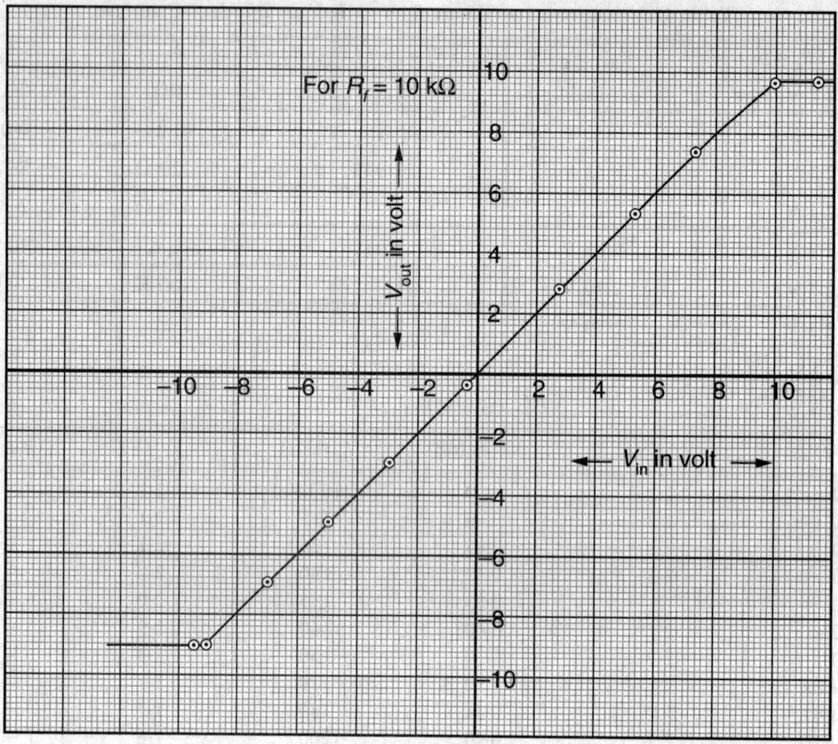
For R_f = 10 kΩ
V_{out} in volt
V_{in} in volt
10
8
6
4
2
−2
−4
−6
−8
−10
−10 −8 −6 −4 −2 2 4 6 8 10

G. 2

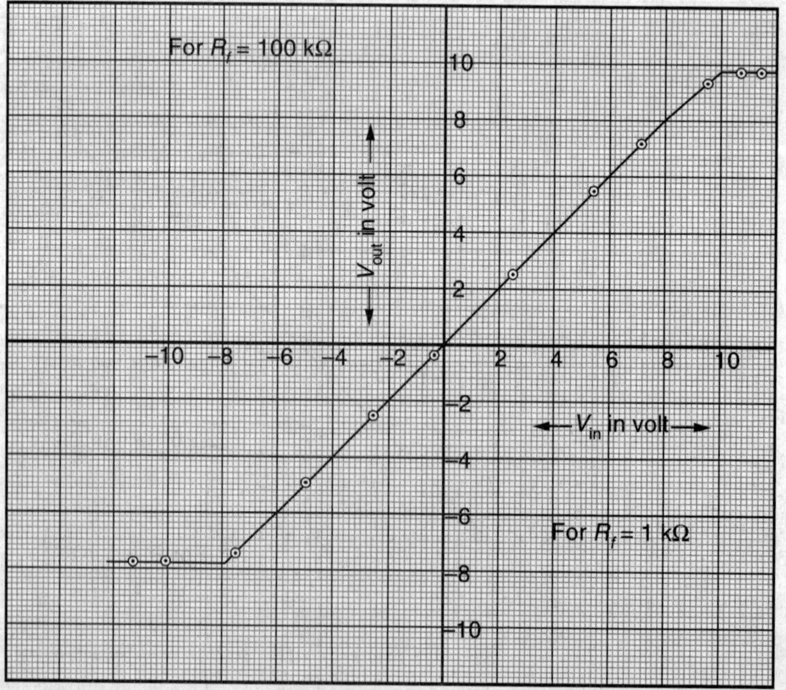
For R_f = 100 kΩ
For R_f = 1 kΩ
V_{out} in volt
V_{in} in volt
10
8
6
4
2
−2
−4
−6
−8
−10
−10 −8 −6 −4 −2 2 4 6 8 10

G. 3

For R_f = 1 MΩ
10
8
6
4
2
–2
–4
–6
–8
–10
–10 –8 –6 –4 –2 2 4 6 8 10
← V_{out} in volt →
← V_{in} in volt →
For R_f = 1 kΩ

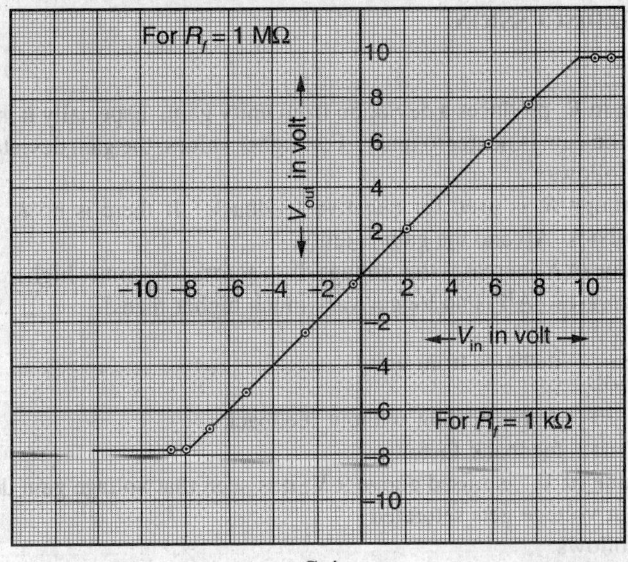

G. 4

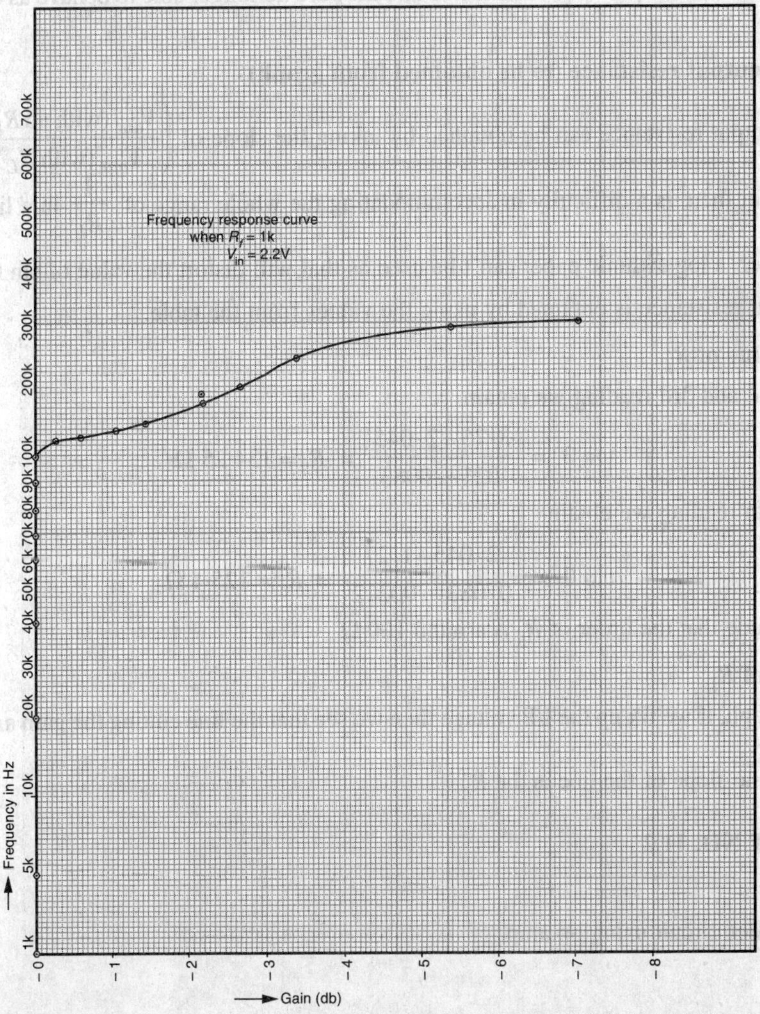

Frequency response curve
when R_f = 1k
V_{in} = 2.2V
→ Frequency in Hz
1k
5k
10k
20k
30k
40k
50k
60k
70k
80k
90k
100k
200k
300k
400k
500k
600k
700k
–0
–1
–2
–3
–4
–5
–6
–7
–8
→ Gain (db)

G. 5

CONCLUSION AND DISCUSSION

Report

(*i*) The variation in R_f produces a deviation from unity gain. Especially it is noted that for low values of R_f the gain is nearer to unity. For higher values, the gain deviates from unity. The reason is as follows:

The path through R_f is used for negative feedback. If there is no R_f then there is total negative feedback $A\beta$ and the gain is unity.

But as the value of R_f increases the voltage drop across it becomes higher. Thus the negative feedback decreases. $A\beta$ is no logger vary much higher than 1.

Thus $\dfrac{A}{1+A\beta}$ deviates from unity

$A \Rightarrow$ Amplification without feedback

$\beta \Rightarrow$ feedback factor.

(*ii*) When the value of V_{in} is raised above 9 V, it is seen that voltage gain deviates from unity and the output voltage gets saturated.

The reason is as follows:

The transistors inside the chip gets saturated and they are no longer able to behave as differential amplifier.

Discussion on output resistance (to be obtained from graph)

The value of output resistance can be obtained by taking the slope of $\left(\dfrac{V_{out}\,(\text{with no } R_L)}{V_{out}\,(\text{with } R_L)}\right)$ versus $\dfrac{1}{R_L}$, $V_s\ \dfrac{1}{R_L}$ ·But there is a difficulty in accommodating the whole range of $\dfrac{1}{R_L}$ in a lineal graph paper. Moreover, a logarithmic paper can't be used as that will distort the value of tan θ (slope).

So the output resistance is obtained by using the values from the table.

Finding the value of R_o

From the second and 3rd reading we obtain

$$\tan\theta = \frac{3\cdot 75 - 2\cdot 045}{\cdot 021 - \cdot 0083} = R_o = 134\cdot 25\ \Omega$$

from 3rd and 4th reading we obtain

$$\tan\theta = \frac{2\cdot 045 - 1\cdot 27}{0\cdot 083\quad \cdot 00212} = R_o = 125\cdot 4\ \Omega$$

So we conclude that the order of R_o is around 100 Ω

Finding value of R_i

In gain Vs R_f graph, if we fix up the I/P voltage then we see that the line cutting the gain axis is unity is a straight line.

The inverse of the slope of the line is the R_i.

EXPERIMENT NO. 11.2

Title

To study the adder circuit using op.amp.

Objective

The object of this experiment is to study the adder circuit by using operational amplifier μA 741.

Components/Equipments Required

(i) Operational amplifier → μA 741.
(ii) Bread-board
(iii) Power supply (± 15V)
(iv) Oscilloscope
(v) Digital/Analog multimeter
(vi) Function generation.
(vii) Resistances – 10 k → three *pcs.*
100 k → three *pcs.*
3·3 k → three *pcs.*
33 k → three *pcs.*

Theory and Circuits

Adder

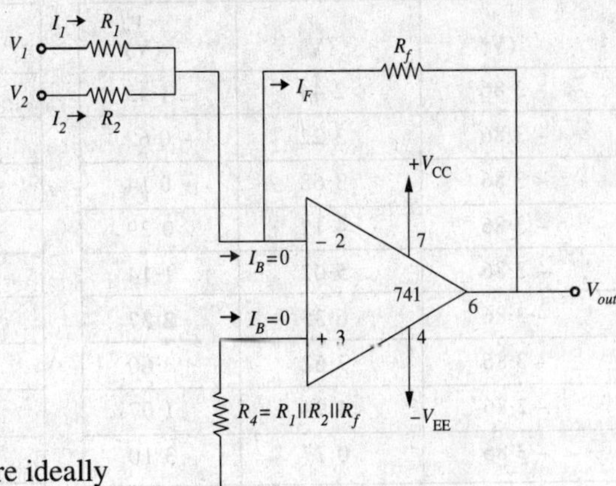

Fig. 11.5.

Theory: From the above circuit

$$I_1 + I_2 = I_B + I_F$$

since R_i and A of the operational amplifier are ideally infinity so $I_B = 0$ and we can write

$$\frac{V_1}{R_1} + \frac{V_2}{R_2} = -\frac{V_o}{R_f} \qquad V_o = -R_f\left(\frac{V_1}{R_1} + \frac{V_2}{R_2}\right)$$

$$V_o = -(V_1 + V_2) \text{ if } R_1 = R_2 = R_f$$

Procedure

(i) Assemble the circuit, as per given pin out diagram on the breadboard.
(ii) Next set the power supply at about ± 10 V. (pin 7 & pin 4)
(iii) The value as considered $R_1 = R_2 = R_f = 10$ K and R_4 as $R_1 \| R_2 \| R_f = 10/3 = 3{\cdot}3$ K firstly and for various values of V_1 & V_2 we get the output as addition of V_1 & V_2.
(iv) We plot the output and input after taking the data in tabular form.
(v) Repeat the experiment with $R_1 = R_2 = R_f = 100$ K and R_4 thus $= \frac{100}{3} = 33{\cdot}33$ K.

$$R_1 = R_2 = R_f = 10 \text{ K} \quad R_4 = 3{\cdot}3 \text{ K}$$

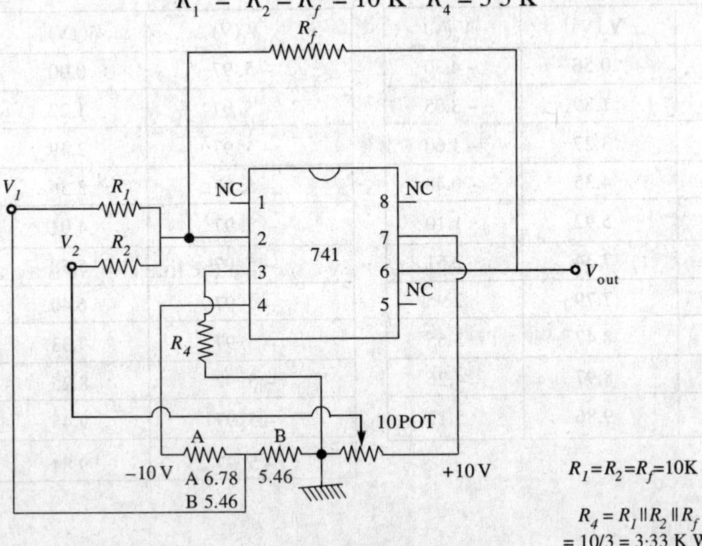

Fig. 11.6.

Records of Data

Observation Table:

Table – 11.3A

v_1 (V)	v_2 (V)	$-v_o$ (V)
– 3·86	2·44	– 1·45
– 3·86	3·22	– 0·62
– 3·86	3·68	– 0·14
– 3·86	4·12	0·29
– 3·86	5·02	1·14
– 3·86	6·35	2·37
– 3·86	7·62	3·60
– 3·86	4·94	1·07
– 3·86	0·77	3·10

Table – 11.3B

v_1 (V)	v_2 (V)	$-v_o$ (V)
– 4·76	0·00	– 4·76
– 4·76	1·20	– 3·60
– 4·76	2·74	– 2·06
– 4·76	3·69	– 1·06
– 4·76	4·42	– 0·35
– 4·76	5·12	0·37
– 4·76	5·14	0·38
– 4·76	6·13	1·33
– 4·76	7·46	2·70
– 4·76	8·62	3·84

v_1 (V)	v_2 (V)	$-v_o$ (V)
All the value of V_1	all +ve values of V_2	

v_1 (V)	v_2 (V)	$-v_o$ (V)
all negative value of V_1	all negative values of V_2	

Observation Table:

$$R_1 = R_2 = R_f = 100\text{ K} \quad R_4 = 3{\cdot}3\text{ K}$$

V_1 (V)	V_2(V)	$-V_o$(V)
– 4.84	0.56	– 4.30
– 4.84	1.89	– 3.05
– 4.84	3.27	– 1.60
– 4.84	4.35	– 0.48
– 4.84	5.92	1.10
– 4.84	7.34	2.51
– 4.84	7.79	2.95
– 4 4	8.47	3.65
– 4.84	8.97	4.26
– 4.84	9.86	5.12

V_1(V)	V_2(V)	$-V_o$(V)
– 5. 97	0.00	– 5.97
– 5. 97	1.22	– 4.75
– 5. 97	2.49	– 3.50
– 5. 97	3.56	– 2.49
– 5. 97	4.01	– 1.40
– 5. 97	5.58	– 0.39
– 5. 97	6.40	0.44
– 5. 97	7.33	1.38
– 5. 97	8.25	2.30
– 5. 97	9.45	3.47
– 5. 97	9.84	3.90

Conclusion

From the data table, we see that the output is the algebric sum of all inputs and a negative sign appears. This negative sign appears due to inverting inputs. And also there is a phase change between input and output. So, this acts as an adder circuit.

EXPERIMENT NO. 11.3

Title

To study the integrator circuit using operational amplifier.

Objective

The object of this experiment is to study the integrator circuit by using operational amplifier μA 741.

Components/Equipments Required

(*i*) Operational amplifier – μA 741.
(*ii*) Bread-board
(*iii*) Power supply (± 15V)
(*iv*) Oscilloscope
(*v*) Digital/Analog multimeter
(*vi*) Function generation.
(*vii*) Resistances – 10 k → three *Pcs*.
1 k → two *Pcs*.
100 k → one *Pcs*.
Capacitor – 0.1 μ R.

Theory and Circuits

Integrator

Theory: $I = \dfrac{V_1 - 0}{R_1}$

$$V_C = -\frac{1}{C}\int_o^t idt$$

$$= -\frac{1}{C}\int_o^t \frac{V_1}{R}dt$$

$$= -\frac{1}{CR}\int_o^t V_1 dt$$

output is the integral of the input. So it is an integrator

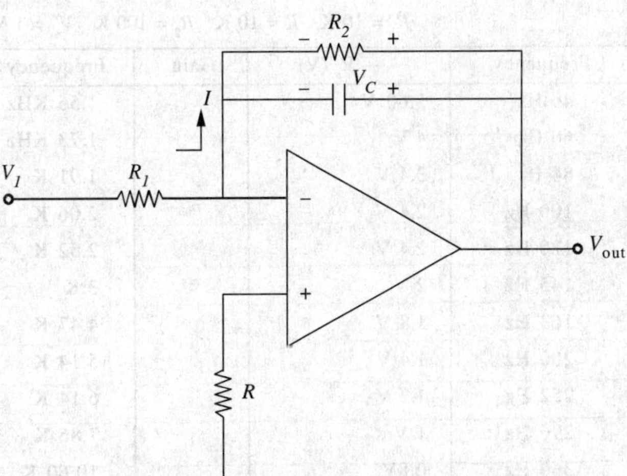

Fig. 11.7

C = 0·1 μ F $\quad R_1 = 10$ K

$f >> \dfrac{1}{2\pi R_2 C}$ $\quad R_2 = 100$ K

$f >> 160$ Hz $\quad R = \dfrac{10 \times 100}{110} = 9{\cdot}11$ K

PROCEDURE

Procedure (Integrator)

(*i*) Make connection of the circuit diagram on the breadboard.

(*ii*) Set the power supply ± 10 V between the pin no. 7 & 4.

(*iii*) Take $R_1 = 10$ K, $R_2 = 100$ and R = 10 K and set the input signal V_{in} as 1V peak to peak.

(*iv*) We check whether it is performing integration by applying various types of signals at input ( ).

(*v*) Then vary the input frequency and plot the V_o vs Varying frequency of the input signal.

(*vi*) Repeat the procedure with R_1 = 1 K, R_2 = 10 K, $R = \frac{10}{11} = 0.9 \cong 1$ K, $C = 0.1\ \mu$, V_{in} = 1V (P_k to P_k)

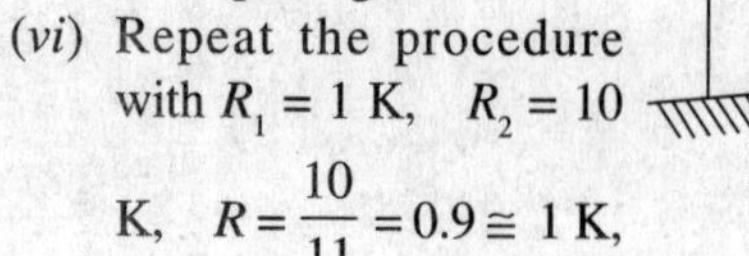

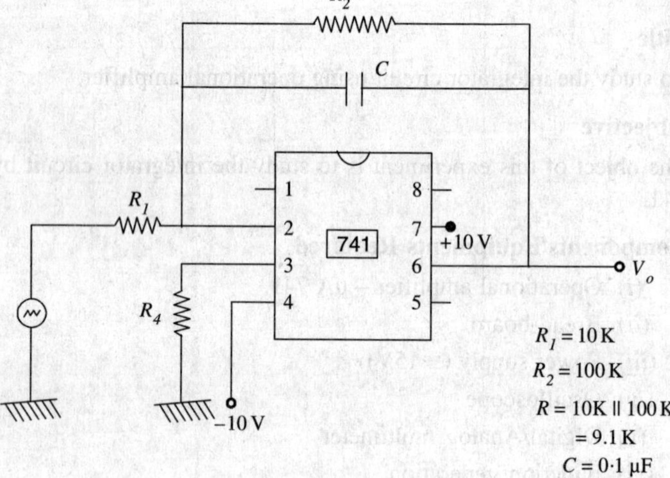

Fig. 11.8

Records of Data

Table 11.4

R_1 = 10 K R = 10 K R_2 = 100 K V_{in} = 1 V (P_k to P_k) C = 0·1 μF

Frequency	— V_o (V)	Gain	Frequency	— V_o (V)	Gain
40 Hz	5.60 V		1.56 KHz	0 .22 (4.450 × mV)	
60 Hz	4 V		1.73 KHz	0 .18 (3.6 × 50 mV)	
84 Hz	3.4 V		1.91 K	0 .16 (3.2 × 50 mV)	
100 Hz	2.6 V		2.06 K	0 .14 (2.8 × 50 mV)	
120 Hz	2.4 V		2.52 K	0 .10 (20 × 50 mV)	
145 Hz	2 V		3 K	0 .9 (1.80 × 50 mV)	
163 Hz	1.8 V		4.47 K	0 .07 (1.4 × 50 mV)	
200 Hz	1.4 V		5.14 K	0 .05 (1 × 50 mV)	
252 Hz	1.2 V		6.14 K	0 .04 (0.8 × 50 mV)	
296 Hz	1 V		7.86 K	0 .03 (0.6 × 50 mV)	
360 Hz	0.8V		10.60 K	0 .02 (0 .4 × 50 mV)	
402 Hz	0.7 V		22.20 K	0 .012 (0 .6 × 20 mV)	
514 Hz	0.6 V		27.70 K	0 .008 (0 .4 × 20 mV)	
611 Hz	0.5 V		38 K		
869 Hz	0.4 V				
920 Hz	00.3 V				
1.14 KHz	0.26 (5.2 × 50 μ)				

Table 11.5

$R_1 = 1$ K, $R = 1$ K, $R_2 = 10$ K, C = 0·1 μ F, $V_{in} = 1$ V (P_k to P_k)

Frequency	V_o	Gain	Frequency	V_o	Gain
88.1 Hz	8 V		1.97 kHz	1.4 V	
202 Hz	7.6 V		2.85 kHz	1 V	
323 Hz	6 V		3.54 kHz	0.8 V	
456 Hz	4.8 V		4.51 kHz	0.6 V	
515 Hz	4.4 V		6.09 kHz	0.5V	
630 Hz	3.6 V		8.01 kHz	0.4 V	
743 Hz	3.2 V		10.84 kHz	240 mV	
885 Hz	2.8 V		20 kHz	140 mV	
990 HZ	2.6 V		33 kHz	60 mV	
1.34 kHz	1 V		69.1 kHz	40 mV	
1.07 kHz	2.4 V				

Results

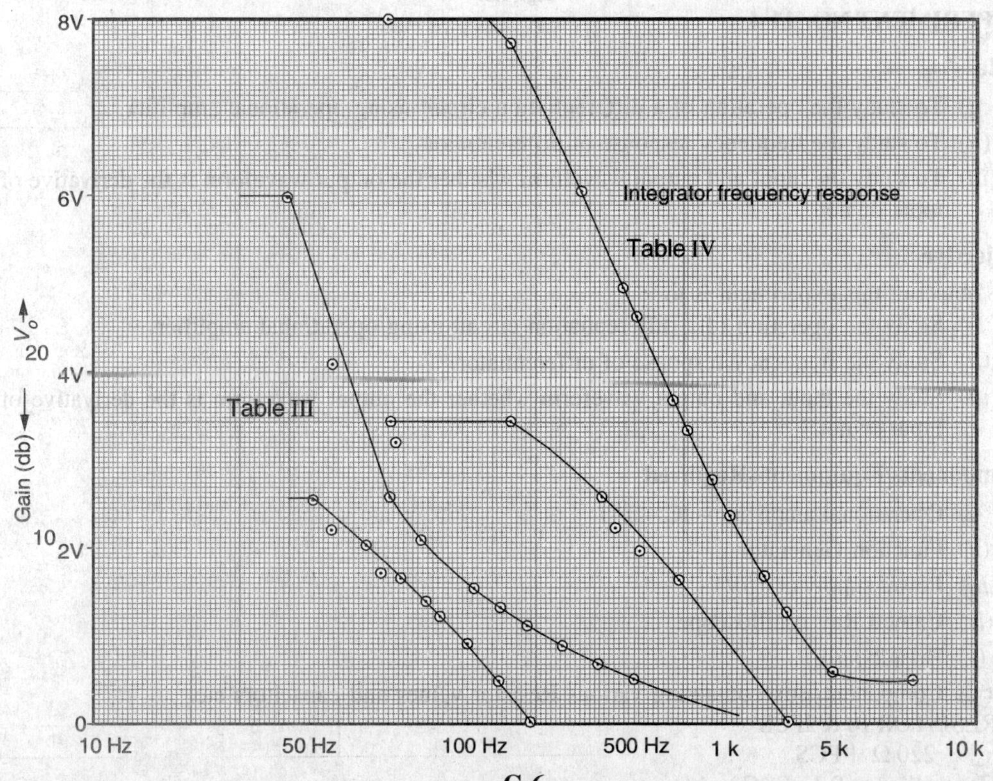

G-6

Conclusion

Comments on Integrator

In integrator the output voltage is directly proportional to the negative integral of the input voltage and inversely proportional to the time constant $R_1 C$ as $V_o = -\frac{1}{R_1 C}\int V_{in}\, dt$.

Now when $V_{in} = 0$ or in case of dc voltage the capacitor is open circuited due to infinite capacitive reactance and the integrator acts as an open loop amplifier. In other words, the input offset voltage V_{io} and the part of the input current charging capacitor C produce the error voltage at the output of the integrator. Therefore practically to reduce the error voltage at the output a resistor R_2 is connected across the feedback capacitor C such that $R_2 = 10\, R_1$ for proper integration. Thus, R_2 limits the low frequency gain and hence minimises the variations in the output voltage.

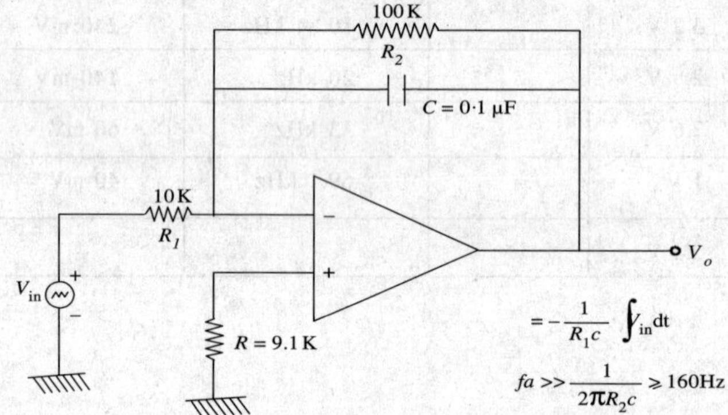

Fig. 11.9

EXPERIMENT NO. 11·4

Title

(*i*) To study the operation of a differentiation circuit using operational amplifier.
(*ii*) To study the frequency response of differentiator.
(*iii*) To study the input and output waveform whether the output waveform is the derivative of input or not.

Objective

The object of this experiment is to:

(*i*) Study the operation of a differentiation circuit using operational amplifier.
(*ii*) Study the frequency response of differentiator.
(*iii*) Study the input and output waveform whether the output waveform is the derivative of input or not.

Components/Equipments Required

(*i*) Operational amplifier – IC – 741
(*ii*) Function Generator
(*iii*) Power supply (± 15V)
(*iv*) Cathod Ray oscilloscope
(*v*) Breadboard
(*vi*) Component Box containing various Resistor values and capacitors etc.

RESISTOR 10 K 2PCS
220 Ω 1 PCS
Capacitance: 0.1 μF (C_1)
0.001 μF (C_2)

Theory and Circuits

The expression for the output voltage can the obtained from the Kirchoff's current law written at node V_2 as follows: (Fig. 11.10)

$$i_c = i_f + i_b \quad \text{since } i_b = 0$$

$$i_c = i_f$$

$$c_1 \frac{d}{dt}(V_{in} - V_2) = \frac{V_2 - V_o}{R_f}$$

As gain A is very large so $V_i \cong 0 \cong V_2$

$$\therefore \; C_1 \frac{d}{dt} V_{in} = -\frac{V_o}{R_f}$$

$$\Rightarrow \quad V_o = -R_f\, C_1 \frac{d}{dt} V_{in}$$

Thus we easily see that the output is the derivative of the input which agrees with differentiator circuits.

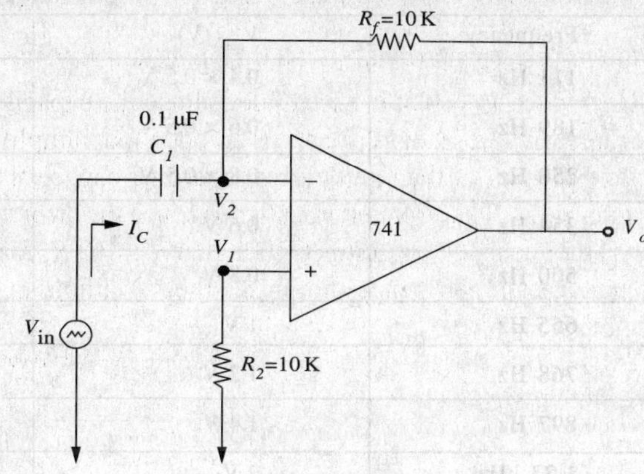

Fig. 11.11(*a*)

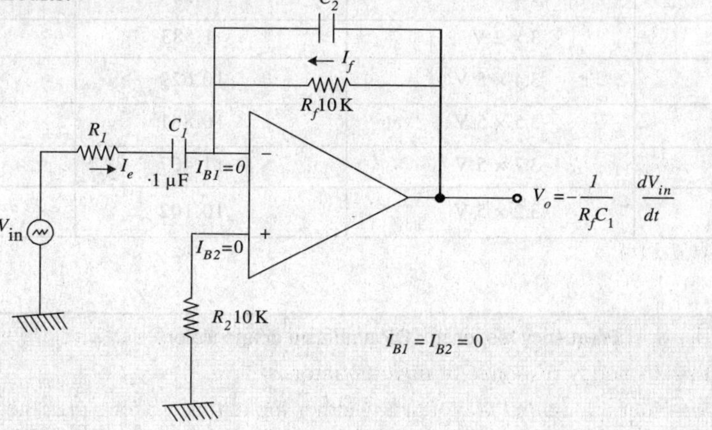

Fig. 11.11(*b*)

Procedure

(*i*) Assemble the circuit on the breadboard (Fig. 11.11)

(*ii*) Set the power supply ± 10 V between pins 7 and 4.

(*iii*) Take R_1 = 220 – 300 Ω, C_1 = 0·1 µ F, C_2 = 0·0027 µF, R_r = 10 K = R_2 and set the V_{in} as 5V P_k to P_k.

(*iv*) Then vary the input frequency and plot the output V_o vs frequency.

(*v*) Check whether it is performing or serving our goal by applying at input various types of signal.

(*vi*) Repeat the same by taking another set of values of R_1, R_2 *and*, C_1 and C_2.

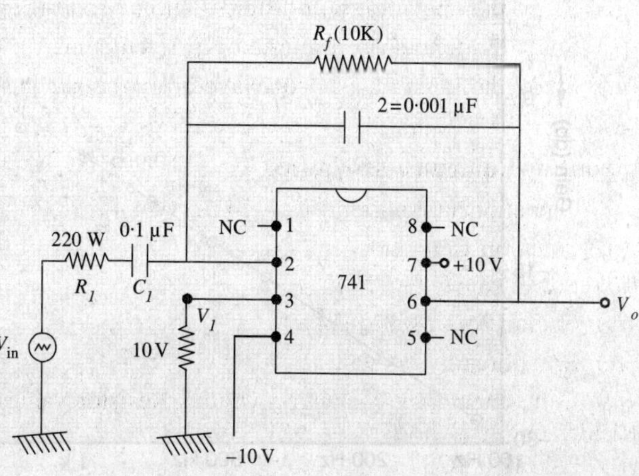

Fig. 11.12

Records of data

Table 11.6

V_{in} = 5V (P_k to P_k)

Frequency	V_{out} (V)	Gain in dB	
111 Hz	0.4 × 0.5 V	– 27.958	—
189 Hz	0.6 × 0.5 V	– 24.436	—
250 Hz	0.8 × 0.5 V	– 21.938	—
354 Hz	0.6 V	– 18.416	—
500 Hz	0.8 V	– 15.917	—
655 Hz	1 V	– 13.979	—
768 Hz	1.2 V	– 12.395	—
897 Hz	1.4 V	– 11.051	—
1.33 kHz	2 V	– 7.958	—
2.99 kHz	4 V	–1.98	—
4.12 kHz	3 × 2 V	1.583	—
5.41 kHz	3.4 × 5 V	10.629	—
10.85 kHz	3.5 × 5 V	10.881	—
14.5 kHz	3.7 × 5 V	11.407	—
16.4 kHz	3.2 × 5 V	10.102	—

Results

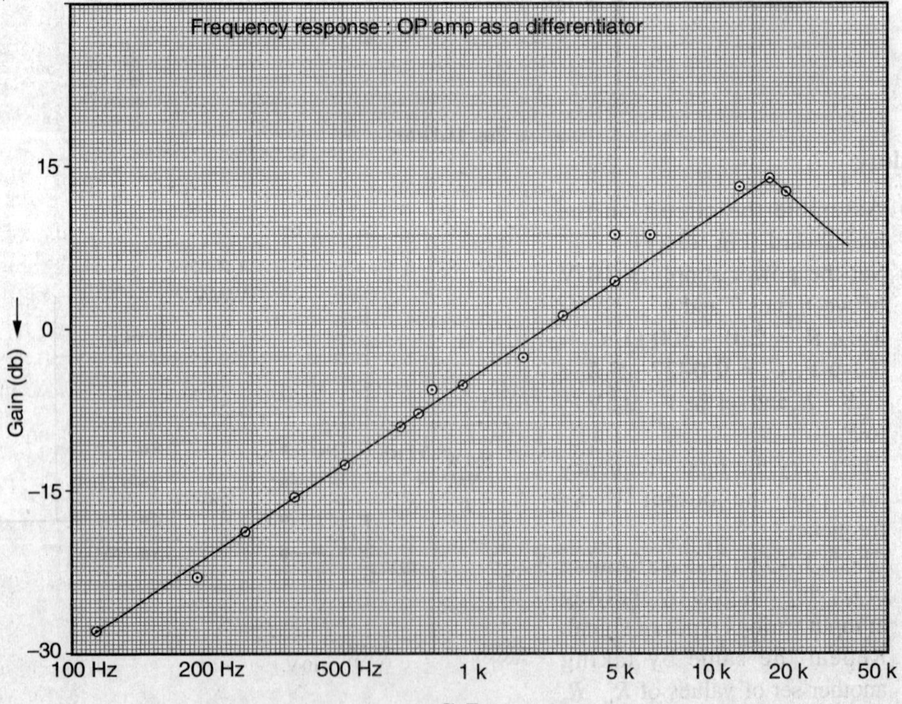

G-7

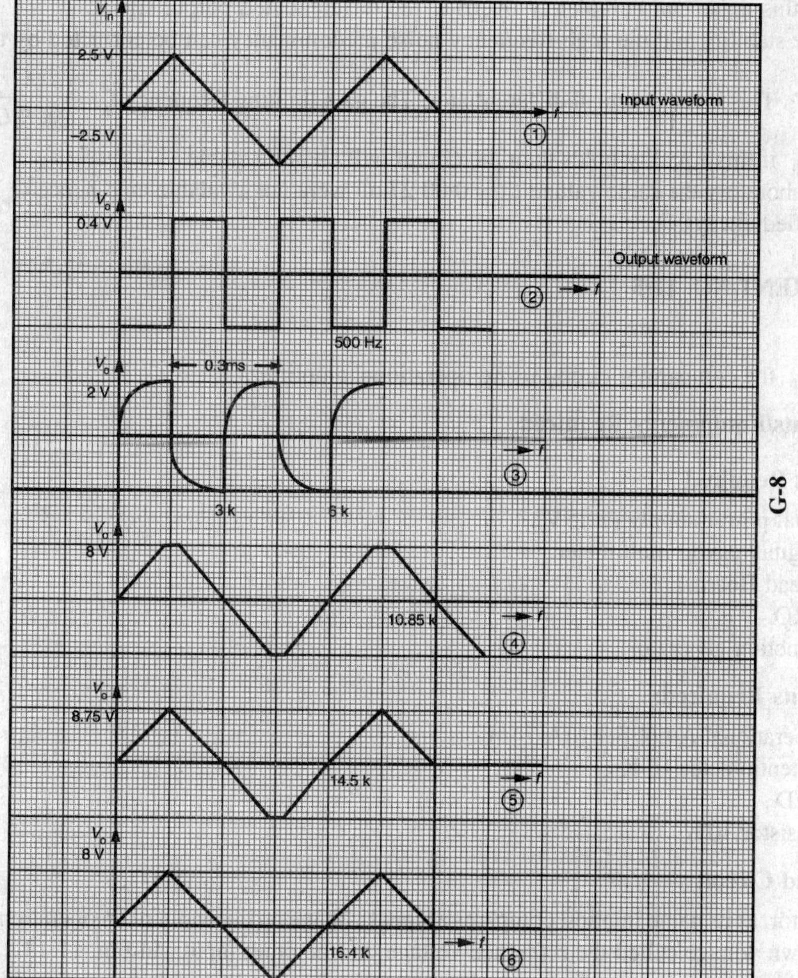

Conclusion

The circuit has some practical problem since the ratio $R_f\ /X_c$ rises with higher frequencies, the circuits gain increases with frequency. This tends to amplify the high frequency noise generated in the system. Another Problem is its tendency to be unstable. The problem is solved by using a resistance and a capacitance.

Also at high frequency X_c becomes so low that, instead of differentiator it acts as a voltage follower with some attenuation and the input waveform would in a similar form at the output .

Comments on Differentiator

$$V_o = -R_f\ C_1 \frac{dv_{\text{in}}}{dt}$$

The output is equal to the $R_f\ C_1$ times the negative instantaneous rate of change of the input voltage V_{in} with time sine the differentiator performs the reverse of the integrator's function, a triangular input will produce a square wave output.

The gain of the circuit with out C_2 $\dfrac{R_f}{X_{C_1}}$ increases with increase in frequency. This makes the circuit unstable and causes distortion at output. Also the input impedance X_{C_1} decreases with increasing frequency which makes the circuits very susceptible to high frequency noise when amplified, this noise can completely override the differentiated output signal.

Both the stability and the high frequency noise predominancy can be corrected by the addition of R_1 and C_2. This is the practical differentiator. The gain limiting frequency $f_b = \frac{1}{2\pi R_1 C_1}$ where R_1 $C_1 = R_f\ C_2$, if this equality holds then the circuit will be more stable.

But in laboratory the same valued $C_2 = 0{\cdot}00\ 27\ \mu F$ were not available and hence $C_1\ R_1 = R_f\ C_2$ is not satisfied always.

EXPERIMENT NO. 11·5

Title

To study the comparator circuit using operational amplifier.

Components/Equipments Required

Apparatus Required

(*i*) Dual power supply (± 15V).
(*ii*) Digital/analog multimeter.
(*iii*) Bread Board.
(*iv*) CRO.
(*v*) Function generator.

Components Required:

(*i*) Operational Amplifier (µA 741)
(*ii*) Potentiometer 10 K
(*iii*) LED
(*iv*) Resistor 10 K

Theory and Circuit

A comparator, as its name implies, compares a signal voltage on one input of an operational amplifier with a known voltage called the reference voltage on the other input. In Fig. 11.13 a comparator circuit has shown. A fixed reference voltage say V when applied at the inverting input through potentiometer that focus a voltage divider with the dc supply and at the same time in other terminal we vary the voltage by wiper yet to get the output 'LED' in glows (ON) condition. Here we show that the inverting terminal voltage is compared by other terminal voltage. We see this by changing the output 'LED' condition.

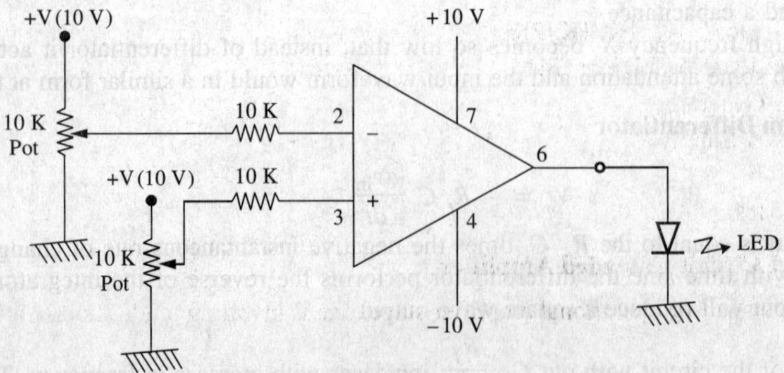

Fig. 11.13

Procedure

(*i*) The given circuit diagram should be implemented on the breadboard.
(*ii*) Set the power supply to drive the operational amplifier at ± 10 V.
(*iii*) Use R_1 and R_2 as 10 K each.
(*iv*) Vary the inverting and non-inverting input to observe the LED (output) condition which denotes the comparison.

Records of Data

V_1 (– Terminal)	V_2 (+ Terminal)	Remarks (LED)
1 V	1.01 V	Glows (ON)
2 V	2 V	ON
3 V	3 V	ON
4 V	4.01 V	ON
5 V	5.00 V	ON
1.8 mV	1.4 mV	ON
2.6 mV	2.3 mV	ON
10.8 mV	10.4 mV	ON
79.3 mV	79 mV	ON

Conclusion

So, we see that from the data table, that it compares two inputs and if two inputs are equal, then only the LED is ON condition. So, it compares two inputs.

EXPERIMENT NO. 11·6

Title

To study the cascade amplifier by using operational amplifier.

Components/Equipments Required

4 Resistances: 1K, 1K, 1K, 2K
2 Operational Amplifier: 741
Function Generator
D.C. Power Supply
CRO
Bread-board.

Theory and Circuit Caseaded Amplifier

In cascaded stage two operational amplifier stage, one is inverting mode another is in non inverting mode.

The Gain of 1st amplifier stage is given by

$$\left(1+\frac{R_f}{R_i}\right) = \left(1+\frac{1}{1}\right) = 2$$

and the gain of 2nd stage is given by

$$\left|\frac{2}{1}\right| = 2$$

Now if these two stages are connected in cascaded form then the overall gain will be 2 × 2 = 4. The necessary circuit has been shown in Fig. 11.14.

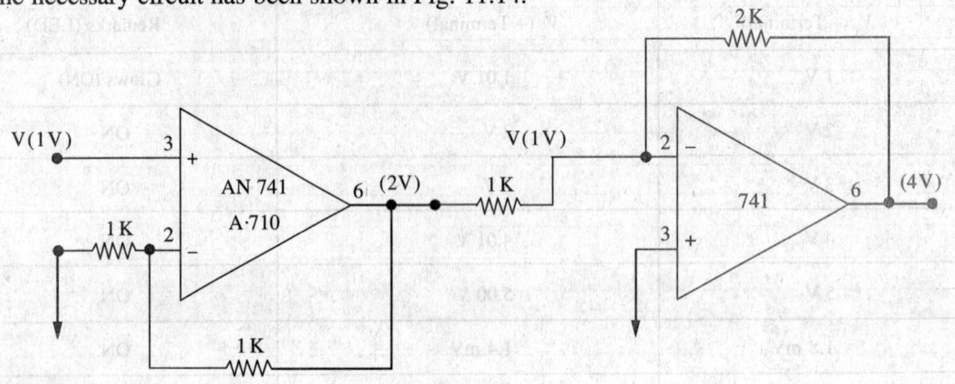

Fig. 11.14

Procedure:

(*i*) Make connection of the given circuit diagram carefully on the breadboard.

(*ii*) Set the power supply as about ± 10 V between pins 7 & 4 of each chip.

(*iii*) Set the input voltage V_{in} as 1V (peak to peak)

(*iv*) Firstly we take output of each individual stages with varying input frequency to plot the frequency response curve.

(*v*) Then we take the output of over all stages with varying frequency and Plot gain vs frequency.

(*vi*) Calculate the Band width (BW) for all stages mentioned above and prove the GBW remains constant. (gain Band width product).

Records of data

Table 11.7

Input Voltage (V_i)	Output Voltage (V_{o1})	Gain of first stage $G_1 = \left(\frac{V_{o1}}{V_i}\right)$	Second stage (V_{o2}) Output	Gain of overall stage (V_{o2}/V_i)	Theo overall gain $\left(\frac{V_{o2}}{V_i}\right) = G_1 G_2$	Practical gain (V_{o2}/V_i)	Remark (if any)
1V (P_k to P_k)	2V (P_k to P_k)	2	4.1V	4.1	$G_1 = 1 + \frac{1}{1} = 2$ $G_2 = 2 + \frac{1}{1} = 2$ $G_1 = G_2 = 2 \times 2 = 4$ Theoretical	4.1 = 4	more or less same but should be decreased because of loading

FREQUENCY RESPONSE TABLE: (INDIVIDUAL STAGE)

Input Frequency	Input Voltage (V_{in}) (P_k to P_k)	Output Voltage (V_o) in (Volt)	Gain in dB= 20 log 10 (V_o / V_{in})
33.7 Hz	1 V	2	6.02
100 Hz	1 V	2	6.02
1 KHz	1 V	2	6.02
10 K	1 V	2	6.02
107.2 K	1 V	3.8 × 0.5	5.58
121 K	1 V	3.6 × 0.5	5.11
133 K	1 V	3.4 × 0.5	4.61
150 K	1 V	3 × 0.5	3.52
142 K	1 V	3.2 × 0.5	4.08
167 K	1 V	2.8 × 0.5	2.92
202 K	1 V	2.4 × 0.5	1.58
217 K	1 V	2.2 × 0.5	0.83
237 K	1 V	2 × 0.5	0
277 K	1 V	1.8 × 0.5	– 0.92
320 K	1 V	1.8 × 0.5	– 0.92
475 K	1 V	0.6	– 4.44
685 K	1 V	0.4	– 7.96
1 MEG.	1 V	0.3	– 10.46

FREQUENCY RESPONSE TABLE: (OVERALL STAGE)

Input Frequency	Input Voltage V_{in} (Pk to Pk)	Output Voltage (V_o) (Pk to Pk)	Gain in dB = 20 log 10 (V_o / V_{in})
50.8 Hz	1 V	2 V × 2	12.04
100 Hz	1 V	2 V × 2	12.04
1 kHz	1 V	2 V × 2	12.04
10 kHz	1 V	2 V × 2	12.04
50 kHz	1 V	2 V × 2	12.04
61.5 kHz	1 V	2 V × 2	12.04
64.9 kHz	1 V	3.8 × 1	11.59
70.3 kHz	1 V	3.6 × 1	11.12
77.1 kHz	1 V	3.4 × 1	10.62
84.0 kHz	1 V	3.2 × 1	10.10
90 kHz	1 V	3 × 1	9.54
96.6 kHz	1 V	2.8 × 1	8.94
105.8 kHz	1 V	2.6 × 1	8.29
112.2 kHz	1 V	2.4 × 1	7.60
122 kHz	1 V	2.2 × 1	6.84
134 kHz	1 V	2	6.02
148 kHz	1 V	1.8	5.11
165 kHz	1 V	1.6	4.08
189 kHz	1 V	1.4	2.92
214 kHz	1 V	1.2	1.58
250 kHz	1 V	1.0	0
295 kHz	1 V	0.8	– 1.94
374 kHz	1 V	0.6	– 4.44
900 kHz	1 V	0.2	– 13.9
1018 kHz	1 V	0.12	– 18.42

Results

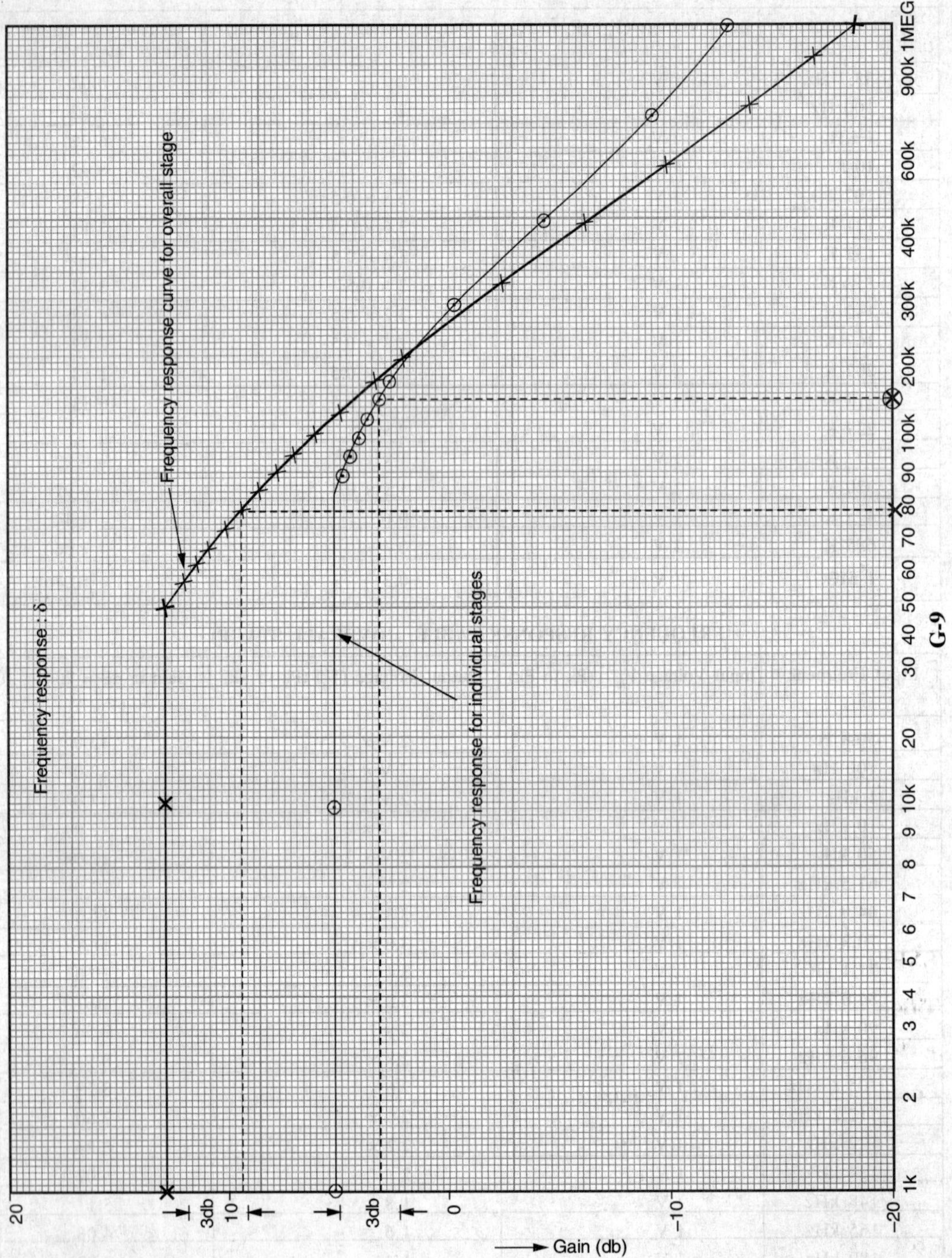

G-9

Conclusion

We find from the table that the theoretical overall gain and practical overall gain are nearly same. Actually what happens here is that in case of operational amplifier practically the input impedance is very high and that's why the loading effect on the preceding stage is not so important. It can be. So we get same theoretical gain practically.

A gain from frequency response curve we see that when we cascade, then the gain is increased as we model the system but at the same time the frequency has been reduced so that the gain-bandwidth product remains always constant which assures us that the gain-bandwidth product is stable in this case and which is demandable in many application.

Calculation of Bandwidth and Gain of each and overall stage

From the graph, the bandwith of the individual stages is f_c = 160 KHZ and the gain of individual stages in dB = 6 dB = A (Say)

So the gain-bandwith produced = 160 × 6

$$Af_c = 960 \text{ kHz} \cong \cdot 96 \text{ MHz} \cong 1 \text{ M}$$

Again from the same graph, the bandwidth of the overall stage is $f_c' = 96$ KHZ and the gain in db is $A' = 1\,2$ dB.

So the gain-bandwidth Produced = $A'f_c'$ = 12 × 96

= 1152 kHz

= 1·1 MHZ ≅ 1 M

Hence we can conclude that

$$A'f_c' \approx Af_c$$

Calculation of BW & Gain of each and overall Stages in tabular form and comparison between them.

INDIVIDUAL STAGES			OVERALL STAGE			REMARKS (if any)
Gain (A) in dB	Bandwidth (Δf_c) KHz	A of GBW pdt.	Gain (A') dB	Bandwidth ($\Delta f_c'$)	$A' \Delta f_c$ GBW Pdt.	
6 dB	160 KHz	960 KHz ≅ 1M	12 dB	96 KHz	1152 K ≅ 1M	More or less both approaches 1 MHz which is fixed band-width product of 741 operational amplifier.

EXPERIMENT NO. 11·7

Title

To study Schmitt Trigger circuit by using operational amplifier.

Components/Equipments Required

Resistance: (4) (≈ 100 Ω, 100 Ω, 56 K, 10 K)

Operational Amplifier: (1) 741

Function Generator

CRO

Bread Board

DC Regulated Power Supply

Theory and Circuit

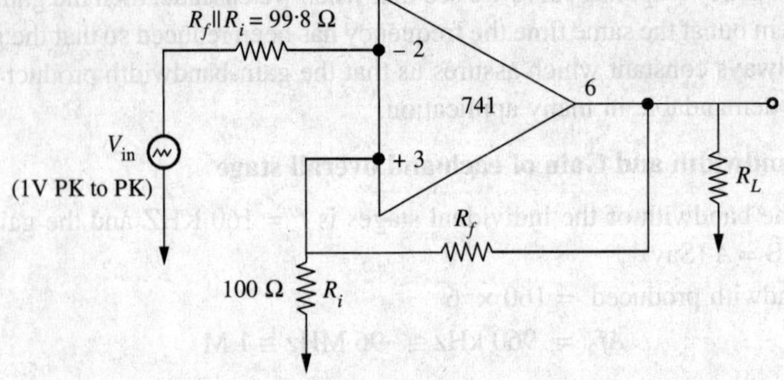

Fig. 11.15

The schmitt trigger circuit converts an irregular shaped waveform to a square wave or pulse. The input voltage V_{in} triggers the output V_o every time it exceeds certain voltage levels called the upper threshold voltage V_{ut} and lower threshold voltage V_{lt} as shown in Fig. 11.15 (*a*) and (*b*).

These threshold voltages are obtained by using the voltage divide $R_i - R_f$.

$$V_{ut} = +V_{sat} \frac{R_i}{R_i + R_f} = 10 \frac{100}{100+56000} = 0{\cdot}018 \text{ volt.}$$

and V_o is at $+ V_{sat}$

On the other hand when $V_o = - V_{sat}$ the lower threshold voltage

$$V_{lt} = \frac{R_i}{R_i + R_f} (-V_{sat}) = -0{\cdot}018 \text{ V}$$

SCHMITT TRIGGER

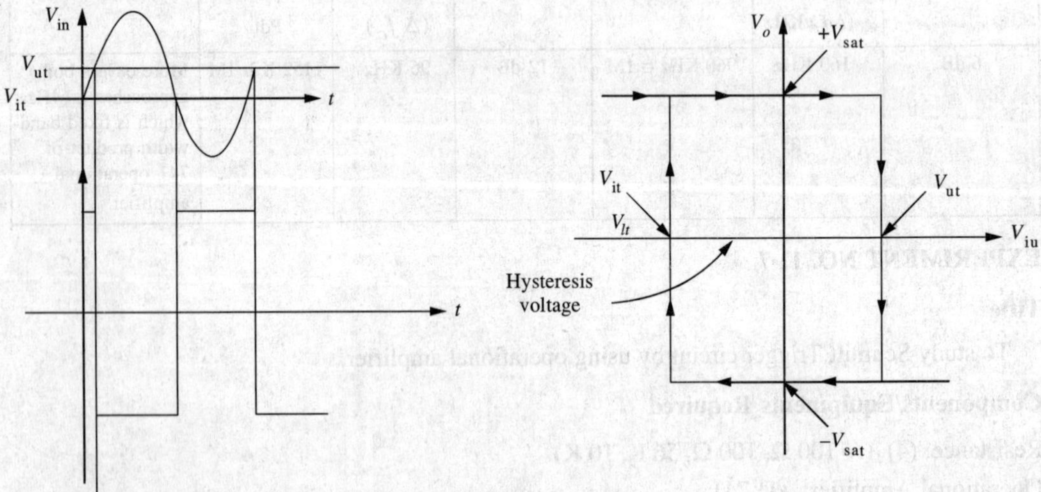

Fig. 11.16 (*a*) **and** (*b*)

Procedure

(*i*) Make connection according to the circuit diagram.

(*ii*) Set the power supply ± 10 V between the pins 7 and 4.

(*iii*) Take R_i =100 Ω, R_f = 56K and $R = R_f \| R_i = 99{\cdot}8\ \Omega$.

(*iv*) Set the V_{in} = 1 V P_k to P_k (~).

(*v*) Plot the output amplitude and frequency with input varying frequency.

(*vi*) Observe the waveform.

Results

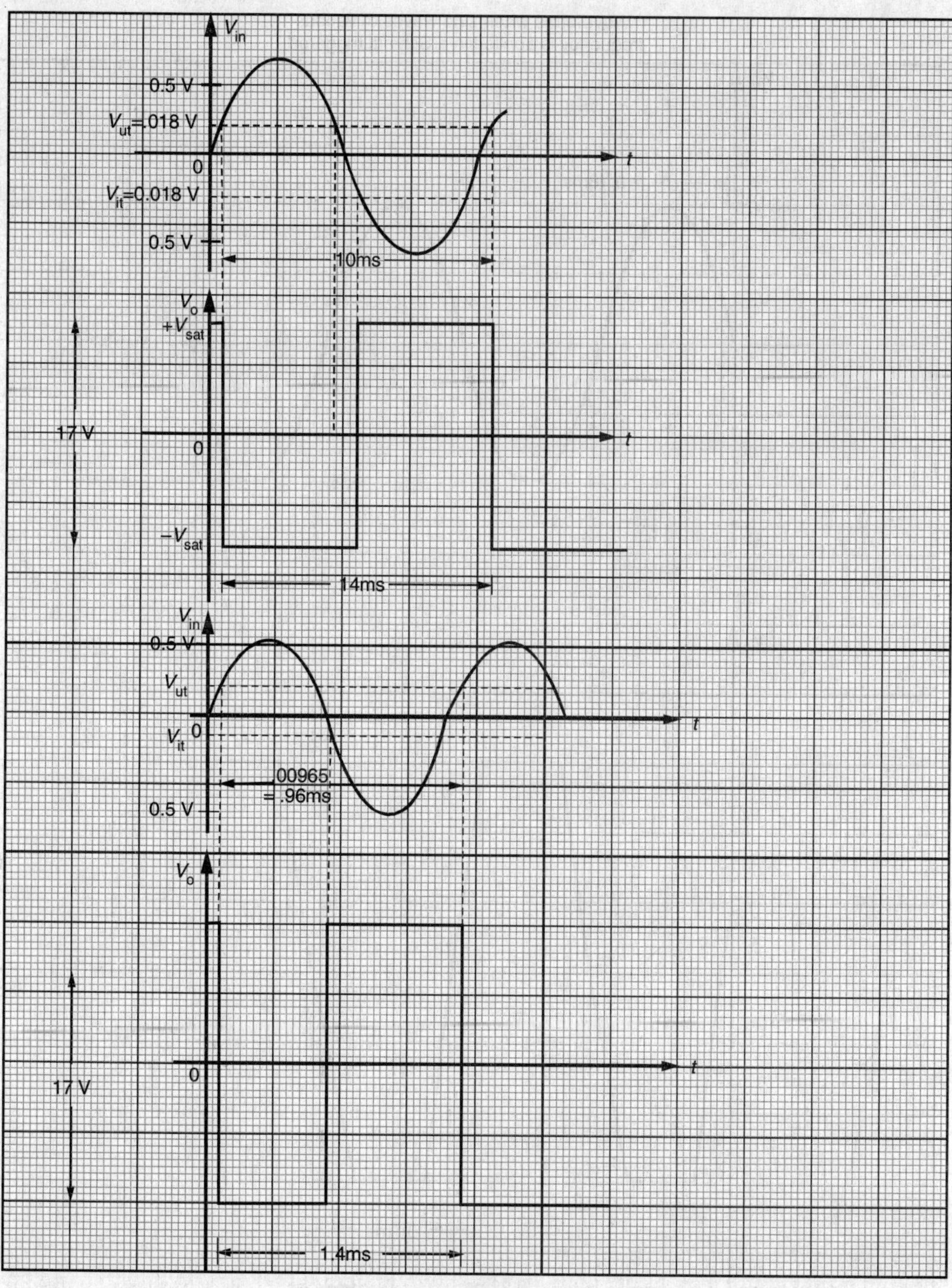
V_{in}
0.5 V
V_{ut}=.018 V
0
V_{lt}=0.018 V
0.5 V
10ms
t
V_o
$+V_{sat}$
17 V
0
$-V_{sat}$
14ms
t
V_{in}
0.5 V
V_{ut}
0
V_{lt}
.00965
= .96ms
0.5 V
t
V_o
0
17 V
1.4ms
t

G-10

Results

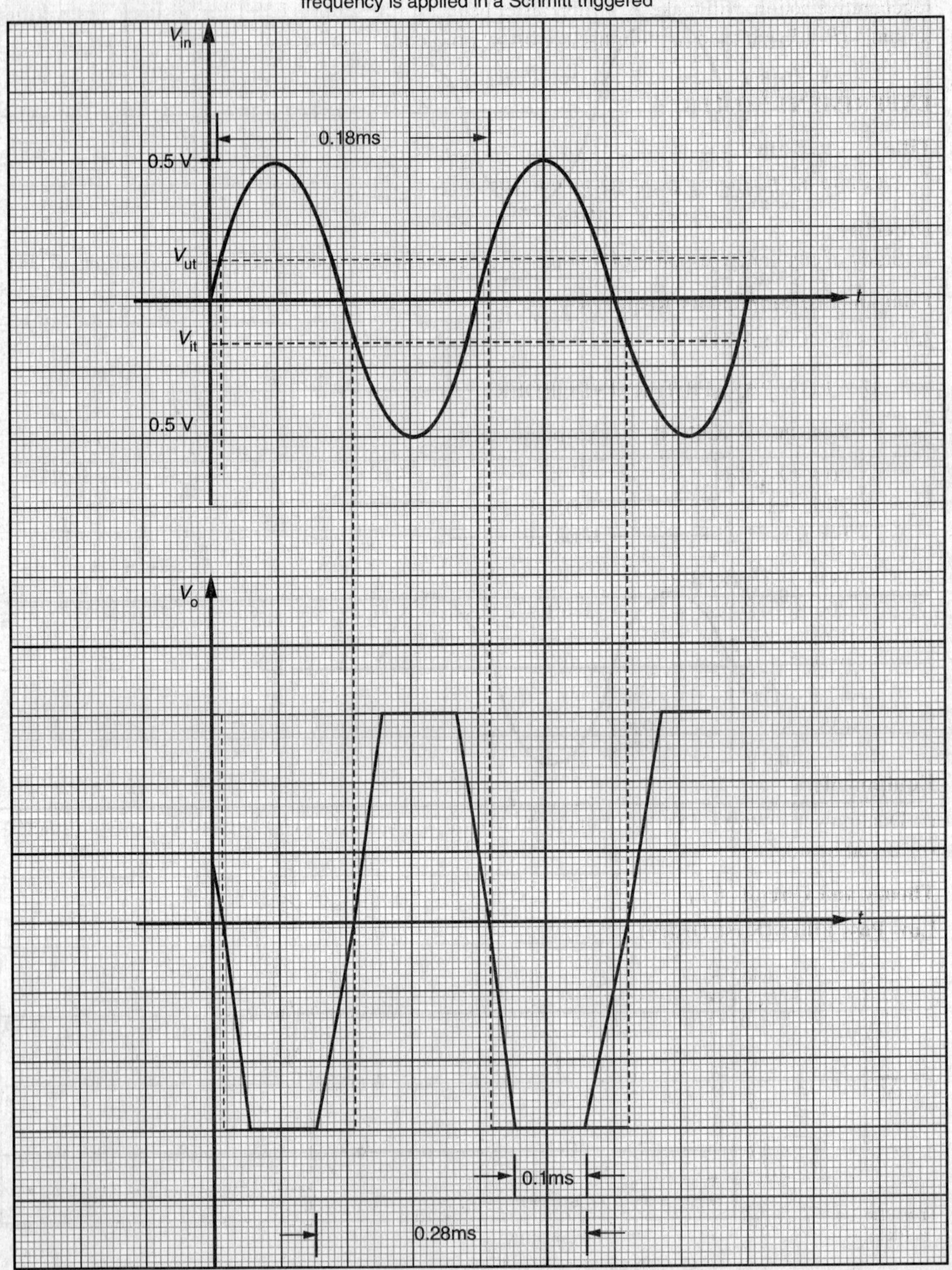
Waveforms when sine waves of various frequency is applied in a Schmitt triggered
V_{in}
0.18ms
0.5 V
V_{ut}
t
V_{lt}
0.5 V
V_o
t
0.1ms
0.28ms

Conclusion

If the threshold voltages V_{ut} and V_{lt} are made larger than the input noise voltages, the positive feedback will eliminate the false output transitions. Also, the positive feedback, because of its regenerative action, will make V_o switch faster between $+V_{sat}$ and $-V_{sat}$. The resistance in inverting terminal ($R_i \parallel R_f$) is used to minimise the offset problems.

EXPERIMENT NO. 11·8

Title

To study the frequency response of low pass filter.

Objective

Study of frequency response of low pass Butter worth filter using operational amplifier μA 741.

Components/components Required

All uses the IC's μA 741

LOW PASS FILTER (1ST ORDER)	
Resistances & POT	**Capacitances**
10 K Ω-3 No. 20 K Pot For R = 15.94 K	 .007 μF .008 μF
FOR 2ND ORDER 200 K – 20 Pcs 10 K – 1 Pcs 27 K – 1 Pcs 47 K – Pot (35.4 K)	 .8 μ F – 2 Pcs.

Equipments:

(*i*) Dual power supply ± 15V (*ii*) Function Generator (*iii*) CRO (*iv*) Digital/Analog multimeter (*v*) Bread board.

Theory and Circuit

Low Pass Filter (First Order)

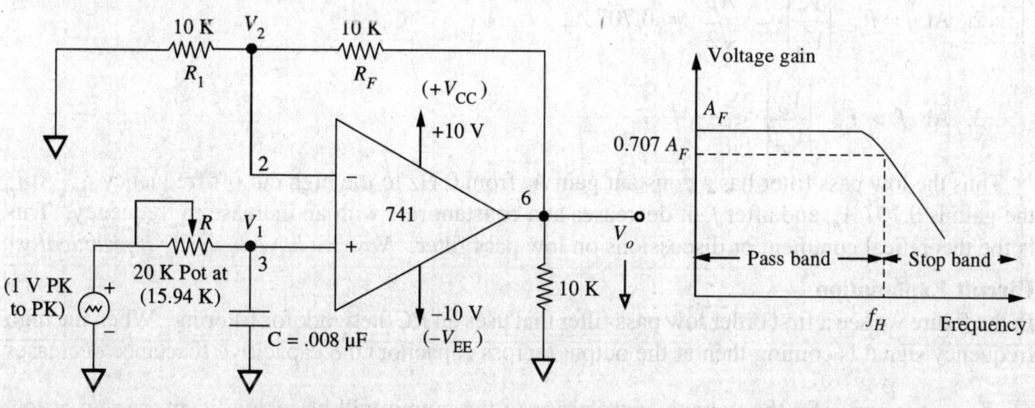

Fig. 11.17 **Fig. 11.18**

BRIEF THEORY OF FIRST ORDER LOW PASS ACTIVE FILTER

According to the voltage divider rule, the voltage at the non-inverting terminal (across capacitor C) is

$$V_1 = \frac{-JX_C}{R-jX_C} V_{in} \text{ where } -jX_c = \frac{1}{j2\pi f_C}$$

Simplifying the equation we get,

$$V_1 = \frac{V_{in}}{1+j\pi f RC}$$

and the output voltage

$$V_o = \left(1+\frac{R_f}{R_1}\right) V_1$$

That is,

$$V_o = \left(1+\frac{R_f}{R_1}\right) \frac{V_{in}}{1+j2\pi f RC}$$

$$\Rightarrow \quad \frac{V_O}{V_{in}} = \frac{A_F}{1+j(f/f_H)}$$

Where V_o/V_{in} = gain of the filters as a function of frequency.

$A_F = 1 + \frac{R_f}{R_1}$ = Pass band gain of the filters.

f = frequency of the input signal.

$f_H = \frac{1}{2\pi RC}$ = high cut-off frequency of the filter.

The gain magnitude and phase angle eqn. of low pass filter can be obtained by converting eqn. above into polar form.

$$\left|\frac{V_o}{V_{in}}\right| = \frac{A_F}{\sqrt{1+(f/f_H)^2}} \text{ and } \phi = -\tan^{-1}\left(\frac{f}{f_H}\right)$$

ϕ is the phase angle in degrees.

The operation of the low pass filter can be verified from the gain magnitude equation.

1. At very low frequencies, *i.e.*, $f < f_H$

$$\left|\frac{V_o}{V_{in}}\right| \cong A_F$$

2. At $f = f_H$, $\left|\frac{V_o}{V_{in}}\right| = \frac{A_F}{\sqrt{2}} = 0{\cdot}707\, A_F$

3. At $f > f_H$, $\left|\frac{V_o}{V_{in}}\right| < A_F$

Thus the low pass filter has a constant gain A_F from 0 Hz to the high cut off frequency f_H. At f_H the gain is 0.707 A_F, and after f_H it decreases at a constant rate with an increase in frequency. This is the theoretical comment or discussions on low pass filter. *Now we have to verify it practically.*

Circuit Explanation

In the figure we see a first order low pass filter that uses an RC network for filtering. When the high frequency signal is coming then at the output (across capacitor) the capacitive reactance decreases as $X_c = \frac{1}{j2\pi f_C}$. So the voltage contribution at the output will be insignificant. Again at low frequency the capacitive reactance increases causing an increment in output voltage. So large frequency signal attenuated whereas low frequency signal are at the output with voltage gain.

Actually here *RC* Network acts for filtering. But due to presence of active component *i.e.,* 741 *IC* it is undoubtedly a low pass active filter.

Again note that the operational amplifier is used in the non-inverting configuration, hence it does not load down the *RC* Network. Because it donates the high input-resistance. Resistors R_1 and R_F determine the gain of the filters.

CIRCUIT OF 2ND ORDER L.P.F.

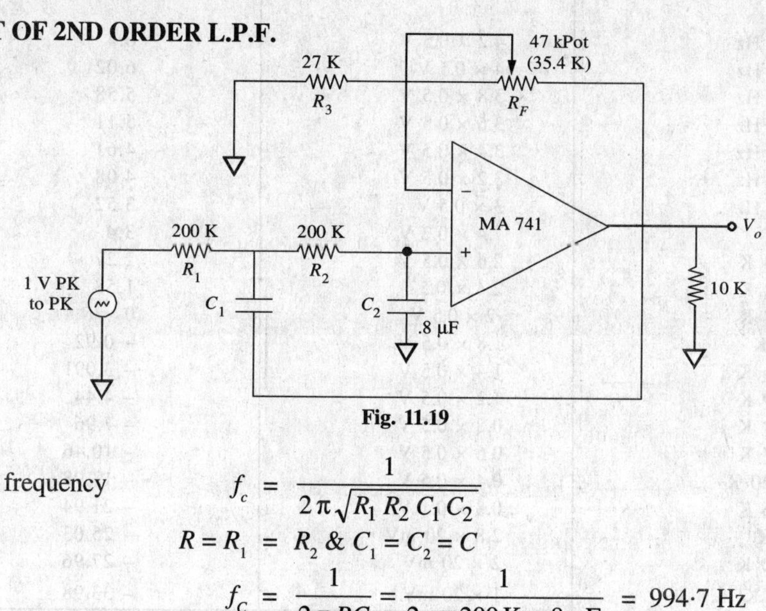

Fig. 11.19

Cut off frequency
$$f_c = \frac{1}{2\pi\sqrt{R_1 R_2 C_1 C_2}}$$
$$R = R_1 = R_2 \;\&\; C_1 = C_2 = C$$
$$f_C = \frac{1}{2\pi RC} = \frac{1}{2\pi\times 200\,\text{K}\times \cdot 8\,\mu\text{F}} = 994{\cdot}7\ \text{Hz}$$

Design Procedure

A low pass filter can be designed by implementing the following steps:

1. Choose a value of high cut off frequency = 1.25 kHz
2. Select a value of *C* less than or equal to 1 μF. Let *C* = ·008 μF (available in Lab.)
3. Calculate the values of *R* using
$$R = \frac{1}{2\pi\times f_H\, C} = \frac{1}{2\pi\times 1.25\,\text{kHz}\times \cdot 008\,\mu\text{F}} = 15{\cdot}94\ \text{k}\Omega$$
for this resistance we use a 20 kΩ potentiometer.
4 Finally select values R_1 and R_F dependent on the desired pass band gain
$$A_F = 1 + \frac{R_f}{R_1}$$

Here in our experiment we have used R_1 = R_F = 10 kΩ just to make the band pass gain?

Experiment Procedure

A low pass filter can be designed by implementing the following steps:

(*i*) Assemble the CKT on bread-board.
(*ii*) Connect the power supply to pin 7 & pin 4.
(*iii*) Set the supply to ± 15V.
(*iv*) Vary the frequency in function generation.
(*v*) Measure I/P and O/P voltage from CRO.
(*vi*) Calculate the gain in dB.
(*vii*) Plot the graph gain Vs frequency.

Records of Data

Data Table for 1st Order L.P.F.

Frequency (1/p)	V_o (P_k to P_k)	Gain in dB [20 $\log_{10}$ (V_o / V_i)]
10 Hz	4.2 × 0.5 V	6.4
100 Hz	4.2 × 0.5 V	6.4
228 Hz	4 × 0.5 V	6.02
419 Hz	3.8 × 0.5 V	5.58
530 Hz	3.6 × 0.5 V	5.11
634 Hz	3.4 × 0.5 V	4.61
800 Hz	3.2 × 0.5 V	4.08
900 Hz	3 × 0.5 V	3.52
1 K	7.4 × 0.2 V	3.4
1.13 K	2.6 × 0.5 V	2.27
1.42 K	2.4 × 0.5	1.58
1.87 K	2 × 0.5 V	0
2.1 K	1.8 × 0.5 V	– 0.92
2.84 K	1.4 × 0.5 V	– 3.091
3.49 K	1.2 × 0.5 V	– 4.44
5.28 K	0.8 × 0.5 V	– 7.96
7.17 K	0.6 × 0.5 V	– 10.46
11.20 K	0.4 × 0.5 V	– 13.98
24.6 K	0.8 × 0.1 V	– 21.94
36 K	2.8 × 20 mV	– 25.03
54.2 K	2 × 20 mV	– 27.96
100 K	1 × 20 mV	– 33.98

DATA TABLE FOR SECOND ORDER LOW PASS FILTER

f_C = 994 Hz ≈ 1 K
FOR V_{in} = 1 V (P_k to P_k)

Frequency (1/p)	V_o (P_k to P_k)	Gain in dB [20 $\log_{10}$ (V_o / V_i)]
200 Hz	4.2 × 0.5 V	6.4
400 Hz	4.2 × 0.5 V	6.4
373 Hz	3 V	9.5
800 Hz	4 × 0.5 V	6.02
830 Hz	3.8 × 0.5	5.58
870 Hz	3.6 × 0.5 V	5.11
900 Hz	3.4 × 0.5 V	4.61
930 Hz	3.2 × 0.5 V	4.08
950 Hz	3 × 0.5 V	3.52
1.04 K	2.6 × 0.5 V	2.27
1.11 K	2.2 × 0.5 V	0.82
1.24 K	1.6 × 0.5 V	– 1.94
1.53 K	1 × 0.5 V	– 6.02
1.92 K	0.6 × 0.5 V	– 10.46
3.5 K	0.2 × 0.5 V	– 20
4 K	0.2 × 0.5 V	– 20
10 K	0.1 × 5 V	– 26.94

Results

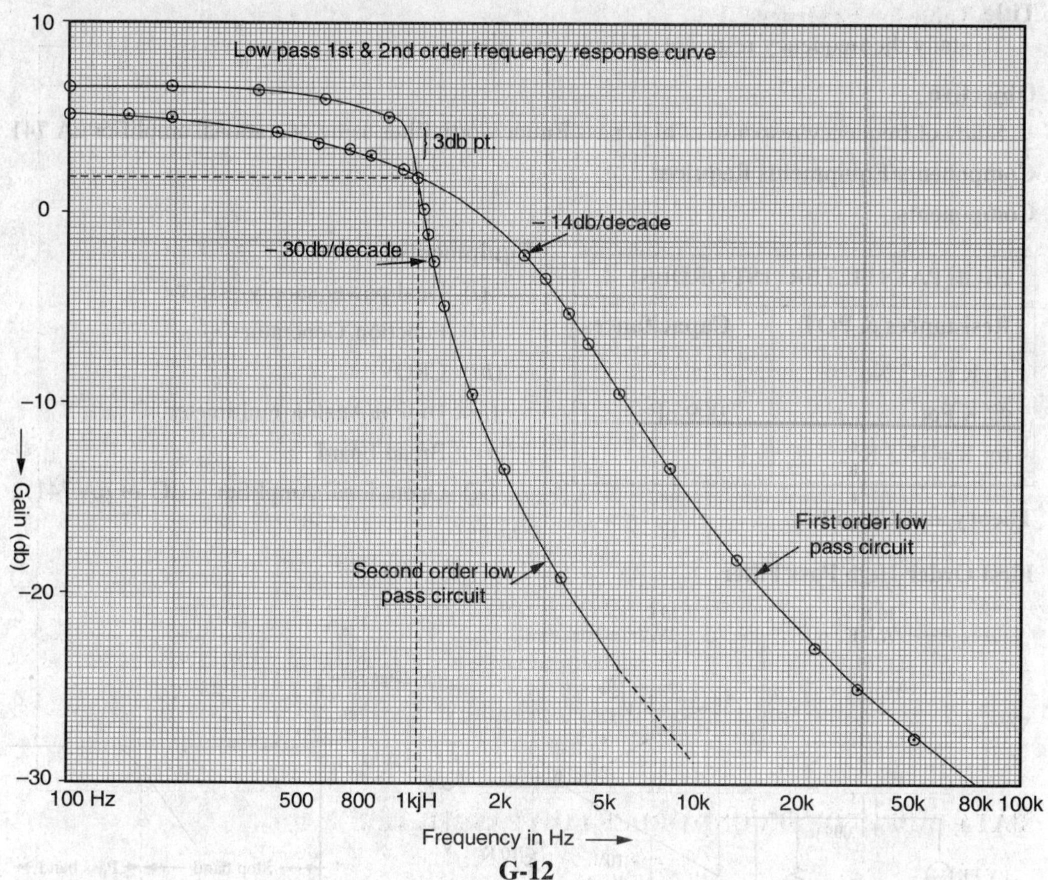

G-12

Conclusion

(1st Order) Cut-off frequency theoretically,

$$f_H = \frac{1}{2\pi RC} = \frac{1}{2\pi \times 13{\cdot}94 \times 0{\cdot}008\,\mu\text{F}} = 1.2\text{ k}$$

& Practically, f_H = 1k.

(2nd Order) f_H (theoretically) = 994·7 Hz ~ 1k.

f_H (Practically) = 1k.

Actually we have performed this for better response. We see that the fall rate after 3 dB frequency from response curve

– 14 dB/decade (1st order)

& – 30 dB/decade (2nd order)

So, we conclude that the 2nd order filter gives the better response.

EXPERIMENT NO. 11·9

Title

To study the frequency response of High pass filter.

Objective

Study of frequency response of high pass Butter worth filter using operational amplifier μA 741.

Components/Equipments Required

Components

HIGH PASS FILTER (1ST ORDER)	
Resistances & POT	**Capacitances**
10 K Ω – 3 No. 47 K Pot for R = 35.3 K	.009 μF

Equipments:

(*i*) Dual power supply ± 15V
(*ii*) Function Generator
(*iii*) CRO
(*iv*) Digital/Analog multimeter
(*v*) Bread board
(*vi*) Operational Amplifier – (IC → μA 741)

Theory and Circuits

First Order High Pass Filter

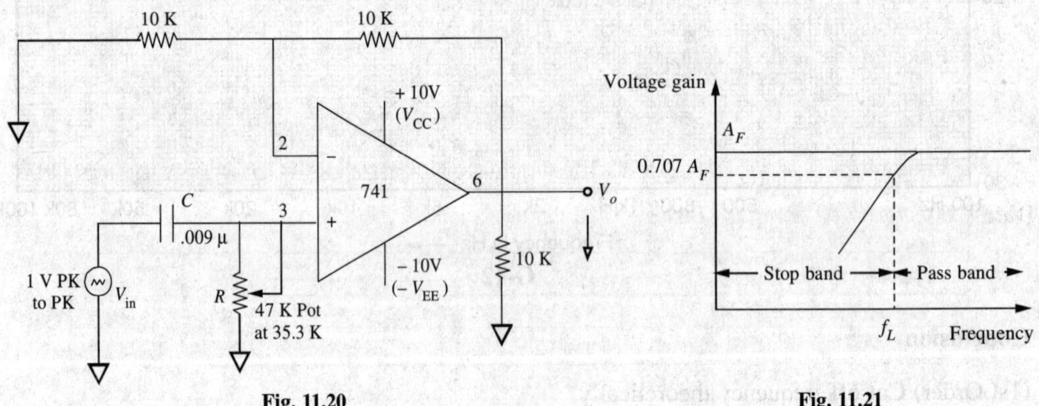

Fig. 11.20 Fig. 11.21

FIRST ORDER HIGH-PASS ACTIVE FILTER

Brief Theory

High pass filters are often formed simply by interchanging frequency determining resistors and capacitors in low pass filters. That is, a first order high pass filters is formed from a first order low-pass type by interchanging components *R* and *C*.

For first order high pass filter of figure the output voltage is

$$V_o = \left(1+\frac{R_F}{R_1}\right)\frac{j2\pi f RC}{1+j2\pi f RC}V_{in}$$

$$\frac{V_o}{V_{in}} = A_F\left[\frac{j(f/f_L)}{1+j(f/f_L)}\right]$$

where $A_F = 1+\frac{R_F}{R_1}$ = pass band gain of the filter.

f = frequency of the input signal (Hz)

$f_L = \frac{1}{2\pi RC}$ = Low cut-off frequency (Hz)

Hence the magnitude of voltage gain

$$\left|\frac{V_o}{V_{in}}\right| = \frac{A_F(f/f_L)}{\sqrt{1+(f/f_L)^2}}$$

Circuit Explanation

Here at low frequency the capacitive reactance of the $R - C$. Network which is actually responsible for the filtering action is greater. So the low freq. signals are blocked. They couterible in signal *i.e.*, and voltage at the output.

On the other hand the high frequency signals reach to the output due to low capacitive reactance of the $R - C$ filtering network. Hence high frequency gain occurs.

Procedure

(*a*) Experiment Procedure

(*i*) Assemble the ckt in bread board.

(*ii*) Connect the pow`er supply to the pin 7 & 4.

(*iii*) Set the supply about ± 15V.

(*iv*) Measure the o/p at CRO from the actual pin of the IC according to figure.

DESIGN PROCEDURE (H.P.F.)

(*i*) Choose a low frequency $f_1 \cong 500$ Hz (Cut off Frequency)

(*ii*) Choose small values capacitance $c = 0{\cdot}009$ μF.

(*iii*) Find out the value of R using

$$R = \frac{1}{2\pi f_L c} \cong 35{\cdot}3 \text{ K}.$$

(*iv*) Fixing the V_{in} at 1V P_k to P_k vary the input frequency to plot the frequency response curve.

Data Collection of High Pass Filter

Frequency (1/P)	V_o (P_k to P_k)	Gain in db [20 $\log_{10}$ (V_o /V_i)]
50 Hz	2.8 × 0.1 V	– 11.06
99.3 Hz	2.8 × 0.2 V	– 5.04
200 Hz	2 × 0.5 V	– 0
300 Hz	2.8 × 0.5 V	2.92
400 Hz	3.2 × 0.5 V	4.08
500 Hz	3.4 × 0.5 V	4.61
600 Hz	3.6 × 0.5 V	5.11
700 Hz	1.8 × 1 V	5.11
800 Hz	2 × 1 V	6.02
900 Hz	2 × 1 V	6.02
1 K	2 × 1 V	6.02
3 K	4.2 × 0.5	6.4
5 K	4.2 × 0.5	6.4
7 K	4.2 × 0.5	6.4
10 K	4.2 × 0.5	6.4
20 K	4.2 × 0.5	6.4
50 K	4.2 × 0.5	6.4
115 K	4.2 × 0.5	6.4

Results

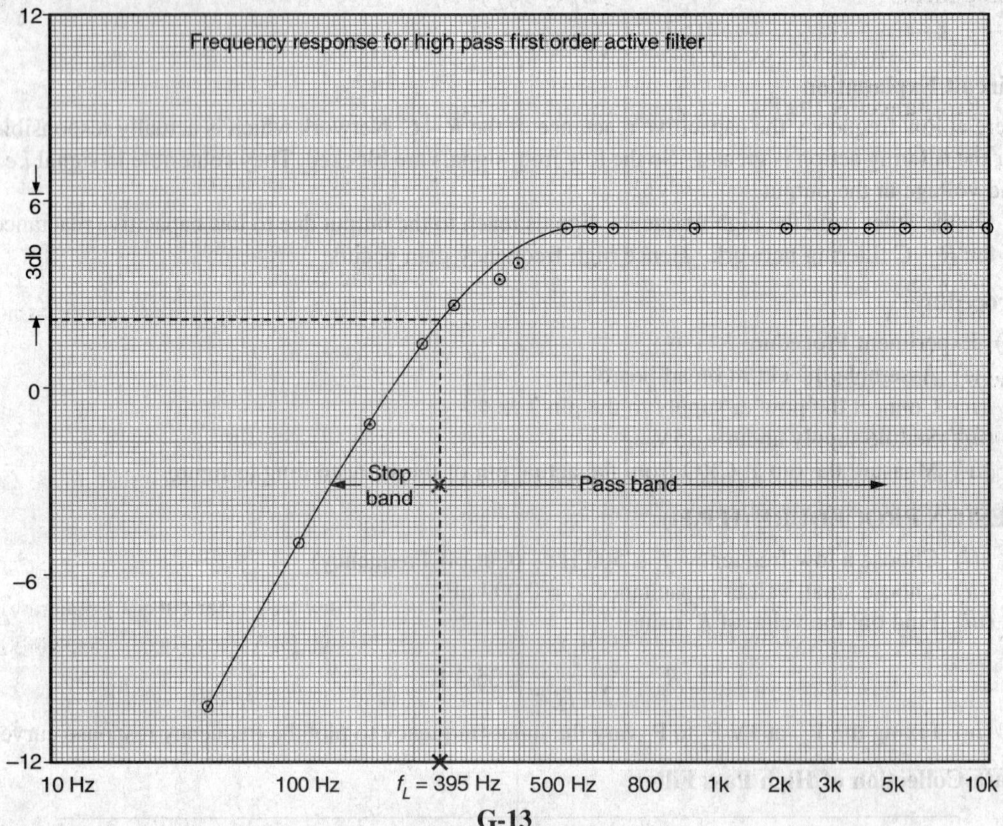

G-13

Conclusion

Cut off frequency (theoretically),

$$f_L = \frac{1}{2\pi \times 35{\cdot}3\,\text{K} \times 0{\cdot}009\,\mu\text{F}} = 500{\cdot}9 \text{ Hz}$$

Practically, $f_L = 335$ Hz

So, we see that this is a response of high pass filter. Because after some value of frequency, the gain is constant.

EXPERIMENT NO. 11·10

Title

To study the frequency response of Band-pass filter.

Objective

Study of frequency response of Band pass filter using operational amplifier μA 741.

Components/Equipments Required

Components

BAND PASS FILTER	
Resistances & POT	**Capacitances**
10 K Ω – 5 No. 20 K Pot for 1.94 K & 47 K pot for 35.3 K	.008 μF .009μF

Equipments:

(*i*) Dual power supply
(*ii*) Function Generator
(*iii*) CRO
(*iv*) Digital/Analog multimeter
(*v*) Bread Board
(*vi*) IC – μ A 741 (operational amplifier)

Theory and Circuits

Band Pass Filter

A band pass filter has a pass band between two cut off frequency f_H and f_L such that $f_H > f_L$. Any input frequency outside this passband is attenuated.

And the band width of this filter is given by

$BW = (f_H - f_L)$

f_H = high cut off frequency (low pass filter cut off frequency)

f_L = Low cut off frequency. (High pass filter cut off frequency)

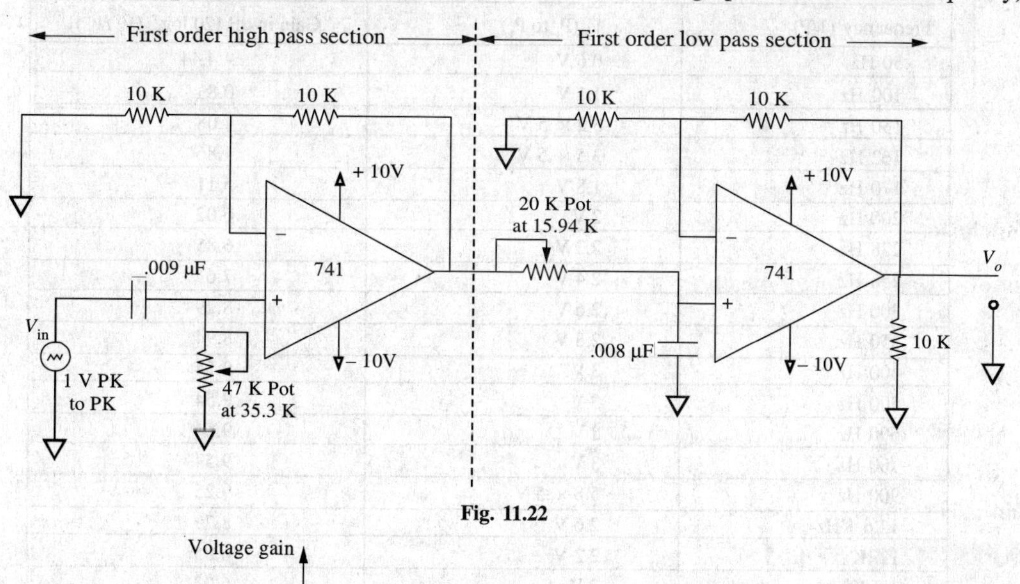

Fig. 11.22

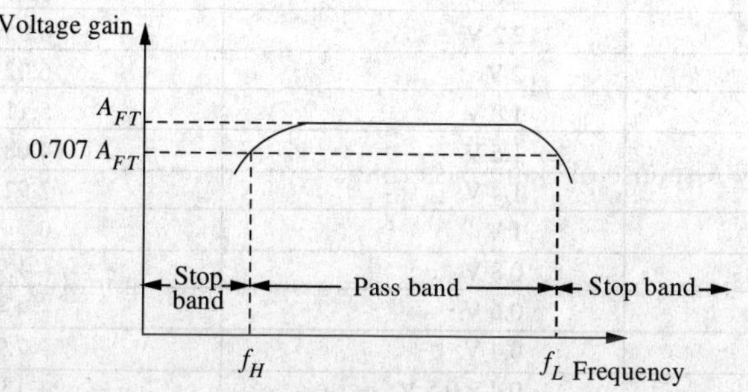

Fig. 11.23

Procedure

DESIGN STEPS (B.P.F.)

(*i*) Here we assumed $f_L > f_H$ as given

(*ii*) Take $f_L = 1.6$ KHz and $f_H = 230$ Hz we set the circuit.

(*iii*) Vary the input frequency (setting the input amplitude at 1V P_k to P_k) to plot the frequency response curve.

The Bandwidth of Band pass filter

$$= 1600 - 230 \text{ Hz}$$

$$= 1370 \text{ Hz} = 1{\cdot}3 \text{ K}.$$

Experiment Procedure

(*i*) Assemble the ckt in bread board.

(*ii*) Connect the power supply to pin 7.

(*iii*) Set the supply at ± 15V.

(*iv*) Vary the frequency in function generation.

(*v*) Measure I/P and O/P voltage from CRO.

(*vi*) Calculate the gain in dB.

(*vii*) Plot the graph gain Vs frequency.

(*viii*) Calculate 3-db frequency.

Records of Data

Frequency (I/P)	V_o (P_k to P_k)	Gain in dB [20 $\log_{10}$ (V_o/V_i)]
50 Hz	0.6 V	– 4.44
100 Hz	1.1 V	0.83
150 Hz	3.2 × .5 V	4.08
162 Hz	3.5 × .5 V	4.86
170 Hz	1.8 V	5.11
200 Hz	2 V	6.02
228 Hz	2.2 V	6.85
256 Hz	2.4 V	7.6
300 Hz	2.6 V	8.29
350 Hz	2.8 V	8.94
400 Hz	3 V	9.54
500 Hz	3 V	9.54
600 Hz	3 V	9.54
700 Hz	3 V	9.54
900 Hz	5.8 × .5 V	9.25
1.26 KHz	2.6 V	8.29
1.5 K	2.2 V	6.85
1.8 K	2 V	6.02
2.13 K	1.8 V	5.11
2.5 K	1.6 V	4.08
3 K	1.4 V	2.92
4 K	1 V	0
5 K	0.8 V	– 1.94
6.5 K	0.6 V	– 4.44
10 K	0.4 V	– 7.96
20 K	0.4 × 0.5 V	– 13.98
50 K	0.8 × 0.1 V	– 21.94

Results

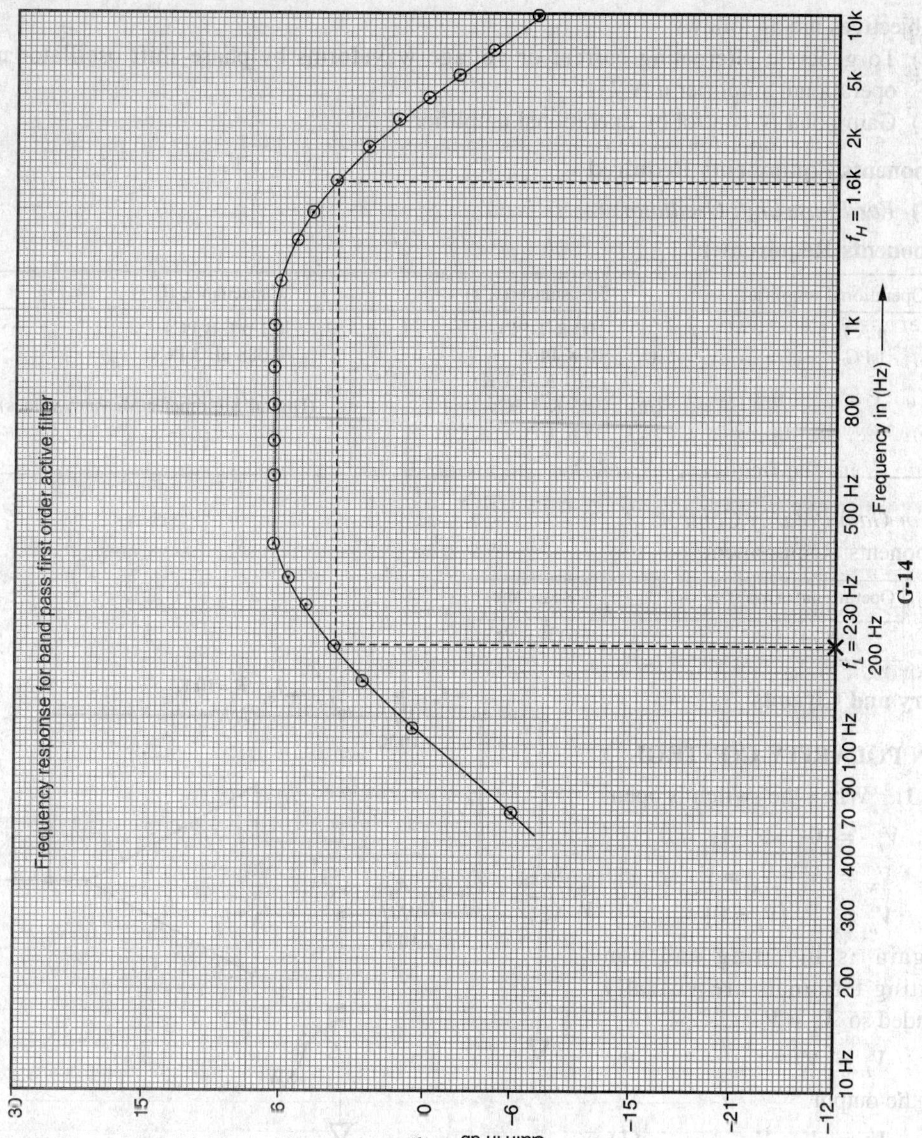

G-14

Conclusion

From the response curve, we see that

$$f_H = 1.6 \text{ K} \quad \& \quad f_L = 230 \text{ Hz}$$

So, we can tell that the above response is a response of Band Pass Filter. Because we get a constant gain within a range of frequency.

EXPERIMENT NO. 11·11

Title

(*i*) To study gain polarity control by operational amplifier.

(*ii*) To study some oscillators (a) phase shift oscillator.

Objectives

The objectives are as follows:

(*i*) To generate alternating current or voltage waveforms by phase-shift oscillator using operational amplifier μ A 741.

(*ii*) Gain polarity control by operational amplifier.

Components/Equipments Required

(*i*) *For Phase Shift Oscillator*

Components Requirement

Operational amplifier	Resistance (R's)	Capacitance (C's)
μ A 741 1 PC	(*i*) 100 K 1 PCs (*ii*) 10 K Plot (2.61 K, 3.1 K) (*iii*) 3.43 K 3 PCs (*iv*) 33 K 1 PCs (*v*) 1 K	0.1 μ F B PCs 0.088 μF 3 PCs (Digital Multimeter Measure values)

(*ii*) *For Gain Polarity Control*

Components Requirement

Operational Amplifier	Resistance
μ A 741 1 PC	10 K 3 PCs.

Theory and Circuits

GAIN POLARITY CONTROL

Case 1: When the switch is open

then $V_{R1} = 0 \Rightarrow 1_{R1} = 0$

$V_N = V_i - V_{R1} = V_i$

$\Rightarrow \quad V_N = V_i \; [V_R = 0]$

Again as inverting and non inverting terminals are virtually grounded so $V_N = V_I$

$\therefore \quad V_I = V_i$

Now the output

$V_o = V_I - V_{Rf} \quad ...(1)$

again $RI_R = V_i - V_I = 0 \Rightarrow I_R = 0$

[as $V_i = V_I$ Proved]

So $\quad I_{Rf} = 0$

So from (1) we get

$V_o = V_I = V_i$

$$\Rightarrow \quad \frac{V_O}{V_i} = 1$$

So the amplifier acts as Non-inverting amplifier.

Case II: When the switch S_w is choosed to ground then it acts as inverting amplifier.

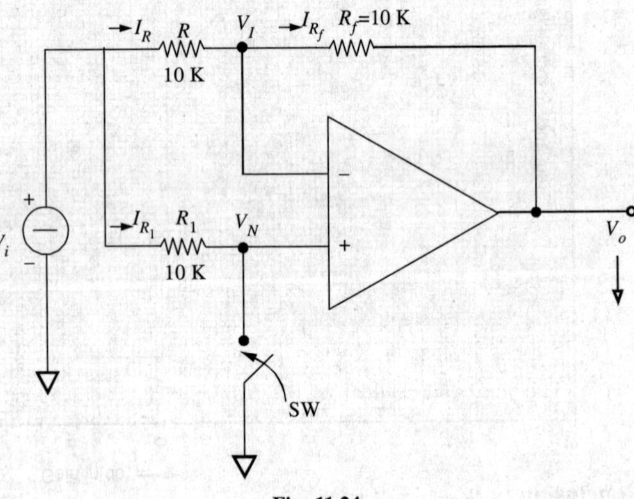

Fig. 11.24

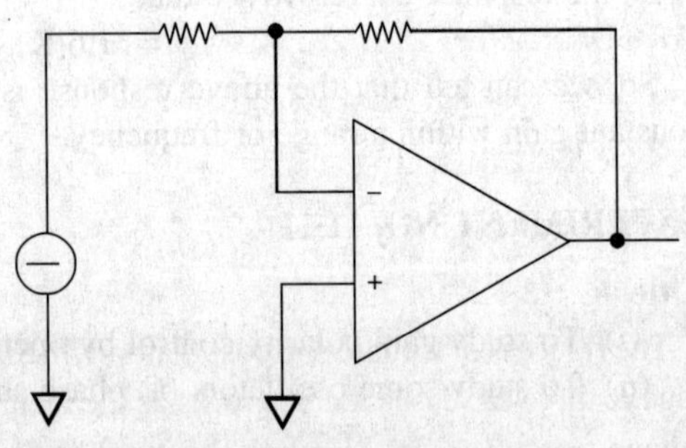

Fig. 11.25

Oscillator Principles and Theory

An oscillator is a type of feedback amplifier in which part of the output is feedback to the input via a feedback circuit if the signal feedback is of proper magnitude and phase, the circuit produces alternating current or voltages. To visvalise the requirements of an oscillator, consider the block diagram of following figure.

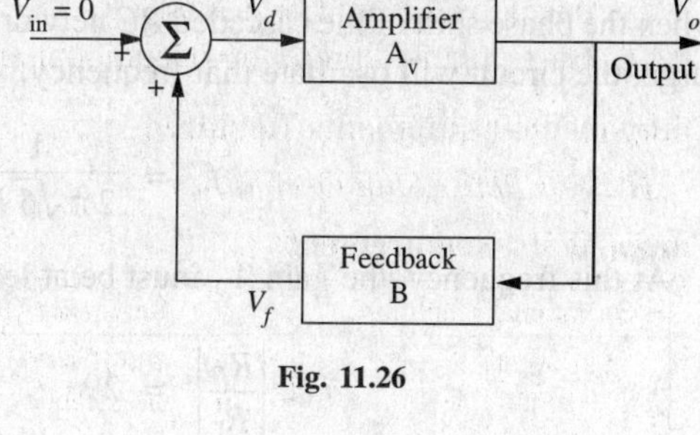

Fig. 11.26

However here the input voltage is zero. (V_{in} = 0). Also *the feedback is positive because oscillators use positive feedback.*

Finally the closed loop gain of the amplifier is denoted by A_v rather than A_F.

From block diagram,

$$V_d = V_{in} + V_f$$

$$V_o = A_V \, V_d$$

$$V_f = \beta \, V_o$$

Using these relationship we get

$$\frac{V_O}{V_i} = \frac{A_V}{1 - A_V \beta}$$

for $V_{in} = 0$ & $V_o \neq 0$ implies that

$$A_V \, \beta = 1$$

represented by polar form

$$A_V \, \beta = 1 \angle 0^\circ \text{ or } 360^\circ$$

So the above equation gives two important requirement for oscillation:–

(1) The magnitude of the loop gain $A_V \beta$ must at least 1.

(2) The total phase shift of the loop gain $A_V \; \beta$ must be equal to 0° or 360°.

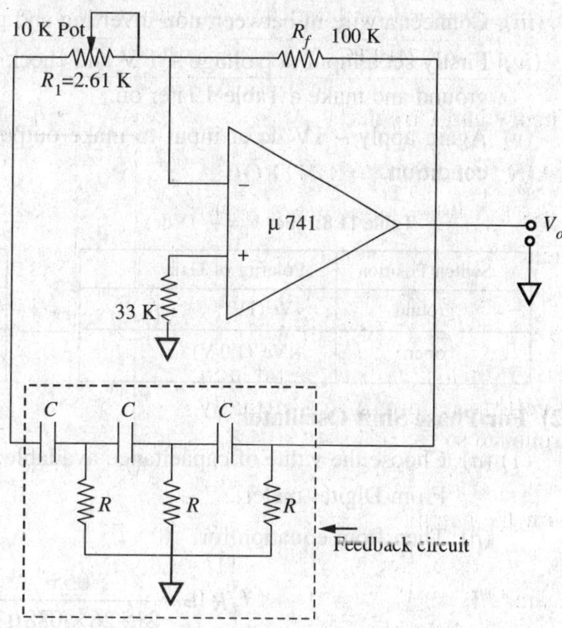

Fig. 11.27

PHASE SHIFT OSCILLATOR CIRCUIT AND ITS EXPLANATION

(*i*) R = 3·4 K, C = ·088 μF,

R_1 = 2·61K

(*ii*) R = 3·1 K, C = 0·1 μF,

R_1 = 3·1 K

The figure is of a phase shift oscillator, which consists of an operational amplifier as the amplifying stage & three *RC* cascaded networks as the feedback circuit. The feedback circuit provides feedback voltage from the output back to the input of the amplifier. The operational amplifier is used in the inverting mode; therefore any signal that appears at the inverting terminal is shifted by 180° at output. An additional 180° phase shift required for oscillation is provided by the cascaded Rc networks. Thus the total phase shift around the loop is 360° (or 0°). At some specific frequency when the phase shift of the cascaded *RC* networks is 180° and the gain of the amplifier is sufficiently large, the circuit will oscillate that frequency. This frequency is given by

$$f_{th} = \frac{1}{2\pi\sqrt{6}\,RC} = \frac{0{\cdot}065}{RC}$$

At this frequency, the gain A_v must be at least 29.

$$i.e., \left|\frac{R_F}{R_1}\right| = 29$$

Procedure

(1) For Gain Polarity Control

(*i*) Assemble the circuitry on the breadboard.

(*ii*) Set the power supply at about ± 10 V.

(*iii*) Connect a wire in between non inverting and ground node terminal to act as switch.

(*iv*) Firstly set a input dc voltage + 1 V and check the output in switch position both open and ground and make a Table 1 later on.

(*v*) Again apply – 1V dc at input to make output Table II at both ground and open switch condition.

Table 11.8: (For V_i = + 1Vdc)

Switch Position	Polarity of Gain
ground	–Ve (1V)
open	+ Ve (1.0 V)

Table 11.9: (For V_i = – 1 V dc)

Switch Position	Polarity of Gain
ground	+ Ve (1V)
open	–Ve (1V)

(2) For Phase Shift Oscillator

(1) (*a*) Choose the value of capacitance available in the laboratory let $C = 0{\cdot}1\ \mu$ F (0·088 μ F From Digital meter).

(*b*) Then from equation for

$$R = \frac{{\cdot}065}{215{\cdot}26 \times {\cdot}088\,\mu\text{F}} = 3{\cdot}4\text{ K}$$

(*c*) Then adjust the values of *R* & *C* of *RC* phase shift Network and the value of R_1 by potentiometer.

(2) Next set the circuitry on the bread board.

(3) Set the power supply at about ± 10 V.

(4) Observe the output waveforms (*r*) at the Cathode Ray Oscilloscope.

(5) Repeat this same for the another set of values of

R, C & R_1 (R = 1 K, C = 0·1 μ F & R_1 = 3·1 K).

Results

For Phase Shift Oscillator

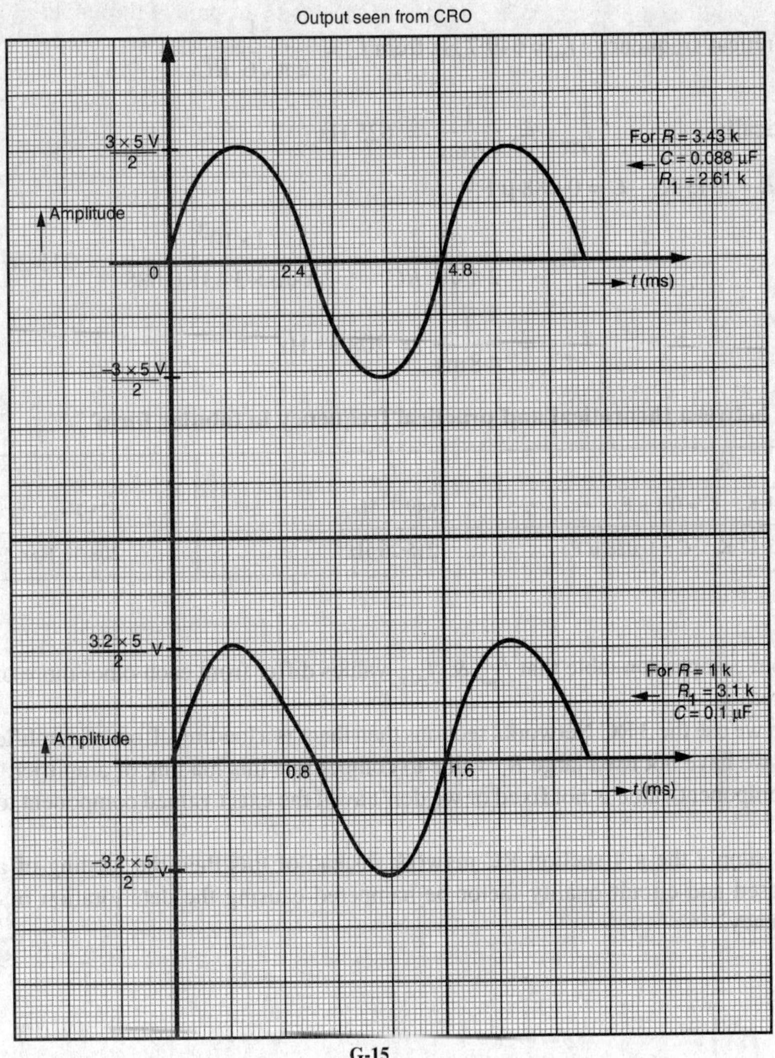

G-15

Conclusion

(1) For Gain Polarity Control

From the above table we find the truth of previous theoritical assumption.

When switch is open then the circuit behaves as a noninverting amplifier and output is noninverting voltage follower output (+ 1V). Again when switch is closed then it behaves as an inverting amplifier.

So at output we get $$-\frac{R_f}{R_L}V_{in} = -\frac{10}{10} \times 1\text{ V}$$

So it supports theoretical values.

(2) For Phase Shift Oscillator

Calculation of Frequency of Output Signal

(*i*) For $R = 1\text{K}, \quad C = 0{\cdot}1\ \mu\text{F}$

Theoretical frequency, $f_{Th} = 649{\cdot}7$ Hz from $f_{Th} = \dfrac{1}{2\pi\sqrt{6}\ RC}$

Practically $\quad f_{prac.} = \dfrac{1}{1{\cdot}6\,\text{ms}} = 625$ Hz

(*ii*) For $R = 3{\cdot}43$ K, $\quad C = 0{\cdot}088\ \mu$F

$$f_{Th} = \frac{1}{2\pi\sqrt{6}\ RC} = \frac{1\times10^3}{2\pi\sqrt{6}\times3{\cdot}43\times0.088} = 215{\cdot}26\ \text{Hz}$$

$$f_{prac.} = \frac{1}{4{\cdot}8\,\text{ms}} = 208{\cdot}33\ \text{Hz}$$

Comparison between theoretical and practical frequency in tabular form

For	f_{theo}	$f_{prac.}$
$R = 1$ K, $C = 0{\cdot}1\ \mu$F	649·7 Hz	625 Hz
$R = 3{\cdot}43$ K, $C = 0{\cdot}088\ \mu$F	215·26 Hz	208·33 Hz

Remarks

We notice from comparison table that f_{prac} & f_{theo} values differ from each other more or less.

- The reason:
  When we use the 3 RC Networks sections then there is a loading effect of amplifier. Another thing we have not used large R_1 value to compensate this loading of amplifier. Moreover, the component value is not fixed or we don't avail the exact valued component to give exact tally.
- If we supply the a 4 section RC network instead of this then the loading of amplifier is increased and circuit quality factor be hampered causing the deterioration of stability of frequency.

EXTRA PROBLEMS ON OPERATIONAL AMPLIFIER CIRCUITS

1. *Show that the effective capacitance at the point X of the following figure is* $C_x = \left(\frac{R_1}{R_2}\right)C$

Ans. In *S*-domain the ckt looks like Fig. 1(*ii*).

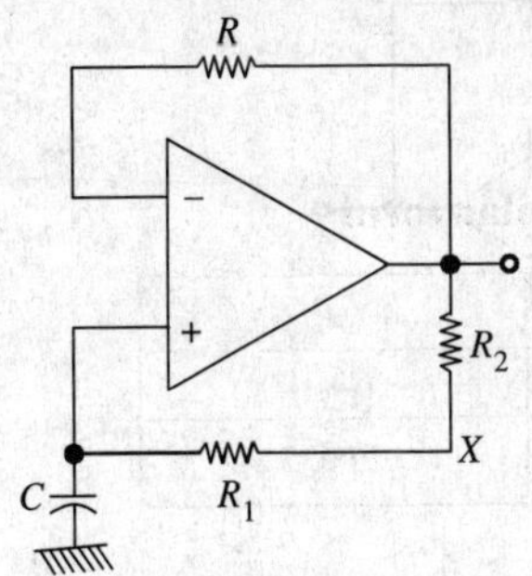

Fig. 1(*i*)

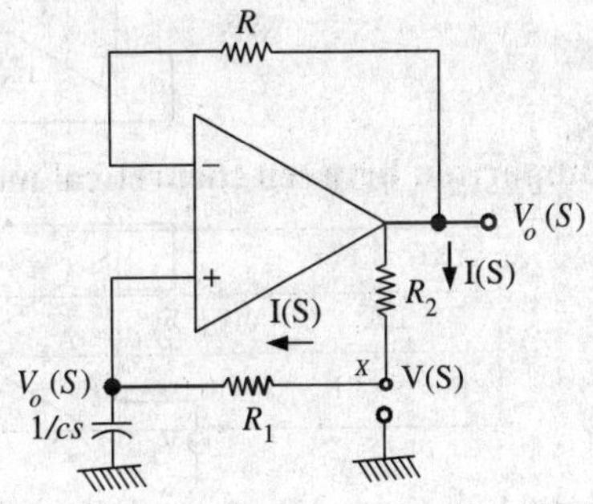

Fig. 1(*ii*)

We have, $V_0(S) = \dfrac{V(S)\left(\dfrac{1}{SC}\right)}{R_1 + \dfrac{1}{SC}}$ Now, $I(S) = \dfrac{V_0(S) - V(S)}{R_2}$

$$= \frac{V(S)\left[\dfrac{\dfrac{1}{SC}}{R_1 + \dfrac{1}{SC}} - 1\right]}{R_2} = V(S)\left[\frac{-R_1}{R_2\left(R_1 + \dfrac{1}{SC}\right)}\right]$$

Considering only the magnitude

$$I(S) = \frac{R_1 V(S)}{\left(R_1 + \dfrac{1}{SC}\right)R_2} \quad \text{[Sign is for the direction of current.]}$$

$$Z(S) = \frac{V(S)}{I(S)} = \frac{\left(R_1 + \dfrac{1}{SC}\right)R_2}{R_1}$$

$$= R_2 + \frac{R_2}{R_1}\left(\frac{1}{SC}\right) = R_2 + \frac{1}{S\left(\dfrac{R_1}{R_2}\right)C} = R_2 + \frac{1}{SC_x}$$

where, $$C_x \cong \left(\frac{R_1}{R_2}\right)C \equiv \text{Capacitance at the point } X$$

2. *Given,*

$$R_1 = R_2 = 15\text{K};\ R_3 = R_4 = 1{\cdot}5\text{K}.$$
$$R_5 = R_7 = 1\text{K};\ R_6 = 5\text{K}.$$

Calculate

(i) The voltage gain
(ii) The I/P resistance seen by each source
(iii) The O/P resistance
(iv) The bandwidth of differential amplifier

Deduce the formula first and then calculate.

Ans.

Fig. 2.

(*i*) Firstly we shall consider the first part of the circuit; [Here we have deviated the circuit into two parts] then we can draw the individual circuit for the operational amplifier A_1 and A_2. Next we shall calculate the voltage levels V_z and V_t from which we can find out the gain of the 1st part.

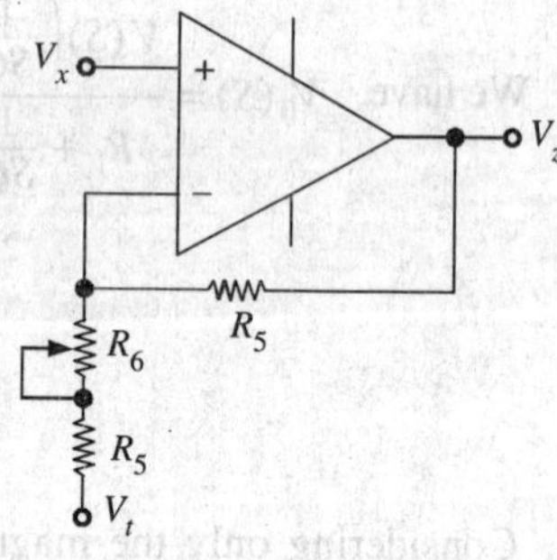

Fig. 3.

From this part we have,

$$V_z = \left(1 + \frac{R_5}{R_5 + R_6}\right) V_x - \frac{R_5}{R_5 + R_6} V_t$$

[Applying the principle of superposition]

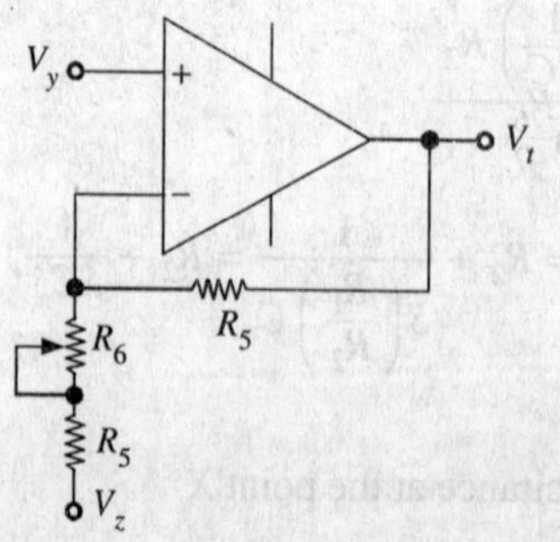

Fig. 4.

$$V_z = \frac{2R_5 + R_6}{R_5 + R_6} V_x - \frac{R_5}{R_5 + R_6} V_t \quad \text{...(1)}$$

Similarly, we have

$$V_t = \left(1 + \frac{R_5}{R_5 + R_6}\right) V_y - \frac{R_5}{R_5 + R_6} V_z$$

$$= \frac{2R_5 + R_6}{R_5 + R_6} V_y - \frac{R_5}{R_5 + R_6} V_z \quad \text{...(2)}$$

Thus, from (1) and (2) we have,

$$V_{zt} = V_z - V_t = \frac{2R_5 + R_6}{R_5 + R_6}(V_x - V_y) + \frac{R_5}{R_5 + R_6}(V_z - V_t)$$

$$= \frac{2R_5 + R_6}{R_5 + R_6} V_{xy} + \frac{R_5}{R_5 + R_6} V_{zt}$$

$$V_{zt}\left[1 - \frac{R_5}{R_5 + R_6}\right] = \frac{2R_5 + R_6}{R_5 + R_6} V_{xy}$$

$$V_{zt} = \left(\frac{2R_5 + R_6}{R_5 + R_6}\right)\left(\frac{R_5 + R_6}{R_6}\right) V_{xy}$$

$$= \left(\frac{2R_5 + R_6}{R_6}\right) V_{xy} \quad ...(3)$$

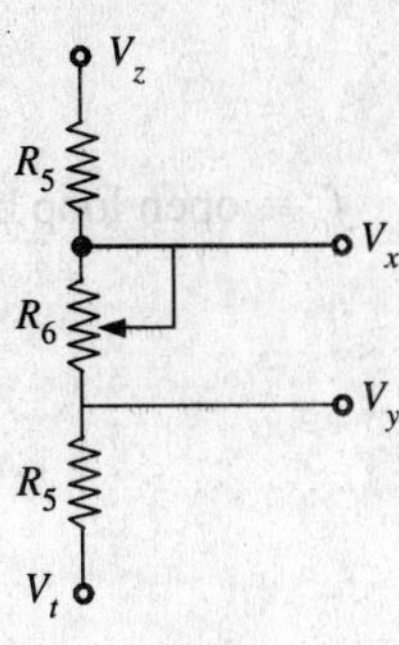

Fig. 5.

Also, the circuit of the second stage is given by

We have,

$$V_0 = -\frac{R_2}{R_4}(V_z - V_t) \quad [\because V_{xy} = V_x - V_y]$$

$$= -\frac{R_2}{R_4} V_{zt} \quad ...(4)$$

From the equations (3) and (4) we get

$$V_0 = -\left(1 + \frac{2R_5}{R_6}\right)\left(\frac{R_2}{R_4}\right) V_{xy}$$

Thus the overall voltage gain

$$A_D = \frac{V_0}{V_{xy}} = -\left(1 + \frac{2R_5}{R_6}\right)\left(\frac{R_2}{R_4}\right) \quad ...(5)$$

(*ii*) The input resistance of the ckt is the input resistance of the 1st stage

We have, $R_{iF} = R_i(1 + AB)$

where, $R_i \equiv$ input resistance of 741

$A \equiv$ open loop gain of 741

$B \equiv$ gain of the feedback circuit

$$= \frac{R_5 + R_6}{2R_5 + R_6}$$

Hence, we have

$$R_{IF} = R_i\left[1 + A\frac{R_5 + R_6}{2R_5 + R_6}\right] \quad ....(6)$$

(*iii*) The output resistance is given by

$$R_{oF} = \frac{R_0}{1 + \dfrac{A}{A_D}} \quad ...(7)$$

As it is the o/p resistance of the second stage

(*iv*) The bandwith of the circuit is given by

$$f_F = \frac{\text{unity gain bandwidth}}{\text{closed loop gain}}$$

$$= \frac{Af_o}{A_D} \qquad ...(8)$$

where, $f_o \equiv$ open loop break frequency of 741.

We have,

$$R_1 = R_2 = 15\,\text{K} \qquad A = 200{,}000$$

$$R_3 = R_4 = 1.5\,\text{K} \qquad R_{in} = 2\,\text{M}\Omega$$

$$R_5 = 1\,\text{K} \qquad f_o = 5\,\text{Hz}$$

$$R_6 = 5\,\text{K}. \qquad R_o = 75\,\Omega$$

Hence

(*i*) Voltage gain

$$A_D = -\left(1 + \frac{2R_5}{R_6}\right)\left(\frac{R_2}{R_4}\right)$$

$$= -\left[1 + \frac{2\times 1}{5}\right]\left[\frac{15}{1\cdot 5}\right] = -14.$$

(*ii*) I/P resistence

$$R_{IF} = R_i\left[1 + A\,\frac{R_5 + R_6}{2R_5 + R_6}\right]$$

$$= 2\times 10^6\left[1 + (2\times 10^5)\frac{(5+1)}{(5+2)}\right] \text{ ohms.}$$

$$= 342.86\ \text{G}\Omega.$$

(*iii*) O/P resistence

$$R_{OF} = \frac{R_0}{1 + \frac{A}{A_D}} = \frac{75}{1 + 2\times 10^5/14} = 5.25\,\text{m}\Omega.$$

(*iv*) Bandwidth

$$B_W = \frac{f_0 A}{A_D} = \frac{2\times 10^5 \times 5}{14} = H_t = 71.42\ \text{KHz}$$

PROBLEMS ON TRANSIENT RESPONSE

Problem 1:

Find out, if V_{in} is a 5V positive going step and the top plate of C has an initial voltage 1V, the natural, forced and transient and steady state response.

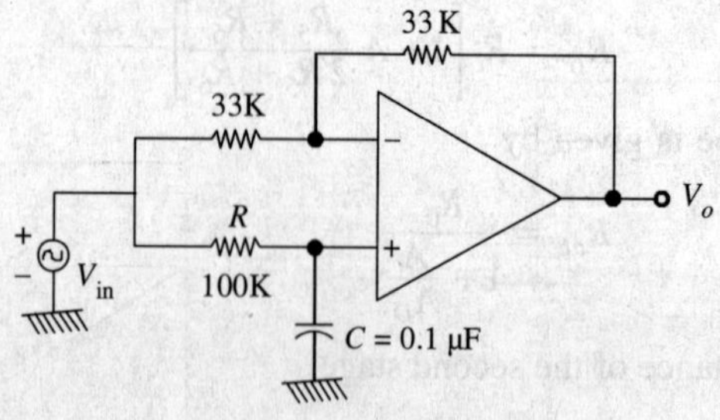

Fig. 6.

Ans.

Now we consider the S-domain representation of the above circuit:—

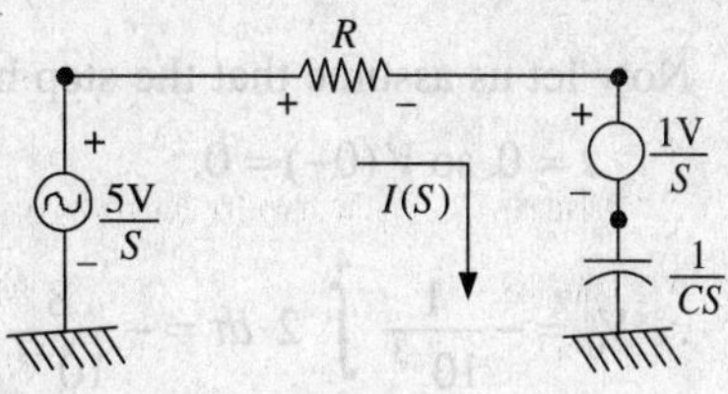

Fig. 7.

$$\therefore \quad V_C(S) = \frac{1}{S} + RI(S) + \frac{I(S)}{CS}$$

$$\therefore \quad I(S) = \frac{4/S}{R + \frac{1}{SC}} = \frac{4C}{RSC + 1}$$

$$\therefore \quad V_C(S) = \frac{1}{S} + \left(\frac{4C}{RSC+1} \times \frac{1}{SC}\right)$$

$$= \frac{1}{S} + 4\frac{1}{RC\left(S + \frac{1}{CR}\right)S}$$

$$= \frac{1}{S} + 4\frac{\frac{1}{RC}}{S\left(S + \frac{1}{RC}\right)} = \frac{1}{S} + 4\left[\frac{1}{S} - \frac{1}{S + \frac{1}{RC}}\right]$$

$$\therefore \quad V_c(t) = 1 + 4\left[1 - e^{-t/RC}\right]$$

The output voltage $= 2V_C(t) - V_{in}$

$$= 2\left[1 + 4\left(1 - e^{-t/RC}\right)\right] - 5 = 5 - 8e^{-t/RC}$$

$$= 5\left[1 - e^{-t/RC}\right] - 3\,e^{-t/RC}$$

$$CR = 0.1 \times 10^{-6} \times 100 \times 10^{3} = 10\,\text{ms}$$

$$\therefore \quad V_0(t \geq 10+) = 5\left[1 - e^{-t/10\,\text{ms}}\right] - 3e^{-t/10\,\text{ms}}$$

Natural component $= (-3e^{-t/10\,\text{ms}})$ V

Forced response $= 5[1 - e^{-t/10\,\text{ms}}]$ V

Transient component $= (-8\,e^{-t/10\text{ms}})$ V

Steady state component $= 5$ V

Problem 2:

Assume the capacitor be initially discharged. Sketch and label V_0 if V_{in} is a 2V positive going step.

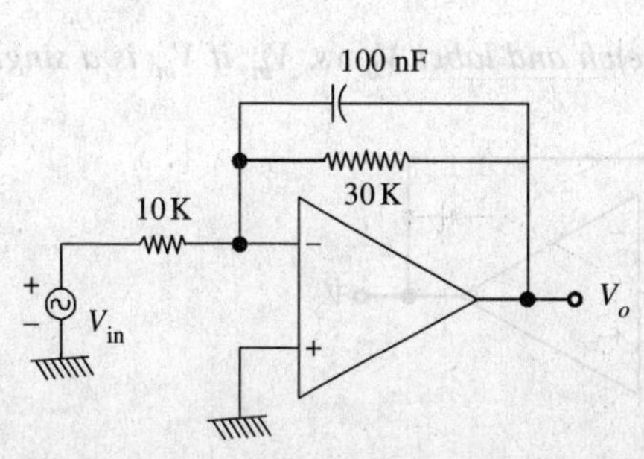

Fig. 8.

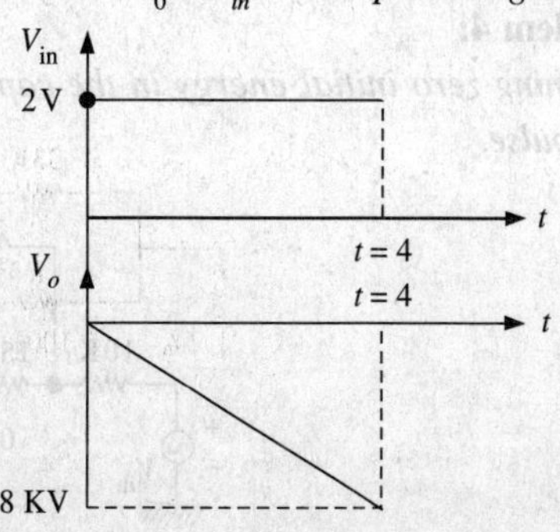

Fig. 9.

Ans.

$$R_1\ C_F = \left(10 \times 10^3 \times 100 \times 10^{-9}\right) = 10^{-3}\ \text{S}.$$

Now let us assume that the step begins at

$t = 0$, so $V(0-) = 0$.

$$\therefore\ V_0 = -\frac{1}{10^{-3}} \int_0^4 2 \cdot dt = -\frac{8}{10^{-3}}\ V$$

We are considering the output voltage upto $t = 4$ sec.

$V_0 = -\ 8$ KV at $t = 4$ sec.

Problem 3:

For the circuit, sketch and lable V_0 versus t if V_{in} after being at –2V for a long time is changed to 1 V at $t = 0$. At what instant $V_0 = 0$ V?

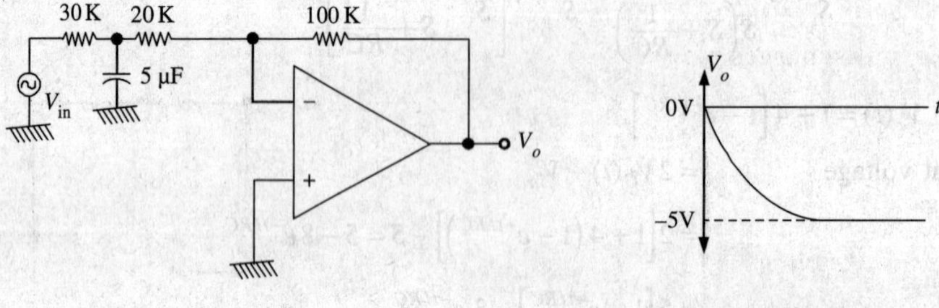

Fig. 10. Fig. 11.

Ans. Now, V_i remains at the level –2V for a long time and hence the capacitor has been charged upto –2V.

$$\therefore \qquad V(0-) = (-2)\,(-5) = 10\,V$$

Now the input voltage changes abruptly to +1V, the capacitor holds at the –2V level and then charges toward +1V.

$$\therefore \qquad V_C(t \geq 0+) = -\,2 + (1+2)\,(1 - e^{-t/30\,\text{K} \times 5n})$$

$$= -\,2 + 3\,(1 - e^{-t/150\,\mu s}) = (1 - 3e^{-t/150\mu s})\ V$$

Now, $\qquad V_0\,(t \geq 0+) = (-5)\,(1 - 3e^{-t/150\mu s})\,V = 5[3e^{-t/150\mu s} - 1]\ V$

$V_0 = 0$ sat at $t = T$. $\quad \therefore \quad 3e^{T/150\mu s} = 1 \quad$ or, $\quad T = -\left(150 \ln \frac{1}{3}\right) \mu s = 165\ \mu s$

Problem 4:

Assuming zero initial energy in the capacitor sketch and label V_0 vs. V_{in} if V_{in} is a single 5V, 0.5 ms pulse.

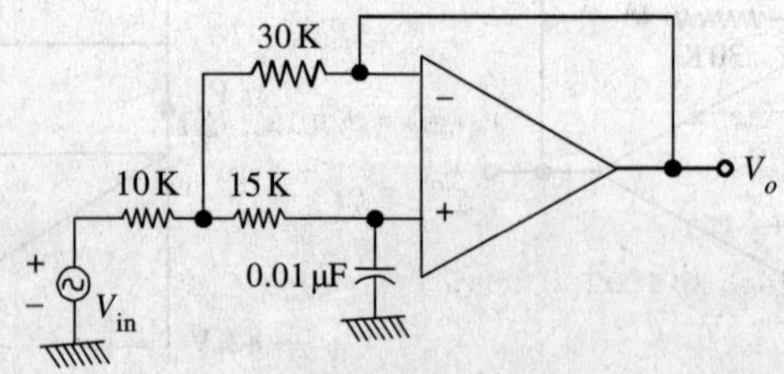

Fig. 12.

Ans.

The gain of the inverts amplifier is zero as the feedback is a short circuit. The gain of the noniverting amplifier is $1\left[1+\frac{0}{30\,K}=1\right]$ i.e., the circuit behaves as unity follower to the input V_C.

The capacitor has no stored energy. So when the pulse is +ve then the capacitor charges towards 5V.

$$V_C\,(0<t<0.5\,\text{ms}) = 5[1-e^{-t/25\text{k}\times 10ns}]\,\text{V}$$

$$= 5[1-e^{-t/250\mu s}]\,\text{V}$$

Fig. 13.

at $t = 0.5$ ms

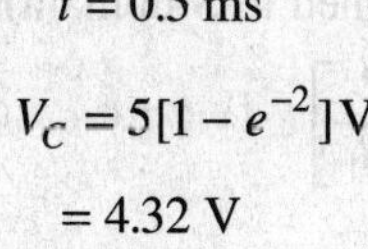

$$V_C = 5[1-e^{-2}]\,\text{V}$$

$$= 4.32\ \text{V}$$

When t > 0.5 ms, the capacitor now discharges toward 0V.

$$V_C = 4.32\,e^{-t/250\mu s}\,\text{V}$$

Problem 5:

(*a*) *Show that the circuit is a noninverting differentiator with* $V_0 = 2RCjwV_i$

(*b*) *Specify component for* $V_0 = 10\,|\,V_{in}\,|$ *at* $\omega = 1\ K$ *rad/sec.*

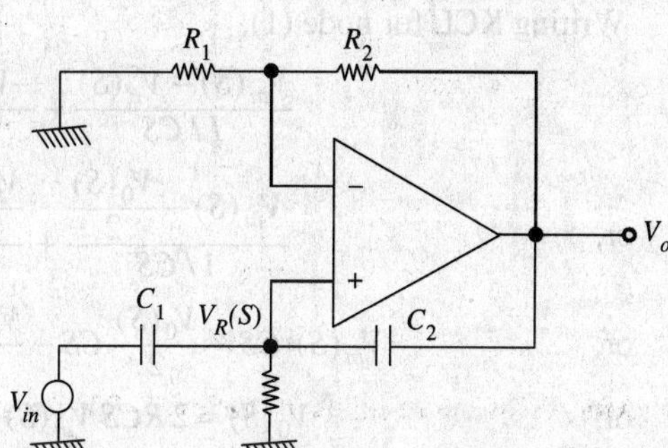

Fig. 14.

Ans.

(*a*) Now in case of a differentiator we have to show

$$V_0 = K\cdot\frac{d\,V_{in}}{dt}.$$

where K is any system constant depends on the value of R and C.

Now, if we consider the case in s-domain then,

$$V_0\,(S) = K\,S\,V_{in}\,(S) - K\,V_{in}\,(0-)$$

Assuming, $V_{in}\,(0-) = 0$

and putting $S = j\omega,$

$$V_0\,(S) = Kj\omega\,V_{in}\,(S)$$

We have to show $K = 2RC.$

The equivalent circuit in S-domain.

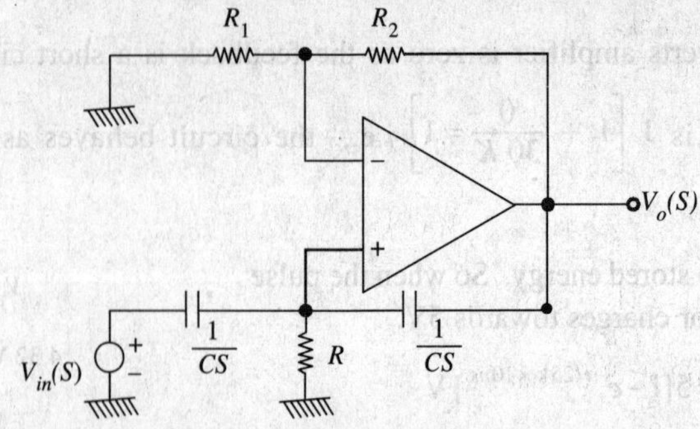

Fig. 15.

The voltage across the resistance $R = V_R(S)$ (when transformed to S-domain).

$$V_0(S) = V_R(S)\left[1 + \frac{R_2}{R_1}\right]$$

Say $R_1 = R_2$, thus

$$V_0(S) = 2\,V_R(S)$$

Writing KCL for node (1),

$$\frac{V_{in}(S) - V_R(S)}{I/CS} + \frac{-V_R(S)}{R} + \frac{V_0(S) - V_R(S)}{1/CS} = 0$$

or,
$$\frac{V_{in}(S) - \frac{V_0(S)}{2}}{1/CS} + \frac{\frac{V_0(S)}{2}}{R} + \frac{V_0(S) - \frac{V_0(S)}{2}}{1/CS} = 0$$

or,
$$V_{in}(S)\cdot CS - \frac{V_0(S)}{2}CS - \frac{V_0(S)}{2}CS - \frac{V_0(S)}{2R} + \frac{V_0(S)}{2}CS = 0$$

or,
$$V_0(S) = 2\,RCS\,V_{in}(S)$$

$\therefore$
$$V_0(S) = j\omega\,2\,RC\,V_{in}(S).$$

The circuit behaves as non-inverting differentiator.

(*b*) As $R_2 = R_1 = R$ say,

$\therefore$ $10 = 2\,RCW$

Considering, $C = 10\,nF$

and having $\omega = 10^3$ rad/sec. $2R \times 10 \times 10^{-9} \times 10^3 = 10$ or, $2R \times 10^{-6} = 1$ or, $R = 500\,\text{K}\Omega$.

Problem 6:

(*a*) *Show that the circuit is a non inverting integrator with*

$$V_0(S) = \frac{1}{j\omega CR}V_{in}(S)$$

(*b*) *Specify component values so that*

$$|V_0| = |V_{in}| \text{ for } \omega = 10^3 \text{ rad/sec.}$$

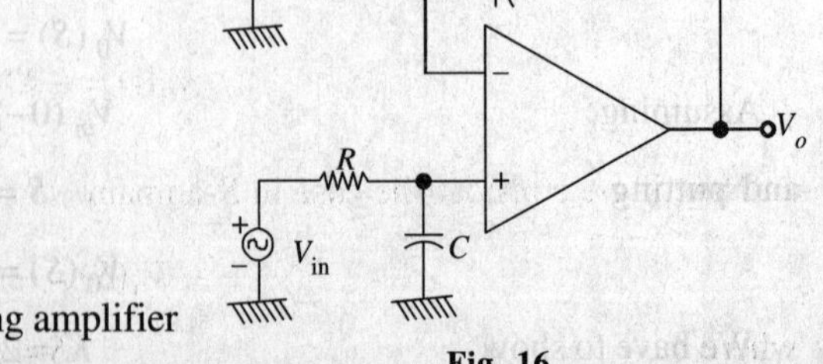

Fig. 16.

Ans.

Now when the circuit behaves as non-inverting amplifier integrator then

$$V_0(t) = K\int_0^t V_{in}(t)\,dt$$

where k is the gain constant.

In S-domain notation,

$$V_0(S) = \frac{K}{S} V_{in}(S)$$

or

$$V_0(S) = \frac{K}{j\omega} V_{in}(S)$$

We have to show $K = \frac{1}{CR}$.

The equivalent circuit in S-domain is

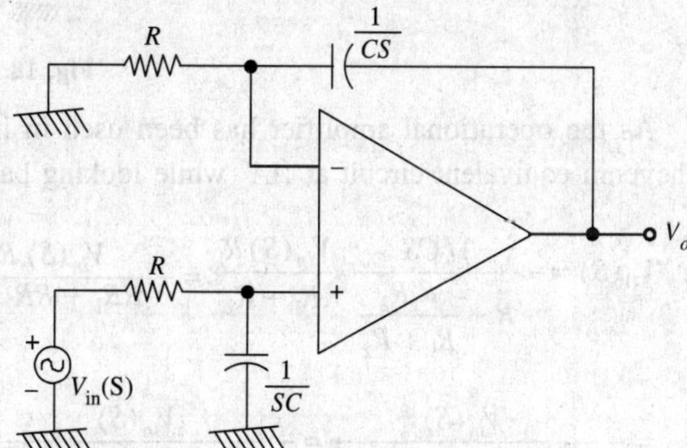

Fig. 17.

$$V_0(S) = \frac{\frac{V_{in}(S)}{SC}}{R + \frac{1}{SC}} \left(1 + \frac{1}{SCR}\right)$$

$$= \frac{V_{in}(S)}{SCR}$$

or,

$$V_0(S) = \frac{1}{j\omega CR} V_{in}(S)$$

(*b*) When $|V_0| = |V_{in}|$,

$$1 = \frac{1}{\omega CR}$$

We select $C = 10\,n\text{F}$ [and $\omega = 10^3$ rad / S]

$$\therefore\ R = \frac{1}{10^3 \times 10 \times 10^{-9}}\ \Omega = 100\ \text{K}\ \Omega.$$

Problem 7:

(*a*) *Show that the circuit is an inverting integrator with* $V_0(S) = \frac{1}{j\omega CRK} V_{in}(S)$ *where*

$$K = 1 + \frac{R_2}{R_1} + \frac{R_2}{R}$$

(*b*) *If C = 0.1 μ F, select resistance not greater then 100 K Ω to yield* $V_0 = -\frac{1}{j\omega} V_{in}$.

Ans.

(*a*) For an inverting amplifier integrator relation between input and output signal is given by

$$V_0(t) = -K' \int_0^t V_{in}(t)\, dt$$

Now if we consider the case in S-domain

$$V_0(S) = -\frac{K'}{S} V_{in}(S)$$

where

$$S = j\omega$$

and K' is the system constant.

The equivalent circuit in S-domain.

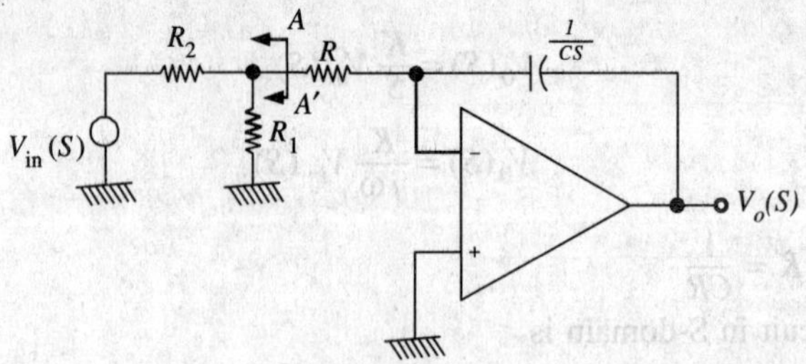

Fig. 18.

As the operational amplifier has been used in inverting mode, we proceed first to find the thevenin equivalent circuit at AA' while looking back.

$$\therefore\ V_0(S) = -\frac{1/CS}{R + \dfrac{R_1 R_2}{R_1 + R_2}} \cdot \frac{V_{in}(S) R_1}{R_1 + R_2} = -\frac{V_{in}(S)\, R_1 / CS}{RR_1 + RR_2 + R_1\, R_2}$$

$$= -\frac{V_{in}(S)}{CS\left[R + \dfrac{RR_2}{R_1} + R_2\right]} = -\frac{V_{in}(S)}{CSR\left[1 + \dfrac{R_2}{R_1} + \dfrac{R_2}{R}\right]}$$

Fig. 19.

or, $$V_0(S) = \frac{-V_{in}(S)}{j\,\omega\, CRK}$$

where, $$K = 1 + \frac{R_2}{R_1} + \frac{R_2}{R}.$$

$\therefore$ The circuit behaves as an inverting integrator.

(b) Considering $R_2 = 100\ R_1$; $V_0(S) = -\dfrac{1}{j\omega} V_{in}(S)$; $\therefore\ 1 = \dfrac{1}{CRK}$

or, $$CRK = 1$$

or, $$RK = \frac{1}{C} = \frac{1}{0.1 \times 10^{-6}} = 10^7$$

or, $$R\left[1 + 100 + \frac{R_2}{R}\right] = 10^7$$

or, $$(R \times 101) + R_2 = 10^7$$

or, $$R = \frac{1}{101}\left[10^7 - R_2\right]$$

Taking $R_2 = 100\ \text{K}\Omega$

thus, $R_1 = 1\ \text{K}\Omega$

We get, $$R = \frac{1}{101}\left[10^7 - 10^5\right]\Omega$$

$$= 98.02\ \text{K}\Omega$$

$\therefore$ Calculated values of the components

$$R_1 = 1\ \text{K}\Omega,\quad R_2 = 100\ \text{K}\Omega,\ R = 98.02\ \text{K}\Omega,\ C = 0.1\mu F$$

Problem 8:

(*a*) *Show that the ckt is an Inductor simulator with* $Z = j\omega L_{eq}$ *where,* $L_{eq} = \dfrac{R_1 R_2 R_4 C}{R_3}$

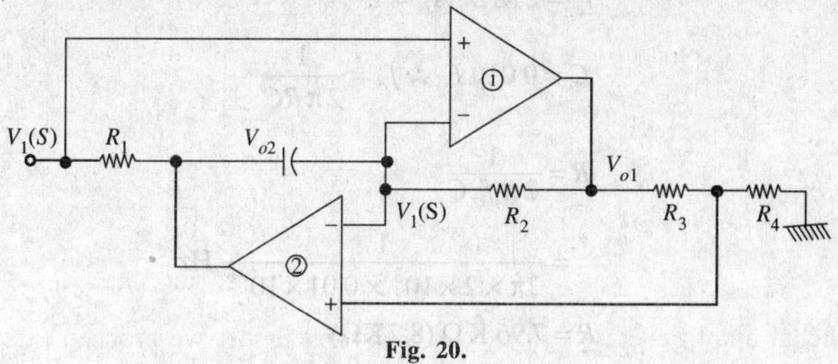

Fig. 20.

(*b*) *If C = 1 μF, specify suitable resistance to synthesis a 10 mH inductance.*

Ans.

Here, we have,
$$V_1(S) = \frac{V_{01}(S)\,R_4}{R_3 + R_4}[1] = \frac{V_{01}(S)\,R_4}{R_3 + R_4}$$

$$V_{01}(S) = V_1(S)\left[1 + \frac{R_2}{\frac{1}{SC}}\right] = V_1(S)\,[1 + R_2 CS]$$

Applying KCL at node $V_1(S)$

$$\frac{V_{02}(S) - V_1(S)}{\frac{1}{SC}} + \frac{V_{01}(S) - V_1(S)}{R_2} = 0$$

or
$$\{V_1(S) - V_{01}(S)\}\,\frac{R_4 R_2 CS}{R_3} = V_1(S)$$

Now,
$$I_1 = \frac{V_1(S) - V_{02}(S)}{R_1} = \frac{V_1(S)\,R_3}{R_1 R_2 R_4 CS}$$

∴
$$Z(S) = \frac{V_1(S)}{I_1(S)} = \frac{S\,R_1 R_2 R_4 C}{R_3}$$

∴
$$Z = j\omega L_{eq} \quad \text{where} \quad L_{eq} = \frac{R_1 R_2 R_4 C}{R_3}.$$

PROBLEMS ON FILTERS

Problem 1:

Design a 1st-order low-pass filter so that it has a cutoff frequency of 2 KHz and pass-band gain is 1.

Solution.

For this ckt we have, cut off frequency,

$$f_c = \frac{1}{2\pi RC}$$

Fig. 21.

Pass band gain $A_F = 1 + \frac{R_F}{R_1}$

Now, given $f_c = 2\,\text{KHz},\ A_F = 1.$

Let $C = 0.01\mu F \ \therefore f_c = \frac{1}{2\pi RC}$

$$R = \frac{1}{2\pi f_c C}$$

$$= \frac{1}{2\pi \times 2 \times 10^3 \times 0.01 \times 10^{-6}} \text{Hz}$$

$$R = 7.96\ \text{K}\Omega\ (8.2\ \text{K}\Omega)$$

Also, $A_F = 1 + \frac{R_F}{R_1} = 1$

$$R_1 >> R_F$$

Let, $R_1 = 10\,\text{K}$

$$R_F = 150\,\Omega$$

$\therefore$ $R_1 = 10\,\text{K}\Omega$

$$C = 0.01\mu\,\text{F}$$

$$R_F = 150\,\Omega\ R = 7.96\,\text{K}\Omega\ (10\,\text{K pot})$$

Problem 2:

Design a second order low pass filter at cutoff frequency of 1.2 KHz.

Solution.

For this ckt $f_c = \frac{1}{2\pi\sqrt{R_1 C_1 R_2 C_2}}$

We assume, $R_1 = R_2 = R$

$$C_1 = C_2 = C$$

$\therefore$ $f_c = \frac{1}{2\pi RC}$

$$A_F = 1.586$$

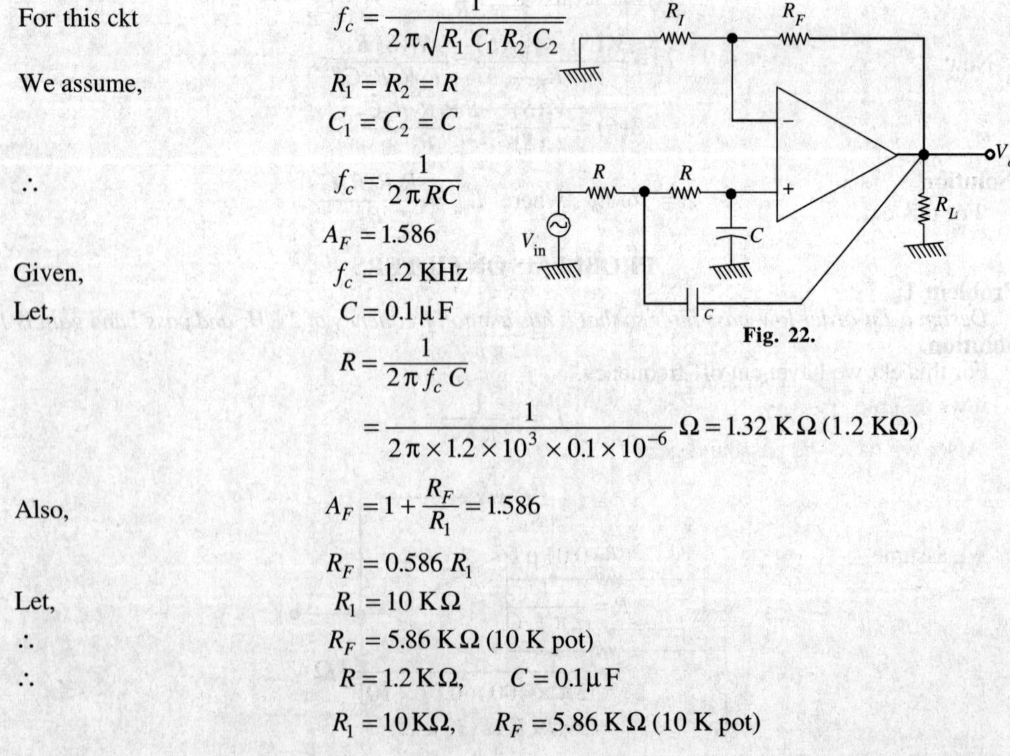

Fig. 22.

Given, $f_c = 1.2\,\text{KHz}$

Let, $C = 0.1\,\mu\,\text{F}$

$$R = \frac{1}{2\pi f_c C}$$

$$= \frac{1}{2\pi \times 1.2 \times 10^3 \times 0.1 \times 10^{-6}}\,\Omega = 1.32\,\text{K}\Omega\ (1.2\ \text{K}\Omega)$$

Also, $A_F = 1 + \frac{R_F}{R_1} = 1.586$

$$R_F = 0.586\,R_1$$

Let, $R_1 = 10\,\text{K}\Omega$

$\therefore$ $R_F = 5.86\,\text{K}\Omega$ (10 K pot)

$\therefore$ $R = 1.2\,\text{K}\Omega, \quad C = 0.1\mu\,\text{F}$

$$R_1 = 10\text{K}\Omega, \quad R_F = 5.86\,\text{K}\Omega\ (10\ \text{K pot})$$

Problem 3:

Design a 1st order highpass filter at a cut-off frequency of 1 KHz.

Solution.

We use a voltage follower ckt as the pass band gain is given to be 1. $\left[R_1 = R_F\right]$

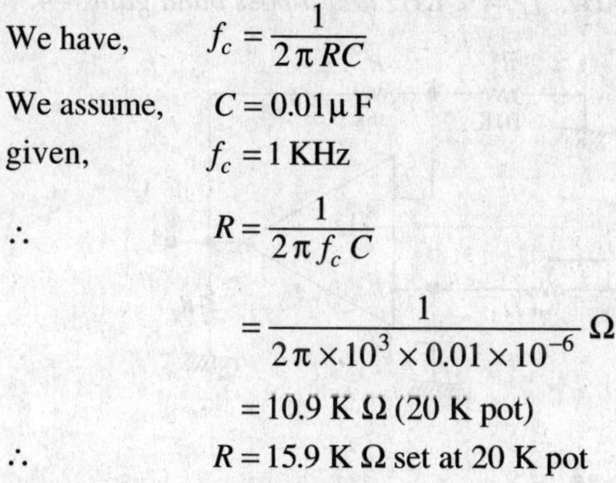

We have, $f_c = \dfrac{1}{2\pi RC}$

We assume, $C = 0.01\,\mu\text{F}$

given, $f_c = 1\,\text{KHz}$

$\therefore$ $R = \dfrac{1}{2\pi f_c C}$

$= \dfrac{1}{2\pi \times 10^3 \times 0.01 \times 10^{-6}}\,\Omega$

$= 10.9\,\text{K}\,\Omega$ (20 K pot)

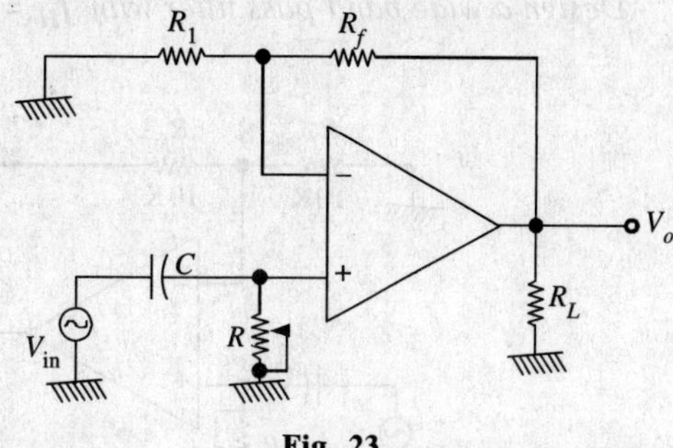

Fig. 23.

$\therefore$ $R = 15.9\,\text{K}\,\Omega$ set at 20 K pot

$C = 0.01\,\mu\text{F}$

Problem 4:

Design a second-order high-pass filter at a cut-off frequency of 400 KHz.

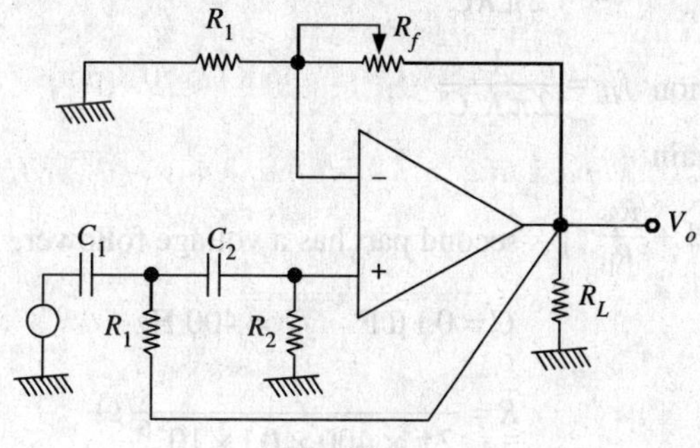

Fig. 24.

Solution.

For this ckt,

$$f_c = \frac{1}{2\pi\sqrt{R_1C_1R_2C_2}}$$

$$= \frac{1}{2\pi RC}$$

if we assume, $\begin{cases} R_1 = R_2 = R \\ C_1 = C_2 = C \end{cases}$

Also, we have the passband gain

$$A_F = 1 + \frac{R_F}{R_1} = 1.586$$

We assume, $C = 0.01\,\mu\text{F}$

$$\therefore \quad R = \frac{1}{2\pi f_c C}$$

$$= \frac{1}{2\pi \times 400 \times 0.01 \times 10^{-6}}\,\Omega$$

$$= 39.79\,\text{K}\Omega\ (39\,\text{k}\,\Omega)$$

Also, $1 + \frac{R_F}{R_1} = 1.586 \quad R_F = 0.586\ R_1$

Let, $R_1 = 10\,\text{K}\Omega \quad R_F = 5.86\ \text{K}\Omega\ (10\,\text{K}\Omega \text{ pot})$

Problem 5:

Design a wide band-pass filter with f_H = 400 Hz, f_L = 2 KHz and a pass band gain = 4.

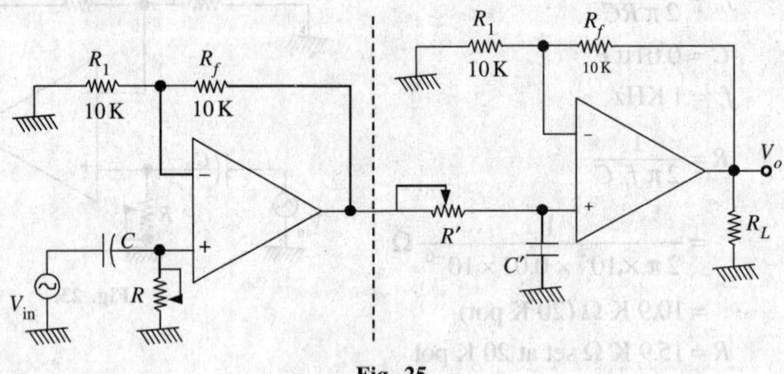

Fig. 25.

Solution.

For the highpass portion $f_L = \frac{1}{2\pi RC}$

For the lowpass portion $f_H = \frac{1}{2\pi R'C'}$

Also, total voltage gain

$$A_{FT} = 1 + \frac{R_F}{R_1} \quad [\because \text{ second part has a voltage follower, } \therefore A_{F2} = 1]$$

Let, $C = 0.1\,\mu\text{F} \quad f_L = 400\ \text{Hz}$

$$\therefore \quad R = \frac{1}{2\pi \times 400 \times 0.1 \times 10^{-6}}\ \Omega$$

$$= 3.98\ \text{K}\Omega\ (5 \text{ pot})$$

Let, $$R' = \frac{1}{2\pi \times 2 \times 10^3 \times 0.01 \times 10^{-6}}\ \Omega$$

$$= 7.96\ \text{K}\,\Omega\ (10 \text{ pot})$$

Also, $1 + \frac{R_F}{R_1} = 4 \quad R_F = 3\,R_1$

Let, $R_1 = 1.5\ \text{K}\Omega$

$\therefore \quad R_F = 4.5\ \text{K}\Omega\ (4.7\ \text{K}\ \Omega)$

$\therefore \quad R = 3.988\ \text{K}\Omega\ (5 \text{ pot})$

$R' = 7.96\ \text{K}\Omega\ (10\ \text{K pot}) \quad R_1 = 1.5\,\text{K}\ \Omega$

$C = 0.1\mu\ F \quad R_F = 4.5\ \text{K}\Omega$

$C' = 0.01\mu\ F$

Problem 6:

Design a narrow bandpass fitter so that, $f_C = 2$ KHz, $Q = 20$, $A_F = 10$

Solution.

We assume

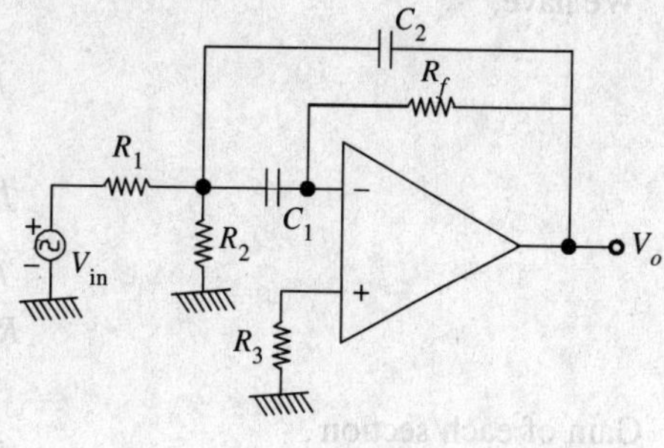

Fig. 26.

$$C_1 = C_2 = C$$

$$\therefore \quad R_1 = \frac{Q}{2\pi f_c C A_F}$$

$$R_2 = \frac{Q}{2\pi f_c C(2Q^2 - A_F)}$$

$$R_3 = \frac{Q}{\pi f_c C}$$

and, $$A_F = \frac{R_3}{2R_1}$$

We assume,

$$C_1 = C_2 = C = 0.1\mu\text{F}$$

$$Q = 20,\ f_c = 2\,\text{KHz},\ A_F = 10$$

$$\therefore \quad R_1 = \frac{Q}{2\pi f_c C A_F} = \frac{20}{2\pi \times '2' \times 10^3 \times 0.1 \times 10^{-6} \times 10}\ \Omega = 1.59\ \text{K}\Omega (1.5\text{K})$$

$$R_2 = \frac{Q}{2\pi f_c (2Q^2 - A_F) C}$$

$$= \frac{20}{2\pi \times 2 \times 10^3\ (800 - 10) \times 0.1 \times 10^{-6} \times 10}\ \Omega = 20\,\Omega = (22\,\Omega)$$

$$R_3 = \frac{Q}{\pi f_c C} = \frac{20}{\pi \times 2 \times 10^3 \times 0.1 \times 10^{-6}}\ \Omega = 31.8\ \text{K}\Omega\ (33\ \text{K}\Omega)$$

$$\therefore \quad R_1 = 1.5\,\text{K}\Omega,\ R_2 = 22\,\Omega,\ R_3 = 33\ \text{K}\Omega,\ C_1 = C_2 = 0.1\mu\text{F}$$

Problem 7:

Design a wide band reject filter using 1st order high-pass & low-pass filters having $f_L = 2KHz$, $f_H = 400$ Hz.

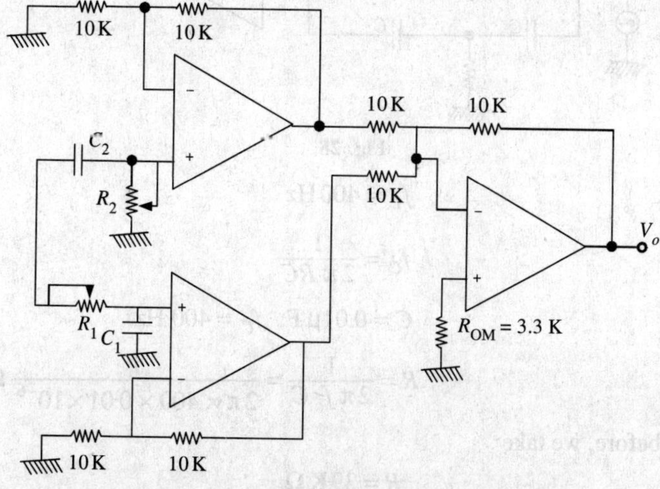

Fig. 27.

Solution.

We have,

$$f_L = \frac{1}{2\pi RC}$$

$$f_H = \frac{1}{2\pi R'C'}$$

$$R_1 = R_2 = R_3$$

$$R_4 = R_1 \,||\, R_2 \,||\, R_3$$

Gain of each section $= 1 + \frac{R_F}{R_1} \;\&\; 1 + \frac{R_F'}{R_1'}$

Let $C = 0.01\mu\text{F},\ R = \frac{1}{2\pi f_L C} = \frac{1}{2\pi \times 2 \times 10^3 \times 0.01 \times 10^{-6}}\ \Omega$

$$R = 7.96\ \text{K}\Omega$$

Let, $C' = 0.1\mu\text{F},\ R' = \frac{1}{2\pi f_H C} = \frac{1}{2\pi \times 400 \times 0.1 \times 10^{-6}}\ \Omega$

$$R' = 3.98\ \text{K}\Omega$$

Let, $R_1 = R_2 = R_3 = 10\,\text{K}\Omega$

$$R_4 = R_1 \,||\, R_2 \,||\, R_3 = 3.3\ \text{K}\Omega$$

There is no restriction for gain; we take it 2 for each section.

$\therefore \quad R_1 = R_F = R_1' = R_F' = 10\,\text{K}$

Problem 8:

Design a narrow band reject notch filter for the frequency.

Solution.

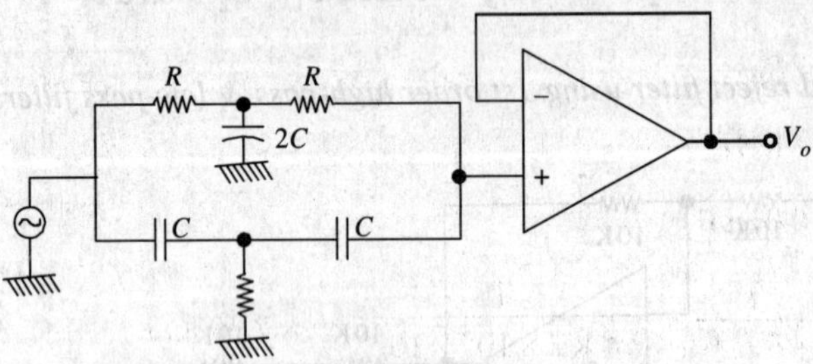

Fig. 28.

$$f_L = 400\,\text{Hz}$$

Here, $f_C = \frac{1}{2\pi\, RC}$

Let, $C = 0.01\mu\text{F};\ f_C = 400\ \text{Hz}$

$\therefore \quad R = \frac{1}{2\pi f_c C} = \frac{1}{2\pi \times 400 \times 0.01 \times 10^{-6}}\ \Omega = 39.79\,\text{K}\Omega$

For commercial before, we take

$$R = 39\,\text{K}\Omega$$

$\therefore \quad \begin{cases} R = 39\,\text{K}\Omega \\ C = 0.01\mu\text{F} \end{cases}$

Problem 9:

Design a phase-shift oscillation

$f_0 = 1\ KHz$

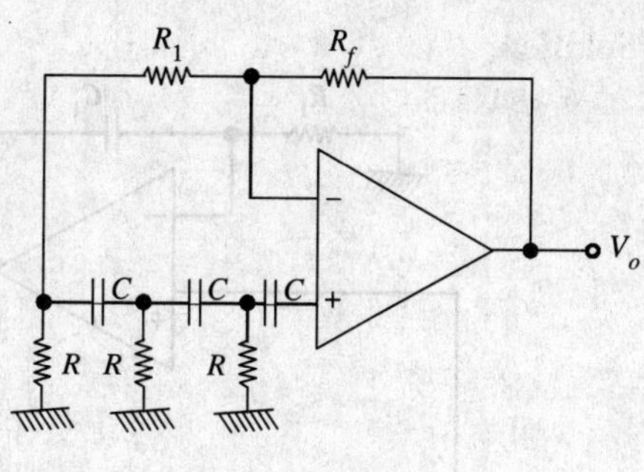

Fig. 29.

Solution.

Here, we have

$$f_0 = \frac{1}{2\pi\sqrt{6}\,RC} \ \& \ \left|\frac{R_F}{R_1}\right| = 29$$

We have, $f_0 = 1\ \text{KHz}$

Let, $C = 0.1\,\mu\text{F}$

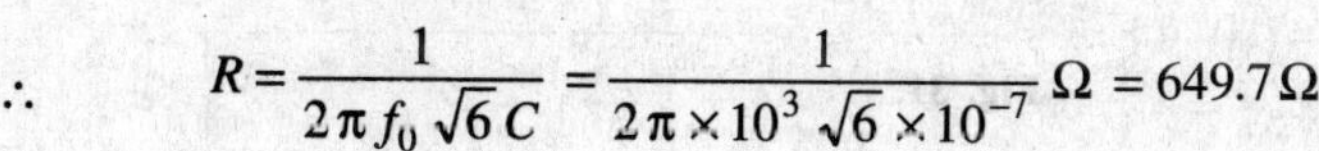

$$\therefore \quad R = \frac{1}{2\pi f_0 \sqrt{6}\, C} = \frac{1}{2\pi\times 10^3\sqrt{6}\times 10^{-7}}\,\Omega = 649.7\,\Omega$$

$\therefore$ $R = 680\,\Omega$, Also, $R_F = 29\,R_1$ Let, $R_1 = 33\,\text{K}\,\Omega$

$\therefore$ $R_F = 33\times 29\ \text{K}\Omega = 957\ \text{K}\Omega\ (1\ \text{M}\ \Omega\ \text{pot})$

Problem 10:

Design a Wain bridge oscillator that will oscillate at 2 KHz

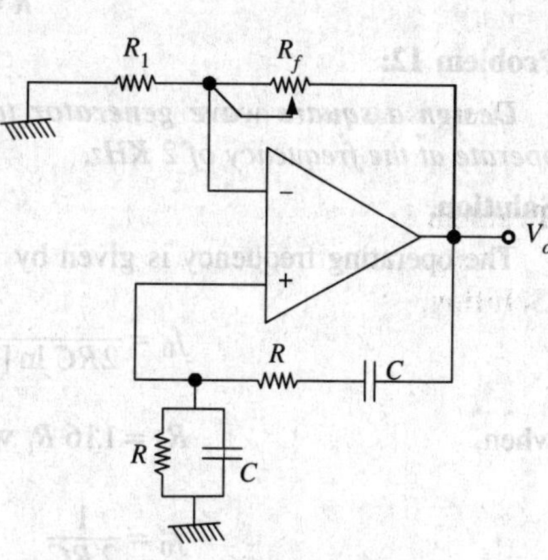

Fig. 30.

Solution.

We have,

$$f_0 = \frac{1}{2\pi\,RC},\quad A_V = 1 + \frac{R_F}{R_1} = 3$$

$R_F = 2R_1$

Given, $f_0 = 2\ \text{KHz}$,

Let, $C = 0.01\,\mu\text{F}$

$$\therefore \quad R = \frac{1}{2\pi f_0 C} = \frac{1}{2\pi\times 2\times 10^3\times 10^{-8}}\,\Omega = 7.96\ \text{K}\Omega$$

$\therefore$ $R = 82\ \text{K}\Omega$

Also, $R_F = 2R_1$ Let $R_1 = 33\,\text{K}\Omega$ $\therefore\ R_F = 68\ \text{K}\Omega$

$\therefore$ $R = 8.2\ \text{K}\Omega$ $C = 0.01\,\mu\text{F}$ $R_1 = 33\ \text{K}\Omega$ $R_F = 68\ \text{K}\Omega$

Problem 11:

Design a quadrature oscillator to operate at the frequency of 1.5 KHz.

Solution. Here, we have, $R_1 = R_2 = R_3 = R$ (say)

$C_1 = C_2 = C_3 = C$ (say)

$$\therefore \quad f_0 = \frac{1}{2\pi\,RC}$$

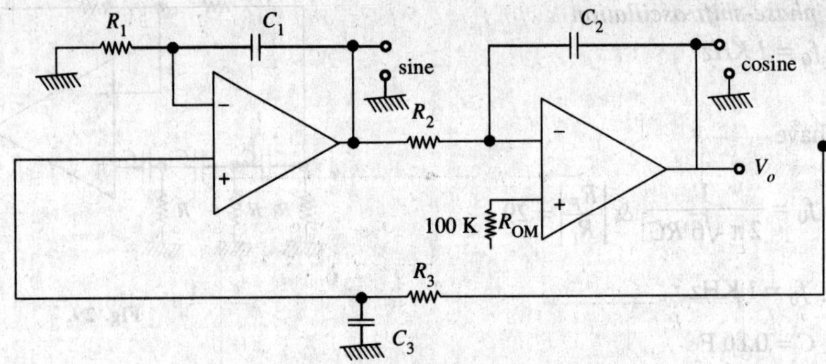

Fig. 31.

Let, $C = 0.1\,\mu\text{F}, \quad f_0 = 1.5\,\text{KHz}$

$$\therefore \quad R = \frac{1}{2\pi f_0 C} = \frac{1}{2\pi \times 1.5 \times 10^3 \times 10^{-7}}\,\Omega = 1.06\,\text{K}\Omega$$

$$\therefore \quad R = 1\,\text{K}\Omega$$

Problem 12:

Design a square wave generator to operate at the frequency of 2 KHz.

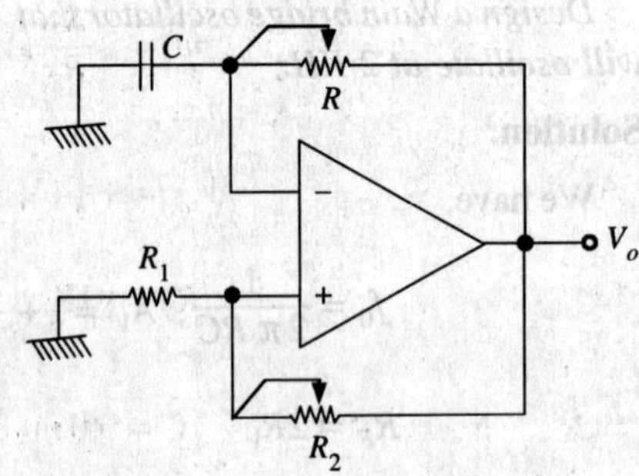

Fig. 32.

Solution.

The operating frequency is given by

$$f_0 = \frac{1}{2RC \ln [(2R_1 + R_2)/R_2]}$$

when, $R_2 = 1.16\, R_1$ we get

$$f_0 = \frac{1}{2RC}$$

Let, $R_1 = 10\,\text{K}\Omega$

Then $R_2 = 1.16 \times 10\text{K} = 11.6\,\text{K}\Omega$

(20 K pot)

Let, $C = 0.05\,\mu\text{F}$

$$\therefore \quad R = \frac{1}{2 f_0 C} = \frac{1}{2 \times 2 \times 10^3 \times 0.05 \times 10^{-6}} = 5.0\,\text{K}\Omega$$

$\therefore \quad R = 5.0\,\text{K}\Omega$ (10 K pot)

$C = 0.05\,\mu\text{F}$

$R_1 = 10\,\text{K}\Omega, \quad R_2 = 11.6\,\text{K}\Omega$ (20 K pot)

Problem 13:

Design a triangular wave generator with $f_0 = 1.5$ KHz and $V_0\ (p-p) = 5V$

Solution.

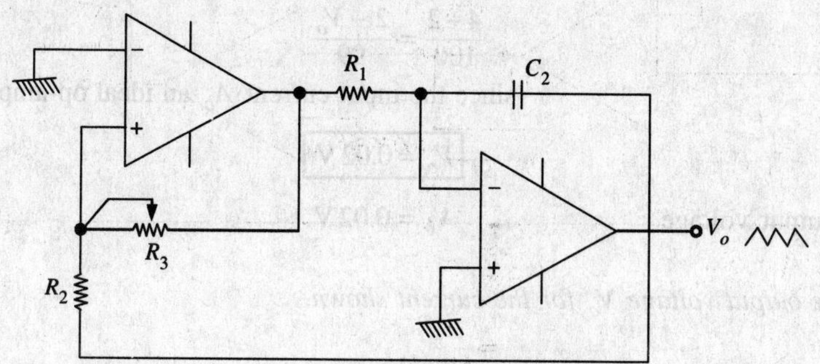

Fig. 33.

Considering supply voltage $= \pm 15V$.

Here, we have used a operational amplifier 772.

So, $V_{sat} = 14\,V$.

$\therefore \quad V_o\,(pp) = 2\dfrac{R_2}{R_3}(V_{sat}) \qquad f_0 = \dfrac{R_3}{4 R_1 C_1 R_2}$

As, $\quad V_{sat} = +14\,V \qquad \therefore \dfrac{R_2}{R_3} = \dfrac{5}{2 \times 14} = 0.1786$

Let, $\quad R_3 = 10\,K \qquad \therefore R_2 = 1.78\,K\Omega\ (1.8\,K\Omega)$

Let, $\quad C = 0.05\,\mu F. \qquad \therefore 1.5 \times 10^3 = \dfrac{10 \times 10^3}{4(R_1 C_1) \times 1.8}$

$$R_1 C_1 = 0.926$$

$$\therefore \quad R_1 = \frac{0.926}{0.05 \times 10^{-6}}\ \Omega = 18.5\ M\Omega\ (18\ H\Omega)$$

$$\therefore \quad R_1 = 18\ H\Omega,\ \ R_2 = 1.8\,K\Omega,\ \ R_3 = 10\ K\Omega,\ \ C = 0.05\,\mu F$$

Problem 14:

Calculate the output voltage V_o.

Solution.

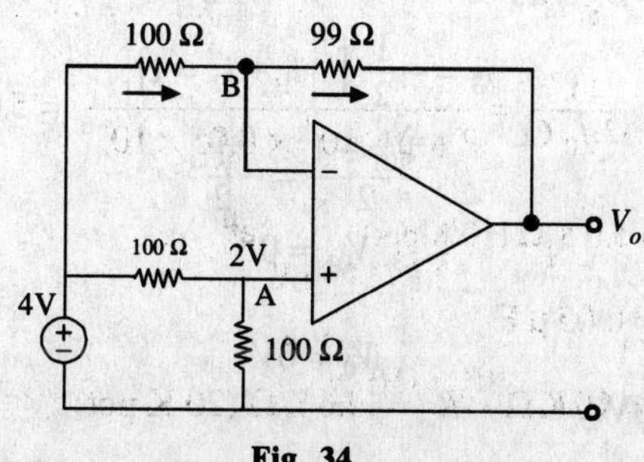

Fig. 34.

The potential at $pt. A = V_A = \frac{4 \times 100}{100 + 100} = 2V$

Similarly, potential at $pt. B = V_B = 2V$

$\therefore \quad \frac{4-2}{100} = \frac{2 - V_o}{99}$

(since the input current A_o an ideal op-amp is negligible).

$$\boxed{V_o = 0.02 \text{ V}}$$

Hence the output voltage $V_o = 0.02 \text{ V}$.

Problem 15:

Compute the output voltage V_o for the current shown.

Solution.

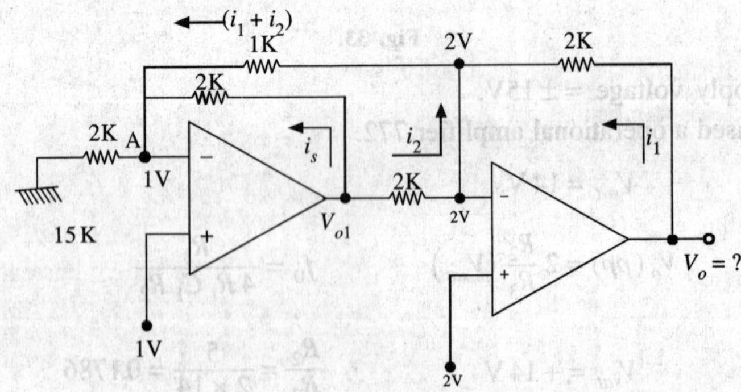

Fig. 35.

From the above figure we can write,

$$i_1 = \frac{V_o - 2}{2}$$

$$i_2 = \frac{V_{01} - 2}{2}$$

and, $$1 = (i_1 + i_2) \times 1 = \frac{V_o - 2}{2} + \frac{V_{01} - 2}{2}$$

or $$V_o + V_{01} = 6 \quad \ldots(1)$$

$$i_3 = \frac{V_{01} - 1}{2}$$

Applying KCL at mode A,

$$i_1 + i_2 + i_3 = \frac{1}{2}$$

or $$i_3 = -\frac{1}{2} \; [\because i_1 + i_2 = 1]$$

$\therefore$ $$\frac{V_{01} - 1}{2} = -\frac{1}{2}$$

or $$V_{01} = 0 \quad \ldots(2)$$

From 1 and 2 we get

$$V_0 = 6V$$

Hence the *o/p* voltage is 6V.

Problem 16:

Calculate the output voltage (V_o).

Solution.

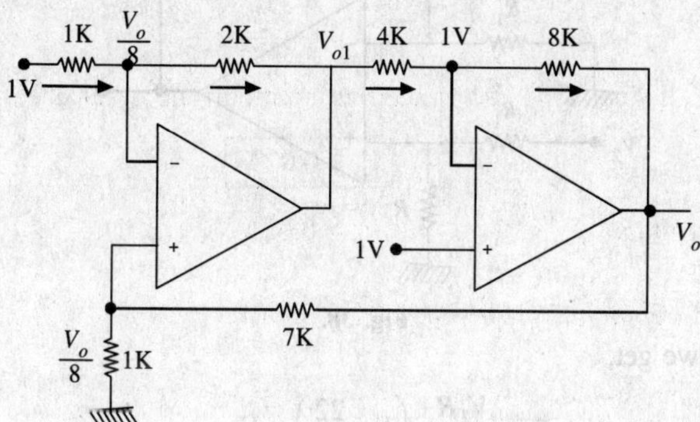

Fig. 36.

From the above ckf we can write,

$$\frac{1-\frac{V_o}{8}}{1} = \frac{V_{01} - V_o/8}{2}$$

(since the *yp* current for ideal op-amp)

or $$V_{01} = \frac{3V_0}{8} - 2$$

Similarly,

$$\frac{V_{01} - 1}{4} = \frac{1 - V_o}{8}$$

or $$V_o = 3 - 2V_{01}$$

or $$V_o = 3 - 2\left(\frac{3V_o}{8} - 2\right)$$

or $$V_o = \frac{3}{4} V_o = 7$$

or $$V_o = 4V$$

Output voltage $= 4V$

Problem 17:

Calculate the value of resistor R as if the gains in two modes (inverting or noninvertor) are equal.

Solution.

Considering the effect of V_1 only and short ckt the V_2 the ckting reducing to

From figure,

$$\frac{V_1 - 0}{R_1} = \frac{0 - V_{01}}{22}$$

or $$\frac{V_{01}}{V_1} = \frac{-22}{R_1} \quad \ldots(1)$$

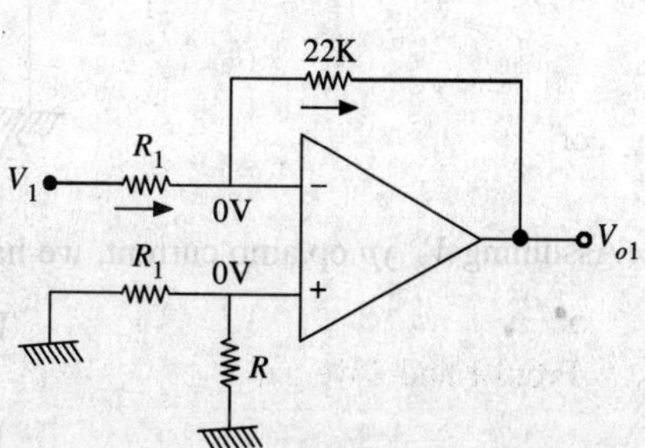

Fig. 37.

Considering the effect of V_2 only and short ckting the V_1 we get,

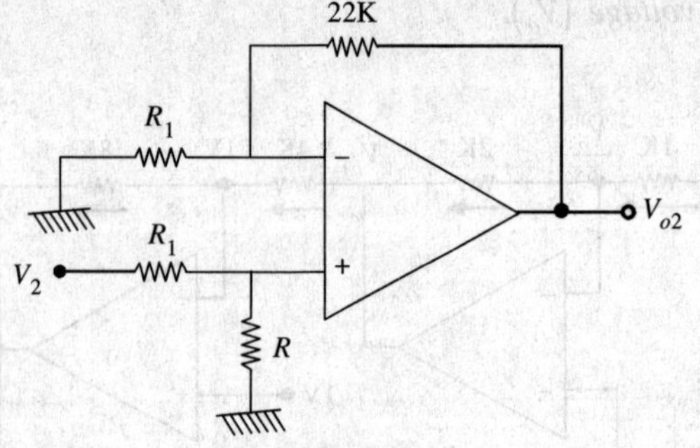

Fig. 38.

From the above ckt we get,

$$\frac{V_2 R}{R+R_1}\left(1+\frac{22}{R}\right) = V_{02}$$

or
$$\frac{V_{02}}{V_2} = \frac{R}{R+R_1}\left(1+\frac{22}{R}\right) \quad \ldots(2)$$

Since the gain in both the cases are equal, we can write using (1) and (2),

$$\frac{+22}{R_1} = \frac{R}{R_1+R}\left(1+\frac{22}{R_1}\right)$$

$$22\,(R+R_1) = R\,(R_1+22)$$

$$22\,R_1 = RR_1$$

$$\boxed{R = 22\,\text{K}}$$

Hence the reanvied value of $R = 22\,\text{K}$.

Problem 18:

Draw and explain the output wave form for sinusoidal and triangle waveform.

Solution.

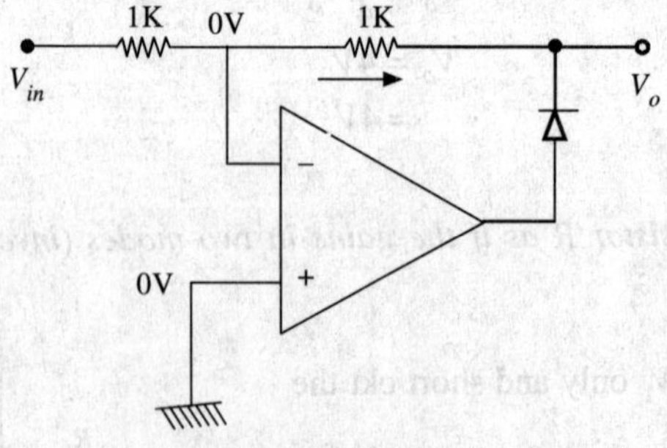

Fig. 39.

Assuming V_o *yp* op.amp current, we have,

$$\frac{V_{in}-0}{1} = \frac{0-V_o}{1}$$

or
$$\boxed{V_o = -\,V_{in}}$$

V_o should be 180° out of phase w.r.t. V_{in}

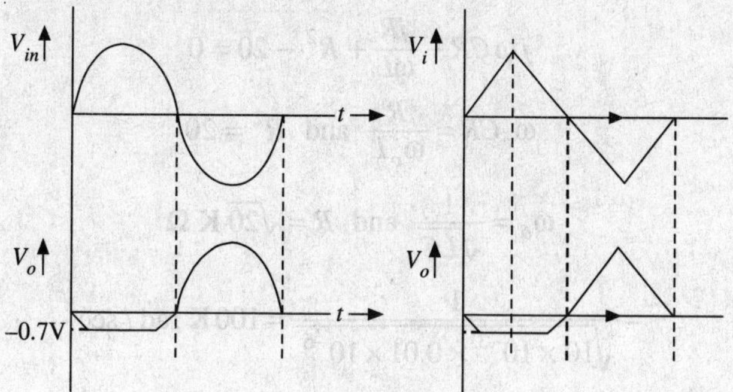

Fig. 40.

For –ve half cycle of V_{in}, V_o is +ve, but when V_{in} is positive, *i.e.*, V_o is –ve and if this –ve voltage (V_o) is less than – 0.7V the diode will be forward biased. Hence the o/p voltage will stay at = – 0.7V for +ve half cycle of the *yp* signal.

Problem 19:

Calculate the frequency of oscillation of the circuit.

Solution.

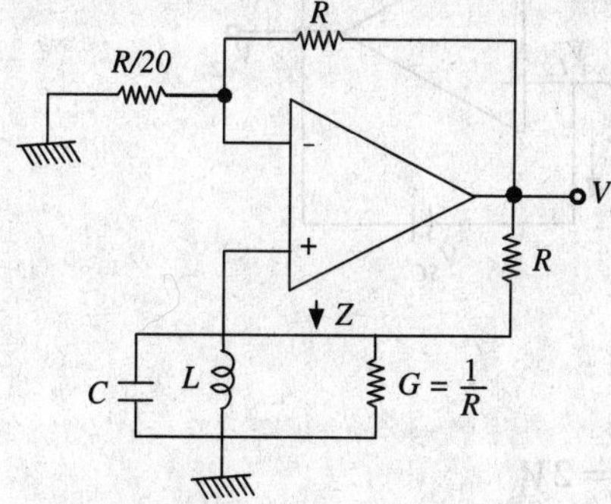

Fig. 41.

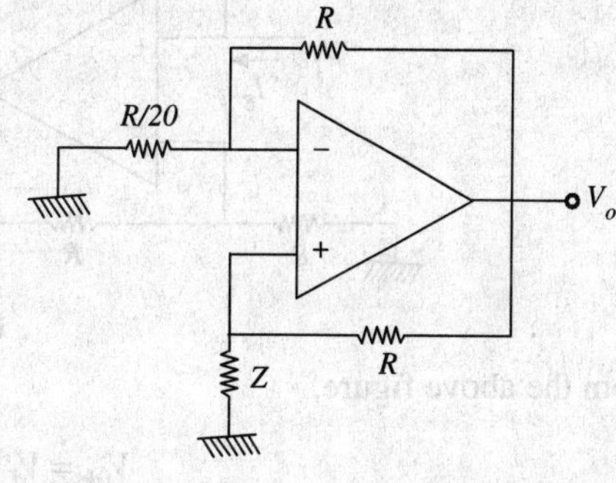

Fig. 42.

$$C = 0.01\mu\,\text{F}$$

$$L = 10\ \text{mH}$$

$$Z = \frac{1}{SC + \dfrac{1}{LS} + \dfrac{1}{R}}$$

From the ckt we can write,

$$\frac{V_o \times Z}{Z + R}\left(1 + \frac{R}{R/20}\right) = V_o$$

or
$$Z \times 21 = R + Z$$

or
$$R = 20Z$$

or
$$R = \frac{20}{SC + \dfrac{1}{SC} + \dfrac{1}{R}}$$

or $$SCR + \frac{R}{SL} + R^2 = 20$$

or $$j\omega CR - \frac{jR}{\omega L} + R^2 - 20 = 0$$

$$\omega_o CR = \frac{R}{\omega_o L} \text{ and } R^2 = 20$$

or $$\omega_o = \frac{1}{\sqrt{LC}} \text{ and } R = \sqrt{20}\text{ K}\Omega$$

$$= \frac{1}{\sqrt{10 \times 10^{-3} \times 0.01 \times 10^{-6}}} = 100\text{ K rad/sec}$$

Hence the frequency of $osc^n = 100\text{ K rad/sec}$

$$= 15.91\text{ KHz.}$$

Problem 20:

Show that the circuit simulates an inductor. Calculate its equivalent inductor value.

Solution.

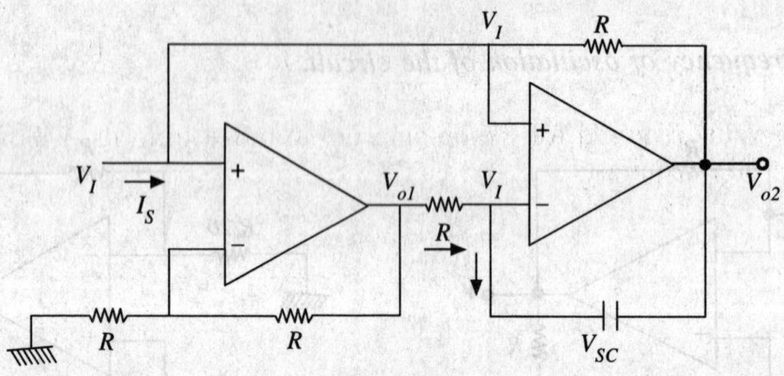

Fig. 43.

From the above figure,

$$V_{01} = V_I\left(1 + \frac{R}{R}\right) = 2V_1$$

again $$\frac{2V_I - V_I}{R} = \frac{V_I - V_{02}}{1/SC}$$

or $$V_{02} = \frac{V_I(SCR - 1)}{SCR}$$

again $$I_s = \frac{V_I - V_{02}}{R}$$

$$= \frac{V_I - \frac{V_I(SCR-1)}{SCR}}{R}$$

$$= \frac{V_I}{SCR^2}$$

or $$\frac{V_I}{I_s} = SCR^2$$

Hence the ckt simulates inductance

and $$L_{eq} = CR^2.$$

Problem 21:

An opamp voltage follower is to operate with a minimum input signal of 200 mV. If the error in the output voltage due to amplifier gain is not to exceed 0.005%, determine the minimum voltage gain required for the opamp.

Solution.

For voltage follower, $\beta = 1$

we know that, $\frac{V_{sat}}{1 + A\beta}$ = error in amplification.

$$\frac{14}{1+A} \geq 0.2 \times 0.005$$

taking $V_{sat} = 14V$ for the op.amp.

or $14000 \geq 1 + A$

or $A \leq 13999$

Hence minimum voltage gain required for the operational amp. − 13999.

Problem 22:

The slew rate of an opamp is 0.5V/μ second. The saturation voltages are +15 and −15. Calculate the minimum time required to move its output from one saturation to the other saturation state.

Solution.

Slew rate $= 0.5V / \mu$ sec. (typical value for A 741)

Power suply $\pm 15V$

Hence the typical value required for the op-amp *o/p* to move from its –ve extreme to its +ve extreme is change of 30V requires

$$= \frac{30}{0.5} = 60\mu \text{ sec.}$$

Problem 23:

Calculate V_o.

Solution.

From $V - I$ characteristic of diode,

$$I_f = I_o\left(e^{V_{f1}/\eta V_T} - 1\right) \cong I_c\, e^{V_{f1}/\eta V_T} \quad \ldots(1)$$

provided $\frac{V_{f1}}{\eta V_T} >> 1$ is $I_f >> I_o$

where, I_o = rev. sat. current

V_T = temp. cqn of V

η = multiplying faitor

= 1 (for large ct.)

= 2 (for small ct.)

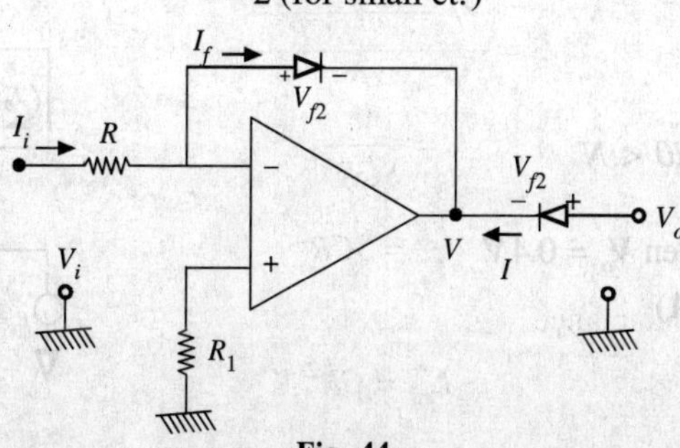

Fig. 44.

Taking 'log' of (1).

$$\frac{V_{f1}}{\eta V_T} = \ln I_f - \ln I_o$$

$$V_{f1} = \eta\, V_T \left(\ln I_f - \ln I_o\right)$$

Since, $I_{f1} = I_i = \frac{V_i}{R}$ due to virtual ground.

$$V = -V_{f1} = -\eta\, V_T \left(\ln I_f - \ln I_o\right)$$

$$= -\,\eta\, V_T \left(\ln \frac{V_i}{R} - \ln I_o\right)$$

$$= -\,\eta\, V_T \ln \frac{V_i}{IR}$$

The *o/p* voltage, $V_o = V_{fe} + V$

$$= \eta\, V_T \left(\ln I - \ln I_o - \ln \frac{V_i}{R} + \ln I_o\right)$$

$$= -\,\eta\, V_T \ln \frac{V_i}{IR}.$$

$\therefore$ The *o/p* voltage $= -\,\eta\, V_T \ln \frac{V_i}{IR}$

Problem 24:

The jksdf vnmefhj Ljizfgi0 <:N

Solution.

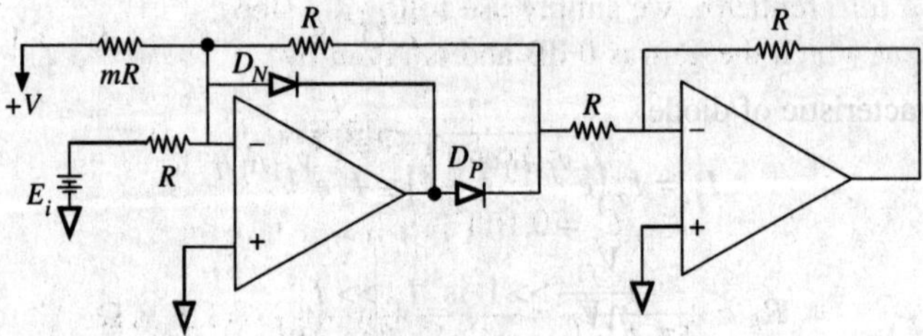

Fig. 45.

In the circuit 6(*a*), +ve = 15*V*, *mR* = 30 KΩ and *R* = 10 K Ω, so that *m* = 3. Find (*a*) V_{ref}; (*b*) V_{oA} when $E_i = 10V$; (*c*) V_{oB} when $E_i = -10V$

$\left(\textbf{Ans. } (a) \rightarrow 5V,\ (b) \rightarrow 5V,\ (c) \rightarrow V_{oB} = -5V\right)$

Problem 25:

The jksdf vnmefhj Ljizfgi0 <:N

Solution.

In the figure find I_B when $V_o = 0.4\,V$

(**Ans.** $\rightarrow 0.4\,\mu A$)

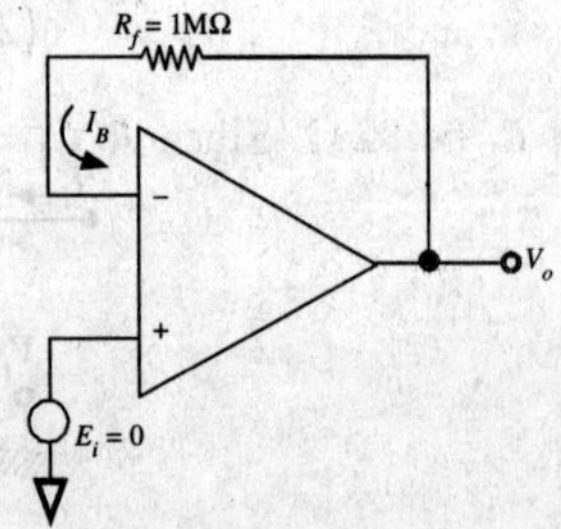

Fig. 46.

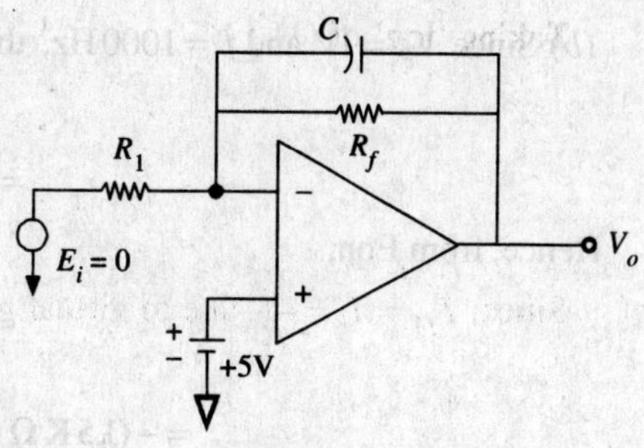

Fig. 47.

Problem 26:

The jksdf vnmefhj Ljizfgi0 <:N

Solution.

Calculate V_o when $R_1 = R_f = 5\,\text{K}\Omega$ and $C = 1\,\mu\text{F}$.

Problem 27:

(a) Design a differentiator to differentiate an input signal. That varies in frequency from 10 Hz to about 1 KHz.

(b) If a sine wave of 1V peak at 1000 Hz is applied to the differentiator of part (a), draw its O/P waveform.

Solution.

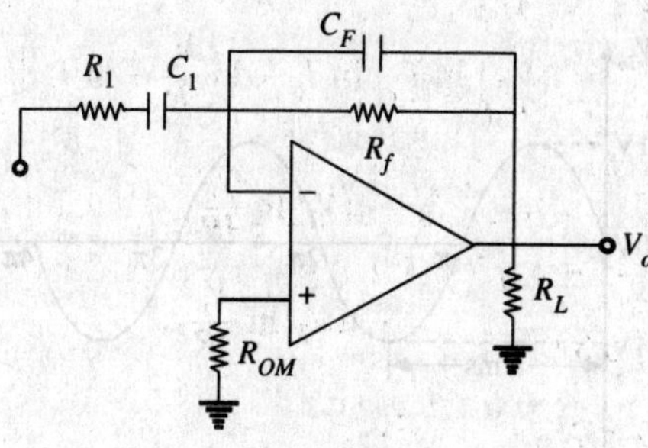

Fig. 48.

(*a*) To design a differentiator, we simply use following steps.

The frequency at which the gain is 0 dB and is given by

$$f_a = \frac{1}{2\pi R_F C_1} = 1\,\text{KHz}$$

Let $$C_1 = 0.1\,\mu\text{F}$$

Then $$R_F = \frac{1}{2\pi f_a C_1} = \frac{1}{(2\pi)(10^3)(10^{-7})} = 1.59\,\text{K}\Omega$$

$\therefore$ The gain limiting frequency,

$$f_b = \frac{1}{2\pi R_1 C_1} = 20\,\text{KHz}$$

$$\therefore \quad R_1 = \frac{1}{(2\pi)(f_b)(C_1)} = \frac{1}{(2\pi)(2)(10^4)(10^{-7})} = 79 \cdot 5\,\Omega$$

Let R_1 be $82\,\Omega$. Since $R_1 C_1 = R_F C_F$

$$\therefore \quad C_F = \frac{R_1 C_1}{R_F}$$

$$= \frac{(82)(10^{-7})}{1 \cdot 5\,\text{K}\Omega} = 0 \cdot 0055\,\mu\text{F}$$

Let $C_F = 0 \cdot 005\,\mu\text{F}$. Finally, $R_{em} = R_F = 1 \cdot 5\,\text{K}\Omega$

(*b*) Since $V_P = 1V$ and $f = 1000\,\text{Hz}$, the input voltage is,

$$V_{in} = V_p \sin \omega_L$$

$$= \sin (2\pi)\left(10^3\right) - L$$

Hence, from Eqn,

$$V_o = R_F\, C_1 \frac{dv_{in}}{dt}$$

$$= -(1.5\,\text{K}\Omega)\,(0.1\,\mu\text{F})\frac{d}{dt}\left[\sin (2\pi)\left(10^3\right)t\right]$$

$$= -(1 \cdot 5\,\text{K}\Omega)\,(0 \cdot 1\,\mu\text{F})\,(2\pi)\left(10^3\right)\cos\left[(2\pi)\left(10^3\right)L\right]$$

$$= -\,0.94 \cos\left[(2\pi)\left(10^3\right) - L\right]$$

The *I/P* and differentiated *o/p* waveforms are given below,

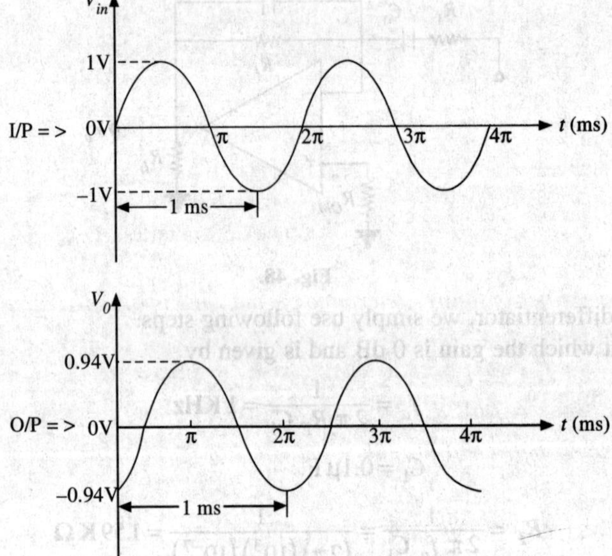

Fig. 49.

Problem 28:

In the ckt, if $R_1 = R_2 = 1\,\text{K}\Omega$, $R_F = R_3 = 10\,\text{K}\Omega$, $V_d = 5\,mV$ *since wave at 1 KHz, and* $V_{ni} = 2mV$ *at 60 Hz. Calculate (a) the o/p voltage at 1 KHz and (b) The amplitude of the induced 60 Hz noise at the output. The op-amp is the μA 741 with CMRR = 90 (dB).*

Solution.

The closed loop differential gain of the ckt is

$$A_D = \frac{R_F}{R_1} = \frac{10\,\text{K}\Omega}{1\,\text{K}\Omega} = 10$$

Since, the input signal is applied, in a differential mode, it is amplified by the differential gain A_D. Therefore, at 1 KHz, the *o/p* signal is

$$V_o = A_D V_d = (10)(5 mV) = 50 mV$$

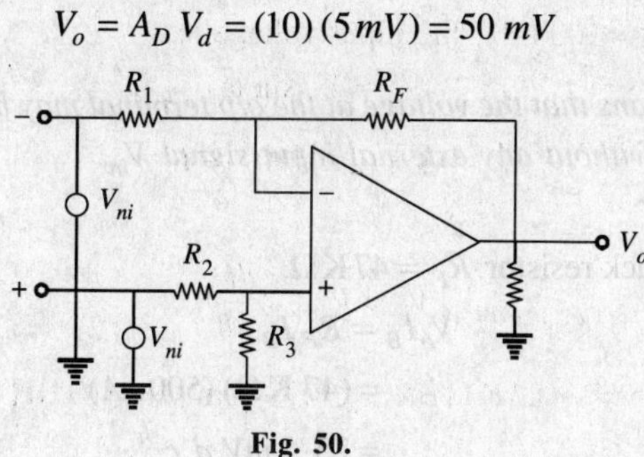

Fig. 50.

(*b*) The 60-Hz noise voltage V_{ni} appears in common mode at the *I/P* terminals of the op-amp; therefore, $V_{ni} = V_{cm}$. Thus we can calculate the value of the *o/p* common-mode voltage V_{ocm}.

$\therefore$ $$20 \log CMRR = 90\ dB$$

or, $$\log CMRR = \frac{90}{20}$$

or, $$CMRR = (10)^{4 \cdot 5}$$

or, $$CMRR = 31622 \cdot 78$$

Therefore, $$V_{ocm} = \frac{A_D V_{cm}}{CMRR}$$

$$= \frac{(10)(2 mV)}{31622 \cdot 78}$$

$$= 0 \cdot 63 \mu V \text{ at } 60 \text{ Hz.}$$

Problem 29:

For the inverting amplifier of figure, determine the maximum possible output offset voltage due to

(i) Input offset voltage V_{io}.

(ii) Input bias current I_B.

The op-amp has V_{io} *max* $= 6 mV$ *d.c.,* I_B *max* $= 500$ *nA dc at* $T_A = 25° C$ *and* $V_S = \pm 15V$.

(b) What value of R_{OM} *is needed to reduce the effect of input bias current* I_B*?*

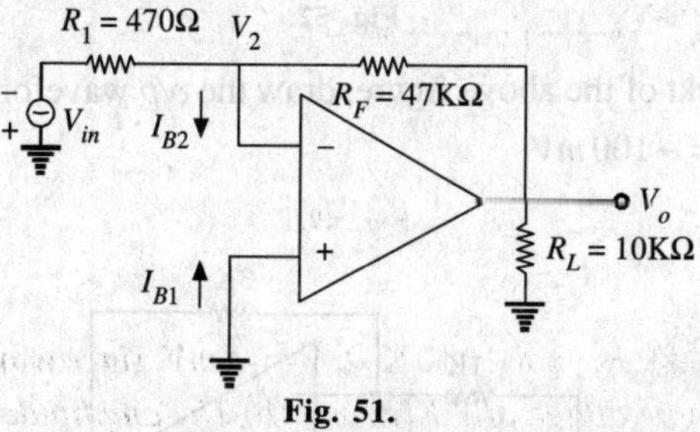

Fig. 51.

Solution.

(*a*) (*i*) Since $R_1 = 470\,\Omega$ and $R_2 = 47\,K\Omega$, the *o/p* voltage offset due to V_{io} might be as large as

$$V_{oo} = \left(1 + \frac{R_F}{R_1}\right) V_{io}$$

$$= \left(1 + \frac{47 \times 103}{470}\right)(6 \times 10^{-3})$$

$$= 606\ mV\ dc$$

Problem 30:

Remember that this means that the voltage at the o/p terminal may be below or above the ground potential by 606 mV dc without any external input signal V_{in}.

Solution.

(*a*) The value of feedback resistor $R_F = 47\,\text{K}\Omega$,

$$\therefore \quad V_o I_B = R_F\, I_B$$
$$= (47\ \text{K}\Omega)\,(500\ nA)$$
$$= 23{\cdot}5\ mV\ d.c.$$

From this result, it is obvious that, $V_o >> V_{OIB}$.

(*b*) The value of R_{OM} to be used is

$$R_{OM} = \frac{R_1\, R_F}{R_1 + R_F}$$
$$= \frac{(470\,\Omega)\,(47\ \text{K}\Omega)}{(470\ \Omega + 47\ \text{K}\Omega)}$$
$$= 470\ \Omega.$$

Problem 31:

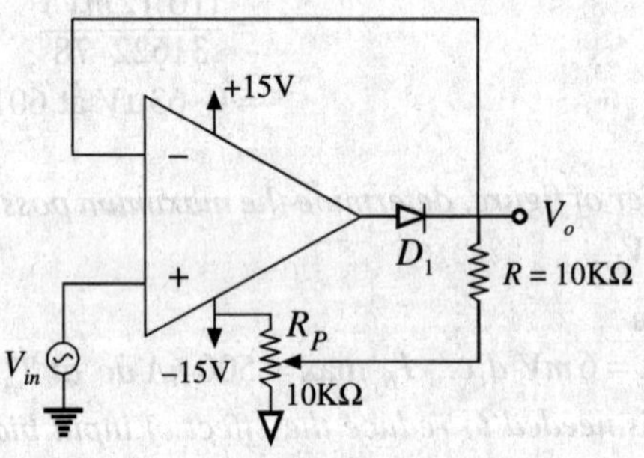

Fig. 52.

For the negative clipper ckt of the above figure, draw the *o/p* waveform if V_{in} is 350 *mV* peak sine wave at 500 Hz and $-V_{ref} = -100\,mV$.

Problem 32:

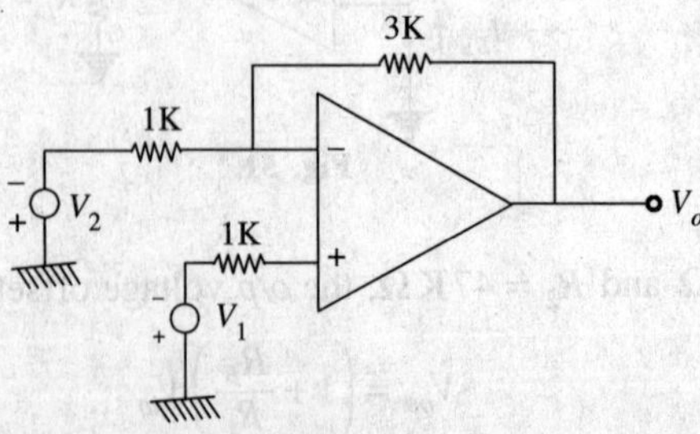

Fig. 53.

The op-amp used in the ckt is ideal. Then calculate V_o.

Ans. $(2V_1 - 3V_2)$.

Problem 33:

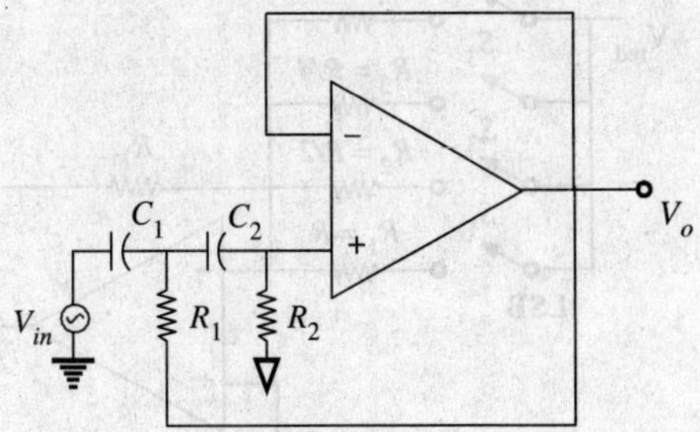

Fig. 54.

Using sealing techniques, determine the component values required for the given circuit.

Given that $R_1 = 7 \cdot 07\,\text{K}; R_2 = 14 \cdot 14\,\text{K}, f_c = 500$ Hz

$(\textbf{Ans.} \to C_1 = C_2 = 0 \cdot 008\,\mu\text{F})$

Problem 34:

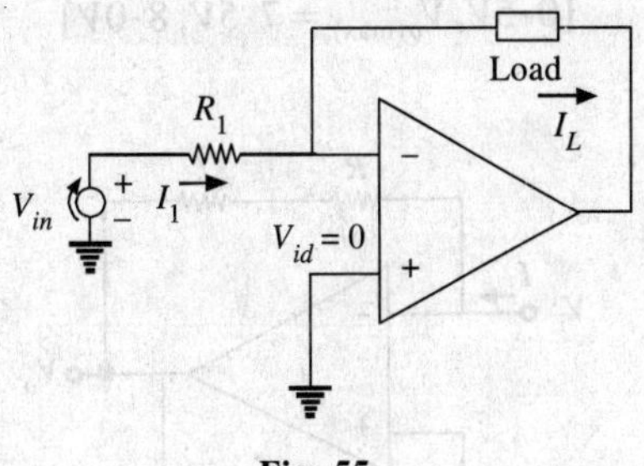

Fig. 55.

Solution.

Assume $R_1 = 1\,\text{K}\Omega, V_{in} = +2V$, and the op-amp has the following limitations: $V_{o(\max)} = \pm 12V$, $I_{o(\max)} = \pm 10\,mA$. Determine the following: (*a*) *gm*, (*b*) I_L, (*c*) the maximum load resistance that may be used; and (*d*) the maximum value of V_{in} that may be used, given $R_1 = 1\,\text{K}\Omega$ and $R_L = 0\,\Omega$.

[**Ans.** $-1\,mS, -2\,mA, 6\,\text{K}\Omega, 110V$]

Problem 35:

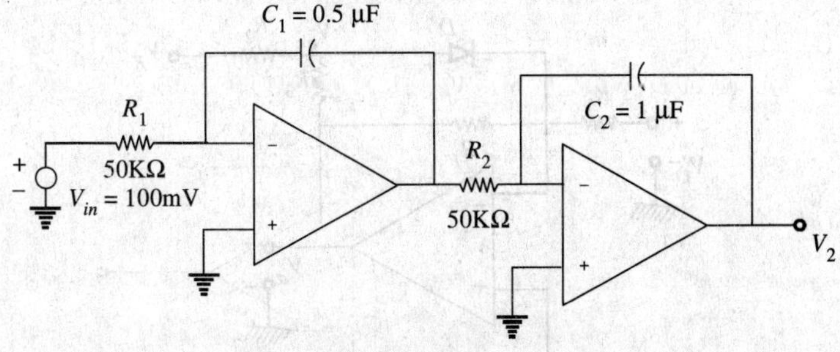

Fig. 56.

Solution.

Determine the output voltage produced by the cascaded integrations in figure at $t = 0 \cdot 5s$. Assume that the integrators are reset to OV at the starts of the operation.

[**Ans.** $V_2 = 10V$]

Problem 36:

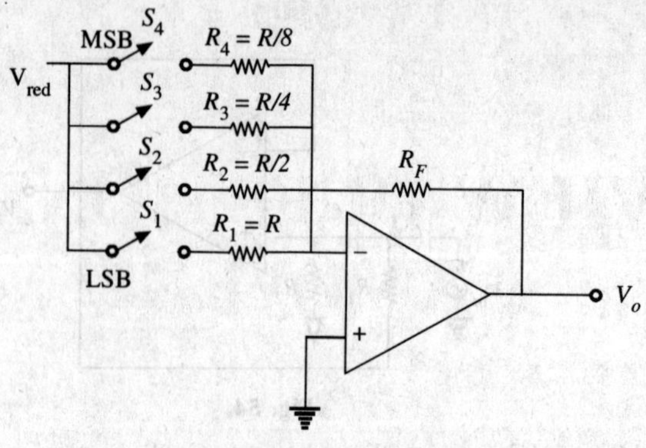

Fig. 57.

Solution.

The crt of figure has the following component values: $R = 80\,\text{K}\Omega$, $R_F = 8\,\text{K}\Omega$. Assuming that $V_{ref} = -5\cdot 00\,V$, determine the LSB size, $V_{o(\max)}$ and V_{FS}.

$$[0\cdot 5V,\ V_{o(\max)} = 7\cdot 5V,\ 8\cdot 0V]$$

Problem 37:

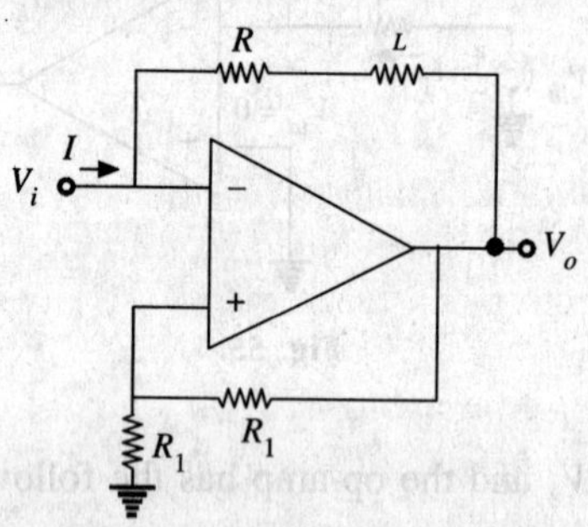

Fig. 58.

Solution.

Calculate I from the given ckt.

$$(\textbf{Ans.} \rightarrow I = -(R + SL))$$

Problem 38:

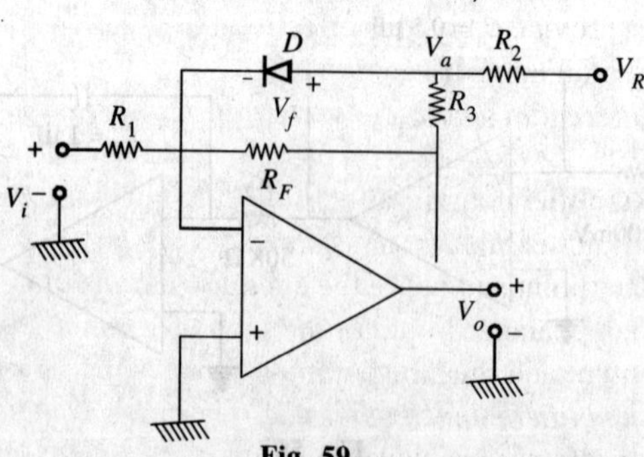

Fig. 59.

Solution.

For this ckt show that

$$A_{CL}\ (gain) = -\frac{R_F\, R_3}{(R_F + R_3)\, R_1}$$

REVIEW QUESTIONS AND ANSWERS

Q. 1. *How may the voltage gain of a differential amplifier be increased without the increase of very high voltage collector resistors?*

Ans. The gain of a Diff. Amp. is given by $Ad = \frac{R_C}{r_e}$. and the CMRR is given by $(\rho) = \frac{Ad}{Ac}$. As emitter resistance is increased, CMRR will also increase. As R_E is increased, voltage drop across R_E will cause I_{EQ} to decrease. So to maintain the same Q-point, V_{EE} must be increased $g_m = \frac{h_{fe}}{h_{ie}} = 40$ I_{CQ}. If I_{EQ} decreases, $\frac{h_{fe}}{h_{ie}}$ will decrease. Now, $Ad = \frac{R_C}{r_e}$. If h_{ie} increases, $\left(\frac{R_e}{r_e}\right)$ will decrease, and Ad will decrease.

So, to keep h_{ie} (or r_e) constant, I_{EQ} is to be kept constant by adjusting V_{EE} We want that during operation dc current through R_E will not change. So, instead of increasing R_e (which causes Joule heating, power loss and lowers CMRR), we should replace the emitter resistance R_E by an active device producing very high effective resistance but physically resistance of the circuit will be moderate.

Q. 2. *State two advantages of using active current sources, as opposed to passive (resistive) current sources, to provide emitter biasing differential amplifier design.*

Ans. Two advantages of using active current sources instead of passive ones are:

(*i*) In active current sources the circuit can adjust itself properly to compensate for thermal changes. In passive current sources the passive ϕ circuit parameters all vary with temperature and so, as temperature increases, the current supplied by the current source and its effective impedance change. In active sources, we can use zener diodes or ρ-*n* junction diodes to compensate against change in V_{BE}.

(*ii*) Active current source provides very high effective resistance and thereby improves the CMRR i.e. makes the differential amplifier more ideal.

Q. 3. *Of the four basic differential amplifier configurations which one(s) will not exhibit common mode rejection?*

Ans. Of the four basic amplifier configurations, (1) dual input unbalanced output and (2) single input unbalanced output will not exhibit common mode rejection. In these configurations we take output from only one collector point and hence the common mode signal is not nullified as only one output is taken. When we take balanced output, the output from the two collectors are taken and their difference is the net output and thus the common-mode signal is rejected.

Q. 4. *Why are push-pull amplifiers sometimes used to provide the output of differential amplifiers?*

Ans. Push-pull amplifiers are used as power amplifiers to increase the amplitude or magnitude of the signal transmitted after it has passed through two or more differential-amplifier stages. Earlier in diff.amp. stages, there is power loss (due to dissipation & I^2R loss) across collectors resistances.

Class A mode of operation also has maximum efficiency of 50%. So wastage of power occurs. So to compensate for power loss in earlier system and to provide large-signal, class B push-pull amplifiers are used.

Q. 5. *What term is given to the gain that is associated with offset components produced at the input of an op.amp?*

Ans. Input offset voltage and input offset current.

Q. 6. *In BJT-based op.amp. designs, what is primarily responsible for the presence of input offset voltage? Input offset current?*

Ans. Input offset voltage results from the mismatch between the V_{BE}, I_B & h_{fe} values of two transistors constituting a differential amplifier. If the two transistors are identical, then as $V_{BE_1} = V_{BE_2}$, $I_{B_1} \simeq I_{B_2}$ and consequently $I_{c1} \simeq I_{c2}$, will cause the dc level $V_{c1} = V_{CC} - I_{c1} R_C$, to be same as V_{c2}. But due to mismatch of BJT parameters, even with input voltage is zero, $V_{c1} \neq V_{c2}$ and so output offset voltage results. So, some input dc voltage is applied at one terminal to make the output voltage equal to zero.

Q. 7. *Which frequency-related op.amp. parameters is of greater significance under large-signal operating conditions?*

Ans. Frequency-related op.amp. parameter used for large-signal operating conditions is *slew rate* which is defined as the maximum rate of change of output signal w.r.t. to time.

Let the output signal be $V_o = V_m \sin \omega t$.

$$\therefore \quad \frac{dV_o}{dt} / \max = \omega V_m \cos \omega t / \max = \omega V_m = 2 \pi f V_m.$$

Slew rate depends on both frequency and amplitude of the output waveform. So if frequency or amplitude is too high or both are high and their product ($\omega \times V_m$) exceeds the slew rate, then output signal will be distorted.

Q. 8. *Explain why high CMRR is important in instrumentation amplifier applications.*

Ans. In instrumentation amplifier, the aim is to amplify the difference signal such that the variation of the difference signal is linearly proportional to certain physical quantity, which we want to measure i.e. if difference of the two input voltage is directly proportional to change in resistance (ΔR) in an ac bridge, then by observing the output voltage we can directly compute ΔR and thus instrumentation amplifier is used as a transducer. So if common mode signal is not rejected, then this linear relation (between ΔV_i and ΔR) will not be obtained. So, we must make CMRR very high, so that A_c is negligible compared to A_d.

Q. 9. *List and draw the four types of amplifiers that may be implemented using op.amp.*

Ans. (1) Transconductance amplifier, (2) Transresistance amplifier, (3) Instrumentation amplifier, (4) Inverting or non-inverting amplifiers (Drawings given in the box).

Q. 10. *The slew rate of an op. amp. is 50V/μ second. The I/P signal V_i is a ramp which rises from 0 to 5V at a rate which is very fast in comparison with the slew rate so that the input can be considered to be a voltage step. If R_f = R = 10K. sketch the output waveform V_i and V_o. For how long will the amplifier be overloaded. ?*

Ans.

It is a non-inverting amplifier, hence.

$$V_o = \left(1 + \frac{R_f}{R}\right) V_N = (1 + 1)\, V_N = 2V_N.$$

Slew rate is $\left(\frac{dV_o}{dt}\right)_{\max}$.

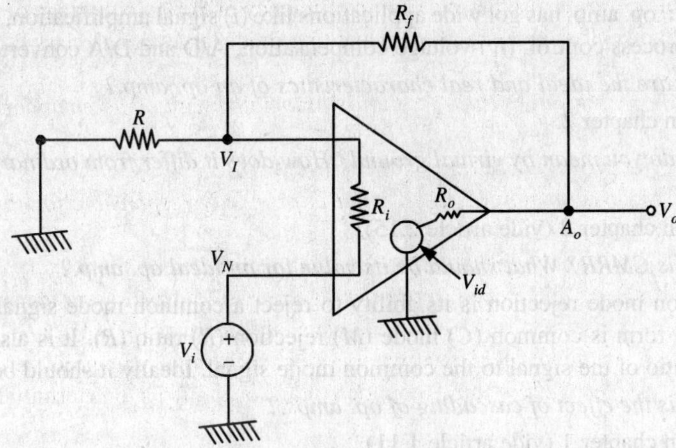

Fig. 1.

The input voltage is a ramp function rising from 0 to 5 V at a rate which is very fast in comparison to SR.

So we can take it as a step input function which rises from 0 to 5V.

When $V_i = 5V$, $V_o = 2V_i = 10V$.

$$\text{S.R.} = \frac{dV_o}{dt}/\text{max} \quad \therefore \quad dt = \frac{dV_o}{SR}$$

$$\therefore \quad dt = \frac{5\times2}{50\times10^{+6}} \rightarrow (0 \text{ to } 10V)$$

$$= .2\ \mu \text{ second.}$$

The amplifier will be overloaded for 0.2 μ second.

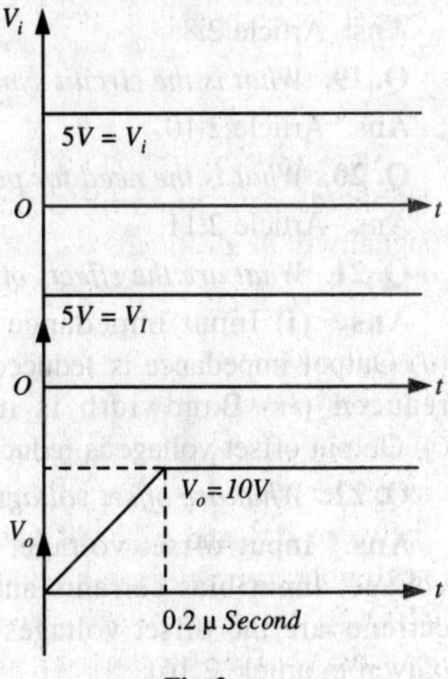

Fig. 2.

Q. 11. *When a low frequency sinusoidal waveform is applied to an input of the op.amp. the amplifier responds linearly over an output range from – 10 to + 10V. If $R_f = R$ and the slew rate is 50V/μ s, then what is the maximum allowable frequency of a sinusoidal if the output signal swing is to be maintained from – 10V to + 10V without distortion?*

Ans. Let the input waveform be $V_{in} = V_m \sin \omega t$ and the output waveform be $V_o = V_{om} \sin \omega t$.

$$\therefore \text{Slew rate} = \frac{dV_o}{dt}/\text{max} = V_{om}\,\omega \cos \omega t/\text{max}.$$

$$\therefore \text{Slew rate} = V_{om}\,\omega.$$

$$\therefore \quad f = \frac{\text{Slew rate}}{V_{om}\times2\pi}$$

$$= \frac{5\times10^6}{2\times3.14\times10}\ \text{Hz} = 795\ \text{KHz}.$$

Q. 12. *What do you mean by an op. amp? Write some of its applications.*

Ans. An operational amplifier is basically a direct coupled high gain differential amplifier with high input impedance and low output impedance.

Applications: op. amp. has got wide applications like (*i*) signal amplification, (*ii*) wave shaping, (*iii*) Servo and process control, (*iv*) voltage compensation, A/D and D/A converter etc.

Q. 13. *What are the ideal and real characteristics of an op. amp.*?

Ans. Given in chapter 2.

Q. 14. *What do you mean by virtual ground? How does it differ from ordinary ground? Why is it so named?*

Ans. Given in chapter 2 (vide article 2.15).

Q. 15. *What is CMRR? What should be its value for an ideal op. amp.*?

Ans. Common mode rejection is its ability to reject a common mode signal–one common to both inputs. Full form is common (*C*) mode (*M*) rejection (*R*) ratio (*R*). It is also called figure of merit. It is the ratio of the signal to the common mode signal. Ideally it should be infinity.

Q. 16. *What is the effect of cascading of op. amps.*?

Ans. Given in chapter 1 (vide article 1.11).

Q. 17. *What is the ordering information for IC op. amp.*?

Ans. Article 2.6.

Q. 18. *How can you select a right op. amp. for a right job*?

Ans. Article 2.8.

Q. 19. *What is the circuit symbol of op. amp.*?

Ans. Article 2.10.

Q. 20. *What is the need for power supplies for of op. amp.*?

Ans. Article 2.11.

Q. 21. *What are the effects of feedback in op. amp.*?

Ans. (*i*) Input impedance is enhanced, (*ii*) Output impedance is reduced, (*iii*) Gain is reduced (*iv*) Bandwidth is increased and (*v*) Output offset voltage is reduced.

Q. 22. *What are offset voltages and currents*?

Ans. Input offset voltage, output offset voltage, Input bias currents and input offset currents are the offset voltages and currents. (Given in article 2.16).

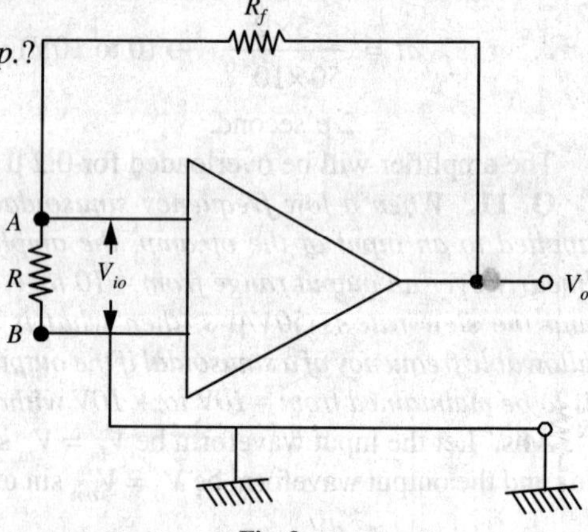

Fig. 3.

Q. 23. *How can you measure them*?

(*a*) *Measurement of input offset voltage* (v_{io})

Applying *KCL* at node *A*:

$$\frac{V_o - V_A}{R_f} - \frac{V_A - V_B}{R} = 0.$$

V_A and V_B are the voltages at *A* and *B*, respectively,

where $V_A = V_{io}$ and $V_B = 0$

$$\frac{V_o - V_{io}}{R_f} = \frac{V_{io}}{R}$$

$$V_{io}\left(\frac{1}{R_f} + \frac{1}{R}\right) = \frac{V_{io}}{R_f}$$

$$V_o = 1 + \frac{R_f}{R}\ V_{io}$$

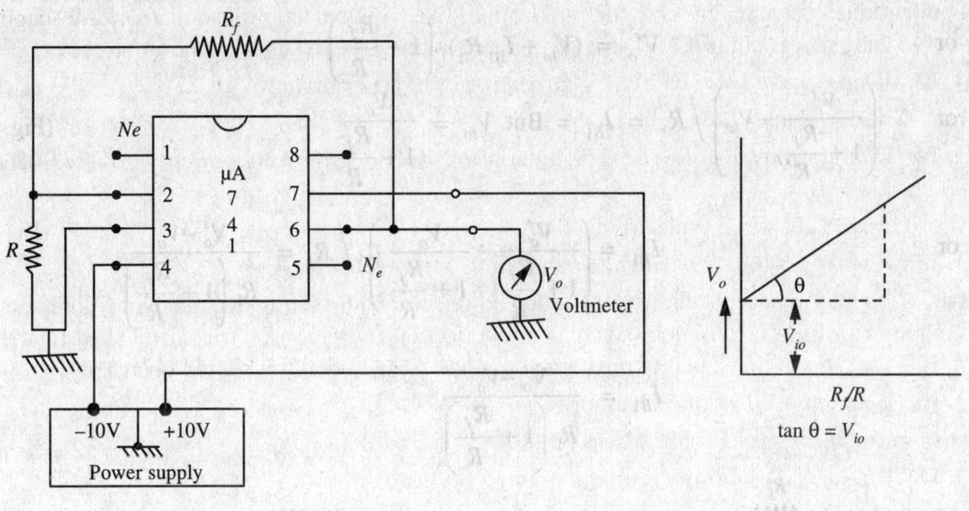

Fig. 4. **Fig. 5.**

Hence $$V_o = V_{io}\left(\frac{R_f}{R}+1\right) \quad ... \quad V_o = V_{io} + \frac{R_f}{R}\cdot V_{io}$$

If we vary R_f keeping R constant or vice versa and draw a curve showing the variation of V_o and $\frac{R_f}{R}$ we will get a straight line curve as shown in Fig. C. The **intercept on the** V_o-axis also the slope of the curve will give the input offset voltage.

(*b*) Measurement of biasing current (I_{B1}, & I_{B2})

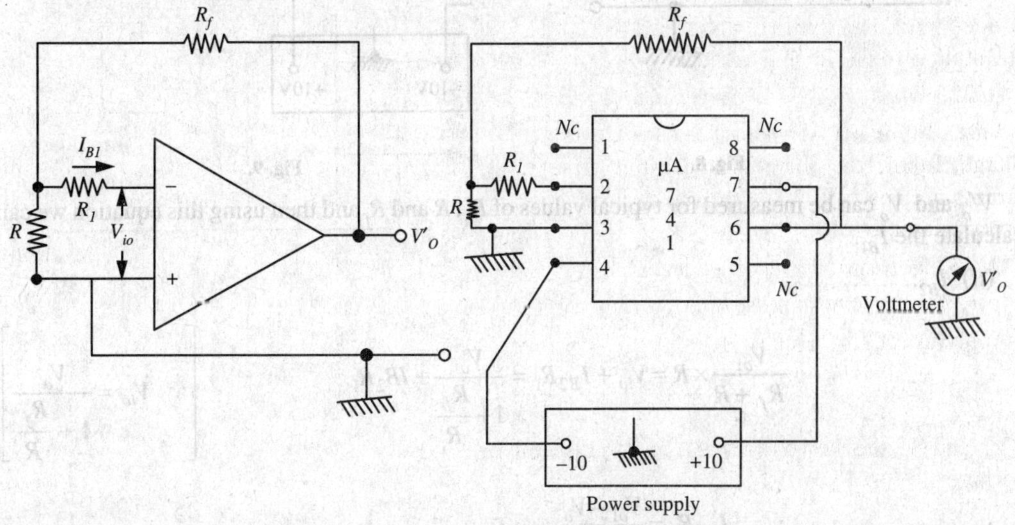

Fig. 6. **Fig. 7.**

(*i*) I_{B1}:

From Fig. (4)

$$\frac{V'_o}{R+R_f}\times R = 1_{B1}\, R_1 + V_{io}$$

or $$V'_o = (V_{io} + I_{B1} R_1)\left(1 + \frac{R_f}{R}\right)$$

or $$\left(\frac{V'_o}{1 + \frac{R_f}{R}} - V_{io}\right) \Big/ R_1 = I_{B1} = \text{But } V_{io} = \frac{V_o}{1 + \frac{R_f}{R}} \quad \text{(Fig. (1))}$$

or $$I_{B1} = \left(\frac{V'_o}{1 + \frac{R_f}{R}} - \frac{V_o}{1 + \frac{R_f}{R}}\right) \Big/ R_1 = \frac{V'_o - V_o}{R_1\left(1 + \frac{R_f}{R}\right)}$$

$$I_{B1} = \frac{V'_o - V_o}{R_1\left(1 + \frac{R_f}{R}\right)}$$

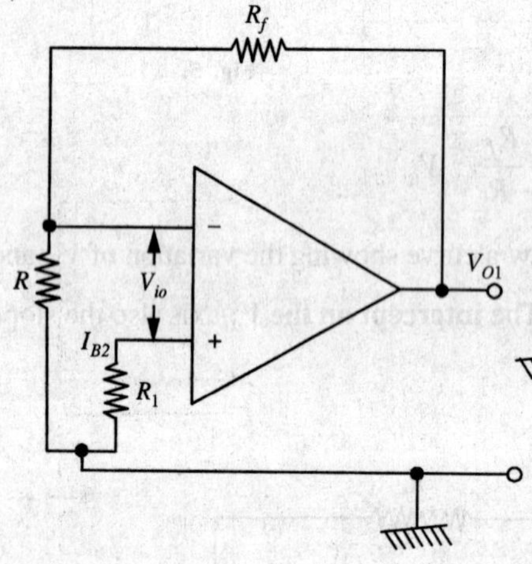

Fig. 8.

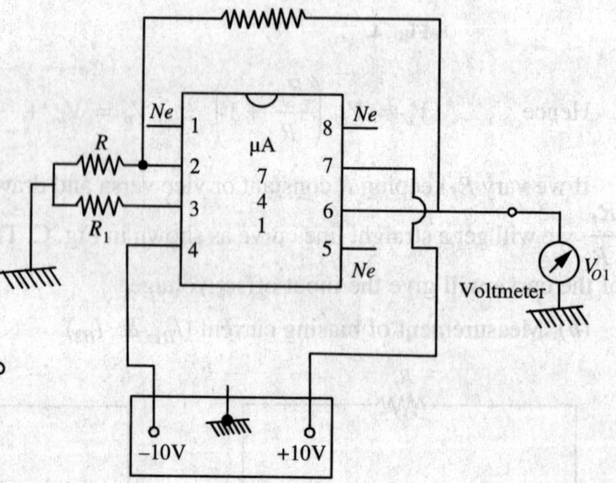

Fig. 9.

V'_o and V_o can be measured for typical values of R_1, R and R_f and then using this equation we can calculate the I_{B1}.

(*ii*) I_{B2}:

$$\frac{V_{o1}}{R_f + R} \times R = V_{io} + I_{B2} R_1 = \frac{V_o}{1 + \frac{R_f}{R}} + IB_2 R_1. \qquad \left[\because \; V_{io} = \frac{V_o}{1 + \frac{R_f}{R}}\right]$$

$$\therefore \quad I_{B2} R_1 = \frac{V_{o1} - V_o}{1 + \frac{R_f}{R}}$$

$$I_{B2} = \frac{V_{o1} - V_o}{R_1\left(1 + \frac{R_f}{R}\right)}$$

Measurement input offset current I_{io} ($= I_{B1} - I_{B2}$)

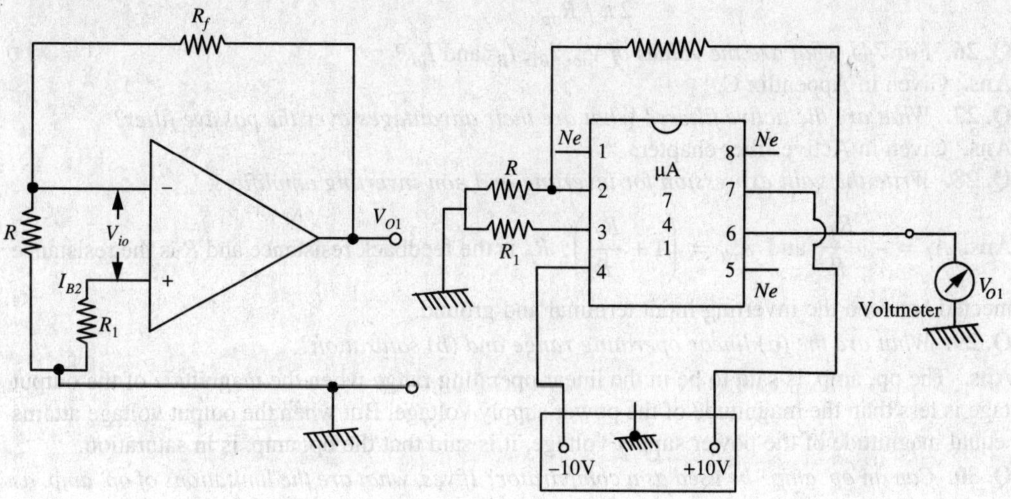

Fig. 10. Fig. 11.

$$\frac{O - V_{o1}}{R_f + R}\, R = - V_{io} + I_{B2}\, R_1 - I_{B1}\, R_1$$

or
$$V_{o1} = \left(1 + \frac{R_f}{R}\right) \{V_{io} + R_1\,(I_{B1} - I_{B2})\}$$

or
$$I_{B1} - I_{B2} = I_{io} = \left(\frac{V_{o1}}{1 + \frac{R_f}{R}} - V_{io}\right) \Big/ R_1, \quad \left[\because\ v_{io} = \left(\frac{V_o}{1 + \frac{R_f}{R}}\right)\right]$$

$$I_{io} = \left(\frac{V_{o1}}{1 + \frac{R_f}{R}} - \frac{V_o}{1 + \frac{R_f}{R}}\right) \Big/ R_1 = \frac{V_{o1} - V_o}{R_1\left(1 + \frac{R_f}{R}\right)}$$

$$\therefore \quad I_{io} = \frac{V_{o1} - V_o}{R_1\left(1 + \frac{R_f}{R}\right)}$$

Q. 24. *How can you measure the input and output impedance of an op. amp.?*

Ans. Answer given in Ch. 10.

Q. 25. *How can you measure an unknown value of a capacitor using op. amp. circuit?*

Ans. We can take the result of the integrator circuit of chapter 10 where we should consider that the capacitor value is unknown. We can employ a sinusoidal voltage of known amplitude and frequency.

$$V_{in} = V_P \sin 2\,\pi ft$$

$$V_o \text{ (output voltage)} = -\frac{V_P}{RC\,2\pi f} \cos 2\pi ft, \quad \left[\because V_o = -\frac{1}{RC}\int V_{in}\, dt\right]$$

Hence the amplitude of the output signal is

$$V_{op} = \frac{V_P}{2\,\pi\, f\, RC}.$$

If V_P, f, R are known, then we can get c from the amplitude of the output

$$C = \frac{V_P}{2\pi f R_{op}}$$

Q. 26. *For 741 what are the values of* V_{io}, I_{B1}, I_{B2} and I_{io} ?

Ans. Given in Appendix C.

Q. 27. *What are the active filters? What are their advantages over the passive filter?*

Ans. Given in Active filter chapter.

Q. 28. *Write the gain expression for inverting and non-inverting amplifiers.*

Ans. $A_I = -\frac{R_f}{R}$ and $A_{NI} = \left(1 + \frac{R_f}{R}\right)$; R_f is the feedback resistance and R is the resistance connected between the inverting input terminal and ground.

Q. 29. *What are the (a) linear operating range and (b) saturation?*

Ans. The op. amp. is said to be in the linear operating range when the magnitude of the output voltage is less than the magnitude of the power supply voltage. But when the output voltage attains the equal magnitude of the power supply voltage, it is said that the op. amp. is in saturation.

Q. 30. *Can an op. amp. be used as a comparator? If yes, what are the limitations of op. amp. as comparators?*

Ans. Yes, rest you can get from chapter 3 (vide article 3.14).

Q. 31. *Is it possible to get double integration using op. amp(s)?*

Ans. Yes, rest in chapter 4 (vide article 4.9).

Q. 32. *What is called frequency scaling?*

Ans. Chapter 5 (vide article 5.7).

Q. 33. *What are the drawbacks of active filters?*

Ans. Chapter 5 (vide article 5.2).

Q. 34. *Explain why there is no such term like characteristics impedance in active filter?*

Ans. Chapter 5 (vide article 5.14)

Q. 35. *What are the important noises associated with op. amp.?*

Ans. Chapter 6 (vide article 6.2).

Q. 36. *What do you mean by the optimum noise preference conditions in op. amps.?*

Ans. Chapter 6 (vide article 6.6)

Q. 37. *Give the examples of op. amp. applications in domestic appliances?*

Ans. Radio, TV., Taperecorder etc.

Q. 38. *Give an example where op. amp. has been used as an oscillator.*

Ans. (*i*) Quadrature oscillator or (*ii*) Wien bridge oscillator or (*iii*) Phase shift oscillator.

Q. 39. *Give one example where op. amp. has been used in digital circuit.*

Ans. D/A or A/D converts.

Q. 40. *What is SPICE?*

Ans. Chapter 9 (vide article 9.2)

Q. 41. *What do you mean by the gain bandwidth product of an op. amp.? Is it a constant quantity?*

Ans. Keeping gain equal to unity the bardwidth of the op. amp. is called the gain band width product. Yes, it is a constant quantity.

Q. 42. *What is the cause of input offset voltage?*

Ans. The input offset voltage error is caused by a mismatch in transistor base-emitter voltages in the input DIFF. AMP. combined with different unbalances in the other stages.

Q. 43. *What does basically determine the number of pins in an op. amp.*?

Ans. Number of components in the *IC* determines the number of pins *i.e.,* it determines the packing density of the components.

Q. 44. *What is the main problem with the input offset voltage*?

Ans. The main problem with this input error is that it gets amplified right along with the input signal.

Q. 45. *What is the important application of a unity gain or voltage follower using op. amp.*?

Ans. The output impedance of the op. amp. is very low and the input impedance being very high, this circuit (unity gain) is frequently used as a buffer amplifier to reduce voltage error caused by source loading and to isolate high-impedance sources from the following circuity.

Q. 46. *Derive the expression for the output of the circuit and comment on its nature.*

Ans. For an ideal op-amp.

$$V_0 = A(e_2 - e_1) \quad \text{and} \quad A \to \infty$$

or $$e_2 - e_1 = \frac{V_0}{A} \to 0$$

or $$e_2 \approx e_1, \text{ here, } e_2 = e_1 = 0$$

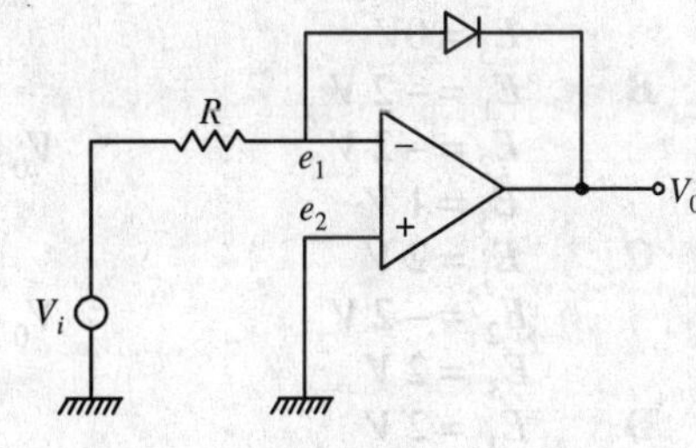

Fig. 12

Also, ideal op.amps have infinite *i/p* impedance

Bias analysis

Now, when the diode is forward biased. Let r_f = forward bias resistance of diode.

Then at node e_1,

$$\frac{V_i - 0}{R} = \frac{0 - V_o}{r_f}$$

or $$\boxed{V_o = -\frac{r_f}{R} V_i}$$

So, diode is forward biased only when V_0 is – ve i.e. $\boldsymbol{V_i}$ **is +ve**. When V_0 is –ve, feedback path is off and $\boldsymbol{V_0 = + V_{sat}}$.

Actually, considering V_i +ve, $I_{diode} = \log\left(\frac{qV}{kT}\right)$ and if we place a resistor at load, *o/p* voltage is logarithmic version of *i/p* voltage.

∴ Answer is **logarithmic amplifier**.

Q. 47. *If input* V_i *is a sine wave, what will be its output when* $V_G = 0V$?

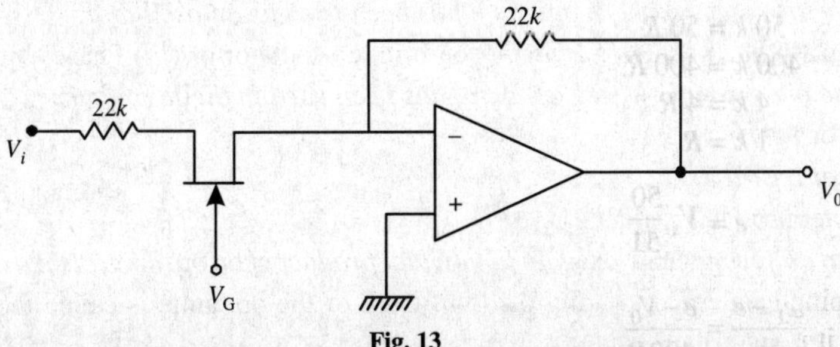

Fig. 13

Ans. When $V_G = 0V$, the channel is fully open, then current flows through it. So, at *o/p* we will get an exact but scaled (scale = 1) replica of *i/p*.

However, the *o/p* voltage is an inverted version of *i/p*.

∴ *o/p* is sine wave (2 *Vp* – *p*).

Q. 48. *Calculate its output for different conditions given in A, B, C and D.*

Ans. $\dfrac{E_1 - e}{10} = \dfrac{e - E_3}{10}$

or $e = \dfrac{E_1 + E_3}{2}$

Again, $\dfrac{E_2 e}{10} = \dfrac{e - V_0}{10} - \dfrac{V_0}{10}$

or $\boxed{V_0 = -E_2 + E_1 + E_3}$

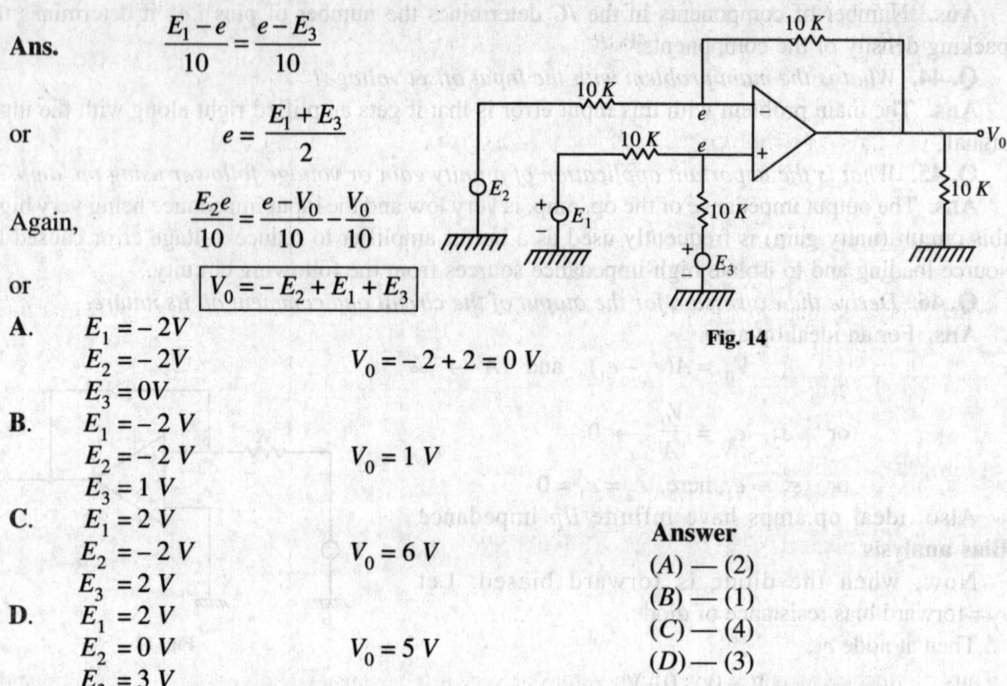

Fig. 14

A. $E_1 = -2V$, $E_2 = -2V$, $E_3 = 0V$ $\quad V_0 = -2 + 2 = 0\ V$

B. $E_1 = -2\ V$, $E_2 = -2\ V$, $E_3 = 1\ V$ $\quad V_0 = 1\ V$

C. $E_1 = 2\ V$, $E_2 = -2\ V$, $E_3 = 2\ V$ $\quad V_0 = 6\ V$

D. $E_1 = 2\ V$, $E_2 = 0\ V$, $E_3 = 3\ V$ $\quad V_0 = 5\ V$

Answer

(*A*) — (2)
(*B*) — (1)
(*C*) — (4)
(*D*) — (3)

Q. 49. *Derive the output of the circuit given:*

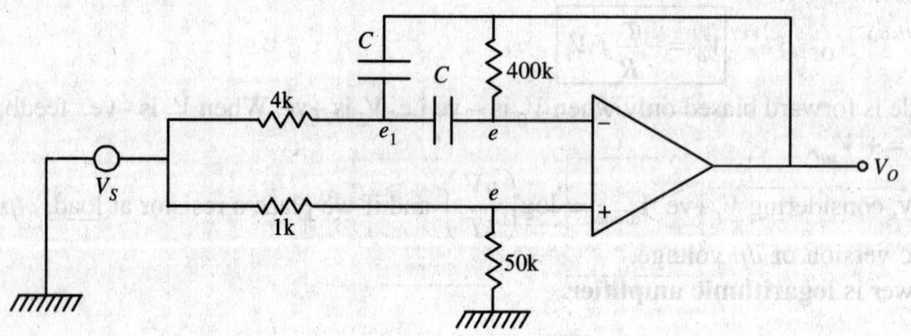

Fig. 15

Let
$$50\ k = 50\ R$$
$$400\ k = 400\ R$$
$$4\ k = 4\ R$$
$$1\ k = R$$

$$e = V_s \frac{50}{51}$$

$$\frac{e_1 - e}{\frac{1}{SC}} = \frac{e - V_0}{400R}$$

or
$$e_1 = \frac{(400SCR + 1)e - V_0}{400SRC}$$

$$\frac{V_s - e_1}{4R} + \frac{V_0 - e_1}{\frac{1}{SC}} = \frac{e_1 - e}{\frac{1}{SC}} = \frac{e - V_0}{400R}$$

or $$V_s\left[400SCR - (400SRC+1)\frac{50}{51}\right] + V_0 = 4SCR\left[V_s\frac{50}{51} - V_0\right](400\,SCR + 2)$$

or $$\frac{V_0}{V_s} = -\frac{50}{51} - \frac{1600S^2R^2C^2 + 1}{1 + 1600S^2R^2C^2 + 8SRC}$$

When S is very small *i.e.*, low freq. response

$$\frac{V_0}{V_s} = -\frac{50}{51}$$

Again $5 >> 1$, $\frac{V_0}{V_s} = -\frac{50}{51}$

Also, we can neglect $S^2R^2C^2$ w.r.t. 1 but not SRC

Then, $\frac{V_0}{V_s} = -\frac{50}{51} - \frac{1}{1 + 8SRC}$.

Thus, frequency response gives high values at very low frequency and very high frequency and in between where at slightly high frequency response decreases.

$\therefore$ ***o/p* is a notch filter.**

Q. 50. *Analyze the given circuit.*

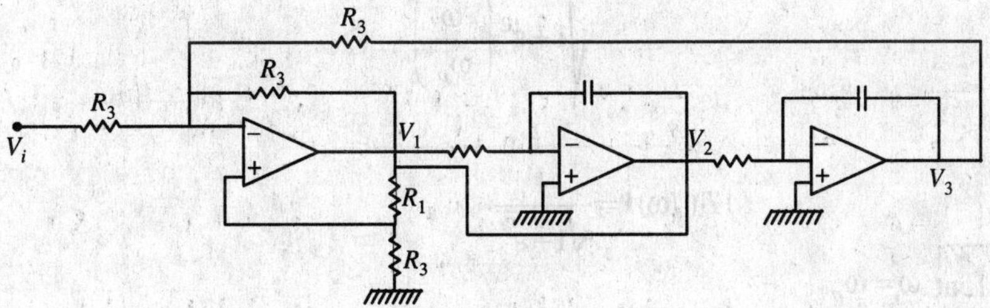

Fig. 16.

Ans. For the first summer block,

$$V_1 = V_i\left(-\frac{R_3}{R_3}\right) + V_3\left(-\frac{R_3}{R_3}\right) + \frac{V_2R_2}{R_1 + R_2}\left(1 + \frac{R_3}{\frac{R_3}{2}}\right)$$

or $$V_1 = -V_i - V_3 + \frac{3R_2}{R_1 + R_2}V_2$$

$$= -V_i - V_3 + k\,V_2, \text{ where } k = \frac{3R_2}{R_1 + R_2}$$

Now, $V_2 = -\frac{1}{SRC}V_1$

$$V_3 = -\frac{1}{SRC}V_2 = \frac{1}{S^2R^2C^2}V_1$$

$$\therefore \quad V_1 + \frac{1}{S^2R^2C^2}V_1 + \frac{k}{SRC}V_1 = V_i$$

or $$\boxed{V_1 = \frac{S^2R^2C^2}{S^2R^2C^2 + kSRC + 1}Vi}$$

$$V_2 = -\frac{SRC}{S^2R^2C^2 + kSRC + 1}V_i$$

$$V_3 = \frac{1}{S^2R^2C^2 + kSRC + 1}V_i$$

V_1 represents a high pass *o/p*
V_3 represents a low pass *o/p*
V_2 represents a band pass *o/p*

Q. 51. *Design an analog circuit to solve the equation $d^2y/dt^2 + 4.dy/dt + 3.y = 2.\ V_1$. Design a second order low-pass Butterworth filter at a high cut-off frequency of 1 kHz. Derive necessary working formulae.*

Note: The necessary relations are derived first, then the circuit diagram using op. amps. is shown.

Ans: The Butterworth filter exhibits a monotonically decreasing transmission with all the transmission zeros at $\omega = \infty$, making it an all pole filter. The magnitude function of an N-th order low pass Butterworth filter with a pass band edge of ω_p is given by:

$$|T(j\omega)| = \frac{1}{\sqrt{1+\varepsilon^2\left(\frac{\omega}{\omega_p}\right)^{2N}}}$$

At $\omega = \omega_{p'}$

$$|T(j\omega)| = \frac{1}{\sqrt{1+\varepsilon^2}}$$

For $\varepsilon = 1$, at $\omega = \omega_{p'}$

$$|T(j\omega)| = \frac{1}{\sqrt{2}}$$

The magnitude response of a Butterworth filter is as shown:

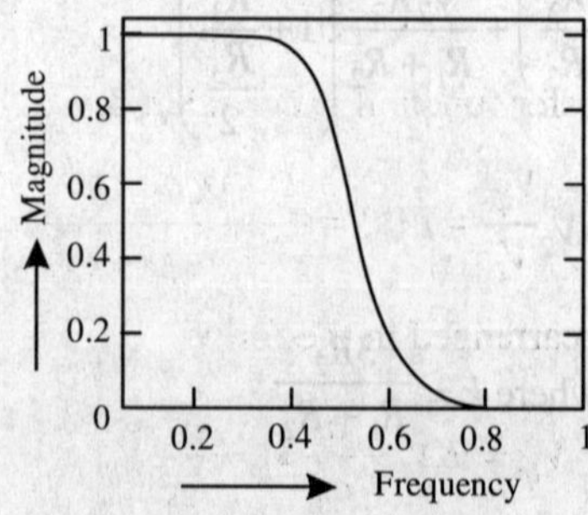

Fig. 17. Magnitude response of a Butterworth filter

The natural modes of an N-th order Butterworth filter lie on a circle of radius $\omega_0 = \omega_p\left(\frac{1}{\varepsilon}\right)^{\frac{1}{N}}$ and are spaced by equal angles of $\frac{\pi}{N}$, with the first mode at an angle of $\frac{\pi}{2N}$ from + $j\omega$ axis. Since the poles all have equal radial distances from the origin, they all have the same frequency given by, $\omega_0 = \omega_p\left(\frac{1}{\varepsilon}\right)^{\frac{1}{N}}$. Once the N natural modes $p_1, p_2, \ldots, p_N$ are found, the transfer function can be expressed as:

$$T(s) = \frac{K\omega_0^N}{(s-p_1)(s-p_2)\ldots(s-p_N)} \qquad \ldots(i)$$

where k is a constant, equal to the dc gain of the filter.

In the given problem, $\omega_p = 2\pi\times10^3$ rad/s. As $\varepsilon = 1$, the poles have the same frequency given by, $\omega_0 = \omega_p = 2\pi\times10^3$ rad/s.

The two poles are given by:

$$p_1 = \omega_0(-\cos 45° + j\sin 45°)$$

$$p_2 = \omega_0(-\cos 45° - j\sin 45°)$$

From equation (*i*), the transfer function is given by:

$$T(s) = \frac{K\omega_0^2}{\left[s-\omega_0(-\cos 45° + j\sin 45°)s - \omega_0(-\cos 45° - j\sin 45°)\right]}$$

Substituting cos 45° = sin 45° = $\frac{1}{\sqrt{2}}$, we get,

$$T(s) = \frac{K\omega_0^2}{\left(s+\frac{\omega_0}{\sqrt{2}}\right)^2 + \left(\frac{\omega_0}{\sqrt{2}}\right)^2}$$

or,

$$T(s) = \frac{K\omega_0^2}{s^2+\sqrt{2}\omega_0 s+\omega_0^2}$$

A second order low pass transfer function is considered:

$$\frac{V_{lp}}{V_i} = T(s) = \frac{K\omega_0^2}{s^2+a\omega_0 s+\omega_0^2}$$

The above equation may be rearranged in the form:

$$V_{lp} = KV_i - \frac{as}{\omega_0}V_{lp} - \frac{s^2}{\omega_0^2}V_{lp}$$

The following diagram is constructed from the above equation:

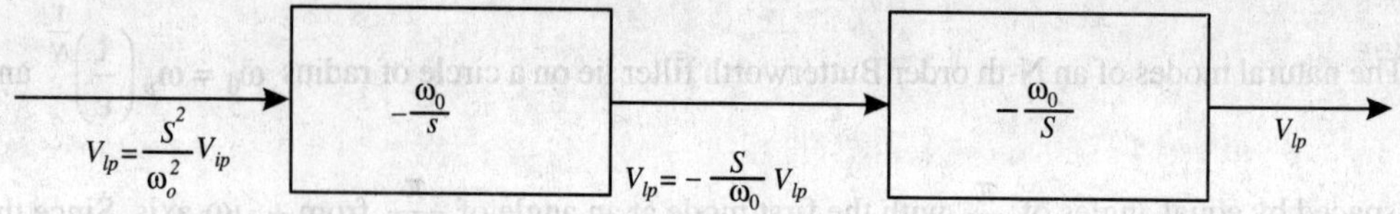

Fig. 18

Following is the circuit realization of the above block diagram:

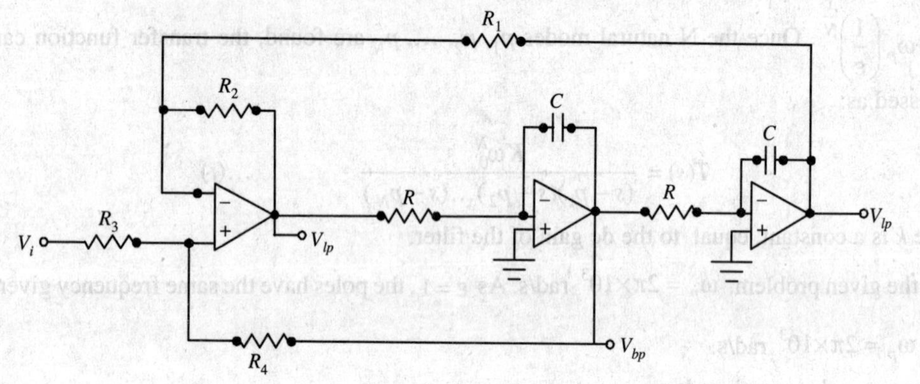

Fig.19

From the above circuit,

$$V_{hp}=\frac{s^2}{\omega_0^2}V_{lp}=\left(\frac{R_4}{R_3+R_4}\right)\left(1+\frac{R_2}{R_1}\right)V_i+\left(\frac{R_3}{R_3+R_4}\right)\left(1+\frac{R_2}{R_1}\right)\left(-\frac{s}{\omega_0}V_{lp}\right)-\left(\frac{R_2}{R_1}\right)V_{lp} \quad \ldots (ii)$$

$$\text{Again, we know, } V_{hp}=\frac{s^2}{\omega_0^2}V_{lp}=KV_i-\frac{as}{\omega_0}V_{lp}-V_{lp} \quad \ldots (iii)$$

Comparing the coefficients of various powers of s in the equation (*ii*) and (*iii*), we get the following:
(*i*) Equating the coefficient of V_{lp}, $R_1 = R_2$. Both R_1 and R_2 are chosen to be equal to 2.2 *K*.
(*ii*) Equating the coefficient of sV_{lp} and setting $R_1 = R_2$, we get,

$$\frac{2R_3}{R_3+R_4}=a$$

or
$$(2-a)R_3=aR_4$$

or
$$\frac{R_3}{R_4}=\frac{a}{2-a}$$

In this case, $a=\sqrt{2}$. Therefore, $\frac{R_3}{R_4}=2.414$. Setting $R_4 = 3.3\ K$, $R_3 = 7.9662\ K$.

The closest value of the standard resistor that matches with the calculated value is 7.8 *K*.
Equating the coefficients of V_i, we get,

$$\frac{2R_4}{R_3 + R_4} = K$$

Using the value of a and simplifying, we get, $K = 2 - a$, or $K = 0.5857$.

Again, it is given that, $\omega_0 = 2\pi \times 10^3 = \frac{1}{RC}$. Setting C to be equal to $1\mu F$, $R = 0.15915\ K$.

The following second-order low-pass Butterworth filter circuit is designed:

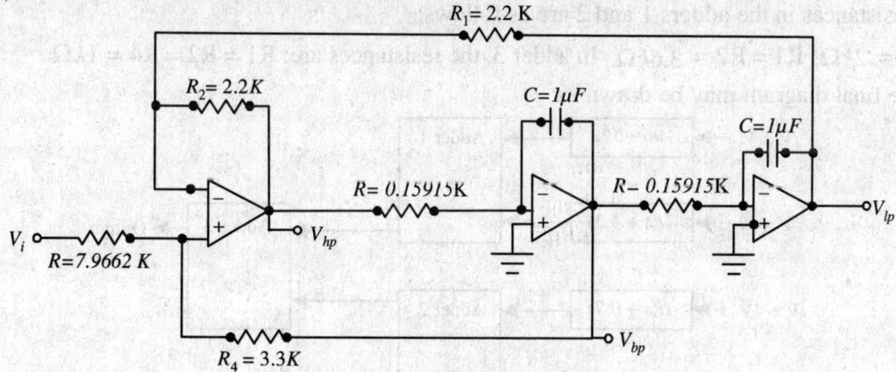

Fig.20

From Eq. (*ii*), taking Laplace transform of the differential equation and putting initial condition of $y(0) = -1$, we can write $(s^2 + 5.s + 3).V_0(s) = V_i(s) - 4$, where $y = V_0$.

Solving the equation $s^2 + 5.s + 3 = 0$, we get the roots as: $s = -0.7, -4.3$.

$s^2 + 5.s + 3 = (s + 0.7)\ (s + 4.3)$.

$V_0(s) = 2.V_i(s)/[(s + 0.7)(s + 4.3)] - 4/[(s + 0.7)\ (s + 4.3)]$.

Decomposing into partial fractions:

$1/[(s+0.7)(s+4.3)] = (1/3.6).[1/(s+0.7) + 1/(s+4.3)]$.

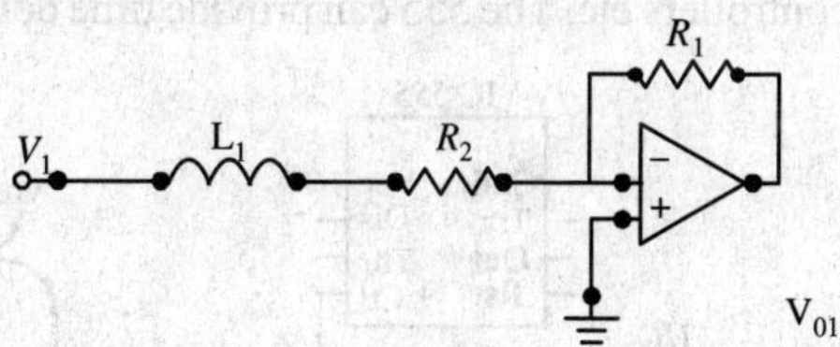

Fig.21

$V_{01} = V_{i1}.R_1/(R_2 + sL_1)$

If $R_1 = 1\Omega$, $R_2 = 0.7\Omega$ and $L_1 = 1H$, then we can write: $V_{01} = V_{i1}/(s + 0.7)$.

If $R_1 = 1\Omega$, $R_2 = 4.3\Omega$ and $L_1 = 1H$, then we can write: $V_{01} = V_{i1}/(s + 4.3)$.

An op-amp summer can be drawn as:

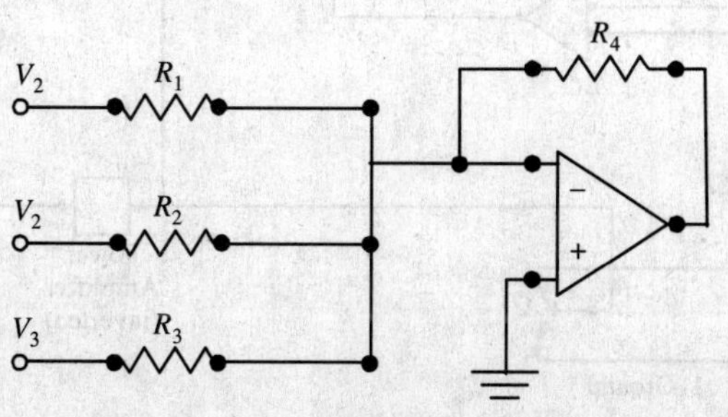

Fig.22

Using block diagram representation to draw the system:

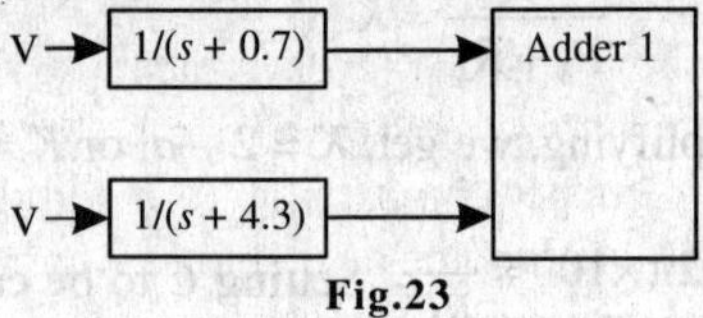

Fig.23

In one case, we use $V = V_i$ and in the second case we use $V = -2V$.

The outputs of these 2 adders are fed to another adder (adder 3) and finally we obtain the output. The resistances in the adders 1 and 2 are as follows:

R4 = $2k\Omega$, R1 = R2 = $3.6k\Omega$. In adder 3, the resistances are: R1 = R2 = R4 = $1k\Omega$.

The final diagram may be drawn as:

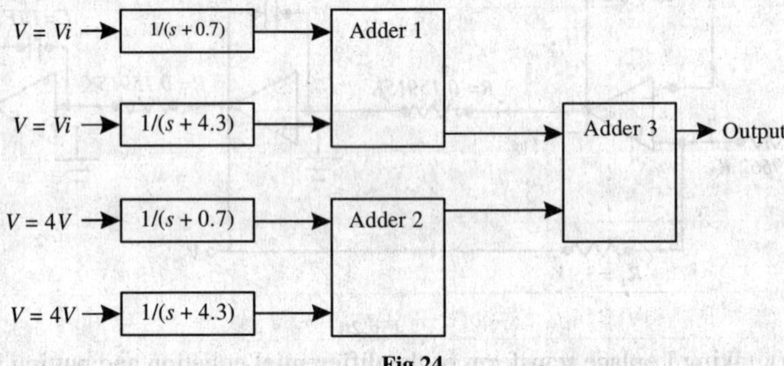

Fig.24

Q. 52. *Write configuration of IC 555.*

The **IC 555 timer** can be used as a pulse generator, a square-wave generator, a linear saw tooth generator, a time-delay generator etc. It can be operated with a dc supply voltage ranging from $+5V$ to $+18V$. This feature makes the IC highly compatible to TTL/CMOS logic circuits and also the op-amp based circuits. The IC 555 timer is very versatile and can be used in applications like oscillator, pulse generator, square and ramp wave generators, one-shot multivibrator, and safety alarm and timer circuits, traffic light controllers etc. The 555 can provide time delay ranging from microseconds to hours.

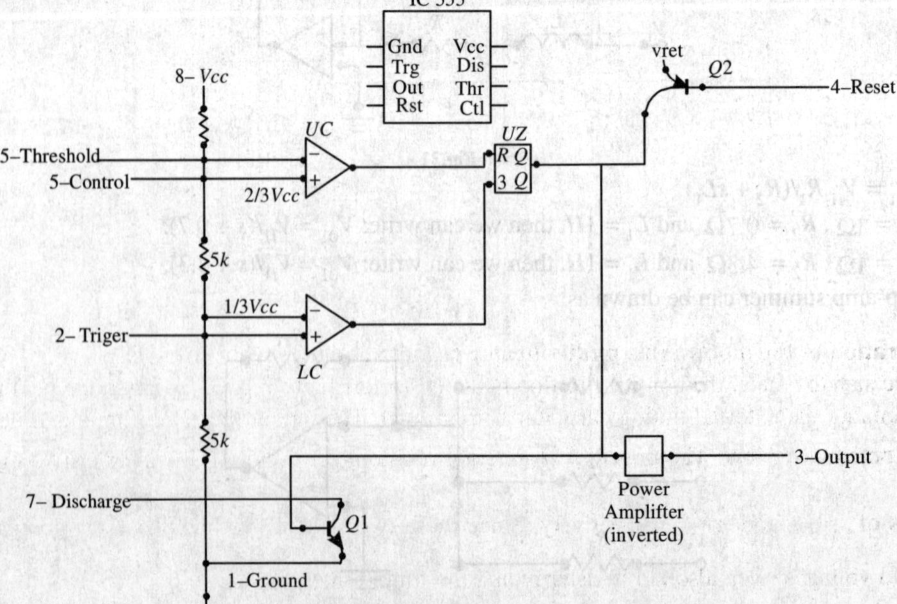

Fig.25. Fundamental Block Diagram of IC 555 Timer

Fig. (23) shows the functional block diagram of a typical IC 555 timer circuit. The positive dc power supply terminal is connected to pin 8(Vcc) and the negative terminal is connected to pin (Gnd). The output pin 3 can assume a HIGH level (typically 0.5 *V* less than Vcc) or a LOW level (approximately 0.1 *V*).

There are two comparators, the upper comparator (UC) and the lower comparator (LC), used in this circuit. Three 5*k* internal resistors provide a potential divider arrangement. It provides a voltage of (2/3) Vcc to the (-) terminal of the upper comparator and (1/3) Vcc to the positive terminal of the lower comparator. A control voltage input terminal pin 5 accepts a modulation control voltage applied externally. Pin 5 is connected to ground using a bypassing capacitor of 0.1uF. It bypasses the noise or ripple from supply. The (+) input terminal of UC is known as the threshold terminal (pin 6) and the (-) terminal of LC is known as the trigger terminal (pin 2). The operation of the IC can be summarized in the following table.

S. No.	Trigger (pin 2)	Threshold (pin 6)	Output state (pin 3)	Discharge state (pin 7)
1.	Below (1/3)Vcc	Below (2/3)Vcc	High	Open
2.	Below (1/3)Vcc	Above (2/3)Vcc	Last state remains	Last state remains
3.	Above (1/3)Vcc	Below (2/3)Vcc	Last state remains	Last state remains
4.	Above (1/3)Vcc	Above (2/3)Vcc	Low	Ground

The reset terminal (pin 4) allows the resetting of the timer by grounding pin 4. This makes output pin 3 low overriding operation of the lower comparator. When not used the reset terminal is connected to Vcc. Transistor Q_2 isolates the reset input from FF and transistor Q_1. Transistor Q_1 acts as a discharge transistor. When pin 3 is HIGH, Q_1 is OFF making discharge terminal 7 open. When the output is LOW Q_1 is forward biased to ON condition. Then the Discharge terminal appears as a short-circuit to ground.

Monostable multivibrator circuit using 555 IC:

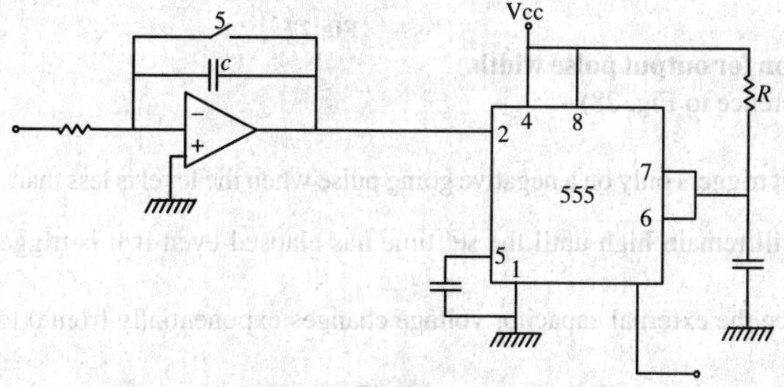

Fig.26

Operation of the monostable multivibrator circuit shown above:-

In the standby state, the control flip flop holds Q_1 (referring to Fig. 27 given on the next page) thus clamping the external timing capacitor *C* to ground. The output (pin 3) during this time is at ground potential or low. The three 5 $K\Omega$ internal resistors act as voltage dividers providing bias voltages of $\frac{2}{3}V_{cc}$ and $\frac{1}{3}V_{cc}$ respectively. Since these two voltages fix the necessary comparator threshold voltages, they also aid in determining the timing interval.

Since the 'lower' comparator is biased at $\frac{1}{3}V_{cc}$ it remains in the steady state so long as the trigger input is held above $\frac{1}{3}V_{cc}$. When triggered only by a –ve going pulse, the lower comparator sets the internal flip flop which releases the short-circuit across the timing capacitor, thus turning Q_1 off and the output goes high (approx. equal to + V_{cc}). Since the timing capacitor is now unclamped, the voltage across it now rises exponentially through R towards V_{cc} with a time constant Re. After a period of time, the capacitor voltage will equal $\frac{2}{3}V_{cc}$ and the upper comparator resets the internal flip flop which in turn discharges the capacitor rapidly to ground potential turning Q_1 ON. As a consequence, the *o/p* now returns to the standby state or ground.

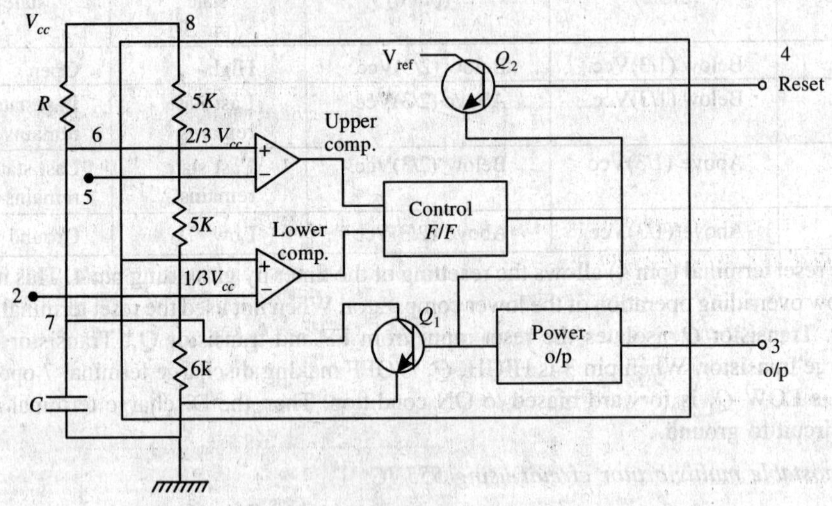

Fig.27

Expression for output pulse width
(with reference to Fig. 28)

The circuit triggers only on a negative going pulse when the level is less than $\frac{1}{3}V_{cc}$. Once triggered, the output will remain high until the set time has elapsed even if it is triggered again during this interval. Since the external capacitor voltage changes exponentially from 0 to $\frac{2}{3}V_{cc}$.

$$\Delta V = V_{cc}\left(1-e^{-t/Rc}\right)$$

$$\frac{2}{3}V_{cc} = V_{cc}\left(1-e^{-t/Rc}\right)$$

or $t = -\text{RC}\ln\left(\frac{1}{3}\right)$ or t = RC ln (3) = 1.1 RC.

When output is high the interval becomes t = 1.1 RC

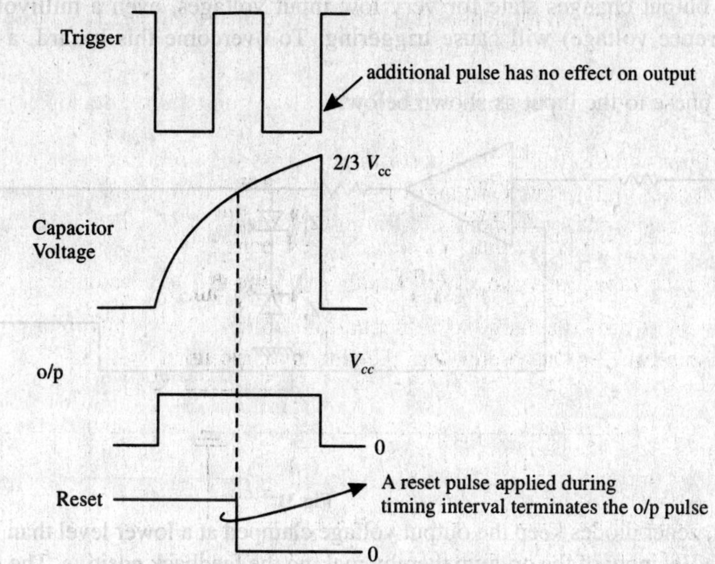

Fig.28. Timing pulses of monostable multivibrator using IC 555 timer

Comparator using op-amp:

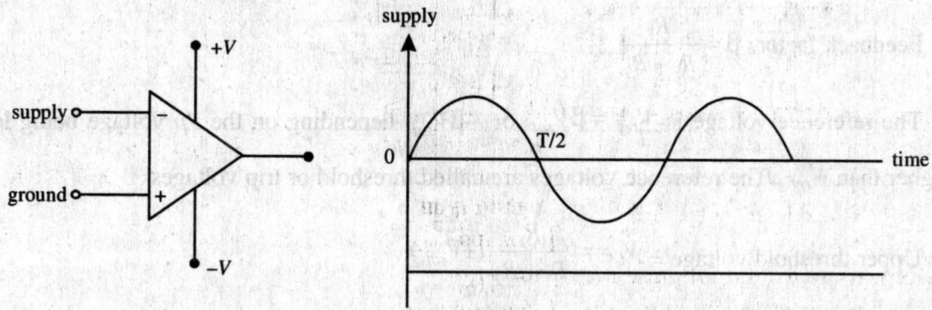

Fig.29

The sinusoid input is given to the supply terminal. The op-amp is in open loop condition and hence it has very large gain. So, the output will have very large amplitude. But in practice the output is limited by the supply voltage and hence the output is saturated to a constant voltage (proportional to the supply voltage). Hence, the output will be as follows:

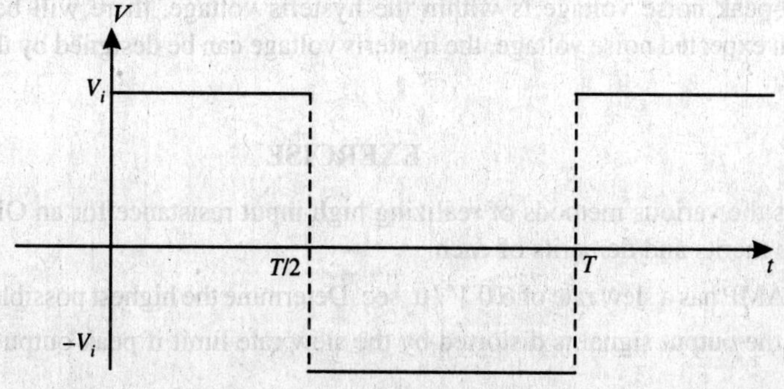

Fig.30

A major defect of the comparator studied is its unwanted response to noise voltages. As the comparator output changes state for very low input voltages, even a millivolt of noise voltage (above reference voltage) will cause triggering. To overcome this hazard, a part of the output voltage is fed-back in phase to the input as shown below.

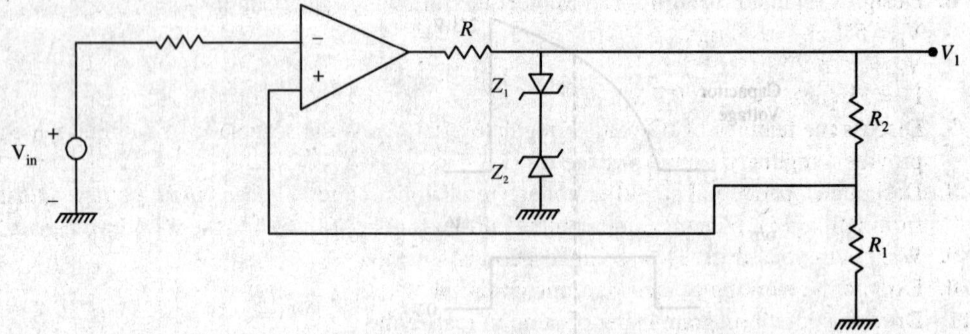

Fig.31

As noted, zener diodes keep the output voltage clamped at a lower level than $\pm V_{sat}$. A voltage is fed-back to +Ve, input of the op-amp thereby making the feedback positive. The feedback voltage is

$$V_f = \frac{R_1}{R_1 + R_2} V_0$$

Feedback factor, $\beta = \frac{R_1}{R_1 + R_2}$

The reference voltage is $V_{ref} = \beta V_{sat}$ or $-\beta V_{sat}$ depending on the *i/p* voltage being lower or higher than V_{ref}. The reference voltages are called threshold or trip voltages.

Upper threshold voltage = $V_{UT} = \frac{R_1}{R_1 + R_2}(+V_{sat.})$

Lower threshold voltage $V_{LT} = \frac{R_1}{R_1 + R_2}(-V_{sat})$

When $V_{in} < V_{LT}$, $V_0 = +V_{sat}$

$V_{in} > V_{UT}$, $V_0 = -V_{sat}$.

The difference in voltage between V_{UT} and V_{LT} is called hysteresis voltage (V_H), $V_H = V_{UT} - V_{LT}$

If peak-to-peak noise voltage is within the hysteris voltage, there will be no false triggering. Depending on expected noise voltage, the hysteris voltage can be designed by the feedback resistors, R_1 and R_2.

EXERCISE

1. Discuss the various methods of realizing high input resistance for an OPAMP. Highlight the relative merits and demerits of each.
2. An OPAMP has a slew rate of 6.0 V/μ sec. Determine the highest possible operating frequency before the output signal is distorted by the slew rate limit if peak output is (i) 1 *V*; (ii) 10 *V*.

3. Sketch the sample and Hold circuit and explain the principle of working.
4. Draw the circuit of temperature compensated log. amplifier and obtain the expression for output voltage.
5. Draw the circuit diagram of a stable multivibrator using op-amp. Explain its operation with neat waveforms. Obtain the expression for frequency of oscillations.
6. Design a regulator using IC 723 to meet the following specifications:–
   $V_0 = 5V$; $I_0 = 100$ mA.
   $V_{in} = 15 \pm 20\%$
   $I_{sc} = 150$ mA ; $V_{sense} = 0.7$ V
7. Discuss the features of IC voltage regulator 723. Draw the schematic of a circuit which can provide a regulated output voltage of $3V$.
8. Design the operational amplifier voltage regulator circuit to give an output voltage adjustable from $10V$ to $15V$. The maximum output current is to be 100 mA and the supply voltage is $20V$.
9. What is thermal drift? How compensation is obtained ?
10. Explain the working of a current mirror circuit.
11. Draw the circuit diagram using op-amp to realize the

    $V_0 = [2V_1 + 0.5V_2 + 3V_3]$
12. Explain the working of free running multivibrator using opamp. Design the same to generate a frequency of 1KHz and derive any expression used.
13. For the circuit given below, write the I/p and O/p waveform and plot the transfer characteristic (showing suitable calculation) for $V_i = 20\sin\,\omega t$.

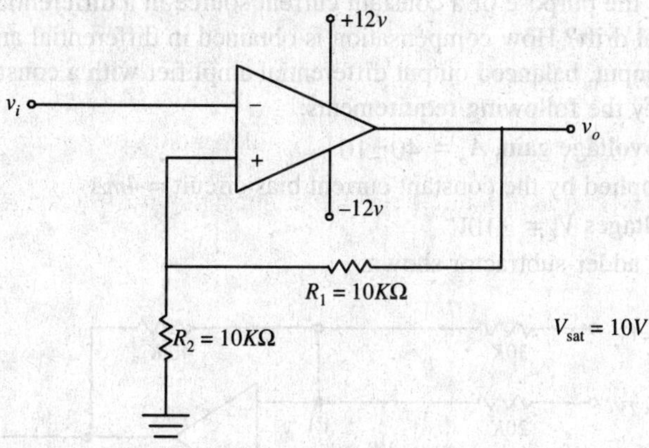

Fig.32

14. How do you achieve offset nulling in the general purpose like $\mu A741$?
15. Design an all pass filter to have a phase angle of + 60° if the frequency of V_{in} is 1 KHz. Write I/p and O/p waveforms.
16. The slow rate for an op-amp is $0.5\,V/\mu\text{sec}$. At what maximum frequency can you get an undistorted o/p voltage of $1V$ peak.
17. Explain how temperature compensation is achieved in a diode based antilog amplifier.
18. Design an op-amp inverting Schmitt trigger with UTP = 4V, LTP = $2V$, supply voltages = $\pm 15\,V$ and $V_{sat} = \pm 13V$. Draw the circuit and incorporate the designed values.
19. Design $a \pm 20dB/decade$ active wide band pass filter with $f_L = 200$ Hz and $J_H = 1$kHz and a pass band gain of 4. Calculate the value of Q for the filter.
20. What are the requirements of the output stage of an OPAMP? Write the basic circuit of a complementary emitter follower output stage and describe its voltage - transfer characteristics.

Describe the technique commonly used to remove the cross-over distortion in the transfer characteristics.

21. A non-inverting amplifier with a gain of 100 is nulled at 25°C. What will happen to the output voltage, if the temperature rises to 50°C for an offset voltage drift of 0.15 *mV/°C.* ?

22. For the OPAMP circuit shown in figure 33, find the output voltage.

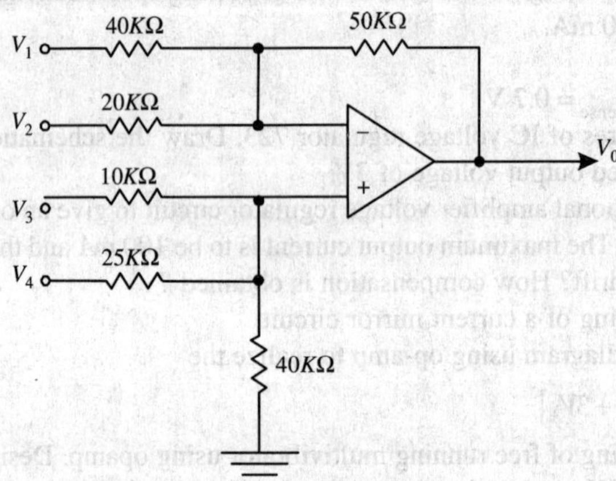

Fig. 33

23. What is an instrumentation amplifier? Where is it often used? List its features.

24. Briefly explain the purpose of a constant current source in a differential amplifier.

25. What is thermal drift? How compensation is obtained in differential amplifier ?

26. Design a dual input, balanced output differential amplifier with a constant current bias using diodes to satisfy the following requirements:

(*i*) Differential voltage gain, $A_d = 40 \pm 10$

(*ii*) Current supplied by the constant current bias circuit = 4*mA*

(*iii*) Supply voltages $V_s = \pm 10V$

27. Find V_0 for the adder-subtractor shown.

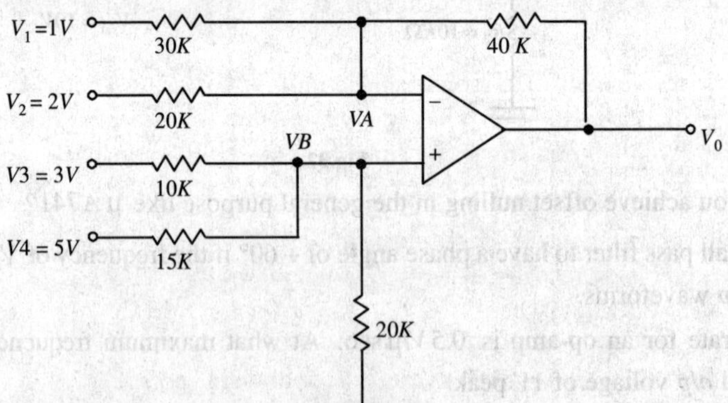

Fig. 34

28. With suitable circuit diagrams, show how OP-Amp can be used as log and anti-log amplifiers. Derive the expression for output voltages in both cases.

29. Draw the circuit diagram of 3 OP-Amp instrumentation amplifier & explain its features. Also derive the expression for output voltage.

30. Design a second order high-pass filter with a cut-off frequency of 10kHz and a pass band gain of 1.5. Assume $C = C_3 = C_2 = 0.02\mu F$ and $R_f = 100k\Omega$

31. Explain the working of sample Hold Circuit.

32. Design an amp. Schmitt trigger circuit with UTP = 2*V*. LTP = IV, supply voltage = $\pm 15V$, $V_{sat} = \pm 12V$

33. Draw the circuit diagram of a monostable multivibrator using op.amp and derive an expression for the output pulse width, giving the waveforms.

34. Design an active high pass filter to meet the following specifications:
(*i*) Butterworth response
(*ii*) Cutoff frequency = 4 kHz
(*iii*) Decay rate in the stop band = 40*dB*/decase.

35. Explain the working of Successive Approximation ADC.

36. Design an Op-Amp series voltage regulator to meet the following specification:
$V_i = 18 \pm 3V$, $V_0 = 9V$ at $I_0 = 10$ to $15mA$.
Zener available, $V_z = 5.6V, P_z = 0.5\,\omega$.

37. An Op-Amp has a feedback factor of 0.1 $Z_i = 4\ M\Omega, Z_0 = 50\Omega,$ = B.W = 1 MHz, A_{VOL} = 200,000. Compute
(*i*) The gain.
(*ii*) – 3dB bandwidth.
(*iii*) Effective input impedance.
(*iv*) Effective output impedance.

38. Discuss the effect of conventional compensation and feed forward compensation on the frequency response of an Op-Amp.

39. For a non-inverting amplifier $R_1 = 1K\Omega$ and $R_f = 10k\Omega$, calculate the maximum output offset voltage due to V_{0s} and I_B and for an Op-Amp $V_{0s} = 10\,mV$; $I_B = 300\,nA$, $I_{0s} = 50\,nA$. Calculate
(*i*) The value of R_{comp} needed to reduce the effect of I_B.
(*ii*) The maximum output offset voltage of R_{comp} as calculated in (*i*) is connected in the circuit.

40. Draw the circuit diagram of a monostable multivibrator using Op.Amp. With the help of waveforms, explain its operation. Obtain an expression for the output pulse width.

41. Design an Op-Amp Schmitt triggering for following specifications:-
$V_0 = \pm 10V$, tripping voltage are 4 *V* and [– 2] *V*.

42. With the help of the circuit diagrams, circuits,
(*i*) Half-wave precision rectifier explain the working of the following
(*ii*) Sample and hold circuit.
Mention its area of application.

43. Design a wideband bandpass filter to meet the following specifications:-
$f_1 = 5$ kHz; $f_2 = 15$ kHz.
Passband gain = 2.

44. Design an stable multivibrator using 555 timer to generate a clock of 1 kHz with 60 % duty cycle. Modify the circuit designed to obtain a clock of 1 kHz with 40 % duty cycle.

45. Draw the equivalent circuit of OPAMP at high frequency.

46. Define CMRR.

47. Refer to Fig. 35 given the ideal OPAMP circuit. Draw the voltage transfer characteristics, assuming ideal diodes, with zero cut in voltage

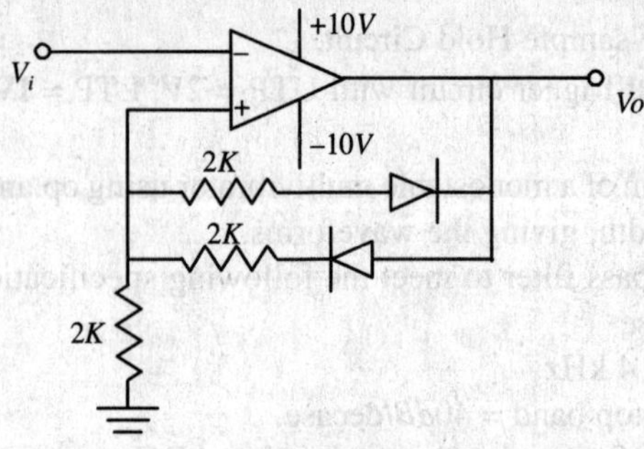

Fig. 35

48. Why open loop OPAMP is not used in linear application?

49. Find the Hysteresis voltage for the Schmitt trigger circuit shown in Fig. 36.

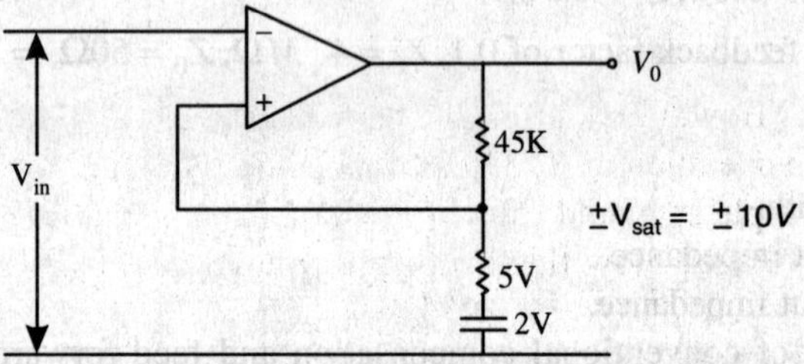

Fig. 36

50. If the differential voltage gain is 48 dB and the common mode voltage gain is 2 dB, then find the value of CMRR.

51. Briefly explain about all the internal stages of OPAMP.

52. Discuss the general properties of OPAMP.

53. What is slew rate? What is the cause of it? What is its significance in operational amplifier?

54. Find the voltage gain (V_0/V_s) for the differential amplifier shown in Fig. 37.

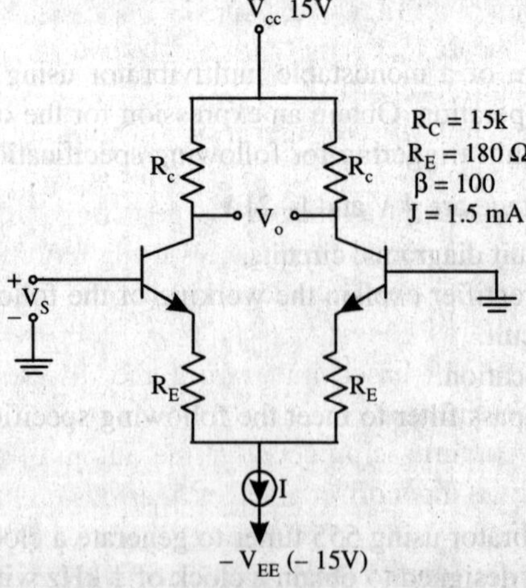

Fig. 37

55. What is an Instrumentation Amplifier? Discuss it's application. Find the *o/p* voltage(V_0) for the circuit shown in Fig. 38.

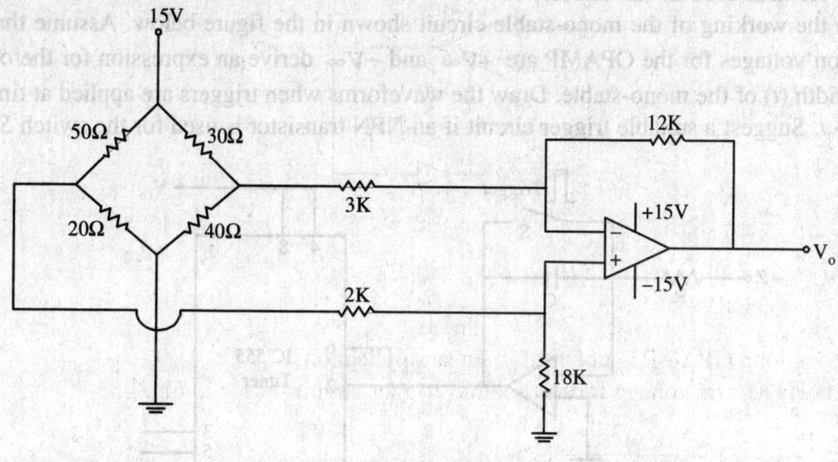

Fig. 38

56. What is thermal drift? How does it affect the performance of OPAMP circuit?

57. Draw and explain the operation of IC 555 as astable multivibrate.

58. Draw and explain Sample and Hold Circuit. Mention its application.

59. What is *i/p* offset voltage? How the *o/p* offset voltage due to *i/p* offset voltage can be minimized?

60. What is the need of frequency compensation in OPAMP? Discuss pol-zero method of compensation.

61. A Schmitt trigger with upper threshold level V_{ut} = OV and hysteresis voltage $V_H = 0.5H$, converts a 1 kHz sine wave of amplitude 4V (p-p) into rectangular pulses. Calculate the duty cycle of the *o/p* pulses.

62. What are the trip points and what is the value of hysteresis? If the stray capacitance across R_1 is 1.5pF, what size should the speed-up capacitor C be?

63. Name a member of the logic family you know which gives the highest speed and describe its working with a neat diagram

64. Draw a simple block diagram of a PLL and explain the basic idea how it remains locked on to the incoming frequency. What are lock range and capture range of a PLL? What type of VCO is used in PLL? Mention application of PLL.

65. Why is the non-inverting OPAMP configuration unsuitable for use in integrator and differentiator application?

66. In the non-inverting configuration, if a reactive device is to be used in the feedback loop of the OPAMP and a resistor is connected from the inverting terminal to ground, what type of reactive component is required to produce a leading phase at the output of the circuit? Give proper explanation.

67. How do the outputs of OPAMP based integrators and differentiators differ from their mathematically derived counterparts?

68. In general, what type of waveform is produced at the output of an integrator when square wave input is applied? Why are input offset voltages a serious problem in the realization of an OPAMP integrator?

69. In case of an antilog amplifier does voltage gain effectively increase or decrease as input voltage is increased in magnitude? Give explanation.

70. A certain logarithmic amplifier produces an output voltage that changes at rate of 120mv/decade with Vin. What can be said about the equation describing the Transconductance of the logging element used in this circuit?

71. Explain the working of the mono-stable circuit shown in the figure below. Assume that the saturation voltages for the OPAMP are $+V\infty$ and $-V\infty$ derive an expression for the output pulse width (t) of the mono-stable. Draw the waveforms when triggers are applied at times t_1 and $t_2 > t$. Suggest a suitable trigger circuit if an NPN transistor is used for the switch S.

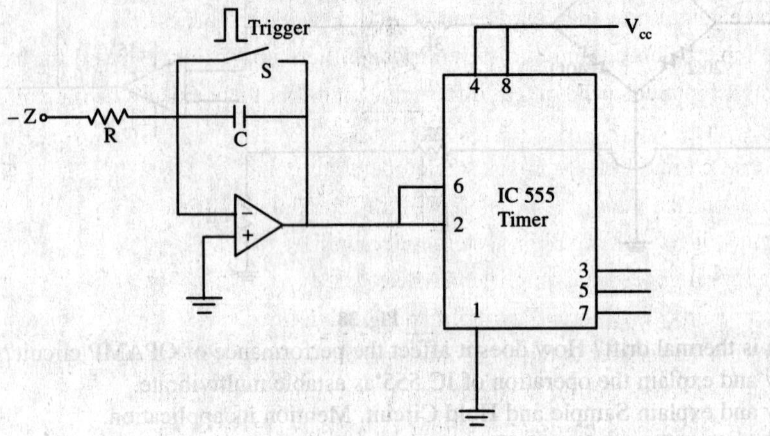

Fig. 39

72. A sine wave with peak value 6 volts drives one of the inverters in a 741 chip. Sketch the output voltage.

73. How can a noisy input be prevented from triggering a comparator? What is the function of a speed-up capacitor?

MULTIPLE CHOICE QUESTIONS

TRUE / FALSE

1. For differential amplifier, output voltage is the differentiation of input voltage.
2. Voltage gain of the differential amplifier is dependent on R_E.
3. Dual input balanced output differential amplifier support, undesired disturbances.
4. In single input balanced output differential amplifier there exists a dc out voltage without any input signal.
5. Constant current bias improves stable operating point.
6. Automatic gain control is possible with differential amplifier.
7. Schmitt trigger is basically a differential amplifier.
8. For an ideal differential amplifier CMRR = 0.
9. Current gain of a differential amplifier is well defined.
10. Operational amplifier is the basic building block of differential amplifier.
11. The differential amplifier is suitable only for amplifying ac signals.
12. At high frequencies, cascode amplifier fails to provide high gain.
13. Flat pack ICs are ideal for bread board circuits.
14. Military grade ICs have maximum temperature tolerance.
15. CC-CB connection is called a cascode amplifier.
16. In a current mirrors circuit, the output current is forced to equal the input current.
17. For ac analysis of differential amplifier we use *h* parameters.
18. Differential amplifier is not used for power or current amplification.
19. The differential amplifier is generally used as a current amplifier.
20. The voltage gain of dual I/p, unbalanced o/p differential amplifier is half the gain of the dual I/p balanced o/p differential amplifier.
21. The current mirror is a special case of constant current bias.
22. In differential amplifier power gain is undefined.
23. Differential amplifier can be used as phase splitter.
24. The differential amplifier is capable of amplifying dc as well as ac input signals.
25. Differential amplifiers are widely used to compare more than one signals.
26. For ideal different amplifier CMRR should be low.
27. For ideal differential amplifier R_{in} should be low.
28. Cascode amplifier mainly for high frequency application.
29. Level translator shifts dc level to supply.
30. Operational amplifier of differential amplifier also depends on average I/P voltage.
31. Constant current ckt gives very high I/P resistance.
32. B.W is a low signal phenomenon, but slew rate is a high signal phenomenon.

33. The gain of an operational amplifier varies with frequency.
34. Slew rate can't change with temperature.
35. O/p impedance of an ideal op amp is zero.
36. Transformer coupling is used in differential amplifier.
37. 180° phase shift occurs in differential amplifier.
38. Increase in Bandwidth increases gains.
39. Instrumentation Amplifier shows high I/P low o/p amplifier resistance.
40. The power gain of a differential amplifier is well defined.
41. The overall output impedance of the *m* cascaded differential amplifier is the output resistance of the last stage.
42. The differential amplifier is the basic building block of their processors.
43. Differential amplifiers are only for small signal analysis.
44. The R_E value should be large enough to make a differential amplifier ideal one.
45. I/p offset voltage for an operational amplifier changes with supply voltage.
46. Operational amplifiers input offset voltage and current are constant with time.
47. Any unwanted signal associated with the operational amplifier desired operational amplifier signal is noise.
48. Common mode rejection ratio of an operational amplifier is the ratio of differential gain and common mode gain.
49. In negative feedback operational amplifier the feedback network is connected in inverting input terminals.
50. Slew rate is large signal phenomenon.
51. μ A - 709 is an internally compensated operational amplifier. The operation amplifier is a direct couple high gain amplifier.
52. Input impedance of an ideal operational amplifier is finite.
53. The output resistance of an ideal operational amplifier is zero.
54. The input resistance of dual input unbalance output differential amplifier is $\beta_{ac}\,\gamma_e$.
55. The operational amplifier is direct coupled high gain amplifier.
56. Most linear IC_S need both positive and negative power supply.
57. By introducing negative feedback, the gain of the amplifier is the reciprocal of the open loop voltage gain.
58. Automatic gain control (AGC) is possible with the differential amplifier.
59. Differential gain of dual input unbalanced output differential amplifier is $\frac{R_c}{\gamma_e}$.
60. Differential amplifier is used as a power amplifier.
61. Differential amplifier can be used as phase splitter.
62. The output resistance of differential amplifier is always R_C.

FILL UP THE BLANKS

1. The basic building block of operational amplifier is ________________.
2. Input impedance of an ideal operational amplifier is ________________.
3. The slew rate of an operational amplifier is ________________ signal phenomenon.

4. The input offset current is the ____________ on separate current entering the input terminal at a balanced amplifier.
5. The voltage gain of dual input balance output differential amplifier is A_d = ____________.
6. The differential amplifier consists of two ____________ common emitter transistor.
7. The differential amplifier can amplify ac as well as dc input signal because it employs ____________ coupling.
8. In case of differential amplifier, input resistances at both transistors are ____________.
9. For single input, unbalanced output differential amplifier, output is ____________.
10. A differential amplifier is sometimes called a ____________ because it consists of two transistors connected to a single resistor.
11. ____________ current is defined as the difference between the base currents.
12. One of the reasons of the differential amplifier is so popular (1) because it discriminates against ____________ signals.

101 μV, +, 100 μV, −, V_o, 10 K

13. The amplifier of the figure has r_{in} = ____________.
14. If both the transistors of differential amplifier is similar, input offset current is ____________.
15. Generally in a cascaded differential amplifier, the last dual input unbalanced output stage is followed by a ____________.
16. A good quality operational amplifier must have low ____________ impedance.
17. Direct coupling is used in ____________.
18. Voltage gain of differential amplifier is ____________.
19. μ A 741 is an ____________ and it belongs to ____________ generation.
20. The differential amplifier amplifies the ____________ of two signals applied at the I/Ps.
21. The four types of differential amplifiers are ____________, ____________, ____________ and ____________.
22. The input impedance of BJT differential amplifier is ____________ than the I/P impedance of FET differential amplifier.
23. The figure of merit of a differential amplifier is its ____________.
24. The CE-CB configuration is referred to as the ____________.
25. Ideally the gain bandwidth product of an operational amplifier is ____________.
26. The function of the level translator is to make the dc voltage at o/p terminal ____________.
27. For dual I/P balanced operational amplifier differential amplifier operational amplifier is taken across ____________.
28. This cascode amplifier provides a large amount of ____________ at higher frequencies.
29. To improve the thermal stability in constant bias the resistor is replaced by ____________.
30. The voltage transfer characteristics curve of operational amplifier is the graph of ____________ versus differential input voltage.
31. A differential amplifier amplifies the ____________ between two input signals.

32. CMRR of a differential amplifier ideally equal to ______________.
33. By using ______________ in series with each emitter the dependence of voltage gain of the differential amplifier on variations in R_C can be reduced.
34. The differential amplifier can amplify ac as well as dc input signals because it employs ______________.
35. Constant current bias ckt is better because it provides better ______________.
36. The cascode amplifier is composed of direct coupled ______________ and ______________ configuration.
37. Input impedance of a Dual input balanced output amplifier is ______________.
38. Differential gains of an JFET differential amplifier are ______________.
39. In cascaded differential amplifier overall input impedance is equal to ______________ & overall operational amplifier impedance is equal to ______________.
40. Transfer conductance g_{md} is proportional to ______________.
41. In operational amplifier ckt, if input is square wave then output will be ______________ wave.
42. The integrator and differentiation are most commonly used in ______________.
43. Slew rate limiting occurs with all large, fast-changing signals. If slew rate is exceeded, ______________ of the output waveform results.
44. ______________ are used to control the phase shift and thus improve the stability of the operational amplifier.
45. It is advantageous to use a differential amplifier with higher CMRR since its ability to reject ______________.
46. Voltage gain of single input unbalanced output differential amplifier is ______________ the gain of dual input balanced output.
47. The voltage gain of the differential amplifier is independent of ______________.
48. There are ______________ different types of differential amplifier.
49. If the operational amplifier voltage is measured between two collectors, then the configuration is called as ______________.
50. The cascode amplifier is composed of direct coupled ______________ and ______________ configurations.
51. Output offset voltage occurs due to ______________.
52. If, $V_1 = V_0 \cos \omega t$ then maximum slew rate is ______________.
53. The circuit in which the operational amplifier is forced to equal the input ckt is called ______________.
54. Generally in a cascaded differential amplifier the last dual I/P unbalanced operational amplifier stage is followed by ______________.
55. The dual I/P unbalanced operational amplifier differential amplifier R_i = ______________ and R_o = ______________ .
56. The differential amplifier offers the best ______________ to induce noise.
57. The input resistance power consumption and output short circuit current of an operational amplifier are ______________ parameter.
58. Voltage follower is ______________ gain amplifier.

59. Voltage series negative feedback configuration is commonly called ______________ with feedback.

60. Voltage shunt feedback configuration is called an ______________ amplifier.

61. To reduce the effect of γ_e or gain we can use a resistor (R_E) reflected to as a ______________.

62. In a current mirror ckt the operational amplifier is ______________ of the input.

63. To reduce the undesired d.c. voltage the differential amplifier is generally followed by ______________.

64. In a zener constant current bias circuit the value of R_2 should be such that ______________.

65. Because of ______________ the dc level at the emitters rise from stage to stage.

66. If we want to obtain a very large voltage or power gain we use ______________ configuration.

MULTIPLE CHOICE QUESTIONS

1. The first stage of any operational amplifier is dual input balanced output/signal input balanced output.

2. If the output is measured at one of the collectors w.r to ground, the configuration is called balanced output/unbalanced output.

3. The swapping resistor R_E' of differential amplifier decreases/increases in the linearity range.

4. Noise of input signal in differential amplifier
(*a*) increases (*b*) decreases (*c*) remains the same (*d*) is cancelled out.

5. If CMRR is high, the wide variation of input within the tolerable limits of the equipment, makes output
(*a*) high (*b*) low (*c*) same (*d*) almost same

6. Output resistance of differential amplifier can be reduced by decreasing
(*a*) R_E (*b*) I_C (*c*) R_C

7. Cascaded differential amplifier requires level translator because of
(*a*) Impedance matching (*b*) Isolating each stage (*c*) D.C. shift.

8. Offset voltage is generated due to
(*a*) Noise (*b*) Mismatch of T_1 & T_2 (*c*) Supply.

9. LM 324 operational amplifier needs for biasing
(*a*) one power supply (*b*) two power supplies (*c*) no power supply.

10. For package type identification of an operational amplifier '*T*' indicates the package type is
(*a*) Mini dip (*b*) Flat pack (*c*) Plastic dip. (*d*) None of these.

11. With negative feedback in operational amplifier the bandwidth will
(*a*) increase (*b*) decrease (*c*) remain the same.

12. Feedback is done in an operational amplifier due to
(*a*) increase gain (*b*) increase i/p impedance
(*c*) for unsuitability of open loop operational amplifier in linear application.

13. For high frequency amplification the better configuration is
(*a*) CC-CE (*b*) CC-CB (*c*) CE-CB (*d*) CE-CF

14. Input resistance of dual input balance output differential amplifier is
(*a*) $a_c\ r_e$ (*b*) $2\ \beta\ a_c\ r_e$ (*c*) $\beta\ a_e\ r_e$ (*d*) $Rd_e\ r_e$
15. The swamping resistor R_E of differential amplifier decreases/increases the effecting of r_c on voltage gain.
16. For high frequency amplification the better configuration is
(*a*) CC-CF (*b*) CC-CB (*c*) CE-CB (*d*) CE-CE
17. The voltage gain of single input balanced output differential amplifier is
(*a*) $R_C\ /\ R_E$ (*b*) $\dfrac{2R_C}{r_e}$ (*c*) $\dfrac{R_C}{r_e}$ (*d*) $\dfrac{R_E}{2r_e}$
18. The operational amplifier is used to amplify
(*a*) a.c signal (*b*) D.C. (*c*) d.c as well as a.c. (*d*) None of these.
19. The cascode amplifier is composed of direct coupled
(*a*) CE-CB configuration (*b*) CC-CC configuration
(*c*) CC-CB configuration (*d*) CE-CF configuration.
20. For a.c analysis of differential amplifier we use
(*a*) h-parameters (*b*) *r*-parameters (*c*) None of these
21. The constant current bias circuit is better because.
(*a*) it provides current stabilisation (*b*) it increases input impedance
(*c*) it decreases input impedance (*d*) (*a*) & (*b*) (e) (*a*) & (*c*)
22. The voltage gain of dual I/P unbalanced operational amplifier is
(*a*) $R_C\ /\ r_e$ (*b*) $2R_C\ /\ r_e$ (*c*) $R_C\ /\ 2r_e$ (*d*) None of these.
23. If the output is measured between two collectors the differential amplifier is said to have
(*a*) balanced output (*b*) unbalanced output (*c*) None of these.
24. While cooking in a highly noise-prone environment, you will require an operational amplifier with
(*a*) high CMRR (*b*) low CMRR (*c*) The operation will not be affected by CMRR
25. Noise of input signal at differential amplifier output
(*a*) Increases (*b*) Decreases (*c*) remains the same (*d*) is cancelled out.
26. In case of dual-input balanced output differential amplifier output impedance is
(*a*) equal to collector resistance (*b*) greater than collector resistance
(*c*) equal to twice the collector resistor (*d*) less than collector resistance.
27. In all types of differential amplifier DC operating point
(*a*) is not equal (*b*) is equal (*c*) is dependent on application
(*d*) None of these
28. Constant current bias is required to
(*a*) stabilise the operating point
(*b*) variate the operating point to get satisfactory result.
(*c*) increase operational amplifier impedance and decrease I/P impedance.
(*d*) equate I/P and operational amplifier impedance.
29. In case of constant current bias, R_1 is replaced by diode D_1 & D_2 to
(*a*) increase the I/P impedance (*b*) improve thermal stability
(*c*) increase gain (*d*) decrease thermal stability

30. The cascode amplifier is
(*a*) CC-CC configuration (*b*) CC-CE configuration
(*c*) CE-CB configuration (*d*) none of these
31. In cascaded differential amplifier
(*a*) direct coupling is used (*b*) capacitive coupling is used
(*c*) Both of these
32. I/P resistance of a practical differential amplifier is
(*a*) infinity (*b*) low
33. If $V_{ind} = 0$ the A_d = (indues-input balance operational amplifier different)
(*a*) α (*b*) 0 (*c*) Positive (*d*) Negative.
34. If $R_E > r_e$ then R_{i1} = (In dues input balance operational amplifier different)
(*a*) $2\beta_{ac}\, r_e$ (*b*) $\dfrac{\beta_{ac}\, r_e\,(2R_E)}{R_E + r_e}$ (*c*) $\dfrac{\beta_{ac}\, r_e\,(r_e + 2R_E)}{(R_E + r_e)}$
35. FET differential amplifier, A_d = ?
(*a*) $\dfrac{V_o}{1/g_m}$ (*b*) $\dfrac{R_0}{g_m^{-1}}$ (*c*) $\dfrac{1}{g_m}$ (*d*) $R_c\, g_m$
36. The differential input resistance of a single stage differential amplifier is
(*a*) $2\beta_{ac}\, r_e$ (*b*) R_C / r_e (*c*) $2\beta_{ac}\,(r_e + R_E)$
(*d*) None of these (*e*) both (*a*) and (*c*)
37. Differential voltage gain is a function of
(*a*) emitter resistance (*b*) collector resistance (*c*) both emitter and collector resistances
(*d*) input impedance (*e*) None of these
38. Differential amplifier can amplify the difference of the two-signals of
(*a*) a.c. (*b*) d.c. (*c*) both a.c. & d.c. signals (*d*) None of these
39. Differential amplifier makes noise component
(*a*) increased (*b*) same (*c*) decreased
40. O/p of differential amplifier can be reduced by decreasing
(*a*) collector resistor (*b*) collector current (*c*) emitter resistor
41. The input impedance of a differential amplifier decreased by
(*a*) shorting output terminal (*b*) shorting another input terminal
(*c*) keeping open ckt another input terminal
(*d*) keeping open ckt operational amplifier terminals
42. In differential amplifier, the supply voltage V_{CC} and V_{EE} must be
(*a*) $V_{CC} > V_{EE}$ (*b*) $V_{CC} < V_{EE}$ (*c*) $|V_{CC}| = |V_{EE}|$ (*d*) None of these
43. In an emitter biased differential amplifier the emitter or collector current depends on
(*a*) The negative power supply (*b*) Emitter resistor
(*c*) The base emitter voltage (*d*) The β-value of the transistor.
44. The desired characteristics of an operational amplifier is:
(*a*) high gain (*b*) high bandwidth
(*c*) high i/p impedance (*d*) high operational amplifier impedance.
45. Instrumentation amplifier is preferred for
(*a*) high CMRR (*b*) low Z_{in} (*c*) low distortion

46. A single supply operational amplifier is
(*a*) LM 318 (*b*) MC 414 (*c*) LM 324 (*d*) μA 741
47. Howland ckt gives
(*a*) Constant Voltage (*b*) Constant Current (*c*) CE & CB (*d*) $R_0 = \alpha$

OBJECTIVE TYPE QUESTIONS

1) In the op amp circuit V_o is given by

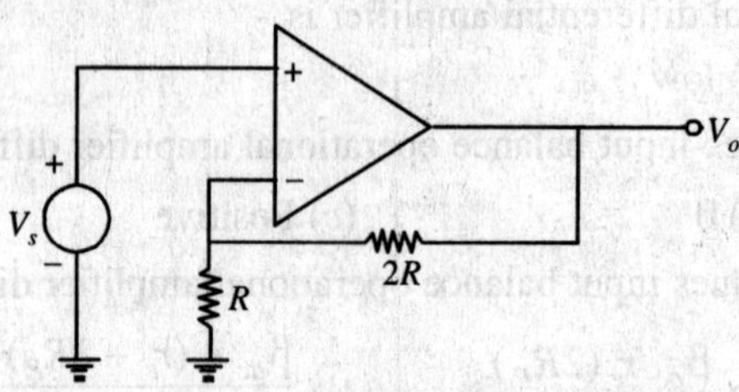

Fig. 1.

(Ans. $\rightarrow 3V_s$**)**

2) Value of V_o is given by

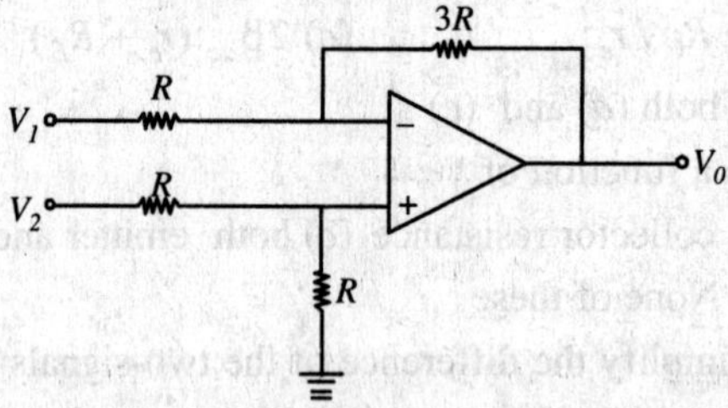

Fig. 2.

(Ans. $(2V_2 - 3V_1)$**)**

3) In the ckt value of V_o is given by—

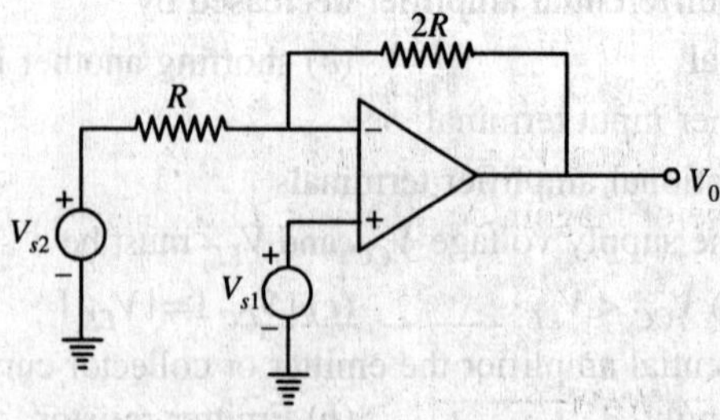

Fig. 3.

(Ans. $(3V_{s1} - 2V_{s2})$**)**

4) In the practical differenciator ckt C_F is used for

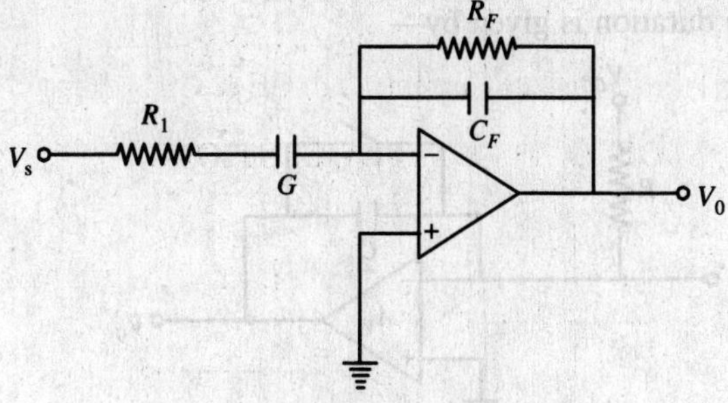

Fig. 4.

(**Ans.** C_F insures stable operation)

5) In the ckt I is given by—

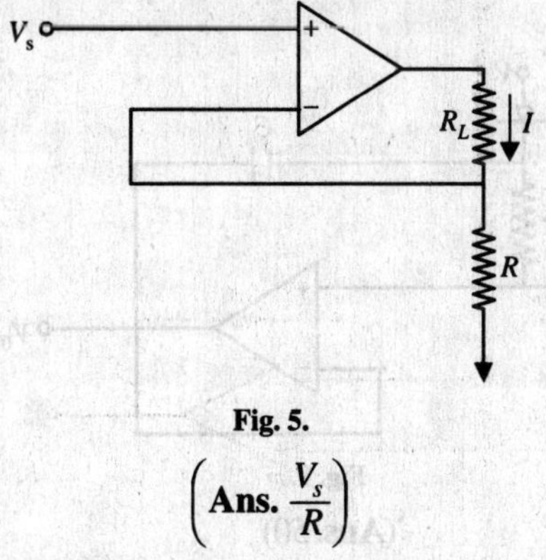

Fig. 5.

$\left(\textbf{Ans. } \frac{V_s}{R}\right)$

6) In the ckt V_z = zenor voltage; V_i = input signal, V_R = reference voltage. Calculate V_o.

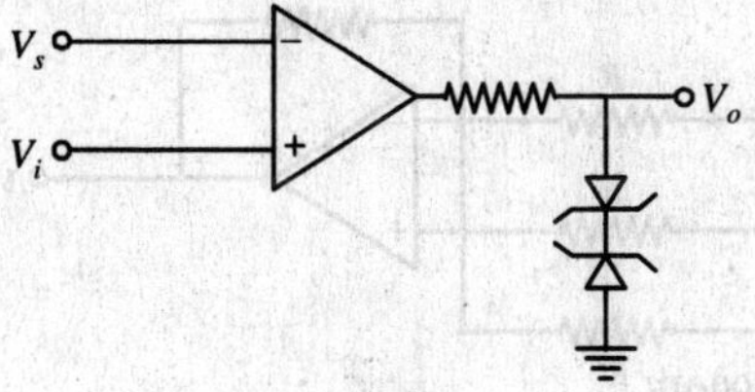

Fig. 6.

(**Ans.** $V_o = +V_z$ for $V_i > V_R$)

7) In the ckt, is a step voltage of magnitude –0·5 volt. Calculate V_o.

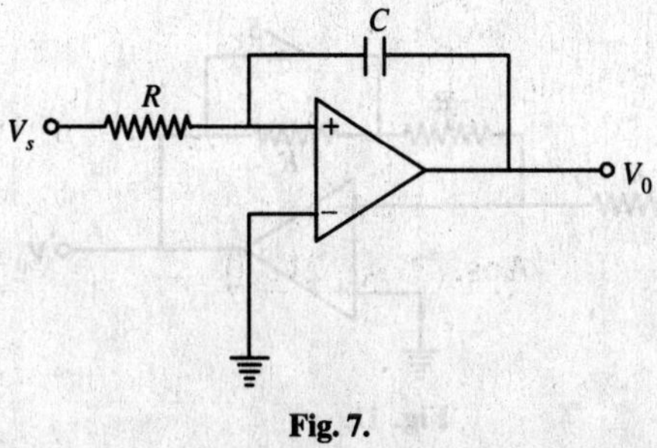

Fig. 7.

(**Ans.** $+t$ volt)

8) Figure shows a Miller's sweep, $V_{cc} = 45V$, $R = M\ ohm$, $C = 9\mu F$ $A_v = 5\times10^4$, sweep voltage $V_o = 25V$. The sweep duration is given by—

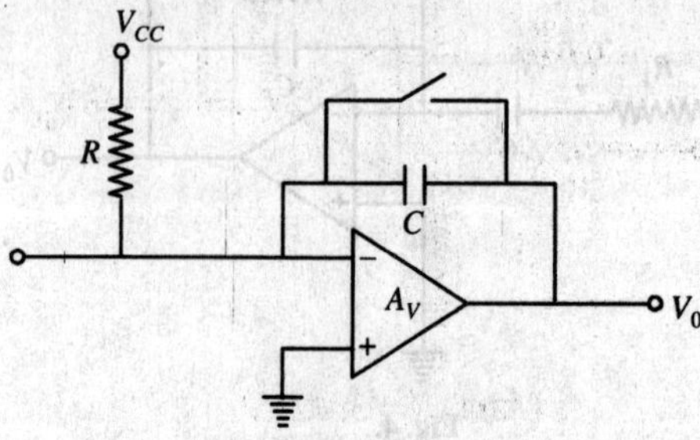

Fig. 8.

(**Ans.** 5 seconds)

9) In the ckt $V = 50$ volts, $R = 1M\Omega$, $C = 1\mu F$, $C_1 = 100\mu F$. The sweep speed is Volts/sec is given by—

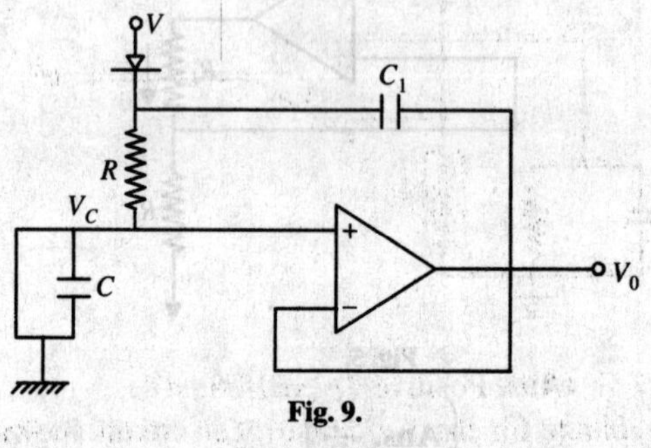

Fig. 9.

(**Ans.** 50)

10) A non-inverting op-amp summer is shown in Figure. The o/p voltage V_o is given by—

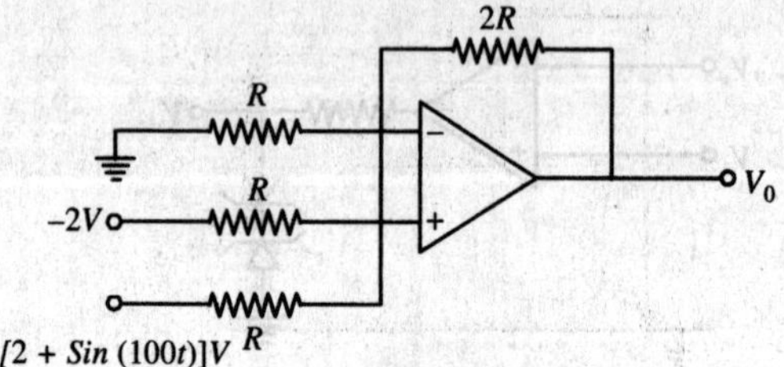

Fig. 10.

(**Ans.** $3\,Sin\,(100t)$)

11) Let, the magnitude of gain is A, when S_1 is open. Then the gain, when S_1 is closed, is given by—

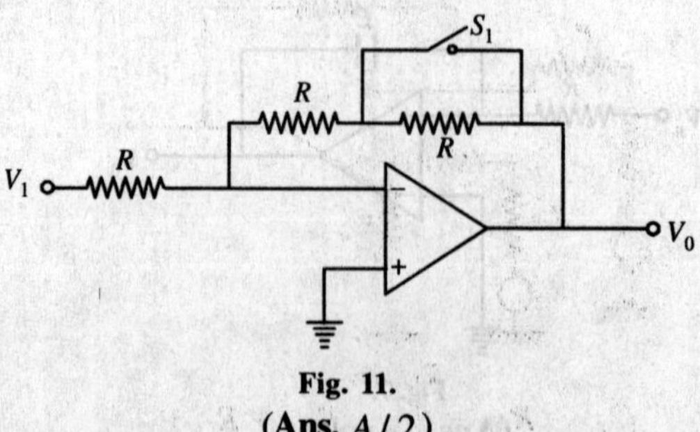

Fig. 11.

(**Ans.** $A/2$)

12) For the same amplification of V_1 and V_2, value of R will be

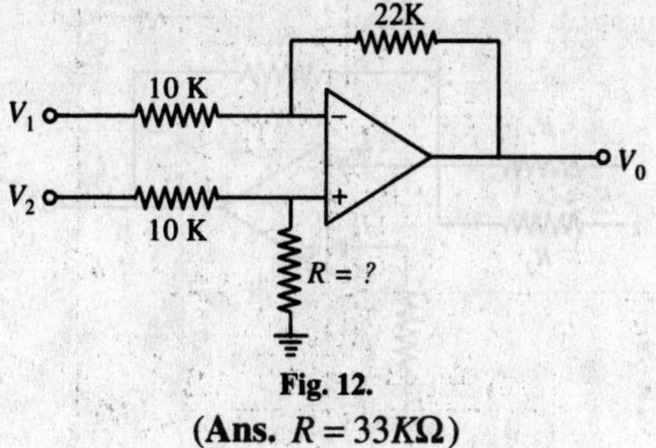

Fig. 12.

(**Ans.** $R = 33K\Omega$)

13) In this op-based Wein-bridge RC-oscillator R_2 is invariably a resistor having.

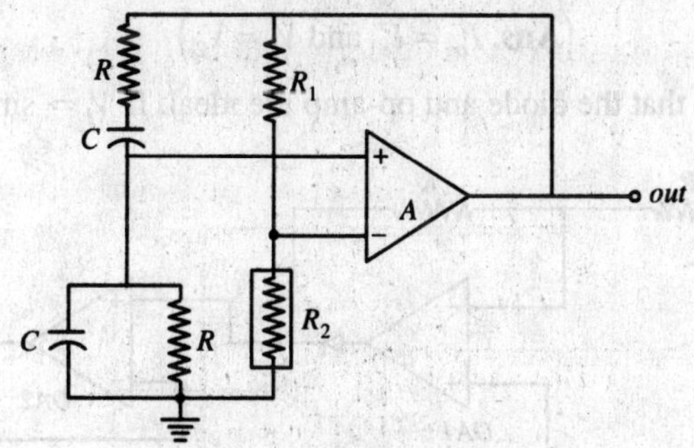

Fig. 13.

(**Ans.** Positive *Te* coefficient)

14) What is the hysteresis voltage for the Schmitt trigger circuit shown in the given figure, if $V_{sat} = \pm 10V$?

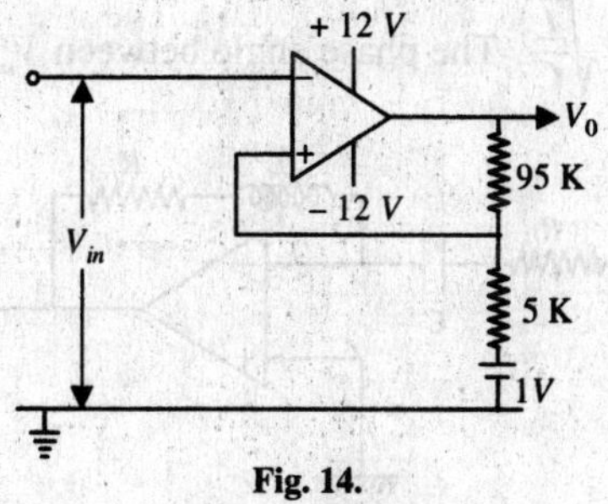

Fig. 14.

(**Ans.** 1.00 volt)

15) For which condition the instrumentation amplifier will give highest CMRR?

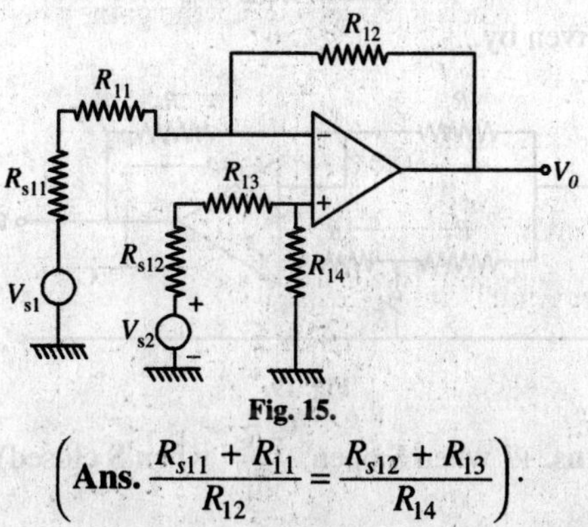

Fig. 15.

$$\left(\textbf{Ans.}\ \frac{R_{s11} + R_{11}}{R_{12}} = \frac{R_{s12} + R_{13}}{R_{14}}\right).$$

16) For the given ckt output offset will be zero?

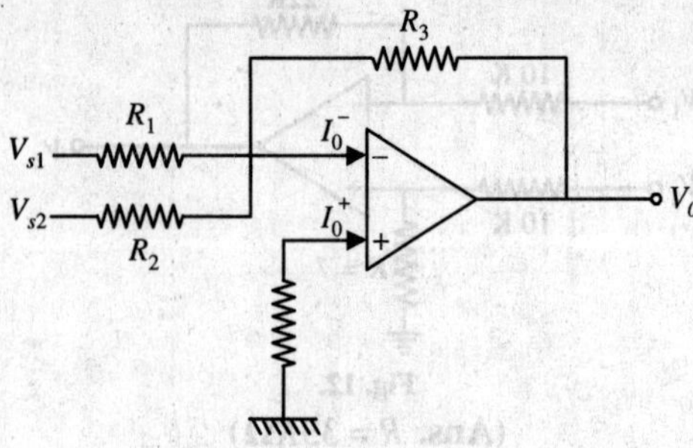

Fig. 16.

(**Ans.** $I_o^- = I_o^+$ and $V_1 = V_2$)·

17) In the figure, assume that the diode and op-amp are ideal. If V_i = sin ωt, then V_o is.........

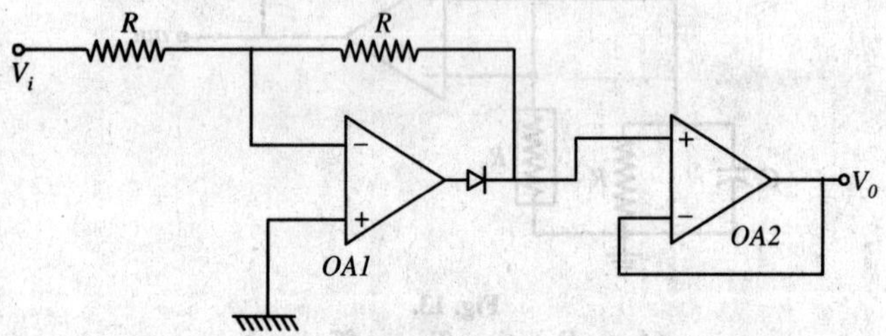

Fig. 17.

(**Ans.** half-wave rectified with peak value 1*V*)

18) Given op-amp is ideal. $R = \sqrt{\frac{L}{C}}$. The phase angle between V_o and V_i at $\omega = 1\sqrt{LC}$ is...........

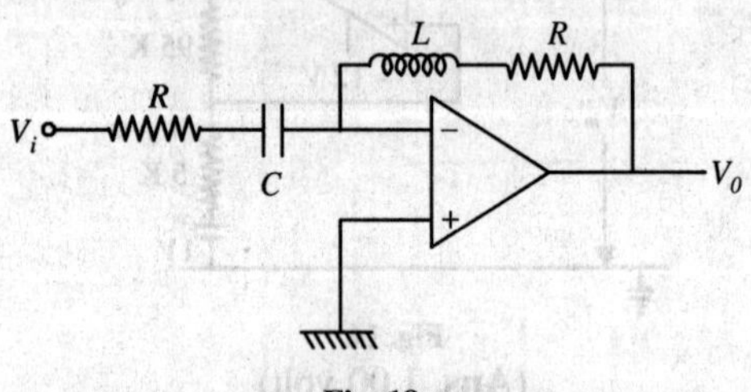

Fig. 18.

(**Ans.** $\pi/2$)

19) The gain of the ckt is given by...

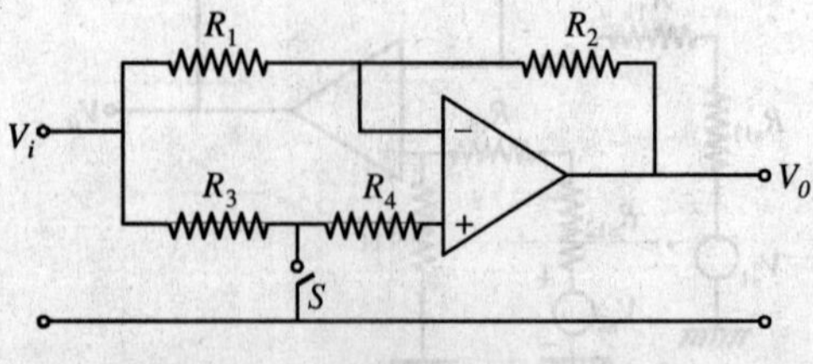

Fig. 19.

(**Ans.** +1 when S open, $\frac{-R_2}{R_1}$ when S closed).

20) In this Schmitt trigger circuit V_o is limited to $+10V$ and $-5V$. The lower and upper trigger voltages are respectively...

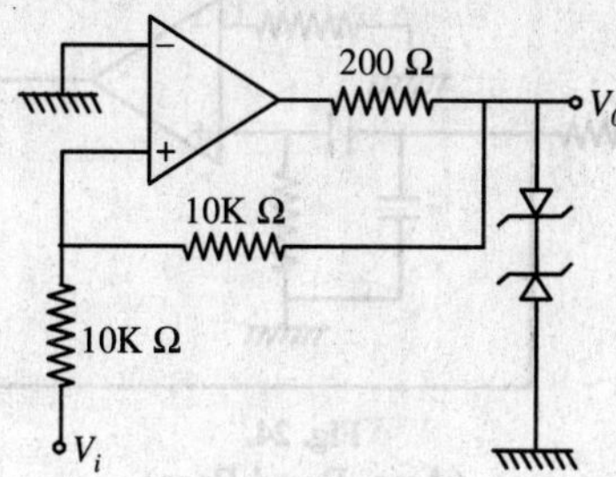

Fig. 20.

(**Ans.** $-1V$ and $+0{\cdot}5V$)

21) In the ckt $V_o(t) = ?$

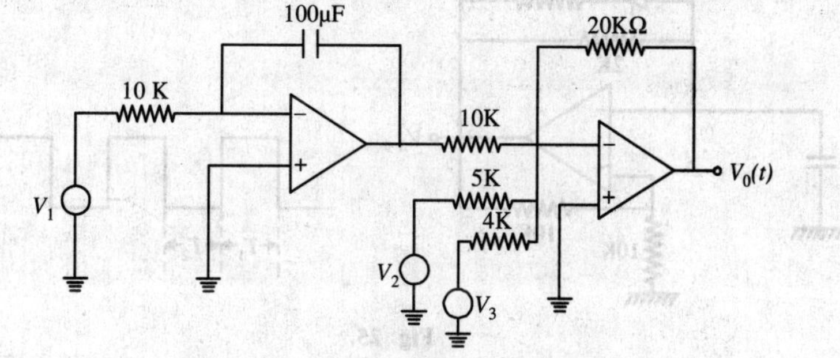

Fig. 21.

(**Ans.** $2V(t) - 4V_2(t) - 5V_3(t)$)

22) The LED will be ON if V_i is

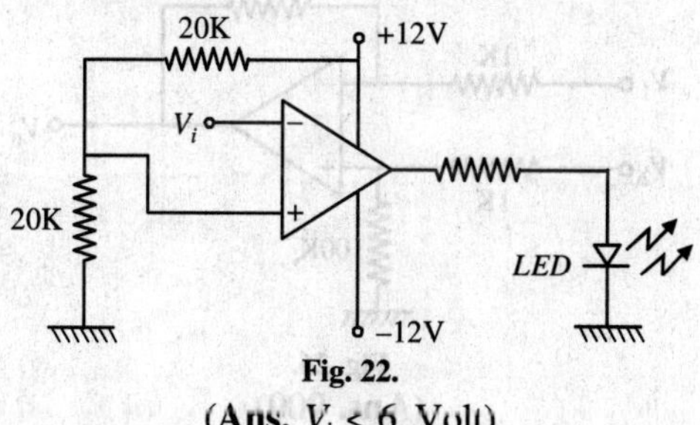

Fig. 22.

(**Ans.** $V_i < 6$ Volt)

23) In this Wein bridge oscillator if $R = 1K$, $C = \frac{1}{2\pi}$μF, then calculate $f = ?$

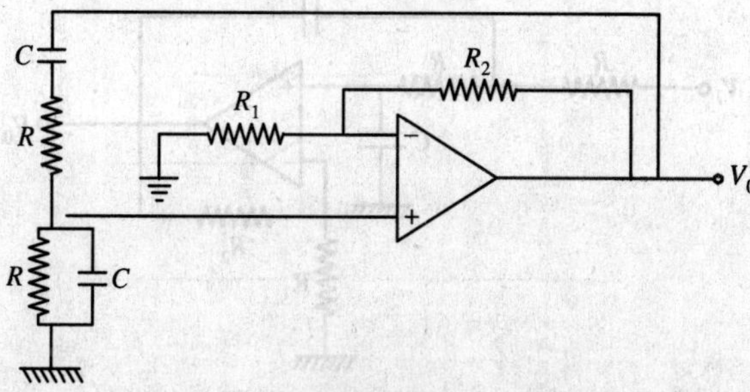

Fig. 23.

(**Ans.** 1 KHz)

24) What kind of response do you get from the ckt?

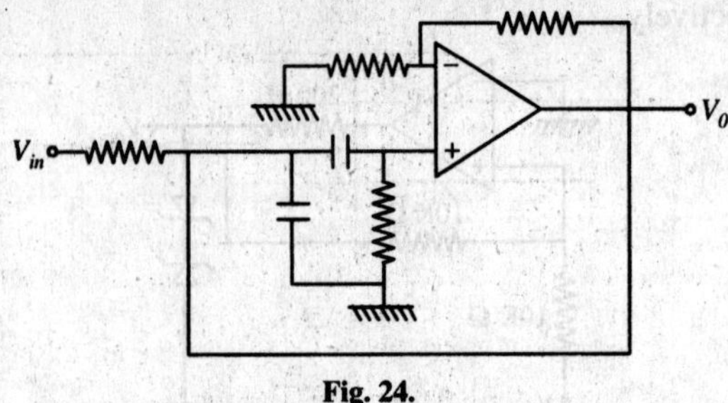

Fig. 24.

(**Ans.** Band Pass)

25) If the diode is ideal then calculate T_1 / T_2

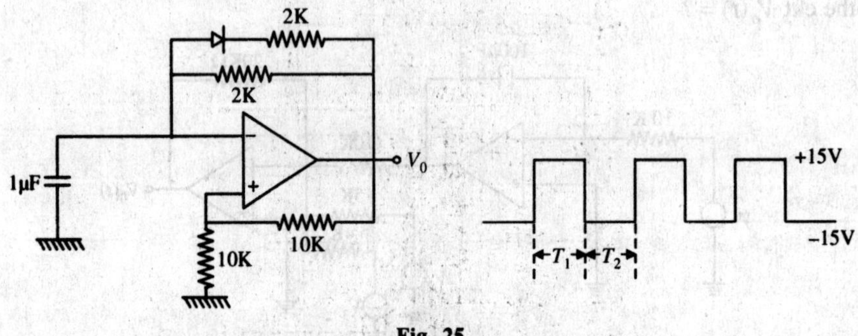

Fig. 25.

(**Ans.** 2)

26) The CMRR of this differential amplifier is...

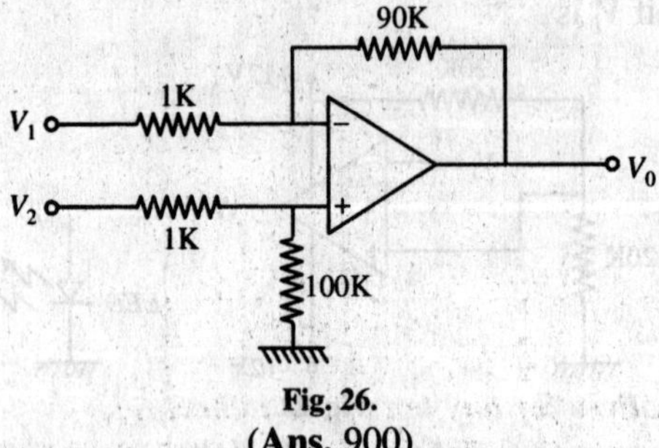

Fig. 26.

(**Ans.** 900)

27) This circuit represents...

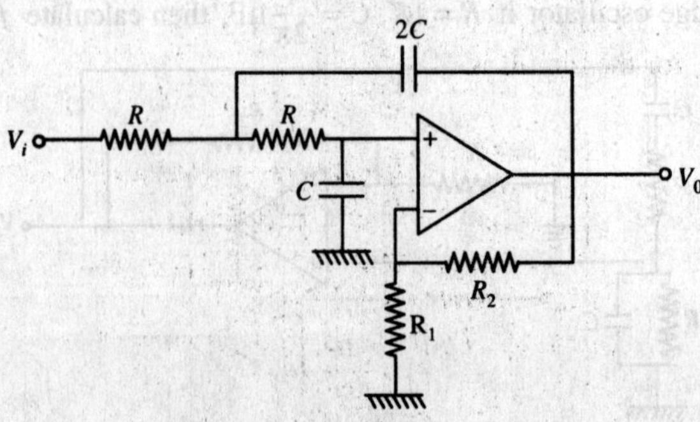

Fig. 27.

(**Ans.** an active 2nd order LP filter)

28) In the ckt above I_o / I_i is....

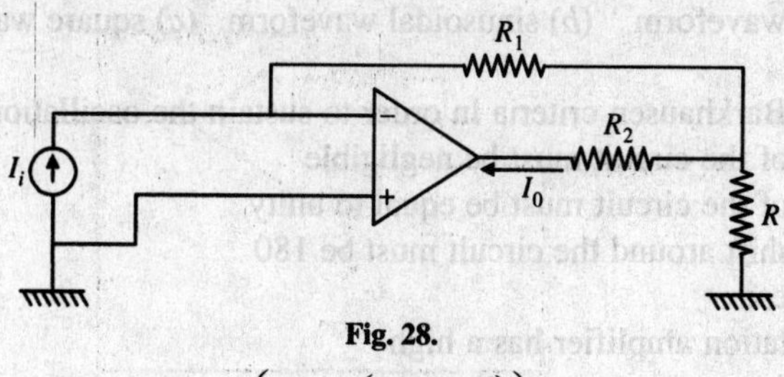

Fig. 28.

$\left(\textbf{Ans.}\ \left(1+R_1/R\right)\right)$

29) The o/p Voltage V_o is given by....

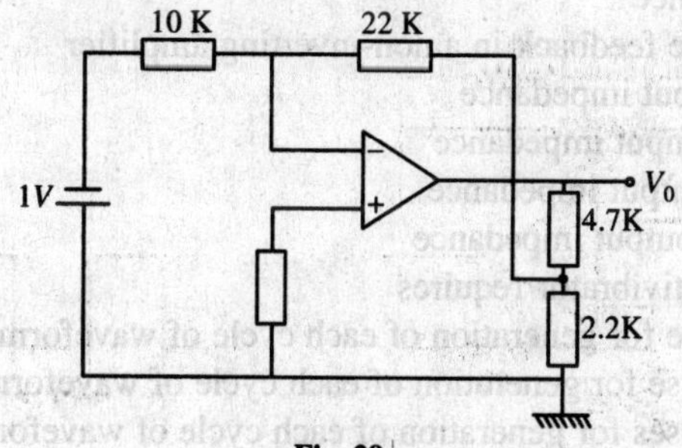

Fig. 29.

(Ans. 7·37*V***)**

30) Given that $V_z = 10$, $V_D = 0 \cdot 7$, $V_R = 4V$. Draw the transfer characteristic. (gain = ∞)

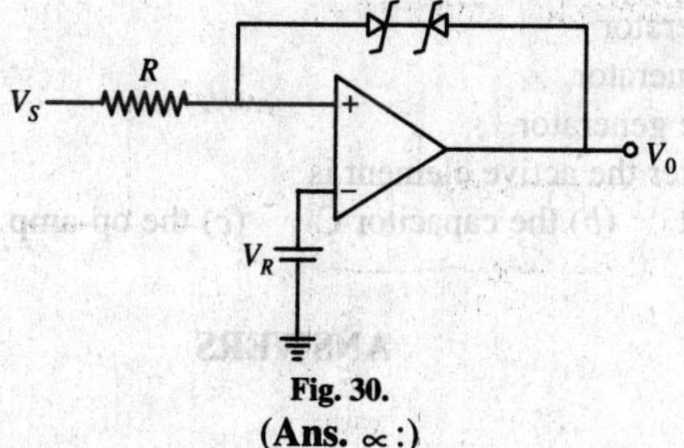

Fig. 30.

(Ans. ∞ **:)**

Choose the correct alternatives for any ten of the following:

31) A differential amplifier has a differential gain of 20,000. CMRR = 80dB. The common mode gain is given by
(*a*) 2 (*b*) 1 (*c*) ½ (*d*) 0 **[Ans. (*a*)]**

32) The gain V_0/V_{in} for the circuit is

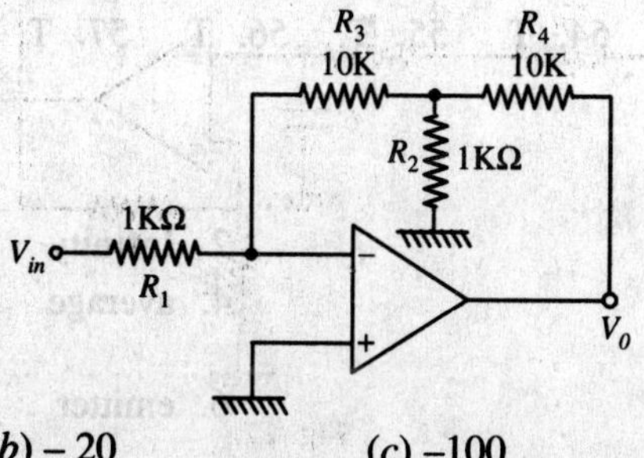

(*a*) –1 (*b*) – 20 (*c*) –100 (*d*) – 120 **[Ans. (*d*)]**

33) An a stable multivibrator generates
(*a*) triangular waveform (*b*) sinusoidal waveform (*c*) square waveform (*d*) none of these
[Ans. (*c*)]

34) According to Barkhausen criteria in order to sustain the oscillations
(*a*) loop gain of the circuit must be negligible
(*b*) loop gain of the circuit must be equal to unity
(*c*) the phase shift around the circuit must be 180
(*d*) none of these **[Ans. (*b*), (*c*)]**

35) An instrumentation amplifier has a high
(*a*) Supply voltage
(*b*) Power gain
(*c*) CMRR
(*d*) Output impedance **[Ans. (*c*)]**

36) The use of negative feedback in a non-inverting amplifier
(*a*) Increase the input impedance
(*b*) Decreases the input impedance
(*c*) Increases the output impedance
(*d*) Decreases the output impedance **[Ans. (*a*)]**

37) A monostable multivibrator requires
(*a*) no driving pulse for generation of each cycle of waveform
(*b*) one driving pulse for generation of each cycle of waveform
(*c*) two driving pulses for generation of each cycle of waveform
(*d*) four driving pulses for generation of each cycle of waveform **[Ans. (*b*)]**

38) Wien-bridge oscillator is basically a
(*a*) pulse generator
(*b*) sine wave generator
(*c*) square wave generator
(*d*) triangular wave generator **[Ans. (*b*)]**

39) In an active RC filter the active element is
(*a*) the resistance R (*b*) the capacitor C (*c*) the op-amp (*d*) none of these
[Ans. (*c*)]

ANSWERS

True/False

1. F	2. F	3. T	4. F	5. T	6. T	7. T	8. F	9. F	10. F
11. F	12. T	13. F	14. T	15. T	16. T	17. T	18. T	19. F	20. T
21. T	22. T	23. T	24. T	25. T	26. F	27. F	28. F	29. F	30. T
31. T	32. T	33. T	34. T	35. T	36. F	37. F	38. F	39. T	40. F
41. T	42. F	43. F	44. T	45. F	46. F	47. T	48. T	49. T	50. T
51. T	52. T	53. T	54. T	55. T	56. T	57. T	58. T	59. F	60. F
61. T	62. T								

Fill up the blanks

1. Diff. Amplifier
2. Infinity
3. large
4. average
5. $\frac{R_c}{r_e}$
6. emitter
7. direct
8. same

9. $\frac{R_C}{2r_e}$
10. long tail pair
11. I/P offset current
12. common mode
13. 100 μV
14. Zero
15. level shifting stage
16. output
17. operational amplifier
18. $\frac{R_C}{r_e}$
19. operational amplifier
20. Difference
21. Dual input (1) balanced output, and (2) unbalanced output, single input (3) balanced and (4) unbalanced output.
22. higher
23. CMRR
24. Cascode
25. infinity
26. Zero
27. Collector
28. voltage gain
29. diodes
30. output voltage
31. Difference
32. infinity
33. Swamping resistor
34. Direct coupling
35. performance
36. CE & CB
37. $2\,\beta_{ac}\,r_e$
38. $A_d = g_{md}\,R_d$
39. Input impedance of 1st stage overall o/p impedance of the last stage.
40. I_K (constant current)
41. triangle
42. Filter circuits
43. Distortion
44. Negative feedback
45. common mode signals
46. half
47. R_E
48. four
49. Balanced output
50. CE & CB
51. non-equality of the transistor
52. $V_0\,\omega$
53. level shifter
54. level shifter
55. $2\,\beta_{ac}\,r_e$ & R_c
56. rejection/elimination
57. Push-Pull configuration.
58. unity gain.

ADDITIONAL MULTIPLE CHOICE QUESTIONS

1. Feedback in an operational amplifier done due to unsuitability of open loop operational amplifier linear application
   (*a*) to increase I/P impedance
   (*b*) to increase gain.
2. Slew rate is (*a*) large signal phenomena (*b*) low signal phenomena (*c*) a medium signal phenomena.
3. I/P bias current is always (*a*) greater (*b*) equal (*c*) less than input offset current.
4. In an ideal operational amplifier the input impedance is
   (*a*) zero (*b*) infinite (*c*) 1kΩ
5. Which of the following needs ckt one supply
   (*a*) μ A F91 (*b*) LM 201 (*c*) LM 324
6. Operational amplifier offset voltage due to input bias ckt can be significantly reduced if we use (*a*) offset compensatory network (*b*) offset minimizing resistance.
7. The bandwidth of closed loop operational amplifier is
   (*a*) $f_F = f_o(1 + A\beta)$ (*b*) $f_F = f_o / (1 + A)$
   (*c*) $f_F = f_o / (1 + A\beta)$ (*d*) none of them.
8. The total output offset voltage of closed loop operational amplifier is
   (*a*) $V_{out} = \pm V_{sat}\ (1 + AB)$ (*b*) $V_{ooT} = \pm V_{sat}\left(1 + \frac{R_F}{R_i}\right)$
   (*c*) $V_{ooT} = \pm \frac{V_{sat}}{1 + A\beta}$ (*d*) none of the above
9. In small scale integration no. of components are
   (*a*) < 10 (*b*) < 20 (*c*) > 10 (*d*) < 100
10. In VLSI no. of components are
   (*a*) > 100 (*b*) > 1000 (*c*) < 1000 (*d*) none
11. Temp. way of unitary operational amplifier
   (*a*) –65°C tr. 125°C (*b*) –55°C tr. 125°C
   (*c*) –75°C tr. 125°C (*d*) –55°C tr. 125°C
12. If I/P frequency exceeds the slew rate the output will be
   (*a*) distorted (*b*) not distorted (*c*) amplified
13. DIP pack is best for experimenting because it is
   (*a*) easy mounting (*b*) manufactured with strong casing (*c*) cheap

13 *a*. Transient response is a
   (*a*) small signal phenomena (*b*) large signal phenomena (*c*) All signal phenomena

14. For a voltage series feedback configuration, gain β of the feedback is
   (*a*) AR_F (*b*) $\frac{R_i}{R_i + R_F}$ (*c*) $\frac{R_F}{R_l + R_F}$

15. The slew rate has
(*a*) positive temp. coefficient
(*b*) negative temperature coefficient
(*c*) none of the above

16. The 1st generation operational amplifier came out in
(*a*) 1978 (*b*) 1968 (*c*) 1965

17. The practical operational amplifier has
(*a*) infinte B.W. (*b*) B.W. of 100 MHz
(*c*) finite B.W. (*d*) none of the above

18. In the current to voltage converter the o/p voltage is given by
(*a*) $-I_{in} R_1$ (*b*) $I_{IN} R_F$ (*c*) $-I_{IN} R_F$

19. μ A 741 is a chip of type
(*a*) industrial (*b*) military (*c*) commercial

20. Which of the following requires different values of power supply ?
(*a*) μ A 702 (*b*) LN 324 (*c*) μ A 714

21. The code SN stands for
(*a*) National semiconductor (*b*) Texas industry (*c*) Fairchild.

22. In the major blocks of an operational amplifier the intermediate stage is followed by
(*a*) differential amplifier stage (*b*) class B push-pull amplifier
(*c*) level shifting stage.

23. Slew rate is defined by
(*a*) $\left.\frac{dV}{dt}\right|_{max}$ (*b*) $\left.\frac{dI}{dt}\right|_{max}$ (*c*) None of the above

24. Bandwidth with unity gain for μu A 741 is
(*a*) 1MHz (*b*) 2 MHz (*c*) 3 MHz

25. In case of shunt voltage feedback the bandwidth with feedback can be given by
(*a*) $BW(1+\beta A)$ (*b*) $\frac{BW}{1+\beta A}$ (*c*) $B.W. \times \beta A$

26. Input bias current is always
(*a*) greater (*b*) less (*c*) equal to transistor's input offset current.

27. The use of negative feedback in non-inverting amplifier increases
(*a*) I/P resistance & B.W. (*b*) I/P and o/p resistance (*c*) bandwidth.

28. The operational amplifier can be nulled by
(*a*) using an offset voltage compensating network
(*b*) using an error minimizing resistance
(*c*) cutting off the power supplies

29. Slew rate limiting occurs with
(*a*) large fast changing signals
(*b*) small signals with big time periods
(*c*) all high frequency signals.

30. For a given operational amplifier $CMRR = 10^5$ at $A_d = 10^5$, then the A_c of the operational amplifier will be
(*a*) 10^{10} (*b*) 10^5 (*c*) 1 (*d*) 10

31. Open loop configuration of operational amplifier is not needed for
(*a*) linear operation (*b*) nonlinear operation (*c*) none of these.

32. In an operational amplifier offset voltage compensatory network the relation among resistances is
(*a*) $R_b > R_c > R_{max}$ (*b*) $R_b > R_{max} > R_a$
(*c*) $R_c > R_{max} > R_s$ (*d*) $R_c < R_a < R_{max}$

33. The gain with feedback of a voltage shunt feedback amplifier is
(*a*) $1+\frac{R_F}{R_i}$ (*b*) $1-\frac{R_F}{R}$ (*c*) $-\frac{R_F}{R_1}$ (*d*) $\frac{R_F}{R_i}$

34. An example of programable operational amplifier is
(*a*) LN 318 (*b*) μ A 791
(*c*) μ A 776 (*d*) μ A 291

35. The type of linear IC package used in μ A 741 is
(*a*) the flat pack
(*b*) the metal cane or transistor pack
(*c*) the dual in line package.

FILL IN THE BLANKS

1. ____________ is the manufacturing company of LN 741.
2. Incase of ideal operational amplifier the CMRR should be ____________.
3. Slew rate ____________ with the increase of temperature.
4. The gain of the inverting amplifiers of an operational amplifier is the ratio of ____________ with the resistance.
5. Because of ____________ with the operational amplifier the gain decreases will frequency ?
6. The input offset voltage ____________ with negative feedback.
7. Voltage follower is a special case of ____________.
8. ____________ is used for military purpose.
9. The standard supply voltage for an ordinary operational amplifier is ____________ .
10. The gain of the differential circuit increases with increase in frequency at a rate of ____.
11. Slew rate is a ____________ phenomenon.
12. If output voltage of a circuit is equal to and in phase with the input then circuit is called ____________.
13. The integration and differentiation are most commonly used in ____________.
14. In operational amplifier differentiator circuit if I/P is a square wave then output will be ____________.
15. Output of an operational amplifier can never exceed ____________.
16. The main advantage of closed loop operational amplifier is ____________.
17. When negative feedback is applied in an operational amplifier the BW decrease ____________.
18. The bendwidth of most open loop operational amplifier is ____________.
19. Total output offset voltage decreases by an amount of ____________ if applying negative feedback.
20. The gain-boodwidth product of the of μ A 741 IC is ____________.

21. The temperature range of military operational amplifier is __________ .
22. The value of feedback factor β is __________ .
23. Operational amplifier with single break frequency is inherently stable because the total phase shift never exceeds __________ .
24. If the slew rate is exceeded __________ of the output waveform results.
25. Open loop gain of an operational amplifier successively decreases at a rate of __________ after each break frequency.
26. For the voltage follower the value of β is __________ .
27. LM 101 is a __________ generation op. amp.
28. IC's are classified is monolithic and __________ .
29. μ A signifies the manufacturer's name of ....
30. The unity gain bandwidth is a __________ phenomenon whereas the slew rate is a __________ phenomenon.
31. As slew rate increases the BW of a operational amplifier __________ .
32. μ A 741 is an __________ compensated operational amplifier.
33. The resistance ROM connected to inverting terminal to compensate for o/p offset voltage caused by I/p bias current is __________ .
34. An operational amplifier which uses different power supplies is __________ .
35. The gain of –ve feedback inverting amplifier is __________ .
36. Bandwidth is a __________ signal phenomena.
37. In practical cascaded operational amplifier the bandwidth is __________ in comparison with one stage.
38. If the capacitor charging current is 15 μ A and capacitor value 3PF, this SR is __________ V/μs.
39. The first introduced operational amplifier was __________ .
40. If $A_d = 10^5$ and $A_c = 1$, then CMMR of operational amplifier is __________ .
41. The third stage of operational amplifier building block is __________ .
42. Slew rate is a function of __________ .
43. Transient response is a __________ phenomena and B.W is a signal phenomena.
44. A special case of three non-inverting amplifier is the voltage follower, while the current to voltage converter and the inverter are two special cases of the __________ amplifier.
45. To achieve a stable current the phase angle of the loop gain must be greater than __________ when its magnitude reaches unity.
46. Most digital IC's are __________ .
47. __________ requires only one power supply.
48. How fast can the o/p of an operational amplifier change by 10 V/μ sec of its slew rate is 1 V/μs (Fill up) __________ .

TRUE OR FALSE

1. Slew rate is a small signal phenomena.
2. Positive feedback is never expected in operational amplifier.

3. The closed loop gain of the operational amplifier is infinity.
4. The ideal operational amplifier has zero offset and zero drift.
5. As slew rate increases the B.W. of operational amplifier decrease.
6. The operational amplifier 324 requires, two different power supplies.
7. The error voltage can be both positive and negative.
8. The current shown in the figure represents an integrator.

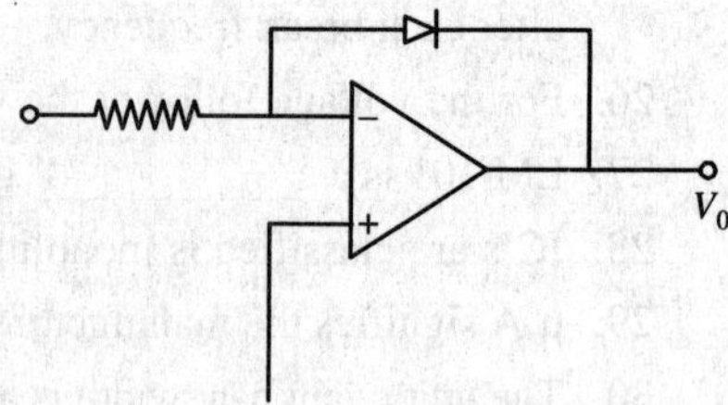

9. The voltage follower is a special case of non-inverting amplifier.
10. Operational amplifier can amplify any ac signal.
11. The first inverted operational amplifier was μ A 709.
12. μ A 741 is an internally frequency compensated operational amplifier.
13. R_{OM} is used to minimize error voltage.
14. Compensated network can control phase shift.
15. Input bias circuit depends on temp.
16. The I/p offset voltage is difference voltage that exists between terminals 2 & 3 of μ A 741 without any external input applied.
17. The input bias current I_b is always equal to I_{b1} & I_{b2}.
18. The value of offset minimizing resistor is $R_1 \parallel R_F$.
19. One of the most common uses of the current to voltage converter is in sensing current from photodetectors.
20. With the increase in input frequency slew rate decreases.
21. PSSR depends on frequency.
22. Transient response is time variant.
23. Input bias current depends upon temperature.
24. Slew rate of an ideal operational amplifier is infinity.
25. The gain of an operational amplifier varies with frequency.
26. O/p impedance of an ideal operational amplifier is zero.
27. The DIP is widely used because it can be mounted easily.
28. Bandwidth is a large signal phenomenon.
29. Introduction of negative feedback decreases gain.
30. If bandwidth exceeded, the O/p voltage is reduced.
31. Lower value of power supply rejection ratio causes smaller amount of offset voltage.

32. Operational amplifiers require two power supplies.
33. μ A 741 is a first generation operational amplifier.
34. For ideal operational amplifier I/p impedance is zero.
35. The temp. range of military operational amplifier is –25°C to –55°C.
36. LM 301 is a commercial variety of operational amplifier.
37. In operational amplifier differentive circuit, if I/p is square wave the O/p will be triangular wave.
38. If positive feedback is applied then the gain decreases.
39. If voltage is concerned with the ordinary and virtual ground are same but if current is concerned with them then they are different.
40. The open loop voltage gain for a high frequency operational amplifier is given by

$$A(f) = \frac{A}{1+(f/f_o)}$$

41. The error voltage is the rate of change of total o/p offset voltage V_{out}.
42. The year of 1st generation operational amplifier is 1967.
43. The operational amplifier is in phase with I/p for an inverting amplifier.
44. For ideal operational amplifier voltage gain is zero.

APPENDIX A

TABLE 1. Typical Electrical Characteristics of the μA 709 Op. Amp.

SPECIFICIATION (AT 25C AND 15V SUPPLIES)	VALUE	UNIT
Input Offset Voltage (10K or less source)	1.0	mV
8 Input Offset Current	50	nA
Input Bias Current	200	nA
Input Resistance	400	kΩ
Output Resistance	150	Ω
Power Dissipation	80	mW
Input Offset-Voltage Drift	6.0	μVC
Voltage Gain (open.-loop)	45.000	
	93	dB
Output Voltage Swing (R_L = 10K or more)	14	V
(R_L = 2K)	13	V
Input Voltage Range	10	V
CMRR (10K or less source resistance)	90	dB

TABLE 2. Typical Electrical Characteristics of the LM101 Op. Amp.

SPECIFICIATION (AT 25C AND 15V SUPPLIES)	VALUE	UNIT
Input Offset Voltage (10K or less source)	1.0	mV
Input Offset Current	40	nA
Input Bias Current	120	nA
Input Resistance	800	kΩ
Power Dissipation	50	mW
Input Offset-Voltage Drift	6.0	μVC
Voltage Gain (open.-loop)	160.000	
	104	dB
Output Voltage Swing (R_L = 10K or more)	14	V
(R_L = 2K)	13	V
Input Voltage Range	13	V
CMRR (10K or less source resistance)	90	dB

TABLE 3. Typical Electrical Characteristics of the μA 741 Op. Amp.

SPECIFICIATION (AT 25C AND 15V SUPPLIES)	VALUE	UNIT
Input Offset Voltage (10K or less source)	2.0	mV
Input Offset Current	20	nA
Input Bias Current	80	nA
Input Resistance	2.0	MΩ
Output Resistance	75	Ω
Power Dissipation	50	mW
Input Offset-Voltage Drift	15	μVC
Voltage Gain (open.-loop)	200.000	
	106	dB
Output Voltage Swing (R_L = 10K or more)	14	V
(R_L = 2K)	13	V
Input Voltage Range	13	V
CMRR (10K or less source resistance)	90	dB

TABLE 4. Output Offset in General-Purpose IC Op. Amps. Due to Typical (20 nA) and Maximum (200 nA) Values of Input Offset Current

FEED BACK RESISTOR R2 (OHMS)	OUTPUT OFFSET: I_{OS} = 20 nA	$E_{OS} = I_{OS} \times R2$ I_{OS} = 200 nA
100	2 μV	20 μV
1K	20 μ V	200 μ V
10K	0.2 mV	2 mV
100K	2 mV	200 mV
1M	20 mV	200 mV

TABLE 5. Output Offset in General-Purpose IC Op. Amps. Due to Typical (80 nA) and Maximum (500 nA) Values of Input Offset Current

FEED BACK RESISTOR R2 (OHMS)	OUTPUT OFFSET: I_{OS} = 20 nA	$E_{OS} = I_B \times R2$ I_B = 500 nA
100	8 μV	50 μV
1K	80 μ V	500 μ V
10K	0.8 mV	5 mV
100K	8 mV	50 mV
1M	80 mV	500 mV

TABLE 6. Effect of Source Resistance on Output in a Noninverter (for R1 = 1K, R2 = 100K, and I_B = 80 nA)

SOURCE RESISTANCE R_S (OHMS)	OUTPUT OFFSET FROM + INPUT $I_2 \times R_s$ (1 + R2R1)	OUTPUT OFFSET FROM – INPUT $I_s \times R2$	TOTAL OUTPUT OFFSET $I_S \times R2$ – $I_s \times R_s$ (1 + R2R1)
10	0.08 mV	8 mV	7.0 mV
100	0.8 mV	8 mV	7.2 mV
600	4.8	8 mV	3.2 mV
1.2 K	9.6 mV	8 mV	– 1.6 mV
2K	16.0 mV	8 mV	– 8.0 mV

TABLE 7. Effects of Negative Feedback

Feedback	Bandwidth	$R_{in}(CL)$	$R_{out}(CL)$	$R_{dist}(CL)$	$R_{oo}(CL)$	Stabilized
Noninverting voltage	Larger	Higher	Lower	Lower	Lower	v_{out}/v_{in}
Noninverting voltage	Larger	Higher	Lower	Lower	Lower	i_{out}/v_{in}
Noninverting voltage	Larger	Higher	Lower	Lower	Lower	v_{out}/v_{in}
Noninverting voltage	Larger	Higher	Lower	Lower	Lower	i_{out}/v_{in}

APPENDIX B

1. Typical Parameters of Popular Op. Amps.

Number	$I_{in(bias)}$ nA	$I_{in(off)}$ nA	$I_{out(max)}$ mA	$V_{in(off)}$ mA	f_{unity} MHz	Slew rate V/μs
LF351	0.05	0.025	20	5	4	13
LF353	0.05	0.025	20	5	4	13
LF355	0.03	0.003	20	3	2.5	5
LF356	0.03	0.003	20	3	5	12
LM10C	12	0.4	20	0.5	0.1	0.12
LM11C	0.025	0.0005	2	0.1	0.5	0.3
LM301C	70	3	10	2	1	0.5
LM307	70	3	10	2	1	0.5
LM308	1.5	0.2	5	2	0.3	0.15
LM312	1.5	0.2	6	2	1	0.1
LM318	150	30	21	4	15	70
LM324	45	5	20	2	1	0.5
LM348	30	4	25	1	1	0.5
LM258	45	5	40	2	1	0.5
LM709	300	100	42	2	*	0.25
LM739	300	50	1.5	1	6	1
LM741C	80	20	25	2	1	0.5
LM747C	80	20	25	2	1	0.5
LM748	80	20	27	2	*	*
LM1458	200	80	20	1	1	0.5
LM4250	*	*	*	3-5	*	*
LM13080	*	*	250	3	1	*
NE531	400	50	20	2	1	35
TL071	0.03	0.005	10	3	3	13
TL072	0.03	0.005	10	3	3	13
TL074	0.05	0.025	17	5	4	13

APPENDIX C

TABLE 1. Chebyshev Polynomials

n	Chebyshev polynomials, $C_s(\omega) = \cos(n \cos^{-1} \omega)$
0	1
1	ω
2	$2\omega^2 - 1$
3	$4\omega^2 - 3\omega$
4	$8\omega^4 - 8\omega^2 + 1$
5	$16\omega^5 - 20\omega^2 + 5\omega$
6	$32\omega^3 - 48\omega^2 + 18\omega^2 - 1$
7	$64\omega^7 - 112\omega^5 + 56\omega^2 - 7\omega$
8	$128\omega^8 - 256\omega^6 + 160\omega^4 - 32\omega^2 + 1$
9	$256\omega^9 - 576\omega^7 + 432\omega^5 - 120\omega^3 + 9\omega$
10	$512\omega^{10} - 1280\omega^8 + 1120\omega^4 - 400\omega^4 + 50\omega^2 - 1$

TABLE 2. Butterworth LP Filter Transfer Function = 1/D(*s*)

n	D(s) [Transfer Function = 1/D(s)]
1	$s + 1$
2	$s^2 + \sqrt{2}\ s + 1$
3	$s^3 + 2s^3 + 2s + 1 = (s + 1)(s^2 + s + 1)$
4	$s^4 + 2.613\ s^3 + 3.414\ s^2 + 2.613\ s + 1 = (s^2 + 0.7653\ s + 1)(s^2 + 1.8477\ s + 1)$
5	$s^5 + 3.2336\ s^4 + 5.236\ s^3 + 5.236\ s^2 + 3.236\ s + 1 = (s + 1)(s^2 + 0.6180\ s + 1)$ $(s^2 + 1.6180\ s)$
6	$s^6 + 3.863\ s^5 + 7.464\ s^4 + 9.141\ s^3 + 7.464\ s^2 + 3.863\ s + 1$ $= (s^2 + 0.5176\ s + 1)(s^2 + \sqrt{2}\ s + 1)(s^2 + 1.9318\ s + 1)$
7	$s^7 + 4.493\ s^6 + 10.097\ s^5 + 14.591\ s^4 + 14.591\ s^3 + 10.097\ s^2 + 4.493\ s + 1)$ $= (s + 1)(s^2 + 0.4450\ s + 1)(s^2 + 1.2470\ s + 1)(s^2 + 1.802\ s + 1)$
8	$s^8 + 5.125\ s^7 + 13.137\ s^4 + 21.846\ s^3 + 25.68\ s^3 + 13.137\ s^2 + 515\ s + 1$ $= (s^2 + 0.3902\ s + 1)(s^2 + 1.1110\ s + 1)(s^2 + 1.6630\ s + 1)(s^2 + 1.9616\ s + 1)$
9	$s^9 + 5.758\ s^8 + 16.581\ s^7 + 31.163\ s^6 + 41.986\ s^5 + 41.986\ s^4$ $+ 31.163\ s^3 + 16.581\ s^2 + 5.758\ s + 1$ $= (s + 1)(s^2 + 0.3474\ s + 1)(s^2 + s + 1)(s^2 + 1.5320\ s + 1)(s^2 + 1.8794\ s + 1)$
10	$s^{10} + 6.392\ s^9 + 20.431\ s^8 + 42.802\ s^7 + 64.882\ s^6 + 74.233\ s^5$ $+ 64.882\ s^4 + 42.802\ s^3 + 20.431\ s^2 + 6.392\ s + 1$ $= (s^2 + 0.3128s + 1)(s^2 + 0.908s + 1)(s^2 + 1.414\ s + 1)(s^2 + 1.781\ s + 1)(s^2 + 1.975\ s + 1)$

APPENDIX D

BoMOS Operational Amplifier

Features

Directly replaces industry type 741 in most applications

Very High Input Impedance : 1.5 T Ω typ

Very Low Input Current : 10 pA typ

: at ± 15 V

Low Input Offset Voltage : 2mV (max)

Wide Bandwidth : 4.5 MHz unity gain at ± 15V

High Slew Rate : 9V/μ s

Internal Compensation

Electrical Characteristics at T_A = 25°C

DC Supply Voltage : 36V (max)

(Between V$^+$ and V$^-$ terminals)

Differential Input Voltage : ± 8V (max)

DC Input Voltage : (V$^+$ + 8 V) to (V$^-$ – 0.5V)

Output Short-circuit Duration : Indefinite

Large Signal Voltage Gain : 100K

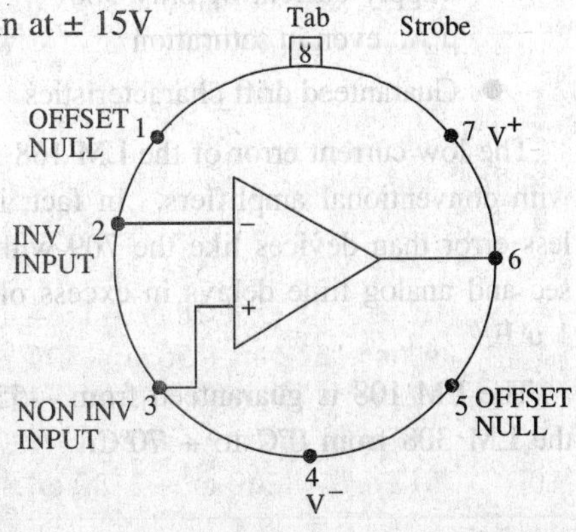

Fig. 1

Applications

Ground referenced single supply amplifiers in automobile and portable instrumentation • Sample and hold amplifiers • Long duration timers multivibrators (Microseconds minutes hours) • Photo current instrumentation • Active filters • All standard operational amplifier applications.

Package	Operating Temp. Range
8 Lead TO-5	– 55 to + 125°C

Operational Amplifier/Buffers

LM108/LM 208/LM308 Operational Amplifier

General Description

The LM108 series are precision operational amplifiers having specifications a factor of ten better than FET amplifiers over a –55°C to +125°C temperature range. Selected units are available with offset voltages less than 1.0 mV and drifts less than 5μV/°C, again over the military temperature range. This makes it possible to eliminate offset adjustments, in most cases, and obtain performance approaching chopper stabilized amplifiers.

The devices operate with supply voltages from ± 2V to ± 20V and have sufficient supply rejection to use unregulated supplies. Although the circuit is interchangeable with and uses the same compensation as the LM 101A, an alternate compensation scheme can be used to make it particularly insensitive to power supply noise and to make supply bypass capacitors unnecessary. Outstanding characteristics include:

- Maximum input bias current of 3.0 nA over temperature
- Offset current less than 400 pA, over temperature
- Supply current of only 300 μ A, even in saturation
- Guaranteed drift characteristics

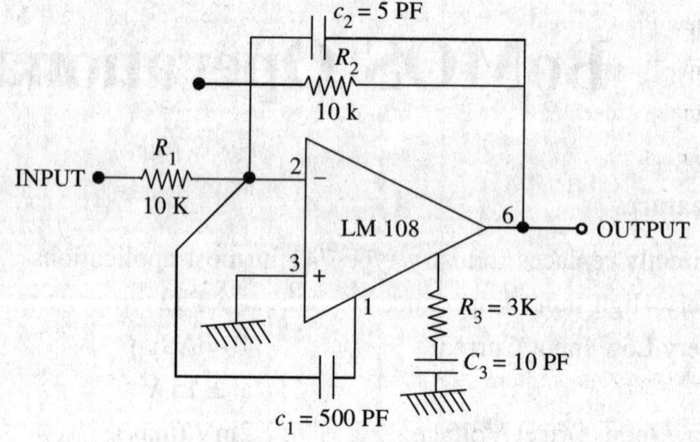

Fig. 2

The low current error of the LM 108 series makes possible many designs that are not practical with conventional amplifiers. In fact, it operates from 10 MΩ source resistance, introducing less error than devices like the 709 with 10Ω sources. Integrators with drifts less than 500μV/sec and analog time delays in excess of one hour can be made using capacitors no larger than 1 μ F.

The LM 108 is guaranteed from – 55°C to + 125°C, the LM 208 from – 25° to + 85°C, and the LM 308 from 0°C to + 70°C.

Absolute maximum ratings

	LM108/LM208	LM308
Supply Voltage	± 20V	± 18V
Power Dissipation (Note 1)	500 mW	500 mW
Differential Input Current (Note 2)	± 10 mA	± 10 mA
Input Voltage (Note 3)	± 15 V	± 15 V
Output Short-Circuit Duration	Indefinite	Indefinite
Operating Temperature Range (LM 108)	– 55° to +125°C	0°C to +70°C
(LM208)	– 25°C to +85°C	
Storage Temperature Range	– 65°C to +150°C	– 65°C to +150°C
Lead Temperature	(Soldering, 10 seconds)	300°C

Electrical characteristics (Note 4)

PARAMETER	CONDITIONS	LM108/LM208			LM308			UNITS
		MIN	TYP	MAX	MIN	TYP	MAX	
Input Offset Voltage	T_A = 25°C		0.7	2.0		2.0	7.5	mV
Input Offset Current	T_A = 25°C		0.05	0.2		0.2	1	nA
Input Bias Current	T_A = 25°C		0.8	2.0		1.5	7	nA
Input Resistance	T_A = 25°C	30	70		10	40		mΩ
Supply Current	T_A = 25°C		0.3	0.6		0.3	0.8	mA
Large Signal Voltage Gain	T_A = 25°C, T_S = ± 15V. V_{OUT} = ± 10 V R_L ≥ 10 k Ω	50	300		25	300		V/mV
Input Offset Voltage				3.0			10	mV
Average Temperature Coefficient of Input Offset Voltage			3.0	15		6.0	30	μV/°C
Input Offset Current				0.4			1.5	nA
Average Temperature Coefficient of Input Offset Current			0.5	2.5		2.0	10	pA/°C
Input Bias Current				30			10	nA
Supply Current	T_A = 125°C		0.15	0.4				mA
Large Signal Voltage Gain	V_S = ± 15 V V_{OUT} = ± 10 V R_L > 10 kΩ	25			15			V/mV
Output Voltage-Swing	V_S = ± 15 V R_L = 10 k Ω	± 13	± 14		± 13	± 14		V

Parameter	Conditions	Min	Typ	Max	Min	Typ	Max	Units
Input Voltage Range	$V_S = \pm 15$ V	± 13.5			± 14			V
Common-Mode Rejection Ratio		85	100		80	100		dB
Supply Voltage Rejection Ratio		80	96		80	96		

Note 1: The maximum junction temperature of the LM 108 is 150°C, for the LM 208, 100°C and for the LM 308, 85°C. For operating at elevated temperature, devices in the TO-5 package must be derated based on a thermal resistance of 150°CC/W, junction to ambient, or 45°C/W, junction to case. For the flat package, the derating is based on a thermal resistance of 185°C/W when mounted on a 1/16 inch thick epoxy glass board with ten, 0.03 inch wide, 2 ounce copper conductors. The thermal resistance of the dual-in-line package is 100°C/W, junction to ambient.

Note 2: The inputs are shunted with back-to-back diodes for overvoltage protection. Therefore, excessive current will flow if a differential input voltage in excess of 1V is applied between the input unless some limiting resistance is used.

Note 3: For supply voltages less than ± 15V, the acute maximum input voltage is equal to the supply voltage.

Note 4: These specifications apply for $\pm 5V \le V_s \le \pm 20$ V and $-55°C \le T_A \le 125°C$, unless otherwise specified. With the LM 208, however, all temperature specifications are limited to $-25°C \le T_A \le 85°C$, and for the LM308 they are limited to $0°C \le T_A \le 70°C$.

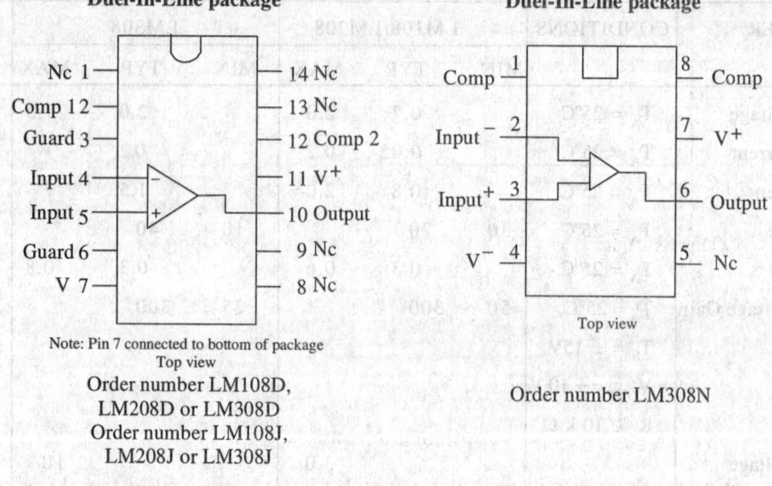

Fig. 3

Operational Amplifiers/Buffers

LM124/LM224/LM324 LM124A/LM224A/LM324A, LM2902

Low power quad operational amplifiers

General Description

The LM124 series consists of four independent, high gain, internally frequency compensated operational amplifiers which were designed specifically to operate from a single power supply over a wide range of voltages. Operation from split power supplies is also possible and the low power supply current drain is independent of the magnitude of the power supply voltage.

Application areas include transducer amplifier, dc gain blocks and all the conventional operational amplifier circuits which now can be more easily implemented in single power supply systems. For example, the LM124 series can be directly operated off of the standard + 5 V_{DC} power supply voltage which is used in digital systems and will easily provide the required interface electronics without requiring the additional ± 15 V_{DC} power supplies.

Unique characteristics

- In the linear mode the input common-mode voltage range includes ground and the output voltage can also swing to ground, even though operated from only a single power supply voltage.
- The unity gain cross frequency is temperature compensated.
- The input bias current is also temperature compensated.

Connection diagram

Duel-In-Line and flat package

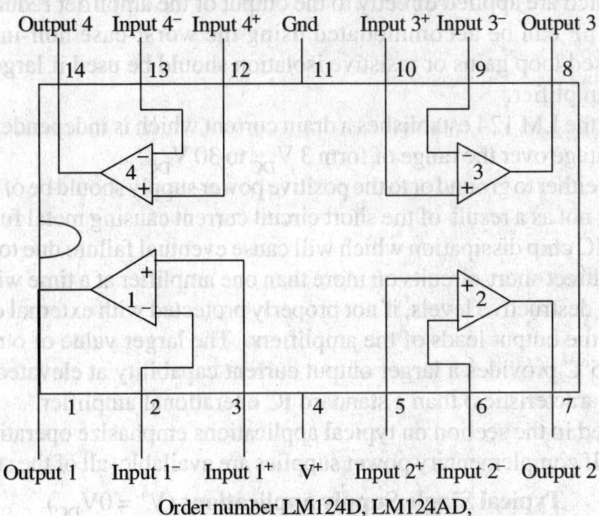

Order number LM124D, LM124AD,
LM224D or LM224AD
Order number LM124F, LM124AF,
LM224F or LM224AF

Fig. 4

Application hints

The LM 124 series are operational amplifiers which operate with only a single power supply voltage, have true-differential inputs, and remain in the linear mode with an input common-mode voltage of 0 V_{DC}. These amplifiers operate over a wide range of power supply voltage with little change in performance characteristics. At 25ºC amplifier operation is possible down to a minimum supply voltage of 2.3 V_{DC}.

The inputs of the package have been designed to simplify. PC board layouts. Inverting inputs are adjacent to outputs for all of the amplifiers and the outputs have also been placed at the corners of the package (pins 1, 7, 8, and 14).

Precautions should be taken to insure that the power supply for the integrated circuit never becomes reversed in polarity or that the unit is not inadvertently installed backwards in a test socket as an unlimited current surge through the resulting forward diode within the IC could cause fusing of the internal conductors and result in a destroyed unit.

Large differential input voltages can be easily accommodated and, as input differential voltage protection diodes are not needed, no large input currents result from large differential input voltages. The differential input voltage may be larger than V^+ without damaging the device. Protection should be provided to prevent the input voltages from going negative more than –0.3 V_{DC} (at 25ºC). An input clamp diode with a resistor to the IC input terminal can be used.

To reduce the power supply current drain, the amplifiers have a class A output stage for small signal levels which converts to class B in a large signal mode. This allows the amplifiers to both source and sink large output currents. Therefore both NPN and PNP external current boost transistors can be used to extend the power capability of the basic amplifiers. The output voltage needs to raise approximately 1 diode drop above ground to bias the on-chip vertical PNP transistor for output current sinking applications.

For ac applications, where the load is capacitively coupled to the output of the amplifier, a resistor should be used, from the output of the amplifier to ground to increase the class A bias current and prevent crossover distortion. Where the load is directly coupled, as in dc applications, there is no crosover distortion.

Capacitive loads which are applied directly to the output of the amplifier reduce the loop stability margin. Values of 50 pF can be accommodated using the worst-case non-inverting unity gain connection. Large closed loop gains or resistive isolation should be used if larger load capacitance must be driven by the amplifier.

The bias network of the LM 124 establishes a drain current which is independent of the magnitude of the power supply voltage over the range of form 3 V_{DC} to 30 V_{DC}.

Output short circuits either to ground or to the positive power supply should be of short time duration. Units can be destroyed, not as a result of the short circuit current causing metal fusing, but rather due to the large increase in IC chip dissipation which will cause eventual failure due to excessive junction temperatures. Putting direct short-circuits on more than one amplifier at a time will increase the total IC power dissipation to destructive levels, if not properly protected with external dissipation limiting resistors in series with the output leads of the amplifiers. The larger value of output source current which is available at 25ºC provides a larger output current capability at elevated temperatures (see typical performance characteristics) than a standard IC operational amplifier.

The circuits presented in the section on typical applications emphasize operation on only a single power supply voltage. If complementary power supplies are available, all of the standard operational

Typical Single Supply applications ($V^+ = 0V_{DC}$)

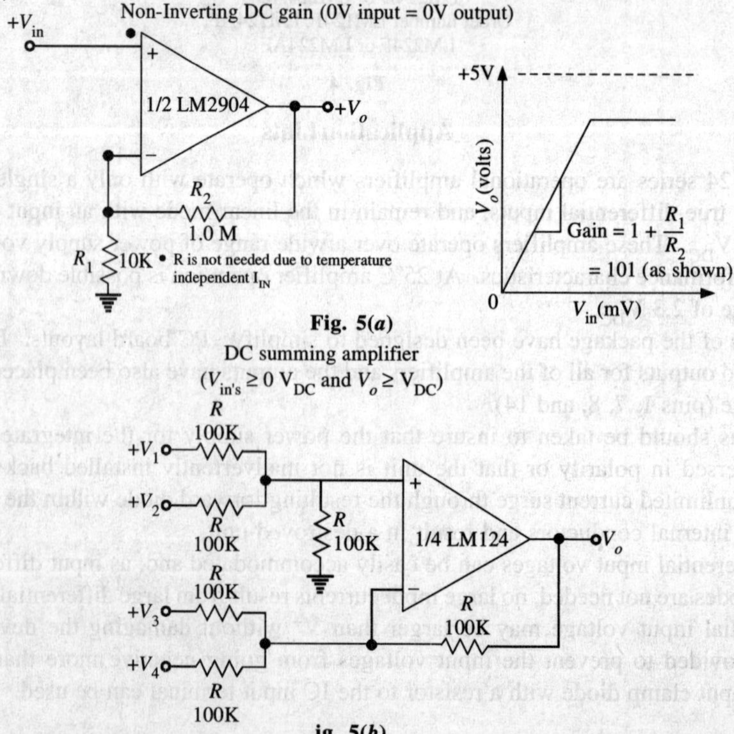

Fig. 5(*a*)

ig. 5(*b*)

When $V_0 = (V_1 + V_2) - (V_3 + V_4)$ $(V_1 + V_2) \geq (V_3 + V_4)$ to keep $V_0 \rangle 0V_{DC}$ amplifier circuits can be used. In general, introducing a pseudo-ground (a bias voltage reference of $V^+/2$) will allow operation above and below this value in single power supply systems. Many application circuits are shown which take advantage of the wide input common-mode voltage range which includes ground. In most cases, input biasing is not required and input voltages which range to ground can easily be accommodated.

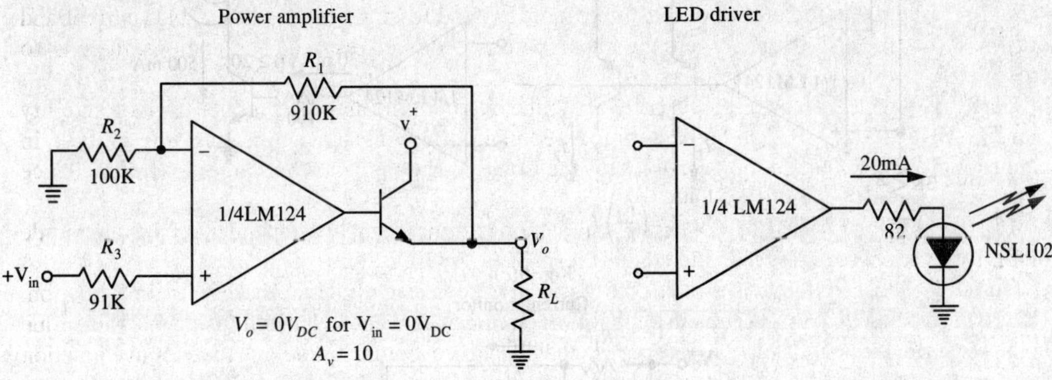

Fig. 6(*a*)

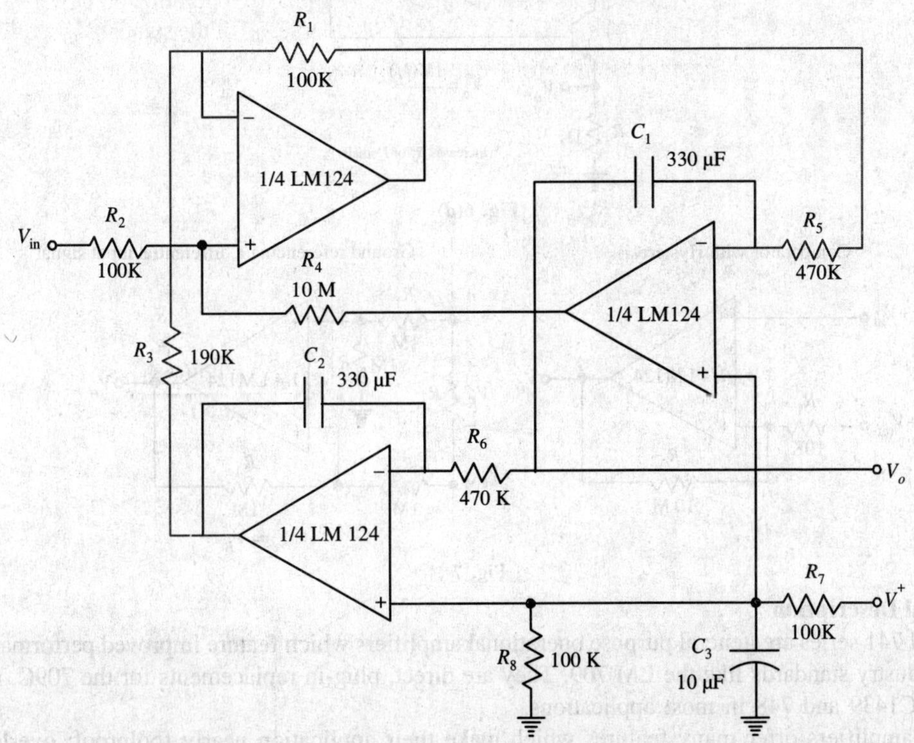

Fig. 6(*b*)

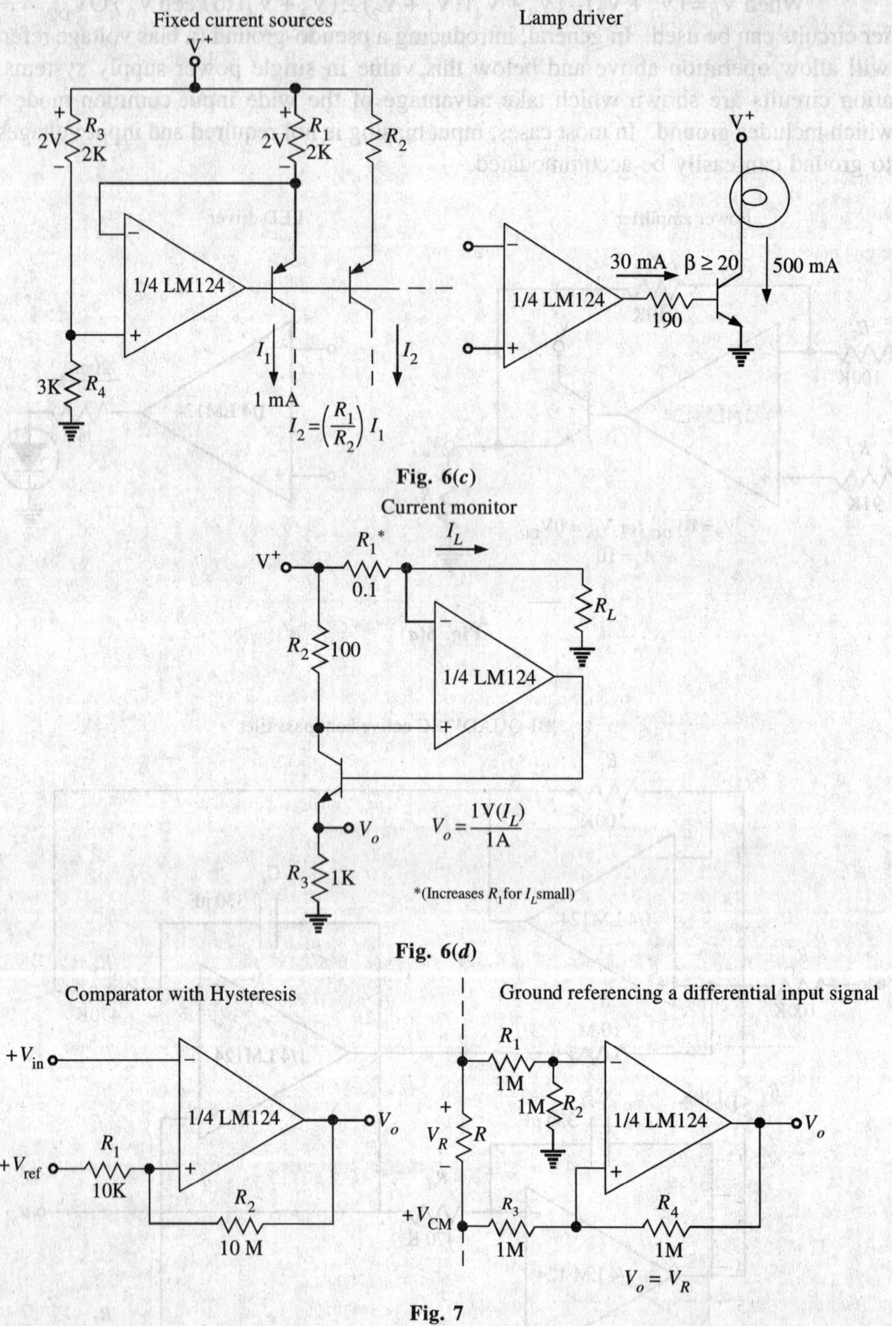

Fig. 6(*c*)

Fig. 6(*d*)

Fig. 7

General Description

The LM 741 series are general purpose operational amplifiers which feature improved performance over industry standards like the LM 709. They are direct, plug-in replacements for the 709C, LM 201, MC1439 and 748 in most applications.

The amplifiers offer many features which make their application nearly foolproof: overload protection on the input and output, no latch-up when the common mode range is exceeded, as well as freedom from oscillations.

The LM741/LM741E are identical to the LM741/LM741A except that the LM741C/LM741E have their performance guaranteed over a 0ºC to 7ºC temperature range, instead of –55º to + 125ºC.

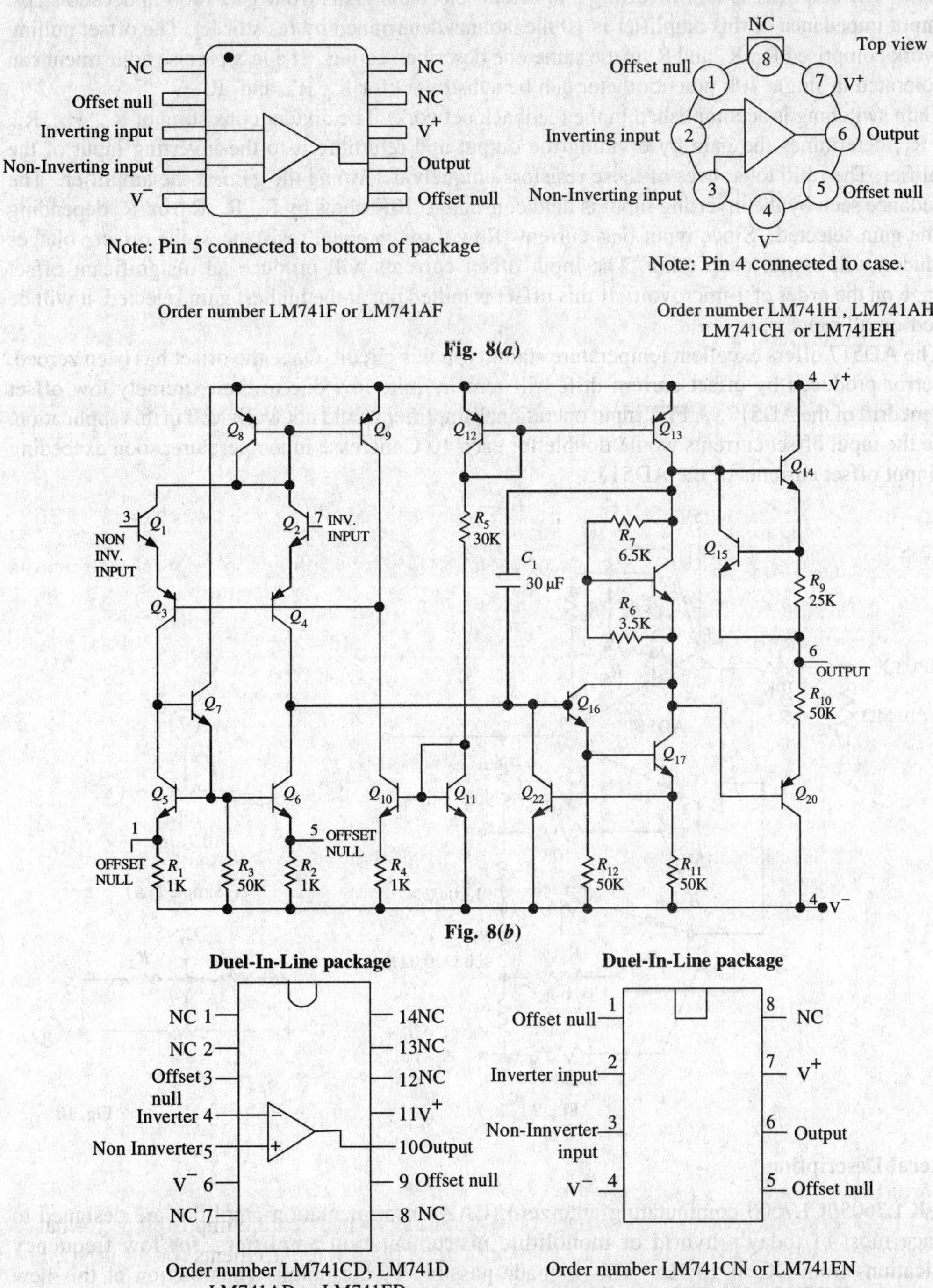

Fig. 8(c)

AN INSTRUMENT INPUT AMPLIFIER USING THE AD517L

The circuit shown in Figure 10 represents a typical input stage for laboratory instruments and panel meters. The amplifier is non-inverting and offers selectable gains from 1 to 1000 in decade steps.

Input impedance of this amplifier is 10 megaohms determined by resistor R_1. The offset nulling network comprised R_3, R_4 and R_5 is the same one described earlier. If a less precise adjustment can be tolerated, a single 10k potentiometer can be substituted for R_3, R_4 and R_5.

Gain switching is accomplished in the feedback network. The divider consisting of R_{10}, R_{11}, R_{12} and R_{13} determines the gain by dividing the output and returning it to the inverting input of the amplifier. The ratio tolerances of these resistors uniquely determine the gain of the amplifier. The impedance seen by the inverting input is held constant to 10K ohms by R_6, R_7, R_8 or R_9 depending on the gain selected. Since input bias currents flow through equal resistances, the offset voltages produced will cancel each other. The input offset currents will produce an insignificant offset voltage on the order of 1 microvolt. If this offset is nulled out at the highest gain selected, it will be nulled on all ranges.

The AD517 offers excellent temperature stability in this circuit. Once the offset has been zeroed, the error produced by offset current drift will remain quite low due to the extremely low offset current drift of the AD517. A FET input operational amplifier would not work well in this application, since the input offset currents would double for each 10°C increase in temperature, soon exceeding the input offset currents of the AD517.

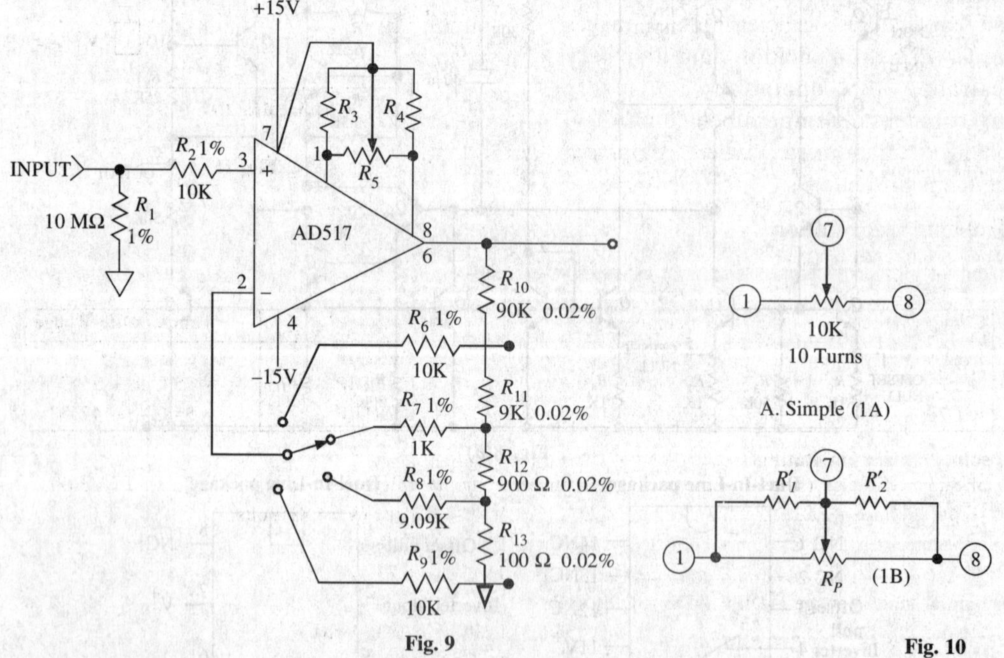

Fig. 9

Fig. 10

General Description

The ICL7605/ICL7606 commutating auto-zero (CAZ) instrumentation amplifier are designed to replace most of today's hybrid or monolithic instrumentation amplifiers, for low frequency applications from DC to 10 Hz. This is made possible by the unique construction of this new internal device, which takes an entirely new design approach to low frequency amplifiers.

Unlike conventional amplifier designs, which employ three operational amplifiers and require ultra-high accuracy in resistor tracking and matching, the CAZ instrumentation amplifier requires no trimming except for gain. The key features of the CAZ principle involve automatic compensation for long term drift phenomena and temperature effects, and a flying capacitor input.

The ICL7605/ICL7606 is a monolithic CMOS chip which consists of two analog sections–a unity gain differential to single-ended voltage convert and a CAZ operational amplifier. The first section senses the differential input and applies it to the CAZ amplifier section. This section consists of an operational amplifier circuit which continuously corrects itself for input voltage errors, such as input offset voltage, temperature effects, and long term drift.

The ICL7605/ICL7606 is intended for low-frequency operation in applications such as strain gauges, which require voltage gains from 1 to 1000 and bandwidth from DC to 10 Hz. Since the CAZ amplifier automatically corrects itself for internal errors, the only periodic adjustment required is that of gain, which is established by two external resistors. The no-adjustment feature, combined with extremely low offset and temperature coefficient figures, makes the CAZ instrumentation amplifier very desirable for operation in severe environments (temperature, humidity, toxicity, radiation, etc.) where equipment service is difficult.

PIN CONFIGURATION

Pin	Name	Pin	Name
1	AZ	18	–DIFT IN
2	–INPUT	17	+DIFT IN
3	C_4	16	C_3
4	C_4	15	C_3
5	C_2	14	C_1
6	C_2	13	C_1
7	Y	12	DR
8	BIAS	11	OSC
9	OUTPUT	10	V^+

(outline dwg JN)

Fig. 11

Ordering Information

Order parts by the following part numbers:

Compensated	Uncompensated	Package	Temperature Range
ICL7605CJN	ICL7606CJN	CERDIP	0ºC to + 70ºC
ICL7605IJN	ICL7606IJN	CERDIP	– 25ºC to + 55ºC
ICL7605MJN	ICL7606MJN	CERDIP	– 55ºC to + 125ºC

Absolute Maximum Ratings

Total Supply Voltage (sum of both positive and negative supply voltages V^+ to V^-) .... 18 Volts

DR Input Voltage .... (V^+ + 0.3) to (V^+ 8) Volts

Input Voltage (C_1, C_2, C_3, C_4 + DIFF IN,– DIFF In, – INPUT, BIAS, OSC)
(Note 1) .... (V^+ + 0.3) to (V^+ – 0.3) Volts

Differntial input Voltage (+DIFF IN to – DIFF IN)
(Note 2) .... (V^+ + 0.3) to (V^+ – 0.3) Volts

Duration of Output Short Circuit (Note 3) .... Unlimited

Continuous Total Power Dissipation (at or below 25ºC free-air temperature) (Note 4) .... 500 mW

Operating Temperature Range:
ICL 7605/ICL7606CJN .... 0 to + 70ºC
ICL 7605/ICL7606IJN .... – 25ºC to + 85ºC
ICL7605/ICL7606MJN .... – 55ºC to + 125ºC

Storage Temperature Range .... – 55ºC to + 150ºC

Load Temperature (soldering 60 second) 300ºC

Stresses above those listed under Absolute Maximum Ratings may cause permanent damage to the device. These are stress rating only, and functional operation of the device at these or any other conditions above those indicated in the operational sections of the specifications is not implied. Exposure to absolute maximum rating conditions for extended periods may affect device reliability.

Note 1: Due to the SCR structure inherent in all CMOS devices, exceeding these limits may cause destructive latchup. For this reason, it is recommended that no inputs from sources operating on a separate power supply be applied to the 7605/6 before its own power supply is established, and that when using multiple supplies, the supply for the 7606/6 should be turned on first.

Note 2: No restrictions are placed on the differential input voltage on either the +DIFF IN or – DIFF IN inputs so long as these voltages do not exceed the power supply voltages by more than 0.3V.

Note 3: The outputs may be shorted to ground (GND) or to either supply (V^+ or V^-). Temperature and/or supply voltages must be limited to insure that the dissipation ratings are not exceeded.

Note 4: For operation above 25°C free-air temperatures, derate 4mW/°C from 500 mW above 25°jC.

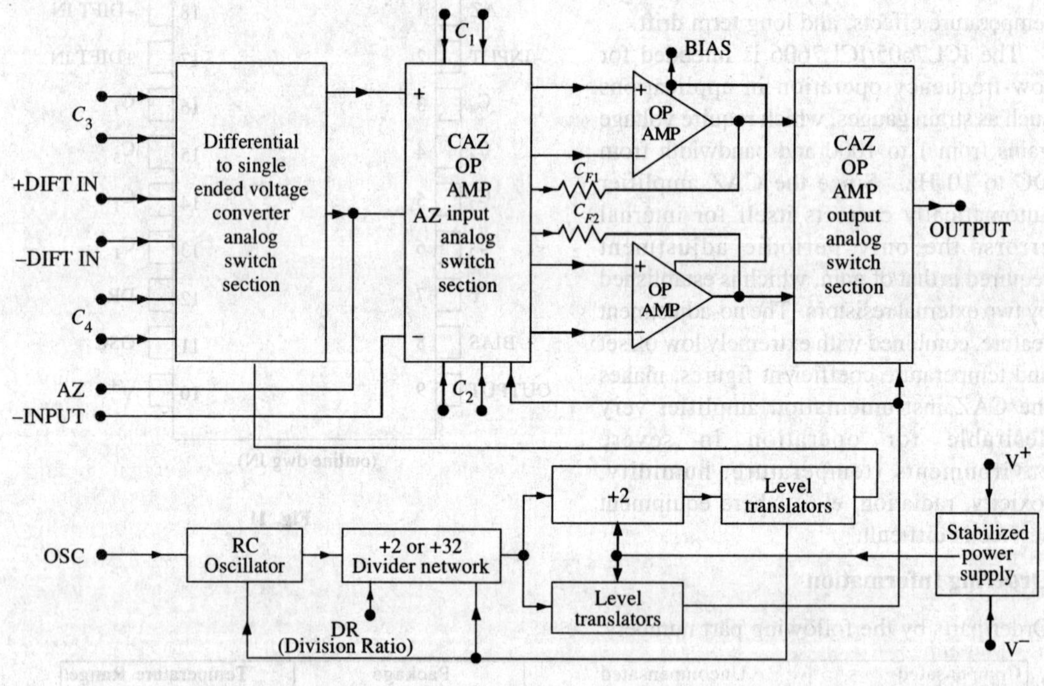

Fig. 12

Operating Characteristics

Conditions: V^+ = +5 votts, V^- = – 5 volts, T_A = + 25°C, DR pin connected to V+ (f_{COM} = 160 Hz, f_{COM} = 160Hz, $f_{COM1} \geq$ 80Hz), $C_1 = C_2 = C_3 = C_4 = 1\ \mu$ F, Tes Circuit 1 unless otherwise specified.

Detailed Description

CAZ Instrumentation Amp. Overview

The CAZ instrumentation amplifier operates on principles which are very different from those of the conventional three operational amplifier designs, which must use ultra-precise trimmed resistor networks in order to achieve acceptable accuracy. An important advantage of the ICL7605/ICL7606 CAZ instrumentation amplifier is the provision for self-compensation for internal error voltages, whether they are derived from steady-state conditions, temperature, supply voltage fluctuations, or are variable over a long term.

The CAZ instrumentation amplifier is constructed with monolithic CMOS technology, and consists of three distinct sections, two analog and one digital. The two analog sections–a differential to single-ended voltage converter, and a CAZ operational amplifier–have on-chip analog switches to steer the input signal. The analog switches are driven from a self-contained digital section which consists of an RC oscillator, a programmable divider, and associated voltage translator. A functional layout of the ICL7605/ICL7606 is shown in Fig. 13.

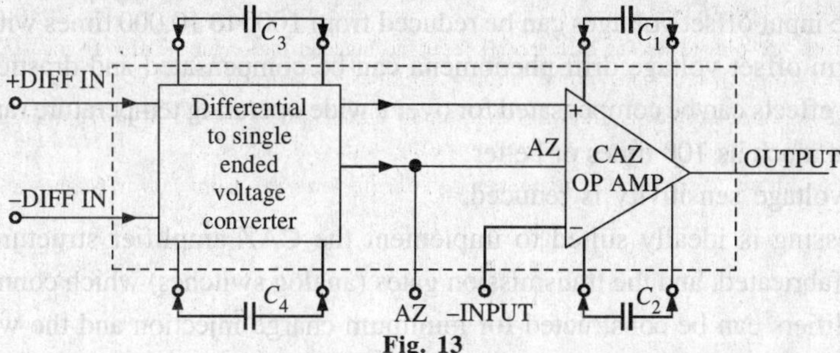

Fig. 13

The ICL 7605/ICL7606 have approximately constant equivalent input noise voltage, CMRR, PSRR, input offset voltage and drift values independent of the gain configuration. By comparison, hybrid-type modules which use the traditional three operational amplifier configuration have relatively poor performance at low gain (1 to 100) with improved performance above a gain of 100.

The only major limitation of the ICL7605/ICL7606 is its low frequency operation (10 to 20 Hz maximum). However in many applications speed is not the most important parameter.

CAZ Operational Amplifier Section

Operation of the CAZ amplifier section of the ICL7605/ICL7606 instrumentation amplifier is best illustrated by referring to Figure 14. The basic amplifier configuration, represented by the large triangles, has one more input than does a regular operational amplifier–the AZ, or auto-zero terminal. The voltage on the AZ input is that level at which each of the internal operational amplifiers will be auto-zeroed. In Mode A, operational amplifier is connected in a unity gain mode through on-chip analog switches. It charges external capacitor C_2 to a voltage equal to the DC input offset voltage of the amplifier plus the instantaneous low-frequency noise voltage. A short time later, the analog switches reconnect the on-chip operational amplifier to the configuration show in Mode B. In this mode, operational amplifier #2 has capacitor C_2 (which is charged to a voltage equal to the offset and noise voltage of operational amplifier #2) connected in series to its non-inverting (+) input in such a manner as to null out the input offset and noise voltages of the amplifier. While one of the on-chip operational amplifiers is processing the input signal, the second operational amplifier is in an auto-zero mode, charging a capacitor to a voltage equal to its equivalent DC and low frequency error voltage. The on-chip amplifiers are connected and reconnected at a rate designated as the commutation frequency (f_{COM}), so that at all times one or the other of the on-chip operational amplifier is processing the input signal, while the voltages on capacitors C_1 and C_2 are being updated to compensate for variables such as low frequency noise voltage and input offset voltage changes due to temperature, drift or supply voltages effects.

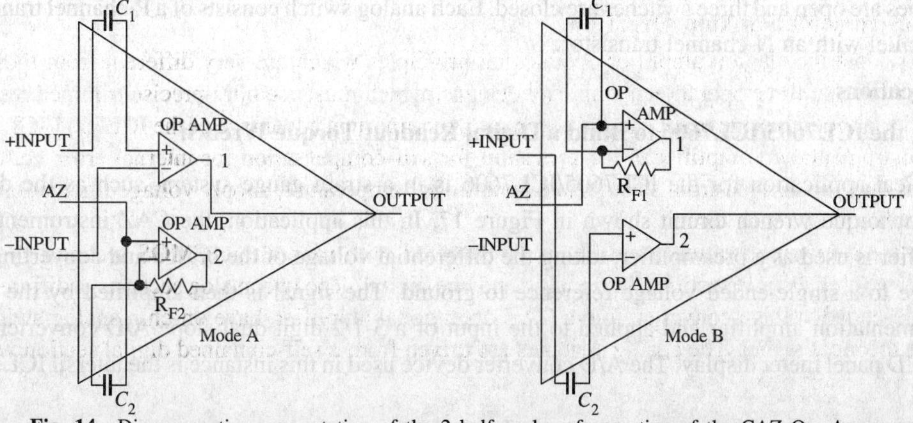

Fig. 14. Diagrammatic representation of the 2 half cycles of operation of the CAZ Op. Amp.

Compared to the standard bipolar of FET input operational amplifier, the CAZ amplifier scheme demonstrates a number of important advantages:

- Effective input offset voltages can be reduced from 1000 to 10,000 times without trimming.
- Long-term offset voltage drift phenomena can be compensated and drastically reduced.
- Thermal effects can be compensated for over a wide operating temperature range. Reduction can be as much as 100 times or better.
- Supply voltage sensitivity is reduced.

CMOS processing is ideally suited to implement the CAZ amplifier structure. The digital section is easily fabricated, and the transmission gates (analog switches) which connect the on-chip operational amplifiers can be constructed for minimum charge injection and the widest operating voltage range. The analog section, which includes the on-chip operational amplifiers, contributes performance figures which are similar to bipolar or FET input designs. CMOS structure provides the CAZ amplifier with open-loop gains of greater than 100 dB, typical input offset voltage of ± 5 mV, and ultra-low leakage currents, typically 1 pa.

The CMOS transmission gates connect the on-chip operational amplifiers to external input and output terminals, as shown in Figure 15. Here, one operational amplifier and its associated analog

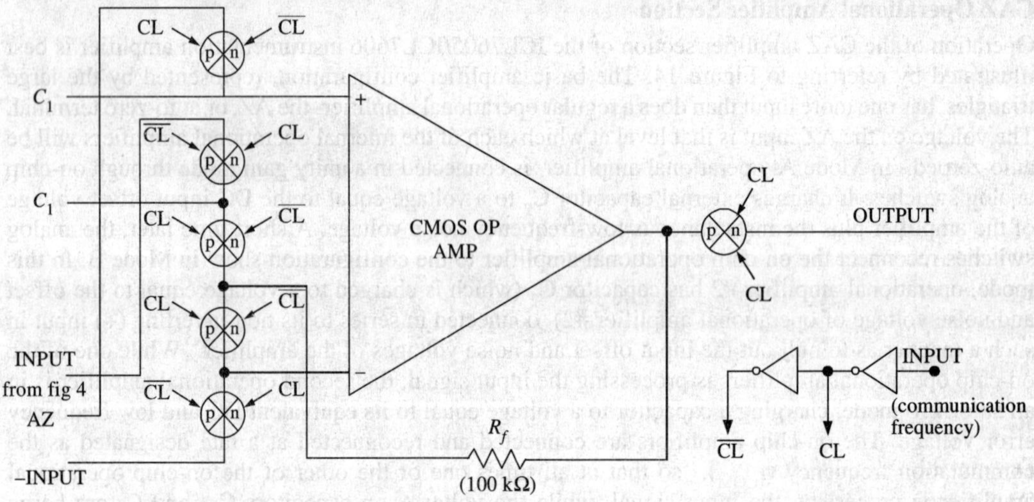

Fig. 15. Diagrammatic representation of the 2 half cycles of operation of the CAZ Op. Amp.

switches are required to connect each on-chip operational amplifier, so that at any time three switches are open and three switches are closed. Each analog switch consists of a P-channel transistor in parallel with an N-channel transistor.

Applications

Using the ICL7605/ICL7606 to Build a Digital Readout Torque Wrench

A typical application for the ICL7605/ICL7606 is in a strain gauge system, such as the digital readout torque wrench circuit shown in Figure 17. In this application, the CAZ instrumentation amplifier is used as a preamplifier, taking the differential voltage of the bridge and converting this voltage to a single-ended voltage reference to ground. The signal is then amplified by the CAZ instrumentation amplifier and applied to the input of a 3-1/2 digit dual-slope A/D converter chip for LCD panel meter display. The A/D converter device used in this instance is the intersil ICL7106.

In the digital readout torque wrench circuit, the reference voltage for the ICL7106 is derived from the stimulus applied to the strain gauge, to utilize the ratiomatric capabilities of the A/D. In order to set the full-scale reading, it is required that, given a certain strain gauge bridge with a defined pressure voltage sensitivity, a value of gain for the ICL7605/ICL7606 instrumentation CAZ amplifier be selected along with an appropriate value for the reference voltage. The gain should be set so that at full scale the output will swing about 8.5V. The reference voltage required is about one-half the maximum output swing, or approximately 0.25V.

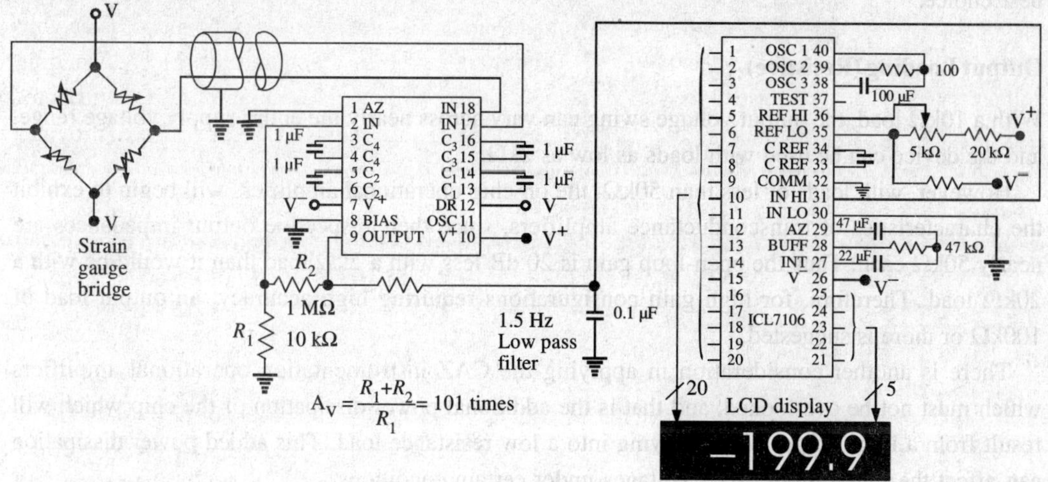

Fig. 16

In this type of system, only one adjustment is required. Either the amplifier gain or the reference voltage must be varied for full-scale adjustment. Total current consumption of all circuitry, less the current through the strain gauge bridge, is typically 2 mA. The accuracy is limited only by resistor ratios and the transducer.

Some Helpful Hints

Testing the ICL7605/ICL7606 CAZ Instrumentation Amplifier

Test Circuits #1 and #2 provide convenient means of measuring most of the important electrical parameters of the CAZ instrumentation amplifier. The output signal can be viewed on an oscilloscope after being fed through a low-pass filter. It is recommended that-for most applications, a low-pass filter of about 1.0 to 1.5 Hz be used to reduce the peak-to-peak noise to about the same level as the input offset voltage.

The output low-pass filter must be of a high-input impedance type-(not simply a capacitor across the feedback resistor R_2) at about 100 kΩ and 10µF so that the output dynamic loading on the CAZ instrumentation is about 100 kΩ.

Bias Control

The on-chip operational amplifiers consume over 90% of the power required by the ICL7605/ ICL7606 instrumentation operational amplifier. For this reason, the internal operational amplifiers have externally programmable bias levels. These levels are set by connecting the BIAS terminal to either V+, GND, orV− for LOW, MED or HIGH BIAS levels, respectively. The difference between each bias setting is about a factor of 3, allowing a 9:1 ratio of power supply versus bias setting. This current programmability provides the user with a choice of device power disspation levels, slew rates (the higher the slew rate, the better the recovery from commutation spikes), and offset errors due to "IR" voltage drops and thermoelectric effects (the higher the power dissipation, the higher the input offset error). In most cases, the medium bias (MED BIAS) setting will be found to be the best choice.

Output Loading (Resistive)

With a 10kΩ load, the output voltage swing can vary across nearly the entire supply voltage range, and the device can be used with loads as low as 2kΩ.

However, with loads of less than 50kΩ, the on-chip operational amplifiers will begin to exhibit the characteristics of transconductance amplifiers, since their respective output impedances are nearly 50kΩ each. Thus the open-loop gain is 20 dB less with a 2kΩ load than it would be with a 20kΩ load. Therefore, for high gain configurations requiring high accuracy, an output load of 100kΩ or more is suggested.

There is another consideration in applying the CAZ instrumentation operational amplifiers which must not be overlooked, and that is the additional power dissipation of the chip which will result from a large output voltage swing into a low resistance load. This added power dissipation can affect the initial input offset voltages under certain conditions.

Output Loading (Capacitive)

In many applications, it is desirable to include a low-pass filter at the output of the CAZ instrumentation operational amplifier to reduce high-frequency noise outside the desired signal passband. An obvious solution when using a conventional operational amplifier would be to place a capacitor across the external feedback resistor and thus produce a low-pass filter.

However, with the CAZ operational amplifier concept this is not possible because of the nature of the commutation spikes. These voltage spikes exhibit a low-impedance characteristic in the direction of the auto-zero voltage and a high-impedance characteristic on the recovery edge. It can be seen that the effect of a large load capacitor produces an area error in the output waveform, and hence an effective gain error. The output low-pass filter must be of a high-impedance type to avoid these area errors. For example, a 1.5 Hz filter will require a 100kΩ resistor and a 1.0 μF capacitor, or a 1mΩ resistor and an 0.1 μF capacitor.

Oscillator and Digital Circuitry Considerations

The oscillator has been designed to run free at about 5.2 kHz when the OSC terminal is open circuit. If the full divider network is used, this will result in a nominal commutation frequency of approximately 150 Hz. The commutation frequency is that frequency at which the on-chip operational amplifiers are switched between the signal processing and the auto-zero modes. A 160 Hz commutation frequency represents the best compromise between input offset voltage and low frequency noise. Other commutation frequencies may provide optimization of some parameters, but always at the expense of others.

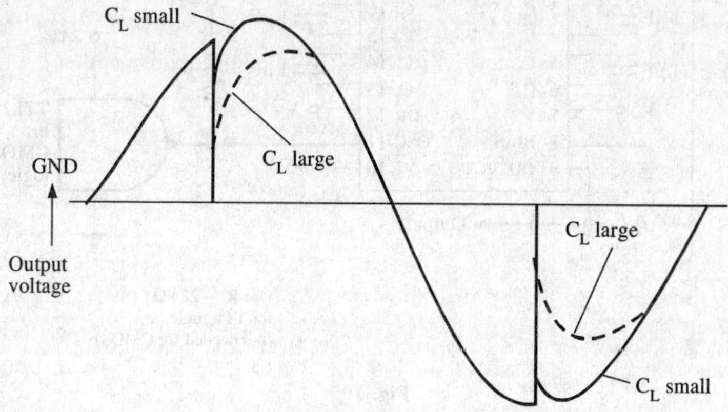

Fig. 17

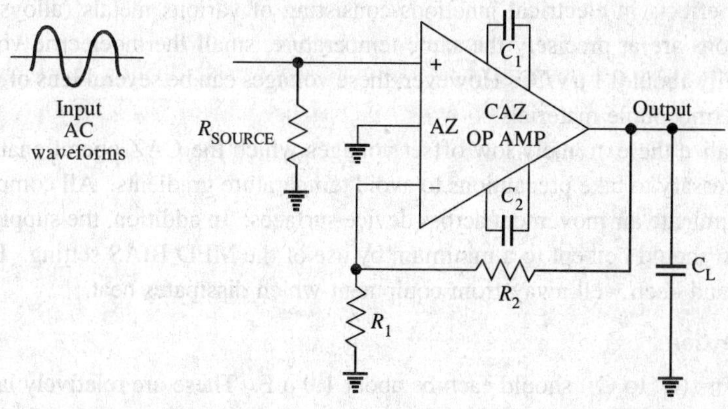

Fig. 18

The oscillator has a very high output impedance, so that a load of only a few picofarads on the OSC terminal will cause a significant shift in frequency. It is therefore recommended that if the natural oscillator frequency is desired (5.2 kHz) the terminal remains open circuit. In other instances, it may be desirable to synchronize the oscillator with an external clock source, or to run it at another frequency. The ICL760 5/ICL7606 CAZ amplifier provides two degrees of flexibility in this respect. First, the DR division (ratio) terminal allows a choice of either dividing the oscillator by 32 (DR terminal to V$^+$) or by 2 (DR terminal to GND) to obtain the commutation frequency. Second, the oscillator may have its frequency lowered by the addition of an external capacitor connected between the OSC terminal and the V$^+$ or system GND terminals. For situations which require that the commutation frequency be synchronized with a master clock, the OSC terminal may be driven from TTL logic (with resistive pull-up) or by CMOS logic, provided that the V$^+$ supply (with respect to ground) is + 5 V (± 10%) and the logic driver also operates from a similar voltage supply. The reason for this requirement is that the logic section (including the oscillator) operates from an internal – 5V supply, referenced to V$^+$ supply, which is not accessible externally.

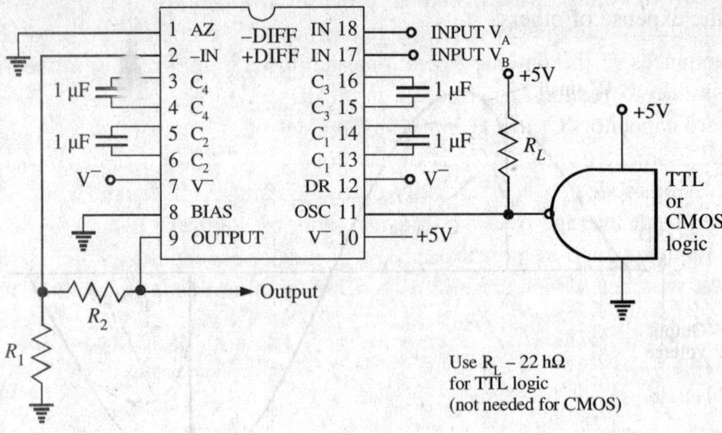

Fig. 19

Thermoelectric Effects

The ultimate limitations to ultra-high-sensitivity DC amplifiers are due to thermoelectric, Peltier, or thermocouple effects in electrical junctions consisting of various metals (alloys, silicon, etc.) Unless all junctions are at precisely the same temperature, small thermoelectric voltages will be produced, generally about 0.1 µV/°C. However, these voltages can be several lens of microvolts per °C for certain thermocouple materials.

In order to realize the extremely low offset voltages which the CAZ operational amplifier can produce, it is necessary to take precautions to avoid temperature gradients. All components should be enclosed to eliminate air movement across device surfaces. In addition, the supply voltages and power dissipation should be kept to a minimum by use of the MED BIAS setting. Employ a high impedance load and keep well away from equipment which dissipates heat.

Component Selection

The four capacitors (C_1 to C_4) should each be about 1.0 µ F. These are relatively large values for non-electrolytic capacitors, but since the voltages stored on them change significantly, problems of dielectric absorption, charge bleed-off and the like are as significant as they would be for integrating dual-slope A/D converter applications. Polypropylene are the best for C_3 and C_4, though Mylar may be adequate for C_1 and C_2.

Excellent results have been obtained for commercial temperature ranges using several of the less-expensive, smaller-size capacitors, since the absolute values of the capacitors are not critical. Even polarized electrolytic capacitors rated at 1.0 µF and 50V have been used successfully at room temperature, although no recommendations are made concerning the use of such capacitors.

Commutation Voltage Transient Effects

Although in most respects the CAZ instrumentation amplifier resembles a conventional operational amplifier, its principal applications will be in very low level, low-frequency preamplifiers limited to DC through 10 Hz. This is due to the finite switching transients which occur at both the input and output terminals because of commutation effects. These transients have a frequency spectrum beginning at the commutation frequency, and including all of the higher harmonics of the commutation frequency. assuming that the commutation frequency is higher than the highest in-band frequency, then the commutation transients can be filtered out with a low-pass filter.

The input commutation transients arise when each of the on-chip operational amplifiers experiences a shift in voltage which is equal to the input offset voltages (about 5-10mV), usually occurring during the transition between the signal processing mode and the auto-zero mode. Since the input capacitances of the on-chip operational amplifiers are typically in the 10 pF range, and since it is desirable to reduce the effective input offset voltage about 10,000 times, the offset voltage auto-zero capacitors C_1 and C_2 must have values of at least 10,000 × 10 pF or 0.1 μ F each. The charge that is injected into the input of each operational amplifier when being switched into the signal processing mode produces a rapidly-decaying voltage spike at the input, plus an equivalent DC input bias current average over a full cycle. This bias current is directly proportional to the commutation frequency, and in most instances will greatly exceed the inherent leakage currents of the input analog switches, which are typically 10 pA at an ambient temperature of 25°C.

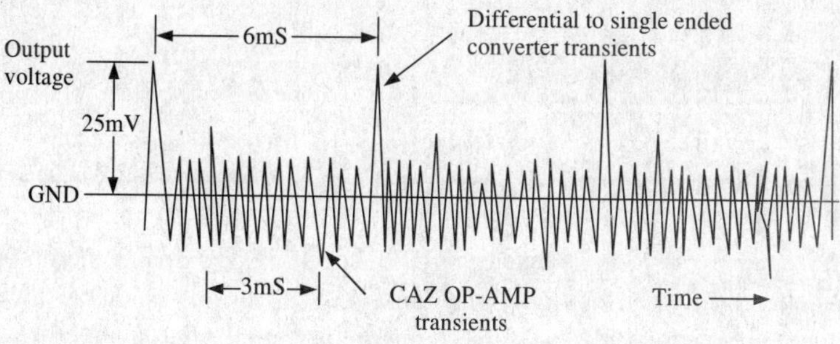

Fig. 20

Layout Considerations

Care should be exercised in positioning components on the PC board, particularly the capacitors C_1, C_2, C_3 and C_4 all of which must be shielded from the OSC terminal. Also parasitic PC board leakage capacitances associated with these four capacitors should be kept as low as possible to minimize charge injection effects.

INDEX

A

Active Filter Circuits, 104-125
— advantages and disadvantages of 104, 105
— applications of, 105
— characteristic impedance of, 121–123

Amplifier
— differential, 1-17

Applications, of Op. Amp., 134-169
— as active voltage divider, 135, 136
— as audio mixer, 134-136
— as audio tone control, 138, 140
— as equalizer in microphone, tape-head and disc-recording, 136-138
— as electric thermometer, 146-149
— as high pressure voltage source, 141
— as high voltage power source, 144
— as medical electronic monitoring system, 148, 149
— as phase detector, 144, 146
— as photo-electric relay, 140
— as photo-volatic light sensor, 140
— as power amplifier, 148, 149
— as quadrature oscillator, 150, 151
— as saw-tooth wave generator, 158, 159
— as sine-wave form square wave generation, 159, 160
— as signal rectifier, 142
— as Schmitt trigger circuit, 160, 161
— as simulator of inductance, 165-169
— as special circuit for capacitive multiplicity, 169
— as waveform generator, 156-158
— as Wien bridge oscillator, 151, 152
— as zero crossing detector, 153-154
— as temperative resistance, 141
— as variable voltage supply, 143
— as phase-shift oscillator, 154
— as four bit D/A and A/D convertor, 161, 162

Automatic d.c. analysis, 173, 174, 175
Appendices (A to D)] 256-354

Band width with feed back (in Op. Amp.), 41
Basic Op. Amp. circuit, 51
Bias
— constant current, 8
— emitter bias, 9

Boltzmann's constant (k), 10

Closed loop gain (A_{ct})
— voltage gain, (of an Op. Amp.), 39, 40
— as open loop gain, 40

Configurations (of Diff. Amp.), 7, 8
Common Mode Rejection Ratio (CMRR) (= δ) or figure of merit of an Op. Amp.
Common Mode Voltage Gain A_c, 7
Control Gain Polarity, 66, 67
Current Drift. effect of, 37, 38

Differential Amplifier, 1-17
— application of, 3
— a.c. analysis of, 4
— as Limiter, 11
— cascading of, 12
— circuit configurations of, 3
— comparison of different configurations of, 12
— common mode rejection ratio (CMRR), (or Figure of Merit = δ)
— definition of, 1
— diode, function in, 9, 12
— dual input, unbalanced output type, 7
— effects of cascading of Diff. Amp., 12
— ideal Diff. Amp. 1, 2
— input-resistance, R_{in} 4-8

— output resistance R_o, 6
— parameters of, 1
— single input, balanced output type of, 7
— symmetrical emitter coupled Diff. Amp., 3, 4
— single input, unbalanced output type of, 7
— transfer characteristics of, 10, 11
— voltage gain, 6-8
— with FET, 11
— with constant current stage, 8, 9
Differentiator Circuits, 99-102
— for triangular input wave form, 100, 102
— practical differentiator, 101, 102
— some specialised differentiators, 101-103
Double Integrator Circuit, 98

END Statement, 171
Effect of Feedback, 42, 43
Extra Problems (on Op. Amp. circuit), 256-272

Families (or Generations of Op. Amps.), 21-24
Feedback (negative) Effect of, 42
Filters
— active filter circuits, 104, 122, 123
— active filters, 104, 105
— advantages of, 104
— applications of, 105
— characteristic impedance, 121-123
drawbacks of, 104, 105
Filter classification of, 105, 106
— all pass, 106, 117
— band pass, 105
— band elimination, 106
— high pass, 105, 114
— low pass, 105
— Butterworth, 113
— Chebysher and Caucer filter, 106, 116
— notch, filters, 118, 119
Filters, high order, advantage of, 114
Frequency, 114
Frequency compensator circuits, 19-21

Input Resistance with feedback (in Op. Amp.), 40, 41
Integrator-differential, 98-100

Johnson (or Thermal or white) Noise; 123, 124, 125

Multiple-choice Questions, 250-298
— Additional Questions, 273-281

Noise eliminator in Diff. Amp. output, 13
Noise control in Operational Amplifier, 124-134
— associated noise, 124
— (in) cascaded Op. Amp. 132, 133
— equivalent input noise for BJT Diff. Amp., 125, 126, 127, 128
— equivalent input noise (for FET Diff. Amp., 129, 130, 131
— Johnson (or Thermal) Noise, 124, 125
— Optimum noise performance conditions, 27, 28
— noise characteristic of BJT Differential stage, 129
— Schottky (or Shot) noise, 124

Operational Amplifier, 18-50
— applications of, 18
— bandwidth (with feed back), 41, 42
— Basic Op. Amp., 30
— block diagram, 26-28
— characteristic features of, 28-30
— circuit symbol of, 26, 27
— common mode rejection ratio, 33
— designations for, 22-24
— different packages of ICs for, 24-25
— detailed circuit of 741, 29-30
— effect of voltage and current drifts, 37, 38
— Generations of, 18, 23
— Gain bandwidth product, 38, 39
— feedback in Op. Amp., 39
— identification (of Op. Amp.), 25, 26
— ideal Op. Amp. 28-30
— input offset voltage, 29, 32, 33
— input bias and offset currents, 33

— ordering information for I.C. Op. Amp., 25
— offset correcting resistor, 35, 36, 37
— non-ideal Op. Amp. characteristics, 38
— output resistance (with feedback), 41
— power supply rejection ratio, 33
— pin configurations, 24, 25
— power supplies for, 26-28
— selection of right Op. Amp., 25, 26
— special Op. Amps. 25
— slew rate, 34, 35
— virtual ground, 30, 31
Operational Amplifier Circuits (Basic), 51-88
— comparators, 64, 65
— controlled source, representation, 62, 63
— current Amplifier, 61, 62
— Differential Amplifier, 55, 56
— Instrumentation Amplifier, 58, 59
— Inverting Op. Amp. Circuit, 52
— Log and Antilog Amplifiers, 65, 66
— Multiplier circuit, using Op. Amp., 56, 57
— Negative Resistance Convertor, 57, 58
— Non-inverting Op. Amp. Circuit, 52, 53
— Summing Amplifier (Adder Subtraction) circuit, 54, 55
— Transconductance Amplifier, 60, 61
— Trans-Resistance Amplifier, 59, 60
— Voltage Follower Circuit (using Op. Amp.), 53, 54

P

Parameters, which control accuracy of Op. Amp., 147-149
Phase characteristics (of Diff. Amp.), 19-21
Power dissipation in Op. Amp., 22
Practical Differentiator, 99-101
Proportional plus Integral Inverting circuit, 99
Practical Experiments (on Op. Amps.), 199-250
— Study of Op. Amp. as Voltage follower, 199-209
— To study (*i*) Adder Circuit (*ii*) Integrated circuit, 209-215
— Study of a Differential Circuit (using Op. Amp.), 216-222
— To study a Comparator Circuit (using Op. Amp.), 222-230
— Study of Active Filters (using Op. Amp.), 230-244
— (*i*) Study of Gain Polarity Control by Op. Amp.
— (*ii*) Study of some Oscillators, 244-249
PSPICE
— application in analysis of Op. Amp., 170-198
— general description, 170, 171
— labelling of nodes; 171
— rules regarding, 171, 175
— scale factors, 172, 173
— some special statements, 175
— working principle, 171-175

— Review Questions, 218, 250-255

Schottky (or Shot) noise, 124
Sensitivity to capacitive loading (in Op. Amp.), 22
Setting of initial condition (in Op. Amp.), 94
Short-circuit Protection (in Op. Amp.), 21-23
Signal gain (*Ad, Ac*), 2
Signal conditioning Circuits, 91-109
— Integrator Circuits, 91-93
— non-integrator, 93, 94
— double integrator, 98
— other practical considerations, 94
— some specialised circuits, 98
— with bias current compensation, 94, 95
— with feed forward frequency compensation, 95-97
— with two Op. Amps., 96-98
Slew rate of (Op. Amp.), 22
SPICE
— use in analysis of Op. Amp., 170-198
— analysis for purely resistive circuit, 175, 176
— general description, 170, 171
— labelling of nodes, 171
— rules regarding, 171- 174
— scale factors, 172, 173
— some special statements, 175
— working principle of, 171
— to get Thevenin & Norton Equivalents across terminals, 176-178

Thermal (or Johnson Noise), 124, 125
Transconductance (of Diff. Amp.) (g_{md}), 10, 11

Unity Gain Bandwidth Product (Op. Amp.), 19-21, 41

Virtual ground, 21, 30
Voltage drift, effect of (on Op. Amp.), 37, 38
Voltage gain (A_d) (of Diff. Amp.), 6, 7

White (or Thermal or Johnson) Noise, 17, 125.